Woman's Power, Man's Game

Essays on Classical Antiquity in Honor of

Joy K. King

Joy K. King

Woman's Power, Man's Game

Essays on Classical Antiquity in Honor of

Joy K. King

BOLCHAZY-CARDUCCI PUBLISHERS

Cover illustration by Bob Johnson
Cover design by David Van Delinder

© Copyright 1993

Bolchazy-Carducci Publishers
1000 Brown Street
Wauconda, IL 60084 U.S.A.

Printed in the United States of America

International Standard Book Number:
Softbound 0-86516-258-1

Library of Congress Cataloging-in-Publication Data

Woman's power, man's game: essays on classical antiquity in honor of Joy K. King / edited by Mary DeForest.
   p. cm.
   Includes bibliographical references (p.) and index.
   ISBN 0-86516-258-1 : $35.00
      1. Classical literature--History and criticism. 2. Women and literature--Greece--History. 3. Women and literature--Rome--History. 4. Sex role in literature. 5. Women--Greece--History. 6. Women--Rome--History. I. King, Joy K. II. DeForest, Mary, 1946- .
PA3016.W7W65 1993
880.9'352042--dc20   93-17713
                                                                                 CIP

Contents

Preface ii
Acknowledgments xvii
Tabula Gratulatoria xviii
Abbreviations xix
Ernest J. Ament, *Aspects of Androgyny in Classical Greece* 1
Bella Zweig, *The Only Women Who Give Birth to Men: A Gynocentric, Cross-Cultural View of Women in Ancient Sparta* 32
Kristina Passman, *Re(de)fining Woman: Language and Power in the Homeric Hymn to Demeter* 54
Jody Rubin Pinault, *Women, Fat, and Fertility: Hippocratic Theorizing and Treatment* 78
Jon Solomon, *The Wandering Womb of Delos* 91
Joan O'Brien, *Hera, Nurse of Monsters* 109
Mary DeForest, *Clytemnestra's Breast and the Evil Eye* 129
Patricia A. Marquardt, *Penelope as Weaver of Words* 149
Richard Minadeo, *A Hero's Wife* 159
Lena Hatzichronoglou, *Euripides' Medea: Woman or Fiend?* 178
K. R. Walters, *Women and Power in Classical Athens* 194
Kathleen McNamee, *Propertius, Poetry, and Love* 215
Brenda H. Fineberg, *From a Sure Foot to Faltering Meters: The Dark Ladies of Tibullan Elegy* 249
Barbara Hill, *Horace, Satire 1.8: Whence the Witches? Thematic Unity within the Satire and within the Satires of Book 1* 257
Emily E. Batinski, *Julia in Lucan's Tripartite Vision of the Dead Republic* 264
Barbara K. Gold, *"The Master Mistress of My Passion": The Lady as Patron in Ancient and Renaissance Literature* 279
Judith de Luce, *"O for a Thousand Tongues to Sing": A Footnote on Metamorphosis, Silence, and Power* 305
Judith P. Hallett, *Martial's Sulpicia and Propertius' Cynthia* 322
Georgia L. Irby-Massie, *Women in Ancient Science* 354
Hazel E. Barnes, *Images of Iphigenia* 373
Elizabeth A. Holtze, *Sirens and their Song* 392
Bibliography 415
Index 425

Preface

"I do not think I ever opened a book in my life which had not something to say upon a woman's inconstancy. Songs and proverbs, all talk of woman's fickleness. But perhaps you will say, these were all written by men."

"Perhaps I shall.—Yes, yes, if you please, no reference to examples in books. Men have had every advantage of us in telling their own story. Education has been theirs in so much higher a degree; the pen has been in their hands. I will not allow books to prove any thing."

"But how shall we prove any thing?"

"We never shall."

(Jane Austen, *Persuasion*, 234)

The chorus of Euripides' *Medea*, composed in 431 B.C., like the speakers of Jane Austen's *Persuasion* some twenty-two centuries later, points out that the songs about women's infidelity were made by men:

> Cease now, you muses of the ancient singers,
> To tell of my unfaithfulness;
> For not on us did Phoebus, lord of music,
> Bestow the lyre's divine
> Power, for otherwise I should have sung an answer
> To the other sex. Long time
> Has much to tell of us, and much of them.
> (*Medea* 421–30, trans. Rex Warner)

Medea, deserted by her ungrateful husband and exiled by the country's king, finds a chorus of sympathetic listeners in the women of Corinth who perceive her as a victim in a world run by men. Unaware of the horrible crimes she will soon perform, they sing that women have a bad reputation because men write the songs. Innovative in many respects, Euripides recognized the bias of literature composed by men and for men.

The hand that rocks the cradle, despite the old cliché, does not rule the world; the hand that wields the pen controls the only representation of the world that endures. The western literary tradition is a dialogue carried down through the span of time, with writers of each generation answering earlier generations and hoping to be answered by the generations that follow. Unfortunately, women's contribution to this dialogue has been largely lost. Almost everything we know about women in Greco-Roman antiquity has been passed down through the writings of men. With few exceptions, the authors and authorities discussed in this volume—poets, playwrights, historians, orators, grammarians, and philosophers—are male. Consequently, the women discussed in these articles are discerned only through the distortions of a male lens, their voices heard under the voices of the men transmitting them. Despite the pervasive bias of our sources, the articles reveal significant aspects about the situation of women in antiquity, several focusing directly on women's access to speech and writing.

The first two articles consider two widely different approaches to ancient gender difference. Ernest Ament's article on androgyny shows that the Greek obsession with these differences was countered in myth and ritual, which created, at least in metaphor, a union of the masculine and feminine. This state was associated with the legendary Golden Age, and, in mythic terms, the "Fall" means the division into gender, procreation, and death. Greek myth pointed to a prelapsarian state, with androgynous gods and heroes, a state in which ritual maintained the fantasy of merging into an androgynous whole.

On the other hand, Bella Zweig discusses Sparta, where men and women lived almost entirely in single-sex communities. Adopting a comparative approach, she offers an alternative model to the usual western one for understanding the character of Spartan women. She argues that in Spartan society men and women lived as separate groups, with the members of each group deriving self-esteem from their contributions to society as a whole. By drawing an analogy with Native American societies, she makes a powerful argument for connecting the

Spartan women's strength and patriotic pride with their living almost exclusively in the society of other women. A Spartan woman takes credit for the military excellence of her son because she produced him. Zweig's comparative approach helps to balance the overemphasis on Athenian social structures passed down in the literary and scholarly tradition.

In *The Creation of Patriarchy*, Gerda Lerner argues that as society adjusts the relationships between men and women, with symbols of power transferred to the dominant group, the myths accommodate themselves to ratify the new order of things.[1] The next few articles show how in various areas the powers of females were transferred to males. In her study of the *Homeric Hymn to Demeter*, Kristina Passman shows how co-optation underlies the story of Demeter's search for her lost daughter. The version of the story told in the *Hymn* reflects a cognitive pattern (found also in Hesiod) according to which the earth goddesses' powers of fertility and reproduction are transferred from the female to the male.

Greek scientific thought, profoundly influenced by mythic patterns, devised apparently scientific reasons to deny women access to their own fertility. Jody Pinault's article on Greek men's theories of female fertility shows that ancient scientists would not have viewed the fat earth goddesses, known to us from prehistoric figurines, as the ideal of feminine fecundity. Instead, they maintain that thinner, more masculine women had bodies suitable for childbearing. In science, as in myth, women's power of reproduction was taken over by men and male paradigms.

Earth's shrines, too, were taken over by male gods. Delos, the wandering island said to have became fixed with Apollo's birth, was originally—like Delphi—sacred to a goddess. In his explanation for the choice of Delos as a sacred site, Jon Solomon takes the reader from the classroom to modern Delos and back to the beliefs underlying the myths. His article represents a powerful new approach in scholarly inquiry (compare Thomas van Nortwick's study of Homer, *Somewhere I Have Never Travelled: The Second Self and the Hero's Journey in Ancient Epic* [Oxford, 1992]), in that he employs the autobiographical perspective and the personal voice, simultaneously presenting his idea and the experiences through which the idea was born in him.

Another mythic expression of the cosmic victory of male over female is the marriage of Zeus and Hera. In her article, excerpted from her book on Hera, Joan O'Brien shows how the images and diction of the *Iliad* point to an older stratum of Argolic myth in which Hera is the preeminent goddess of the early Argolid, the mother, nurse, and tamer of life and the one who brings fulfillment in marriage and death. In the present article, O'Brien reads through Homer's account of the battle between Achilles and the River Xanthus to the cosmic battle between Zeus and Typhon, the snake-headed monster created by Earth in her final rebellion against Zeus. Under Hephaestus, the mildest and most reasonable of the gods on Olympus, lurks Typhon, the symbol of blind destruction.

Aeschylus' *Oresteia*, as Froma Zeitlin has pointed out, describes the mythical transition of power from female to male as son kills mother under orders from Apollo, slayer of the snake.[2] In this transfer of power, Clytemnestra bears significant resemblances to the earth mother. Like Hera, she rebels against her husband; like the angry Demeter, she avenges her daughter; like Earth herself, she makes war on her son. Drawing on psychological theory and popular culture, I discuss the implications of the scene where Clytemnestra exposes her breast to Orestes. At that moment, I argue, she assumes the iconographical identity of the goddess in both her nourishing and destructive aspects.

Few wives of mythology, however, rebel against husbands, and the next two articles analyze Greek literary portrayals of virtuous wives married to heroes: Homer's Penelope and Sophocles' Deianeira. Patricia Marquardt proposes a bold, new theory that augments Penelope's repertoire of skills. She suggests that Penelope outwits the suitors by resorting to writing, a technology new in Homer's day and one that was at a later time kept from women.

Deianeira, the heroine described by Richard Minadeo, in contrast to Penelope, is limited intellectually. Treated by Heracles with an all too typical callousness, Deianeira tries to win back his love by a magical cloak. Sophocles' heroine is, except for one blunder into deceit, the Homeric ideal—noble, generous, and brave. Like many Sophoclean heroes, she is destroyed by her best qualities, whereas her monstrous husband achieves apotheosis. Perhaps because of his indifference to the sufferings he imposes on others, Heracles belongs with the gods, or at least with the gods of Sophocles' pantheon, while Deianeira represents suffering humanity.

The best known example of women's resistance to unequal sexual dynamics is Euripides' Medea. Unlike Deianeira, she does not try to win back the love of the husband who abandons her for another woman. Instead, she destroys him, first by killing his bride and father-in-law, and then by killing her sons by him. Lena Hatzichronoglou draws significant parallels between Medea and another of Euripides' characters, Dionysus of the *Bacchae*. Her discussion extends the discourse of oppression, showing how the symbols of superiority are extended to subsume barbarians as well as women under the rubric of Other in Athenian male ideology.

In Athenian society where exemplary women were never mentioned and respectable women were nameless, Medea might be regarded as the first self-realized woman. Whereas Athenian women were identified by their fathers, husbands, brothers, and sons, Medea betrays her father, murders her brother, and destroys her husband by killing their sons, thus creating a separate identity for herself independent of male attachments. The women of fifth- and fourth-century Athens lacked her powers, but Kenneth Walters corrects the bleak picture of their helpless passivity by providing evidence about certain women who achieved their goals by manipulating the law even though they were barred direct access to the law-court.

When we pass from Greek literature to Roman, particularly to the love poets, we read about women who seem vital and more modern. The literary antecedents of such women lie in a period not covered by the essays in this volume, and are rooted in the literary theories of the Alexandrian poet Callimachus, who devised a literary program in opposition to Homeric epic poetry. His student Apollonius deconstructed epic poetry by centering an epic poem, the *Argonautica*, on Medea, a girl in love, who overshadows both Jason and his Argonauts. The Roman love poets set themselves in the tradition of Callimachus when they rejected the theme of epic poetry in favor of love poetry, but they followed Apollonius in writing about powerful women. Probably Apollonius and the Roman love poets intended to ridicule heroic poetry rather than to elevate women, but, because of their writings, women were set at the center of serious narrative fiction. The Roman poets added a new dimension to literature by often casting the "implied reader" as female, the addressee of love poems. When the gender of the reader becomes indeterminate, so do the enshrined roles of male and female. In an anti-heroic setting, in the realm of words written and read, men and women meet on equal terms.

Both in her lectures and in her published work, Joy King has described the ambivalence of the Roman poets to the sophistication of their mistresses.[3] Learned in Greek, these women are portrayed as understanding the resonance of their lovers' poetry with Greek literature, but as not allowing themselves to be dominated by their lovers. Intellectual sophistication was accompanied by emotional independence and a disregard for chastity. According to Greek thought, women have a natural propensity for mischief, particularly sexual mischief, which is aggravated by an ability to think.[4] In Roman literature, although it portrays some intellectual women as leading lives of exemplary virtue, the sexual misconduct of the educated woman is a commonplace. Among the associates of the revolutionary Catiline was a noblewoman, Sempronia, whom Sallust describes as well-educated in Greek and Latin literature, and, not coincidently, as sexually forward (*Catiline* 25). As a stereotype, Sempronia resembles the female characters described by the Roman love poets: Catullus' Lesbia, Propertius' Cynthia, Tibullus' Delia, and Ovid's Corinna.

The articles of Kathleen McNamee and Brenda Fineberg also discuss the women described by the elegiac poets. These women are realistically portrayed as living in contemporary Rome rather than mythological Greece, but they work as symbols for literature and life. Lacking an independent voice, they have only the power to inspire others. McNamee argues that *all* Cynthia's charms are literary, that she is merely an allegory for Propertius' Alexandrian poetry. Fineberg describes Tibullus' gloomy progression of mistresses implied in the replacement of Delia by Nemesis. The dark meaning of the latter is reinforced by feminine abstract nouns clustering around her that signify wasting away and death.

Some of the women of elegy have a magical quality that connects them to Medea. It is tempting to speculate that Horace, who, like Vergil, did not write anti-establishment love poetry, intentionally counters the idealized image of the elegists' *domina* by the witches of

Satire 1.8, discussed by Barbara Hill. These witches, on first sight terrifying, invade Maecenas' garden with their grisly rituals, but the poet exposes the artificiality of their power by sending them scuttling off without their false teeth and hair. Their ominous, female power is revealed to be, like their beauty-aids, a hollow shell.

Emily Batinski discusses the women of Lucan's epic poem on the Civil War, who were historical figures and connected to Rome's most powerful men. Their principal importance for the poem, however, is symbolic, because the image of Rome stands behind them, infusing their personalities with abstract meaning. Through the women of the poem Lucan shows how the major figures of the era—Caesar, Pompey, and Cato—responded to the Republic.

Possibly it is coincidence that powerful women existed simultaneously in Roman history and Roman poetry. Whether or not the women we encounter in poetry could have been encountered in the real world is open to debate. Certainly women of the Roman upper class had more power than their Athenian counterparts. Although she is skeptical about Cynthia's existence on the physical plane, Barbara Gold introduces us to powerful women who were patrons of cities and instrumental in initiating policy through the male members of their families. Gold argues that the Roman love poets apply the language of patronage to their beloveds, thus turning them into patrons and investing them with a seeming power. This power, however, proves insubstantial as the women in question have no substance apart from the poetry about them and no power over the poet who constructs them. The theme of the lover's patronage is also prominent in Shakespeare, who, however, changes the hierarchies of power by applying the idea of patron/lover to a man.

Like some of his Greek literary predecessors, Ovid, it seems, was sensitive to the issue of women's right to speech and the significance of their being denied access to speech. Many of the narrators of the *Metamorphoses* are women, and the character most like Ovid in the poem is the woman Arachne. Judith de Luce discusses the silence imposed upon women in the *Metamorphoses*, particularly in connection with rape. The cruelty of their fate deprives them at once of innocence, of humanity, and of voice.

The few examples of women's poetry surviving from classical

antiquity were transmitted, assembled, and—until recently—edited by males. From the Augustan period a few poems of a Roman woman named Sulpicia are preserved in the collection of Tibullus' poetry. Most of our information about the poetry of another Sulpicia (first century A.D.) we owe to two poems written about her by her contemporary, Martial. Joining a discussion recently begun in *Classical World* by a young Canadian scholar, Carol Merriam, Judith Hallett examines Martial's portrayal of Sulpicia and her writing. In pointing up the similarities between Martial's representation of Sulpicia and Propertius' depiction of his beloved Cynthia, Hallett locates the surviving fragment of Sulpicia's verse in the tradition of erotic poetry composed by men. She interprets Sulpicia's use of masculine language and literary conventions as "affording women greater opportunity to conduct themselves as men did in the spheres of marital relations and artistic production."

Martial's contemporary Juvenal found fault with learned women, dividing them into two groups—the promiscuous and the pedantic.[5] The educated women of the sort described by Catullus and Propertius, he claimed, adopt Greek for the language of sex, and even fornicate in that language.[6] Juvenal was just as hostile to intellectual women when their sexuality was not impugned (*Satire* 6.434–56). Echoing Euripides' Hippolytus (*Hippolytus* 640), Juvenal "hated" the clever woman, even when she was engaged in the apparently harmless pursuits of philosophy, history, and grammar (*Satire* 6.451). As Juvenal's angry remarks make clear, however, women who lived during the Roman Empire had opportunities for intellectual achievement in many areas. Georgia Irby-Massie gives an account of women who excelled as scientists and philosophers.

As western society continually reformed itself along the traditionally heroic lines, women were repeatedly submerged within the dominating male ideologies. Throughout the historical length of western culture, female figures have been moulded into symbols of men's concerns. Hazel Barnes' discussion of the treatments of Iphigenia, the maiden sacrificed at Aulis, shows how writers from Euripides to the modern Greek filmmaker Cacoyannis have employed this heroine to represent a feminine quality valued by men, namely, self-sacrificing devotion. Standing out against this trend, the androgynous heroine of

Goethe's *Iphigenia in Tauris* combines women's traditional role of peacemaker with the chivalry associated with men.

At the time Goethe wrote, the issue of gender roles came under scrutiny, particularly in the study of the classical languages.[7] Before the nineteenth century, women were simultaneously barred from learning Greek and Latin and scorned for not knowing them. Samuel Johnson warned of the invasion of the Amazons, women who would invade the intellectual territories of males.[8] Entering a conversation swinging classical allusions like tire-irons, such women threatened the calm surface of men's superiority. Even when learned women were accepted, they were expected to retain their domestic virtues. Johnson praised the translator of Epictetus, Mrs. Carter, for making a pudding.[9]

In the eighteenth century, women began to read classical mythology from a consciously feminine perspective. In her novel *Persuasion*, Austen rewrites the *Odyssey* as a *Penelopeia* by focusing on the woman left behind and by giving the sea-captain a subordinate role in what should—classically speaking of course—have been his story.[10] In the past two centuries, the rules governing men's and women's behavior have changed. Women, who have entered the fields of classical learning, science, and politics, have also appropriated the roles of classical male heroes for their heroines.

Elizabeth Holtze's article about the Sirens, the seductive monsters of mythology, discusses the modulations of their song as the song is given words by male and female writers. Until this century, she argues, the imagined auditor—and victim—of the Sirens was male, but in the twentieth century, women writers have endowed the Sirens with new voices to be heard by women navigators. Shattered by the break-down of gender dynamics, the Greek myths have been hammered into new shapes for exciting, new voyages.

Just as individuals need to come to terms with the memories of childhood, so writers do not deny their literary past even when they reject its values.[11] Plunging into the depths of the classical tradition, women writers have found in the ancient stories a vitality that transcends the assumptions concerning gender and power that underlie the stories. To illustrate the continuum between the old and new worlds, I will conclude this section of the preface by pointing out the recent re-emergence of Medea, who, in antiquity, inspired writers most sympathetic to women—Euripides, Apollonius, and Ovid. After the close of classical antiquity, Medea has found defenders among intellectual women all too aware of men's resentment. In 1405, Christine de Pisan found in her the prototype of the female scientific pioneer; the eighteenth-century bluestocking Elizabeth Montagu playfully suggested Medea was another bluestocking slandered by men, jealous of her intellect.[12]

As a woman who sacrificed her children and had a career, Medea has something to say to women of our century. How the centuries have changed her, we learn from Fay Weldon, who, in *The Life and Loves of a She-Devil* (New York, 1983), gives the ancient story of Medea a new and optimistic twist.[13] The heroine of the story, Ruth, is abandoned by her husband Bobbo in favor of the beautiful Mary Fisher, a wealthy writer of popular romances. Like Jason, Bobbo is handsome and faithless; like Jason too, he resents his wife because he mistreats her. In angry self-justification, Bobbo packs to leave:

> "What about me?" asked Ruth, and the words sped out into the universe, to join myriad other "what about me"s uttered by myriad other women, abandoned that very day by their husbands. Women in Korea and Buenos Aires and Stockholm and Detroit and Dubai and Tashkent, but seldom in China, where it is a punishable offense. Sound waves do not die out. They travel forever and forever. All our sentences are immortal. Our useless bleatings circle the universe for all eternity. (46)

Real life and myth meet in the eternal cry of the abandoned wife transmitted through literature.

Until recently, a woman's career has been marriage, a successful career being marriage to a good man. Euripides' Medea clearly sets forth the plight of women, who must rest every hope on marriage (*Med.* 231–51). Her eloquence on the subject, however, is specious because, unlike most other women of antiquity, she has a career. As a witch, she is invited to Corinth because she can prevent earthquakes; in Athens, the king gives her a position as a fertility counselor. The plight of normal women is illustrated by the fate of the intelligent Charlotte Lucas of Austen's *Pride and Prejudice*. She found it necessary to marry stupid, boring, odious men because, as Medea says, "Not to take a master is even worse" (*Med.* 234). Charlotte marries Mr. Collins in the same spirit that a young woman with a college degree will work as a waitress. The modern young woman can hope for change, but Charlotte takes on a life sentence.

Medea, having beguiled the women of Corinth with her appeal to feminine solidarity, flies off to Athens and leaves them crushed with horror. Ruth, however, enriches the lives of women by starting an employment agency.[14]

> The women ... —and they emerged out of the suburbs on bus and train by the hundreds—were grateful, patient, responsible, and hardworking; and for the most part, after a little training by Ruth, regarded office work as simplicity itself; as should anyone who has dealt daily with the intricacy of sibling rivalry and the subtleties of marital accord, or discord. (122)

Medea's famous claim that it is easier to stand in the first row of battle than to bear one child finds a twentieth-century response.

At the end of the novel, Ruth achieves her goals: she avenges herself on her husband, she has money, power, and she is loved without loving in return. Bobbo, broken by misfortunes, watches her numbly.

> I cause him as much misery as he ever caused me, and more. I try not to, but somehow it is not a matter of male or female, after all; it never was: merely of power. I have all, and he has none. As I was, so he is now.
> (241)

She has attained a bleak form of happiness, almost as bleak as Medea's. Yet the contrast between Ruth and Medea shows how far we have come. Looking back we can see that the women of classical antiquity—the victims and monsters—form part of the dialectic of oppression that has universal human application. As Ruth comes to realize, the issue of power does not depend on gender.

When the novel opens, Ruth is only one of many discarded wives, but, like Medea, immensely powerful. Instinctively, she turns to witchcraft, burning her rival in effigy, but she gains only momentary satisfaction.

> I make puff pastry for the chicken vol-au-vents, and when I have finished circling out the dough with the brim of a wine-glass, making wafer rounds, I take the thin curved strips the cutter left behind and mould them into a shape much like the shape of Mary Fisher, and turn the oven high, high, and crisp the figure in it until such a stench fills the kitchen that even the fan cannot remove it. Good.
>
> I hope the tower burns and Mary Fisher with it, sending the smell of burning flesh over the waves. I would go and fire the place myself, but I don't drive. (10)

Weldon's allusion to the dreadful death of the princess in *Medea* exists in Ruth's fantasy; Medea's other form of revenge appears in Bobbo's guilty dreams:

> Children open up exquisite nerves and twang them daily, painfully. He wished they had never been born, even while he loved them. They stood between him and Mary Fisher and he had strange dreams in which they came to sorry ends. (20)

He may well be troubled by an unconscious memory of Euripides' play.

Instead of killing her children Ruth leaves them to sabotage her husband's affair. Their vile teenage habits fill Mary Fisher's palace with bad music, television, and dirt. Horrified, Mary sees

> Nicola's casual heel grinding crisps into the Persian rug, and Andy's spurting Coca-Cola from his mouth all over the whitewashed walls, as he accidentally sneezed.
> (74)

Mary Fisher soon feels that other inhabitants of her beautiful tower are devouring her living flesh (97). She eventually dies of cancer, the equivalent in modern fiction for Medea's poisoned robe.

Ruth pays the price for abandoning her children:

> I am a woman learning to be without her children. I am a snake shedding its skin. It makes no difference that the children are Nicola and Andy, that they lack charm. A child is a child: a mother, a moth. I twist and squirm with guilt and pain, even knowing that the quieter I stay the quicker I will heal, slip the old skin, and slither off renewed into the world.　　(77–78)

These words evoke Euripides' play, the contest in Medea's soul between love of her children and hatred of their father. Having triumphed over her maternal feelings, she hisses her hatred of Jason in sibilants as she stands in a chariot drawn by serpents. Yet Ruth, who feels herself turning into a snake, would not have killed her children. Rather than committing infanticide, she becomes a powerful advocate of birth control.

※

Joy King is as heroic as Medea, but her hallmarks are gentleness and concern for others. Like a skilled pilot, she has repeatedly steered her course through Clashing Rocks without swerving from the beacon of professional excellence. Unlike the heroes of old, she works through cooperation, rather than competitiveness. The successes that have crowned her efforts demonstrate the power of the "feminine" virtues.

Joy was my professor at the University of Colorado. She was very demanding of her students, yet she demanded infinitely more of herself. At the same time, she nurtured our spirits with encouragement, constructive criticism, and delight in the literature. We came away with a solid foundation of the texts and the scholarship, but her greatest gift was the sense of wonder and discovery that only the best teachers inspire in their students.

Joy's scholarship, like her teaching, is precise, imaginative, and elegant.

She has, moreover, integrated her scholarship with the major interests of her life. Her attraction to Propertius may well be founded on his rejection of war and on respect for women. In her more recent work, she has found a kindred spirit in Lucretius, who stressed the importance of personal friendship.

Joy is ever willing to fight hard for good causes. At the University of Colorado, where she was repeatedly honored for her services, she pioneered a course on Women in Antiquity and offered much needed support for Latin teachers in secondary schools. In the world outside, she has also found recognition. As President of the Classical Association of the Middle West and South in 1991–92, she orchestrated a huge cooperative movement to preserve at least one classics department about to fall under the axe. In those causes, as in others, her reason and diligence have made the world of classical scholarship a richer place. We offer her this volume of essays as a small thanks for the endless labors she has undertaken on behalf of men and women in the profession.

Mary DeForest

Notes

[1] Gerda Lerner, *The Creation of Patriarchy* (Oxford, 1986), 192–93, 201.

[2] Froma I. Zeitlin, "The Dynamics of Misogyny: Myth and Mythmaking in the *Oresteia*," *Arethusa*, 11 (1978), 149–84.

[3] "Sophistication vs. Chastity in Propertius' Latin Love Elegy," *Helios*, 4 (1976), 69–76; see also Sarah Pomeroy, *Goddesses, Whores, Wives, and Slaves* (New York, 1975), 170–76; Plato, *Republic* 5.454d–61e, *Laws* 7.804c–806c; cf. Plutarch, *Moralia* 145b–d, *Pompey* 55; Quintilian 1.1.6 recommended that women be educated, as did the Stoic philosopher, Musonius Rufus, frag. 4.

[4] Theophrastus, in Stobaeus 4.193; [Menander] 703 Koch, cited by Susan Guettel Cole, "Could Greek Women Read and Write?" in *Reflections of Women in Antiquity*, ed. Helene P. Foley (New York, 1981), 219–45.

[5] Juvenal, *Satire* 6.184–99, 434–56; see Amy Richlin, "Invective against Women in Roman Satire," *Arethusa*, 17 (1984), 67–80.

[6] Juvenal, *Satire* 6.191; cf. Martial, *Epigram* 10.68.

[7] See my "Eighteenth-Century Women and the Language of Power," *Classical and Modern Literature*, 12 (1992), 191–207.

[8] Samuel Johnson, *Adventurer*, No. 115, 11 Dec. 1753, quoted by Roger Londsdale, *Eighteenth-Century Women Poets: An Oxford Anthology* (Oxford,

1989), xxx.

[9] Boswell's *Journal of a Tour to the Hebrides with Samuel Johnson, LL.D*, ed. Frederick A. Pottle and Charles H. Bennett (New York, 1936), 118; Mrs. Thrale, *Thraliana: The Diary of Mrs. Hester Lynch Thrale (Later Mrs. Piozzi) 1776–1809*, ed. Katharine C. Balderston, 2d ed. (Oxford, 1951), vol. 1, 171–72.

[10] See my "Jane Austen and the Anti-Heroic Tradition," *Persuasions*, 10 (1988), 11–21. For the kindred idea that Austen's *Mansfield Park* is a retelling of *Lear*, see Margaret Kirkham, *Jane Austen, Feminism and Fiction* (New York, 1986), 112–16.

[11] Margaret Atwood said, "You can't study English literature without knowing something about the Bible, and Greek and Roman Mythology, and you have to know it because it comes up in so much literature that was written in English," in a 1983 interview, *Margaret Atwood: Vision and Forms* (Carbondale, 1988), 215.

[12] De Pisan is quoted by Diane Purkiss, "Women's Rewriting of Myth," in *The Feminist Companion to Mythology*, ed. Carolyne Larrington (London, 1992), 442; Elizabeth Montagu, in *Mrs. Montagu, "Queen of the Blues": Her Letters and Friendships from 1762 to 1800*, ed. Reginald Blunt (London, 1906), vol. 2, 68.

[13] Alan Wilde, "'Bold, but not too bold': Fay Weldon and the Limits of Poststructuralist Criticism," *Contemporary Literature*, 29 (1988), 413, points out the allusions in the novel to Mary Shelley's *Frankenstein* and to Hans Christian Andersen's *The Little Mermaid*.

[14] Cf. Wilde, who points out that Ruth improves the lot of almost everyone she encounters (ibid., 404).

Acknowledgments

This book has come about through the financial generosity of institutions and individuals listed in the *Tabula Gratulatoria*, through private subvention, and through the intellectual generosity of the contributors. Barbara Gold, Judith Hallett, Bella Zweig, and Elizabeth Holtze read the preface more than once and considerably strengthened it with their suggestions. On behalf of the publisher, Aaron Baker read the whole book carefully and eradicated many errors. I would also like to express my appreciation to Gilbert Lawall for printing the book.

I am especially grateful to Elizabeth Holtze, who took time off from her busy schedule to copy-edit the essays in this volume. Her careful attention to detail and her piercing questions improved the book and at the same time she gave me valuable instructions in the art of editing.

Tabula Gratulatoria

Gilbert Lawall
David Traill
William M. Calder, III
Marilyn Skinner
Ardith Tjossem
Kristin K. Tracy
Susan Pedersen
Mrs. Farrand Baker
Steven Ostrow
John W. Greppin
Edward V. George
Charles R. Beye
Daniel F. Margolies
Virginia Greenwald
James Ring
Catherine Boden
Daniel Jackson

Wayne State University
Miami University
Hamilton College
Knox College
Marquette University
Dean's Office, University of Colorado
University of Maryland, Department of Classics
University of Arizona

Abbreviations

Scholarship

CIL	*Corpus Inscriptionum Latinarum*
CJ	*Classical Journal*
CP	*Classical Philology*
CQ	*Classical Quarterly*
CR	*Classical Review*
CW	*Classical World*
FGrHist	F. Jacoby, *Fragmente der griechischen Historiker* (Berlin, 1923–)
TAPA	*Transactions and Proceedings of the American Philological Association*
RE	A. Pauly–G. Wissowa–W. Kroll, *Real-Encyclopädie der klassischen Altertumswissenschaft* (Stuttgart, 1884–)

Literature

Aen.	Vergil, *Aeneid*
Ag.	Aeschylus, *Agamemnon*
Apollodorus	Apollodorus, *Library*
Choe.	Aeschylus, *Choephori*
Del.	Callimachus, *Hymn to Delos*
Ecl.	Vergil, *Eclogues*
Eum.	Aeschylus, *Eumenides*
Hom. Hymn Ap.	*Homeric Hymn to Apollo*
Hom. Hymn Aph.	*Homeric Hymn to Aphrodite*
Hom. Hymn Dem.	*Homeric Hymn to Demeter*
Il.	Homer, *Iliad*
Met.	Ovid, *Metamorphoses*
Od.	Homer, *Odyssey*
Theog.	Hesiod, *Theogony*

Aspects of Androgyny in Classical Greece

It has long been known and frequently pointed out that ancient Greek civilization was strongly masculine in its orientation, and never more so than in the so-called Golden Age of fifth-century Athens. Pericles' *Funeral Oration*, as presented by Thucydides (2.45), which many have considered the noblest declaration of the best Greek values, concludes with the statement that women should not be talked about among men for good or evil. I do not intend to dispute the existence of this masculine bias. What I would like to suggest is that there persisted at the same time in Greek culture a substantial element of androgyny from their past; that the Greeks overrode this androgynous tradition in favor of a wholly masculine approach to reality; but that some few, such as Euripides, Plato, and Aristophanes, recognized and accepted the concept of androgyny and promoted its ideals, many of which are being rediscovered and evaluated today.[1]

The concept of androgyny has a long history and great breadth and complexity, and one who approaches the subject quickly finds that examples and meanings proliferate. One can easily trace a history of male-female interdependence of mind and body stretching all the way through Virginia Woolf, German and French Romanticism, medieval mysticism, first- and second-century neoplatonism, Christian and pre-Christian gnosticism to the Classical civilization itself and beyond; while a glance at the religion and philosophy of the Far East (Kundalini Yoga, Hindu and Buddhist Tantric rites and practices, Taoism, Tai-Chi) where bisexuality is too common even to summarize confirms the opinions of Marie Delcourt, Herman Baumann, Mircea Eliade, A. J. L. Busst, Carl Jung, and numerous others that androgyny is one of the most basic human concepts, figuring "prominently in almost every religion and mythology of practically every country and age."[2]

Moreover, androgyny is a concept of enormous breadth, running a gamut of meanings from the ultimate spiritual reality of the philosophers and mystics to the coarsest, most detailed, physical hermaphrodite reclining on its pedestal in the museum or decorating Pompeian walls of A.D. 79. Christ has been seen as androgynous, as has Adam before him, as have Eros and Priapus. Androgyny has meant everything from the brotherhood of man and the hope of the future to onanism, sadism, demonality, and, what A. J. L. Busst calls the consummate vice, cerebral lechery.[3] As Eliade remarks, "When the mind is no longer capable of perceiving the metaphysical significance of a symbol, it is understood at levels which become increasingly coarse."[4]

In our own time, Freud and Jung have restored a great measure of authority to androgyny by incorporating into psychological systems the androgynous element they believed exists, latent or overt, in each person. Freud made bisexuality central to his theory of psychoanalysis and felt that the unconscious rejection of sexual differentiation and the concomitant desire to recover the bisexuality of childhood was one of the most persistent causes of neurosis.[5] Jung also felt that awareness of the duality of human sexuality within the individual was central to psychological well-being. Androgyny for him was an archetype of the collective unconscious, and the human psyche itself androgynous; he lamented the split consciousness and polarity in the modern mind whereby we have lost a sense of wholeness.[6]

Yet, the concept of androgyny has seldom occupied center stage in the thinking of the West—an indication perhaps of the sexual disbalance of our culture as inherited from ancient Greece and Rome. Androgyny threatens patriarchy and a patriarchal god. But even when acknowledged, androgyny has not always been understood in its fullest sense. In spite of their emphasis on psychic bisexuality, Freud and Jung have been criticized by followers for perpetuating the stereotype of female inferiority; but these critics, in turn, often fail themselves to grasp the higher aspects of androgyny, which is raised to new and transcendent heights in some ancient myths and in such thinkers as Plato.[7]

I will distinguish the two-fold aspect of bisexuality by restricting the term "androgyny" to its abstract, spiritual and mythical qualities, while keeping "hermaphroditism" for the purely physical aspects. In practice, of course, the terms are often used loosely and interchangeably. Delcourt has described androgyny as an example of "pure myth," springing entirely from the mind and not from the existence of people with the attributes of both sexes (hermaphrodites).[8] Androgyny does not derive from the physical phenomena that mythology traditionally tries to explain, but is rather a concept that arises in and from the mind alone and owes nothing to the existence of any biological entity. Indeed, representations of male-females in antiquity, says Delcourt, are invariably mental, not physical, conceptions, and in Western civilization at least, usually arrive late, the product of a sensationalizing, decadent age. Whoever wants to behold an androgyne has already lost both the idea and the ideal. Nowhere, according to Delcourt, is the ambivalence of sacred things so striking as here: as physical entities, hermaphrodites were persecuted as abominations of god; as an abstraction, androgyny was an attribute of god and an ideal for humanity.[9]

Androgyny may be defined, then, as the state of being both male and female, or, conversely, of being *neither* male *nor* female—that is, transcending the distinctions of gender. The androgyne has within its single person the powers and potentialities of both sexes. The significance of this sexual blend differed in various ages and presentations, but in ancient Greece and Rome androgyny appeared primarily as an ideal condition which certain gods possessed and humans tried to attain. Its basic characteristics are perfection, immortality (or health and longevity in the case of mortals), wisdom, and creativity.

The Creation Myth

Androgyny is often present in creation myths, as the undifferentiated state of reality before creation begins through division into opposites. Sometimes this initial reality is represented impersonally as the simple material of the world—the "pre-chaos" of Hesiod,[10] the "formless waste" of Genesis; more often it is personified as two opposing principles, male and female, locked in eternal embrace—Earth and Sky, Tiamat and Apsu, Rangi and Pappa—and far removed from our world of changing phenomena. Creation begins when that matter or those principles separate into distinct deities; creation proceeds thenceforth by means of procreation. "Not mine the tale," says Euripides in his lost play *Melanippe*,

> ... but of my mother:
> How sky and earth were once one form,

> But once divided from each other
> Brought all things to light in birth—
> The trees and winged-things and beasts
> Of the sea, and the race of those who die.
>
> (Nauck, frag. 484)

Or again:

> When on high the heaven had not been named,
> Firm ground below had not been called by name,
> Naught but primordial Apsu, their begetter,
> [And] Mummu-Tiamat, she who bore them all,
> Their waters commingling as a single body ...
>
> (*Enuma Elish*, tablet 1; trans. Speiser)

This initial, cosmic androgyny represents, of course, far more than the mere totality of male and female; it represents the totality of all opposites, all elements, all creatures that male and female ever will bring forth into the world. Although any pair of opposites could represent this initial totality, the sexual pair is chosen through its anthropomorphic significance as best representing the fervid and fecund development of the world we see about us. Androgyny, therefore, in the creation myth represents wholeness, a synthesis of opposites, an unchanging immortality as opposed to the world that followed, incomplete and subject to change and death. Androgyny thus becomes a hallmark of greatness for god or mortal in myth and religion, just as its loss represents their fall.

There have been various explanations offered for this presumption of an initial, cosmic wholeness. For Jung it marks the human condition before evolution from unconsciousness to consciousness and reveals a primitive and largely unconscious state of mind: "a twilight where differences and contrasts were either barely separated or completely merged."[11] As consciousness increased, the blended opposites drew more sharply and irrevocably apart. And yet not irrevocably, according to Jung, for the concept of androgyny did not disappear with the arrival of consciousness and differentiation, but merely retreated again to the unconscious. Once restored to consciousness, it looks forward as well as backwards toward a new and creative *conjunctio oppositorum*—a return to the unity of the beginning, this time with consciousness and freedom. For Eliade, also, androgyny is "now-oriented" and reflects our dissatisfaction with a world of opposites and its contradictions as well as our desire to transcend these opposites and recover a lost paradise where contraries exist side by side without conflict. Our efforts to do this will lead us toward "metaphysical knowledge" of ultimate reality.[12]

The Androgyny of the Gods

The concept of androgyny envisioned in Greek and Near Eastern creation myths carried over to numerous divinities in Greece and Rome even after they were clearly identified in human worship as male or female. For there is, as Eliade remarks, "the traditional conception that one cannot be anything *par excellence* unless one is at the same time the opposite or, to be more precise, if one is not many other things at the same time."[13] Divinity, in other words, in implying perfection, implies also the possession of opposites.

The primary androgynous deity is Earth-Mother, for although the product of the initial separation in Greek creation and designated female from the start, her essential androgyny is inescapable, since Earth is the ultimate source, who needs no male consort to create. From this conception of her wholeness follows, in turn, that of her androgynous wisdom, and historically as well as mythically most, if not all, oracular sites and shrines were, at least in origin, those of Earth-Mother. Who else should know the future if not the one who has produced it all before and will again? In Hesiod's *Theogony*, her sagacity directs Cronus to overthrow Sky, Zeus to overthrow Cronus and the Titans, and the Olympians to make Zeus their king (*Theog.* 160–75, 468–91, 494, 626, 884).

The Greeks' historical development is reflected in the evolution of their mythology away from the androgynous ideal. Earth and her successors declined in prestige and power, whereas Zeus grew strong. In the end, Hera, as wife of Zeus, with her scant brood of children, is a mere shadow of her predecessor Earth. And yet even to Hera tradition accredits parthenogenic deliveries of Hephaestus (Hesiod, *Theog.* 927–29; *Hom. Hymn Aph.* 316–21), Ares (Ovid, *Fasti* 5.229–60), and

Typhon (*Hom. Hymn Aph.* 305ff; Stesichorus, frag. 62).[14] Since Earth is the traditional mother of Typhon (e.g., Hesiod, *Theog.* 820ff), Hera's assumption of Earth's roles—both in producing Typhon and in other myths that she nurtured the Lernean Hydra and Nemean lion (both creatures of Earth, *Theog.* 313–29)—indicates that she has the basic nature of Earth Mother.[15] The Greeks seem to have lost an understanding of androgyny because they accounted for Hera's parthenogenic deliveries of Ares and Hephaestus not by reference to her natural bisexuality as an earth-goddess (which might also explain the lameness of Hephaestus as son-lover), but by such silly inventions as her pique at the birth of Athena from Zeus's head (*Theog.* 927–29)—a motive impugned by Hephaestus' presence himself in some accounts at the birth of Athena (e.g., Apollodorus 1.3.6). Carl Kerényi, on the other hand, sees an element of bisexuality in Hera even in her marriage to her brother Zeus. "The love of a brother and sister couple," he says, "tends, more than normal love, to the restoration of a bisexual totality, which is presupposed by that powerful mutual attraction."[16] Certainly, as we shall observe again, incest is a prominent element of androgyny.

This androgynous fusion of male and female principles is found in Roman religion, with its uncertainty about the gender of certain vegetation and fertility deities. The formulae *sive deus sis, sive dea*, "whether you are god or goddess," and *sive mas, sive femina*, "whether male or female," were frequent in Roman ritual. Still other deities (again usually agricultural) seem to come in pairs and probably represent "later elaborations of a primordial androgynous divinity": Pomo and Pomona, Tellumon and Tellus, Faunus and Fauna, Liber and Libera, Cacus and Caca, Caeculus and Caecilia.[17] These couples are, in fact, always sterile, and represent not wedded couples but totalities.[18]

More startling—and apparently as surprising to the ancient Greek as to us—is the androgyny of Zeus, the epitome of Greek masculinity: god of sky, not earth; hunter, warrior, not agrarian; husband and father, not son-lover. The Greeks themselves were taxed to explain the numerous oddities of Zeus' long career that evince feminine characteristics. In particular his role as male-mother in the births of Athena, Zagreus and Dionysus struck them—as us—as not only unnatural, but absurd; and they gave what, even making allowance for the nature of myth, were scarcely satisfactory explanations. In time they allegorized these birth-legends for service to their mystery religions (of Orpheus, Demeter, and Dionysus), but the myths retained a crudity that strained belief. The very mechanics of axing open a divine head, begetting a heart on Semele, or nurturing an embryo in a thigh invited ridicule, as witness Lucian's account of when Poseidon, upon visiting Zeus, is refused admission on the grounds that Zeus has just given birth:

> "I see," says Poseidon, "Another birth *from* the head, as with Athena. What a fertile head."
> "On the contrary," says Hermes, "it was his thigh this time. He had Semele's baby there."
> "Incredible!" says Poseidon. "He conceives throughout his body, wherever he wants."
> (*Dialogi Deorum* 9)

Modern archaeologists have also proffered explanations of these birth legends, alleging such things as gender-confusion arising from historical arrogation by Zeus of various earth-mother shrines throughout the Greek peninsula (the *hieroi gamoi*). Some confusion of powers and prerogatives no doubt occurred in the shift from an agrarian mother to an Olympian male hierarch, but there is also evidence that some of these feminine characteristics and activities of Zeus bespeak an original and lingering bisexuality on his part from a past that lay outside the Classical Greek experience.

Frazer, for instance, was among the first to note the remarkable similarity between the Zagreus-Dionysus myth and the puberty rites of peoples across the world, in particular those of the Aranda tribes of Central Australia. He has been followed by Jane Harrison, Eliade, Géza Róheim, Joseph Campbell, and others.[19] The similarity is as follows. Among the Aranda, at the time of initiation, boy initiates are removed from the camp and from the women. Numerous rites and rituals are enacted over them for a period of days culminating in a scene where men, masked as animals and covered with the white down of birds (to represent gods) and whirling bull-roarers (the voice of god), attack and "kill" the initiates, who are then covered over or put to sleep and called dead. Later the boys are roused and told that, although they had indeed been killed by divine beings, one of those beings, the Great Spirit

Twanyirika, had reappeared and restored them to life. Thereafter followed circumcision and a roasting or smoking at the fire reminiscent of the treatment of the baby Achilles by Thetis or of Demophoön in the *Homeric Hymn to Demeter*.[20]

The masked monster-men with their whitened bodies and bull-roarers who "destroyed" the children correspond remarkably to the chalk-whitened Titans and their ρόμβοι who set upon the child Zagreus (Dionysus) and tore him to pieces. Equally significant is the fact that the youths were reborn through the agency of a male, not female, god, for in initiation rites the initiate is thought to re-enact the experience of the god himself—in this case the god's own death and resurrection—and so we have here a parallel not only to the death and rebirth of Zagreus-Dionysus from Zeus, but perhaps also to the devouring of Zeus himself (originally at least), together with his brothers and sisters, by their father Cronus, and their subsequent rebirth through him.

And the means (or "motherly-organ," as Joseph Campbell puts it[21]) by which Father Zeus gave birth to Zagreus-Dionysus, and which was apparently unknown to the Classical Greek, becomes clear now from the sequel to the Aranda initiation. For when the circumcision wound had healed—some weeks, months, or even years later—the initiate was offered a second operation, the painful subincision, which gave him the sexual organ of woman and her "magic" to cleanse and refresh her blood and to "make" children. Again, what man imitates symbolically, the god is believed to have achieved in fact, namely, in this case, a "vaginal fatherhood."

Margaret Mead comments on this custom, which she refers to as "womb-envy," as she found it in Pacific Island cultures:

> In the parts of New Guinea I have studied, it is men who envy women their feminine capacities. It is men who spend their ceremonial lives pretending that it was they who had borne the children, that they can "make men." Boys are taught to bleed their penises in imitation of girls' menstruation, which was seen as a salutary bleeding, getting rid of "bad blood."[22]

The relationship of the Greek myth to this rite seems confirmed. The role of the Titans—and in particular their use of the bull-roarer, one of the oldest religious symbols—suggests antiquity. Moreover, the Greeks' retention of the myth, despite their distaste, indicates that it was very old and very sacred.

In the *Bacchae* of Euripides, also, we observe the seer Teiresias' attempt to mitigate the crudeness of the tale for King Pentheus by rationalizing the bit about the "thigh" (*Bac.* 286–97). He suggests a confusion between the Greek word μηρός, "thigh," and ὅμηρος, "hostage," arguing that in reality Dionysus was born not of Zeus' "thigh," but rather, after being born of Semele, was hidden away on Olympus and a "hostage" made of *aither* given to Hera to abuse. It is not the first time that professional religion has been embarrassed by a crude, but sacred, revelation from its past, but in this case the "cleaning up" has removed the most sublime element of the myth, namely, the double-birth (i.e., death and resurrection) of Dionysus.[23] "A squeamish deist," Rosenmeyer rightly calls Teiresias;[24] and yet no doubt both Teiresias and Euripides knew, as we do, that the word "thigh" in the tale is a euphemism for "genitals." An Old Testament expression "to swear with the hand under one's thigh" means to swear by one's genitals, i.e., one's progeny.[25] And it can be no coincidence that Latin similarly uses the word *testis* to mean both "witness" and "testicle."

In these earthy tales, then, of Dionysus and Zagreus, Zeus assumed the power of woman to give birth, and his male and human followers in early times no doubt sought this same power in imitative rites of initiation.[26] And this subsumption of feminine powers continued to be, I believe, a basic trait of Zeus for later Greeks in myth and religion, as we see in the *Theogony*, where he successively appropriates the powers and prerogatives of Earth (procreation and prophecy), Styx (the apportionment of powers and the sanctioning of oaths), Hecate (material prosperity), and Metis (wisdom).[27]

The crudity of these attempts to give Zeus a woman's nature and functions might seem a far cry from that ideal of androgyny discussed at the beginning of this paper. And not surprisingly, anthropologists ask whether they evince a basically negative or positive attitude toward women: a desire to downgrade and supplant their role in society or a positive wish to imitate and share it. There could be, of course, a mix of motives: sympathy with women and envy. Certainly there is envy, but it is mutual; and those who call attention in these rites to man's jealousy of woman often overlook, as Eliade remarks, the complementary jealousy that ancient women displayed toward men—of their magic and lore, power to hunt and fight, understanding of religious mysteries (e.g., shamanism), and relations with the dead. Although less is known of female initiation rites, evidence shows that they paralleled in part at least those of men, using masculine symbols and rituals for similar ends. But the intent for both sexes, however crudely expressed, was essentially positive: to overcome the limits of their own sexual singularity and attain a more total mode of being.[28]

The birth of Athena from Zeus' head may also be interpreted along the lines of "womb-envy," as seen in the sub-incision rites above, for the head also, like the thigh, may symbolize the womb and hence fertility.[29] Campbell and others also see a parallel in this myth to the creation of Eve from Adam (Genesis 2.21–22), where in each instance there is the same inversion of nature—woman taken from man rather than man from woman—and doubtless the same "patriarchal inversion."[30] In each account there is latent androgyny.

> So God created man in his own image;
> in the image of God he created him;
> male and female he created them.
> 	(New English Bible)

This text of Genesis has long suggested for some both an androgynous Adam and God. The Biblical commentator Eusebius, for instance (*Praeparatio Evangelica* 12.12), believed that Plato had seen it and modeled his own myth of androgyny on it. Several Jewish Midrashim are even more explicit, telling of a literal sawing or splitting in half of a bisexual Adam. According to the *Bereshit rabba* (8.1), "Adam and Eve were made back to back, joined at the shoulders; then God divided them with an axe stroke, cutting them in two."[31] Maimonides (twelfth century) also recounts this legend.[32]

The axe occurs in the Greek story of Athena's birth, where Prometheus (Apollodorus 1.3.6; Euripides, *Ion* 458) or Hephaestus (Apollodorus 1.3.6; Pindar, *Olympian* 7.35–38) used a double-axe to open Zeus' head. The double-axe is a prominent symbol of bisexuality, carried traditionally by the bisexual Dionysus and a favorite weapon of the Amazons.[33] Prometheus, also, as trickster figure equates well both in nature and in role with the snake of Genesis. Hence the birth of Athena from Zeus and of Eve from Adam, according to Campbell, are one.[34]

And yet the androgyny of the Athena legend may not involve Athena so much as Metis, i.e., an original and bisexual Zeus-Metis, that divided into Zeus and Metis, whose daughter Athena was clearly a doublet of Metis, though now, of course, inferior to and subservient to the father Zeus. Metis, as wise daughter of the primal water-couple Oceanus and Tethys, is counterpart to Mummu, whose name, "Lord of Truth and Knowledge," refers similarly to wisdom and who was the son of the androgynous Mesopotamian water-couple, Apsu and Tiamat, mentioned earlier. Metis had the power to change shape, and did so unsuccessfully, we are told, to avoid mating with Zeus (Apollodorus 1.3.6), a fact that resembles the creation myth of the Hindu *Brihadaranyaka Upanishad* (1.4.1–5), wherein the initial Atman (World-Self) divides into male and female and the female-half, through dread of incest, changes into successive animal shapes to avoid mating with the male-half, again unsuccessfully. Dread of incest is several times cited for the reluctance of the female-half of the androgyne to mate with the male-half, a dread that could also lie behind the prohibition to Adam and Eve against experiencing the fruit of the Tree of Knowledge, which gave them awareness of sex,[35] and which may also be implicit in Demeter's changing shape on one occasion to avoid mating with her brother Poseidon. Incest is an inherent aspect of androgyny for no two creatures can possibly be more closely related than the divided androgyne. (Jung therefore derived the incest theme from the archetype of the Hermaphrodite.[36]) All of the creation myths we have mentioned here begin with androgyny: Earth and Sky, Apsu and Tiamat, Adam and Eve, and, conceivably now, Zeus and Metis.

The swallowing of the beloved, on the other hand, as Zeus swallows Metis (*Theog.* 899–900), may signify a creation or, as it were, recreation of androgyny (that is, a reunification of the divided androgyne), for the androgynous personality desires even more than other lovers the complete and lasting assimilation of the beloved.[37] Metis, swallowed, is still present and active in the belly of Zeus: they are both two and one. And certainly the wisdom and power that Zeus gains from that union (personified by the wise and warlike Athena) are, as we have seen, among the primary fruits of androgyny.

In Orphic cosmology (Kern, *Orphic Fragments* 72–86) Metis is clearly bisexual, for the offspring of the androgynous (masculofeminine) egg that appears out of Chaos is Phanes, who is not only bisexual (frags. 76, 80, 81), but known, among other names, as Metis—a creature who is said to bear within herself "the renowned seeds of the gods" (frag. 85), that is, all creation. Metis resembles Earth here, as she does also in Apollodorus 1.2.1, where, as Farnell notes,[38] she plays Earth's role of aiding Zeus against Cronus. Zeus subsequently swallowed her (under the name Erekepaius), thus reconciling Orphic with Olympian theogony by giving creation a second beginning under the now all-encompassing person of Zeus: "all that existed then or would exist thereafter was there, co-mingled in the belly of Zeus" (frag. 167).[39] Thus Zeus replaces Earth (Metis) in Orphic cosmology as the matter of creation. Whatever the original relationship between Zeus and Metis, it is clear that they ultimately became one, and that in philosophical-religious myths, as elsewhere, Zeus' power and person were enlarged to encompass both sexes, with cosmological import. In the Orphic hymn quoted in the *De Mundo* attributed to Aristotle (Kern, frags. 21a, 168) we are told, Ζεὺς ἄρσην γένετο, Ζεὺς ἄμβροτος ἔπλετο νύμφη, "Zeus was born male, Zeus was the immortal bride." And in the poet Valerius Saranus, quoted by Augustine (*De Civitate Dei* 7.1; Kern, frag. 21a), Jupiter is *progenitor genetrixque deum*, "father and mother of the gods." Therefore Zeus' bisexual nature is affirmed from many sources.

There was a Zeus Labrandeus, worshipped, says Herodotus (5.119), only in Caria at Labranda, whose statues appeared beardless, with necklaces and multiple breasts. The Greeks called this god Zeus Stratios, and, to Plutarch's surprise (*Quaestiones Graecae* 301f–302a), the god was shown carrying the double-axe and not the scepter and thunderbolt (the axe, according to Plutarch, being the one taken from the Amazon Hippolyte by Heracles and later given to Zeus by the Lydian Gyges). The bisexuality of this Zeus is not accepted by all authorities, for multiple breasts, according to W. Deonna, may be a symbol of power only and not of bisexuality.[40] But the two ideas are not contradictory, for power is of the essence of bisexuality. At Rome the herm of Jupiter Terminalis possessed the symbols of both sexes.[41] Further evidence of Zeus' sexually ambivalent nature is his pederasty with the boy Ganymede and his assumption of women's clothing for the seduction (or rape?) of the nymph Callisto, and, according to a reference in Lactantius,[42] in his affair with the Amazon Antiope. Both of these activities—homosexuality and transvestism—in a mythic context, signal bisexuality.[43]

Lesser gods follow Zeus in lesser ways and evidence of divine bisexuality is scattered throughout Greek and Roman myth and cult: Priapus (becoming more and more closely identified with Hermaphroditus); Eros (always bisexual); and, of course, Dionysus. Some of these gods will be discussed below in treating human bisexuality.

The Androgyny of Mortals

The cosmos began in androgyny and not surprisingly humanity, the microcosm, sees its own initial state, like that of the universe, as androgynous, with similar perfections, and equates its present unhappiness and mortality with the loss of androgyny. The fall of man, says Berdyaev, is the fall of the androgyne.[44] Hence the longing for completeness described by Plato, Augustine, Jung, and so many others. In particular, the fall of man is equated with the advent of sexuality, and sexuality, in turn, is linked with death.[45]

Although this androgynous origin for humanity is explicit in many creation myths,[46] in male-oriented societies, such as the ancient Greek and Judaeo-Christian, humanity's fall from grace was at times restructured to result not from the division of the initial androgyne into male and female, but from the separate creation of woman *from* or *for* man, thus putting upon her the responsibility for human unhappiness and at the same time assuring her an inferior status in society. Instead of an androgynous deity creating human beings in its own image, male and female, the new, wholly masculine god drew woman from man, as Eve was drawn from Adam, and Athena from Zeus, thus reversing both nature and myth. But although belief in humanity's initial androgyny is obscured in Hesiod (as in Genesis), evidence for it there remains. The human condition before Prometheus tricked Zeus into taking the fat and the bones at the sacrifice seems to have been in essence androgynous, for it resembles a typical pre-fall setting in its close association between gods and men (ὥς τε θεοὶ ἔζωον, "they lived like gods," *Works and Days* 112), such as we find also in Genesis before the Fall; and death at least as an evil, rather than a desired transition to a better state was unknown: even work, sorrow, and old age were absent. Thus the "celibacy" (ἀγαθόν, "a good") of the *Theogony* (602) refers in all likelihood not just to an ideal condition, but to the natural human condition in a Golden Age where women did not exist. This condition is in contrast to the celibacy of the subsequent age of sexuality (*Theog.* 602–7) that is associated with women and leaves the celibate to face a childless old age, wretched and uncared for. Moreover, the trickster Prometheus and his trial of food parallel the snake and apple of Genesis and since the result for humanity in each myth is the same—namely, sexuality and death—it appears that the two accounts are close in kind, with an androgynous origin for humanity presumed by each.[47]

All of this is obscured in Hesiod; but elsewhere evidence for early Greek belief in the androgynous origin of humanity is more explicit, one such evidence being found in an element of ancient puberty rites known as "ritual androgynization."

For many early peoples, the non-initiates (i.e., the young) are considered asexual, and admission to sexuality is a major intent of puberty rites, often ignored by researchers, but underscored by the fact that such rites almost invariably include sexual instruction and conclude in marriage—marriage and the assumption of a clearly defined role in society being a culminating goal of initiation. In line, however, with the ancient belief that no qualitative advance in life can be made without a return to the beginning (i.e., death and rebirth), the initiate must first be taken back and made aware of the *totality* of sexuality that existed for him or her in the beginning (i.e., androgyny) before being introduced to his or her new and differentiated sexual role to come in the community, as male or female. As Eliade remarks:

> For mythical thought, a particular mode of being is necessarily preceded by a *total* [his italics] mode of being. The androgyne is considered superior to the two sexes just because it incarnates totality and hence

> perfection. For this reason we are justified in interpreting the ritual transformation of novices into women—whether by assuming women's dress or by subincision—as the desire to recover a primordial situation of totality and perfection.[48]

(Female initiates would of course assume the guise of boys.) There is, in other words, as occurs so often in initiation rites, a re-enactment of the creation scene, where the sexes were at first united, then separated from an original whole.

There were numerous rites among the ancients to bring about this androgynization, the most extreme for males being sub-incision, as practiced in Australia and Pacific Island cultures, but with evidence for it as we have seen in Greek myths also. Other, more common forms, were transvestism (boys dressed as young women, young women as boys), ritual nudity or the wearing of white (a neutral color), eating white food, and homosexuality (when tied to initiatory rites).[49] There is evidence that the ancient Greeks knew and practiced most of these forms, but for transvestism in particular there seems abundant proof, for they practiced it not only as part of puberty rites but also in connection with the great civil and religious κῶμοι and ὄργια celebrated by entire cities, both of which festivities evince through mutual exchange of clothing by men and women an androgynous blurring of roles and values in order to effect community cleansing and regeneration. From this reversal of human behavior, this temporary regression to creation, the citizen returned to his or her individual role in society invigorated because psychologically, and even physically in a sense, reborn.[50]

Thus at the celebration of the *Hybristika* at Argos (the name of which suggests a riotous, Mardi-Gras type of carnival) women and men exchanged dress; and the κῶμος, like the ὄργια, was a regular feature of the feasts of Dionysus during which men dressed and played the role of women and vice versa. Likewise intersexual disguise and role-changing seem to have been a part of the Laconian feasts to Artemis, an original earth-mother and thus androgynous deity, and of the Eleusinian Mysteries also.

The *Hybristika* illustrate how such ritual androgynization in the form of transvestism persisted long after its significance was lost, for

Plutarch, in order to explain the intersexual exchange of dress, relates the festival to the annual celebration of the victory of Telesilla and the Argive women over the Spartan forces of Cleomenes in the war of 494 B.C. (*Mulierum Virtutes* 245d–f). Aside from the doubtful historicity of this victory (Herodotus, in a detailed account of the war [6.76–82], makes no mention of it), it certainly had no connection, at least originally, with the *Hybristika*, for it fails to explain both the name of the festival ("Feast of Wantonness or Impudence") and the fact that *men* exchanged clothing as well as women. In fact, as both the name and the transvestism suggest, the *Hybristika* were a typical carnival of recreation and renewal, characterized by coarse humor and the temporary reversal of social roles typical of such festivals; and it is far more likely that the victory of Telesilla was invented to explain the transvestism than that the transvestism was instituted to honor her. So tenuous, in fact, is the connection between the two events, even for Plutarch, that he cites an alternative date for the commemoration of Telesilla besides the *Hybristika*.

On the individual level, at weddings on the island of Cos, according to Plutarch (*Quaestiones Graecae* 304c–e), the husband donned women's dress to receive his wife. Plutarch connects this custom to a time when Heracles hid out at Cos in women's clothing and then married his benefactress there while wearing a robe embroidered with flowers. Because of this, he explains, Heracles' priests at Cos always wore feminine clothes while sacrificing. But the traditionally virile Heracles also wore feminine dress while serving the Lydian Queen Omphale, daughter of Iardanes, an action which is usually construed to have been part of his punishment (Ovid, *Heroides* 9.55–118, *Fasti* 2.305–58; Lucian, *Dialogi Deorum* 13.2). But how to explain that Omphale also wore the clothing of Heracles? Ovid gives no reason in the *Heroides* (9.55–118), where he relates this myth, but in the *Fasti* he suggests one that is significant:

> sic epulis functi sic dant sua corpora somno,
>   et positis iuxta secubuere toris;
> causa, repertori vitis quia sacra parabant
>   quae facerent pure, cum foret orta dies.
>
>   (*Fasti* 2.327–30)

> Thus [in each other's dress] they dined and thus gave
> their bodies to sleep, and they lay apart from each other
> on the beds made up close by; the reason was because
> they were preparing for the inventor of the vine rites,
> which they would perform properly when day broke.

Ritual continency and transvestism in honor of the bisexual Dionysus! A plausible reason. But the transvestism, as shown above, is equally and perhaps more naturally suggestive of initiatory rites preparatory to marriage; and Diodorus Siculus (4.31.5–8) relates that Omphale and Heracles did, in fact, marry, and that she bore him a son (attested to also by Ovid, *Heroides* 9.53–54). Heracles' experience with Omphale then parallels his transvestism and marriage at Cos, as well as that of the traditional initiatory pattern discussed above.[51]

There may be further significance in this transvestism in the fact that the occasion for Heracles' service to Omphale was his need to rid himself of a debilitating disease brought on by his murder of Iphitus, son of Eurytus (Apollodorus 2.6.2–3; Diodorus Siculus 4.31.4–8). This service was ordered by the oracle of Delphi. Aside from the obvious connection between the worship of the "omphalos" at Delphi and the name "Omphale" (an Amazon name as well), we remember that one of the positive effects of androgyny for mortals is health and longevity (the human equivalent of immortality for the gods); and it is plausible, therefore, that the transvestism of Heracles in this instance was part of the purification rite itself, which incorporated androgyny as an aid to ridding him of his disease. At Rome, it is known that Heracles—under the title of "Hercules Victor"—was venerated as a "Health-Giver," and his image shown as a phallic being in women's clothes.[52] Health and marriage—or rather health *in* marriage—as we will see below, are not unrelated concerns. Therefore, the suggestion of later writers that Heracles' transvestism in his association with Omphale was designed to humiliate him is, in all likelihood, the reverse of its true, beneficent purpose, and a further instance of ancient misunderstanding of ritual androgynization.

We see, then, evidence throughout his career that the super-virility of Heracles, humanity's greatest mythical hero, was androgynous in character and not merely masculine, and had an androgynous, not simply masculine, origin. And in this he reflects, as in so many other respects, the androgyny of his father Zeus.

At Sparta the young bride's head was shaved and she was dressed in men's clothing and laid on a bed in darkness to await her husband's secret visit (Plutarch, *Lycurgus* 15); at Argos the bride wore a false beard for the wedding night (Plutarch, *Mulierum Virtutes* 245f). Once again Plutarch fails to explain customs he no longer understood. The Argive women, he says, were forced to wear the false beard as punishment for sexually slighting the new and socially inferior husbands they received after the loss of their own Argive husbands in the war with Sparta. This non sequitur explains nothing, of course, of what was in reality a traditional wedding ritual of androgynization, and the Spartan and Argive rituals recall rather the bearded and ithyphallic Aphrodite of Cyprus (called "Aphroditus"), whose worshippers wore clothing of the opposite sex, and the bald and bisexual Venus at Rome, guardian of marriage and birth.[53]

Young women of Crete slept on their wedding eve by the image of the bisexual Leucippe, the young maiden who legend said was raised secretly as a boy because of her father's distaste for daughters and later changed into a boy by the goddess Leto (Antoninus Liberalis, *Metamorphoseon Synagoge* 414). Since, as Delcourt notes, this tale purports to explain the Cretan festival *Ekdysia* (i.e., "The Divestment"), it is probable that at this feast boy-initiates wearing feminine clothes discarded them in favor of those of their own sex on being inducted into manhood. "The feminine principle in the candidate," says Jeanmaire, "is affirmed in the initiation at the very moment when he is about to cast it aside."[54]

Legend

The accounts of Heracles above show that ritual androgynization persisted in Greek legend as well as in Greek religion. Since it has long been generally accepted that the lives and exploits of Greek heroes proceed in part along the lines of initiation rites—that is, are elaborations of or heroic exaggerations of original rites of passage from boyhood to manhood—we might expect an element of androgyny to surface, and it is noticeable that a number of the greatest heroes appear at one time or another in feminine dress.[55] Achilles is a typical instance.

After instruction in the mountains by centaurs (tribal monster-men?) and a "roasting at the fire" by his mother Thetis, we find him at puberty at the court of King Lycomedes of Scyros in the dress of a young woman. He is nicknamed Pyrrha; marries Deidamia, one of Lycomedes' daughters (who bears him a son); is given a man's shield and spear; and goes off to fight at Troy. Told in this way, we have a traditional Greek rite of passage, incorporating instruction, purification, and ritual androgynization, and culminating in marriage and soldiery—nothing unusual. The unusual enters when later writers, such as Hyginus, Bion, and the author of the *Cyprian Lays*, no longer understand, hence disapprove of, the element of transvestism in the story and invent more "plausible" reasons for it: Thetis' attempt to forestall Achilles' destiny and Odysseus' ingenious ruse to thwart her. Transvestism here, then, comes to be interpreted exactly opposite its original intent: from a rite directed at *becoming* a man it becomes a ruse to *escape* manhood.

A similar misinterpretation is given an incident in the life of Athens' hero Theseus, as told by Pausanias (1.19.1). On reaching puberty, and after recovering from under a rock the sword and sandals of his father and performing heroic exploits along the road from Troezen to Athens, Theseus was jeered at upon entering Athens, we are told, by men working on the roof of the Delphinium, who called him παρθένος ἐν ὥρᾳ γάμου, "a maiden ripe for marriage," because of his braided hair and foot-length tunic. Whereon he unyoked his oxen and hurled them above the roof of the temple to prove the workmen wrong. Frazer, in his commentary on this passage, refers to "braided hair" as an old Attic custom for young men, as perhaps it was. But in two other instances where Pausanias mentions braided hair, it relates to virgins ready for marriage, one instance in fact narrating the Arcadian legend of Daphne, wherein Leucippus, son of Oenomaus, loved Daphne and gained her friendship by disguising himself as a young woman, "braiding his hair like a girl and wearing women's clothes" (8.20.3). Braided hair, then, seems to signify not simply maidenhood but eligibility and readiness for marriage, and its appearance on young men, along with transvestism, suggests once again a rite of androgynization preparatory to marriage, regardless of how later writers, ancient or modern, construe or misconstrue it. The legend of Leucippus, of course, recalls the tale of the bisexual Leucippe mentioned above, of which it seems a kind of inversion.

Therefore, since all of the previous incidents in the story of Theseus—the receipt of the paternal sword and sandals, the journey and heroic exploits along the road to Athens—are clearly initiatory in nature, we should expect Theseus upon reaching Athens to assume the feminine garb and marry a young woman of his father's choosing, as no doubt he did. But the business of transvestism proved an embarrassment in time and was omitted by Plutarch and misconstrued by Pausanias. Theseus, of course, had other adventures and marriages to attend to, adventures also initiatory in nature, such as the ritualistic descent into the sea to meet his father, the heroic test of the labyrinth and its monster, and the carrying off of Ariadne (the last of which again involves transvestism). We note finally that the Athenian celebration of the Oschophoria, said to be in honor of Theseus' safe return from Crete, featured a race of naked adolescents and a procession led by two boys dressed in women's clothing, who carried a vine-stock laden with grapes, the ὤσχη. Since, as Delcourt remarks, the ὤσχη, whence the event got its name, is a common phallic symbol in Greek art and homonymous to the term ὄσχη, its appearance in the hands of youths dressed up as young women adds up to a prominent bisexuality.[56]

Within the myths of Achilles and Theseus, the persistence of these incidents of transvestism, slight as they are, suggests that they were so imbedded that they had somehow to be explained when they were no longer understood. Along with the parallel adventures of other Greek heroes, they show a pattern of heroic action, sexual disguise, and marriage that suggests ancient rites of passage incorporating ritual or symbolic androgynization. And the purpose of this androgynization was always to promote a positive and lasting benefit on the individual, with each sex taking something of the powers of the other, in particular, health, longevity, and fertility.

Significant as well is the fact that the heroes we can associate with transvestism are those also associated prominently with Amazons: Achilles with Penthesilea; Heracles with Hippolyte (or Melanippe); Theseus with Antiope (or Hippolyte). We can add also, as having Amazon names at least, Omphale, the Lydian Queen whom Heracles served, and Deidamia, Achilles' wife at Scyros—if these women are not in fact Amazons (Scyros, for instance, the island where Achilles wed Deidamia, being early connected with a cult of Ares and his Amazon daughters). Zeus too, as noted above, wore feminine clothing when he deceived the Amazon Antiope; and Dionysus, a favorite god of the Amazons, was linked to them both by transvestism and by a common preference for the double-axe, symbol of bisexuality. We are tempted to see, then, in these examples further androgynous pairings: the man in feminine clothes, the woman in masculine. But on inspection the details appear extreme and unpleasant. The women wear men's armor, not clothing; are masculine in nature; and cruel to children and men; the heroes seek not to marry the women, but to kill or abandon them. Whatever the origin of the Amazons—and many are suggested—their greatest significance seems to lie in the Greek mind, and it is difficult, I think, not to see in the Greek hero in his connection with Amazons something of that extreme of masculinity that Philip Slater attributes to Heracles and other Greek heroes in his book, *The Glory of Hera* ("exaggerated masculine differentiation, with emphasis on secondary rather than primary characteristics"[57]) and to suspect that the race of Amazons was created largely out of a deep-rooted phobia toward women by Greek males. If this is true, then, the Amazon-hero relationship in Greek myth is a perversion and mockery of the original significance of ritual androgynization.

Two myths of bisexuality in antiquity illustrate well the contrasting significance bisexuality may assume. The cult of the god Hermaphroditus appeared late in Greek history, possibly entering Greece through Athens by way of Cyprian merchants during the Peloponnesian War, although others think its origin native.[58] But while the god's geographical origin is obscure, the association of Hermes and Aphrodite in temples, altars, and on coins was widespread in antiquity, making it plausible that the concept of a single god called Hermaphroditus may have arisen from joint worship of these two deities as protectors of sexual union. Plutarch in fact (*Coniugalia praecepta* 138c–d) confirms how the ancients placed images of Aphrodite and Hermes alongside each other to promote a good marriage.[59] He commends in this practice the "rational" (λόγος) powers of Hermes as important to marriage; but the presence of Aphrodite nearby suggests, as Delcourt notes, that Hermes was honored because of his role as fertility god. Certainly the combined sexuality of this pair would contribute a powerful and welcome impetus to any marriage and the fact that their alleged offspring, Hermaphroditus, was, at least originally, sexually potent is borne out by his gradual association and even confusion with the god Priapus.

Striking, then, is the god's evolution at the hands of the poets, who enlarged the erotic element and dissipated his powers until there was left typically only an effeminate youth, more asexual than bisexual. The process culminates in Ovid (*Met.* 4.285–388), who portrays a naive and youthful Hermaphroditus, lured to the pool of Salmacis and rendered therein not the empowered double-creature of his name, but a *semivir*, "half-man," *mollitaque in illis/ membra*, "his limbs softened in it" (381–82). Small wonder the young man cursed the pool that destroyed him. Here, then, in Ovid's account, is a proclamation of everything that androgyny is not.

The myth of Teiresias, on the other hand, shows an opposing and more profound vision of androgyny, although again with distortion and confusion of detail. His blindness, wisdom (as symbolized by the gift of prophecy), and long life are connected only accidentally to his androgynous experience with the snakes (one of the great symbols of androgyny in myth[60]). Instead, these androgynous qualities are attributed to the anger of Hera and the compensatory pity of Zeus at the time of their quarrel over whether the male or female has the greater pleasure in sex (e.g., Hyginus, *Fabulae* 75; Apollodorus 3.6.7; Antoninus Liberalis, *Metamorphoseon synagoge* 17.5). In fact, Teiresias' wisdom and longevity are the direct result of his androgyny; and his judging the quarrel of Hera and Zeus merely shows in a charming way the clear superiority of the androgyne to even the greatest gods (as pictured here), who know only half of an elemental fact of existence—sexuality.[61]

Luc Brisson has further argued that two variant and seemingly disparate myths of Teiresias—those of his blinding for seeing Athena bathing (Callimachus, *Hymn* 5.75ff; Apollodorus 3.6.7) and a longer narrative wherein he undergoes seven sexual metamorphoses to end up a mouse (Eustathius, *Commentary on the Odyssey* 10.494)—in fact parallel and reinforce the androgynous theme of the first.[62] Teiresias, like Zeus and Apollo before him, is the serpent-killer, who attacks the serpent guardians of the secrets of Earth (represented in the myths by

Hera, Athena, and Aphrodite [in Eustathius' version]), seeking to wrest from her her androgynous wisdom. He succeeds and becomes himself the androgynous intermediary of opposites: heaven and earth, god and mortal, male and female, past and future, the living and the dead. In this myth we return to the fullness of the creation myth.

Conclusion

By the fifth century B.C. a masculine-oriented Greek civilization had become sufficiently unbalanced, I believe, for some thinkers—Euripides, Aristophanes, Plato—to see the need for a kind of androgynous restoration of balance. Repeatedly in his plays Euripides attacks the extreme masculinity of Greek society through his sophistic portrayal of their traditional heroes; and contrary to the charge of misogyny with which antiquity assailed him, laments better than any other writer of his time the lot and treatment of women. In play after play, according to Philip Vellacott, he draws "a clear picture of male cruelty and contempt as a constant factor in the fate of women";[63] and this inhumanity of man towards woman ranks for him (along with the inhumanity of war) as one of the two great moral evils of his age. His feeling towards women's treatment, Vellacott suggests, approaches guilt; but Vellacott correctly eschews the title of "feminist" for Euripides, stressing instead a more profound neutrality towards the sexes: "He was a man who felt himself a member of the whole human race rather than of one half of it."[64] He was, in short, of the androgynous temper.

Certainly his last play, *The Bacchae*, is, among other things, an androgynous statement, centering as it does on the most androgynous deity of all[65] and dramatizing the destructiveness of both the traditional, one-sided, rationality of man, as represented by Pentheus, and the equally one-sided, instinctive and irrational behavior of woman, represented by Agave and the maddened women of Thebes. Meanwhile, in the midst of that destruction, undisturbed, is the ever-smiling, androgynous personality of Dionysus: aggressive and passive, tender and harsh, rational and intuitive, creative and destructive, natural yet refined: "the unlimited personality," Rosenmeyer calls him, and continues, "To follow him or to comprehend him we must ourselves give up our precariously controlled, socially desirable sexual limitations."[66]

Θηλύμορφος, "women-shaped," Pentheus calls Dionysus (*Bac.* 353); and in the end he adopts the bisexuality of the god, but too late and for his destruction, not salvation. "The man," says Rosenmeyer, "has been found out, in the god's image."[67]

Plato also, I believe, attempted a similar rebalancing of Greek society in his *Republic*, where men and women at the highest levels share education, power, and roles. While aware that the higher status he assigned women was more for civic goals than out of sympathy for their plight, Sarah Pomeroy nonetheless characterizes Plato's provisions for the female guardians of his ideal state as "remarkable," and says that his "critique of marriage and the nuclear family, coupled with his provisions for an androgynous life style accessible through equal education and state-supported child care, foreshadows the ideas of modern radical feminists such as Shulamith Firestone and Simone de Beauvoir."[68] Even his *Laws*, written toward the end of his life and notably less utopian than the *Republic*, offers a vastly superior private and public role to women than that of their real world. Certainly his *Symposium* represents the greatest statement on androgyny of all, as speech and action progress above and beyond the physical, psychological, and individualized androgyny of Aristophanes' myth toward the intellectual, spiritual, and universal androgyny of Socrates and Diotima, leaving us with the unforgettable picture of those two conversing together—eternally, it seems—both splendidly whole and complete in themselves, fully equal and at ease with each other. The guide toward this perfection is the daimon Eros, itself an androgynous synthesis of opposites, directing lovers beyond the contradictions of flesh towards wholeness and immortality.

The myth of the androgyne in the *Symposium* was put by Plato in the mouth of Aristophanes, three of whose surviving plays—*Lysistrata, Thesmophoriazusae, Ecclesiazusae*—treat at length the androgynous interdependence of men and women. Elements of transvestism, male effeminacy, and female masculinity in these plays, plus parodies in the *Birds, Frogs,* and *Clouds,* of the Orphic creation myth of the bisexual Phanes, and a general and keen awareness throughout his works of the lowered position of women in Athens, reveal in Aristophanes a spirit kindred to both Plato and Euripides in recognizing the disbalance between the sexes and in proclaiming the androgynous mind.[69]

Androgyny is never far below the surface of the human mind and never more so than in a society that forces men and women to live by rigid and artificial stereotypes of masculine and feminine behavior, with sharply defined boundaries. Such a society was ancient Greece, particularly during its so-called "golden age." Nonetheless, there persisted throughout its masculine tradition another tradition that pointed to androgyny as the way of salvation and suggested (what modern psychology now teaches) an ideal wherein woman is not the cause of humanity's unhappiness so much as one-half of its cure.

Ernest J. Ament
Wayne State University

Notes

This paper is an elaboration of a talk given in December, 1977, to the Women's Classical Caucus at the Convention of the American Philological Association in Atlanta, Georgia. Translations, unless otherwise attributed, are my own.

[1] Carolyn Heilbrun, *Toward a Recognition of Androgyny* (New York, 1973); June Singer, *Androgyny: Toward a New Theory of Sexuality* (New York, 1976). A negative and, to my mind, unduly pessimistic view is that of Robert May, *Sex and Fantasy: Patterns of Male and Female Development* (New York, 1980), who criticizes the purely psychological approach commonly taken toward androgyny that minimizes the importance of the body and its genetic traits.

[2] Quotation from A. J. L. Busst, "The Image of the Androgyne in the Nineteenth Century," *Romantic Mythologies*, ed. Ian Fletcher (London, 1967), 4. Basic works covering androgyny in Classical cultures are Marie Delcourt, *Hermaphrodite: Myths and Rites of the Bisexual Figure in Classical Antiquity* (London 1961), from whom many examples in this text are taken; Hermann Baumann, *Das Doppelte Geschlecht* (Berlin, 1955), which covers non-Classical cultures also; and Mircea Eliade, *Mephistopheles and the Androgyne* (New York, 1965), chap. 2, and *Birth and Rebirth* (New York, 1958).

[3] Busst, "The Image of the Androgyne," 38–49.

[4] Eliade, *Mephistopheles and the Androgyne*, 100.

[5] For a discussion of Freud's understanding of bisexuality see Robert J. Stoller, "Facts and Fancies: An Examination of Freud's Concept of Bisexuality," in *Women and Analysis: Dialogues on Psychoanalytic Views of Femininity*, ed. Jean Strouse (New York, 1974), 343–64. For Freud's view that sexual

differentiation leads to neurosis, see Norman O. Brown, *Life Against Death* (Middletown, 1959), 131–34.

[6] Jung's views on androgyny (often given under the term "hermaphrodite") are widespread throughout his writings; for example, *Psychology and Alchemy*, in *Collected Works* 12 (Princeton, 1968), passim. For a summation and critique of his views, see Singer, *Androgyny*, 40–54.

[7] Margaret Mead, "On Freud's View of Female Psychology," in *Women and Analysis*, ed. Strouse, 96–98, criticizes Freud's concept that "ideally every child should be a boy," but herself misconstrues, in my opinion, aboriginal androgyny among males as mere envy of women, with no higher transformative purpose. Singer criticizes Jung's masculine bias (*Androgyny*, 47–50), but her own definition of androgyny, "the shifting back and forth from the constellated opposites" (277), resembles a type of alternating current more than a profound synthesis of opposites.

[8] Delcourt, *Hermaphrodite*, xi–xiii and 43–46.

[9] Delcourt, *Hermaphrodite*, 43–46 includes examples of and sources for the ancient punishment of hermaphroditism.

[10] I understand the word Χάος in the *Theogony* (116) to mean "separation," or "the principle of separation," and not, as is usually understood, the material flux itself that was separated. Both the etymology of the word and a comparison with similar creation myths seem to me to support this interpretation.

[11] Carl Jung, *The Archetypes and the Collective Unconscious*, in *Collected Works*, 9, Part 1, 2d ed. (Princeton, 1968), 173.

[12] Eliade, *Mephistopheles and the Androgyne*, 95–97, 122–24.

[13] Ibid., 110.

[14] For Hera and Typhon, see the essay of Joan O'Brien in this volume.

[15] Lewis R. Farnell, *The Cults of the Greek States*, vol. 1 (Oxford, 1896), 183–94, while admitting the direction of this and other evidence, nonetheless rejects the conclusion, citing Hera's unprolific marriage, her lack of oracular powers, and her lack of association with the underworld as being uncharacteristic of Earth, as they certainly are.

[16] Carl Kerényi, *Zeus and Hera, Archetypal Image of Father, Husband and Wife* (Princeton, 1975), 113.

[17] Eliade, *Mephistopheles and the Androgyne*, 110–11.

[18] Delcourt, *Hermaphrodite*, 29.

[19] J. G. Frazer, *On Some Ceremonies of the Central Australian Tribes* (Melbourne, 1901), cited and elaborated upon by Jane Harrison, *Themis: A Study of the Social Origins of Greek Religion*, 2d ed. rev. (Cambridge, 1927), 14–20. For a more recent account, see Joseph Campbell, *The Masks of God: Primitive Mythology* (New York, 1970), 93–103. The following summary of Australian initiation rites follows in general the account of Campbell.

[20] Frazer (Loeb ed., Apollodorus, vol. 2, Appendix 1) saw no sexual symbolism in the fire element of initiation rites, but others have. Mircea Eliade, *Birth and Rebirth*, 17, and Bruno Bettelheim, *Symbolic Wounds* (Glencoe, 1954), 180–88, see it basically as representing feminine power over men in connection with the rites of circumcision and subincision. At the end of the fire ceremony, says Bettelheim, the novices feel safe with women, who then offer themselves to them as sexual objects (187).

[21] Campbell, *Primitive Mythology*, 102.

[22] Mead, "On Freud's View of Female Psychology," 96–97; cf. also Bettelheim, *Symbolic Wounds*, 173–206, for a longer account of the same rite.

[23] Equally embarrassed seem to have been the editors Dindorf, Tyrrell, Wecklein, and Boeckh, each of whom rejected the passage about the thigh as spurious.

[24] Thomas Rosenmeyer, "Tragedy and Religion: *The Bacchae*," in *Euripides: A Collection of Critical Essays*, ed. Erich Segal (Englewood Cliffs, 1968), 166.

[25] Ad de Vries, *Dictionary of Symbols and Imagery* (London, 1974), s.v. thigh 3a. Richard B. Onians, *The Origins of European Thought* (Cambridge, 1951) Part 2, chaps. 1 and 4, argues that the head, spinal fluid, marrow of the thigh, and, in particular, the knee (but not the testicles, 109, n. 4) were thought in antiquity to hold the seed of life. Hence, according to Onians, the thigh of Zeus, as a seat of life, might be intended literally here rather than used euphemistically for the genitals (109, n. 1); but I think otherwise. Compare the *Epic of Gilgamesh* (tablet 6. 168–69), where the thigh of the bull of heaven which Enkidu throws in disgust at Ishtar, goddess of love, seems clearly "a euphemism," as G. S. Kirk suggests, *Myth: Its Meaning and Function* (Cambridge, 1970), 137.

[26] Bettelheim, in discussing subincision and similarly directed rites of initiation, suggests that perhaps all rites of puberty, at least psychologically, are concerned with the desire of men to give birth (*Symbolic Wounds*, 204–26).

[27] Although Hesiod states that Zeus did no violence to the earlier rights and prerogatives of Hecate and Styx, it is clear from his very stamp of approval that he has subordinated their powers to himself and made them effectively his own (for more on this, see Passman's essay in this volume). As Cornford argues, *From Religion to Philosophy* (New York, 1957), Zeus, who at one time had only one-third of the province of the world, came in time to be the dispenser of all powers, wealth, and honors (25–27).

[28] Eliade, *Birth and Rebirth*, 41–47, 78–80.

[29] Onians, *The Origins of European Thought*, 108–12.

[30] Joseph Campbell, *The Masks of God: Occidental Mythology* (New York, 1970), 29–30, 151–52 (quotation, 30). Otto Rank, *Psychoanalytische Beiträge*

zur Mythenforschung (Leipzig, 1919), cited by Theodor Reik, *Myth and Guilt* (New York, 1957), 95–96, sees three inversions in the Genesis myth: Adam was originally taken from Eve, the primal mother (i.e., earth); he gave her the apple in seducing her; the snake was the guardian of the tree and its fruit, not the intruder. The original story, then, and the nature of original sin for Rank (and Freud later) is Adam's incest with his mother Eve.

[31] Eliade, *Mephistopheles and the Androgyne*, 104.

[32] Delcourt, *Hermaphrodite*, 74.

[33] The association of Dionysus with the double-axe is confirmed in both myth and ritual. See C. Kerényi, *Dionysos: Archetypal Image of the Indestructible Life* (Princeton, 1976), who points out that Dionysus is called *pelekus*, "double-axe," at Thessalian Pagasae (190–93). For the Amazonian association, see, for example, Ovid, *Metamorphoses* 12.611, who describes the Amazon Penthesilea as having a double-axe. The connection of the double-axe to androgyny is less explicit, being inferred largely from its use by androgynous persons; but see de Vries, *Dictionary of Symbols*, under *axe*: G. the double-axe: 3. phallic: "the waxing and waning moon separated by the phallic shaft." He also points out that the double-axe was an instrument of Dionysus and the Amazons.

[34] Campbell, *Occidental Mythology*, 152. For Prometheus' guile, see Kathleen McNamee, "Guile in Aeschylus' Prometheus," *La Parola del Passato*, 225 (1985), 401–13.

[35] See Edmund Leach, *Genesis as Myth and other Essays* (London, 1969), 7–23, for the incest theme in the Adam and Eve story and throughout Genesis.

[36] Jung, *The Archetypes and the Collective Unconscious*, 68 n. 27, cited by Delcourt, *Hermaphrodite*, 81 n.

[37] Busst, "The Image of the Androgyne," 61–62.

[38] Farnell, *Cults of the Greek States*, vol. 1, 284 n. a.

[39] Delcourt, *Hermaphrodite*, 69–70; cf. W. K. C. Guthrie, *Orpheus and Greek Religion* (New York, 1966), 104–7.

[40] W. Deonna, *Revue des Études Grecques*, 28 (1915), 341, cited by Delcourt, *Hermaphrodite*, 19.

[41] Delcourt, *Hermaphrodite*, 20.

[42] Schol. Statius, *Achilleid* 1.263, cited by Delcourt, *Hermaphrodite*, 20.

[43] In a typical homosexual affair there are combined the natures and roles of both sexes, the physical characteristics of the one and the psychological characteristics of the other. Hence the lover-beloved roles. It is significant that Freud identified both overt and latent homosexuality as bisexuality (Singer, *Androgyny*, 30–31).

[44] N. Berdyaev, *The Destiny of Man* (London, 1948), 64, quoted by Norman O. Brown, 133.

[45] Not only ancient myth but modern science links sex inseparably with

death—death, in the words of a modern biologist, being the price paid for sex. Sexuality for biology, therefore, is a capability designed by nature to insure the survival of the species at the expense of the individual. This being so, the necessity, even desirability, of the androgyne's fall into sexuality (as distinct from its occasion: disobedience in Genesis; impiety in Plato; loneliness in the *Brihadaranyaka Upanishad*) must be explained. Division into sexes, of course, gives an experience of opposites, without which, as Jung says, there can be "no experience of wholeness" (*Psychology and Alchemy*, 19–20). A human being (that is, "the self") for Jung is in fact "a union of opposites *par excellence*" (19). For the French mystic and novelist, Joseph Peladan (Busst, "The Image of the Androgyne," 67–69), the initial wholeness of the human being was that of the child—unconscious; whereas experience of opposites brought consciousness and self-knowledge. Through the creation of his opposite, Eve, Adam became an adult. Nonetheless, human problems are not over. Jung warns: "Although insight into the problem of opposites is absolutely imperative, there are very few people who can stand it in practice" (*Psychology and Alchemy*, 20).

[46] Tuisto, for example, the first human in German mythology, was not only bisexual, but his name is akin to the old Norwegian word *tvistr*, meaning "dual," and the Latin *bis* (Eliade, *Mephistopheles and the Androgyne*, 111).

[47] See William B. Tyrrell's discussion of the paradisical motifs in the fall of man episode in Hesiod and of the role of Prometheus as intermediator between gods and man, "Greek Myth and *Star Trek*," *Classical Bulletin*, 53 (1977), 38 and 39, n. 17. At least one scholar, James Adam, *The Religious Teachers of Greece* (Edinburgh, 1908), 76, saw an explicit reference to androgyny in Hesiod by taking πόδας καὶ χεῖρας ὁμοῖοι (*Works and Days* 114) to refer to the same androgynous structure of early humans as that described by Plato (*Symposium* 189e). Although subsequent scholars—Mair, West, Sinclair, Pucci—reject this interpretation, they do generally agree that the phrase signifies the unchanging (therefore unaging) condition of humanity before the advent of woman, a blessed condition characteristic of androgyny.

[48] Eliade, *Birth and Rebirth*, 26.

[49] Eliade, *Mephistopheles and the Androgyne*, 112; see also his *Birth and Rebirth*, 26, 44. Homosexuality during initiation may signify that the initiate acquires both sexes (Eliade, *Mephistopheles and the Androgyne*, 112) or may be a means "to convey manliness from a man to a boy" (Stoller, "Facts and Fancies," 350, citing Vanggaard). In either case it is a ritualistic and not typical act of homosexuality.

[50] Examples of transvestism that follow are taken largely from Delcourt, *Hermaphrodite*, 1–16, but ancient sources for them are cited also.

[51] Although Lewis R. Farnell, *Greek Hero Cults and Ideas of Immortality* (Oxford, 1921), 140–41, discounts the suggestion that the "effeminacy" (as he

calls it) of Heracles in connection with Omphale arose from a sacerdotal ceremony of Lydian religion—citing its relatively late, i.e., post fifth-century B.C. entry into the legend—he does not account for its entry into the legend in the first place nor its consistency with other feminine traits of Heracles.

[52] Delcourt, *Hermaphrodite*, 21–22.

[53] Ibid., 27–29.

[54] Henri Jeanmaire, *Couroi et Courètes* (Lille, 1939), 153, 321, quoted by Delcourt, 6.

[55] Cf. Walter Burkert, *Greek Religion*, trans. John Raffan (Cambridge, 1985), 261.

[56] Delcourt, *Hermaphrodite*, 8–9. Plutarch again misconstrues (*Theseus* 22), in the words of Jane Harrison, "by an aetiological myth of more than usual foolishness" (*Themis*, 324). Two of the seven maidens, Plutarch explains, that Theseus took with him to Crete as offerings to the Minotaur were in reality boys disguised as young women, a trick Theseus devised to assist himself in Crete. On his safe return these two boys, still in feminine disguise, led the procession that celebrated his victory. Modern interpreters, Harrison suggests, fare little better in understanding the ritual, as note her own suggestion (324 n. 2) that the pair of youths may have been in reality a mother and son whose dress was not clearly distinguishable. Certainly the *Oschophoria* had become by historical times a mix of rites, dedicated to Athena Skiras, but honoring Dionysus and Theseus as well. But whether it centered originally on a vintage-festival and added Athena, Dionysus, and Theseus later (as H. W. Parke argues, *Festivals of the Athenians* [Ithaca, 1977], 79–80) or arose from initiation rites—a return of the youth to the city after initiation in the bush—and added Theseus later (as Delcourt claims, *Hermaphrodite*, 8–9), the element of androgyny is clear, and appropriate to either case.

[57] Philip Slater, *The Glory of Hera* (Boston, 1968), 339. See also William B. Tyrrell, "A View of the Amazons," *Classical Bulletin*, 57 (1981), 1–5, who sees Amazon culture as a mirror reversal of Athenian patriarchy, protected by men to vindicate and reinforce their claimed superiority over women.

[58] On the origin and nature of Hermaphroditus see Delcourt, *Hermaphrodite*, 45–54, and her annotated bibliography, 102–3.

[59] Japan's bisexual god of fertility, Dosojin, though one god in concept, is regularly portrayed by two separate images placed side by side, one male, one female. Carl Kerényi, on the other hand, thinks that Hermes and Aphrodite were originally twins, *The Gods of the Greeks*, trans. Norman Cameron (New York, 1960), 171–72.

[60] See deVries, *Dictionary of Symbols*, under *serpent* A. 2 and 4.

[61] Campbell, *Occidental Mythology*, 26–27.

[62] Luc Brisson, *Le Mythe de Tirésias* (Leiden, 1976). Teiresias' androgyny

also relates in kind and intent to the bisexuality attempted by the shamans of Siberia, Australia, and elsewhere; cf. Mircea Eliade, *Shamanism* (Princeton, 1972), 351–52, 395; *Birth and Rebirth*, chap. 5, and his *Mephistopheles and the Androgyne*, 116–17.

[63] Philip Vellacott, *Ironic Drama* (Cambridge, 1975), 17; cf. 6–19 and chap. 4. See also Sarah B. Pomeroy's favorable evaluation of Euripides' attitude toward women in *Goddesses, Whores, Wives, and Slaves: Women in Classical Antiquity* (New York, 1975), 103–12: "Euripides shows us women victimized by patriarchy in almost every possible way" (110).

[64] Vellacott, *Ironic Drama*, 125.

[65] Dionysus, as suggested above, is everywhere presented and celebrated as androgynous. The κῶμος, wherein men and women exchanged clothing and function, characterized all of his festivals, and those who danced the "Ithyphallos" or escorted the phallos in his honor also wore clothing of the opposite sex (so Delcourt, *Hermaphrodite*, 11). Aeschylus (Nauck, frag. 61) calls him ὁ γύννις and Euripides θηλύμορφος (*Bac.* 353).

[66] Rosenmeyer, "Tragedy and Religion," 134.

[67] Ibid., 169–70.

[68] Pomeroy, *Goddesses, Whores, Wives, and Slaves*, 117–18.

[69] *Lysistrata* has a special affinity to the speech of Aristophanes in Plato's *Symposium* both in its burlesque of the effeminate Agathon and in its use of the simile of the flatfish (ψῆττα) to portray the divided human (*Lysistrata* 115–16, 131; *Symposium* 191d).

The Only Women Who Give Birth to Men: A Gynocentric, Cross-Cultural View of Women in Ancient Sparta

The Problem

Classical scholars have long recognized the independence, rights, and esteem that women in ancient Sparta of the archaic and classical periods enjoyed, especially as compared with the highly restricted roles of women in ancient Athens.[1] Even while acknowledging these greater privileges, many scholars still conclude that these apparent rights only masked a Spartan woman's subjection to the "State" which resulted in her being no less oppressed than her Athenian counterpart.[2] Typically, contemporary male scholarly bias reinscribes ancient biases. Just notes that Aristotle's descriptions of Spartan women echo Greek, misogynistic stereotypes, such as dramatized by the tragic characters Eteocles in Aeschylus' *Seven against Thebes*, or Creon in Sophocles' *Antigone*.[3] In this same vein of thinking, modern scholars frequently interpret the concept of women's independence as denoting a state of her being "out of control," meaning out of male control.[4] Thus, for example, Michell comments that "[Spartan women] evidently got completely out of hand," "meddl[ing] in the affairs of state," and thereby helping to bring about Sparta's decay.[5] Or, controverting Cartledge's earlier analysis that apparently shows Spartan women's rights, privileges, and importance to the Spartan community, Cartledge and Spawforth subsequently bring forward evidence that they believe shows Spartan women of at least the mid-fourth century "behaving just like any other Greek women for once, rather than as the viragos of laconizing mythology."[6]

While the obvious bias of these remarks limits their analytic value, it also reveals a major part of the problem. The researcher into ancient Sparta must unmask the various layers of ancient and modern mythologizing, these overlaid cobwebs of biases, that have created these "viragos of laconizing mythology," before we can appreciate the roles and ideological constructs of ancient Spartan women. The first of these biases is the moralizing tone that pervades virtually all discussions on ancient Sparta. By and large scholars still view ancient Sparta through an Atheno-inherited lens, whereby the limited Athenian democracy of the fifth century appears as the ultimate social ideal from which any divergence stands out as deviation.

Exacerbating this problem is the recent antagonism (now largely dissolving) between the "democratic west" and the "Communist bloc" that has led scholars, at least the western ones here considered, to condemn all features of Spartan society as serving the monolithic interests of a superimposed "State" that denies Spartan men the freedoms enjoyed by their Athenian brothers; thus, David's somber account even of the role of laughter in Spartan society.[7] This notion of a capitalized, alienated "State" is as much a modern construct as the Orwellian superstructure it fearfully imitates. In fact, both ancient Athens and Sparta show evidence of comparable restraints upon the notion of individual freedom, which is a very modern, western concept in any case. These restraints, however, are played out quite differently in the differing economic and social conditions of the two societies.[8] The Spartan πόλις, "community," was no more removed from the citizens comprising it than the Athenian one. Both were developments of community-oriented strategies that aimed at maintaining the integrity of their community as a whole, and both closely regulated much of the familial, social, religious, political, and military life of its inhabitants, as the strict rules of *teknopoiia*, "child-production," and citizenship testify.[9] Socrates still views his Athens as an integral community, the stated basis for his gadfly-like annoyance of his countrymen (Plato, *Apology* 30e), and it is precisely this notion of community solidarity that appealed to the Lakonophilic elements in Athens as they witnessed their own πόλις disintegrating before their eyes at the end of the fifth century. To claim that the Athenian citizen male is "free" in a modern rendering of that term does as much disservice to the real conditions of ancient Athens, as to believe that the Spartan citizen male is mechanically bound to some distanced "State."

Michell's language, that "[Spartan women] meddled in the affairs of state," reveals another complex of obfuscating webs.[10] The scholarly literature commonly interprets the separation of women's and men's realms of activity as (1) excluding women from public, community-oriented ("political") activities, the domain solely of men, and (2) according primary value to men's roles and spheres of activity while regarding women's activities as derivative. For the first point, the modern structuralist dichotomy of two opposed spheres of activity—a female, private one versus a male, public one, each gender having primary or total control within its own sphere—appeared for a time to offer an apparently neutral scholarly approach to the issue of realms of appropriate male and female activities, especially since it appeared analogous to the ancient οἶκος ("household")/πόλις complex. Anthropological literature has long determined that this construct of a private/public dichotomy distorts perceptions of women's and men's realms in a society, since for many societies a sharp division does not exist between these western notions of domestic and public spheres, but areas of activity tend rather to be interactive or may even coincide.[11] Similarly, for both ancient Athens and Sparta, Just and Kunstler, respectively, find that the οἶκος and the πόλις are not separated and opposed spheres, but highly interactive and fluid categories, and that women's activities in the οἶκος are critical for men's status within and for the well-functioning of the community.[12] Nor does the ancient evidence support the idea that women's activities of significance for the πόλις are enacted only through the realm of the οἶκος. Rather than describing women's and men's activities, this theoretical dichotomy reflects instead the fundamental, hierarchical opposition in western thinking that determines the construction of epistemological dualities.

Murray, quoting from a 1913 article of H. Jeanmaire, reveals the force of the second point when he states that the Spartan social structure *freed* the women to "constitute a society which *copied* that of the men, *imitated* their system of education and initiation rites, and which had a place *beside* male institutions in cult ceremonies and in social life" (emphasis added).[13] This notion of the primacy of male activities pervades every analysis of Spartan women's roles, including the otherwise positive assessment by Kunstler.[14] This androcentric evaluation, by assuming that male activities and discourse constitute the society, while female activities and discourse are a tumorous adjunct, itself an Aristotelian notion, ignores the possibility that women can be integral members of their society who also contribute to its ideological and social constructions and who are valued for their contributions. As feminist scholarship is making increasingly clear, we must look at women as active participants in their societies and examine just how women and men in any given society work out their particular roles.

These constraints of multi-leveled biases and of imposing theoretical paradigms that mask rather than elucidate the nature of women's and men's roles and their interaction within the society have produced, with rare exceptions, analyses of Spartan women's roles that reiterate in modern scholarly discourse the stereotypes already old in the ancient misogynistic tradition. Moreover, they inject into descriptions of antiquity the unequal sexual dynamics of contemporary western society while revealing little of the actual conditions that may have obtained in ancient societies. As the anthropological literature reminds us, it is essential to approach the study of another society without predefined, preconceived categories that attach modern, western meanings and significations to these categories; the literature urges instead that we examine features of another society within the total context of that society.[15] Consequently, we must examine how the relative spheres of women and men are defined and assessed, and to what extent women's affairs are coincident with or significant for the community as a whole.

Theoretical Approach

The premise for my approach is that archaic Sparta, like much of archaic Greece, was fundamentally non-western, and that in particular, as a pre-state civilization, ancient Sparta probably shares more features with other pre-state societies than it does with the super-developed state institutions of contemporary western society.[16] This view of early Greece has long formed the basis for cross-cultural comparisons in studies of antiquity, recently regaining respectability after a long period of hiatus.[17] Many of these cross-cultural studies concentrate on particular activities that are strikingly non-western in form and function: the role of male, same-sex practices for ritual, social, political, and military purposes in the ancient Greek world;[18] the role of ritual and religion in the lives of the ancient Greeks;[19] or the significance of female ritual initiation practices.[20]

In order to better appreciate women's roles in the ancient Spartan community, it is important not only to look for those manifestly non-western features, but also to examine the society as a whole in order to place women into their full societal context. Consequently, my use of cross-cultural material differs significantly from that of many other researchers, because I am seeking to find out how patterns of social organization, interaction, and ideological discourse can shed light upon women's roles and status in their community. For this purpose I examine roles, status, and images of women in other pre-state, sex-segregated societies that demonstrate certain affinities with ancient Sparta.[21] In addition, I bring to this analysis a gynocentric approach, one that not only focuses upon women's activities, but consciously does so from a woman's point of view.[22] Consequently, in the following analysis, I both present some of these cross-cultural paradigms as well as establish the conceptual basis for a gynocentric approach to the understanding of these paradigms. Native American sources provide the primary models for these different evaluations of women's roles in society and for the particular study of women in ancient Sparta.[23]

Research on gender dynamics in sex-segregated societies shows that in many, women and men enjoy a great deal of autonomy and control over their lives, and where sex segregation is especially pronounced, with the men away at war or at the hunt, the women are in charge of the economy and social organization of the community. Women's roles, status, and importance in these communities are evidenced in numerous ways. Economically, women control their own labor, resources, tools, and products.[24] Women also tend to be in charge of the distribution of all goods, both the products of their own labor and those of men's labor as well, and the distribution itself is usually equitable among all members of the society.[25] Those societies where women's economic contribution to the society is recognized, and where women control their own economic production and distribution, are societies generally characterized by women's important roles in the decision-making process for the society, and where women are regarded as autonomous individuals with their own inherent rights, duties, and privileges.[26] Brown and Jensen demonstrate that Iroquoian societies reflect a sexual division of labor where women have benefited from their roles in the home, in horticulture and agriculture and from the men's absences by solidifying their power economically, socially, politically, and by receiving high social status and prestige for their activities.[27]

Furthermore, women's influence upon societal matters cannot be well appreciated if one is seeking women's participation in formal economic or political structures, which may not exist according to western forms of social organization.[28] Rather, we must be open to varied forms of influence and decision-making in the society by both women and men, and examine the relative importance of the roles of each gender. To begin with, women's activities are no less important if they appear to western observers as "informal" or "in the background." Allen notes the different perceptual lenses by which Native and western Americans perceive their surroundings.[29] She sees westerners as focusing on a foreground that is highlighted by surrounding shadows, to the exclusion or even denigration of background. In contrast, the background "is of ultimate importance in a tribal context" forming part of "a living web" created by the interplay between light and shadow. The most important aspects of background, the earth and women's activities, devalued and dismissed in western perceptions, are in contrast perceived and respected as the basic, indispensable foundation for life in tribal matters.

In Native American societies, women's activities *are* community activities. Women exert their influence and authority on the society by speaking out and acting directly in any situations affecting their lives and the well-being of the community, by taking charge as they deem necessary and by controlling essential goods and services, thereby controlling the behavior of anyone who requires them.[30] In the Iroquoian societies in particular all these translate into women's formal control through the leadership of the clan grandmothers who make the important decisions for the community, who appoint the men they empower to execute their decisions, and who maintain the authority to remove from his duties any man not carrying out his assigned tasks.[31]

However, economic power alone does not account for the social and political power of women in Native American societies, and as Schlegel remarks, one must also consider the share ideology plays in determining actual roles and status in the society.[32] While western researchers ground women's societal importance in her economic role,

Native American researchers regard women's social roles as reflecting her centrality in the metaphysical constructs, both sacred and secular, of the society. These often revolve around the centrality of female deity as both creative and procreative forces. Central to the sacralized imaging of woman is her primary role as childbearer.[33] For the Laguna Pueblo, Thought Woman is the original creatrix whose spirit informs everything and who brings into being both material and non-material reality.[34] Changing Woman is regarded as the supreme mother of the Navajo, most blessed and revered of all the Holy People, and consequently the most important bond in Navajo society is the mother-child bond, which symbolizes giving life and sharing sustenance.[35] This mother-child bond is the ideal pattern for all social interaction, leading to the major emphasis on generosity, caring, and helping one another as central values in diverse Native American societies.[36] In Iroquoian and Hopi societies, the mother-daughter dyad is the dominant social pattern, and daughters are more highly valued than sons.[37]

The primacy of women's values and concerns forms the central matrix for community and social action, refuting the notion that women's activities are formed in imitation of or as an adjunct to the men's. Acknowledging that differing forces can account for any particular social phenomenon, Murphy and Murphy posit three possible reasons for the sex segregation of the Amazonian Mundurucu society: that the men refuse to live in the women's houses; that the men abdicated their dwellings along with control over women; or that the women threw the men out.[38] While the first two possibilities reflect male-oriented interpretations, the third emphasizes women's roles as active agents in their own lives.

For Yurok society, Buckley found that the women's menstrual practices profoundly shaped the society's calendrical and spiritual rhythms. Concluding his detailed discussion, Buckley states,

> If we are anywhere near the mark in these speculations, we realize that the menstrual power of Yurok women did not manifest itself only on a gender-specific, esoteric level of knowledge and practice—one that paralleled identical features of opposite-gender life—but *that it had profound, pragmatic implications as well in dictating*

> the temporal structuring of activities for entire households on a monthly basis [emphasis added].[39]

Buckley discovered that it was the women's biological rhythms, their perceptions of the world and of themselves, and the rituals that they had developed to mark their distinctive functions that established the pattern for the rhythms and activities of the entire society, including, of course, the men.

This primacy of women's values also leads to the view that child rearing is the most important activity of the community, so that men's activities are often formed to support women's fundamental roles. This includes men's roles as protector (warrior) and food provider (hunter and/or farmer), and it means that men too are socialized to be child-rearers and nurturers. Thus, it is Hopi men's responsibility to insure that women enjoy the physical and spiritual safety to carry out their roles with an untroubled mind.[40] Lakota women's activities sustain the society spiritually and literally, while the men's activities are regarded as secondary to the women's, and for the benefit of the children Cheyenne and Lakota men must curb their sexual desires.[41] Often, to balance the primacy of women's activities, a greater emphasis may be placed on men's symbolic achievements.[42] Likewise, because women are regarded as being imbued naturally with spiritual power, men must develop rituals in order to attain some of the spiritual power that women possess naturally.[43]

This centrality of women in Native American societies, which Native Americans, both women and men, call matriarchal, does not mean the domination of men by women in some mythically feared inversions of western, patriarchal, gender power dynamics. It results instead in concepts of balance and complementarity within which both genders are seen as essential to the continuity of life and to the ongoing, harmonious functioning of the society.[44] Rather than opposing women's and men's realms, researchers emphasize the complementary balance in Native American societies between the spheres of activities engaged in by women and those by men: each gender has its appropriate realm, each controls the activities, products, and proceeds of that realm, each receives value and respect,[45] without one assuming precedence over the other.[46]

Allen draws attention to the distinctively feminine character of these features typifying Native American societies: primacy of spiritual values, recognition of women's elemental power, equitable distribution of goods, interacting notions of consensus and autonomy, respect for all individuals within the society according to both age and gender, and flexibility in societal roles permitted each individual.[47] The feminine modes of perception that underlie these social manifestations emphasize the qualities of care, respect, and value for life in its many forms. Allen calls this feminine orientation in perception and action by the etymologically Greek term, "gynocentric."

Researchers in other disciplines further affirm the significance of gynocentric values in shaping women's and men's roles in society.[48] Ethnic scholars, and the language they use, "gynocentric," "womanist," "woman consciousness," affirm the distinctiveness of women's perceptions as they are interwoven with the distinctiveness of ethnic identity.[49] In social psychology, Ruddick, in her analysis of "maternal thinking," and Gilligan, through her research on the moral and psychological development of young girls, find distinctive women's epistemologies centered on values of caring and concern for others.[50] In theology, Daly, Reuther, and Christ and Plaskow demonstrate the significance for women's sense of self, of female images in divinity and of the sacralization of female values.[51]

These analyses demonstrate that in these sex-segregated societies, interactive complexes of social and ideological processes reveal women to be strong, independent, and valued agents in their societies. Importantly, women both determine their own roles and images and help shape the values and activities of the whole society. Women enjoy considerable power and authority throughout their social environment. Nor are their rights derived from men, but they more likely form part of a complementary balance, and in some cases women's activities provide the basis for those of the men. This overview of women's roles and status in certain Native American societies, which views women as active agents within the fuller social and ideological context of their community, and which approaches their roles from a woman-oriented, gynocentric perspective, bears directly on our understanding of the familial, economic, societal, and spiritual activities engaged in by Spartan women, as I will show in the next section.

Women in Ancient Sparta

"And what is the difference if women rule or if the rulers are ruled by the women?"
(Aristotle, *Politics* 1269b23)

My analysis focuses on the lives of the Spartiate, that is upper-class, citizen women during the archaic (eighth to sixth centuries, B.C.E.) and classical periods (fifth to fourth centuries). Complicating the paucity of direct sources for almost any study of women in antiquity is the fact that much of our information regarding ancient Sparta comes from non-Spartan sources, sometimes quite late, that allude to features of Spartan society often for ideological purposes, whether the utopian mythologizing of Plato, Xenophon, or Plutarch, or the unique condemnations of Aristotle. The apparently impartial discussions by Herodotus, Thucydides, Strabo, and Pausanias corroborate the descriptions of social features found in the more ideologically grounded analyses.[52]

Direct artistic and poetic evidence from Sparta that dates primarily to the archaic period provides an important foundation for the analysis. Modern scholars largely agree on these basic points:[53] that archaic Sparta flourished in and was renowned throughout the eastern Mediterranean for its artistic and musical production at the same time that it was engaged in a program of conquest and hegemony over much of the Peloponnesus; that Spartan society exhibited features characteristic of earlier and/or Doric societies that were transformed by Sparta's specific responses to the historical and economic forces of the time; that the concept of Spartan "austerity" began to emerge in the early fifth century due to the strain of foreign wars and of constant control over the enslaved Helot and other subject populations, and that this move to austerity was exacerbated by the earthquake of 464 and the subsequent series of slave revolts; that Spartans, female and male, rigorously adhered to their religious, educational, and musical traditions, at least until the early fourth century, and in some cases well into the Roman period; that women's position and their activities within Spartan society were relatively untouched by the vagaries of the Spartan male's political and military activities in the larger Greek world or by their measures of austerity within Sparta; and that women's economic power, at least, grew ever stronger throughout the archaic and classical periods.

The economic record makes it clear that a woman in Sparta could own and inherit land whether or not there were sons in the family, the inheritance often being presented at time of marriage, and that she could own land outright and not only in trust for male heirs. In this she appears in a comparable economic stance to her sisters in Gortyn and probably many other parts of the ancient Greek world, and especially contrasted with the situation of her Athenian sister.[54] The Spartan woman also owned her own movable property, although at Sparta, even more than elsewhere in the ancient Greek world, land was the most significant asset of wealth. It is likely that Spartan women used their economic base to influence their husbands' behavior, by regulating, for instance, the Spartan man's monthly contribution to his communal mess, and thereby controlling his ability to participate as a citizen in the Spartan polity.[55] Aristotle denounces the fact that Spartan women's wealth and their owning two-fifths of the land [notice that this is not even half] enable them to affect the policies of the rulers (*Politics* 1270a20). His criticism is all the more revealing of the extent of Spartan women's importance in their community since this reference to women's economic power is unique in the *Politics*.[56]

Of especial importance for the women, as well as for the men, would have been their system of education, carried out largely through choral bands of song and dance, organized by age group, recognized early in this century by Nilsson and studied extensively by Calame, who explores the pedagogical, ritual, and social importance of girl choruses in archaic Greece, with a focus on Sparta.[57] Bringing together increased critical appreciation of both the role of choral education and of religion in the lives of women in antiquity, Calame shows that the girls' cultural rearing, experienced through these age-divided choral bands, led to their full integration into adult Spartan society, and that the community recognized the girls' importance to the society as being greater than that of the boys.[58] Cantarella further notes that this all-female choral education by age both contributed to forming the girls' personalities and, "more important, to giving them the means with which to express those personalities."[59]

It bears emphasizing that the educational system functions as a far more integral part of a woman's life in ancient Sparta than any modern educational system does. Adult women in the community, some probably as professional *choregai*, "chorus leaders," others perhaps assuming this role because of their experience and skill for particular occasions, would have been actively involved in the educational process. Besides learning cultural, historical, and familial lore through the songs, the choruses were an essential component of all Spartan rituals. This choral system of education fully integrated every aspect of life for Spartan girls and women, leading no doubt to the exuberance displayed in artistic and poetic evidence extant from the archaic period. To sing and dance one's way through life can only intensify one's appreciation of oneself and the world around.[60]

Choral activity also formed a major part of ritual celebrations, for which the Spartans were also renowned throughout the ancient Hellenic world. As women elsewhere in ancient Greek communities, Spartan girls and women marked numerous occasions with ceremony and celebration, most notably of course the transitions from girlhood to adolescence and from adolescence to adulthood. Apparently unique, at least according to the extant evidence, a Spartan woman's acceptance as an adult member of her community is not merged into marriage rites but merits its own ceremony, the Hyacinthia, which recognize the adult status of both women and men, and which, according to Calame, accord greater recognition to the women than the men.[61] Alcman's *Partheneion* provides a singular glimpse into the celebratory nature of some of these rites. Altogether, these rituals spiritually connect women with divine powers, they ritually and socially integrate women into the community, and they provide divine and community sanction for women's roles.

Using the concept of networks of dyadic relationships as his critical lens, modeled in part on McCall's work on the significance of the mother-daughter dyad in Iroquoian societies, Kunstler finds that women's importance in ancient Sparta stems from the strong mother-daughter dyad that dominates the patterns of personal interaction in ancient Spartan society.[62] Kunstler brings out these important points: girls grow up with a strong sense of self-esteem from the educational system and from their bonds with their mothers and other female relations; women maintain a large measure of control and of independence in their lives economically, sexually, and probably politically; family and public spheres are not distinct or opposed, but probably form part of an interactive complex; and sacred, cultural, and social institutions affirm women's value to the community. In addition, the essentially homosocial nature of Spartan society enabled the women to form strong ties of family and friendship that would provide them with a solid and stable foundation for their sense of self worth and for mutual support.[63] It is likely that women developed strong bonds with each other within the family, from their educational *agoge*, "training," and from residential proximity, all of which would have provided the bases for networks of mutual support for a variety of purposes, as Lamphere shows for Navajo society.[64]

By all accounts, the sex-segregated organization of ancient Spartan society was highly advantageous for Spartan women. Nor does the evidence support the contention that women's structures developed in imitation of or as adjuncts to the men's social practices. Plutarch tells us that the women refused to abide by Lycurgus' political and social reforms, yet both he and Xenophon claim that many rituals and practices of Spartan women were instituted by that legendary lawgiver. We may view Spartan women's hostility to the Lycurgan reforms as derived from a long-standing sense of power and authority the women had enjoyed, which they were not willing to relinquish and which additional changes in their social environment permitted them to consolidate. It appears that what the women refused to accept were encroachments upon or male-decreed political changes in their own long-established practices. It is certainly possible that the legendary lawgiver's reforms so transformed earlier structures as to enable the women to strongly consolidate their rights and privileges. The similarity of certain laws and practices of Sparta to those elsewhere in Greek lands suggests the continuation of certain rights and privileges the women had long enjoyed, which the reforms very likely augmented, rather than the women's sudden acquisition of these rights by fiat.

This gynocentric view of Sparta's societal structure can illuminate the meaning attached to the concept of motherhood for ancient Spartan women. Scholars often decry the constriction upon Spartan women's roles resulting from the community-oriented concept of *teknopoiia*, "child-production," as if their Athenian sisters were any "freer" because their motherhood role was at the command of an individual man and a patriarchal family. Moreover, with rare exceptions (e.g., Cantarella), scholars interpret the very emphasis upon motherhood as reflecting the Spartan woman's inferior status to that of men.[65] This negative scholarly valuation of the role of motherhood unmasks the severe depreciation of women and of the institution of motherhood in western society, but it tells us nothing about what motherhood may have meant to Spartan women themselves.

Plutarch fortunately provides us with a few clues, valid despite their anecdotal nature. He three times attributes to Gorgo, wife of the Spartan leader Leonidas, the following saying. In response to the query by an Athenian woman as to why Spartan women are the only ones who rule their men, Gorgo quips, "Because we are the only ones who give birth to men."[66] Comparable remarks from other cultures help to provide the context missing from the Spartan citations. Underhill's (1985) classic *The Autobiography of a Papago Woman*, first published in 1936, presents the life of Chona, an elder Papago woman, both as told by her informant and appended with some accompanying analysis by Underhill. Much like Gorgo's ancient Athenian inquirer, Underhill asks Chona if the women resent not participating in the men's ceremonials. And much like Gorgo, Chona responds, "Why should we envy men? We *made* the men."[67] Chona expresses quite clearly the true priorities of her society: women's roles in childbearing and rearing are valued as primary and men's activities are perceived as secondarily supportive and compensatory. Consequently, the context Underhill provides for Chona's remarks reveals that gynocentric sense of self, self worth, and self-assuredness *as a woman* within her culture that lies at the heart of all of these remarks. We may clearly see this sense of pride, indeed fierce pride, in motherhood attributed to Spartan women as stemming from the acknowledged importance to the community of women's role in motherhood, reinforced, as French argues, by the primacy of the mother-daughter bond.[68]

On the other hand, the preponderance of sayings that attribute fierce derision, to the point of death, by Spartan mothers against their sons whom they believe to be not manly or brave enough in the defense of Sparta, leads scholars to judgments of the cruelty, insensitivity, and plain old unmaternal feelings of Spartan women. From a gynocentric point of view, if the society is to be maintained, and if the women's role is essentially that of procreation and the men's role essentially that of defense, it becomes appropriate for the women who produced the men to inspire, inflame, and even whip them up to their task. This need not intend lack of feeling between mother and son, though it probably does mean the absence of romantic sentimentality in their relationship. It may more simply be an acknowledgment of their different spheres of activity and the right of the mother *qua* mother to chastise or castigate her son to his community-approved role.[69]

Something of this sort may be observed in the response of the Kayapo Indians, an Amazonian people of Brazil, to the building of a hydro-electric dam on the River Xingu by European engineers, a construction that would destroy their river environment. Like the other societies discussed above, the Kayapo also bear striking organizational parallels to ancient Spartan society, the men cohabiting primarily in the men's quarters in town and often away hunting or at war, the women living in extended matrilineal, matrilocal, and matrifocal family groups. On one occasion when the men returned without having secured the agreement to put an end to the dam project, the women rounded upon the men in a manner no less vigorous than the Spartan woman upbraiding her husband or son for daring to return while Sparta was still in military danger. Yet on another occasion the women wept profusely when one man returned after a relatively brief absence. Significantly, when the whole community confronted the European engineers and planners at an international forum, one Kayapo woman accosted this group of foreign white men seated on their dais, and waving a machete at them, she inquired, "Didn't your mothers love you enough? Is that why you treat us this way?"[70]

These questions provide a strong corrective to the notion that men's symbolic and/or public personae define the values of importance for society, revealing instead the profound woman-centered basis of the culture. Clearly, the Kayapo women perceive their power and authority as deriving from their roles as mothers, and they unhesitatingly assume the centrality of maternal actions and values for the well-functioning of the society, recognizing that a disruption of these maternal acts results in inhumane, non-caring actions among human beings, such as those carried out by the European engineers. These remarks also shed light on Spartan women's concepts of motherhood, because they show that the "fierce" comments attributed to them do not automatically mark Spartan women as a-maternal viragos. Rather, this interpretation reflects scholars' derisive judgments and betrays a western male desire for a sorrowing, Christocentric, pietà-esque image of motherhood. Women's pride in their own motherhood may lead to notions of the fulfillment of women's and men's roles differing from the saccharine-sweet ones the Victorian hold upon our psyches leads us to expect.

While all other evidence indicates strong portrayals of Spartan women, one anomaly seems to exist, the marriage custom. Again, most scholars proclaim that the bride's transvestism, waiting alone in a dark room until her husband sneaks in to carry her off to their secret wedding bed, appears to function to ease the transition into marriage for the male, while stigmatizing that institution for the traumatized bride.[71] For Michell the fact that all features of the Spartan wedding ceremony find parallels both in other ancient practices as well as in those of other cultures—the cutting of the hair that is offered to Artemis; the transvestism, which, like the veil, reverses and marginalizes the role of the bride at this moment—mitigates the general scholarly revulsion.[72] Kunstler, who concludes that a one-night ritual cannot contraindicate the entire structure of male-female relations, finds further that the marriage custom may ease the emotional threat to the Spartan male during this ritual transfer from the men's solidarity group to that of the woman-dominated household.[73] Indeed, the women's ceremonial celebrations of the bride stand out in sharp contrast to the purported avoidance of celebration of this occasion by the men. The women's celebrations in fact suggest that the women's deeply rooted sense of self worth incorporates this custom into their confident perceptions of themselves in the society, whatever its origins or whatever range of meanings this custom may entail. The general secrecy surrounding the sexual consummation of the marriage and the subsequent sexual meetings of the young couple also support the notion that not marriage, but motherhood marks woman's critical transition into adult Spartan society.

This gynocentric description of women in ancient Sparta should enable us to better appreciate the reality of women's lives. It ought to emerge that elite citizen women of ancient Sparta enjoyed considerable independence, power, and societal privileges that derived from their economic and procreative roles in the community, that the community highly regarded their value to the society, and that these were built upon a strong foundation of the women's sense of self worth. Spotty as the evidentiary record is, the few clues that do exist reveal strong, self-assured, power-wielding women, whom weak-willed and fearful men have mythologized into bitch-like viragos. It may even be that women enjoyed their independence not because of the men's attention elsewhere, but at the expense of the men's concerns.

In retrospect, one may perhaps see both the women and the men as myopic in their views as far as the community as a whole is concerned. For from this analysis, the women, perhaps even more than the men, may have benefited from the oft-reported harshness of Sparta's control over their slave populations, condemned, by and large, by democratically enlightened scholars. My re-evaluation here of the women's roles in ancient Sparta does not, of course, change the overall nature of Spartan society, nor is my intention to reconstruct condemnable institutions. I do, however, challenge scholars to condemn equally the anti-female and anti-slave practices of ancient Athenian society. In addition, I hope my present analysis provides a challenge to the scholarly smugness that assumes a secondary and inferior status for women whose roles are deemed to exist only for the advantage of men. It is more likely that Sparta's social construction of gender roles developed from a complex exchange of powers for both women and men that over time seems to have concentrated greater power in the hands of the women. And just as elements of ancient Athenian society provide potential sources for creative conceptualizations of self and society, so may our understanding of the roles of women in ancient Sparta from a gynocentric standpoint provide a source for creative re-conceptualizations of women's and men's roles in society.

Bella Zweig
University of Arizona

Notes

This paper is dedicated to Joy King for her inspiration and ceaseless work on behalf of women and equity in the profession, and to the Native American people I have met whose respectful ways and teachings have made this analysis possible: in the hopes of achieving better understanding and respect among all peoples.

[1] Sarah B. Pomeroy, *Goddesses, Whores, Wives, and Slaves: Women in Classical Antiquity* (New York, 1975); Barton Kunstler, "Family Dynamics and Female Power in Ancient Sparta," in *Rescuing Creusa: New Methodological Approaches to Women in Antiquity*, ed. Marilyn Skinner, *Helios*, 13.2 (1986), 31-48; Eva Cantarella, *Pandora's Daughters*, trans. Maureen B. Fant (Baltimore, 1987).

[2] Paul Cartledge, "Spartan Wives: Liberation or Licence?" *CQ*, 31 (1981), 105.

[3] Roger Just, *Women in Athenian Law and Life* (London, 1989), 208–9.

[4] G. L. Huxley, *Early Sparta* (London, 1962), 133, n. 409.

[5] H. Michell, *Sparta* (1952; rpt., Cambridge, 1964), 50–53.

[6] Cartledge, "Spartan Wives"; Paul Cartledge and Antony Spawforth, *Hellenistic and Roman Sparta: A Tale of Two Cities* (London, 1989), 13.

[7] Ephraim David, "Laughter in Spartan Society," in *Classical Sparta: Techniques Behind Her Success*, ed. Anton Powell (London, 1989), 1–25.

[8] Pavel Oliva, *Sparta and Her Social Problems* (Amsterdam, 1971), 11; M. I. Finley, *The Use and Abuse of History* (London, 1975), 175; Sally Humphreys, *Anthropology and the Greeks* (London, 1978), 171–72.

[9] Just, *Women in Athenian Law*, 24; James Redfield, "The Women of Sparta," *CJ*, 73 (1977/78), 158.

[10] Michell, *Sparta*, 50.

[11] Rayna Reiter, ed., *Toward an Anthropology of Women* (New York, 1975), Intro., 15; Alice Schlegel, "Toward a Theory of Sexual Stratification," in *Sexual Stratification: A Cross-Cultural View*, ed. Alice Schlegel (New York, 1977), 15–17; Peggy R. Sanday and R. G. Goodenough, eds., *Beyond the Second Sex: New Directions in the Anthropology of Gender* (Philadelphia, 1990), Intro., 12.

[12] Just, *Women in Athenian Law*, 39, 55; and Kunstler, "Family Dynamics," 32.

[13] Oswyn Murray, *Early Greece* (Stanford, 1980), 169, citing Jeanmaire, "La cryptie lacédémonienne," *Revue des Études Grecques*, 26 (1913).

[14] Kunstler, "Family Dynamics," 34.

[15] Schlegel, "Toward a Theory of Sexual Stratification," 14–17; Humphreys, *Anthropology and the Greeks*, 26.

[16] Claude Calame, *Les chœurs de jeunes filles en Grèce archaïque*, (Rome,

1977), vol. 1, 33.

[17] See Humphreys, *Anthropology and the Greeks*, chap. 1, for overview.

[18] Bernard Sergent, *Homosexuality in Greek Myth*, trans. Arthur Goldhammer (Boston, 1986); John J. Winkler, *The Constraints of Desire: The Anthropology of Sex and Gender in Ancient Greece* (New York, 1990), chap. 2.

[19] Walter Burkert, *Homo Necans: The Anthropology of Ancient Greek Sacrificial Ritual and Myth*, trans. P. Bing (Berkeley, 1983); and Burkert, *Greek Religion*, trans. J. Raffan (Cambridge, 1985).

[20] Bruce Lincoln, *Emerging from the Chrysalis: Studies in Rituals of Women's Initiation* (Cambridge, 1981).

[21] Modern researchers studying such diverse cultures as the Nayar on the Malabar coast of India, the Mundurucu in Amazonia, and the Atjehnese in Sumatra have noted structural similarities between the sex-segregated social organization of these societies and that of ancient Spartan society. See Robert F. Murphy and Yolanda Murphy, "Women, Work and Property in a South American Tribe," in *Theory and Practice: Essays Presented to Gene Weltfish*, ed. Stanley Diamond (The Hague, 1980), 184; and Joan Kelly, *Women, History and Theory* (Chicago, 1984), 112. Nineteenth-century theorists noted affinities with Native American societies.

[22] Although there exists some controversy over the concept of distinctive, gender-based perceptions, scholarship across a spectrum of disciplines affirms the validity of women's distinctive perceptions and epistemologies. The essays in *Explorations in Feminist Ethics: Theory and Practice*, eds. Eve Browning Cole and Susan Coultrap-McQuin (Bloomington, 1992), review some of the issues involved in this debate as they also affirm the concept of a distinctive women's ethics.

[23] I present a more detailed analysis of the perceptual and epistemological correspondences between Native American and early Greek societies in my "The Primal Mind: Using Native American Models to Approach the Study of Women in Ancient Greece," in *Feminist Theory and the Classics*, eds. Amy Richlin and Nancy Rabinowitz (New York, 1993).

[24] Dan McCall, "The Dominant Dyad: Mother Right and the Iroquois Case," in *Theory and Practice*, ed. Diamond, 250; Janet Spector, "Male/Female Task Differentiation among the Hidatsa: Toward the Development of an Archaeological Approach to the Study of Gender," in *The Hidden Half: Studies of Plains Indian Women*, eds. Patricia Albers and Beatrice Medicine (Lanham, 1983), 93–94.

[25] Judith K. Brown, "Iroquois Women: An Ethnohistoric Note," in *Toward an Anthropology of Women*, 247; Patricia Albers, "Sioux Women in Transition: A Study of Their Changing Status in a Domestic and Capitalist Sector of Production," in *The Hidden Half*, 213; Alice Schlegel, "Gender

Meanings: General and Specific," in *Beyond the Second Sex*, 28.

[26] Eleanor Leacock, "Women's Status in Egalitarian Societies: Implications for Social Evolution," *Current Anthropology*, 19 (1978), 248, 252.

[27] Brown, "Iroquois Women," 237; and Joan M. Jensen, "Native American Women and Agriculture: A Seneca Case Study," in *Unequal Sisters: A Multi-Cultural Reader in U.S. Women's History*, eds. Ellen C. DuBois and Vicki L. Ruiz (New York, 1990), 51.

[28] Schlegel, "Male and Female in Hopi Thought and Action," in *Sexual Stratification*, 254.

[29] Paula Gunn Allen, *The Sacred Hoop: Recovering the Feminine in American Indian Traditions* (Boston, 1986), 243–44.

[30] Albers, "Sioux Women in Transition," 190–91; Mary Jane Schneider, "Women's Work: An Examination of Women's Roles in Plains Indian Arts and Crafts," in *The Hidden Half*, eds. Albers and Medicine, 117.

[31] Brown, "Iroquois Women," 238–244; Schlegel, "Toward a Theory of Sexual Stratification," 30; Jensen, "Native American Women," 52–54.

[32] Brown, "Iroquois Women," 251; Schlegel, "Toward a Theory of Sexual Stratification," 14, 31.

[33] Schlegel, "Male and Female in Hopi Thought and Action," 245; Leacock, "Women's Status in Egalitarian Societies," 248; Beatrice Medicine, "Indian Women: Tribal Identity as Status Quo," in *Women's Nature: Rationalizations of Inequality*, eds. Marian Lowe and Ruth Hubbard (New York, 1983), 63–73.

[34] Allen, *The Sacred Hoop*, 14–15.

[35] Gary Witherspoon, *Language and Art in the Navajo Universe* (Ann Arbor, 1977), 85, 201.

[36] Pueblo: Alfonso Ortiz, *The Tewa World: Space, Time, Being, and Becoming in a Pueblo Society* (Chicago, 1969), 49; Navajo: Louise Lamphere, *To Run After Them: Cultural and Social Bases of Cooperation in a Navajo Community* (Tucson, 1977), 41–42; Lakota: Albers, "Sioux Women in Transition," 189.

[37] Brown, "Iroquois Women," 241; McCall, "The Dominant Dyad," 228; Schlegel, "Gender Meanings," 32.

[38] Murphy and Murphy, "Women's Work and Property," 183.

[39] Thomas Buckley, "Menstruation and the power of Yurok women: methods in cultural reconstruction," *American Ethnologist*, 9 (1982), 57.

[40] Schlegel, "Male and Female in Hopi Thought and Action," 264.

[41] Beatrice Medicine, *The Native American Woman: A Perspective* (Austin, 1978), 52–53; Raymond J. DeMallie, "Male and Female in Traditional Lakota Culture," in *The Hidden Half*, eds. Albers and Medicine, 256, 261.

[42] Schneider, "Women's Work," 115; Alice Kehoe, "The Shackles of

Tradition," in *The Hidden Half*, eds. Albers and Medicine, 69.

[43] Ruth M. Underhill, *Papago Woman* (Prospect Heights, 1985), 92; Allen, *The Sacred Hoop*, 87.

[44] Schlegel, "Male and Female in Hopi Thought and Action," 246.

[45] Schlegel, "Toward a Theory of Sexual Stratification," 32–33, "Gender Meanings," 28; Leacock, "Women's Status in Egalitarian Societies," 249, 252; Albers, "Sioux Women in Transition," 188–9; Allen, *The Sacred Hoop*, 82.

[46] Medicine, "Indian Women's Tribal Identity," 68; Spector, "Male/Female Task Differentiation, 94–95; Ella Deloria, *Speaking of Indians* (New York, 1945), 39–40.

[47] Allen, *The Sacred Hoop*, 26–28.

[48] See the fuller bibliographies in Sanday and Goodenough, *Beyond the Second Sex*, and Zweig, "'The Primal Mind.'"

[49] Alice Walker, *In Search of Our Mothers' Gardens: Womanist Prose* (New York, 1983); Katie G. Cannon, *Black Womanist Ethics* (Atlanta, 1988); Carol B. Davies and A. Fido, eds., *Women's Literature of the Caribbean* (Ithaca, 1990), "Introduction."

[50] Sara Ruddick, *Maternal Thinking: Toward a Politics of Peace* (Boston, 1989); Carol Gilligan, *In a Different Voice: Psychological Theory and Women's Development* (Cambridge, 1982).

[51] Mary Daly, *Gyn/Ecology: A Metaphysics of Radical Feminism* (Boston, 1978); Rosemary R. Reuther, ed., *Religion and Sexism: Images of Women in the Jewish and Christian Traditions* (New York, 1974); Reuther, *Sexism and God-Talk: Toward a Feminist Theology* (Boston, 1983); Carol Christ and Judith Plaskow, eds., *Womanspirit Rising: A Feminist Reader in Religion* (New York, 1979).

[52] On the reliability of the ancient sources, see E. N. Tigerstedt, *The Legend of Sparta in Classical Antiquity*, (Stockholm, 1974), passim; Michell, *Sparta*, 45; and Kunstler, "Family Dynamics," 33.

[53] Major sources on ancient Sparta include: Huxley, *Early Sparta*; W. G. Forrest, *A History of Sparta: 950–192 B.C.* (London, 1968); Oliva, *Sparta and Her Social Problems*; Paul Cartledge, *Sparta and Laconia: A Regional History 1300–362 B.C.* (London, 1979); L. F. Fitzhardinge, *The Spartans* (London, 1980); J. T. Hooker, *The Ancient Spartans* (London, 1980); Michell, *Sparta*; Maria Pipili, *Laconian Iconography of the Sixth Century B.C.* (Oxford University Committee for Archaeology, 1987), Monograph No. 12; Powell, *Classical Sparta*.

[54] David M. Schaps, *Economic Rights of Women in Ancient Greece* (Edinburgh, 1979), 6–7; Stephen Hodkinson, "Inheritance, Marriage, and Demography: Perspectives upon the Success and Decline of Classical Sparta," in *Classical Sparta*, ed. Powell, 79–121.

⁵⁵ Hodkinson, "Inheritance, Marriage, and Demography," 112.
⁵⁶ Cartledge and Spawforth, *Hellenistic and Roman Sparta*, 43.
⁵⁷ Calame, *Les choeurs de jeunes filles*; Martin P. Nilsson, "Die Grundlagen des spartanischen Lebens," *Klio*, 12 (1912), 308–40.
⁵⁸ Calame, *Les choeurs de jeunes filles*, vol. 1, 39.
⁵⁹ Cantarella, *Pandora's Daughters*, 72.
⁶⁰ Robert Parker, "Spartan Religion," in *Classical Sparta*, ed. Powell, 150.
⁶¹ Calame, *Les choeurs de jeunes filles*, vol. 1, 39, 411.
⁶² McCall, "The Dominant Dyad"; Kunstler, "Family Dynamics."
⁶³ Carroll Smith-Rosenberg notes that the homosociality of women's and men's lives in sex-segregated societies itself encourages greater self-esteem by gender group. See her "The Female World of Love and Ritual: Relations between Women in Nineteenth Century America," in *A Heritage of Her Own: Toward a New Social History of American Women*, eds. Nancy F. Cott and Elizabeth H. Pleck (New York, 1979), 311–42.
⁶⁴ Lamphere, *To Run After Them*.
⁶⁵ Cantarella, *Pandora's Daughters*, 43.
⁶⁶ Plutarch, *Lycurgus* 14, 47e–48b, *Apophthegmata Laconica* (*Sayings of the Spartans*) 227e13, *Apophthegmata Lacaenarum* (*Sayings of Spartan Women*) 240e5.
⁶⁷ *The Autobiography of a Papago Woman*, 92–93.
⁶⁸ Valerie French, "The Spartan Family and the Spartan Decline: Changes in Child-Rearing Practices and Failure to Reform" (unpublished manuscript, personal communication to the author).

In her earlier article, "Maternal Thinking," *Feminist Studies*, 6 (1980), 345, Ruddick notes the appeal to the powers and authority emanating from the role of motherhood in feminist utopian literature, citing, for example, Charlotte Perkins Gilman's *Herland*. We may also see the same principle at work in Goethe's evocation of the Mothers in the latter part of *Faust*.
⁶⁹ Ruddick, *Maternal Thinking*, 51–57, discusses how different societal constructions or different positions within a particular social framework can lead to differing notions of the concept of motherhood.
⁷⁰ *The Kapayo: Out of the Forest*, 1989 documentary produced by Michael Beckham, distributed by Pennsylvania State University, 1/2"VHS videocassette tape.
⁷¹ Especially Cartledge, "Spartan Wives," 101.
⁷² Michell, *Sparta*, 53
⁷³ Kunstler, "Family Dynamics," 40.

Re(de)fining Woman: Language and Power in the *Homeric Hymn to Demeter*

> Once swallowed, goddesses can be regurgitated
> and made to speak ... in the voice of the new gods.
> Annis Pratt

The *Homeric Hymn to Demeter* is a poem of the phenomenology of domination.[1] I focus on the *Homeric Hymn to Demeter* and its ideological connections to the *Theogony*: my design is to conjure up possibilities of interpretation that apply to diverse literary and cultural environments, suggesting possibilities for further feminist interpretation(s) of mythology.[2]

My discussion focuses on several areas designed to elucidate the mechanics of oppression. These constitute a partial "inventory" of key areas of investigation, made up of phenomena that come together as interconnected and interwoven "fields" all having to do with the symbolic order of the social economy. These are best expressed through a discussion of the sociology of Greek gender relations, and the use of Hecate as a model of the redefinition of "woman" in the *Theogony* and the subsequent use of this same strategy in the Hymn.[3]

Sex-Gender-History

The period of cultural development from which the *Homeric Hymn to Demeter* dates embraces simultaneously an historical moment and a period in the myth-history of the Greeks. From the information in the myth (and from information from other Mediterranean cultures that underwent this change) the myth appears to refer to an historical era when matrilineality and, quite likely, matrilocality were normative.[4] Cultural memories of this period (embedded in myth) are viewed through the lens of the seventh-sixth century.[5] During the seventh-sixth centuries (and into the classical period), Greek societal assumptions regarding changes in the status of women held that in the pre-Olympian period female deities controlled their sexuality and reproduction, and power and goods were passed down through the maternal line (matrilineality).[6] During this pre-patriarchal period, it was commonly held that the goddess chose her consort(s), who then dwelt with her (matrilocality).[7]

The chief tension within the myth is between the assumption of ownership and disposal of the daughter by the patriarchal father, and the (perceived) traditional prerogatives of women regarding their own fates and the fates of their daughters. Demeter's search for Kore and her refusal of immediate compliance with the archpatriarch, Zeus, mirrors a perceived resistance to the imposition of asymmetrical gender relations within Greek culture. The mythological pattern of the resistance of the goddess, with its accompanying social commentary, is common throughout the Mediterranean. As Lerner and Göttner-Abendroth have shown, the myth reflects the moment in the development of Western patriarchy associated with the loss of gender complementarity, division of labor but equality in the culture.[8]

Gender studies dealing with Greek society, particularly Athenian Greek society, have established this culture as being a major source for the Western ideology of asymmetrical gender relations.[9] Athenian marriage patterns, where young girls at menarche were given by their fathers or male guardians to their prospective husbands, often with little or no warning, accompanied by the maternal mortality consequent upon premature marriage, restricted physical activity, and insufficient nutrition, frequently resulted in the death of young girls before they were out of their teens. Marriage repeatedly was equivalent to death, and the symbol of Kore, the bride of Hades, ruler of the realm of the dead, played out in reality.[10]

In the ongoing colonization of the female body and character due to the essentialized and eternalized nature of the female as depicted in ritual practice,[11] we find a series of redefinitions reflective of the double ideological necessity of renaming woman as inferior and dangerous, and of arrogating to the male those "female" characteristics conceived of as emblemizing power and therefore desirable. The primary erasure woman experiences through this process includes her traditional function as life-giver and her right to make decisions about the life she has produced.[12] The *Theogony*, as

Arthur has demonstrated, is a primary document in this process; much of its importance has to do with the work's medial position as religious or spiritual history (eternalizing, essentializing) along with its ideological content.[13] The Homeric Hymns continue this tradition of redefinition, with much the same purpose.[14]

Redefining Women
Justice

Marilyn Arthur demonstrates that the narrative progression in the Theogony moves from the hubris of the non-patriarchal, pre-Olympian world, signified by the violence of Uranus, to the affirmation and establishment of δίκη, the "justice of Zeus," the purpose being the creation of a "morally and socially complex model for regulating the interactions among the members of the cosmic family."[15] She notes that much of the subtext of the Theogony deals with the redefinition of the status of women, particularly in relation to men, and the justification of patriarchal practices through this redefinition. Arthur summarizes the dual teleological goal of the poem: the establishment of the justice of Zeus and the establishment of the patriarchal family.[16] Thus, the poem mirrors the elementary social realities of the Greek cultural field: the definition of the patriarchal οἶκος, "household," as the primary social unit, transmitted from father to son (as seen in the succession myth) and the use of women as a medium of exchange.[17] In the Homeric Hymn to Demeter, the definition of οἶκος is further developed through the antagonism between two "types" of families: the perceived non-pre-patriarchal dyad of mother and child and the patriarchal family.[18]

The conflict within the Homeric Hymn, as in the Theogony, involves struggle between male and female; in this case, there are two "justices" at odds. Resolution is achieved through the establishment of Zeus' justice as essential to the well-being of the community of human beings and gods, making Demeter's justice by implication dangerous to the survival of human beings and gods. In the Theogony, continuity from father to son is a major issue; in the Homeric Hymn, the prerogative of the head of the patriarchal household to bestow his daughter upon whomever he chooses (and all this implies in terms of the sex-gender system) is the principle concern. What the author must do is justify this practice, that is, effectively reveal how the practice resulted in/ results in great benefit to humanity, while its implied converse, the mother's right to retain her daughter, with its implication of female sexual determination, results in great harm to humanity. This right signifies the right of the male to use "his" daughter to strengthen his power and his influence, and involves the reification of the female. The consequences of a world without this aspect of "the justice of Zeus" must therefore be delineated and shown as fatal to human (i.e., patriarchal) cultural and physical survival.

Fragmentation/Displacement

An important strategy in the colonization of woman and her consequent disempowerment is fragmentation of her body/being. Beginning with the *Theogony*, as Arthur and Bergren have noted, women's sexual activity is fragmented into the oppositional categories of erotic desire and fecundity, emblematized through the alteration of goddesses who stand for what Göttner-Abendroth and Pomeroy have termed "the feminine."[19] In work that builds on that of Detienne, both show that in patriarchal marriage female erotic desire and fertility must be kept separate.[20]

An important key to the alteration of pre-Olympian goddesses of regeneration, who embodied fertility *and* erotic desire, is found in the transformation of the powerful goddess Hecate, brilliantly detailed by Arthur.[21] Hecate is the first major female figure in the *Theogony* presented in a completely positive manner from the patriarchal perspective: within the internal logic of the poem, she poses no threat to the male. Arthur's discussion of the "Hymn to Hecate" (*Theog.* 411–52) shows how the character and attributes of the goddess are coopted to the new order. This is accomplished by establishing Hecate as the first lawful offspring of a patriarchal/patrilocal marriage: "She is the child of the social order which subordinates *genetrix* to *genitor*, as Metis is subsumed/consumed by Zeus."[22] In the reworking of her character, she is presented as the only child (μουνογενής, *Theog.* 426) of a lawful, patriarchal marriage, and therefore ἐπίκληρος, i.e., the conduit for the transmission of the estate, which, as a woman, she could not inherit.[23]

Hecate is under the guardianship of Zeus, and takes her place as his "daughter" (other traditions make Hecate Zeus' biological daughter: Callimachus, *Hymn* 4.36–38; Musaeus, frag. 16). Furthermore, as ἐπίκληρος, Hecate's interests are "protected" by Zeus: she transmits her patrimony to Zeus and from Zeus receives special τιμαί: i.e., her honors are only hers *in relation to Zeus*.[24] Regardless of her earlier prerogatives, in the *Theogony* it is through Zeus that Hecate has a portion in each realm of the cosmos (*Theog.* 412–14).[25]

Hecate's share in the τιμαί of the Titans, bestowed by the first Olympian, has the function of emphasizing Zeus' continuity with the old order while establishing the new; he lays claim to all that Hecate represents, making her power his own. This redefinition of a powerful goddess with connections to the old order confirms and eternalizes Zeus' power and status, while the rewriting of her character as virgin and highly esteemed ἐπίκληρος underscores the fact that the goddess no longer possesses autonomous power.[26]

In addition to her (implied) virginal status, Hecate receives the significant epithet κουροτρόφος, "nourisher of the youth" (*Theog.* 450, 452), which further reinforces her transformation as a life-giving goddess, or goddess of regeneration, into a life-sustaining goddess.[27] This practice removes the goddess—and the female—from their most vexing power, that of producing human life, leaving woman under patriarchy party to "a form of sublimated female fertility which, inasmuch as it is not directly and literally expressed, poses no threat to the divine patriarchy."[28]

In the *Homeric Hymn*, there is a similar progression in the treatment of Demeter and Kore.[29] Demeter must be rendered less powerful and threatening by showing her as no longer the Mother Goddess embodying the "wild zone" of untamed nature and fertility, but as a representation of female fertility "drawn away" from direct association with motherhood.[30] As noted previously, in the patriarchal world, erotic desire and marriage are too dangerous to be joined. The implication is that the only proper marriage will be rape, because it *must* be against the desire of the woman; the only proper bride is the intact virgin; the only proper motherhood is that which comes about as a result of rape. Desire (on the part of the woman) and reproduction are incompatible.

This change is accomplished through a series of redefinitions. At the outset, Demeter is represented as a mother connected to her abducted child by her cries, cries which precipitate her search for Kore (*Hom. Hymn Dem.* 38–39). No one, gods or mortals, will tell her the truth, nor will the auguries yield the truth of her daughter's fate; this situation initiates Demeter's dislodgement from her prepatriarchal role.[31] This silence (and silencing) of the Mother Goddess from every realm results in her alienation; Demeter wanders the earth for nine days with torches, and separates herself from the Olympian community through her refusal to partake of the food of the gods and her refusal to bathe (*Hom. Hymn Dem.* 47–50).[32] On the tenth day, Hecate appears and foreshadows Demeter's coming transformation: both goddesses carry torches, both heard the girl's cries (*Hom. Hymn Dem.* 51–61). It is Hecate who articulates the experience of hearing Kore, doubling for Demeter; Demeter herself does not speak. Richardson and Arthur point out Hecate's limitations in this episode, noting that Helius, symbolic of patriarchy, and, in Richardson's analysis, equivalent to Zeus, tells the "truth" of Kore's abduction (*Hom. Hymn Dem.* 74–81).[33] Helius also delivers the first sermon on patriarchal marriage and its benefits for Kore, pointing out the τιμαί *she will receive from her husband* (*Hom. Hymn Dem.* 82–87).[34]

Demeter does not accept the fate of her daughter, nor does she rejoice at Helius' words. Filled with a terrible grief and now angered at Zeus, she continues to refuse participation in the community of the gods, seeking a place now among mortals: "[she] went into the towns and rich fields of men, disfiguring her form a long while (εἶδος ἀμαλδύνουσα πολὺν χρόνον)" (*Hom. Hymn Dem.* 93–94).

Several purposes are served by Demeter's taking on the mortal persona she does. Driven by anger and grief at her (unexpected) impotence, Demeter accurately incarnates the phenomenology of oppression, her mortal body expressive of the extent of her disempowerment.[35] The internalization process emblematic of the process of marginalization is externalized in Demeter's disguise as an old woman accompanied by her "position" beside the Virgin Well (*Hom. Hymn Dem.* 99). In this place Demeter articulates a "lying" history that describes the true history of many women under patriarchy (*Hom. Hymn Dem.* 122ff.), one of loss of country and family, rape, and homelessness.[36]

With the apparent destruction of the prepatriarchal dyad through abduction, rape, and alienation from community, the need for new definitions arise. Demeter, as Doso, describes the role of the woman who is no longer a mother (actual or potential) under patriarchy, i.e., the woman past childbearing who is unattached to a male:

> Well could I nurse a new born child, holding him in my arms, or keep house, or spread my masters' bed in a recess of the well-built chamber, or teach the women their work. (*Hom. Hymn Dem.* 141–44)

Her functionality is to tend to the needs of the patriarchal family.

Furthermore, Demeter's equivalence in this persona is that of a virgin, hence her place beside the "Virgin Well."[37] According to Sissa, a woman who has borne children as a proper matron, i.e., behaving as a "chaste wife," effectively becomes "virginalized" at the close of childbearing years, cyclically meeting herself as intact and impermeable, beyond potential motherhood, and the threat it offers.[38]

Demeter has by no means lost the sense of her own power, as her attempt to make Demophoön immortal illustrates.[39] This incident subtly reinforces the subversion of the goddess, through presenting her as being as capricious and dangerous to mothers as Hades. Felson Rubin and Deal convincingly show the structural similarities between Demeter's reaction to Hades' abduction of Kore and Metaneira's reaction to Demeter's "cooking" of Demophoön, noting, "From the point of view of the bereft mother the narrative chain follows the same sequence, with specific events varying slightly."[40]

The poet shows Demeter's role as κουροτρόφος to be unworkable under patriarchy because she retains the ability and desire to bestow (physical) immortality. Too dangerous even as a life-sustainer, Demeter's "damage" to Demophoön is shown in his inability to be incorporated into the human community as an ordinary infant. Upon Demeter's withdrawal, he cannot be comforted (*Hom. Hymn Dem.* 290), and he grows "like an immortal" (*Hom. Hymn Dem.* 241). There is a chiastic relationship between Demeter/Demophoön and Hades/Kore exceeding the obvious one of inverted relationship (Demophoön is in the place of a son to Demeter; Kore, as Greek wife, is equivalent to Hades' minor child, i.e., his daughter). Both deities separate children from the world of their mothers, but Demophoön's bond with Demeter results in great physical and emotional benefit for the child, appropriate to Demeter's character as Great Mother, whereas Kore's bond with Hades produces fear and terror in the girl.[41] This strategy, wherein Demeter is represented as homologous to Hades, prepares for the next stage of her redefinition, where the uncontained wrath of the goddess leads to the potential destruction of the cosmic order.

The Semiotics of Demeter/Kore

As when she heard the truth about Kore from Helius (*Hom. Hymn Dem.* 90–94), the goddess' grief is renewed and intensified upon being thwarted in her plan for Demophoön. Still a goddess, but a goddess whose chief function has been denied her, Demeter is now alienated from all community: "golden-haired Demeter sat there apart ... and stayed, wasting (μινύθουσα, i.e., diminished, lessened) with yearning for her deep-bosomed daughter" (*Hom. Hymn Dem.* 302–4). As she wastes, so wastes the earth, and the resulting famine causes humanity and the gods to suffer for one year (*Hom. Hymn Dem.* 305–13), initiating the second direct action of Zeus in the Hymn, his summons to Demeter (*Hom. Hymn Dem.* 314–23).[42]

It is useful at this point to briefly discuss the semiotics involved in the abduction of Kore. DuBois points out the equivalence of Demeter to the earth. The Mother Goddess without her daughter is the earth without her fruits.[43] A further connection of Kore to the products of the earth is the triple relation of Kore, Demophoön, and the narcissus, discussed by Felson Rubin and Deal.[44] Demeter's child is the sign of her fertility and Demeter's fertility is the fertility of the earth:[45]

> The earth responds to Demeter's emotions, even though she herself is not the goddess of the earth. As the earth keeps her daughter hidden in the house of Hades, so she keeps the seeds hidden. It is only when Kore is restored to her mother that the earth becomes fertile once again.[46]

Detienne demonstrated that human beings shared an equivalence to barley in the alimentary code, thus establishing the direct relation of Demeter's suppression of barley to her suppression of the means to human life and human life itself.[47] This action along with her already established homology to Hades affirms that Demeter uncontrolled is a goddess fatal to the cosmic order.[48]

Swallowing the Goddess

Arthur observes that in the process of redefining Hecate in the *Theogony*, one of Zeus' most effective methods of consolidating his power lay in his co-optation and (re)distribution of the τιμαί the goddess already possessed.[49] In the same article, she points out that Cronus' ingestion and withholding of the Olympians functions simultaneously as an arrogation to the male deity of female procreative ability and an erasure of Rhea's maternal role, as Gaia becomes κουροτρόφος at this point in the narrative.[50] Cronus' forced disgorgement and the "delivery" of the Olympians by Zeus and Gaia (*Theog.* 501) represent Zeus' further cooptation of the female role as midwife as well as his victory over his father in the literal "bringing to birth" of the new order, thus gaining for himself the power of redistribution of τιμαί. Arthur notes that "the struggle is now condensed so that withholding the child is homologous to withholding the βασιληὶς τιμή; to force Cronus to disgorge the children is at one and the same time to force him to yield up his *timê* ... the right to rule is identified with control over procreation."[51]

Following this logic, in the *Homeric Hymn to Demeter* Hades' withholding of Kore is equivalent to the theft of Demeter's τιμή. Zeus' negotiation with Hades places him in a position analogous to the position he was in with Gaia, regardless of the fact (actually, because of the fact) that he created the crisis in the first place.[52] In the course of the narrative, Demeter has been stripped of all her τιμαί, as has her daughter.

Zeus is now in a position to dispense justice. When Demeter reasserts to Iris that the only way to appease her wrath is to return her daughter, Zeus dispatches Hermes to Hades, where he finds the king of the dead with Persephone, "much unwilling through desire for her mother" (*Hom. Hymn Dem.* 344). Hades agrees to his brother's command, Zeus' argument being that he must act thus because Demeter's wrath is causing the destruction of the human tribe and is wasting away (καταφθινύθουσα) the τιμαί of the gods (Hom. Hymn Dem. 347–56).[53]

Hades, nicely answering Helius' earlier statement (Hom. Hymn Dem. 82–7), now bestows τιμαί upon Persephone:[54]

> Go now, Persephone, to your dark-robed mother, go, and feel kindly in your heart towards me: be not so exceedingly cast down; for I shall be no unfitting husband for you among the deathless gods, that am own brother to father Zeus. And while you are here, you shall rule all that lives and moves and shall have the greatest rights (τιμάς) among the deathless gods: those who defraud you and do not appease your power with offerings, reverently performing rite and paying fit gifts, shall be punished for evermore.
> (Hom. Hymn Dem. 360–69)

At the same time, Hades binds Persephone to the world of the dead through the pomegranate seed.[55] Upon Persephone's return, Demeter's terrible silencing is broken: she hears the truth from her daughter's lips (Hom. Hymn Dem. 405–33). First, however, Demeter states that if she has not eaten, Persephone may return and she will spend her days with Demeter and Zeus and the gods with honor (τετιμένη, Hom. Hymn Dem. 395–97).[56] This is presumably the τιμή the girl had prior to her rape, the prepatriarchal honor that was hers alone. In the event that Persephone has eaten, she must spend one third of the year "beneath the secret places of the earth" (Hom. Hymn Dem. 398–400) and presumably receive her τιμή from Hades.[57] Like Hecate in the Theogony, the τιμή that is inherently Persephone's has been coopted by a stratagem only to be reassigned and redistributed by the male under whose guardianship she now is.

Hecate reappears and embraces Persephone: "From that time the lady Hecate was minister and companion to Persephone" (Hom. Hymn Dem. 440). This phrase completes the redefinition of Hecate begun in the Theogony. Hecate, in her peripheral role as κουροτρόφος, a role still threatening in a goddess, is further translated into that servant or minister (πρόπολος) and attendant (ὀπάων) to the wife of the lord of the dead.[58] The figure who was once a goddess of life and regeneration is, through her own *choice*, shown to be a chthonic goddess acknowledging the sovereignty of another goddess and placing herself in servitude to her. In terms of the patriarchal system, this new hierarchy neatly reaffirms the paradigm for the proper οἶκος, with the role of unmarried, respectable female filled now by Hecate.

It is no surprise that it is Demeter's mother Rhea whom Zeus sends in his final summons to Demeter, bidding her to (re)join the community of the gods (*Hom. Hymn Dem.* 441–58). Rhea's role in the *Theogony* is one of persuasion and supplication, in that she acts not on her own behalf, but for others, and always within the context of the family.[59] As the mother of Zeus and Demeter, completely assimilated into the new order, she is the final and most effective "peacemaker."[60]

> Come, my daughter; for far-seeing Zeus the loud-thunderer calls you to join the families of the gods, and has promised to give you what rights (τιμάς) you please among the deathless gods.
> (*Hom. Hymn Dem.* 460–62)

Zeus demands three concessions of Demeter, using arguments of reciprocation. (1) She must (re)join the company of the gods, incorporating herself into the community, in return for whatever τιμαί she pleases, i.e., in return for *his* bestowal of τιμαί upon the goddess, in keeping with his agenda of gathering and redistributing the τιμαί of the gods. This concession is essentially Demeter's consent to become part of the new order. (2) She must accept the new conditions of Persephone's life. (3) She must give up her wrath and restore the fertility of the earth (*Hom. Hymn Dem.* 460–69).[61]

Demeter agrees and immediately restores fertility to the earth; she then teaches humanity her mysteries. Finally, Demeter and Persephone (re)join the community of the gods in Olympus, "And there they dwell beside Zeus who delights in thunder, awful and reverend goddesses" (*Hom. Hymn Dem.* 485–86).

Transcendence/Regurgitating Patriarchy

> Happy (ὄλβιος) is he among men upon earth who has seen the mysteries, but he who is uninitiate, never has lot of good things once he is dead, down in the darkness and gloom.
> (*Hom. Hymn Dem.* 480–82)

In the final redefinition of Demeter, it was necessary to restore her to a position of beneficence to humanity, for her potency as the Great Mother goddess would not allow her complete erasure. Thus, Demeter must be reformed and revised to serve the new order. Her translation to the realm of the spiritual serves two purposes: as a spiritual κουροτρόφος for humankind, she is removed from active physical participation in the human world, becoming a Mystery goddess whose working occurs in mortal afterlife. Her function as fertility goddess, or goddess of regeneration is thus redefined as mystical regeneration after death. And she has now been disciplined enough to become the example of fertility tamed, of the goddess/female tamed. This final point is illustrated through *Demeter's own bestowal* of the mysteries of agriculture, which are the mysteries of the control of fertility, homologous to the earth and to women. Although *never* a wife, she is made the goddess of "chaste wifehood," a role linked with her maternal experiences and as symbol of the earth, as Detienne so effectively and completely describes.[62]

Summary and Conclusion

The *Homeric Hymn to Demeter* reflects a double crisis of survival for the Greeks: human survival of the conditions of famine, and cultural survival when faced with the new way of life demanded by the sociopolitical institution of patriarchy. Demeter, a pre-Olympian goddess, provides a key to the crisis and its resolution. Her wrath at the changed status of women, expressed in her anger and sorrow over the loss of her daughter to patriarchal marriage, precipitates her alienation and withdrawal from the society of the gods and leads to her vengeance through the creation of famine. Upon the (partial) return of her daughter,

Demeter agrees to put aside her anger, allows the earth to produce grain, and rejoins the society of the gods, healing the breach in Olympian society, and serving as a model for healing Greek society. In teaching humanity control over the fertility of the earth, Demeter *de facto* agrees to patriarchal marriage, becoming emblematic of "chaste wifehood" as she once was emblematic of the untamed procreative abilities of women.

Ideological analysis of the *Homeric Hymn to Demeter* illustrates the continuation of the displacement of female functions onto male figures begun in the *Theogony*. The purpose of this action is two-fold: the consolidation of all power into the figure of the male sovereign and the control of the group considered most threatening to the patriarchal order: unincorporated female figures. The treatment of Hecate serves as a "way in" to understanding the process of the oppression of women during this period.

In the *Theogony*, Zeus' reign is represented as the reign of justice, interpreted as the emergence of symbolic exchange and balanced reciprocity. In order for woman to become the medium of exchange, she must be redefined into a bestowable commodity. In the case of Hecate, Arthur has illustrated a metonymic process whereby the goddess was assimilated into the Olympic pantheon: she enters the Olympic pantheon through the process of redefinition (ἐπίκληρος, κουροτρόφος) and exchange (her identity as a Titan for τιμή and a place in the new order).[63]

The incorporation of the Demeter/Kore dyad required greater effort; the dyad represented fertility and regeneration believed to be necessary for human survival. Thus a complex process of the acquisition of women's power was brought into play utilizing physical force, as in the rapes of Demeter and the abduction and rape of Kore, coupled with the psychological processes of betrayal, silencing, and alienation, as in the process detailed in this paper whereby Demeter and Kore are systematically stripped of their inherent τιμαί and then doled out new τιμαί by Zeus and Hades.

Demeter must be shown to be dangerous if not controlled; furthermore, it must be made clear that only when she is controlled by Zeus does she become beneficent to humanity.[64] Ironically, the mother who resisted patriarchy after her own rape and the rape and abduction of her child is the very woman who is finally made to show men the means to control the earth, to control woman, to control (re)production. Thus the great honors paid to Demeter in the Thesmophoria and the Eleusinian Mysteries: through her redefinition she becomes the key to the colonization of women and the earth, and is forever removed from active intervention in the affairs of humanity through her elevation as a Mystery goddess. The story of Demeter and Kore is a story of appropriation, reminding us again that the fate of women is the fate of the earth.[65] The poem presents an absolute congruence between sexual and political spheres, revising the semiology of "woman" throughout.

The ideological effectiveness of the poem lies in its character as religious myth, thereby possessing, through its genre, an eternalizing quality, which lifts Demeter and Kore and Hecate out of time, making them *types* for all women. Thus, whatever is said about these three who represent the three patriarchal fragmentations/options for women's lives also applies to all women, for "woman" has been essentialized and eternalized through the process of redefinition in the poem.

Kristina Passman
University of Maine, Orono

Notes

For Joy King: *soror, alma mater, amica*.
Translations of the *Hymn to Demeter* are those of Hugh G. Evelyn-White, *Hesiod, The Homeric Hymns, and Homerica*, Loeb Classical Library (Cambridge, 1924).

[1] Other scholars refer to the poem as one of reconciliation; reconciliation, however, implies an earlier situation of harmony (or compliance): Nancy Felson Rubin and Harriet M. Deal, "Some Functions of the Demophon Episode in the *Homeric Hymn to Demeter*," *Quaderni Urbinati di Cultura Classica*, 5 (1980), 7–21; N. J. Richardson, ed., *The Homeric Hymn to Demeter*, (Oxford, 1974); C. G. Jung, and Karl Kerényi, *Essays on a Science of Mythology: The Myth of the Divine Child and the Mysteries of Eleusis*, trans. R. F. C. Hull, Bollingen 22 (Princeton, 1963); Karl Kerényi, *Eleusis: Archetypal Image of Mother and Daughter*, trans. Ralph Manheim, Bollingen 65/4 (New York, 1967). It is my contention that under patriarchy there could not be this period of harmony between men and women in Greek myth-history because of the

threat that the perceived "Otherness" of women outside of patriarchy presented (Nicole Loraux, *Tragic Ways of Killing a Woman*, trans. Anthony Forster [Cambridge, 1987]). The *Homeric Hymn to Demeter* continues the process of the consolidation of patriarchal ideology through rewriting the category "woman."

² In a manifesto concerning the need for risk-taking among feminist scholars, Annis Pratt, "Spinning Among the Fields: Jung, Frye, Lévi-Strauss and Feminist Archetypal Theory," in *Feminist Archetypal Theory: Interdisciplinary Re-Visions of Jungian Thought*, eds. Estella Lauter and Carol Schreier Rupprecht (Knoxville, 1985), maintains that the best in feminist theory comes from "spinning between the fields," producing coalescences of thought and insight impossible without an interdisciplinary and (one hopes) playfully outrageous perspective (93–96).

³ Recognition that the role of the poet in this period included carrying on the "shamanic" or mediating function of the early storyteller is closely connected to analysis of the ideological function of the *Theogony* and the *Homeric Hymn to Demeter*. See Francis Cornford, *Principium Sapientiae* (Cambridge, 1952); Passman, "Literary Shamanism and Augustan Poetry," forthcoming, *Augustan Age* (1993). These factors combined to bestow the status of "truth" upon such works, as Ann L. T. Bergren, "Language and the Female in Early Greek Thought," *Arethusa*, 16 (1983), 69–95, points out.

I assume the author of the *Homeric Hymn to Demeter* was familiar with the *Theogony*. In this I follow Richardson, *The Homeric Hymn to Demeter*, 5ff.

⁴ Margaret Ehrenberg, *Women in Prehistory* (Norman, 1989); Marija Gimbutas, *The Goddesses and Gods of Old Europe, 6500–3500 B.C.: Myths and Cult Images* (Berkeley, 1982); Gerda Lerner, *The Creation of Patriarchy* (Oxford, 1986), 36–53.

⁵ Richardson, *The Homeric Hymn to Demeter*, 5–12.

⁶ Marilyn B. Arthur, "Early Greece: The Origins of the Western Attitude Toward Women," in *Women in the Ancient World: The Arethusa Papers*, eds. John Peradotto and J. P. Sullivan (Albany, 1984), 7–58; Page duBois, *Centaurs and Amazons: Women and the Pre-History of the Great Chain of Being* (Ann Arbor, 1982); duBois, *Sowing the Body: Psychoanalysis and Ancient Representations of Women* (Chicago, 1988); William Blake Tyrrell, *Amazons: A Study in Athenian Mythmaking* (Baltimore, 1984).

⁷ Marcel Detienne, *The Gardens of Adonis: Spices in Greek Mythology*, trans. Janet Lloyd, (Atlantic Highlands, 1977); Heide Göttner-Abendroth, *Matriarchal Mythology in Former Times and Today*, trans. Lise Weil (Freedom, 1987); Miriam Robbins Dexter, *Whence the Goddesses: A Source Book*, (New York, 1990).

⁸ Lerner, *The Creation of Patriarchy*; Göttner-Abendroth, *Matriarchal*

Mythology.

For a discussion of the historical implications of the change from matrilocality to patrilocality for the status of women, see Stephanie Coontz and Peta Henderson, "Property Forms, Political Power and Female Labour in the Origins of Class and State Societies," in *Women's Work, Men's Property: The Origins of Gender and Class*, eds. Stephanie Coontz and Peta Henderson (London, 1986), 108–55.

[9] Arthur, "Early Greece"; duBois, *Centaurs and Amazons*, and *Sowing the Body*; Sarah B. Pomeroy, *Goddesses, Whores, Wives, and Slaves: Women in Classical Antiquity* (New York, 1975); Monique Saliou, "The Processes of Women's Subordination in Primitive and Archaic Greece," in *Women's Work, Men's Property*, eds. Coontz and Henderson, 169–206.

[10] Eva C. Keuls, *The Reign of the Phallus: Sexual Politics in Ancient Athens* (New York, 1985), 129–47; Loraux, *Tragic Ways of Killing a Woman*. Recent studies have shifted the focus to women's self-assertion in the spheres where they had status (and possibly power): domestic and religious life. See, for example, John J. Winkler, *The Constraints of Desire: The Anthropology of Sex and Gender in Ancient Greece* (New York, 1990), 188–209. Women were always essential in Greek religion for the health and well-being of household and *polis* (Pomeroy, *Goddesses, Whores, Wives, and Slaves*, 75–78). In Athens there were important ritual occasions which could only be celebrated by women, and many which required women for their proper observance. These ritual occasions hearkened back to a time traditional in Greek myth-history when women and men were believed to have had a different relationship; they also acknowledged the very real and essential role that women continued to hold in the community even with the change in their civil status. See Lerner, *The Creation of Patriarchy*, 160.

[11] Froma I. Zeitlin, "Cultic Models of the Female: Rites of Dionysus and Demeter," *Arethusa*, 15.1/2 (1982), 141–42.

[12] See Marilyn Arthur's three articles, "Cultural Strategies in Hesiod's *Theogony*: Law, Family, Society," *Arethusa*, 15.1/2 (1982), 63–82; "The Dream of a World without Women: Poetics and the Circles of Order in the *Theogony* Proemium," *Arethusa*, 16 (1983), 97–116; and "Early Greece." See also duBois, *Sowing the Body*; Keuls, *The Reign of the Phallus*.

[13] Arthur, "Cultural Strategies," "The Dream of a World without Women."

[14] Richardson, *The Homeric Hymn to Demeter*, 30–61, discusses the linguistic affinities between the *Theogony* and the Homeric Hymn; Ann L. T. Bergren, "Sacred Apostrophe: Re-Presentation and Imitation in the *Homeric Hymns*," *Arethusa*, 15.1/2 (1982), 83–108, shows how the *Homeric Hymns* to Apollo and Hermes illuminate the "family drama" of brother and sons.

[15] Arthur, "Cultural Strategies," 63.

[16] Jane Harrison, *Prolegomena to the Study of Greek Religion* (Cambridge, 1903), 285, defined the challenge of redefinition:

> Zeus the Father will have no great Earth-goddess, Mother and Maid in one, in his man-fashioned Olympus, but her figure *is* from the beginning, so he remakes it; woman, who was the inspirer, becomes the temptress; she who made all things, gods and mortals alike, is become their plaything, their slave, dowered only with personal beauty and with a slave's tricks and blandishments. To Zeus, the archpatriarchal *bourgeois*, the birth of the first woman is but a huge Olympian jest.

[17] Arthur, "Cultural Strategies," views the problematic of the *Theogony* as the struggle between men and women for power and justice. The male is assigned a place in the cosmos and replaces his predecessor, thus treated "metaphorically." The female is successively redefined through synecdoche and metonymy until she is successfully neutralized and no longer poses a threat to the patriarchal order nor can she interrogate by her presence and power the "justice of Zeus."

[18] Göttner-Abendroth defines the non-patriarchal family:

> The relationship between mother and daughter is the core relationship ... , followed by the relationship between a mother's brother and her son. A father-son relationship does not exist because there is no knowledge of biological fatherhood or, if there is any, the notion is of no importance. ... There exists no permanent bond between mates, and permanent marriage is unknown. ... There are many occasions for free sexual encounters. Men are well-accepted and integrated as sons, brothers and uncles, but they have no importance as husbands or fathers.
>
> (*Matriarchal Mythology*, 2)

Compare the tale of Cecrops' establishment of marriage at Athens:

> At Athens Cecrops first yoked one woman to one man. Before then mating was at random and promiscuous. ... He discovered many laws for humans and led them from savagery [or bestiality] to tameness [or civilization]. ... Men had intercourse with women as it chanced and so the son was not

known to the father nor the father to the son. Cecrops laid down laws so that men had intercourse with them openly and were contented with one wife. He also discovered the two natures of the father and the mother. Cecrops legislated that women, who before mated like beasts, be given in marriage to one man.
(collected and trans. by Tyrrell, *Amazons*, 30)

[19] Arthur, "Cultural Strategies," 67; Bergren, "Language and the Female," 71–75; Göttner-Abendroth, *Matriarchal Mythology*; and Pomeroy, *Goddesses, Whores, Wives, and Slaves*, 8–9.

[20] Vernant, in Detienne, *The Gardens of Adonis*, vii, states the case:

If the wife abandons herself to the call of desire she rejects her status of matron and assumes that of courtesan, thus deflecting marriage from its normal end and turning it into an instrument of sensuous enjoyment. Pleasure is not the object of marriage. Its function is quite different: to unite two family groups within the same city, so that a man can have legitimate children who "resemble their father" despite being the issue of their mother's womb, and who will thus be able, on the social and religious level, to continue the line of their father's house to which they belong.

[21] Arthur, "Cultural Strategies"; cf. Dexter, *Whence the Goddesses*, 128.
[22] Arthur, "Cultural Strategies," 68–69.
[23] Pomeroy, *Goddesses, Whores, Wives, and Slaves*, 60–66.
[24] Arthur, "Cultural Strategies," 69.
[25] Dexter, *Whence the Goddesses*, notes that "[t]he potency of Hecate was reflected in her transformation into a *transfunctional* goddess" (124). She goes on to say that "the transformation of a goddess who reigned over heaven, earth, and sea, into a witch of the Netherworld, was not uncommon. In particular, the 'goddess of regeneration,' who could deprive a person or animal of life, was often relegated by the Indo-European to the place of death, the Underworld" (126). By the end of the *Homeric Hymn*, Hecate is transformed directly into a goddess associated with the Underworld, along with Persephone.
[26] Arthur, "Cultural Strategies," 69–70.
[27] Cf. Dexter, *Whence the Goddesses*, supra; Giulia Sissa's recent work, *Greek Virginity*, trans. Arthur Goldhammer (Cambridge, 1990), has much to say about attitudes toward and definition of virginity in the historical period. The point here is the process of the redefinition of virginity, from the non-

patriarchal meaning of an autonomous woman who has not committed to becoming a matron, a state that does not preclude sexual activity or even childbirth, to the patriarchal definition of *vagina intacta*. For the non-patriarchal definition of virginity, see Nor Hall's discussion, *The Moon and the Virgin: Reflections on the Archetypal Feminine* (New York, 1980), 11ff.

[28] Arthur, "Cultural Strategies," 70; Bergren, "Language and the Female," sees the fundamental struggle in the *Theogony* as the struggle over women's reproduction; the appropriation of women's reproductive capacity is emblematic of the attempt of Greek patriarchy to completely colonize the female, erasing her identity as an autonomous human being through language in the service of ideology. Arthur, "The Dream of a World without Women," speaks of how the Greek "dream of a world without women" becomes more possible through the eradication of women's direct participation in the creation of life.

[29] As noted earlier, it is likely that the composer of the *Homeric Hymn* was aware of the early history of Demeter, as detailed in the *Theogony* and other mythological material and also assumed the audience's knowledge of this material: Demeter's consort, Iasion (*Theog.* 969–75; *Od.* 5.125–28); Zeus as father to Persephone (*Theog.* 912–14); Demeter's transformation into a mare during her mourning-period for Persephone and Poseidon's pursuit and rape of her—used to explain the epithet "Demeter Erinyes" (Pindar, *Pythian* 6.50; Pausanias 8.25. 3–5; Apollodorus 3.6.8—the last two citations are, of course, late; it is impossible to determine whether these accounts were known to the audience of the *Homeric Hymn*).

[30] Zeus' murder of Iasion symbolizes the initiation of patriarchal marriage just as his bestowal of Kore upon Hades indicates its completion. Iasion was the last consort of the Great Mother: she desired him, joining with him in a thrice-ploughed field, reflecting the earlier priority of fertility united with erotic desire.

[31] For language and truth as an original and appropriated prerogative of woman in prepatriarchal Greek culture, see Bergren, "Language and the Female," 69–71.

[32] Richardson, *The Homeric Hymn to Demeter*, 165–67.

[33] Richardson, ibid., 156–57, and Marilyn Arthur, "Politics and Pomegranates: An Interpretation of the *Homeric Hymn to Demeter*," *Arethusa*, 10 (1977), 13.

[34] Because Kore, like her mother, already possesses τιμαί independently from the Olympian order (Dexter, *Whence the Goddesses*, 128), she must be brought into the Olympian fold through a process similar to that of Hecate in the *Theogony*, i.e., the "bestowal" not only of her person in marriage but also of τιμαί from Zeus, through her husband.

Helius speaks:

> Yet, goddess, cease your loud lament and keep not vain anger unrelentingly: Aïdoneus, the Ruler of Many, is no unfitting (ἀεικής) husband among the deathless gods for your child, being your own brother and borne of the same stock: also, for honor (τιμή), he has that third share which he received when division was made at the first, and is appointed lord of those among whom he dwells.
> (Hom. Hymn Dem. 82–87)

[35] Sandra Lee Bartky, *Femininity and Domination: Studies in the Phenomenology of Oppression* (New York, 1990), 22–32; Bergren, "Sacred Apostrophe," 83–108.

[36] This is a syntagmic "lie," paralleling Kore's experience of rape and abduction and Demeter's wanderings. Another way of viewing it is that Demeter, through her lie, is metonymically experiencing Kore's rape and separation and her own wandering, simultaneously. There are other important features of this tale. (1) Her name, although problematical (see Richardson, *The Homeric Hymn to Demeter*, 188), refers to her divinity or to her "gifting" quality. (2) "Doso" was named *by her mother* indicating a matrilineal, dyadic relation, paralleling Demeter's with her daughter. (3) She is from Crete, which certainly is the site of many a "lying tale" (as Richardson, *The Homeric Hymn to Demeter*, 188, points out); however, Crete was also the location of pre-patriarchal traditions, including the birth of Zeus (Martin P. Nilsson, *A History of Greek Religion*, trans. F. J. Fielden, 2d ed. [New York, 1964], 30–33; Richardson loc. cit.). (4) The language of abduction and rape, as well as the distance from home, parallels the story of Kore. (5) Demeter/Doso refuses food, an important aspect of Demeter's continuing refusal to be incorporated into the Olympian and human communities, foreshadowing the reason why Kore may not be completely restored to her mother. Through ingestion of the pomegranate, she is partially incorporated into the realm of the dead. (6) Kore is "unpurchased," but Demeter/Doso flees through the darkness so she will not be taken unpurchased, and win a profit for her captors, a situation she tries to change for her daughter. (7) Her persona and her reality come together when she describes herself as having wandered to the Maiden Well.

[37] Richardson, *The Homeric Hymn to Demeter*, 179–82.

[38] Sissa, *Greek Virginity*, 122–23. A complicit old woman is the least threatening of all women under patriarchy, because she can only ever be a foster-mother; patriarchal logic dictates that this woman is often held in the greatest esteem, as seen in the discussion of Hecate above, and significant works from the classical period reinforce this (Plato, *Theaetetus* 149b–c, *Laws* 6.759b9). She must, however, be held under tight patriarchal supervision:

note the ambiguous position of Hecate in the *Theogony* and *Homeric Hymn to Demeter* as opposed to her popular (and enduring) attributes as "goddess of the witches." The label of "witch" is, of course, the label which continues to keep older (and younger) women with aspirations of autonomy or visions of an alternative lifestyle in submission to patriarchy through the threat and actuality of rape, murder, and incarceration (Starhawk, *The Spiral Dance* [San Francisco, 1979], 183–219).

[39] Richardson, *The Homeric Hymn to Demeter*, 231–36. This is a typical activity for goddesses who wish to make their own or their foster sons immortal, cf. Isis and Thetis. In all cases the goddesses are unable to bestow immortality on human beings; in Greek myth as we have it, under patriarchy, only male gods bestow immortality, and although goddesses continue to have the ability to bestow life, i.e., Aphrodite in the Pygmalion tale, most of their activity as goddesses of regeneration is shifted to the death-bringing aspect of the cycle. Dexter, *Whence the Goddesses*, discusses this process as part of the transformation of "woman" under patriarchy (177–83).

[40] Felson Rubin and Deal, "Some Functions of the Demophon Episode in the *Homeric Hymn to Demeter*." I quote the passage in full:

> In the outsider's request for her child the mother is not fully informed—either not consulted at all in Demeter's case or duped by disguise and deceit in Metaneira's. Each mother remains ignorant of the violent or apparently violent act committed by the outsider upon her child. Each, discovering this act, believes the child has been or will be annihilated at the hands of the stranger. Grief and anger lead each to obstruct a divine plan (Demeter, the will of Zeus; Metaneira, the plan of Demeter). This interference eventually causes the outsider to return, or promise to return, the child (Demeter voluntarily, Hades under constraint). Each mother then partially yields to the outsider (Demeter by a resigned acceptance of Persephone's intermittent residence with Hades, Metaneira by a silent and awed acceptance of Demophon's ritual bond with Demeter). (9–10)

This article contains much that is useful for an understanding of the redefinition of power relations as articulated in the *Homeric Hymn*; where we differ is in my analysis of these relations as contributing to the subversion of female power and the imposition of the ideology of patriarchal dominance.

[41] Felson Rubin and Deal, "Some Functions of the Demophon Episode in the *Homeric Hymn to Demeter*," 15–17.

⁴² For the connection between human society, sacrifice, and the gods, see Marcel Detienne and Jean-Pierre Vernant, et al., *The Cuisine of Sacrifice among the Greeks*, trans. Paula Wissing (Chicago, 1989).

⁴³ DuBois, *Sowing the Body*, 52.

⁴⁴ Felson Rubin and Deal, "Some Functions of the Demophon Episode in the *Homeric Hymn to Demeter*," 11, 15.

⁴⁵ Mythic logic is operative here: as long as she could be mother/foster-mother, Demeter retained her function as fertility-bringer to the earth; with all possibility of nurturing taken from her, the goddess is barren on every level. Maternity denied is fertility denied. With the vestiges of the prepatriarchal world represented by Demeter/Kore now completely destroyed, the stage is set for Zeus to remake it—on his terms.

⁴⁶ DuBois, *Sowing the Body*, 52.

⁴⁷ Detienne, *The Gardens of Adonis*.

⁴⁸ As in all ideologies of oppression, it does not matter that Demeter was driven to this point; what matters is that she is shown to be destructive and therefore unreliable, in need of "taming."

⁴⁹ Arthur, "Cultural Strategies," 68–70.

⁵⁰ Ibid., 71.

⁵¹ Ibid., 71.

⁵² Zeus' consumption of Metis at the close of his battle with the Titans is foundational to this entire process. It is with Metis that Zeus interrupts for all time the possibility of violent overthrow of the rule he has labored to establish. She is Zeus' first "wife" and thus the symbol of his primary process of controlling procreation and taking on that function for himself. The (re)birth (redefinition) of Athena as the quintessential "Daddy's girl" proclaims this function. The ingestion of his wife gives Zeus μῆτις for eternity. See the remarks of Marcel Detienne and Jean-Pierre Vernant, *Cunning Intelligence in Greek Culture and Society*, trans. Janet Lloyd (Atlantic Highlands, 1978):

> There can be no μῆτις possible without Zeus or directed against him. Not a single cunning trick can be plotted in the universe without first passing through his mind. There can no longer be any risk to threaten the duration of the power of the sovereign god. Nothing can surprise him, cheat his vigilance or frustrate his designs. Thanks to the μῆτις within him Zeus is now forewarned of everything, whether good or bad, that is in store for him. For him there is no gap between a plan and its fulfillment such as enables the unexpected to intervene in the lives of other gods and mortals. (14)

Thus when Demeter uses μῆτις, as she does at 345 (with the implication that she has been using it all along), it does not help her: Zeus is aware of her attempts to gain the upper hand through her cunning and is using her stratagems to his advantage, to further and consolidate his sovereignty.

⁵³ The same verb is used in addressing Hades as lord of the departed, καταφθιμένοισιν (346) and the effect of Demeter upon the τιμαί of the gods, καταφθινύθουσα (353). This reinforces the homology between Hades and his activities and Demeter and her activities.

⁵⁴ Richardson, *The Homeric Hymn to Demeter*, 269–75.

⁵⁵ Marilyn Arthur, "Politics and Pomegranates," 28–29; Felson Rubin and Deal, "Some Functions of the Demophon Episode in the *Homeric Hymn to Demeter*," 13, 21; Kerényi, *Eleusis*, 130–44; Richardson, *The Homeric Hymn to Demeter*, 276.

⁵⁶ Eating food from another realm binds one to that realm. Through her ministrations to Demophoön, he now belongs partially to the human world and partly to the world of the immortals. Persephone also belongs to two realms, that of her mother and that of Hades. Because she has sought to accomplish with Demophoön what Hades succeeded in doing, Demeter understands that Persephone is bound to the world of the dead. Her own refusal to eat the food of the gods indicated her separation from that realm, as did her refusal to eat the food of humanity, except in the ritual drink *kykeon*. *Kykeon*, a mixture of barley, mint, and water, mingles the world of humanity (barley) and the world of the dead. Mintha was Hades' lover until destroyed by Demeter to make room for Persephone. The implications of this tradition have yet to be worked out in the larger context of the establishment of patriarchal marriage and the process of assimilation and acceptance of the prepatriarchal goddesses. Detienne's discussion is foundational for this task (*The Gardens of Adonis*, 71–98).

⁵⁷ As noted, patriarchal marriage becomes equivalent to rape, and in both the woman historically has no choice in procreation. Demeter was raped by both Zeus and Poseidon, giving birth to Kore and the horse Arion; ironically, in the next generation Kore was raped by the remaining brother of the trio and gave birth to a son, variously named Plutus (Wealth) and Dionysus. (Kerényi, *Eleusis*, 105–74, discusses these latter offspring.)

⁵⁸ Richardson, *The Homeric Hymn to Demeter*, 294–95.

⁵⁹ Arthur, "Cultural Strategies," 70–71.

⁶⁰ Richardson, *The Homeric Hymn to Demeter*, 295–96.

⁶¹ Arthur, "Cultural Strategies," discusses how the cycle of reciprocity is essential in the establishment of the "justice of Zeus." See also the general discussion of how μῆτις supports Zeus' ability to command and bind in Marcel Detienne and Jean-Pierre Vernant's *Cunning Intelligence*, 279–318.

[62] The spiritual is an essential component of cultural redefinition and social control, and the *Homeric Hymn to Demeter* gave rise to important spiritual practices, such as the Thesmophoria and the Eleusinian Mysteries, that reiterated and reinforced the oppression of women while obfuscating this reality through rhetoric. The purpose of the Thesmophoria was the promotion and generation of crops and human beings; during the festival, gardens signifying both crops and human beings were planted and quickly sprouted, then were allowed to die (Detienne, *The Gardens of Adonis*, 102–4; Winkler, *The Constraints of Desire*, 189–205). Winkler's reconstruction of the Thesmophoria from the women's perspective captures the insidiousness I describe:

> Men's role ... is to plow and to plant the seed. It is human mothers who carry the long burden of human generation. It is women who civilize Demeter's wheat, turning it first into flour, then into bread; it is women who nurture and train children. ... What the gardens with their quickly rising and quickly wilting sprouts symbolize is the marginal role that men play in both agriculture (vis-a-vis the earth) and human generation (vis-a-vis wives and mothers). (205)

Men may have a marginal role in these activities, but through the arrogation of women's power and the suppression of women's identity, men's literal marginality counted for very little; men received the credit and status of parenthood and personhood, and that reality, regardless of the use of language, or the change in present culture towards the power relations between men and women, cannot be denied.

[63] Arthur, "Cultural Strategies," 69–70.

[64] Arthur, ibid., 74, notes that the violent or repressive aspects of male figures do not suffer any such transformation. In fact, they all learn to behave the same way. This establishes male succession: all men metaphorically become Zeus and his followers, replicating in their particularities the patriarchal οἶκος and all it implies in terms of dominance, submission, and complicity.

[65] Demeter's goal is the return of her daughter and all she represents. She resists all Olympus as best she can and Zeus acknowledges her power and subverts it through a series of stratagems. In the end, Demeter, too, is consumed by Zeus as her daughter has been consumed by the Underworld. I do perceive an area of resistance. Nowhere is it stated that Demeter eats with the gods, and she does not appear in Olympus again except in this poem. This suggests that the redefinition of Demeter's power, like the redefinition of Hecate's, did not completely succeed.

Women, Fat, and Fertility: Hippocratic Theorizing and Treatment

Judging women's ideal body image from a society's art is a complex business. In our own late twentieth-century American culture, for example, the women shown on television, in fashion magazines, and in movies are far slimmer than their actual flesh-and-blood counterparts whom we meet and know and work with every day. Despite this discrepancy between image and reality, the ideal of slimness for women continues to dominate our age—fueled afresh by a concern with staying healthy. Dieting is now linked with health, as fat has become our number one dietary villain.[1]

Thin women were not always the ideal, as a glance at the hefty nudes in Peter Paul Rubens' paintings reveal.[2] And traveling back to the dawn of Greek antiquity, we find Cycladic female figures (whether they were representations of goddesses or of women) endowed with massive breasts, thighs, and buttocks—seemingly attributes of female fertility. But how are we to interpret the slender women on classical Greek vases? In some female nudes there is even an assimilation of the female form to the masculine, with an intriguing similarity of the shoulders, hips, and pectoral muscles in *hetairai*, men, and youths.[3] From the evidence of Greek vase painting, at least, one could infer that the ideal of classical Greek feminine beauty was slimness and, even further, the slimness of the adolescent male. But one cannot help wondering if a discrepancy existed between the classical Greek ideal female body image and reality, a discrepancy similar to that which exists today in our own culture. In addition, one would like to know what factors other than the aesthetic may have contributed to the classical ideal of slenderness. Was fertility in ancient Greece associated with female slimness, rather than plumpness?

In this paper I offer the evidence of the classical Greek medical writings to attempt an answer to these questions. As I will show, their concern with female fleshiness suggests that not many classical Greek women matched their images on Greek vases. Dating from the fifth and fourth centuries B.C., this anonymous body of medical writings was collected under the name of Hippocrates, most probably at the Library of Alexandria in the early third century B.C. From that time on it has provided the scientific basis for the care of women all through the rest of antiquity, the Middle Ages, the Renaissance, into the nineteenth century in the West, and up to the present day in Unani medicine practiced in India and Pakistan.[4]

There are no specific treatises in the Hippocratic writings on weight control for women. The information I am presenting here is culled from general works about regimen (a term that includes diet, exercise, baths, and clothing, and really should be translated as *life style*). In addition to strictly gynecological works, I have also looked at general Hippocratic works about the relation of climate to physique and character. In such treatises there are many theoretical passages on the different nature of men's and women's flesh and on the connection between excessive weight and infertility as well as prescriptive passages on special diets for women, for different age groups of both sexes, and for overweight men. From these we can form some impression of fifth- and fourth-century B.C. medical views about women, fat, and fertility.

The anonymous Hippocratic treatise *A Regimen for Health* is a short and lively popular account of the principles of staying healthy throughout the year by adjusting diet and life style to counterbalance the seasons.[5] The underlying assumptions are first, that human beings are combinations of the qualities of hot, cold, dry, and wet; second, that a state of health exists when these qualities are balanced, allowing, of course, for individual variations; and third, that to maintain health or to restore health one must adopt a diet and life style opposite to the prevailing conditions of the season and opposite to any unhealthy condition of one's own. Each season is characterized by a pair of these qualities—hot, cold, dry, and wet—which affect the components of the human body.

Winter, for example, which is cold and wet, chills and moistens the body. Thus the body will take on the characteristics of the season, which, in turn, will distort the innate balance of its components, unless the individual prepares for and counteracts the effects of the season by a rational diet and life style. Accordingly, to keep the body dry and warm, *Regimen for Health* recommends decreasing fluids, drinking undiluted wine, eating roasted meat and fish instead of boiled, substituting wheat bread for barley cake, and avoiding vegetables as much as possible.[6]

Not only were these qualities of hot, cold, dry, and wet predominant in turn in each season, but over the course of a human life first one pair of qualities prevailed, then another. We can reconstruct the full schema on the basis of *A Regimen for Health*, cited above, and another Hippocratic treatise from the late fifth century entitled simply *Regimen*.[7] Male babies start off warm and moist, like the environment of the uterus. As they grow toward their prime, male children dry out, becoming drier as adults, while still remaining warm. As men advance in years they cool off, ending up in old age cold and moist.[8] And women, you are wondering? Women start off in life cooler and moister than men and stay cooler and moister all their lives. *Regimen* attributes this to their diet, which is moister, and their life style, which is less active.[9]

This view of women as moister and cooler than men is characteristic of the Hippocratic dietetic treatises, such as *Regimen*, Book 1,[10] and works like *Airs, Waters, Places*.[11] On the other hand, the Hippocratic gynecological treatises depict women as moister and warmer than men.[12] For example, in the gynecological work *Diseases of Women*, Book 1, the author claims that a woman's body is moister because her flesh is fundamentally different from that of men. Using a famous thought experiment that equates unspun fleece to women's porous flesh and tightly woven woolen cloth to men's more solid flesh, the author concludes that a woman's softer and more spongelike flesh "draws moisture with more speed and in greater quantity from the belly than does the body of a man."[13] The plethora of moisture in a woman is blood. And, according to this same first chapter of *Diseases of Women*, Book 1, "a woman has warmer blood, and therefore she is warmer than a man."[14] The moist female body is at risk, however, if this blood is not properly drained by monthly menstruation or absorbed in pregnancies. Should this occur, a woman's uterus "is heated by the blood that lingers in it and in turn heats the rest of the body," according to the author of another gynecological treatise, *On the Nature of the Child*.[15] Yet there are inconsistencies even in this work. Later in chapters 18 and 31 of *On the Nature of the Child*, the author seems to be thinking of women as moister and colder than men, stating that male fetuses coagulate in thirty days as opposed to forty-two days for female fetuses and that female seed is "more fluid and weaker."[16]

The inconsistencies in whether women were warmer or colder than men arose, I suggest, from attempts to reconcile deeply rooted popular conceptions about the differences between men and women with rational explanations. In this question of temperature, the theory that women were moister and colder won out, for a number of complicated reasons. One was Aristotle, whose reproductive theory held that women did not contribute semen to conception, but rather menses, an unconcocted residue which was unable to form itself into an embryo without male agency. This he likened to a potter's action on clay or a carpenter's action in shaping wood into a house. The crucial aspect of the male's role in conception was his greater heat, which "cooked" female matter into a fetus. Women, in contrast, lacked this ability because they were innately colder.[17] Another factor that established women as colder than men was a deeply rooted system of analogies and polarities, which are evidenced in Greek literature and philosophy dating back to Homer and the Presocratics, and which portrayed the superior quality of body and mind as warm and dry and early on associated these qualities with men. Women, by the habit of thinking in terms of binary pairs, were wetter and colder.[18] So despite inconsistencies in the temperature of women, the consensus in classical Greek medical and non-medical writings was that women were wetter.

But how is this wet nature related to fat? I suggest that a certain confusion or vagueness about the end product of *plethos* ("excess") was responsible. As we have seen in the gynecological works, such as *Diseases of Women*, Book 1, women's soft flesh draws from their bellies a plethora of moisture. This moisture becomes a plethora of blood, which must be drained off in menstruation or used to nourish the fetus in pregnancy, if a woman is to avoid serious disease states. In the dietetic treatises the moisture that makes women's bodies fleshier than men's can be controlled by diet and a drying regimen. A *Regimen for Health* recommends the following diet for women, who are all colder and moister than men by nature: "Women do best on a drier diet as dry foods are most suited to the softness of their flesh (πρὸς τὴν μαλθακότητα τῶν σαρκῶν), and the less diluted drinks are better for the womb and for pregnancy."[19] Note the connection between fleshiness and moisture. Note, also, that the author's concern about women's natural fleshiness is not due to asthetics or longevity or fitness, but rather to their ability to conceive and carry pregnancies to term.[20]

Already one can see the easy or, if you will, imprecise association between wetness and softness of flesh. This kind of associative thinking is, of course, linked to binary or polar thinking, that is, thinking in terms of opposites, which is a distinctive mental habit of fifth-century Greeks, whether medically minded or not. Thus the correct medical response to soft, wet flesh is a preventive regimen or a treatment program characterized as opposite to the condition—that is, in a dietetic context, a dry diet.[21]

Now that I've sketched the Hippocratic connection between female moistness and fleshiness, let me relate this fat/moist/female association to a wider Greek cultural pattern linking fat, moist, and female with barbarian. Like other fifth-century Greeks, Hippocratic physicians were influenced by their habit of seeing the world in pairs of opposites, such as female/male, cold/hot, wet/dry, fleshy/lean, barbarian/Greek.[22] Certain members of these pairs came to be associated with each other through another powerful habit of thinking—analogy, by which one thing is explained by or linked with another thing that is already familiar.[23] In the list above, classical Greeks would have readily assented to the analogous relation of female, cold, wet, fleshy, barbarian. Such a conceptual cluster associating soft flesh with females and Persian barbarians is evidenced by Xenophon's anecdote about the Spartan King Agesilaus. To fill his Spartan soldiers with courage, Agesilaus ordered that "Persian barbarians captured in the raids should be exposed for sale naked. So when his soldiers saw them white because they never stripped, and fat (πίονες) and lazy through constant riding in carriages, they [the Spartans] believed that the war would be exactly like fighting with women."[24]

We can see this cultural pattern associating fat with cold, wet, female, barbarian, <u>and</u> infertility in a very interesting fifth-century Hippocratic work: *Airs, Waters, Places*.[25] This treatise contrasts several distant ethnic groups with the Greeks in order to establish Greek physique and character as the norm. Recall that this is exactly the same goal of Herodotus, also writing in the fifth century B.C., when he presented the Egyptians as doing everything opposite to the Greeks, thereby establishing the Greeks as normal and the Egyptians as the "Other."[26] Similarly, the anonymous Hippocratic author of *Airs, Waters, Places* showed the Egyptians and Libyans in the far south (in a section now lost), then the Scythians in the far north, as extreme opposites of the Greeks. The thesis of *Airs, Waters, Places* is that climate and terrain determine physique and character. The anonymous author explains the mental and physical vigor and versatility of the Greeks as resulting from their exposure to a variety of temperatures in a climate with four seasons. In addition, the Greeks are tempered by the rugged variety of their geography. In contrast, people like the Scythians must be less healthy because they live in a land with only one unvarying climate and in terrain that is uniformly flat. The Scythians, subject to unvarying cold and moist, are depicted as uniformly taking on the qualities of their environment. Accordingly, their bodies are "gross, fleshy, showing no joints, moist and flabby, and the lower bowels are as moist as bowels can be."[27] The Hippocratic author then gives proof of the extreme moistness of the Scythians, noting that they cauterize their shoulder and other joints to strengthen them because their joints are weak as a result of their moistness and softness (διὰ τὴν ὑγρότητα τῆς φύσιος καὶ τὴν μαλακίην).[28] Note how the author associates moistness and softness of flesh by pairing up moistness and lack of muscle tone in this same section.[29] As for the young women, they are extraordinarily flabby and sluggish.[30]

At this point, the author describes how such a physical type or constitution prevents fertility: "[for women] the fatness and moistness of their flesh ... are such that the womb cannot absorb the seed."[31] What is striking here is the linking of fatness with moistness in preventing conception. Elsewhere in the Hippocratic corpus, a woman who is filled with blood does not conceive.[32] But fat? Could not fat as easily be thought of as providing a rich nutrient bed for the seed? But here, at the beginning of the Western medical tradition, fatness is given a negative value, specifically in regard to fertility. The author goes on to relate the Scythian women's fat, moist physique with their scant and delayed menstrual flows. Such a menstrual pattern is ominous. The author of *Airs, Waters, Places*, like other Hippocratic writers, views menstruation as essential to keeping women healthy and fertile by purging them monthly of surplus moisture and of moisture turned into blood. A woman overfilled with blood cannot conceive.[33] Furthermore, the author notes that in Scythian women "the mouth of the womb is closed by fat and does not admit the seed."[34] This is followed by a characterization of Scythian women as fat and lazy, before the conclusion that their bellies are cold and soft.[35] The author concludes with a contrast to prove the theory that the Scythian women's excessive moistness and fatness make them infertile: unlike their mistresses, the Scythians' female slaves readily conceive as a result of their thinness and the hard work they do.[36]

The purpose of the author of *Airs, Waters, Places* in describing the physiques and characters of different people lying to the east, south, and north of Greece (namely the Asians, Egyptians, and Scythians) was to affirm the Greeks as the norm, by showing these other groups as inferior. Unlike the Greeks, with their clear distinctions between male and female, the Scythians lacked gender distinction; male and female alike they were flabby, sedentary, unshapely, lazy, and infertile. Even worse, the Scythian males tended to become assimilated to the female. The author tells us, "The great majority among the Scythians become impotent, do women's work, live like women, and converse accordingly."[37] To Greek males, at least those who had the leisure to read such works, who spent much of their lives outdoors participating in public and military life while, in Athens at least, citizen women stayed indoors out of sight and lived their lives among woman, to these Greek males, such a description could bring only scorn—scorn, and some uneasiness at the idea of men turning into women.

The Scythians in *Airs, Waters, Places*, I suggest, challenged Greek ideas about what was masculine and what feminine almost as much as another group of Scythians who lived far away in the north, namely the Amazons. Much scholarly attention has been recently paid to the Amazons as a mythic threat to the Greek polis.[38] As women who spent active lives outdoors, not only living without men, but also engaging in battle with them, the Amazons obviously violated Greek norms. Greek men saw the proper place of women as inside the male-defined space of the home, using their energy for the benefit of their husbands and the polis by managing the household, weaving valuable textiles at their looms, and, most important, by producing children, especially sons. The author of Airs, Waters, Places in fact introduces the discussion of the Scythians by describing the Sauromatae, another Scythian people living around Lake Maeotis.³⁹ Unlike the other Scythian males, who, as we have seen, become uniformly fat and flabby like women, the women of the Sauromatae, descendants of the Amazons, are masculinized:

> Their women, so long as they are virgins, ride, shoot, throw the javelin while mounted, and fight with their enemies. They do not lay aside their virginity until they have killed three of their enemies. ... They have no right breast; for while they are yet babies their mothers make red-hot a bronze instrument constructed for this very purpose and apply it to the right breast and cauterize it, so that its growth is arrested, and all its strength and bulk are diverted to the right shoulder and right arm.⁴⁰

One can see now that the author of Airs, Waters, Places presented both extremes of the Scythians to Greek readers as disturbingly "other." The Sauromatae women were overly masculine, and the other Scythians were overly feminine. And to the author of Airs, Waters, Places, feminized meant fat, and a fat and soft physique was identified with the naturally cold, moist nature of women. The combination of fat and cold with moist resulted in infertility. This does not mean that the author thought all Greek women were fat and infertile, but was rather presenting a distorted mirror image of Greek norms. If Greek women were meant (at least in the ideal) to represent opposites of the Scythians, they would be slim and fertile. Was this merely an ideal, or was there some basis for this image of classical Greek women? Paleoarchaeology can help us by confirming that Athenian women had a very high birth rate.⁴¹ In addition, the analysis of skeletons also shows the Greeks' remarkable genetic diversity, which verifies the physical hardiness and variety that the author of Airs, Waters, Places claims for the Greeks, in contrast to the Scythians.⁴² Yet a consistent osteoarchaeological pattern does emerge that contradicts the implied characteristics of Greek women in

Airs, Waters, Places. The skeletons of Greek women of the classical period reveal that they were shorter and stockier than their images in Greek art.[43] Stocky does not mean fat. Still, without exercise (and, in Athens at least, respectable women stayed in their small houses most of their lives), female bodies tend to be softer and fleshier than men's.

I conclude that the author of *Airs, Waters, Places* casts in a negative light soft, fatty flesh, which was more typical of women and which was so different from the hard, muscled bodies of well-exercised Greek men. Yet our author is not calling on women to become more like men. We can be sure of that from the inclusion of the fit Amazon Sauromatae with the flabby Scythians as negative models. For this fifth-century Greek medical writer, female fat was a threat because it compromised fertility.

Jody Rubin Pinault
Hamilton College

Notes

I would like to thank Mary DeForest for her helpful suggestions, which added to the clarity of this paper, and Barbara Baltzer, R.N., M.S., C.A.N.P., for providing me with a late twentieth-century medical perspective on the effects of obesity on fertility and pregnancy.

[1] See, for example, Richard A. Gordon, *Anorexia and Bulimia: Anatomy of a Social Epidemic* (Oxford, 1992); "Behind the New Faces: How the New Group of Supermodels-in-waiting Stay Camera-ready," *Fashions of the Times, New York Times Magazine*, Part II, February 23, 1992, 38, 42; the recent movies, "Eating" (1991) and "The Famine Within" (1991), both deal with American women's obsession with body image, weight, and eating (see *NYT*, C 13, July 17, 1991). For dieting linked with health, see, e.g., "Huge Study of Diet Indicts Fat and Meat," *NYT*, C1, 14, May 8, 1990; "How to Calculate the Fat You Consume Without Going into Higher Mathematics," *NYT*, C4, Aug. 15, 1990; "Animal Fat Is Tied to Colon Cancer," *NYT*, A1, B20, Dec. 13, 1990; "Fat's in the Fire: A Guide for the Wary," *NYT*, C7, March 27, 1991; "Rethink 4 Food Groups, Doctors Tell U.S.," *NYT*, C1, 4, April 10, 1991; "Experts Agree on One Thing at Least: Even Less Fat Is Better," *NYT*, C4, July 31, 1991; "Riddle for Healthful Cooks: How to Leave Out the Fat?" *NYT*, C1, 6, Oct. 9, 1991.

[2] See, e.g., his Cupid and the Three Graces, detail from the *Ascent of Psyche*

to *Olympus* (1625–28) and *The Three Graces* (c. 1638).

³ See, e.g., female figure on Athenian red-figure squat *lekythos* by the Eretria Painter, c. 430 B.C. (New York, Metropolitan Museum of Art, Fletcher Fund, 1930.11.8, photograph in John Boardman, *Greek Art* [New York, 1964], 193); kneeling girl in late sixth-century Athenian red-figure cup (Athens, Agora Museum, P 24102, photograph in Boardman, 104); bearded men and youth feasting with *hetairai*, cup (Basel Kä 4, photograph in Eva C. Keuls, *The Reign of the Phallus* [New York, 1985], 169).

⁴ The Hippocratic Corpus contains sixty or so writings, mostly dating back to the fifth and fourth centuries B.C. These writings vary considerably in length, purpose, style, and authorship. Although they have come down to us under the name, "Hippocrates," there is nothing to tie any of these writings irrefutably with a historical Hippocrates. For recent discussions of the authorship and formation of the Hippocratic Corpus, see G. E. R. Lloyd, "The Hippocratic Question," *CQ*, n. s. 25, (1975), 171–92; Lloyd, "Introduction," *Hippocratic Writings* (Harmondsworth, 1978), 9–12; and Wesley D. Smith, ed., *Hippocrates: Pseudepigraphic Writings* (Leiden, 1990), 6–13. For the scientific influence of Hippocratic medicine in the West, see Smith, *The Hippocratic Tradition* (Ithaca, 1979).

⁵ In the still most convenient reference edition, *Oeuvres complètes d' Hippocrate*, ed. Emile Littré, with French trans., 10 vols. (Paris, 1839–1861; rpt., Amsterdam, 1961–1962), vol. 6, 70–87. For the most recent critical edition, see Jacques Jouanna, *Hippocrate. La nature de l'homme*, with French trans. and comm. in *Corpus Medicorum Graecorum* I 1, 3 (Berlin, 1975), 204–20. For the English translation on facing pages with the Greek text, see *Regimen for Health*, eds. W. H. S. Jones (vols. 1, 2, 4), E. T. Withington (vol. 3), P. Potter (vols. 5, 6), in *Hippocrates*, 6 vols. (London, 1923–1931, 1988), vol. 4, 43–59. For an English translation in an accessible paperback edition, see *Hippocratic Writings*, ed. G. E. R. Lloyd, (above, n. 4), 272–76.

⁶ The ancient Greek nutritional principle here was that wheat bread was more drying and warming than barley cake. For barley, see the Hippocratic work *Regimen*, chap. 40, Jones, *Hippocrates*, vol. 4, 306–307, and for wheat, chap. 42, Jones, 310–13.

⁷ Hippocrates, *De diaeta* = *De victu* = *De victus ratione*. Littré, vol. 6, 466–662, reedited by Robert Joly, *Hippocrate: Du régime, Corpus Medicorum Graecorum* I 2, 4 (Berlin, 1984); Jones, vol. 4, 224–447. Cf. the Hippocratic work, *Nature of Man* 12: "A person is warmest the day he is born and the coldest the day he dies," Greek text edited with French trans., J. Jouanna, *Hippocrate. La nature de l'homme, Corpus Medicorum Graecorum*, I 1, 3 (Berlin, 1975), 164–204; English trans. G. E. R. Lloyd, 269.

⁸ *Regimen* 1.33, Jones, vol. 4, 278–81; *Regimen for Health*, chap. 2, Jones,

vol. 4, 46–47. For Aristotle's contrasting view, that old men end up cold and dry, see, e.g., *Generation of Animals* 5.3, 783b7–9; 5.4, 784a34.

[9] *Regimen* 1.34, Jones, vol. 4, 280–81.

[10] See also *Regimen* 1.27. Iain M. Llonie, *The Hippocratic Treatises "On Generation," "On the Nature of the Child," "Diseases 4"* (Berlin, 1981), 172–73, discusses the inconsistencies between the depiction of women as moist and cold, on the one hand, and moist and warm, on the other, in the Hippocratic corpus.

[11] See, e.g., *Airs, Waters, Places* 10.85. For editions, see below, n. 25.

[12] A distinction pointed out by A. E. Hanson between the gynecological treatises and the dietetic treatise, *Regimen*, Book 1, in "The Medical Writers' Woman," in *Before Sexuality*, eds. D. M. Halperin, J. J. Winkler, F. I. Zeitlin (Princeton, 1990), 332. We can go further and add *A Regimen for Health* in viewing a woman as moist and cool. See below.

[13] *Diseases of Women* 1.1, ed. Littré, 8.12; Eng. trans. A. E. Hanson, "Hippocrates: Diseases of Women 1," *Signs*, 1 (1975), 572.

[14] *Diseases of Women* 1.1, Littré 8.12; Hanson, "Hippocrates," 572.

[15] *On Generation/On the Nature of the Child* 15, ed. Littré, 7.496; Eng. trans. Llonie, *The Hippocratic Treatises*, 8.

[16] *On Generation/On the Nature of the Child* 18 and 31, Littré 7.500, 542; Eng. trans. Llonie, *The Hippocratic Treatises*, 9, 21. On the inconsistencies, see Llonie, *The Hippocratic Treatises*, 172–73.

[17] See, e.g., Aristotle, *Generation of Animals* 1.19, 726b3–727b; 1.20, 728a; 1.21–22, 729b–730b; 4.1, 765b; Greek text with Eng. trans. A. L. Peck, ed., *Aristotle XII: Generation of Animals* (London, 1942), 81–101; 112–21; 102–3; 386–87. For the changes this shift made in later gynecological theory, see Hanson, "The Medical Writers' Woman," 332.

[18] For the linked physiological and psychological implications of female wetness (especially wantonness) in contrast to the Greek ideal of male dryness, see Anne Carson, "Putting Her in Her Place: Woman, Dirt, and Desire," in *Before Sexuality*, 137–45.

[19] *A Regimen for Health* 6, Jones, 4.52–53; Eng. trans. Lloyd, 275. In fact, men with this same constitution (a fleshy, flabby, ruddy physique—Τοῖσι δὲ εἴδεσι τοῖσι σαρκώδεσι καὶ μαλακοῖσι καὶ ἐρυθροῖσι) are advised to follow a similar dry diet and life style for most of the year, instead of varying it with the season, as *A Regimen for Health* advises most men. See *A Regimen for Health* 2, Jones, 4.46–47; Eng. trans. Lloyd, 273, and *A Regimen for Health* 1, Jones, 4.44–47; Eng. trans. Lloyd, 272–73.

[20] For the pronatalist stance of the Hippocratic gynecologies, see Hanson, "The Medical Writers' Woman," 316. This same goal of "protecting woman's fertility" can be seen here in *A Regimen for Health*.

[21] In contrast to the dietetic works, the gynecological works and *Epidemics* reduce excess fluid, now thought of as blood, through induced menstruation, nosebleeds, bleeding, or pregnancy.

[22] For the powerful grip this habit of thinking in pairs of opposites or polarities had on fifth-century Greek thought, see G. E. R. Lloyd, *Polarity and Analogy: Two Types of Argumentation in Early Greek Thought* (Cambridge, 1966), 15–384, especially 15–26, 57–85.

[23] Ibid., 172–84.

[24] Xenophon, *Agesilaus* 1.28, Greek text with Eng. trans. in *Xenophon's Scripta Minora*, ed. E. C. Marchant (London, 1925), 72–73.

[25] *Airs, Waters, Places*, ed. Littré, 2.12–92; reedited by H. Diller, *Hippokrates: Über die Umwelt. Corpus Medicorum Graecorum* I 1, 2 (Berlin, 1970); Greek text with Eng. trans., Jones, *Regimen*, vol. 1.70–137; Eng. trans. Lloyd, 148–69.

[26] See Herodotus, e.g., 2.35, 36, 37, 47, 91; cf. Sophocles, *Oedipus at Colonus* 337–41.

[27] *Airs, Waters, Places* 19, Littré, 2.72; Jones, *Regimen*, 1.122–23: διὰ ταύτας τὰς ἀνάγκας τὰ εἴδεα αὐτῶν παχέα ἐστὶ καὶ σαρκώδεα καὶ ἄναρθρα καὶ ὑγρὰ καὶ ἄτονα, αἵ τε κοιλίαι ὑγρόταται πασέων κοιλιῶν αἱ κάτω.

[28] *Airs, Waters, Places* 20, Littré, 2.74; Jones, *Regimen*, 1.122–23.

[29] *Airs, Waters, Places* 20, Littré, 2.74; Jones, *Regimen*, 1.122–23: οὐ γὰρ δύνανται οὔτε τοῖς τόξοις συντείνειν οὔτε τῷ ἀκοντίῳ ἐμπίπτειν τῷ ὤμῳ ὑπὸ ὑγρότητος καὶ ἀτονίης.

[30] *Airs, Waters, Places* 20, Littré, 2.74; Jones, *Regimen*, 1.124–25: τὰ δὲ θήλεα θαυμαστὸν οἷον ῥοϊκά ἐστι τε καὶ βραδέα τὰ εἴδεα.

[31] *Airs, Waters, Places* 21, Littré, 2.76; Jones, *Regimen*, 1.124–25: τῇσι δὲ γυναιξὶν ἥ τε πιότης τῆς σαρκὸς καὶ ὑγρότης· οὐ γὰρ δύνανται ἔτι συναρπάζειν αἱ μῆτραι τὸν γόνον.

[32] See, e.g., *On Generation/The Nature of the Child* 15.4, Littré, 7.494; Eng. trans. Lloyd, 327; *Diseases of Women* 1.24, Littré 8.62.19–64.5; Eng. trans. Hanson, "The Medical Writers' Woman," 316.

[33] For the dangers that will befall a woman if she does not menstruate, see, e.g., *Diseases of Women*, Book 1, chaps. 1–4, Littré, 8.10, 12, 14, 16, 18, 20, 22, 24, 26, 28; trans. of chaps. 1–2 in Hanson, "Hippocrates," 1, 570–75; *On Generation, The Nature of the Child*, chap. 15, Littré, 7.494; trans. Lloyd, 326–27.

[34] *Airs, Waters, Places* 21, Littré, 2.76; Jones, *Regimen*, 124–25. The author may have developed the idea that fat can interfere with conception from thinking of it as a kind of humor, which, when it was in excess, could do just that, according to Hippocratic physicians. See, e.g., *Diseases of Women* 1.11, where the author explains how to determine if excessive phlegm or brine and bile are preventing conception, Littré, 8.42, 44; Hanson, "Hippocrates," 577–

78. Yet there are closer parallels in the Corpus for this mechanical view of the way fat prevents conception. See, e.g., *Aphorisms* 5.46: "When unusually fat women cannot conceive, it is because the fat presses the mouth of the womb and conception is impossible until they grow thinner," Jones, *Regimen*, 4.171. Lloyd, 225, translates *fat* (ἐπίπλοον) as *omentum*. In late twentieth-century medicine these internal fat deposits around the inlet of the uterus in obese women are blamed for complicating delivery. See "Obesity in Pregnancy," published by NAACOG Update Series, from the Continuing Professional Education Center, P. O. Box 305, Skillman, N.J. 08558. Perhaps the Hippocratics, aware of these fat deposits in delivery, hypothesized a role for them in preventing conception.

[35] *Airs, Water, Places* 21, Littré, 2.76; Jones, *Regimen*, 124–27: αὐταί τε ἀταλαίπωροι καὶ πίεραι καὶ αἱ κοιλίαι ψυχραὶ καὶ μαλθακαί.

[36] *Airs, Waters, Places* 21, Littré, 2.76; Jones, *Regimen*, 126–27: οὐ γὰρ φθάνουσι παρά ἄνδρα ἀφικνεύμεναι καὶ ἐν γαστρὶ ἴσχουσιν διὰ τὴν ταλαιπωρίην καὶ ἰσχνότητα τῆς σαρκός.

[37] *Airs, Waters, Places* 22, Littré, 2.77; Jones, *Regimen*, 126–27: Ἔτι τε πρὸς τούτοισιν εὐνουχίαι γίνονται οἱ πλεῖστοι ἐν Σκύθῃσι καὶ γυναικεῖα ἐργάζονται καὶ ὡς αἱ γυναῖκες διαιτεῦνται διαλέγονταί τε ὁμοίως.

[38] See, e.g., Page DuBois, *Centaurs and Amazons* (Ann Arbor, 1982), and William B. Tyrrell, *Amazons: A Study in Athenian Myth Making* (Baltimore, 1984). For a good short summary of the meaning of the Amazon myth, see Mary R. Lefkowitz, "Princess Ida and the Amazons," in *Women in Greek Myth* (Baltimore, 1986), 15–29.

[39] Herodotus, 4.110–17, discusses the relationship of the Sauromatae to the Amazons and the Scythians.

[40] *Airs, Waters, Places*, 17, Littré, 2.66, 68; Jones, *Regimen*, 117–19.

[41] According to M. D. Grmek, *Diseases in the Ancient Greek World*, trans. M. Muellner and L. Muellner (Baltimore, 1989), on the basis of pelvic scars, women during the archaic and classical periods bore an average of 4.3 children during a period of fertility that did not exceed at most a dozen years (97).

[42] Ibid., 90, 91, and especially 94.

[43] Ibid., 110.

The Wandering Womb of Delos

There are three stages in the study of Greek mythology. The first is learning the basic characters and mythological narratives—Zeus, Heracles, Achilles, the Trojan Cycle, such stories from Ovid's *Metamorphoses* as Daedalus and Icarus, Diana and Acteon, Jupiter and Io, and the like. The second stage is learning that all these "basic" myths are merely pre-selected, popular versions of myths that have countless variants in numerous different tellings of the stories. Sophocles (*Oedipus Tyrannus* 1034) and Euripides (*Phoenissae* 25–26), for example, have made it well known that baby Oedipus was exposed on the slopes of Mt. Cithaeron with a pin through his ankles, but a later, more humane source tells us that it was because of swaddling clothes that young Oedipus' feet were swollen.[1] Still other variants have him not exposed at all on the slopes of Cithaeron but cast adrift on the sea, like Perseus and Moses.[2]

The third stage requires sorting out the historical strata and relative importance of all the variants to search for their origins. Acteon and Semele, known generally as characters in Ovidian episodes, Titian paintings, and a Handel opera, have now been identified as more ancient mythical characters from Levantine Ugarit of the Bronze Age.[3] Acteon is the West Semitic hunter *Aqht*, and Semele, *Sml*, the eagle who destroys him.[4] Ovid's tale of Daedalus and Icarus derives its original importance not from the creation of aerodynamically tested feather and wax wings but from the death of son Icarus. The earlier stratum of this myth consists of the myth of Icarus, a Bronze-Age or even neolithic mortal, solar progeny who plunges into the sea, like Phaethon or Ixion/Peirithous, in an eternal return of the primordial sunset.[5] The later stratum concerns the Athenian inventor, Daedalus, who seems to have been contrived or at least developed in a burst of archaic Athenian chauvinism in the seventh and sixth centuries B.C.[6]

The career of the classical scholar who spends his or her career studying such myths, their variants, and their origins, parallels these three stages in the ontogenetic learning process. Beginning with a classical education in school, one is introduced to the ancient languages, history, and culture. Simultaneously or even before schooling begins, there are other avenues of influence—children's books about Greek mythology, films, television, advertisements, and even toy products. Somewhere along the way one is bitten by a bug, snagged by a genuinely Petrarchian passion that fills the waking hours with thoughts of and references to a civilization that flourished over 2000 years ago. Many years of study ensue, after which the scholar emerges with a doctoral degree and various scholarly methods for not only studying antiquity but also making new discoveries about its various aspects.

Some of the questions scholars ask about classical antiquity they find themselves continually pondering their whole career. Because of the perpetual nature of some of these questions, and because of the enveloping devotion and passion a classical scholar has for the subject, hints at a problem's solution might appear at any time and in the oddest source, and the scholar is open to any and all suggestions. The classical information is already there; what is needed sometimes is a different kind of stimulus.

Take as an example the god Poseidon. I learned in childhood that Poseidon, whom I knew then by his Roman name Neptune, was the god of the ocean. By the time I got to college this was corrected to god of the sea, the ancient Greek "Ocean" being the mythical, fresh-water river that flows around the earth, not an ocean, i.e., the large, salty sea, as we know it. In graduate school I then read Schachermeyr's work on Poseidon,[7] from which I learned that Poseidon was originally an Indo-European god representative of horses and god not of the sea but of fresh water springs.

Learning this helped to explain a number of myths. Poseidon's association with the horse-rearing Indo-Europeans helped to explain why Poseidon in the form of a stallion impregnated Demeter in the form of a mare (Pausanias 8.25.5), and why Poseidon impregnated Medusa, who in the archaic vase now in the Louvre is depicted as part horse, i.e., a centauress.[8] It also explained why the offspring Poseidon produced via this partially equine Medusa was Pegasus, the winged horse (Apollodorus

2.4.2–3). Pegasus means "he of the spring," which parallels Poseidon's original association with fresh water, and well-known myths support this association. Wherever Pegasus touches the earth, wherever his hoof has broken the surface of the ground, fresh water springs forth (Statius, *Thebaid* 4.61–62). That is what his name implies, and that is why the most famous spring that Pegasus created, that atop lofty, poetic, Mount Helicon in Boiotia, is named Hippocrene, "horse spring" (Hesiod, *Theog.* 6; Ovid, *Met.* 5.254–66; Pausanias 9.31.3; and Strabo 8.6.21).

One question about Poseidon, horses, and springs still plagued me. What was the essential and original relationship between horses and the creation of fresh water springs that caused the Indo-Europeans to identify and worship a god whose functions included both these aspects? I guessed that horses must sense water, find it in the wild, and that the Indo-Europeans depended on their horses for finding freshwater sources in areas of new occupation or even in drought-stricken areas of previous occupation. I had seen enough nature documentaries to know that the Bushmen of the Kalahari will wound a giraffe, elephant, or baboon in the expectation that the wounded animal will be able to seek out a fresh and otherwise unknown source of water. Do horses have the same ability?

I called around my own university, beginning with the Veterinary College. "Can horses sense water?" I asked. The consensus was that if they could, no scientific work had been done to verify it. Referred beyond, I phoned an equine behaviorist at Cornell. She concurred. There is no professional literature on the subject. I turned to the Chemistry Department. "Can horses (or giraffes, elephants, or baboons) smell water?" I asked. "Of course not," they replied. "Water has no odor. Perhaps these animals sense the negative ions emitted from flowing water." But in many instances the water such animals discover is not flowing. During droughts in the Kalahari desert, water levels are so low that pools of water do not "flow" at all. In some cases, water is even a few inches underground.

I asked my students, some of whom were horse aficionados, if they knew anything about horses finding sources of fresh water. One student brought me a copy of the Stephen King novel he was reading at the time and on one page King mentioned his grandfather who excelled at dowsing with a divining rod.[9] At the bottom of the page, in a footnote—an uncharacteristic apparatus for this prolific Gothic novelist—he mentioned that horses were also excellent at finding fresh water. I wrote Stephen King a letter, via his publishers's address, asking him for more information about horses finding sources of fresh water. I received a reply immediately on the most exquisite staionery I have ever seen—very thick bond paper colored mute gray with King's enlarged signature embossed across the entire top half of the page. On the bottom was his brief note: "Dear Professor Solomon, I don't know anything else about it, but good luck with your search."

Several semesters later, one of my students mentioned that he happened to see on cable television a midnight documentary about the Sable Island off the southern coast of Nova Scotia. The documentary mentioned wild horses on the island, and I wondered how they found fresh water. I wrote first the cable company, then the National Film Board of Canada, and I was finally directed to a Susan Zoe, a geologist doing oil exploration and stationed on the island. I wrote her a letter care of a mail drop, an address I thought sure to guarantee non-delivery. But three months later I received a response written on the back side of a discarded computer printout—she had no other material to write on—which explained that the wild horses living on a North Atlantic island will dig in the permafrost with their hooves.[10] They dig as deep as eight inches below the permafrost to reach the source of fresh water.

So there I had it. It took a number of years, and a letter to a mail drop in the North Atlantic, but I now had some evidence that horses do indeed find fresh water sources and that they do it with their hooves. Pegasus had become alive and well somewhere between an American scholar and an oil exploration team on Sable Island. Subsequently, I have found in Kit Carson's journal a clear reference to his depending on pack mules to find fresh water in the American frontier.[11]

The central point in all this is how odd, unexpected, and untraditional the paths followed by the classical scholar can be when attempting to comprehend an ancient myth. Oftentimes we need to escape the comfortable, well-documented confines of the literary and iconographical evidence and ask questions of the real, modern world so that we can understand some aspect of the ancient world.

Of course there is a problem with this kind of methodology, and that is that it does not make exclusive use of the traditional scholarly repertoire of bibliographical and critical tools. One can always doubt the reliability of such non-traditional sources, and there is the question of how to cite them properly. I can tell you that I do not sense a scholarly triumph when I have to write a footnote citing not Hdt. 2.5 or Pl. *Resp.* 398c but Susan Zoe, Sable Island Exploration Team, letter of 8 November, 1984.[12]

For understanding the wandering womb of Delos, there is another informational odyssey involved, onto which we will now embark. We start with level one, the most widely recognized version of the myth that most scholars and artists recognize: Zeus had made Leto pregnant, much to the chagrin of Hera, his wife. When Leto was full term, the jealous Hera, goddess of childbirth and an earth goddess, prevented Leto from giving birth on any earthly place. Only one place on earth was really not on earth, and that was the magical island of Delos that floated around the seas unattached to the land beneath the sea. Leto used the non-earthly Delos to give birth to Artemis and Apollo, the twin Olympian divinities. Thereafter, Delos ceased to be a floating island because it had earned a permanent resting spot in the Aegean.[13]

Sometimes such canonical versions stem from one particular literary source that establishes a permanent version of the myth adapted and imitated by subsequent artists. For Oedipus, for instance, one inevitably turns to Sophocles; for the quest for the Golden Fleece, one most often turns to Apollonius of Rhodes; and for Daedalus and Icarus, one turns to Ovid. In other instances, though, the most popular and influential version of a myth belongs to an amalgam, as assemblage of details collected from more than one source. An example would be the mythical biography of Achilles. We know his military exploits from the Homeric *Iliad*, yet just as famous is the non-Homeric detail that his mother rendered him 98% invulnerable by dipping most of him into the River Styx or all of him into fire (e.g., Hyginus, *Fabulae* 107 and Apollodorus 3.13.6). Another example is the birth of Aphrodite. One immediately thinks of Hesiod's description of the castration of the Sky God Ouranos, whose discarded genitalia fall into the sea and turn into Aphrodite, the goddess of love (Hesiod, *Theog.* 173–206). But we also know of Homer's Iliadic scenario in which Aphrodite, wounded by Diomedes, returns to Olympus to be confronted by her mother Dione (*Il.* 5.370–84). Two sources, two different variants of the myth of her birth.

The myth we are investigating, the birth of Artemis on the island of Delos, is such a myth. Its most characteristic aspects are not to be found in a single source but must be collected from several sources. If we proceed chronologically through our sources, we turn first to the so-called *Homeric Hymn to Delian Apollo*. Scholars have traditionally dated the first part of this archaic hymn to Apollo as early as the eighth century B.C., or at least no later than 548.[14] It tells us that Zeus has made Leto pregnant, and she wishes to honor some place on earth with the birth of their son, Phoebus Apollo. She is refused by the islands and coastal areas of Aegina, Euboia, Athos, Pelion, Scyros, Imbros, Lemnos, Lesbos, Chios, Claros, Samos, Mycale, Miletus, Cos, Cnidos, Carpathos and the Cycladic islands of Naxos, Paros, and rocky Rhenaea.

Finally the personified Cycladic isle of Delos consents so long as Leto will swear an oath that she and Apollo will build a temple, altar, and holy precinct on the island. Delos is a hard, rocky island, and she (it) fears that Apollo, once born, will scorn her, turn her over, and sink her into the sea with his feet. Leto swears an oath that this will not happen, and Leto goes into labor upon the rocky island near a date-palm along the bank of the Inopus River (*Hom. Hymn Ap.* 30–88).

Her labor lasts for nine days and nine nights. A number of sympathetic goddesses accompany her in her travail—Dione, Rhea, Themis, and Amphitrite among them—but absent are Hera and Eileithyia, goddesses of childbirth. Hera's absence is attributed to her jealousy: her husband Zeus was responsible for this pregnancy. Eileithyia is absent because Hera does not let her attend. But Leto and the other goddesses, particularly Iris, contrive to steal Eileithyia away, and once she arrives, Apollo is immediately born (*Hom. Hymn Ap.* 89–122).

Artemis is mentioned only twice in the hymn (*Hom. Hymn Ap.* 15, 165). There is no specific identification of Delos as a floating island, either. But there is the curious fear, which Leto divulges, that Apollo will turn her upside down and sink her into the sea. Delos could not be turned upside down unless it were not rooted to the earth beneath the sea, and Hesiod tells us that the earth had roots (*Theog.* 728), so the author seems to have known of (but chose not to highlight) the detail that Delos was a floating island without roots connecting it to the earth.

The other important poetic source for this myth is Callimachus' fourth hymn, *To Delos*. The third-century B.C. Callimachus, who (unlike the poet of the previous Homeric hymn) had all the collected knowledge of the Library at Alexandria at his disposal, preserves a number of different details. Poseidon had created all the islands in the sea by ripping off pieces of mainland mountains, rolling them into the sea, and fastening them to the earth's foundations. Delos he did not so constrain; she floats freely (*Del.* 36–40). The reader should notice here how Callimachus makes Delos' floatingness an asset, not a punishing aimlessness to be gotten rid of, as we read in other sources.[15]

In those mythical days Delos was supposedly called Asteria, "star," and sailors reported seeing it floating in the Saronic gulf near Corinth, off Sounion in southern Attica, and as far east as Chios near Anatolia.[16] Leto tried in vain to find a place for giving birth to Apollo, but Hera and her henchmen Ares and Iris kept watch everywhere. With all the geographical and mythological detail expected from an Alexandrian poet, Callimachus takes us on a poetic tour of all the cities, lands, and rivers that refused Leto comfort. This episode goes on so long (*Del.* 86–98) that the full-term fetus himself, Apollo, gets angry enough to make threats from inside the womb!

Leto is rejected by all the mainland sites, and then she is equally unsuccessful at such islands as Cos and Corcyra. Finally she rests near the palm tree on the banks of the Inopus on bold, little Asteria. Callimachus makes his narrative a bit fuzzy from this point on, but Hera rather surprisingly forgives Asteria, and before we know it, Apollo is establishing rituals, dances, and sacrifices on her. He allows the island to have its position fixed, and in memory of the days in which it used regularly to float away and disappear from view, it now is called *delos* ("visible," *Del.* 51–54). Artemis is not mentioned at all, save the reference in the third-to-last word of the entire 326-line poem. The mention is oblique, and it is accomplished simply and in passing by use of the objective case of the third-person singular relative pronoun, ἥν, in the closing sentence: "Hail Delos! Hail also both Apollo and she to whom Leto gave birth!"

The same poet/scholar, Callimachus, also composed a *Hymn to Artemis*, and here he makes it quite clear in the prologue (*Del.* 24–25) that Artemis was born without creating labor pains for her mother Leto. This sounds as if her birth and that of her brother Apollo had no connection, that they were separate pregnancies, but he mentions her brother's birth (*Del.* 7–9), and Apollodorus, the first-century collector of mythological material, states quite clearly that Artemis was born first, Apollo shortly thereafter (1.4.1). A Pindaric fragment (Bowra 78–79) states that Delos had previously been a floating island and that the gods eventually fastened it to the bottom of the sea with four pillars. One last series of variants offered in Aelian and others explains that "Asteria" was not only the name of the island but that Asteria was originally Leto's sister and turned herself into a stone, sank in the sea, and stayed invisible (*adelos*) beneath the waters. When Leto needed to give birth, Asteria raised herself ever so slightly above the waters, became visible (*delos*) and thus allowed Leto to give birth on her (Aelian, *De Natura Animalium* 4.29).

I hope that the reader is more confused than when this analysis of the myths of the birth of Artemis began a few pages ago. After all, we are in stage two of our mythological investigation. The first step is education, the second is uneducation.

Now we are ready for the third step, the part of the analysis that presents hypotheses for the origins of these myths and thereby attempts to interrelate them and place them in a historical context. From the looks of things, our first two sources, the Homeric and Callimachean hymns, describe the Delian birth not of Artemis but only of Apollo. Yet a number of our sources, including the very last line of the Callimachean hymn, do include Artemis in this mythical birthing; Artemis has a significantly placed sanctuary on Delos; and the two divinities Apollo and Artemis are often and widely referred to as twins.[17] It is surprising that these two hymns refer almost exclusively to the birth of Apollo and barely even mention that of sister Artemis.

But contemporary scholarship in mythology and the history of Greek religions has repeatedly demonstrated a pattern of occupation and domination by worshippers of Apollo, whereby they subsume or merge with the cult of another divinity and then add Apollo to the myths of the cult.[18] A wave of Apollonian worshippers seems to have come down into Greece from central Europe and imposed its foreign god Apollo on the myths of Sparta in connection with its local, early-Helladic divinity Hyacinth,[19] in Crete with their local, early-Helladic divinity Paiawones (or Paian),[20] in Delphi with their local, early-Helladic earth goddess (Pythia?),[21] and then in Delos with their local, early-Helladic goddess Artemis.[22] This historical pattern certainly explains the otherwise bizarre detail that each winter Apollo abandoned Delphi and returned to his homeland in Hyperborea—the Land of the Far North.[23] It also accounts for the absence of his name from the Linear B tablets of Mycenaean Greece, and it is represented in the mythology of Delphi, where Apollo is said to be a late arrival and heir to the oracle of the earth goddess (e.g., Aeschylus, *Eum.* 1–19).

The independently examined archaeological evidence at Delphi and Delos makes it quite clear that there is no record of the worship of Apollo on these sites until the eighth century, the period just before the *Homeric Hymn to Delian Apollo* was written. Both archaeologists and literary scholars have therefore observed a consistent pattern among Apollonian worshippers of invading or infiltrating a territory rich in ritualistic and mythological tradition and then substituting their god Apollo for some traditional, local, now nameless deity.

That this happened in Delos is beyond question. Apollo has no important connection with childbirth, but everything else about Leto, Artemis, and Delos is connected with childbirth. The only significant myth we hear about Leto has to do with her travail.[24] Of Artemis' birth we hear only that she immediately prepared herself and assisted in the birth of her twin brother Apollo, on Delos. Mt. Cynthus and the sacred, fertile palm teeming with dates belong to sacred goddesses in labor, not the resulting male progeny. Settlement on Delos is traced back to the early Cycladic period, but at that time the worshippers of Apollo are still two millenia away from bringing him into Greece and Delos. Delos is sacred originally to the Bronze-Age Artemis and Leto, not to the first-millennium intruder Apollo.

I traveled to Delos for the first time only several years ago. I had read in irresponsible, long-forgotten sources that Delos stood at the center of the Cycladic islands and, of course, that as a result it had become a magnificently rich trading center in the later Hellenistic period. One look at a map and an on-site visit to Delos shows, however, that Delos became a great commercial and religious center in antiquity not because of its central location[25] or because of its fine harbors; mooring there even today is very difficult, especially in the very strong winds that characterize its summer weather.[26] Quite the contrary, the island accurately described itself in the hymn when it called itself rocky and windswept (*Hom. Hymn Ap.* 72), so it was not natural beauty either that attracted early Bronze-Age worshippers to its rocky shores.

So new questions were posed in my mind. Why did Delos become a sacred island? What was special about Delos? What did Delos have or offer that such other Cycladic islands as Paros, Naxos, and Myconos, and even Santorini did not have?

In discussing the three general stages of understanding myth and my own parallel ontogenetic development—my computer-printout correspondence with Susan Zoe regarding Pegasus, Poseidon, horses, and fresh water sources—I pointed out how clues and answers to multi-year scholarly ponderances might come from non-traditional, personal observations rather than from traditional bibliographical and philological research. As a further example I would like to describe three incidents that set my mind to realizing why Delos had become the sacred island of the Aegean.

Delos, the rocky, desolate island of antiquity that was at times considered so holy that human beings were forbidden to give birth on, die on, or inhabit it,[27] is just as isolated today. The River Inopus runs only as a torrent during a heavy rain, the cisterns are clogged with insects, frogs, and turtles, and save for a few houses built by the French excavation team, there is no occupation there even today. Fortunately for tourists, there are exquisite and anything but desolate accommodations just forty minutes away on the island of Mykonos. Known for its bars, discos, restaurants, an international jet set, and often gay clientele, Mykonos is one of the recreation centers of Europe and the Mediterranean.

People visiting Mykonos are often rich, smartly dressed, and very sophisticated. Even in such a milieu, however, there was one person who made everyone else's head turn. One evening across the main square in view of a few dozen people, including some of my students, came a jet setter of the jet set. A young woman of such striking style and presence that all heads turned. Not just men, but women, everyone looked at this strikingly clothed woman striding confidently across the square with very high spiked heels, magnificently rich, long, perfectly tended dark-brown hair, and a carriage and posture to match. My wife referred to her as "an Aztec Goddess." Remarkably, the next morning my wife and I boarded the small boat for Delos, and the Aztec Goddess was on that boat ... with her twin sister!

As we arrived at Delos, they immediately headed not for the archaic and classical temples or the ancient domestic quarters where the rest of the crowd was going, but up the steep and difficult steps to the sacred peak of Mt. Cynthus. The irony of being on the sacred island of Delos, birthplace of Leto's twins, in the presence of two modern godlike twins heading for the sacred summit, was not lost on us. My wife and I followed them up the mountain, and once they reached the summit they began not to read a guidebook or take a picture of the expansive view. Instead they folded their hands in front of their faces in a ritualistic gesture of prayer, began chanting, praying, and swaying back and forth, all of which went on for quite a while and, ultimately, caused one of them to reach a sexual climax.

We were absolutely dumbfounded by the whole thing; I myself must have been gaping at them. In fact, I feared for my safety when the swarthy male who was accompanying them and who wore a suspicious amount of gold jewelry approached me as I was gawking at the two women. He certainly was not a Greek scholar or enlightened tourist about to ask me a question of historical or mythological import. Sensitive to pagan religious rituals, I thought perhaps I had broken their spell and that he was coming over to throw me off the cliff. He asked something, but at first I did not understand him. He had a strong, unidentifiable accent. Finally, he pointed at me; he wanted ... oh! he wanted to borrow the pen I had placed behind my ear. I gladly gave it to him and scurried away to safety down the mountain.

The entire incident turned out to be one that stuck in my mind and kept me alert to possible solutions to the question of why Delos became sacred. The next winter I took a dozen students to London to study mythology, particularly the Greek vases in the British Museum, but also the mythological paintings in the National Gallery and the pre-Roman ritual sites of Stonehenge and Avebury. The day before our excursion to Wiltshire, while browsing the used bookshops of London, I was fortunate enough to come across a used copy of Michael Dames' book, *The Silbury Treasure*.[28] I read it rapidly that evening and, fascinated, I directed our bus driver to stop not as scheduled just at the pre-historic stone circles of Stonehenge and Avebury, but also at the sacred mound of Silbury.

Silbury had for centuries been a mystery. It is a grass-covered mound that stands just 130 feet high not more than a mile from Avebury in south-central England. It has long been recognized as Europe's largest mound made by human hands, so treasure seekers and eighteenth- and nineteenth-century archaeologists dug exploratory tunnels to find the buried treasure or the body of the buried king or warrior they believed must be lurking inside. They found nothing, however. It was not until 1968 that a modern archaeologist, R. J. C. Atkinson, scientifically explored the mound to find that it was clearly a third-millennium B.C. human-made mound of chalk and organic material that served, like Stonehenge, Avebury, and other neolithic stone circles and henges of northern Europe, a ritualistic purpose. Carbon-14 dating of the unburnt grasses found amidst the chalk construction, corroborated by dendrochronological dating, fixed the year of construction to 2660 B.C., some 600 years before Stonehenge took its semi-final form.[29]

In his book, Dames demonstrates that the monument of Silbury is the neolithic Great Goddess in her pregnant state. From ground level her figure is more difficult to discern, but from atop the hill itself one can see clearly that this is a large neolithic *sculpture* of a female with a stylized head and enlarged buttocks and breasts. Its perspective is bi-fold perpendicular, her pregnant belly extending vertically out from the ground, the rest of her body extending horizontally. In antiquity, there is excellent reason to believe, her body contours were filled by high ground water. Dames cites dozens of examples of such sculptures, most of them on a much smaller scale, but some, for instance the goddess-shaped temple at Skara Brae in Orkney, being much larger than life size.[30]

Unfortunately, a number of scholars still think Dames' interpretation is kooky, but that may be because they have ignored the great shift that has taken place in the scholarship of Western culture over the past twenty years. Beginning with the socio-political-economic movements of the 1960s, scholars have been working towards an increased understanding of ancient women. At first it was almost solely women who worked in this area, but twenty years later this new emphasis and understanding has spilled over into many aspects of Greek studies, including mythology and religious history. The greatest benefits from this new awareness have been bestowed upon the Great (earth/fertility)

Goddess. The Cambridge School at the turn of the century began to recognize just how pervasive her influence was even in classical Greece,[31] for they realized that Hera, Demeter, Eileithyia, and Artemis had originated as neolithic great goddesses, and their work has been thoroughly corroborated by subsequent archaeological work on Bronze-Age and neolithic Greece. By 1992 the Great Goddess has been restored, at least intellectually, to her rightful place.[32]

In addition, scholarship and science have pushed the limits of our knowledge about ancient Greece ever backwards in time. Classical Greece has attracted scholars and artists since the Hellenistic and Roman epochs, but with the discoveries of Troy, Mycenae, and Knossos before or at the turn of the century, interest began to expand backwards towards the Bronze Age. Since then we have learned even more about the chalcolithic, neolithic, and upper paleolithic periods, and what we have learned clearly is that this Great Goddess can be traced back to at least 20,000 B.C. In fact, she was "god" (in our sense) for almost half of the period during which homo sapiens has existed.

Reading about Silbury forced upon me an immediate comparison with Delphi. Even Aeschylus and Ovid knew that historically the earth goddess (Great Goddess) was worshipped at Delphi before Apollo was, so if Silbury hill was built to look like a huge neolithic goddess, then Delphi must have been a goddess sculpted by nature. Her two, projecting cliffs, the Phaedriades (Ovid, *Met.* 1.316), must have been the breasts and/or thighs, the *omphalos* or navel lies nearby, and between the breasts gushes forth the sacred spring of Castalia from the vaginal walls of the cliff. In addition, although even late archaic sources suggest that the name *Delphoi* has some connection with the ancient Greek word for "dolphin" (*Hom. Hymn Ap.* 495–96), Aristotle (*Historia Animalium* 510b13) and Hippocrates (*De Mulierum Affectibus* 222.9) preserve the original meaning of the word *delphus*—"womb."[33]

As the bits and pieces of this puzzle fell into place, I felt quite odd. I was a classical scholar who grew up (intellectually) with Homer, Sophocles, and Plato now busying himself with thousand-foot breasts or thighs, belly buttons, and a vaginal sanctuary, or rather two vaginal sanctuaries. Silbury also has a vagina, as with that at Delphi, a stream issuing from a rock, the name of which is Kennet or, in its more primitive form, 'Cunnt.' Archive material verifies that this latter name was still applied to the area as late as 1723,[34] by which time the term *cunt* had degenerated to an extreme vulgarism, as it remains today. It was not always so, of course.[35]

All the while I continued to wonder just how Delos fit into this emerging picture of neolithic myth and ritual. That spring, I attended the annual meeting of the CAMWS, and there I heard a paper by Barbara Gold; she was discussing Greek festivals related to Dionysus.[36] The room was crowded, so crowded that I had to stand in the back of the room. I could barely hear, but while she was discussing women worshipping Dionysus, she mentioned the word "hysteria." I had never thought about it, but Plato, Aristotle, and the ancient Greek medical writers described *hysteria* as an emotional disorder caused by the part of the female anatomy the Greeks called the *hystera*—"womb." They believed that a woman's womb could become dislodged, travel around in the body, and cause a variety of physical problems, including the blockage of respiratory passages and blood flow; it could even cause madness. The cure for "hysteria," "wombness," was sexual intercourse, the purpose of which was to impregnate the woman, thereby anchoring the womb down with a fetus.[37]

The only conception that occurred that afternoon, however, was in my brain, because it immediately dawned on me that Delos, simply put, is the wandering womb. It was the sanctuary of two fertility goddesses, Leto and Artemis, in which one great mythical event occurred—the travail of Leto with the resulting birth of her offspring. With a parallel neolithic womb at Kennet and Silbury in England, and another parallel womb at Delphi, Delos is the third such sanctuary of an earth/fertility goddess. In each instance the presence of the earthly womb was apparently essential—the mound at Silbury, the name itself of Kennet (Cunnt); the breast-like Phaedriades at Delphi, its vaginal Castalian spring, the omphalos or navel of the earth goddess, and then also the name itself, *delphus*, "womb."[38] Why Delos? Why not Paros or Naxos? Why is Delos the womb? What Delos has that the other Cycladic islands do not have is Mt. Cynthus, a perfectly shaped conical protrusion from an otherwise relatively flat plane, surrounded, like Silbury, elliptically at its base by less than a mile of land in either direction, all of which is then surrounded, again like Silbury, by water. The ancients obviously felt a sacredness in this location, and it may well be that the name of the mountain, despite its pre-Greek -nthos-ending, also means "womb"; at least its stem *cynth** is suspiciously close to the word *Cunnt* that we have had reason to discuss previously.

All this helps to explain the mythology of Delos. It explains why its only event is the travail and birth of divinities, why Mt. Cynthus—a mere 112 meters high—is of such sacred importance, why the prominent rock of Leto rests on its northeast slope,[39] why Delos does not have to have an exceptional harbor, why Delos used to float around the sea, and why it was ultimately fixed to the earth, like the womb to a woman's body, only after Leto gave birth on it. Mythologically, there was little else said about Delos. It was primarily a birth island, the wandering womb that was fixed after the birth of/by the Great Goddess. During a later period, the worshippers of Apollo came to the island and, as usual, substituted Apollo's birth for that of the original goddess Artemis. Perhaps unable to suppress completely the sacredness of Artemis' birth, Apollo's worshippers allowed for a twin birth, although they never gave Artemis' birth the poetic celebrations they gave to Apollo's.

Archaeological finds atop Mt. Cynthus date from the early Cycladic period, the period from which the most commonly found sculpted artifacts in Greece are the flat, violin-shaped "goddesses" made from island marble.[40] Although not neolithic, the third millennium B.C. still precedes the arrival of the male-dominant Indo-Europeans into Greece, and parallel artifacts from Crete, some also from the neolithic cave of Eileithyia, another goddess of childbirth, clearly represent the Great Goddess of fertility. This was an era in which human, plant, and animal fertility was the central focus of sacred concern, a concept so foreign to us, especially because of our preconceptions of male-dominant Bronze-Age and classical Greece, that we find it hard to believe. In fact, we find it, depending on our moral interpretations, somewhere between vulgar and ridiculous. But this is where the evidence has led me, and contemporary scholarship, inspired by a renewed interest in the neolithic Great Goddess, corroborates much of what I came across in my odyssey. Unless my own intellectual womb has been dislodged and traveled to cause a scholarly hysteria for me, this seems to be why the isle of Delos is the wandering womb that floats no more.

Jon Solomon
University of Arizona

Notes

[1] Cf. schol. to Euripides, *Phoenissae* 26 and Nicolaus of Damascus, *FGrH* 90F8. Cf. Lowell Edmunds, *Oedipus: The Ancient Legend and Its Later Analogues* (Baltimore, 1985), 47–57.

[2] Hyginus, *Fabulae* 66. For references to visual evidence, see Edmunds, *Oedipus*, 9, n. 32.

[3] Michael C. Astour, *Hellenosemitica* (Leiden, 1967), 163–73.

[4] James B. Pritchard, ed., *Ancient Near Eastern Texts Relating to the Old Testament* (Princeton, 1955), 149–55.

[5] Cf. Gregory Nagy, *Greek Mythology and Poetics* (Ithaca, 1990), 223–62.

[6] See W. S. Barrett, ed., *Euripides: Hippolytus* (Oxford, 1964), 1–10; Anthony Snodgrass, *Archaic Greece: The Age of Experiment* (Berkeley, 1980), 38–39; and Jeffrey M. Hurwit, *The Art and Culture of Early Greece, 1100–480 B.C.* (Ithaca, 1985), 311–19.

[7] Fritz Schachermeyr, *Poseidon und die Entstehung der griechischen Götterglaubens* (Bern, 1950).

[8] Paris, Musée du Louvre CA 795. Hurwit, *Art and Culture of Early Greece*, thinks the vase sculptor was at a loss as to her appearance and simply imagined her as a centauress (168).

[9] Stephen King, *Danse Macabre* (New York, 1981), 95.

[10] Letter from Susan Zoe, 8 November, 1984.

[11] Milo M. Quaife, ed., *Kit Carson's Autobiography* (Lincoln, 1935), 12. Other examples can be found in Julian Duquid, *Green Hell: Adventures in the Mysterious Jungles of Eastern Bolivia* (Garden City, 1942), 187–88; Loren D. Estleman, *Bloody Season* (Toronto, 1987), 182; and in the behavior of the horses of Assateague Island, Virginia.

[12] Nonetheless, there is plenty of scholarly precedent for this; cf. Denys Page, "Thucydides' Description of the Great Plague at Athens," *CQ*, n.s. 3, 47 (1953), 118, n. 1.

[13] Cf. Carl Kerényi, *The Gods of the Greeks*, trans. Norman Cameron (1951; rpt. New York, 1960), 132–33.

[14] Despite Hippostratus' date of the sixty-ninth Olympiad (504 B.C.).

[15] Cf. Pindar, frag. 78–79 [Bowra] (= *Prosodion to Delos*).

[16] Callimachus, *Del.* 36–37; cf. Pindar, frag. 39 [Bowra] (= *Paian* 5.42).

[17] E.g., Apollodorus 1.4.1, Pausanias 2.41.4 and 7.23.7 (the Temple of Apollo and Artemis at Aigion).

[18] Frederick M. Ahl, "Amber, Avalon, and Apollo's Singing Swan," *AJP*, 103 (1982), especially 394–98 and 410–11; and H. Kothe, "Apollons ethnokulturelle Herkunft," *Klio*, 52 (1970), 205–30.

[19] B. C. Dietrich, "The Dorian Hyacinthia: A Survival From the Bronze

Age," *Kadmos*, 14 (1975), 136.

[20] George Huxley, "Cretan *Paiawones*," *Greek, Roman and Byzantine Studies*, 16 (1975), 119–24.

[21] For the absence of cult activity until the eighth century, see Anthony Snodgrass, *The Dark Age of Greece* (Edinburgh, 1971), 73; and Catherine Morgan, *Athletes and Oracles: The Transformation of Olympia and Delphi in the Eighth Century* B.C. (Cambridge, 1990), passim.

[22] See Snodgrass, *Dark Ages*, 394–96.

[23] See Ahl, "Amber, Avalon, and Apollo's Singing Swan," 373–411.

[24] She has small rock shrines at both Delphi and Delos. The attempted rape by Tityus is a later contrivance to connect the Ugaritic Nether World divinity Tityus with the Greek pantheon.

[25] Naxos is much more central.

[26] The inhabitants of Delos found it necessary to construct a 100-meter mole as early as the eighth century B.C. Cf. Lionel Casson, *Ships and Seamanship in the Ancient World* (Princeton, 1971), 362.

[27] Although largely, no doubt, for political reasons; cf. Thucydides 1.8 and 3.104.

[28] Michael Dames, *The Silbury Treasure: The Great Goddess rediscovered* (London, 1976).

[29] Ibid., 27–47.

[30] Ibid., 63.

[31] See, for example, *The Cambridge Ritualists Reconsidered*, ed. William M. Calder, III, (Atlanta, 1991).

[32] E.g., Miriam R. Dexter, *Whence the Goddesses: A Source Book* (New York, 1990); and Marija Gimbutas, *The Goddesses and Gods of Old Europe, 6500–3500* B.C.: *Myths and Cult Images* (Berkeley, 1982).

[33] Cf. Athenaeus 9.375a. Both Athenaeus and Aristotle remind us that the Greek word for brother (*adelphos*) preserves the same root.

[34] W. Stukeley, *Itinerarium Curiosum* I (London, 1723), 63, followed by Dames, *The Silbury Treasure*, 110.

[35] See *Oxford English Dictionary* 4.130, under *cunt*.

[36] Now published as Barbara Gold, "Dionysus, Greek Festivals, and the Treatment of Hysteria," *Laetaberis*, 6 (1988), 16–28.

[37] E.g., Plato, *Timaeus* 91b–c; see Gold, "Dionysus, Greek Festivals, and the Treatment of Hysteria," 24–26; Ann Ellis Hanson, "Continuity and Change: Three Case Studies in Hippocratic Gynecological Therapy and Theory," in *Women's History and Ancient History*, ed. Sarah B. Pomeroy (Chapel Hill,1991), 81–87; and Mary R. Lefkowitz and Maureen B. Fant, *Women's Life in Greece and Rome: A source book in translation* (Baltimore, 1982), 90–91, 93–95, 225–26, 258.

[38] In addition, the Cretan cave of Eileithyia, which Homer (*Od.* 19.188–89) knew as an important sanctuary and from which neolithic artifacts have been excavated, sits less than a kilometer above the bay of Amnissos. R. F. Willetts, *Cretan Cults and Festivals* (London, 1962), 172, n. 191, suggests "amniotic" as a cognate of Amnissos.

[39] Delos #109 in P. Bruneau and J. Ducat, *Guide de Délos*, 3d ed. (Paris, 1983), 238.

[40] E.g., Christos Doumas, *Cycladic Art* (London, 1983), 9–26.

Hera, Nurse of Monsters

For several years now I have been fascinated by the "early Hera," that is, the goddess whom Homer calls "Argeia" (from Argos) and βοῶπις πότνια, "lady with the look of a cow," but whom he characterizes as "the wife and sister of Zeus," the prototypical bitch whose jealous schemes threaten her lordly spouse.[1] Who was this deity? Did the early Hera achieve her stature because she slept in the arms of great Zeus or because of some other marital scenario? This is the usually accepted scholarly opinion. Martin Nilsson saw Hera as essentially the wife of Zeus. Linguist Walter Pötscher argued consistently for over two decades that Hera was to be defined as the female mature for marriage, wed early to the Mycenaean ἥρως, "hero," and later to Zeus.[2] Archaeologists digging at various Heraia or sanctuaries of Hera generally have tried to fit their finds into the scheme of a divine wife. But the *Iliad*, which is our earliest repository of stories about Hera, contains many anomalies. For instance, the education of a Greek wife is a taming of the woman to her spouse.[3] But Iliadic Hera is not only an untamed wife but also, upon occasion, one who tames others: Heracles, a river-god, and even her own spouse. So the diction and motifs of the *Iliad* made me suspect that Homer transforms a very different goddess of regional cult into Zeus' sister/wife. But what really convinced me that this was the case was the evidence at Hera's earliest sanctuaries, at Samos off the coast of Turkey and at Argos in the Peloponnesus. Neither site contains any concrete sign of Zeus in the early Archaic Period. Instead, both sites suggest a goddess with regional sovereignty—over the island or the Argolid. And both sites suggest continuity with the Bronze-Age Argolid, the "Argos" from which mythical heroes set off with Agamemnon for Troy. Furthermore, we now can surmise from linguistic evidence that Mycenaean Greeks would have linked "lady Hera with the look of a cow" to Heracles ("glory from Hera"), and the ἥρως.

These and other clues sent me off in search of the "Early Hera" from whom Homer shapes his Olympian queen. A rarely noted aspect of this queen is her nursing of rage. In a recent article, "Homer's Savage Hera," I show that Hera provides the *Iliad*'s pattern of ὠμοφαγία, "eating raw flesh," a pattern that begins when she lusts to eat Priam raw and culminates when Achilles lusts to eat the raw flesh of Hector.[4] This present article seeks to explain what in Hera's past gave rise to this aspect of her Homeric personality. I analyze Hera's mythical links to non-Olympian, often serpentine figures like Ocean, Styx, and Typhon, who dwell variously at the rims of the earth, or in the land of the mythical Arimoi. I examine language and motifs associated with Hera: nurturing among nature gods at non-Olympian haunts; chthonic oaths; the eviction of her son and would-be champion from heaven; and the typhonic, bestial character of both mother and son. A series of Iliadic passages are my primary evidence for Hera's links to the serpentine world.

I begin with an overview of two serpentine families. Typhon (called Typhon, Typhaon, and Typhoeus), is known to both Homer's *Iliad* and Hesiod's *Theogony* as a traditional character. He is born into the group of monsters resulting from the consanguineous union of Phorcys and Ceto (*Theog.* 270–306). He is a serpent who dwells among the mythical Arimoi, one whose whirlwinds devastate land and sea (*Theog.* 870–80). He is a chaos demon who is Zeus' ultimate rival for power in the universe. He shares his bed with Echidna, whose very name means viper. She gives birth to a famous brood of monsters: the Hydra, the Nemean lion, Cerberus, Chimaera, and the Sphinx (*Theog.* 311–29). Though fair of face, Echidna is a grisly "eater of raw flesh" (ὠμηστήν, *Theog.* 300). The anatomy of this pair mixes the anthropomorphic and the serpentine. Sometimes Typhon has a hundred serpent heads (*Theog.* 825), though in art he usually resembles Echidna— anthropomorphic atop and serpentine in tail.

Hera's link to the clan is intimate. According to the *Hymn to Apollo*, she mothers Typhon as an ally of Delphi's notorious Python. According to Hesiod, she nurses some of the next generation, specifically the Lernean Hydra and the Nemean lion (*Theog.* 313–14, 327–29). According to Apollodorus, she sends the Sphinx to Thebes with the famous riddle about the three ages of humanity (3.5.8). Since Lerna and Nemea were situated near the Argolid, these stories presumably reflect regional legend.

Another serpentine family, not related to Typhon, is that of Ocean, the great river flowing around the rim or binders of the earth (πείρατα γαίης). He fathers all other rivers and a vast clan of daughters, the most famous of whom is dread Styx (*Theog.* 361). Unlike Typhon and other monstrous descendants of Phorcys and Ceto, he is a benign, creative, even sacral figure, whose daughters' names signify intellectual or moral qualities.[5] The source of all life (γένεσις πάντεσσι, *Il.* 14.246), he and Tethys generate the gods (θεῶν γένεσις, "source of the gods," *Il.* 14.301–2, cf. 14.200–201). These verses have long been recognized as indicating an early theogony in which rivers generate all life.[6]

Hera's link to this cosmogonic clan is also intimate. She talks about visiting Ocean's home, about being nurtured by him and Tethys, and about reconciling the couple. And as to the dread daughter, only twice in the *Iliad* does someone swear by Styx' inviolable waters, and that someone is in both cases Hera, once in the Seduction of Zeus and once in its aftermath (*Il.* 14.271–80, 15.34–38).

With this background we turn to the birth of Typhon in the *Hymn to Apollo*. Enraged at Zeus' parthenogenetic birth of Athena, Hera accosts him:

> "I shall not visit your bed, but far from you, will pass my time among the immortal gods (ἀπὸ σεῖο/ τηλόθεν οὖσα θεοῖσι μετέσσομαι ἀθανάτοισιν, 329–30)." Enraged, cow-faced lady Hera departed from the gods, said a quick prayer, and with hand turned downward, lashed the earth (χειρὶ καταπρηνεῖ δ' ἔλασε χθόνα, 333), saying: "Hear me now, Earth and broad Sky above and you Titan gods who dwell under the earth around great Tartarus from whom are sprung both gods and men. Hearken to me now, all of you, and grant me a child apart from Zeus (νόσφι Διός, 338), in no way inferior to him in strength. Nay, let him be as much stronger than Zeus as far-seeing Zeus is stronger than Cronus." Crying aloud, she smote the ground with her fertile hand, and life-giving Earth was moved (ἵμασε χθόνα χειρὶ παχείῃ ·/ κινήθη δ' ἄρα Γαῖα φερέσβιος, 340–41).   (*Hom. Hymn Ap.* 329–41)

After a few verses and a year's time, she bears "terrible Typhon, a creature unlike gods or mortals to be a bane for mortals," and "immediately presents him" to Delphi's monstrous Python, "bringing one evil to another":

> ἣ δ' ἔτεκ' οὔτε θεοῖς ἐναλίγκιον οὔτε βροτοῖσι
> δεινόν τ' ἀργαλέον τε Τυφάονα, πῆμα βροτοῖσιν.
> αὐτίκα τόνδε λαβοῦσα βοῶπις πότνια Ἥρη
> δῶκεν ἔπειτα φέρουσα κακῷ κακόν ... .
> (Hom. Hymn Ap. 351–54)

The most striking point about this passage is that Hera, not Gaia, the traditional earth goddess (as in *Theog.* 821), is Typhon's mother. She takes on the role that Gaia plays in *Theogony* 166, attempting to destroy the current divine order by initiating a cycle of succession through a son's rebellion.[7] The language supports this theory. First, Hera talks about two sets of gods, on the one hand Zeus and the Olympians, and on the other "the immortals far from him" (*Hom. Hymn Ap.* 329–30, cf. 338). It is among these distant divinities that she will prepare for the birth of Typhon. We are not told who they are, whether the monsters of Arimoi or Ocean and company at the rims of the earth. But this text, like others to come, shows her at home with both these sets of non-Olympian gods and in their respective haunts. It is in their midst that she can plot an Olympian coup, by bearing a chaos monster to reinforce Delphi's Python. Second, the pre-Olympian Titans are to play some role in her revolution since she invokes them in their Tartarian dwelling in a manner resembling her chthonic oaths in the *Iliad* (*Il.* 14.271–79, 15.34–38). Third, the actual oath is proper to a chthonic deity: a fertile hand turned downward, a smiting of the ground, and a loud cry (*Hom. Hymn Ap.* 340–41, cf. 333). These are hardly the gestures of a wife of Zeus or goddess of marriage.

Could this birth of Typhon from Hera be an early story, known to the tradition before the *Iliad* even though it differs from Hesiod's account? I think so—not only because Stesichorus seems to have known the story, but also because a series of Iliadic texts show signs of such knowledge.[8] I refer to five passages in which pre-Olympian figures like Sleep, Styx, Cronus, the Titans, and the cosmogonic serpents appear or are at least discernible: (a) Hera's chthonic oath to the god Sleep in the Seduction of Zeus (14.271–79); (b) Zeus' smiting of Typhon (2.782–83); (c–d) his evictions of would-be champions of Hera from Olympus (1.590–93, 15.16–28); and (e) Hephaestus' Hera-led blitzkrieg against the river-god Xanthus (21.331–41).

The first passage comes from the marvelous episode in which Hera beguiles Zeus on Mt. Ida, thereby diverting his attention from the war raging on the battlefield at Troy. Sleep, twin brother of Death, is her accomplice, though a reluctant one at first, remembering all too well how Zeus almost destroyed him once before when he came to Hera's defense. A bribe from Hera, in the form of a beautiful bride, pleases him. Yet he demands still more:

"ἄγρει νῦν μοι ὄμοσσον ἀάατον Στυγὸς ὕδωρ,
χειρὶ δὲ τῇ ἑτέρῃ μὲν ἕλε χθόνα πουλυβότειραν,
τῇ δ' ἑτέρῃ ἅλα μαρμαρέην, ἵνα νῶϊν ἅπαντες
μάρτυροι ὦσ' οἱ ἔνερθε θεοὶ Κρόνον ἀμφὶς ἐόντες,
ἦ μὲν ἐμοὶ δώσειν Χαρίτων μίαν ὁπλοτεράων,
Πασιθέην, ἧς αὐτὸς ἐέλδομαι ἤματα πάντα."
Ὣς ἔφατ', οὐδ' ἀπίθησε θεὰ λευκώλενος Ἥρη,
ὄμνυε δ' ὡς ἐκέλευε, θεοὺς δ' ὀνόμηνεν ἅπαντας
τοὺς **ὑποταρταρίους**, οἳ **Τιτῆνες** καλέονται.
(Il. 14.271–79 = a)

"Come! Swear by the inviolable water of Styx. Seize the bountiful earth with one hand and the shimmering sea with the other, so all the gods around Cronus below may witness that you are giving me one of the young Graces, Pasithea, whom I have desired all my days." [Sleep] spoke and the goddess white-armed Hera obeyed. She swore as bidden, and named all the hypotartarean gods who are called Titans.

The specificity and solemnity of Sleep's demand that she swear "by the inviolable water of Styx" (14.271) suggest a cultic source with prescribed ritual. One hand is to seize earth and the other the sea, Sleep insists (14.272–73). And she is to do this so that "all the gods around

Cronus below" may witness her mighty oath (273–74), in which she names all the *hypotartareans* (ὑποταρταρίους) who are called Titans (Τιτῆνες 279). I have already noted that Hera is the only Iliadic figure to swear by serpentine Styx. She is also the only one to invoke the Titans or even mention the word Τιτῆνες. But even more telling is the use of ὑποταρταρίους.

What can it mean to be "below Tartarus"? Dank Tartarus is the rock bottom of the cosmos, a place inhabited only by the deposed Titans and Typhon. So ὑποταρτάριοι must mean in Tartarus, possibly in the sense of "below Earth" since Tartara is the name of the earth goddess mother of Typhon in Hyginus' account.[9] But the salient point is that the only other epic attestation of the word comes in Zeus' fight with Typhon in the *Theogony*: "The hypotartarean Titans who live with Cronus (Τιτῆνές θ' ὑποταρτάριοι Κρόνον ἀμφὶς ἐόντες) trembled at the dread, unending encounter [between Zeus and Typhon]" (851–52). The restriction of this strange word to Hera's oath to Sleep in the *Iliad* and to the Typhonomachy in the *Theogony* suggests that her Iliadic oath came from a battle between Zeus and Typhon. It begins to look as though the *Hymn to Apollo* preserves an early tradition: Hera would have been mother of Typhon and ally of the rebel Titans in antecedent tales.

But the *Iliad* virtually ignores Typhon, its only reference coming in an explanation of earthquakes. The ground beneath rumbled:

χωομένῳ, ὅτε τ' ἀμφὶ Τυφωέϊ γαῖαν ἱμάσσῃ
εἰν Ἀρίμοις, ὅθι φασὶ Τυφωέος ἔμμεναι εὐνάς·
(*Il.* 2.782–83 = b)

... as when [Zeus] angry with Typhon smites the earth around him among the Arimoi, where they say Typhon keeps his couch.

Whereas Hera's fertile hand smote the earth to bring about the birth of Typhon in the *Hymn to Apollo* (ἵμασε 340, cf. 333), the only deity to smite (ἱμάσσειν) in the *Iliad* is Zeus. These verses, the only direct reference to Typhon or Typhoeus in the *Iliad*, indicate that the monster and his Ariman couch (presumably a wedding bed shared with Echidna) were already fixtures of myth: the general clause in the first verse and the word φασί, "they say" in the second are the markers. That same rare epic φασί marks Hesiod's account of Typhon joined in love with Echidna among the Arimoi (*Theog.* 304-6). And as Hesiod fills out the story, "the illustrious wife of Zeus" nurses two of the offspring born in that Ariman cave, the Lernean Hydra and the Nemean lion (Νεμειαῖόν τε λέοντα,/ τόν ῥ᾽ Ἥρη θρέψασα Διὸς κυδρὴ παράκοιτις, *Theog.* 327–28, cf. 313-14). Apparently, then, both Homer and Hesiod were drawing on a traditional account in which Typhon, Echidna, and Hera would have dwelt among the Arimoi.

A scholiast on the *Iliad* supports this conclusion by linking Hera to the Arimoi, or at least Mt. Arimon, through the following story.[10] Once, in a rage against Zeus, Hera approaches Cronus for help. He obliges by giving her two eggs smeared with his semen and telling her to bury them underground (κατὰ γῆς). The daimon born from them would dethrone Zeus. After she buries them under Cilicia's Mt. Arimon, Typhon comes forth. What seems to be reconstructed here is another account of Hera, in cahoots with Cronus, giving birth to and/or nursing chthonic, Ariman monsters to rival Zeus—the same motifs we saw in the *Hymn to Apollo*. Strange company and haunts for the wife of Zeus and queen of the gods.

The only other Iliadic reference to a smiting Zeus occurs in the aftermath of the Seduction of Zeus, when he awakens to the realization that Hera has duped him:

"οὐ μὰν οἶδ᾽ εἰ αὖτε κακορραφίης ἀλεγεινῆς
πρώτη ἐπαύρηαι καί σε πληγῇσιν ἱμάσσω.
ἦ οὐ μέμνῃ ὅτε τ᾽ ἐκρέμω ὑψόθεν, ἐκ δὲ ποδοῖιν
ἄκμονας ἧκα δύω, περὶ χερσὶ δὲ δεσμὸν ἴηλα
χρύσεον ἄρρηκτον; σὺ δ᾽ ἐν αἰθέρι καὶ νεφέλῃσιν
ἐκρέμω· ἠλάστεον δὲ θεοὶ κατὰ μακρὸν Ὄλυμπον,
λῦσαι δ᾽ οὐκ ἐδύναντο παρασταδόν· ὃν δὲ λάβοιμι
ῥίπτασκον **τεταγὼν ἀπὸ βηλοῦ**, ὄφρ᾽ ἂν ἵκηται
γῆν ὀλιγηπελέων. ἐμὲ δ᾽ οὐδ᾽ ὣς θυμὸν ἀνίει
ἀζηχὴς ὀδύνη Ἡρακλῆος θείοιο,
τὸν σὺ ξὺν Βορέῃ ἀνέμῳ πεπιθοῦσα θυέλλας
πέμψας ἐπ᾽ ἀτρύγετον πόντον, κακὰ μητιόωσα,

καί μιν ἔπειτα Κόωνδ' εὖ ναιομένην ἀπένεικας."
(*Il.* 15.16–28 = c)

"I'll not be surprised if you catch it this time for your wicked web-spinning and I smite you with thunderbolts. Don't you remember the day you swung aloft, with two great anvils suspended from your feet and an unbreakable golden chain fastened around your wrists? There you dangled in the clouds! The gods in great Olympus were distraught, but could not get near to free you. Anyone I caught, I laid my hands on and threw from the threshold, and down he came to earth with little breath left. Even that did not ease my pain for godly Heracles. In league with Boreas, you and your machinations blasted him across the restless sea, sweeping him off to well-populated Cos."

This passage, together with the previous one (b), contain the epic's only two attestations of Zeus' smiting. He threatens to smite Hera, as he regularly smites Typhon (ἱμάσσω, 15.17, ἱμάσσει, 2.281). So, the only two whom Iliadic Zeus smites or would smite are Typhon and his own wife. A strange way to treat one's wife, one might say, but a lashing with thunderbolts is a perfect punishment for a sky god to inflict on an earth goddess who incites her earthling son to insurrection. And it is a perfect way to revenge the blasts (θύελλαι) that she and her winds sent against the Olympian's son Heracles (15.26–28). Hence this description of Hera's previous punishment—hung up on high amid the clouds, anvils suspended from her feet—appears to have come from an earlier battle of gods in which Hera would have received the punishment of a cosmic slave (bound and hanging in midair) for the rebellion that she and Typhon would have instigated against Zeus. We see hints of the earth goddess and earthling son being punished in diverse ways by the triumphant sky god: one hung aloft in golden chains (c); the other eventually left to rumble forever underground (b). Zeus' thunderbolt proves effective against the mother's blasts and the son's fire.

These hints are confirmed by similarities between this description of the fate of Hera's would-be champion and that in Book 1. Here in Book 15 (c), no god dared help her lest Zeus fling him from the threshold (τεταγὼν ἀπὸ βηλοῦ, 15.23) and the victim hit the earth "with little breath" (ὀλιγηπελέων, 15.24). In Book 1's famous tale, Hephaestus tells how Zeus once evicted him from the threshold of Olympus when he tried to help Hera:

"ἤδη γάρ με καὶ ἄλλοτ' ἀλεξέμεναι μεμαῶτα
ῥῖψε ποδὸς **τεταγὼν ἀπὸ βηλοῦ** θεσπεσίοιο,
πᾶν δ' ἦμαρ φερόμην, ἅμα δ' ἠελίῳ καταδύντι
κάππεσον ἐν Λήμνῳ, ὀλίγος δ' ἔτι θυμὸς ἐνῆεν·"
(Il. 1.590–93 = d)

"Once before when I tried to defend you [Hera], [Zeus] caught me by the foot and flung me from the awesome threshold. I fell all day long! Just as the sun dropped, so did I, onto Lemnos—with little breath left in me."

These two pericopes (c and d) clearly describe the same eviction, as Cedric Whitman showed years ago.[11] Dictional clues include a peculiar phrase used in both to describe Zeus' eviction of Hera's would-be defender (τεταγὼν ἀπὸ βηλοῦ, "seizing from the threshold") and forms of the stem *olig-* to describe the victim's shortness of breath (ὀλίγος δ' ἔτι θυμὸς ἐνῆεν, 1.593, cf. ὀλιγηπελέων, 15.24). Since τεταγὼν ἀπὸ βηλοῦ is not attested elsewhere in the epic and since both scenes ascribe the same fate to Hera's champion, both the language and the motifs suggest a common source.

Taken together, Zeus' smiting of Typhon (b) and the two evictions (c and d) are related: two of them (b and c) concern the only would-be victims of Zeus' smiting in the epic (Hera and Typhon), and two (c and d) concern the eviction of Hera's would-be champion from Olympus. The three passages suggest a common source in which Hera would have been defended against Zeus' wrath not by Hephaestus, as the *Iliad* has it, but by Typhon, one fire-god son replacing another.[12] Tradition gave Hera two parthenogenetic sons, each of whom was a fire-god—Typhon and Hephaestus. Homer replaces the earlier monstrous Typhon with the civilized Hephaestus.[13]

Such an alliance between Hera and Typhon must have been a

source for the mock-heroic Battle of the Gods (e), in which Hera and Hephaestus are engaged in a typhonic struggle, though the rival this time is not Zeus but a river-god (21.331–41). When one recalls that Typhon is the sender of evil whirlwinds (called in *Theog.* 870–80 ἄελλαι, a variant of θύελλαι), winds which scatter havoc and sometimes rivers of fire on sea and land, the typhonic nature of the theomachy of *Iliad* 21 becomes even more apparent.[14] Hera not only urges Hephaestus to display a mighty fire (φλόγα πολλήν, 21.333) in his battle against the river Xanthus but promises that she herself will raise a typhonic firestorm:

> "I'll spread an evil flame (φλέγμα κακὸν φορέουσα) and stir up from the sea a fierce blast (θύελλαν) of Zephyr and white-clouded Notus to consume the Trojan corpses and their battlegear. Meanwhile burn up the trees along Xanthus' banks. Plunge him into fire. Don't let him divert you with honeyed words or threats. Cease not your rage until I cry out with a loud voice (φθέγξομ' ἐγὼν ἰάχουσα). Then withhold your fire.
> (*Il.* 21.337–41 = e)

Scorching firestorms, ill winds, and loud cries are characteristic of the chaos monster Typhon (*Theog.* 869–80), not the normally gentle Hephaestus. And the description leaves no doubt that the son's blitzkrieg is an instrument of the mother's rage, thereby reminding us that, in (c), Hera-sent θύελλαι drove Heracles to Cos (15.26–28). Hera's power over θύελλαι in two scenes (c and e), her preternatural cries here and elsewhere in the epic (φθέγξομ', *Il.* 21.341, cf. 5.784–86)—more reminiscent of Typhon (φθέγγονθ', *Theog.* 831) or the deep-whorling river-god (φθέγξατο, *Il.* 21.212–13) than of Hephaestus—and Hephaestus' uncharacteristic violence here point to Hera's pre-Homeric life as a Greek Tiamat allied with the traditional chaos demon in a primal battle of the elements.

Book 21's battle of the elements ends, you may recall, on a comic note, with the misdemeanors of Hera (boxing Artemis' ears) and of other "wives of Zeus" (*Il.* 21.499, 510–12)—anomalies that have long baffled scholars. But taken as a whole, Book 21's combination of the grotesque and the absurd provides an apt prelude for the death of Hector and the growth of Achilles in the final books. The naked elemental power and the divine comedy bereft of any ethical dimension provide a backdrop for the hero's nadir and growth. Seen in this way, the theomachy (e), like the Seduction of Zeus, its aftermath, and Hephaestus' eviction from Olympus at the end of Book 1 (a, c, and d), comes from a larger unit in which Hera and company provide relief from and perspective on the human tragedy. It is these ironic and/or comic Iliadic passages in which Homer most openly employs motifs drawn from the early Hera. Obviously, Homer's Olympian pantheon has little scope for Hera's monstrous past. Hence, Homer discards inappropriate aspects of her regional mythology, like her mothering of a chaos-monster.[15] But if we review our five Iliadic texts (a–e above) and consciously ignore Homer's contexts, we can perceive the early Hera's elemental power, her chaos-monster son, and some of her pre-Olympian allies or enemies:

    a. At Sleep's urging, Hera snatches the earth and sea, swears by the waters of Styx, and invokes the hypotartarean Titans abiding below in Tartarus;

    b. Typhon is pictured as a traditional monster situated near his viper-wife's couch, rumbling like an earthquake, and smitten by Zeus;

    c. Furiously reacting to Hera's hoodwinking, Zeus threatens to smite her and dangle her in midair like a cosmic slave, as he did before when she blasted Heracles to Cos, and to evict any would-be Olympian defender;

    d. Hephaestus recalls his eviction from Olympus with diction that identifies him with the anonymous champion of Hera in c;

    e. With a typhonic roar and blast, Hera demands and receives her son's obedience to her command; she and Hephaestus use elemental fire storms in a cosmic struggle against the river-god Xanthus, in a battle that ends only when the river-god accepts her terms and she calls off her son's fire (21.369–83).

Hence the early tradition seems to have known Hera as a fearsome figure engaged in battles against elemental rivers, supported by a chaos-monster and the hypotartarean Titans, and enduring punishments appropriate to an earth goddess. Furthermore, supporting evidence from the *Hymn to Apollo* and the *Theogony* link this Hera to monsters renowned in the Argolid and Delphi: the lion of Nemea, the Hydra of Lerna, and Typhon, ally of Delphi's Python.

All this evidence suggests that early tradition identified Hera with the Herois, or the dragoness earth goddess of Delphi. Fontenrose clearly establishes that Herois (an alternate form of Hera) was a Delphic name for the Parnassian dragoness, that Delphic Delphyne is called a *herois*, and that Herois is a name both for the foster mother of Typhon-Python and for a chthonic Delphian festival.[16] Furthermore, Fontenrose cites Servius and other late commentators who allude to a venomous Hera in league with Python to pursue the pregnant Leto and prevent the birth of Apollo (18). Nevertheless, Fontenrose does not identify this Hera with the *Iliad*'s Hera. But we now have seen evidence in early epic passages from the *Iliad* and the *Theogony*, showing that the tradition knew Hera as a chthonic goddess associated with fire-gods, the gentle Hephaestus being the Homeric modification of the serpentine Typhon.

Our literary sleuthing continues. One of Fontenrose's conclusions (255–56), that Delphic Gaia or Hera as mother of Typhon/Python was the nurse of the young (κουροτρόφος), provides an important clue for an understanding of Hera's relationship in the *Iliad* with both Ocean and the sea-nymph Thetis. At Hera's cult sites she is rarely depicted as a nurse of youth.[17] Τρέφειν, "nourish," a word that designates the nurturing of both plants and youths, is used of Iliadic Hera only in relationships with pre-Olympian water-gods: Ocean and Tethys in Book 14 and Nereid Thetis in the epic's finale. In the Seduction, Hera talks, albeit in a couple of lies, of going to visit primordial Ocean:

> "εἶμι γὰρ ὀψομένη **πολυφόρβου πείρατα γαίης**,
> Ὠκεανόν τε, θεῶν γένεσιν, καὶ μητέρα Τηθύν,
> οἵ με σφοῖσι δόμοισιν ἐὺ τρέφον ἠδ' ἀτίταλλον.
> δεξάμενοι Ῥείας, ὅτε τε Κρόνον εὐρύοπα Ζεὺς
> γαίης νέρθε καθεῖσε καὶ ἀτρυγέτοιο θαλάσσης·"
> (*Il.* 14.200–204)[18]

"I'm going to see the binders of the bountiful earth, Ocean and Tethys, father and mother of the gods. They nursed and cherished me in their home, receiving me from Rhea, when Zeus put Cronus deep beneath the earth and barren sea...."

Now the coils of Ocean and Tethys formed the πείρατα γαίης, or "binders of the earth," as Onians showed.[19] Πείρατα binding the world would have been the idea behind mother Tethys and father Ocean generating all things (γένεσις πάντεσσι, Il. 14.246). It can hardly be coincidental that the only Iliadic uses of the phrase πείρατα γαίης or of the word γένεσις, "generation," "source" (of the gods or of all) occur in scenes that specifically involve Hera with cosmogonic forces. The only other use of πείρατα γαίης outside the Seduction of Zeus occurs when Zeus, furious at Hera's military meddling, threatens her with a "visit" to the nethermost binders of the earth where Cronus and the Titans abide (8.479). Whatever the earlier context of that remark, all the epic's uses of πείρατα γαίης both reveal and conceal journeys of the earth goddess, whether to her westernmost or her nethermost binders.[20]

But there is more. Hera claims not only to have been nursed by these binding dragons "in their home" but also to have renewed their love by replacing them on their lovebed (εἰς εὐνὴν ἀνέσαιμι ὁμωθῆναι φιλότητι, "I would replace them on their bed to be joined in lovemaking," Il. 14.209). These notions must have originated under circumstances in which Hera would have been understood as an earth goddess interacting with primordial water dragons. Their coils would have been understood as binding and nourishing her earth. Her return to them and replacement of them on their riverbed (or her earthbed) would have renewed earth, presumably in a rite of spring. This explains Hera's Lesbian title γενέθλη πάντων, female "origin of all things," according to an almost certain reference to her in a fragment of Alcaeus.[21] Whether the poet meant γενέθλη πάντων literally, that is, whether he understood Hera as the cosmogonic mother of all things or just as the preeminent Lesbian goddess, is irrelevant here. Her possession of a title corresponding to Ocean's γένεσις πάντεσσι, "male origin of all things" (Il. 14.246), suggests that she would have been understood during the pre-polis period, locally at least, as the "female origin of all things," or as an earth goddess returning cyclically to primal riverbeds for a sacred renewal of the earth.[22]

Hera's intimacy with these cosmogonic rivers may cast light on

Sleep's enigmatic response to her request for help (*Il.* 14.243–48). Instead of helping her seduce Zeus, Sleep offers to lull to sleep "another (ἄλλον) of the everlasting gods ... even the streams of the river Ocean who is the origin of all things" (καὶ ἂν ποταμοῖο ῥέεθρα/ Ὠκεανοῦ, ὅς περ γένεσις, 245–46). On the plot level, Sleep in effect says that he would risk complicity in Hera's deception of Ocean, the original father of the gods, but not of the now reigning Zeus. But on the level of the chthonic subplot, Sleep's willingness to dupe "streams of the river Ocean" may very well have been calculated to remind Homer's contemporaries of the sacred marriage as it would have been understood at an early Heraion—one at which the goddess would presumably have been understood to have had her union with a local river-god. My work in progress shows Hera's intimacy with the river-gods near her cult sites: the Imbrasus flows through the Samian Heraion and Hera's cult statue was yearly tied to her lugos tree at its banks, where she herself was said to have been born; the Inachus was bridged for the building of the Argive Heraion and the river-god's daughter Io, who was Hera's priestess, was tied to her olive tree nearby. From Homer's Panhellenic perspective, the local river would have been a tributary from the great Ocean. Hence Sleep's playful remark may well have evoked memories among Homer's contemporaries of Hera's spouse in local ritual.[23]

Be that as it may, Hera's nurture by Ocean and Tethys in the Seduction must be related to her argument about nursing Thetis in *Iliad* 24, since the same two verbs occur in both descriptions: "Ocean and Tethys nursed and cherished me in their home" (οἵ με σφοῖσι δόμοισιν εὖ τρέφον ἠδ' ἀτίταλλον, 14.202 = 303); and "I myself nursed and cherished her [Thetis]" (ἣν ἐγὼ αὐτὴ/ θρέψα τε καὶ ἀτίτηλα, 24.59–60). The use of "cherish," ἀτιτάλλειν, along with "nurse," τρέφειν, must be significant since only these passages employ the two words in a phrase concerned with gods nursing gods. The phrase, which the *Theogony* uses to describe Gaia nurturing the young Zeus on Crete, suggests long-term kourotrophic care rather than the limited activity of a wet nurse (*Theog.* 480). Like Ocean, Thetis is a water deity of early cosmic importance.[24] As earth goddess, Hera would appropriately nurture Thetis at the rims of the earth where primordial rivers nurtured her. This also makes sense of Hera's relationship to the Lernean Hydra and Nemean lion in the Ariman cave. She is to these monsters of the

Theogony exactly what Ocean is to her in the *Iliad*—not parent but foster parent. Hera was born of Rhea but nurtured by Ocean and Tethys. The Hydra and Nemean lion are born of Echidna, the raw-eating viper (ὠμηστήν, *Theog.* 300), but nurtured (θρέψα, θρέψασα, *Theog.* 313–14, 328) by the earth goddess Hera.

This chthonic past finally explains Hera's strange line of argument:

"Ἕκτωρ μὲν θνητός τε γυναῖκά τε θήσατο μαζόν·
αὐτὰρ Ἀχιλλεύς ἐστι θεᾶς γόνος, ἣν ἐγὼ αὐτὴ
θρέψα τε καὶ ἀτίτηλα καὶ ἀνδρὶ πόρον παράκοιτιν,
Πηλέϊ...."   (*Il.* 24.58–61)

"Mortal Hector suckled at a woman's breast. But Achilles is born of a goddess [Thetis], one whom I myself nursed, cherished, and made spouse to mortal Peleus...."

She argues that Achilles is superior to Hector because her divine rage (χόλος) flows in him, giving him an innate superiority over someone suckled by a human breast. Her reasoning here, which has previously defied adequate explanation, is now clear. When she rails against giving the same honor to Hector as to Achilles, child of Thetis, "whom I myself nursed and cherished," she is arguing what I call a biological determinism: the transmission of χόλος from one goddess to another and thence to the demi-god Achilles.[25]

Where would Homer have found such an argument? We can now see its origin in Hera's cosmogonic, Argolic past.[26] As Echidna is the *Theogony*'s eater of raw flesh (ὠμηστής), Hera is Homer's psychological raw-eater whose breast could not contain her rage (χόλος 4.23–24 = 8.460–61) and who would "raw-eat Priam and sons" (ὠμὸν βεβρώθοις Πρίαμον Πριάμοιό τε παῖδας, 4.35–36). And her Nemean lion is Achilles, the rage of her breast feeding his. So, as Hesiodic Hera physically nurtures the leonine offspring of the raw-eating Viper-lady (Echidna) in a cave and brings him to the Nemean hills near the Argolid (*Theog.* 328–29), so Iliadic Hera psychologically nurtures the leonine Achilles till he finally outgrows her pattern of raw-eating in *Iliad* 24. In response to Thetis' simple question, "My child, how long will you eat your heart out (σὴν ἔδεαι κραδίην) in tearful sorrow with no thought of food or sleep" (24.128–30), Achilles returns from the self-destructive world of raw-eating and learns compassion at a meal with his archenemy, Priam.

Hera's argument from biological determinism shows the origin of Homer's metaphor of raw-eating. In early Argolic tradition, the transmission of the capacity to raw-eat from Hera to a hero would presumably have been not psychological as Homer makes it but physical as described by the *Iliad*'s Hera. One can surmise, too, that the hero would probably not have been Achilles, but someone like Agamemnon with roots in her Argos.[27] As earth goddess nursing earthlings like the Nemean lion, Hera would be a natural transmitter of the rage that both sustains and bestializes a warrior. This nurse of raw-eating monsters in regional legend becomes for Homer a goddess of bitter bile in the psychological sense.

Where are we, then? We began with the *Hymn to Apollo* in which Hera is clearly an earth goddess, smiting the ground with fertile hand, invoking subterranean Titans, her cry producing Typhon as ally to Delphi's Python. We have now seen that both Homer and Hesiod have these stories in their memory banks, however transmuted they may have been by the constantly shifting perspectives of oral tradition. As Hesiod uses them, their regional, Argolic roots clash with Hera's "new" role in the Olympian family, as when the "illustrious wife of Zeus" nurses the Nemean lion and settles him in the hills near Argos. Nursing a monster would hardly be appropriate behavior for an illustrious wife. As Homer uses them, however, the regional motifs and language are so magnificently woven into the very fabric of the epic that the stitching is discernible only by a careful scrutiny of the language and motifs. In the witty, often ironic context of the Seduction of Zeus and its aftermath, Hera's chthonic oaths invoking the "hypotartareans" lead us ultimately to the unmentioned Typhon and Echidna. The nurturing theme provides Homer with Hera's seductive ruse. Her alleged desire to revisit her primordial nurses and rekindle their love-life arouses Zeus' passion and momentarily tames him to her will. But more important for the structure of the epic, Hera's bestial past provides both a pattern for Achilles' lapse into bestiality and a claim for a biological determinism linking him to her. Homer is equally creative in his use of the theme of πείρατα γαίης. Since the Iliadic uses of "the binders of earth" always involve Hera's journeys, we see that Hera's talk of replacing these earth-binders on their love-bed utilizes an image from her chthonic past.

So Homer's view of Hera's position in the Olympian family of gods leads to his transformation of Hera Argeia. Now she nurtures rage, not Argolic monsters. Now she exercises power only in fleeting moments, when she tames a river, or prevents Heracles from returning to Argos with blasts at sea. Her chthonic roar and fire storms, stolen one presumes from a genuine battle of elemental powers, occurs in a strange theomachy in which her claims appear ultimately as pure bravado. Most crucially, this Hera has no power to smite. However artfully she and Sleep tame Zeus, her machinations never presage cosmic ruin. They amuse, not frighten. Zeus may be hoodwinked, but he has the power to smite again as once before he dealt with her and Typhon. This nurse of monsters has lost her bite.

Are we to conclude, then, that Homer's Hera rises out of the ashes of an earlier embodiment of matriarchal chaos? Surely, the passages considered here establish the existence of such a tradition. But other "Heraian" images in early myth and cult suggest that such an image is only part of the received tradition: that Hera was also regarded as the Mycenaean Argolid's giver—and tamer—of all life. If so, the early tamer of all life degenerates into the tamer of wives to husbands. But that is a story for another day.

Joan V. O'Brien
Southern Illinois University at Carbondale

Notes

[1] My forthcoming work, *The Transformation of Hera* (Rowman and Littlefield, 1993), studies evidence from the three principal early sources, the *Iliad* and the two early Heraia (at Argos and at Samos). The evidence points in two different directions: on the one hand, toward a deity typically Greek in myth, ritual, and Olympian stature, and on the other, toward a pre-polis, regional symbol of all life, human and vegetal, benign and chaotic, a chthonic goddess nourishing earthlings, and a seasonal goddess bringing nature alive and taming it each season. Linguistically, we now know that Hera's Homeric formula βοῶπις πότνια ῞Ηρη, "lady Hera with the look of a cow" could have

been known by the Mycenaean Greeks and that it antedated her wifely formulae. See C. J. Ruijgh, "Le Mycénien et Homère," in *Linear B: A 1984 Survey*, eds. A. Morpurgo Davies and Y. Duhoux (Louvain-la-neuve, 1985), 143–90. Archaeology and mythology suggest that Zeus was relatively unimportant in the early Argolid. For the various meanings of the slippery Homeric word "Argos," see Anne Foley, *The Argolid 800–600 B.C.*, vol. 80 of *Studies in Mediterranean Archaeology* (Göteborg, 1988), 22, Table 1. It can be a name for all Greece, for northern Greece, for the whole Peloponnesus, and especially for the triangular Argolic plain, stretching from Mycenae south to the Gulf of Argos, and including the Bronze Age sites of Argos, Tiryns, Nauplia, Lerna, and Prosymna (where the Late Geometric Heraion was built).

Translations of the Greek are my own.

[2] Walter Pötscher, *Hera: Eine Strukturanalyse im Vergleich mit Athena* (Darmstadt, 1987).

[3] Claude Calame, *Les choeurs de jeunes filles en Grèce archaïque* (Rome, 1977), vol. 1, 409–20.

[4] Joan O'Brien, "Homer's Savage Hera," *CJ*, 86 (1991), 105–25.

[5] Jean Rudhardt, *Le Thème de l'eau primordiale dans la mythologie grecque* (Berne, 1971), 27.

[6] Richard Broxton Onians, *The Origins of European Thought* (Cambridge, 1951), 246–50, 315–16.

[7] Jenny Strauss Clay, *The Politics of Olympus: Form and Meaning in the Major Homeric Hymns* (Princeton 1989), 67–74.

[8] Στησίχορος δὲ (γενεαλογεῖ Τυφωέα) Ἥρας μόνης κατὰ μνησικακίαν Διὸς τεκούσης αὐτόν, "Stesichorus traces Typhoeus' pedigree from Hera alone because of her memory of Zeus' past injury," in Denys L. Page, *Poetae Melici Graeci* (Oxford, 1962), 125 frag. 62.

[9] "*Tartarus ex Tartara procreavit Typhonem*," *Fabulae* 152, in H. J. Rose, *Hygini Fabulae* (Leiden, 1933), 108.

[10] H. Erbse, *Scholia Graeca in Homeri Iliadem* (Berlin, 1969), vol. 1, 337–38.

[11] Cedric Whitman, "Hera's Anvils," *Harvard Studies in Classical Philology*, 74 (1970), 37–39.

[12] That Hera was a traditional mother of fire-gods who rebelled against Zeus is illustrated by the story of Prometheus, her son by the giant Eurymedon (T Scholion on *Il.* 14.296). For evidence that stories of gigantomachy and typhonomachy must have featured Hera and sons seeking to reimpose matriarchal chaos in place of the Olympian patriarchal order, see Clay, *The Politics of Olympus*, 68.

[13] Typhon is Hera's parthenogenetic son in the *Homeric Hymn to Apollo* 300–355 and in Stesichorus frag. 62. Hephaestus is Hera's parthenogenetic

son in Hesiod, *Theog.* 927–28 and in Chrysippus frag. 908 (= [Hesiod] frag. 343). In Homer, however, Hephaestus is son of Zeus and Hera (*Il.* 1.578, 14.338; *Od.* 8.312). In Ovid's *Fasti* 5.229–58, it is Ares, not Hephaestus, whom she bears without Zeus' aid in response to the birth of Athena. According to Hesiod, Hera nurses the offspring of Echidna (the Nemean Lion) but Gaia is the mother of Typhon (*Theog.* 327–29, 821). See Annie Bonnafé, *Eros et Eris. Mariages divins et mythe de succession chez Hésiode* (Lyon, 1985), 87–88 for the way that Hesiod minimizes Hera's role in the cosmogonic tradition.

[14] Of the six Iliadic uses of θύελλα, two are acts of Hera: at 15.26, when with Boreas her blasts prevent Heracles' return to the Argolid; and at 21.335ff., when with Hephaestus she blasts the river Xanthus. In the *Odyssey*, Hera saves Jason and the Argonauts from θύελλαι of fire (12.66–72). These θύελλαι are echoed in Typhon's rivers of fire (e.g., *Theog.* 870–80).

[15] Ares, son of both Hera and Zeus, acquires some typhonic characteristics in the *Iliad*, e.g., at 5.859–61 and 891–98.

[16] Joseph Fontenrose, *Python: A Study of Delphic Myth and Its Origin* (Berkeley, 1959), 119, 377–78.

[17] At her two earliest cult sites, Samos and Argos, there are no statues of Hera with a child in her arms. Hera's kourotrophic character is most clear in Italiote sites (e.g., at Paestum), and scholars have long observed that images of Hera and Demeter at Italiote sites are similar in that both were nurses of the young.

[18] Cf. 14.301–3 (Hera's lie to Zeus).

[19] On the meaning of πεῖραρ, see Onians, 310–42, and Ann L. T. Bergren, *The Etymology and Usage of 'Peirar' in Early Greek Poetry* (New York, 1975), 22–28, 163–64. The πείρατα γαίης, "boundaries of the earth," should be interpreted as the ultimate meeting of land and sea at earth's circumference. In this sense, Ocean binds Earth. Onians understands the mating of Ocean and Tethys as that of two primordial dragons. Since Tethys is distinguished from Ocean only by her sex, the underlying myth apparently indicates a dual origin of fecundity (Rudhardt, *Le Thème de l'eau primordiale*, 64–66; cf. Ament's article in this volume). One suspects, therefore, that Hera would have functioned in earlier myths as an earth goddess reuniting with serpentine Ocean. Epimenides of Crete (by way of Pausanias 8.18.2) says that Styx, the female offspring of Ocean, mates with Πείρας whence comes viperous Echidna, who in turn bears the Nemean lion and the Lernean Hydra. All these non-Olympian chthonic figures are associated with the early Hera.

[20] ... οὐδ' εἴ κε τὰ νείατα πείραθ' ἵκηαι
γαίης καὶ πόντοιο, ἵν' Ἰάπετός τε Κρόνος τε
ἥμενοι οὔτ' αὐγῆς Ὑπερίονος Ἠελίοιο.   (*Il.* 8.478–80)

... not even if you go to the nethermost binders of earth and sea, where Iapetus and Cronus dwell with no rays of Hyperion Helius.

This threatened "visit" to the sunless Titans in the nethermost extremities (τὰ νείατα πείραθ') and her proposed visits to the primordial rivers (14.200, 301) are the only Iliadic uses of "binders of the earth." Similarly, in the *Iliad* Ocean is called the cosmic originator only in the context of Hera's seduction of Zeus (14.200–201, 246, 301–2), about visiting this "begetter of the gods." My work in progress ties these motifs to seasonal journeys of the early Hera.

[21] Alcaeus frag. 129 (see Denys Page, *Sappho and Alcaeus* [Oxford, 1975], 161ff. [Alc. G 1.1–12] and 58ff. for reasons to attribute the phrase to Hera). See Sappho frag. 17.1–12 and *Odyssey* 3.173–74 for the difference between the Lesbian tradition, in which the returning Argives pray to Hera, Zeus, and Dionysus, and the *Odyssey*, where they invoke only Zeus.

[22] In support of this interpretation is another rare epithet that Hera and Ocean share, τέλεια or τελήεις, "complete," "fulfilled." Ocean is τελήεις (*Theog.* 242) because the river comes full circle (Rudhardt, *Le Thème de l'eau primordiale*, 75).

[23] In support of this argument is the fact that most Heraia, from Samos to Paestum, Crotona, Perachora, and Delos, were placed at the confluence of waters. Argive rivers like the Inachus and Asterion and numerous streams long dried up were also important at early Argos. See Richard A. Tomlinson, *Argos and the Argolid* (Ithaca, 1972), 8–11; and Pausanias 2.15.5, 2.17.1.

[24] Laura Slatkin, "The Wrath of Thetis," *TAPA*, 116 (1986), 1–24, especially 13–14.

[25] Cf. my "Homer's Savage Hera," 119.

[26] In ibid., I present the evidence for biological determinism in more detail. Nevertheless, I argue there that the principal link between Hera and raw-eating would have been her son Ares alias Dionysus alias Bronze Age Drimios (122–24). While that argument based on Dionysus' cultic association with omophagia remains valid, the diction and motifs of *Iliad* 24 specifically link her to Typhon and Echidna.

[27] Mycenae, Agamemnon's mythical home, and Argos are two of Hera's "dearest" citadels (πολὺ φίλταται, *Il.* 4.51–52). Hera is said to love both Agamemnon and Jason (θεὰ λευκώλενος Ἥρη,/ ... θυμῷ φιλέουσά τε κηδομένη τε, *Il.* 1.195–96 = 208–9; ἀλλ' Ἥρη παρέπεμψεν, ἐπεὶ φίλος ἦεν Ἰήσων, *Od.* 12.72).

Clytemnestra's Breast and the Evil Eye

In the center of the *Oresteia*, as a kind of centerpiece to the whole trilogy, Clytemnestra checks the murderous attack of Orestes by revealing to him her naked breast:

ἐπίσχες, ὦ παῖ, τόνδε δ' αἴδεσαι, τέκνον,
μαστόν, πρὸς ᾧ σὺ πολλὰ δὴ βρίζων ἅμα
οὔλοισιν ἐξήμελξας εὐτραφὲς γάλα.
(*Choe.* 896–97)

> Stop my son, honor this, child, the breast at which often while dozing you quaffed the nourishing milk with your gums.

Scholars deny that the actor playing Clytemnestra would have revealed a breast at this crucial moment.[1] The actor playing Clytemnestra, they argue, was male, and, consequently, had no breast to reveal. To be sure, the breast revealed by a male actor on the stage would have been artificial, but so was his mask. The actor's torso was as irrelevant to his role as his face. His body was made to conform to the shape demanded by his role, and padding allowed art's triumph over nature (*somatia* and *progastridia* mentioned by Plato Comicus frag. 256, Pollux 2.235, 4.115, and Lucian, *Iuppiter Tragoedus* 41). It is not doubted that male actors revealed breasts in Aristophanes' plays (*Wasps* 1374; *Lysistrata* 83; *Thesmophoriazusae* 638ff.). In that the Athenians had the technology to permit a male actor to reveal an artificial breast, we may presume that Aeschylus composed the scene with the intention that Clytemnestra's breast be revealed on the stage. Otherwise, he would have composed the scene differently.[2]

It may be that our culture does not associate the naked breast with lofty drama. Nevertheless, as commentators have pointed out,

Clytemnestra's gesture would have brought back to the audience one of the most poignant scenes in Homer, when Hecuba urged Hector to escape certain death from Achilles by retreating within the safety of the city walls. As a final, desperate appeal, Hecuba revealed to Hector her naked breast (*Il.* 22.79–85).[3] Even as they are joined in image, however, the two scenes are based on widely different realities. Although each mother tries to compel her son's obedience by a potent reminder of past devotion, Hecuba's sincerity underscores the sinister treachery of Clytemnestra. Hecuba was trying to draw her son to safety. Clytemnestra intends to ward her son off until she can kill him. Before holding out her breast, she has reached for a "man-slaying" axe in order to kill Orestes as she had killed his father (*Choe.* 889).[4] The breast wielded by such a mother is used only in default of another weapon.

As a theatrical image, Clytemnestra's bared breast would have had religious power entirely appropriate to the occasion. In her splendid robes, pointing to her bared breast, Clytemnestra would have looked like the images of the Earth goddess, who, in statues throughout the Aegean, points to her naked breast—indeed, this is a universal image for her as the great κουροτρόφος.[5] Invested with an aura of divinity, Clytemnestra stands at the door immensely powerful both as Orestes' mother and, by transference, as Earth herself, mother of all, who must be respected by all. Her stage presence forces us to view her in archetypal terms.

Contributing to our sense of Clytemnestra's power as a religious image, is her likeness to the incarnations of Earth, Demeter and Hera discussed by Ament, Passman, and O'Brien in this volume. According to myth, both she and Demeter avenged the loss of their daughters. To the parallel established in mythology, Aeschylus contributes others . Clytemnestra's prophetic dream, that she gives birth to a snake, makes her like Hera, mother of Typhon. In her dream, she offers the snake her breast, just as she will her son, and it draws blood instead of milk (*Choe.* 531–33). Hera, too, gave her breast to Heracles, according to some accounts,[6] and was wounded by him in the breast (*Il.* 5.392–94). In the *Eumenides*, Clytemnestra shows the Furies the gashes over her heart (*Eum.* 103). These resemblances to the Earth goddess, however powerful, are specious. As Froma Zeitlin points out, Clytemnestra's treatment of Electra negates her devotion to Iphigenia.[7] At the end of the trilogy, when the horror has begun to recede, we learn that Orestes stabbed Clytemnestra in the throat, not the breast (*Eum.* 592). Clytmnestra only dreamed that she gave birth to a snake. Because of either weakness or guile, Clytemnestra falls short of the archetypal ideal.[8]

Nevertheless, the archetype surrounds her like an aura, magnifying her magnificent gesture to her son. The audience would have felt his awe at violating a sacred image even if under the image there lurked a treacherous, adulterous woman. Contributing to the power of Clytemnestra's image, moreover, is is her resemblance to the Earth goddess in her destructive aspect, the Gorgon.[9] The artificial breast exposed by the actor would have been a powerful image because of the breast's resemblance to the eye, which was—and is—a terrifying symbol. The images of nurture and destruction are fused together in Clytemnestra's gesture because of the coincidental likeness between the breast and the eye in shape and pattern.

Anthropologists tell us that iconographically pictures of eyes and pictures of breasts are identical.[10] The eye goddesses of 3,000 B.C., found in Tel Brak, Syria, display the ambiguity. That breasts resemble eyes has been noticed in antiquity and in modern times. We see this resemblance in Magritte's *Viol*; in the last century Shelley had a nightmare vision that his wife's nipples turned into eyes.[11] The ancients were aware of the likeness between eyes and breasts. On the Greek "Baubo" dolls, a woman's face was imposed upon a woman's torso, with eyes where the breasts would be.[12] Most importantly for my argument, Aeschylus himself evidently pondered on the resemblance. In one of his plays there appear the race of Sternophthalmagoi, whose name indicates that they had eyes in their chests (frag. 431). In the *Choephori*, it is dramatically effective and thematically powerful to combine two dynamically opposed images: the nourishing breast and the evil eye.

In that the *Oresteia* was performed before the eyes of spectators, it is appropriate that allusion be made to the act of seeing. Throughout the trilogy (and indeed in all Aeschylus' plays[13]) φθόνος, "the evil eye," is a major theme because the glance has physical power. At Aulis, the chorus says, Iphigenia smote her sacrificers with her eyes, because her mouth had been gagged to prevent ill-omened curses (*Ag.* 240–41). Aeschylus emphasizes that her glance smote her viewers because he uses the cognate words, ἔβαλλ', "she struck" (*Ag.* 240) and βέλει, "with a blow" (*Ag.* 241) to describe the effect of her eyes.[14] Helen, too, is said to strike others with her gaze. In contrast to the darts sent out by the innocent Iphigenia, however, the gentle shafts from Helen's eyes bite the heart (*Ag.* 741–42). Helen's glance feels sweet, but its effect is destructive. Within the trilogy the eyes' shafts actually affect the person on whom they fall. The spectators' passive role of watching is given a vital role within the drama where the glance is felt like a blow or like a caress. The physical power of the glance reenforces a major theme of the trilogy, namely the manifestations of φθόνος on the divine level, and how this φθόνος is, by the end of the trilogy, transformed into the kindly eyes of the Eumenides. Before entering into discussion of Aeschylus, however, I will give a brief introduction to its prevalence in Greek literature and thought.[15]

The Greeks believed that the glance had power, mainly power to do harm. According to popular optic theory, the eyes emitted rays, which made vision possible.[16] Plutarch (*Quaestiones Convivales* 682f–683a) gives a scientific basis for belief in the evil eye by adapting Democritus' theory of *simulacra*, emanations from the eye (Diels 77). The English language reveals the prevalence of this notion: words for light (flash, flare, gleam, glow) are also used to describe the glance. Moreover, the rays emitted by the eye had physical force in that they could transmit the observer's feelings. That is, the glance had the power to foster or harm the person or object observed. Consequently, a glance charged with envy and malice would naturally hurt what was viewed. For this reason, Plutarch likened φθόνος to poisoned arrows (*Quaestiones Convivales* 681e).

The association of the evil eye and human success permeates Greek literature. The evil eye was believed to be cast upon the prosperous by those who resent their prosperity, both fellow humans and even the gods in heaven. The Greeks, who exalted competition, projected their envy at rivals onto their gods, who, they imagined, put limits on human happiness and who kept Bellerophon from storming their gates (Pindar, *Isthmian* 7.44–47). The two very different responses to the evil eye described in the *Iliad* and *Odyssey* are consistent with the two different strains of the poems themselves.

The heroes of the *Iliad* do not fear the evil eye. Their uninhibited boasting and their assaults on divinity exemplify a spirit that thirsts for immortality, rather than for life.[17] The death of a hero approaches, as Griffin puts it, when Zeus casts his shining eyes upon him.[18] The god's glance endows the hero with his greatest brightness just before his death so that he shines brightly and briefly before vanishing forever. Zeus' shining eyes call a hero to his death, but Patroclus, Hector, and eventually Achilles leave life to enter the eternal life of literature. Had Achilles preferred to live to an old age in obscurity, he would never have been given a role in the *Iliad*, let alone its brightest role.

In the *Odyssey*, which values survival, an existence in the flesh is preferred to legendary immortality. Achilles, when Odysseus meets him in the Underworld, repents his choice, declaring that he would rather be the slave of a migrant laborer, and live, than rule the shades (*Od.* 11.488–91). Pressed forever between the pages of a book, he yearns for the sun. In the *Odyssey*, the eyes of divinity are to be feared. Odysseus falls into overconfidence after he has put out the malignant eye of the Cyclops.[19] Like a hero of the *Iliad*, he boasts over his victim, urging the Cyclops to tell anyone who asks, that it was Odysseus of Ithaca, son of Laertes, who put out his eye (*Od.* 9.502–5). Knowing Odysseus' name, the Cyclops prays to his father Poseidon to punish Odysseus, who still has many miles of sea to cross. At the end of the *Odyssey*, Odysseus has learned his lesson. When his nurse begins to raise the cry of victory over the slain suitors of his wife, he stops her (*Od.* 22.411–12).

Writing in the fifth century B.C., Pindar adopts an Odyssean attitude to greatness in his praise of rich and successful athletes. To brighten his parallel between contemporary patrons and Homeric heroes, Pindar warns his victors to beware of the evil eye: the shadow of φθόνος enhances the brilliance of victory.[20] The athletes had risen so high that even the gods might view them as challengers. They must not emulate the heroes of the *Iliad* in excessive zeal.

The popular belief that the gods envied human success evolved into the sense that the universe is structured in such a way that of itself prosperity brings ruin. Prosperity induces in its victims tendencies towards luxury and arrogance and leads them to acts of folly. Herodotus presents both aspects of φθόνος at work in human affairs. In his *Histories* wise men speak of divine φθόνος, at the same time that overly successful individuals and nations are led to ruin by historical and psychological probability. Solon warns Croesus that divinity is somehow *phthoneros*, "envious" (1.32), but Croesus was brought down by the evils endemic to prosperity.[21]

Like Herodotus, Aeschylus combines the popular and enlightened views of φθόνος. Agamemnon adheres to the former view, that the successful have to tread more carefully, whereas the chorus and the playwright search for a more satisfying meaning. In its first instance, φθόνος sets in motion the tragedy. We learn from the chorus that Iphigenia was sacrificed because of Artemis' φθόνος against Agamemnon and the Greek army for the slaughter foreboded in the eagle omen (*Ag.* 134–35). Giving a greater moral significance to φθόνος, the chorus speculates that it is aroused in the gods against those who win wealth by slaughter. Zeus' thunderbolt, his traditional weapon, is hurled not by his powerful hand, but from his eyes (*Ag.* 469–70).[22] As the visual climax of the first play, when Agamemnon walks on the purple carpet, Aeschylus presents a tableau of a man in the act of drawing φθόνος on his own head (*Ag.* 947).[23]

Agamemnon is, moreover, instinctively aware of his danger, and prays that the eyes of no deity transmit φθόνος against him (*Ag.* 947). His limited vision, however, blinds him. According to the moral view of the trilogy, φθόνος has an ethical basis, being directed against guilty men, rather than fortunate ones. Of the characters in the trilogy, only Agamemnon maintains the lower, amoral view of φθόνος, that losers envy winners, that gods resent those who are too prosperous (*Ag.* 832–37). He cannot see his own crimes when he congratulates himself for punishing others. Accustomed to being envied in Troy, he is not surprised to learn that some citizens of Argos resent him. Unaware of a larger pattern, he can ride up to the palace with a young woman on his arm, with no fear of Clytemnestra, with no sense of her bitter hatred against him for killing their daughter. His inability to grasp the ethical basis of φθόνος makes him vulnerable to her arguments. By his reckoning, as a successful man, he must necessarily arouse φθόνος because success and power attract φθόνος, not the actions by which success and power are secured. By slaying his daughter, Agamemnon trampled down what was holy, and with a pious prayer to any god who may be watching, he symbolically reenacts the crime for which he is to be punished (*Ag.* 369–72, 905–7).[24]

As she stands blocking Agamemnon's entrance into his palace, I suggest, Clytemnestra metaphorically takes on another aspect of the Earth goddess, the Gorgon.[25] Such a creature guarded the threshold of Hades (*Od.* 11.633–35), which is itself an appropriate image for the house of Atreus. Cassandra addresses the palace door as if it were the door of Hades (*Ag.* 1291), and recoils from the door as reeking of the tomb (*Ag.* 1311) Moreover, the houses of ordinary people were guarded by such protective deities, whom Aeschylus evoked in the play's opening scene. In Athens, images of Gorgons stood on rooftops and repelled the invader with their sharp teeth and bulging eyes.[26] The watchman in the first scene of the *Oresteia* is placed on the roof of the palace like one of these protective deities. Moreover, the watchman's speech blurs the distinction between the dog and the Gorgon—because crouched in the position of a dog, as he says (*Ag.* 3), he is set on top of a roof, where the Gorgon should sit. Dogs were used quite loosely for monsters, to be sure: in the second play, Clytemnestra threatens Orestes with "the resentful dogs of his mother" (*Choe.* 924; cf. later where the phrase is repeated by Orestes at 1054). In his loyalty to Agamemnon, the watchman plays the role of protective guardian shared by dog and Gorgon, though, to be sure, he is the unwitting tool of his master's enemy.

The audience would have recalled the watchman's speech when Clytemnestra likens herself to a dog, loyal to those within, hostile to those outside (*Ag.* 607–8). In reality, she is like the hell hound, Cerberus, fawning on those entering the house, by sleeping with Agamemnon's enemy Aegisthus, and biting those within, namely, her husband and children. Keeping Agamemnon from the door, she repels the house's legitimate master. Just before Clytemnestra faces her son, her resemblance to the Gorgon is made explicit, when the chorus likens Orestes to Perseus (*Choe.* 831–32). With Orestes, Clytemnestra hides her Gorgon aspect under the guise of mother; with Agamemnon, she disguises herself as the loving wife.

Yet even here she reveals her hatred. At his entrance, she makes Agamemnon's arrival as ill-omened as possible by extravagance in speech and action. Her welcome speech draws φθόνος on Agamemnon's head by praising him: it was (and is) thought unlucky to praise someone or something excessively (*Ag.* 904).[27] Her actions show the same intent as her words. By strewing his path with lavish purples, as Agamemnon recognizes, she puts him in danger of divine φθόνος (*Ag.* 921). His death, which happens soon after, does not settle the question of divine φθόνος. If he dies in requital of his crimes, what about his murderess, who has also committed crimes against the family?

In the first play of the trilogy, Clytemnestra stands like a Gorgon controlling the door against her husband over whom she prevails. In the second play, she stands against her son, whom she fails to persuade. The pivotal position of the *Choephori*, at the center of the *Oresteia*, is reinforced by the ambivalent force of Orestes' eyes. In joy at their reunion, Electra calls Orestes the sweet eye of the house (*Choe.* 238); his enemies, on the other hand, receive his malignant glare. Orestes' connection with the hostile glance is expressed symbolically in Clytemnestra's prophetic dream, where she gives suck to a snake that bites her breast. The word for *snake*, δράκων (*Choe.* 527), was thought to be etymologically related to the verb *to see*, δέρκομαι (cf. Porphyrius, *De abstinentia* 3.8). With the emphasis on φθόνος in the tragedy, it is significant that Clytemnestra's first sense of doom should come to her through an image of sight. Orestes' gaze, which beams on his friends and glares at his enemies, evokes the sinister fusion of evil and charm in Helen's gaze. In Orestes' case, however, the ambivalence is healthy because both his loving gaze and his baleful gaze are directed towards the proper recipients.

When Clytemnestra bares her breast, in the center of the trilogy, her gesture is pivotal because, despite the horror of the moment and the greater horror to follow, it marks the transition where the evil eye that has glared on the Atreidae begins its transformation into the kindly eye that will beam on the Athenians. On a larger scale, the fiends emanating from the wounded mother's wrath will become the nourishing Eumenides. In fusing the two images together, Aeschylus draws on universal human experience, infancy.

Anyone who has nursed a baby, even with a bottle and even someone else's baby, has found that the infant, as it takes in milk, engages one in eye-contact. This seems deliberate on the part of nature because the early stages of an infant's vision are limited to the space separating a woman's chest and her face. Perhaps in honor of that earliest and most universal memory, the mother and child, connected by the gaze and by the act of nursing, form a compelling and universal image. The archetype of Mother and Child is especially powerful to all humans who have passed through infancy, whether the names given the archetype are Mary and Jesus, or Isis and Horus.

Now the gaze and the mother have presented themselves to the human imagination in two aspects, as bad and good. The good, kindly, creative aspect of the mother is set against the evil, malignant and destructive aspect. Just as the earth symbolizes fertility and death, so the image of mother, Neumann argues, takes on both aspects: nourishing and devouring, creating and destroying.[28] Neumann has argued that the faces of demons found from South America to Tibet are emblematic of the destructive mother who takes us in when we die. For westerners the most familiar example of this demon face is the Gorgon, whose bulging eyes and sharp-toothed jaws are depicted on many pieces of Greek art, but the "terrible deities" of Tibet show the same features. The jaws of the death goddess rend and devour us in gruesome parody of our mothers' wombs which sent us out into the world. Neumann has suggested that the jaws of the demon faces symbolize the *vagina dentata*, which reflects a universal fear that the womb that sends us forth can grow teeth and change into the devouring jaws of the death goddess.[29] He adduces examples from Greek mythology: the seductive monster, Lamia, whose name means gullet, and the demon Scylla, whose loins were girded round by dogs.

I would like to add to Neumann's theory by filling in the torso. He suggested that the mouth of the demon evokes the nourishing womb transformed into its opposite, the devouring jaws. I suggest that the eyes which glare out of the demon's face evoke in our mind the breasts of the mothers from which we drew our first nourishment. Instead of sustenance, however, the bulging eyes emit a malevolent stare. The horror we feel at Medusa is in part derived from the horror we feel when what is familiar and loving is turned into something malignant. Writers of horror stories know how to exploit this terror.

Just as the eye and the mother are envisioned either as kindly or as malign, so, according to the Freudian psychologist Melanie Klein, the same dichotomy exists in the mind of the nursing infant. According to her theory, the infant assigns will to its mother's breasts, so that they give milk or refuse milk as a deliberate act. The infant, in turn, absorbs the images of a good breast, one that gives milk, and of a bad breast, one that withholds milk.[30] Folklore beliefs that women exist whose breasts give out poison or blood tend to support Klein's theory as well as popular expressions such as "cold as a witch's tit."

Following up on Melanie Klein's hypothesis, Michael Carroll suggested a relationship between the good and evil eye and the good and bad breast.[31] He has drawn on the similarity in shape and pattern between the breast and the eye to give a theoretical explanation for the prevalence of the belief in the evil eye. The hateful feelings that the infant conceives towards the breast that rejects it are projected into the rejecting breast, which then becomes the "Bad Breast." Thus, as the infant desires to drain out the liquids from the uncooperative breast, so it projects these hostile and devouring impulses on the "Bad Breast." The traditional means of counteracting the eye (spitting, urinating, defecating), Carroll suggests, derive from the means at the infant's disposal. Consequently, it seems that as adults we project upon the evil eye what as infants we projected upon the breast. Thus, it would seem, the mother, the gaze, and the breast are profoundly joined in the human psyche.

Clearly, Aeschylus could not have been aware of how deeply grounded the fusion of eye and breast may be in the psychology of the infant. Nevertheless, Clytemnestra at the door, her breast exposed, would have conjured up two opposing images in the minds of her spectators: the nourishing mother and the Gorgon with bulging eyes. The audience would have envisioned an angry face superimposed on her torso. As I suggested earlier, the image of Clytemnestra was shaded in the first play with the image of Gorgon. At the end of the ode immediately before the matricide, the chorus urges Orestes to take on the heart of Perseus (*Choe.* 831–32), implicitly likening Clytemnestra to the Gorgon Medusa. Moreover, in the first stanza of the same ode, Aeschylus prepares the viewer to connect Clytemnestra's breast and the hostile eye. The chorus hopes that the eye of the house (or of freedom) will shine out from its dark veil (*Choe.* 808–10), looking ahead to the revelation of the eye-like breast from its garment.[32]

As a Gorgon, Clytemnestra momentarily freezes Orestes. He acts as one struck by the eye of Medusa, paralyzed, unable to do more than cry out to his friend Pylades (*Choe.* 899). At this moment a miracle takes place when a mute character speaks. Kitto has suggested that Apollo speaks through the mouth of Orestes' friend.[33] If this is so, Aeschylus has adapted for the stage the Homeric practice of sending a god in human shape into the realm of mortals, in that the gulf separating the mute role from the speaking role was as profound as the one separating humans from gods.[34] Within the context of drama, the break in dramatic convention is equivalent to a suspension of the laws of the natural universe. Apollo, who in the *Eumenides* will take Orestes' part against the evil-eyed Furies, and who later in Callimachus will be the opponent of Φθόνος (*Hymn* 2.106ff.), speaks from the mask of Pylades, urging Orestes to respect Apollo's oracles. Orestes is freed from paralysis by the god's intervention and manages to commit the matricide.

Orestes' victory over his mother contrasts and is intended to contrast with his father's defeat by her in the previous play. As symbolic spectacle, the purple carpet on which Clytemnestra compels Agamemnon to walk is matched by the breast she directs at her son. The scenes resonate with each other in other ways.[35] In each, a man and woman argue about entrance into the palace. Both scenes are set apart from the texture of the trilogy by the rapid-fire stichomythia. The differences are also significant. Clytemnestra, who persuaded her husband, fails to persuade her son: Agamemnon succumbs in a few lines to Clytemnestra, while Orestes gives her line for line in protracted argument. The similarities between the two sets of murders underscore the ever recurring horror of crime reenacted in each generation with the victor doomed to perish in turn. In each scene the visual imagery is spectacular and integral to the meaning. Each scene offers visual representation for verbal imagery developed in the drama. When Agamemnon walks on a scarlet path, a verbal image comes to life as this man has trampled on more sacred things. About to commit matricide, Orestes, too, fears to trample on what is precious. In the earlier scene we see a man bringing φθόνος on his head; in the later, we see φθόνος itself glaring out of the breast of the injured mother. The anger of the mother killed by her own son is personified in the chorus of Furies, visible to Orestes at the end of the *Choephori*. These figures, whose entrance was said to have caused miscarriages among the pregnant women of the audience (*Life of Aeschylus*; Pollux 4.110), play a major role in the third play of the trilogy. Their conversion to Eumenides, "Kindly Ones," is the dramatic issue that closes the *Oresteia*.

The eyes of the Furies have horrifying power. In the scene with Orestes, Clytemnestra bares her breast. In her dream, she gave the breast to the snake, which drew blood instead of milk (*Choe.* 531-33). Consciously or unconsciously, we expect Orestes to stab her in the breast, in the very place where, according to Homer, Heracles once wounded the Earth goddess in her aspect of Hera (*Il.* 5.392-94). That Orestes stabbed Clytemnestra in the breast is implied in the *Eumenides*, where her ghost shows to the sleeping Furies the wounds over her heart (*Eum.* 103). Once again, she opens her garment revealing to the eyes or the imagination of the horrified spectator her breasts, now dripping with blood. The eyes of the Furies conjured up by her vengeance also drip with blood (*Choe.* 1058), and in art the Gorgons were painted with red eyes so that they might seem to drip with blood.[36] Consequently, when Orestes sees the Furies' eyes, we imagine that he relives the moment when he saw his mother's bleeding breasts. The fiends, who are the embodiment of his mother's curse (*Choe.* 924, 1054), glare at him with eyes that keep alive the horror of the matricide.

In the *Choephori*, where justice and φθόνος begin to merge, Clytemnestra assures Orestes that there are eyes in the house that revere justice (*Choe.* 671). Clytemnestra, who simply means that she and her associates respect the laws governing human conduct, does not know that Orestes is watching her with eyes that revere justice, as he plans to take vengeance for his father. In turn, as Orestes envisions her murder, he does not realize that other eyes inside the house are beginning to open. After the matricide the Furies will persecute him with their vengeful eyes. In the third play, however, the Furies become the Eumenides, and the obsessive malice of their eyes changes so that they beam forth prosperity onto the land of Attica. Φθόνος still exists, but in the service of justice, not of blood-feuds.[37] When the Furies are converted from loving vengeance to loving justice, hope is introduced into the play.

In the larger framework of the trilogy, images of evil are cleansed to become images of healing.[38] Beginning as φθόνος, the gaze is finally transformed into the kindly gaze of the reformed Furies, the Eumenides. Allusions to the kindly eye are only rarely found in Greek literature— by no means as prevalent as they are among Buddhists or the ancient Egyptians.[39] The change in the Furies' glance reflects the change in their nature from Furies to Eumenides. At first, they breathe φθόνος on

Orestes and threaten to do so on Athens as well.[40] The blights and plagues with which they repeatedly threaten Attica are the typical emanations of the evil eye:[41]

> ἐγὼ δ' ἄτιμος ἁ τάλαινα βαρύκοτος
> ἐν γᾷ τᾷδε, φεῦ,
> ἰὸν ἰὸν ἀντιπενθῆ
> μεθεῖσα καρδίας, σταλαγμὸν χθονὶ
> ἄφορον· ἐκ δε τοῦ
> λειχὴν ἄφυλλος, ἄτεκνος,
> ἰὼ δίκα, πέδον ἐπισύμενος
> βροτοφθόρους κηλῖδας ἐν χώρᾳ βαλεῖ.
> (Eum. 780–87, 810–17)

> I dishonored and resentful, the wretched one, dropping
> venom, venom from my heart in requital on the earth,
> a drop unbearable to the earth, from which a disease
> that blights the leaf and blights the child—oh justice—
> will rush, hurling on the ground man-slaying infections.

Athena persuades them, however, to adopt a more favorable attitude so that they send forth prosperity, happiness, and fertility (Eum. 938–48). Their harsh aspect is still present, but their hostility is directed against Athens' enemies, not her citizens.

The story of pregnant women's miscarriages, I suggest, derives from the baleful glare of the evil eye, the threat of the Furies, rather than from the actual presence of women in the audience. The sources for the story are late and reflect contemporary practice rather than historical reality. Pregnant women and nursing mothers, together with the child, are most vulnerable to the eye's attack and so, if there had been women in the theater, as there were in the Roman period, they would have had miscarriages. Aeschylus' audience would have been moved to terror by them.

The discussion of the evil eye in a drama has particular force because the act of seeing, which has so much power in the world on the stage, mirrors the action required by the audience. Seeing involves both power and danger. The two great scenes of the first two plays concern φθόνος and are performed before the eyes of a living audience. When Agamemnon walks the carpet, he is watched not only by the gods and the Argive elders, but also by the male population of Athens. This means that the living population is invited to feel the φθόνος his deed is intended to arouse. In the second play, Clytemnestra's bared breast is directed at Orestes, but again the audience of Athenians is included in its malevolent glare.

With our experience of ancient literature largely confined to literature classes, we occasionally need to be reminded that Greek tragedy was originally composed for a living audience. In the case of the *Oresteia*, we need these reminders less than for any other drama because the verbal images are reaffirmed by the visual images.[42] Because the unity of word and image is integral to Aeschylus' dramatic vision, he incorporates within the trilogy the action of his audience, namely, the gaze. In the theater, literally, "a place for seeing," characters gaze at each other and are gazed at by unseen forces, all the time watched by fifth-century Athenians. I suggest that awareness of the audience is the reason for Aeschylus' frequent allusions, noted by Moreau, to the evil eye in his dramas.[43]

In the first two plays, the eyes of murderers meet the eyes of their victims. Iphigenia smote her slayers with her eyes. When the murder of the daughter by the father has led ultimately to the murder of the mother by the son, Orestes' serpent eye is met by the glaring eye of Clytemnestra's breast. At the end of the trilogy, eyes meet in love, not in hate or retribution. Athena leads forth the Furies to meet the "eye of Athens" (1025–27), the additional chorus of women and children who escort the Eumenides to their new dwelling. The "eye of Athens" comprehends more than the additional chorus. Present at the performance of the *Oresteia* and ratifying the agreement, were the spectators, the adult male citizens who would not include women and children in their number.[44] Together with the male spectators, the women and children presented on the stage would comprise all Athenian citizens, old and young, male and female, past and present. The theater becomes in Aeschylus' imagination the place where the eyes of the audience could meet the eyes of deity as the barrier between the mythological past and the historical present dissolves through the magical arts of the dramatist.

Mary DeForest

Notes

I would like to thank Robert Lamberton, Reuben Cholokian, Jody Pinault, and Barbara Hill for their suggestions. This first and all subsequent translations of the Greek are my own.

[1] How this would have been presented on the Greek stage by a male actor is a matter for speculation. Without saying why an artificial breast could not have been constructed, scholars have contented themselves with asserting that it would have been impossible to stage, or at least very difficult. See Oliver Taplin, *Greek Tragedy in Action* (Berkeley, 1978), 61; J. Michael Walton, *Greek Theater Practice* (Westport, 1981), 191; A. F. Garvie, *Aeschylus: Choephori* (Oxford, 1986), ad loc. As James R. Baron pointed out in his talk, "'Drag' Humor in Aristophanes' Comedy," at CAMWS (Columbia, MO, April 7, 1990), the audience would have been so far away from the stage that the artificiality of the breast would not have been noticed. Memory of the scene may have affected Euripides' treatments of Orestes' matricide, where Clytemnestra is described (though not shown) as bearing her breast in desperate appeal (*Electra* 1206ff.; *Orestes* 526ff., 839ff.).

[2] Oliver Taplin, *The Stagecraft of Aeschylus. The Dramatic Use of Exits and Entrances in Greek Tragedy* (Oxford, 1977), has, in another context, asked rhetorically, "What is the point of the actors *not* doing what they say they are doing, provided it is practicable?" (36).

[3] Sidgwick, Verrall, and Tucker ad loc.

[4] D. J. Conacher, *Aeschylus' Oresteia: A Literary Commentary* (Toronto, 1987), suggests that the reason for the scene where the nurse mourns Orestes is intended to offset the maternal obligations claimed by Clytemnestra (120). According to H. J. Rose, *A Commentary on the Surviving Plays of Aeschylus* (Amsterdam, 1957–58), the story that Clytemnestra attacked Orestes with an axe is more ancient than Aeschylus (at *Choe.* 889). Froma I. Zeitlin, "The Dynamics of Misogyny in the *Oresteia*," *Arethusa*, 11 (1978), has argued that Clytemnestra's gesture has erotic meaning because of the story that Helen deflected the onslaught of Menelaus by baring her breast (157–59).

[5] V. Tran Tam Tinh, *Isis Lactans: Corpus des monuments gréco-romains d'Isis allaitant Harpocrate* (Leiden, 1973); Theodora Hadzisteliou Price, *Kourotrophos: Cults and Representations of the Greek Nursing Deities* (Leiden, 1978); Erich Neumann, *The Great Mother: An Analysis of the Archetype*, trans. Ralph Manheim, Bollingen 47, 2d ed. (Princeton, 1974), 123–25, plates 8–10, 12a, 13, 20.

[6] See Arthur Bernard Cook, *Zeus: A Study in Greek Religion* (Cambridge, 1940), for discussion of Hera's being tricked into acting as though she were

giving birth to Heracles (Diodorus Siculus 4.39) and for representations on ancient mirrors of her giving her breast to the hero (vol. 3, part 1, 89–94). For stories that the hero suckled at her breast (and spat out the Milky Way) see Robert Graves, *The Greek Myths* (New York, 1957), citing Eratosthenes, *Catasterismoi* 44; Hyginus, *Poetic Astronomy* 2.43; Photius 447; and Diodorus Siculus 4.10 (vol. 2, 90).

[7] Froma Zeitlin, "The Dynamics of Misogyny," 168.

[8] For another, satirical, example of a powerful woman discredited by contrast with the underlying reality, see Hill's article in this volume.

[9] That the Gorgon's face was a mask representing the destructive aspect of the Earth goddess was suggested by Jane Harrison, *Prolegomena to the Study of Greek Religion* (New York, 1955), 187–97; cf. Neumann, *The Great Mother*, 22–23, 80, 153, 166, 169.

[10] Erich Neumann, *The Great Mother*, 126–27; Joseph Campbell, *The Masks of God: Occidental Mythology* (New York, 1970), 152–53; Alan Dundes, "Wet and Dry, The Evil Eye: An Essay in Indo-European and Semitic Worldview," in *The Evil Eye*, ed. Dundes, 277; O. G. S. Crawford, *The Eye Goddess* (London, 1957), 41, 48, 98.

[11] Shelley's vision is described in Richard Holmes' *Shelley: The Pursuit* (New York, 1975), 329; cf. Ross MacDonald, *Black Money* (New York, 1966), 230.

[12] For all that is known about these figurines, see Maurice Olender, "Aspects de Baubo," *Revue de l'Histoire des Religions*, 202 (1985), 3–55. The poet Nonnus (sixth century A.D.) uses images to describe breasts that normally describe eyes. They send forth darts and, in obvious allusion to the Medusa story, paralyze the lover's hand (*Dionysiaca* 7.264, 35.43, 35.173, 42.70). See also the illustration of a figurine from Sardinia of the fourth millennium B.C., which has eyes engraved over the breasts, in Marija Gimbutas, *The Language of the Goddess* (London, 1989), 36. I would like to thank Christina Kohos for this reference.

[13] A. Moreau, "L'Oeil Maléfique dans l'Oeuvre d'Eschyle," *Revue des Études Anciennes*, 78–79 (1976–77), 50–64.

[14] James P. Holoka, "The Point of the Simile in Aeschylus *Agamemnon* 241," *CP*, 80 (1985), 228–29, points out that the psychological effect of the gaze on those who feel guilty is like a missile. See the bibliography given by Eduard Fraenkel, *Aeschylus: Agamemnon* (Oxford, 1962), at *Ag.* 742.

[15] For the evil eye in antiquity, see O. Jahn, "Ueber den Auberglauben des böses Blicks bei den Alten," *Bericht über die Verhandlung der königlich sächsischen Gesellschaft der Wissenschaften zu Leipzig*, 7 (1855), 28–110; Edward Dodwell, *A Classical and Topographical Tour through Greece During the Years 1801, 1805, and 1806*, vol. 2 (London, 1819), 31ff.; and Frederick T. Elworthy, *The Evil Eye*:

The Origins and Practices of Superstition (1895; rpt. New York, 1958).

For discussions relating to more recent times, see *The Evil Eye: A Folklore Casebook*, ed. Alan Dundes (New York, 1981); *The Evil Eye*, ed. Clarence Maloney (New York, 1976).

For the identification of φθόνος with the evil eye, see Fritz Wehrli, *Lathe Biosas* (1931; rpt. Stuttgart, 1976), 83–85 and Walter Burkert, *Structure and History in Greek Mythology and Ritual*, Sather Classical Lectures, vol. 47 (Berkeley, 1979), 73. S. Ranulf, *The Jealousy of the Gods and Criminal Law in Athens: A Contribution to the Sociology of Moral Indignation* (London, 1933), 63–84, gives illustrations of φθόνος in literature.

[16] Charles Mugler, *Dictionnaire historique de la terminologie optique des Grecs: Douze siècles de dialogues avec la Lumière* (Paris, 1964), 5.

[17] E. R. Dodds, *The Greeks and the Irrational* (Berkeley, 1951), 29–31.

[18] Jasper Griffin, *Homer on Life and Death* (Oxford, 1980), 87.

[19] Walter Burkert, *Structure and History in Greek Mythology and Ritual* (Berkeley, 1979), 157, note 30.

[20] S. Eitrem, "The Pindaric *Phthonos*," *Studies Presented to David M. Robinson*, edited by G. E. Mylonas and D. Raymond, vol. 2 (St. Louis, 1953), 531–36.

[21] M. P. Nilsson, *Greek Piety*, trans. Herbert J. Rose (Oxford, 1948), describes the transition from a belief in the jealousy of the gods to their resentment against wanton arrogance (52–59). E. R. Dodds, *The Greeks and the Irrational* (Berkeley, 1951), also distinguishes between the two kinds of φθόνος (28–32, 41, 44). For Aeschylus' combination of the popular belief in the evil eye with the more enlightened one, see Fraenkel's commentary *Ag.* 762; R. P. Winnington-Ingram, *Studies in Aeschylus* (Cambridge, 1983), 1–15; and Rose, *A Commentary on the Surviving Plays of Aeschylus* (at *Eum.* 534).

For Herodotus' view of divine envy, see Charles Rowan Beye, *Ancient Greek Literature and Society*, 2d ed., rev. (Ithaca, 1987), 215–17.

[22] For discussion of the connection between the avenging thunderbolt and the evil eye, see Wehrli, *Lathe Biosas*, 84; Fraenkel, on *Ag.* 469f.; Ranulf, *The Jealousy of the Gods*, suggests that the Greeks assimilated their belief in the gods' justice with their belief in the gods' jealousy (111).

[23] For φθόνος in the carpet scene, cf. Fraenkel on *Ag.* 904 and Winnington-Ingram, *Studies in Aeschylus*, 90–93.

[24] Conacher, *Aeschylus' Oresteia*, discusses the connection between Iphigenia's sacrifice and Agamemnon's treading the carpet (37–39).

[25] Moreau, "L'Oeil Maléfique," 56–57, likens Clytemnestra to a Gorgon when she freezes Agamemnon's will.

[26] For Gorgons on the roofs of buildings, see Jane Danforth Belson, "The Gorgoneion in Greek Architecture," Diss. Bryn Mawr, 1981, vol. 1, 14–16. For

the apotropaic eye, see Elworthy, vii–viii, 126–43.

[27] Cf. Eugene S. McCartney, "Praise and Dispraise in Folklore," in *The Evil Eye*, ed. Dundes, 9–38.

[28] Neumann, *The Great Mother*, 147–208.

[29] Ibid., 168–73.

[30] The views of Melanie Klein are written out in "Some Theoretical Conclusions Regarding the Emotional Life of the Infant," in *Developments in Psycho-Analysis*, ed. Joan Rivière (London, 1952), 198–236. Cf. Howard F. Stein, "Envy and the Evil Eye among Slovak-Americans: An Essay in the Psychological Ontogeny of Belief and Ritual," in *The Evil Eye*, ed. Dundes, 223–53.

The infant's ambivalence towards the mother's breast is reflected in the ambivalence we feel towards nourishing itself. The wicked stepmother plays a vital role in the hero's development—even bad breasts can be good! Heracles would never have achieved divinity were it not for Hera's hatred; and she was (above, n. 6) sometimes presented as his mother or foster mother. The overprotective mother is, perhaps, more dangerous, keeping the hero back from achievement. In conscious or unconscious allusion to the dangers of the overnurturing mother, Woody Allen, in *Everything You Always Wanted to Know About Sex (But Were Afraid to Ask)*, created a monstrous breast that escaped from the laboratory of a mad scientist and drowned its victims with milk. This fantasy exemplifies the "Good-Bad Breast," the breast that kills by nourishing. (I would like to thank my friend, Amy O'Neill, for this suggestion.)

[31] Michael P. Carroll, "On the Psychological Origins of the Evil Eye: A Kleinian View," *The Journal of Psychoanalytic Anthropology*, 7 (1984), 171–84.

[32] As Conacher, *Aeschylus' Oresteia*, points out, the text is disputed (135, n. 60). Nancy Rabinowitz, "From Force to Persuasion: Aeschylus' *Oresteia* as Cosmogenic Myth," *Ramus*, 10 (1981), notes that Clytemnestra is like Medusa in the scene where she bares her breast, but does not connect her breast with Medusa's eye, suggesting rather that she resembles the seductive and beautiful Medusa (176). For summaries of interpretations of Medusa's glare (Freudian, existential, and literary), see Hazel Barnes, *The Meddling Gods* (Lincoln, 1974), 3–51.

[33] H. D. F. Kitto, *Form and Meaning in Drama: A Study of Six Greek Plays and of Hamlet* (London, 1956), 53.

[34] For the possibility of other appearances of gods on the stage disguised as human beings, see my "Gods in Livery," *Classical Bulletin*, 69 (1989), 71–76.

[35] Taplin, *Greek Stagecraft*, 356–57, points out that the interchange between Orestes and his mother parallels the one between Clytemnestra and Agamemnon. R. W. Garson, "Observations on Some Recurrent Metaphors in Aeschylus' *Oresteia*," *Acta Classica*, 26 (1983), 33–39, shows how similar

imagery links the victims and their oppressors.

[36] Belson, "The Gorgoneion in Greek Architecture," vol. 2, 4, 19, 31, 35.

[37] Conacher, *Aeschylus' Oresteia*, contends against Hugh Lloyd-Jones that Aeschylus did intend the transition from vendetta to law court (168–69).

[38] Cf. Moreau, "L'Oeil Maléfique," 64, for the kindly gaze of the reformed Eumenides. For the transformation of evil images into good, see Winnington-Ingram, *Studies in Aeschylus*, 166; Conacher, *Aeschylus' Oresteia*, 172–74; and Elizabeth Belfiore, "The Eagles' Feast and the Trojan Horse: Corrupted Fertility in the Agamemnon," *Maia*, 35 (1983), 3–12.

[39] Examples are collected by Headlam in his edition of Herodes, at *Mime* 4.73. For the kindly eye in Egypt and India, see in *The Evil Eye*, ed. Mahoney, the essays of Leonard W. Moss and Stephen C. Cappannari, "Mal' Occhio, Ayin ha ra, Oculus Fascinus, Judenblick: The Evil Eye Hovers Above," 2, and Clarence Mahoney, "Don't Say 'Pretty Baby' Lest You Zap It with Your Eye—The Evil Eye in South Asia," 129–30.

[40] To avert their malevolence, Orestes spits at their words (*Eum.* 303). For spitting as a way to avert the evil eye, see Tibullus, 1.2.56; Petronius, *Satyricon* 131; Persius, *Satire* 2.32; Pliny, *Naturalis Historia* 28.3–4; Seneca, *De Consolatione ad Marciam* 9.4. Kathy Mardikes pointed out the apotropaic function of Orestes' action in her talk, "The Binding Song in Aeschylus' *Eumenides*," CAMWS, 1987.

[41] According to Pliny, *Naturalis Historia* 7.2, trees and children are withered by the effect of the evil eye. The effect of the evil eye was thought to be one of drying up the vital sap, the liquids that keep us alive. Dundes, "Wet and Dry, The Evil Eye," has suggested that cultures that believe in the Evil Eye also have the sense that life is carried in liquids (266–79). Growing old and dying are perceived as a process of drying. Tithonus, the man who grew old but could not die, was imagined as withering away until he became a cricket. At the other end of life, babies seem almost as liquid as their diet. In Greek, the word meaning to raise a child literally means to harden milk into cheese. Beliefs in the Elixir of Life and the Fountain of Youth attest to a belief that life is liquid. To explain the concept of the Evil Eye, Dundes combines the belief that life is liquid with another belief, the doctrine of limited good. Adherents of this doctrine believe that there is only so much to go around. Therefore, if one enjoys the bounty of life, someone else must go short. Since life was conceived as liquid, people who are in the act of drinking are most vulnerable to envy from those who lack. For that reason, Dundes suggests, the custom has grown up to toast one another before drinking, as if to say, though I drink, I do not begrudge you the goods of life (266–67). In some areas, people will not drink while there is an empty glass on the table. Someone thirsty might cast a spell on those who drink.

For the opposite theory, also extant in antiquity, that fertility in women was associated with dryness, see Jody Pinault's essay in this volume.

[42] Thomas G. Rosenmeyer, *The Art of Aeschylus* (Berkeley, 1982), 136–37, comments on the way that images seem to come to life in Aeschylus. Cf. Taplin, *The Stagecraft of Aeschylus*, 39–40, and Rabinowitz, "From Force to Persuasion," for more references to Aeschylus' theatrical imagination (186, n. 1).

[43] Moreau, "L'Oeil Maléfique," 50–64.

[44] Whether women attended Greek theater is controversial. Sir Arthur Pickard-Cambridge, *The Dramatic Festivals of Athens*, 2d ed. (Oxford, 1968), gives discussion and bibliography. More recently it has been argued that women were allowed to watch the plays. See Jeffrey Henderson, "Women and the Athenian Dramatic Festivals," *TAPA*, 121 (1991), 133–47.

Penelope as Weaver of Words

Penelope's δόλος ("ruse") of weaving and unraveling the shroud for Laertes, all the while stringing along the suitors with encouraging messages, bespeaks a devious and self-possessed intelligence. Penelope "sends forth messages" (ἀγγελίας προϊεῖσα, 2.92 and passim) which, although not reflecting her true feelings (we are told), kindle ardent hopes in the suitors and provoke their three-year siege on the palace. Shrewdly manipulating the suitors' presence in Ithaca to secure her own position against increasing pressure to remarry, clever Penelope uses these enigmatic messages, it appears, to great effect.[1]

The precise nature and form of Penelope's messages warrant examination. What scenario can we reasonably offer for their composition and delivery? Since ἀγγελίη in Homer regularly denotes a spoken message (e.g., 2.30, 10.245, 15.314), let us begin with the natural assumption, almost universally held, that Penelope's messages took an exclusively oral form. Are we to imagine, then, a regular relay of spoken messages between Penelope and all 108 suitors, delivered individually by harried handmaidens, scurrying around the palace? Were there, perhaps, only occasional group messages, entrusted to the delivery of a single, discreet messenger, which were powerful nonetheless to raise the hopes of each man? The messages are mentioned directly by Antinous, the spokesman for the suitors, and by Athena, in identical words:

> πάντας μὲν ἔλπει, καὶ ὑπίσχεται ἀνδρὶ ἑκάστῳ
> ἀγγελίας προϊεῖσα· νόος δέ οἱ ἄλλα μενοινᾷ.
> (2.91–92, 13.380–81)

> She causes all to hope and makes promises to each man by sending forth messages, but her mind devises other things.

It is clear from the text that Penelope, at least initially, encouraged the courtship of all of her noble suitors. Folktale elements have colored the depiction of the suitors to such a degree, however, that it seems almost plausible that these greedy and arrogant men, with little or no encouragement, would have wanted to hang around the palace, for years running, feasting daily at Odysseus' expense and carousing with the serving girls (e.g., 18.304–5).[2] But, if that were the case, why would Penelope have felt it necessary in the first place to encourage such gluttonous rowdies with messages? The suitors, we are told, were wealthy and important men (ἄνδρες ἄριστοι, e.g., 15.521) from Ithaca and the surrounding islands, who presumably had their own kingdoms and concerns (e.g., 18.357–59). The prospect of controlling Odysseus' estates was no doubt attractive, but such wide-scale courtship in the beginning can only have been the result of significant encouragement, in one form or another.

It is important to remember, too, that we are glimpsing the situation at Ithaca in its final stages. The encouragement and courtship, such as it was, had gone on for almost four years. Things have reached an ugly pass. The suitors know that Penelope has deceived them with her ruse of weaving and by her messages. Penelope knows that the suitors know. Consequently, when she appears before them in Book 18 in a rare, spirited mood to declare that she has now resigned herself to the prospect of remarriage and expects to receive suitable courtship presents from her potential bridegrooms, there is little effort at pretense. She says flatly that the prospect of marriage is hateful to her but inevitable (18.272–73). But, even at this late hour, Penelope holds out the promise of marriage to each of the suitors, presumably as she had done previously through her messages, and she demonstrates that she has lost none of her extraordinary powers of persuasion:

> τῶν μὲν δῶρα παρέλκετο, θέλγε δὲ θυμὸν
> μειλιχίοις ἐπέεσσι, νόος δέ οἱ ἄλλα μενοίνα.
> (18.282–83)

> She drew from them gifts for herself and bewitched their souls with honeyed words, but her mind devised other things.

More of the original tone of the messages can be glimpsed in Penelope's recounting to Odysseus, disguised as a beggar (19.141–47), of her earlier deception of the suitors. She remembers saying, "Young men (κοῦροι), my suitors since Odysseus' death, wait awhile, though you are eager to marry me, until I finish the shroud for Laertes, so that my weaving may not be in vain" (19.141–44).³ She also appeals to the suitors' sense of propriety by mentioning the criticism she could expect to receive from her countrywomen if she should rush into a new marriage and neglect her filial duty. Penelope's accurate memory of this scenario is confirmed by Antinous (2.96–104), as he complains of Penelope's delaying tactics to Telemachus. We might note that Penelope, at this earlier time, does not say to the suitors that the prospect of remarriage is hateful or even unwelcome. She implies only that it is untimely.

Whatever direct contact Penelope had originally with the suitors no doubt decreased as the situation at the palace became more strained (e.g., 15.516–17). One can imagine Penelope resorting more and more to the sending of messages as she sensed the increasingly impatient mood of the suitors. Now, an ἀγγελίη, by its very nature, demands some medium of communication. Who are we to imagine delivered these messages of encouragement to the suitors? The obvious candidate is the herald Medon who, although popular with the suitors (17.172–73), is spared in the end by Telemachus' plea on his behalf (22.356–58; cf. 4.679–702). Penelope, however, seems to regard Medon with cool disdain and suspicion, as a man who is only too ready to do the suitors' bidding and to join willingly in their plunder of Odysseus' property (e.g., 4.681–87). Although Medon undoubtedly served in his capacity of herald in a perfunctory way, it is hard to imagine that Penelope would readily entrust him with messages of such a personal nature.

Might Penelope's chosen messenger have been the old nurse Eurycleia or the housekeeper Eurynome, who obviously was devoted to Penelope and something of a confidant (e.g., 18.164–84)? Or perhaps the messenger was one or more of the handmaidens, who had regular contact with both Penelope and the suitors, and with whom a number of them did become involved. One thinks immediately of Melantho (18.321ff), whom Penelope "reared and cared for as her own child, and gave her playthings which delighted her heart" (18.322–23). Melantho eventually turned against Penelope (e.g., she felt no "sadness" [πένθος] for the queen, 18.324), fell in love with the suitor Eurymachus, and became his mistress. It is Melantho who berates the disguised Odysseus when he dares to suggest that the maids favor Penelope, instead of the suitors, with their presence (18.313–36; cf. 19.65–69). Such a handmaiden as Melantho may initially have been Penelope's trusted messenger, who could have been expected to be unfailingly loyal to Penelope and, because of her youth, more sympathetic than Eurycleia or Eurynome to Penelope's emotional dilemma. We may speculate further that it was Melantho's role as Penelope's messenger which brought her into close contact with the suitors in the first place and prompted her infatuation with Eurymachus.

Penelope tells the disguised Odysseus simply that she was betrayed by her female slaves, good-for-nothing bitches (κύνες οὐκ ἀλέγουσαι), who permitted the suitors to catch her unawares at her loom (19.154). Antinous' account of the suitors' discovery of Penelope's deception differs in one important respect from Penelope's account. He says that one of her women in particular (τις γυναικῶν), who knew the situation clearly (ἣ σάφα ᾔδη), revealed all to them, and that they accordingly caught Penelope in the act of unraveling her weaving (2.108–9). If Penelope were embarrassed or wounded by Melantho's betrayal of her, as she surely must have been by the girl's impertinence and obvious hostility, it would help to explain why she attributes the disclosure of her deception to her female slaves, in general, and does not allude to the betrayal of any one in particular, as Antinous does. It is also possible that Penelope did not know for certain who betrayed her. When, for example, she learns that Telemachus has sailed secretly from Ithaca to learn of Odysseus' fate, she immediately suspects a conspiracy of silence among all of her handmaidens to keep her uninformed (4.729–31). We may remember that, in the end, twelve of her maids *are* killed, on the advice of Eurycleia, for their flagrant disloyalty (22.421–25; cf. 22.151–52). Clearly, Penelope could not confidently have entrusted her messages to any of these women.

The messages demand our further attention. Homer does not bother to explain how these messages might be conveyed to so many different recipients under such constrained circumstances, but it must be presumed that here, as elsewhere in the poem, he has created a situation with an inner logic which his audience can readily comprehend. His audience will permit the poet the improbable situation on Ithaca, I believe, only if it can imagine that the situation is handled in a plausible way. Even if we are to consider Penelope's messages to the suitors in the same category as Odysseus' fantastic adventures on his journey home, we are permitted to expect the characters and situations to have an air of verisimilitude about them. On the face of it, the circumstances surrounding Penelope's communication with the suitors are puzzling, to say the least. If Penelope's ἀγγελίαι were exclusively spoken messages, entrusted to the delivery of one or more handmaidens, we might expect them to cease after Penelope's deception of weaving was uncovered, through treachery in her own quarters. The messages apparently continued, however, judging from the fact that Athena and Antinous speak of them in the present tense. "She causes all to hope (ἔλπει) and makes promises (ὑπίσχεται) to each man by sending forth (προϊεῖσα) messages" (2.91–92; 13.380–81). The fact that the messages continued in an atmosphere of mistrust and hostility argues for a form of communication which is private and perhaps even clandestine. Even if we are wrong to interpret the present tense literally in Homer, other details seem to point to the desirability of a more private form of communication.

First, the content of the messages would seem to require the kind of delicacy and confidentiality which "prudent" (περίφρων) Penelope herself could best provide. Second, even in earlier days, when the atmosphere in the palace was no doubt more relaxed, it is unlikely that Penelope, in her esteemed position as queen, would ever have been permitted much direct contact with the suitors—and almost certainly she would never have been totally alone with them. Whenever Penelope so much as emerges from her private rooms in the palace, she is accompanied by at least two handmaidens to signal her propriety (18.182–84).[4] In this restricted atmosphere, it is difficult to imagine how Penelope could effectively have communicated delicate matters at all to the suitors, either in person or through the second-hand spoken account of a discreet messenger, especially since she had reason to mistrust her immediate associates. And yet, we are asked to believe that the suitors are so persuaded to a man that each is her favorite that they stayed around Ithaca for almost four years awaiting an imminent decision. Moreover, it is difficult to see how Antinous could accuse Penelope of actually "inciting" (ἀνίημι, 2.115) the suitors through her promising messages (2.89–95) unless their contents and source were unimpeachable. Dare we to suppose that the messages on occasion took a written form?

The only clear reference to writing in Homer occurs in the story of Bellerophon in the sixth book of the *Iliad* (6.155–197). Proteus, king of Argos, believing his wife's charge against Bellerophon's character, sends the hero to the King of Lycia, his father-in-law, with tablets containing orders for Bellerophon's death. The tablets are received and the message understood by the king, who consequently sends Bellerophon on a series of life-threatening missions. Homer says that Proteus personally carved (γράπτω) signs or symbols (σήματα) on a folded wooden tablet (πίναξ πτυκτός), which conveyed his message to his father-in-law (6.168–69). The symbols are called "sad" or "mournful" (λυγρά) because of the unhappy fate they portend for Bellerophon (θυμοφθόρα πολλά, 6.169).

It matters little whether or not these σήματα refer to Linear B or some other script. The important thing is that Homer has imagined the art of written communication in use in the Greek world before the Trojan War, even if only on a very limited basis and not clearly defined.[5] After successfully completing his trials, Bellerophon marries the king's daughter and sires, among other offspring, Laodameia, who in turn gives birth to Sarpedon, a warrior at Troy (6.197–99). If Homer could imagine a form of written communication in use in Bellerophon's day, he almost certainly would have supposed that such an art was available to the generation of the Trojan War as well, particularly to the nobility. Intelligent Penelope, we should remember, was placed totally in charge of affairs at Ithaca in Odysseus' absence (18.266) and would have been cognizant of, if not versed in, the record keeping of Odysseus' extensive estates.[6] Homer's audience is likely to have assumed that a woman as famously clever as Penelope would have had at her disposal a broad repertoire of communication, both oral and written, which she could use as the occasion demanded.

Let us imagine for a moment that Penelope did, from time to time, resort to a private, written sort of communication with some of her more learned suitors, messages in sealed tablets for example, delivered by her handmaidens or Medon. Amphinomus, reputedly Penelope's favorite among the suitors (16.397–98), comes immediately to mind. Amphinomus, we are told, had a good mind (φρένες ἀγαθαι), like Penelope, and pleased her with his μῦθοι ("spoken words," cf. 18.412–21, 20.245–46). Although the use of μῦθοι in this context can be taken as a statement of Amphinomus' courteous demeanor in comparison with his more rowdy peers, it may also hint at a broader verbal dexterity. Penelope may have found it convenient, on occasion, to convey privately to some suitors messages intended for themselves alone, thereby doing away with the need for an intermediary who may or may not be relied upon to report her words faithfully.[7] Sometimes these messages might have been of a wholly private nature. At other times, they might have contained information intended for some or all of the other suitors. Penelope's written messages to intellectuals, such as Amphinomus, would have confused and angered the less refined suitors, such as Antinous, who, already infuriated by Penelope's attempts at delay, would be further annoyed by receiving her "encouraging" messages second-hand from several sources. Written messages by their very nature would have the added advantage of generating suspicion and jealousy among the suitors as Penelope played for more time, once the ruse of the shroud had been removed. Clever Penelope is not without another δόλος, however. In the place of Laertes' shroud, Penelope weaves with her messages a web of confusion and suspicion in the minds of the suitors that effectively keeps them in check. Such a scenario would give added meaning to Antinous' exasperated declaration that Penelope surpassed *all the women who ever lived* in intelligence (φρένες) and cunning arts (κέρδεα, 2.117–18)![8]

Since the traditional formulaic language of Homer, reflecting a preliterate society, evidently did not have a regular word to designate written message, I see no good reason why ἀγγελίαι could not also carry the sense of written messages if the context required it to.[9] The word σήματα ("signs"), used in the story of Bellerophon, may have been too specific and limited for Homer's use in a situation in which both oral and written messages were intended. To argue that Homer intended his audience to understand that Penelope's messages, at least some of the time, were written, it is not necessary to suppose that either Homer himself or his audience was literate, but only that he and his audience believed that such a thing as written communication existed in the

Heroic Age, as we know they did from the reference to Bellerophon's tablets in the *Iliad*.[10] The deeds of the *Odyssey* are played out against a background no less fabulous than that of the slaying of the Chimera. The assumption of writing would have enabled Homer's audience to unravel the absurdly complex situation at Ithaca we have described above and to lift Penelope's dealings with the suitors to that high plane of wonderment and mystery for which the *Odyssey* is justly famous.

Patricia A. Marquardt
Marquette University

Notes

Some of the ideas contained in this article were presented at the 1986 CAMWS Meeting in Tampa, Florida. The translations of the Greek are my own.

[1] For a detailed study of Penelope's motives in encouraging wide-scale courtship and her emotional dilemma, see my "Penelope Πολύτροπος," *AJP*, 106.1 (1985), 32–48. The ambiguity of Penelope's character is examined from the perspective of narrative function by Marylin Katz, *Penelope's Renown: Meaning and Indeterminacy in the Odyssey* (Princeton, 1991). The text throughout is that of W. B. Stanford, *The Odyssey of Homer*, 2 vols., 2d ed. (London, 1965).

[2] For the folklore tradition underlying the suitors' waste and profligacy (the unjust-guest tale), see H. L. Levy, "The Odyssean Suitors and the Host-Guest Relationship," *TAPA*, 94 (1963), 145–53. Comic aspects of the suitors are noted by Douglas Stewart, *The Disguised Guest* (Cranbury, 1976), 100–101. The suitors' foolishness is highlighted by Daniel Levine in "*Odyssey* 18: Iros as Paradigm for the Suitors," *CJ*, 77 (1982), 200–204; and their baseness in "Homeric Laughter and the Unsmiling Suitors," *CJ*, 78 (1982–83), 97–104.

[3] For the suggestion that the object of Penelope's weaving may more appropriately have been a wedding veil, see S. West's comments in A. Heubeck, S. West, and J. B. Hainsworth, *A Commentary on Homer's Odyssey* (Oxford, 1988), vol. 1, 137–38.

[4] Cf. Telemachus' words to Theoclymenus regarding Penelope's inaccessibility: "She does not often appear before the suitors in the house" (15.516). The position of women in general in Homeric Society is discussed by Sarah B. Pomeroy, *Goddesses, Whores, Wives, and Slaves: Women in Classical Antiquity* (New York, 1975), 16–31, especially 27; and James Redfield, *Nature and Culture in the Iliad*

(Chicago, 1975), 119–23.

⁵ Several recent studies of this passage have concluded that Homer is likely alluding to alphabetic writing. See, for example, Walter Burkert, "Oriental Myth and Literature in the *Iliad*," in *The Greek Renaissance of the Eighth Century* B.C., ed. Robin Hagg (Stockholm, 1983), 51–52; Rufus Bellamy, "Bellerophon's Tablet," *CJ*, 84 (1989), 289–307 ("writing tablets were ... well known in eighth-century Greek courts; no Aegean state of any consequence could have been unacquainted with them, nor any citizen of consequence," 293); and G. S. Kirk, *The Iliad: A Commentary* (Cambridge, 1990), who claims, "The balance may be tipped towards alphabetic writing by the 'folded tablet' ... something familiar from Assyrian reliefs and in developed uses of the alphabet" (vol. 2, 181); Barry B. Powell, *Homer and the Origin of the Greek Alphabet* (Cambridge, 1991), 18–20, following the lead of Alan J. B. Wace and Frank H. Stubbings, *A Companion to Homer* (London, 1962), 555, asserts that the Bellerophon story is wholly an Eastern import and that Homer himself is ignorant of writing of any kind. Noting that the σήματα at *Iliad* 7.181–89 appear to be merely signs on lots, Powell argues unconvincingly that the σήματα in the Bellerophon story are also "semasiographic" and not "lexigraphic" (199–200). It is difficult to imagine how Bellerophon could have communicated complex and specific information through only pictographic means (cf. Burkert, 51). Also it is possible to argue that the word σήματα, depending on the context, could designate both semantic and non-semantic signs, as the oral vocabulary available to Homer probably lacked separate words to indicate each concept. Compelling evidence for the "literate" nature of Homer's compositional style is provided by David Shive, *Naming Achilles* (Oxford, 1987).

⁶ For the Mycenaean Greeks' use of writing (Linear B) for administrative and commercial purposes, see John Chadwick, *The Mycenaean World* (Cambridge, 1976), 69–83 and 102–33. Penelope's assumption of power at Ithaca is discussed by Helene P. Foley, "Reverse Similes and Sex Roles in the *Odyssey*," *Arethusa*, 11 (1978), 7–26.

⁷ The suitors, being noblemen with estates and property back home, must themselves have sent and received messages of various sorts during their four years on Ithaca. Cf. 18.357–59, where Eurymachus offers to hire Odysseus to work on one of his farms.

⁸ For an interesting discussion of the meaning of φρένες in this context, see Shirley D. Sullivan, *Psychological Activity in Homer: A Study of Phren* (Ottawa, 1988), 115–17.

⁹ The ordinary word for written message, γράμμα, appears for the first time in Herodotus (e.g., 1.124). Some of the verbs used in context with ἀγγελίη would permit the sense of written communication. Homer uses the vivid word

προίημι ("send forth"), to describe Penelope's issuing of messages (2.92, 13.381). Appearing elsewhere in the *Odyssey* with ἀγγελίη are φέρω ("bring," 1.408) ὀτρύνω ("send forth," 15.40, 16.355), and ἐποτρύνω ("prompt," 24.355). An undeniably oral sense of ἀγγελίη appears with such verbs as ἐρέω and εἶπον ("speak," 16.329, 15.314) and κλύω ("hear," 2.30, 42). Cf. also the use of προίημι with ἔπος and φήμη ("word," "voice," 14.466, 20.105).

[10] All the more is this the case if the innovation of alphabetic writing was becoming known in their own day or already gaining currency, as some scholars believe, e.g., Dorothea Wender, *The Last Scenes of the Odyssey* (Leiden, 1978), 5–9; and Martin Mueller, *The Iliad* (London, 1984), 163–66. Conservative estimates would place the introduction of the alphabet into the Greek world around 750 B.C., roughly contemporary with Homer. Powell, *Homer and the Origin of the Greek Alphabet*, 20, sets the date around 800 B.C., and Kirk, *The Iliad: A Commentary*, 181, likewise argues for a late ninth century date. A somewhat later date is posited by Eric A. Havelock, *The Literate Revolution in Greece and Its Cultural Consequences* (Princeton, 1982), 168–82. Cf. Bellamy, "Bellerophon's Tablet," who argues boldly not only for the literacy of Homer but also for the "literate" nature of the hexameter itself: "Far from being preliterate, the hexameter was actually hyperliterate, arbitrarily tied to the alphabet to an extent unmatched in any modern poetic tradition. The composer of the *Iliad* and *Odyssey* was therefore literate" and could not have "composed before the introduction of the Semitic alphabet" (305).

A Hero's Wife

The *Trachiniae* centers on a dominating male of vast egocentric drive and a female lead who is a model of sympathetic sensibility. It turns on the inadequacy of the human intellect, and both principals come to see themselves as victims of that condition. Deianeira ends a suicide; Heracles, already wracked with terrible pains, can see no sweeter prospect at the close of the action than death by fire. Deianeira, despite subtle misdeeds, wins our sympathy and even our praise. As it turns out, however, Heracles' real prospects transcend praise and blame alike. Cold, tyrannical, and altogether inhuman, he stands before our astonished eyes at the play's end as nothing less than a divinity in the making. As this last is a rare, not to say unexampled, contention, its establishment dictates our first order of business. We may start with the large probability that Sophocles was familiar with the tradition of Heracles' assumption into Olympus on the occasion of his live cremation, which is about to be enacted at play's end, atop Mt. Oeta.[1] Jebb, assuming such familiarity, notes that Hyllus' observation at the close, "No one can foresee the future" (1270), constitutes the play's single hint of Heracles' apotheosis.[2] If some deny even this much, others acknowledge further hints of deification.[3] Fuqua aptly sums these up, together with certain misgivings for their effect on the play:

> When one considers the abundant references to Heracles' end, Mt. Oeta, and finally to the pyre itself, it is hard to think how thought of the hero's prospective apotheosis would not have been conjured up (even if the dramatist does suppress its positive aspects in favor of the grim costs involved).[4]

If, so far, it is safe to say that Sophocles takes no pains to exclude suggestions of deification, the most decisive evidence remains to be explored. A little reflection indicates that he signals the apotheosis from the play's very beginning, in architectonic terms, in fact, at two of the work's most vital junctures, the start and close of the prologue. Deianeira opens the play with the "old saying" that no one can adjudge a life well or ill spent until death brings it to a close. She pointedly excludes her own experience from the scope of the *gnome*, remarking that it is heavy and grievous, and the play's action unmistakably bears her out. To whose life, then, might the saying apply? To no one's, plainly, save Heracles' as it hangs in the balance at the drama's end.

If this does not yet spell out apotheosis, the close of the prologue makes it all but certain. There, Deianeira comments to Hyllus that knowledge of good fortune is profitable even if acquired late. It has been widely recognized that late learning is a fundamental issue of the play, but—witness Deianeira's own horrendous experience—in the sense of futile realization of error. Where does profitable late learning of good fortune come into play, especially with Hyllus as the beneficiary? Surely, indeed exclusively, with the cremation of Heracles atop Mt. Oeta. Such a delayed epiphany, we must appreciate, is enormously dramatic, not the least for its radical irony, after Hyllus' fretful denunciation of heaven in the final verses and his closing, plaintive observation, "Nothing is here that is not Zeus."[5]

Sophocles furnishes other such intimations of deification. Soon after his anguished entrance (1000ff.), Heracles exclaims that no singer or healer can charm away his agonies save Zeus himself. If we do not take the hint, Hyllus presently remarks that he is powerless to render his father's life "forgetful of pains" (1021f.). In straightforward speech, this means that he cannot heal him, but the Delphic convolution of the phrase is deliberate and meaningful. Just such a tranquil life has been proposed for Heracles by the very oracle that is universally understood to be coming true at this very moment. Hence, when Hyllus adds, "Such things Zeus alone can bestow" (1023), we cannot but surmise that, here again, Sophocles is preparing the way for a resolution in apotheosis.[6] Heracles' "cure" will be transferral to a pain-free life among the gods.

If we hang back, there is another avenue of approach to the same conclusion. As has been broadly recognized, Deianeira's opening reference to the mutability of human fortune, far from going unsupported, constitutes a major motif of the drama. First, the notion, stated in an uncharacteristically optimistic vein, permeates the parados: day ever succeeds night (94f.); the sea-billows of Heracles' trials now overwhelm him, now exalt him (112ff.); sorrow and joy come in turns akin to the turning of the Bear (129f.); and, as night does not abide forever, so ought Deianeira to have fairer hope concerning her husband's fortune. Next, after she has learned of Heracles' triumph at Oichalia, the seeming vindication of the chorus' advice, the heroine chooses to be wary (296f.); good fortune, she fears, many portend the reverse. Then come the tremendous reversals: of Deianeira's expectations concerning the robe and of Hyllus' convictions concerning her guilt. Mother and son both "learn too late." All of this is crowned by the nurse's solemn *gnome* after Deianeira's suicide (943ff.): rash it is to reckon upon tomorrow or thereafter, for there is no tomorrow before one closes the present day in good stead. Together with Deianeira's kindred opening comment, then, this sentiment encloses the heroine's entire, sad history, and there, for all intents and purpose, the critics lay the question of fortune's mutability to rest.[7]

Sophocles, however, does not. The exodus remains, the balance of the day remains, and, above all, Hyllus' observation concerning the future's unpredictability lies in wait. Anything still can happen. Hyllus, to be sure, does not believe in his own observation. He "knows" that Heracles' fate is evil. But who is Hyllus to have the last, conclusive word on so grave a matter? He enters the play expressing an infantile and, in view of his final verdict, deeply ironic trust in Heracles' "wonted good fortune" (88f.); and his entire education between that point and the end consists in a series of stunning blows to the intellect. No, anything can indeed still happen, and, as Hyllus' comment has already been recognized to hint at apotheosis, it would seem perverse to continue to resist the most evident of conclusions: Sophocles wished his audience to understand that the resplendent, all-unexpected reward of divine immortality lay in store for Heracles. This is the play's ultimate reversal of fortune, an understanding that at one blow transforms the *Trachiniae* from among the most sombre to one of the most radiant of his extant works.

A result of such an ending, happy indeed for the criticism of the play, is to corroborate the chorus' reassurance of Deianeira early on

(139f.) that, in effect, Zeus is never careless of his children. Hitherto, critics have been persuaded either to deny the proposition or to hold that it is indeed authenticated, but ironically.[8] Now it stands as an incontestable verity. Other consequences, admittedly, seem only to aggravate inveterate problems of interpretation. Why, for example, if he is to be so grandly rewarded, is Heracles portrayed so unattractively? And what part are we to assign amid all these ultimately felicitous reversals to the sad, magnificent Deianeira? These and other difficulties must await detailed analysis of the action for their relief. We may say at the outset, however, that, as fundamentally as it engages the gulf between divine and human knowledge (which opposition, after all, subsumes its stress on the mutability of human fortune), the drama meditates on the difference between divine and human nature. It is against this difference that the fates of both principal characters are most aptly studied.

*

The heroine is introduced as a passive, pessimistic innocent. Her opening judgment upon the tenor of her life reveals a sense of hopelessness, while both innocence and hapless passivity shine through her account of her "wooing" by Heracles and a spectacularly monstrous river god (9ff.). Then, even as he introduces a leading aspect of her naivete, a childlike openness to the counsel of others, Sophocles adumbrates her undoing. Receiving a piece of helpful advice from her nurse, she marvels that such words should issue from the mouth of a slave (61ff.). This is the same innocent who keeps stored in her memory the advice of a centaur.

Her pessimistic turn of mind, which constitutes, ironically, her whole acquaintance with wisdom, again surfaces when she learns that Heracles is, after all, safe and triumphant. There is every reason to rejoice, she concedes (293ff.), but, understanding how the fragility of fortune urges prudence, she yields to vague misgivings. The immediate catalyst is the presence of a group of young slave women, whom Lichas has conveyed to Trachis as part of the spoils of Oichalia. The sight affects Deianeira with wholehearted pity, which, typically of the enlightened Sophoclean character, entails cognizance of the universal human lot. Her appeal to Zeus (302ff.) beseeching death before she sees any of her children brought so low shows that, like the Odysseus of the *Ajax*, Deianeira understands the lessons of misfortune.

For the play as a whole, such sympathy and understanding have weight significantly beyond her schooling in pessimistic misgiving. Clearly, these human qualities set her diametrically apart from the callous and egoistic Heracles. The play has already touched upon aspects of his temperament by citing his seemingly perpetual indifference to Deianeira's cares throughout the course of their long marriage and is destined to record so many more that the antithesis between heroine and hero might seem to mark the gulf between the human and sub-human sensibility. If we are right in our approach, however, we shall see that the play's more genuine and far more interesting contrast lies between the human (the exquisitely human at that) and the divine.

When Iole in particular among the captives catches Deianeira's eye, the theme of *logos* and *ergon*, which, as we shall see, is pervasive in the play, undergoes its first movement on the side of deceit. Lichas claims falsely that he does not know the girl's identity. Indeed, she has been silent throughout the entire journey, save for a constant weeping (322ff.). Here Sophocles fashions an ironic, fateful link between the two women. Deianeira will likewise remain silent when she learns of her own catastrophe (813f.), and she will also weep. For the moment, however, she maintains a tactful solicitude, forbearing to add more trouble to the pitiable girl's store.

Lichas is the only messenger in Sophocles who displays a three-dimensional characterization, doubtless because he is the only one whose behavior materially affects the action. I refer, of course, to his prevarications, which cause a short-lived joy in Trachis and so pave the way for the play's first pathetic reversals of fortune. The most absorbing aspect of his role, however, lies in its relationship, including a curious affinity, to Deianeira's. As he confesses (401f.), he lies concerning Iole's identity in order to spare Deianeira's feelings, and he then becomes her victim when she essays a benign misrepresentation of her own. From another perspective, he is no less an innocent victim of her machinations than she is of Nessus' or, perchance, of a higher power's. The parallelism will prove crucial when we come to assess the implications of the play's monumental last line.

Lichas' deception soon comes to light as Deianeira learns from the old man who first reported Heracles' triumph that the messenger has concealed not only Iole's identity but Heracles' real motive in storming Oichalia. The true reason was his overwhelming passion for the girl. We must not fail to note that Deianeira reacts with unconditional dismay (375f.).[9] Nor may we dismiss her shock as the entirely natural response which it surely is. It must be measured against her claim only a short time later to a sophisticated tolerance where Heracles' infatuations are concerned (441ff.). If she speaks *vera voce* there, we cannot but wonder at her behavior here. In light of such a discrepancy, the chorus' outburst immediately after Deianeira's groans of dismay is destined to take on an unexpectedly ironic cast: "Damned beyond all others is the man who practices secret villainies to his disgrace" (383f.). And the irony will be nothing forced. Such practice, as we shall see, constitutes substantially the same charge that the heroine will bring against herself. Lichas' lie meanwhile constitutes the drama's first play upon the discrepancy between *logos*, "word," and *ergon*, "deed," an opposition that permeates and informs the play, as, indeed, it does the whole of the extant Sophoclean corpus.[10]

Deianeira's main participation in the *logos-ergon* theme consists in her deception in the stratagem of the robe. If duly remarked by the critics, this piece of guile itself has been much too lightly dismissed. The fact, however, is that she implicates herself even more extensively in deception. In order to deceive Heracles, she must first beguile Lichas, and this, despite massive critical opinion to the contrary, she sets about to accomplish with calculated intent.

Her purpose becomes clear at the close of the first episode. After being prepared to send Lichas away earlier without mention of gifts (332ff.), she now orders him to await her preparation of the same. The reason for her change of heart is transparent. She has since learned Iole's identity and inevitable role, and the "gifts," of course, amount to the anointed robe. Not only can we thus conclude that Deianeira has settled upon her intention by the episode's end; we can also deduce when she most probably conceives it. By far the most likely point arrives soon after Lichas' return to the stage (393). Deianeira begins the interrogation of the messenger, but when he again promptly denies knowledge of Iole's identity, the old man angrily takes up the questioning.

Critics once faulted Deianeira for irresolution at this point, a peculiar judgment in view of the concentrated vigor that she will show when she rejoins the dialogue. She remains silent for some 35 lines, and it is, I suggest, in this interlude that she resolves upon her plan of guile. How better to explain the fact that her long ensuing speech (436ff.) is flawed with numerous deceptive assurances? Importantly, it starts with a plea in the name of Zeus of Oeta not to cheat her of the truth. Since she is about to cozen Lichas in the very manner which she here deplores, her self-compromise, despite her ultimately innocuous purpose, is not trivial. The identical irony taints her following assertion that the name of liar is a deadly reproach to a free man.

The mildest case that can be brought against Deianeira on the basis of this speech is that her subsequent actions fail to bear out her unsolicited claims. She is lenient, she avers, regarding the vagaries of the human heart (439f.); she will not enter into conflict with Eros (441f.); she feels no sense of being wronged (448) and none of hurt, so long as she learns the truth (458f.).[11] Everything here not already forfeit will be nullified by acts to come. Her obvious purpose, to elicit the truth from Lichas, easily succeeds, whereupon she pledges her word openly for the first time. Having promised to remain steadfast in her admirable claims (486f.), she makes guileful mention of gifts, a certain indication that she intends nothing of the sort.[12]

Ergon will conform to *logos*, then, no more closely here than in the presentation of the robe. The effect on Heracles aside, the catastrophic result of these virgin excursions into guileful manipulation by Deianeira is Lichas' untimely death and her own. Nor does this lamentable outcome tell the pair's piteous tale in full, for behind it all looms a tangle of pathetic ironies. Lichas, as we have noted, deceives Deianeira only to spare her pain, while her secret purpose, the salvation of her marriage, is also honorably intended. Though both reversals are well grounded in the play's theme of uncertain human knowledge, they are not thereby softened. On a higher plane, meanwhile, engulfing all, there resides an utmost force to which attaches an even more painful irony. Both Lichas and Deianeira are blind players within a vast, inexorable heavenly design. They count for little in that context and will count for even less. If we can pity them already their warm, feckless humanity, how much more so when their histories are all but lost amid the events that consummate Heracles' destiny.

The play ends, as we know, with an indictment of Zeus, but Hyllus has the justice of Heracles' fate in mind, not that of these lesser mortals. Perhaps, nonetheless, we are already verging upon a question of theodicy. There are two designs at work in the play, Deianeira's hapless stratagem and Zeus' imperial plan. Is each flawed in its own way? Difficult questions await resolution, to be sure, but at this point we do well to remind ourselves that Sophocles is not in the habit of impeaching heaven.

When Deianeira returns to the stage, she confirms that she cannot abide Iole's rivalry and that, as a consequence, she has resorted to the deception of the robe. Both admissions, of course, violate her word to Lichas, which leads us again to challenge the play's traditional interpretation of seamless innocence on her part. Deianeira has carefully prepared the robe according to the centaur's prescription, but she now informs the chorus of a moral qualm:

> May I neither know nor learn wicked daring, and I
> abhor women who undertake it. But if I can prevail
> over this girl by love charms, the deed has been
> devised, unless I act rashly. If so, I shall desist.
> (582ff.)

Critics have regularly understood "wicked daring" to signify the use of love-charms pure and simple, but this is too narrow a view.

The use of love magic is reprehensible, after all, specifically because it is a deceitful enterprise. Such a soul as Deianeira, alien till this crisis to both guile and enterprise, must upon reflection inevitably be disturbed by qualms of wicked daring. She has forfeited her word already and now stands on the brink of an irrevocable deceit. Hence she reverts to her habitual dependency on outside counsel. Not love magic alone, however, but the audacious guile that it entails gives her pause. For their part, the Trachinian women see nothing amiss in principle:

> No, you do not seem to us to have designed wrongly,
> if there is some ground of confidence in these
> measures. (588f.)

It has not been noted that Deianeira later contradicts the chorus' judgment measure for measure. Contemplating suicide when her plan threatens to explode disastrously, she declares her design ugly, βουλεύμασιν (725) corresponding with βεβουλεῦσθαι (589), μὴ καλοῖς, corresponding to οὐ κακῶς. We must doubt that the issue addressed, obviously identical in both places, pertains exclusively to love-charms. From the first it is the essential design that troubles her, the whole dubious enterprise of wicked daring.

The chorus' advice emboldens Deianeira to see her deception through, but her conspiratorial call for secrecy just before Lichas returns introduces new moral complexities:

> Only keep my secret well sheltered. For even if you
> commit ugly deeds, you will escape shame so long as
> they are kept in the dark.   (596f.)

This is Deianeira's first open endorsement of deceit, and, it is fair to say, critics have greeted it with shocked dismissal.[13] We must understand, nonetheless, that, more than the heroine's, the statement is Sophocles' work. Why does he place such astonishing words in her mouth at this point?

Limited to its intended scope, it is true, the sense is innocuous enough. Expecting her ruse to succeed, Deianeira simply wishes the world never to learn of her shameful means. This is to compound guile with guile, no doubt, but without real dishonor given a felicitous outcome. At the same time, the word αἰσχρά, "ugly," "disgraceful" (597), indicates lingering misgivings regarding the deception, which, as we have seen, will be confirmed at the brink of catastrophe by μὴ καλοῖς, "not pretty," "ugly," "disgraceful" (725). Still, thus far, we detect little more than the continuing stress of moral anxiety.

But Lichas, who now leaves the palace to join the party, enters eminently into the number of those to be kept "in the dark." In this connection, Deianeira's sermon on honest candor addressed to that same messenger earlier comes ironically home to roost.[14] Her deceptive manipulations thus suddenly illuminated, the comparative innocence of her words begins to fade. If she does not intend their cynical overtones, her acts confound her intention. It is, I suggest, just this ironic jolt to her moral authority at the moment she implements her stratagem that Sophocles sought in crafting her speech.[15]

Her ensuing instructions to Lichas include, fittingly, a clever lie. She sends the robe, she claims (610ff.), in result of a vow she had taken to adorn Heracles splendidly for divine sacrifice if ever she learned of his safety. We know the true genesis of the gift. Her implication of the divine in her deceit, besides aggravating the perjury, raises another aspect of her misadventure. At the play's beginning, Deianeira's whole concern for Heracles' safety was entrusted to divine will as she awaited the outcome of oracles. Now she has taken matters so far into her own hands as to enlist heaven in a deception that she herself fears is ethically dubious. Add her earlier glib invocation of Zeus in her sophistic plea to Lichas in the name of truth and we may conclude that, along with her moral restraint, she has lost much of her religious sensibility.

After Lichas' dismissal and a misguided choral ode to love triumphant, the heroine reports a reversal portending, in her judgment, inevitable disaster (674ff.). Left in the sun, the tuft of wool with which she has smeared the robe has disintegrated. It was for this reason, as she now grasps, the centaur had commanded the charm be kept in darkness, and she deduces both his murderous guile and Heracles' certain destruction. Twice (672f., 693f.), as is appropriate in a play so given to blind reversals, she underscores the unpredictable wonder of the event. But the scene's most gripping interest is her vow to commit suicide if her fears of Heracles' death are borne out in fact.

Deianeira has abused her word no doubt, but we are not invited to judge her at all because, as Gellie understands, she passes sufficient judgment against herself.[16] And a Draconian verdict it is: death for accidental homicide. Moreover, she is swayed by neither the fact that she has never before resorted to guile nor that her intention was benign, much less by any argument that her ulterior purpose, the salvation of her marriage, was blameless.[17] Her precise case against herself, despite the rare ethical sensibility that it reflects, has meanwhile not much exercised the play's critics.

Her reasoning is that "no women could bear to live with an evil name, if she rejoices that her nature is not evil" (721f., trans. Jebb). Far from attempting to exonerate herself on grounds of her virtuous intentions, she finds, in effect, that her virtue condemns her to death:

she is by nature good, and so she must die. At the same time, as we have seen, she pronounces her guileful design sorry, incapable of offering even the breath of a hope that Heracles will survive (725f.). Not a sense of guilt, however, but loyalty to inveterate heroic principles of pride and shame, both redolent with honor, steer her toward death. We must pay her her due. Awesomely transcending her errors, she ends in moral magnificence, a study in human dignity.

When Hyllus enters to ply her with savage recriminations for causing Heracles' destruction, Sophocles drives home the *logos-ergon* theme. "What word do you speak, my son," she asks (741). "One that cannot but be fulfilled," is his answer. Again, she requests his authority for charging her with so terrible an *ergon* (744f.), and he answers, "I have seen my father's heavy suffering with my own eyes and do not speak from hearsay." An unimpeachable word, then, which Deianeira is left to compare, amid the ruins of her deception, with her own. Importantly, while describing the deadly investiture, Hyllus lays stress on the murdered Lichas' innocence, "in no way guilty of your crime" (733). When he has done, she departs without a word. We remember Iole's silence when Deianeira first espies her and the heroine's own silence once the old man interrupts the interrogation of Lichas. But among the pitiable ironies there also resides a poignant justice. Deianeira's word, though distorted just once in a lifetime of virtue, has not served her well.

To complete the thematic scheme of *logos-ergon*, we must recall that Deianeira herself is the victim of a perjured word, the centaur's. Nessus' essential victim, however, is Heracles and behind Nessus stands Zeus. All that has happened has been foretold in prophecy, and, on the principle that divine *logos* must always become *ergon*, everything so predicted must come to pass. Zeus, then, is effecting the end of Heracles. Nessus, Deianeira, and Lichas are but incidental functionaries in a great and inevitable design that turns on the misrepresentation of word. We have remarked that a question of theodicy attaches hereto, but, for the moment, we merely record the thematic amplitude.

The nurse's report of Deianeira's death (899ff) restores her to the chaste and tender humanity with which we became familiar before she learned of her threatening circumstances. She fondles household articles she had known and used in her long stretches of loneliness. She embraces maidservants whom she happens upon. She mounts the marital bed and addresses it ruefully before running herself through with a sword. Gentle goodness, and, equally, courage shine through everywhere, unmixed with any further word of self-recrimination. Those touches are functionally vital. Deianeira will become a fading memory in the play, but Sophocles has provided everything necessary to ensure that it remains, even at its lowest ebb, an image of precisely that humanity which Heracles never shared or, perhaps, even recognized. Sophocles' aim is more than the merely pathetic. We are on the verge of seeing that the play's fundamental opposition lies not between woman and man or human and hero, but between the human in all of its tragic contingency and the divine.

The nurse's report also contains an account of Hyllus' entrance into the bed chamber after the suicide. He sorely regrets his accusations of villainy, having "learned too late" from the household folk of Deianeira's real intention (934). The heroine's exhortation at the close of the prologue thus seems to have gone awry, but, as I have suggested, a profitable piece of late learning still lies in store. More, it will keep to a pattern, coming after a second outburst of recrimination, now against the gods, and founded in a similar misconstrual of intent.

Spontaneously then, in a gesture, as Easterling detects, no different from that of a lover, he throws himself down beside Deianeira and showers her lips with kisses (936ff).[18] If we are puzzled by a Sophoclean effect, our surest recourse is to seek its meaning in irony. Hyllus, accordingly, is assuming Heracles' "connubial" place, not only with the sadly neglected Deianeira, but, in anticipation of his explicit call to surrogacy, more ironically still, with Iole as well. Hence, even as he lingers on the scene between son and mother, Sophocles gestures toward the relationship between father and son, which, properly understood, will provide the last clues to the difficulties of the exodus.

"Now the portrayal of Heracles," says Kamerbeek, "whatever else we may call it, is not human."[19] His character, in fact, is a mixture of the superhuman and the subhuman, the latter, if anything, more intrusive in his portrayal. In certain inessential ways, we are already familiar with his type. He is a blind egocentric, the kind of personality in whom Sophocles ordinarily lays bare a tacit but substantial *kakia*. Selfishly indifferent to the bonds of *philia* and of human kindness, he is a law unto himself, rivaling in this respect even the tyrannical Creon.

But he also has gifts of courage and endurance that beggar comparison. More germane to our thematic interests, he is all but a stranger to deception, a man of straightforward honor, deceiving neither others nor himself.[20] Finally, and most important, he is pious. His whole life has been spent, it may be said, in painful execution of his father's unbending will, and, certainly, the Athenian stage never saw a filial courage more respectful and enduring than that which permits him, already racked with searing pains, to face the torture of live cremation without complaint and with no other reward in view than the welcome release of death.

This is the Heracles who cites to Hyllus, "the fairest of laws, obedience to a father" (1177f.). Narrow as this sentiment may be, we must respect it without reservation in view of his own superlative fealty to the same law. His wretched state, moreover, has been brought about through unsuspected misrepresentations on the part of others. We must, therefore, also respect his determined wish for the largest assurance possible in the execution of his remaining wishes.

Let us examine these. The first, that he must be conveyed to Oeta and there be cremated constitutes in all probability nothing other than the execution of his own father's command. When, still in Euboea, Heracles first fears that he is seized with mortal throes (797ff.), he makes no mention of Oeta, nor, by any reasonable standard, can his treatment of Hyllus be considered abusive. Everything changes with the mention of Nessus, which now leaves no doubt that he must die.[21] Oeta becomes an imperative necessity and, concomitantly, the father's relationship toward the son turns despotic. Surely the most prudent way to explain these abrupt changes is to suppose that Nessus and Oeta were linked in Zeus' oracle (1059ff.). Just as the mention of Nessus authenticates the truth of the prophecy, so must Oeta now be faced in order to fulfill its every demand. As for the oblivion that intervenes between the oracle's enunciation and its implementation, the case of Oedipus assures us that we face nothing rare in Sophocles. The alternative to such a line of reasoning, it seems to me, is to reduce Oeta and its inhuman rigors to a bizarre trial by torture of the hero's own invention. Heracles in his despotic hardness, accordingly, is merely implementing his filial, pious duty of obedience.

But why, we may ask, Hyllus? Why is he singled out for the task of—

as he sees it (1207f.)—murdering his father, and that not only by his own hand, but without the shedding of a tear (1198f.)? The first reason we have already seen. Heracles wants to leave no room for incompletion, and what better agent than one already bound to him by ties of blood? The second is that Sophocles obviously seeks to exploit those ties, which he elaborates, as we must understand, on a double plane—in the relationship both between Zeus and Heracles and between Heracles and Hyllus. As for the igniting of the pyre, Heracles relents (1211), and so must we in our perception of his callousness. He does not utterly lack the milk of human kindness.[22]

But, if Heracles' first demand reflects nothing more reprehensible than the discharge of a sacred obligation, his second can, on its face, lay claim to no such transcendency. Lest anyone else claim the woman who has lain by his side, he asks Hyllus to add "one small favor" to the larger already granted by consenting to marry Iole after his death. Strikingly, if by all appearances, preposterously, he encourages Hyllus' compliance as an act of piety (1222). Meanwhile, the youth is subject to the same dire oath and threat of reprisal as applied in the first request. When Hyllus rejoins with the grave objection that to assent would require his union with his own worst enemy (1237)—which he, for his part, regards as impious (1245)—Heracles answers simply that there is no impiety if the youth gladdens his heart. Again, ordinarily in Sophocles such self-serving attitudes are symptoms of infamy. Ajax takes his own life to "please himself" and thus, ignominiously, since he abridges the very moral law which Hyllus, in effect, cites—the obligation to support one's friends and harm one's enemies.[23] What justification exists for Heracles' spurning of such principles?

There is, of course, none, except by reference to his idiosyncratic logic and the unique world of thought to which he has always been subject. Compliance, he has stated, is not only not impious so long as it serves his pleasure but positively pious. We can grasp his logic only by observing that Heracles has himself always served his own father's pleasure, which is, *ipso facto*, piety. Manifestly, he transfers the same principle and obligation to Hyllus.[24] Morality aside, the very mentality that inheres conforms in its absolutism to no human standard, but reflects the divine; and, by extension, Heracles himself demands unquestioning subservience as if endowed in his own right with divine status. He is not conscious of any temerity in his attitude but merely thinks as he acts. A son must serve his father's pleasure in recognition of "the fairest of laws," and that is all, for this has been the all in all of his own life of toilsome obedience.

We reap the benefit of all this when we reflect how deeply in other elements of his narrow severity Heracles resembles the divine. For the gods too, besides demanding unquestioning service, are proud, distant, pitiless, jealous of their dignity, and terrible in their wrath. It is not entirely facetious to add that even in his incessant womanizing, the root force of the plot's calamities, Heracles resembles his divine father. We see in our hero, then, nothing less than a semblance of the divine; indeed, if our analysis is right, a divinity in the making.

As Hyllus detects nothing of this, his denunciation of heaven (1264ff.) reverberates with irony.[25] The gods, he protests, are uncaring, for they beget sons and, though called fathers, can look placidly upon such sufferings as Heracles'. How abruptly he has lost sight of the imperviousness displayed by his father to his own cruel sufferings! Once again the motif of resemblance: Heracles is like the gods—the gods, at least, as Hyllus understands them. Here we may also fold in Heracles' notorious indifference toward Deianeira, not merely his long connubial unconcern, but its culmination in the heroine's abrupt and complete disappearance from his consciousness once he hears the name of Nessus. Any thought of her actual motives, not to mention her sufferings, of course, vanishes with her. This supreme void of care tallies remarkably with Hyllus' conception of the divine mind.

Heracles, then, is a likeness of the very gods whom Hyllus finds ugly (αἰσχρά, 1272) in their dealings, and a god he will become by virtue of the miracle atop Oeta.[26] Zeus shows himself at long last anything but careless of his children; and, equally vital, his *logos* concerning Heracles' attainment of eternal peace becomes resplendent *ergon*.

A further irony, to be sure, is that the god proves to be vastly more indulgent toward Heracles than is the latter toward Hyllus. There is little danger, nonetheless, that the principle of divine rigor in the governance of universal affairs will seem to need drastic revision as a result of the joyful ending. Consider the case of Deianeira. Nothing happens in the play that is not Zeus (1278)—not the result, that is, of his wisdom and justice. Hence, her unwilled, yet self-annihilating mediation in Heracles' death is also Zeus. This is difficult enough to reconcile to a sense of justice even if the result of the divine plan is, as critics have generally found, universal suffering. In that case, at least, Deianeira's debacle is but a fragment of a whole. An outcome, however, in which she alone suffers amid an explosion of universal joy seems to belong to a queer world of justice indeed. A pawn in heaven's design by any interpretation, she becomes wantonly so if Heracles' reward is to be won at the cost of her splendid humanity. The basic honor of her intentions is rendered more pathetic, the divine plan more arbitrary, the unconcern of heaven no less acute than before. Indeed, the bitter resentment of godly indifference that Hyllus wastes in regard to Heracles comes to seem, by a final fillip of irony, entirely appropriate in regard to Deianeira.

Sophocles, I think, meant to alleviate even these misgivings in the play's final impress. It is true that, if Heracles' end is to be effected by the guile of Nessus, Deianeira is a helpless pawn of Zeus in the process. Still, a number of considerations rooted in her will to independent action combine to restore the gods to their wonted majesty.

First, there is the simple fact that the gods do not require Deianeira's death. Here above all she is her own agent. Next, as we have noted, Deianeira abandons the gods, and that, it seems, without the least reflection. The evidence, in truth, gives scant indication of a pious nature. Virtually her whole relationship to the divine is limited to her early concern over the oracle regarding Heracles' fate, but so swiftly does she transfer her hopes to the resources of magic that the oracle, the question of its meaning, and the whole of Olympus seem to have escaped her mind instantaneously.[27] Even her fears concerning wicked daring bear no connection with the divine. Granted, she can scarcely fulfill the gods' design without abandoning piety, but elements of *authaudia* manifest themselves nonetheless, and her carelessness of heaven in assuming her independent course cannot count in her favor.

Also, Deianeira's abandonment of her better self finds an instructive parallel in a transgression of Heracles. As Lichas reports (270ff.), the hero was forced by Zeus (*Zeus praktor*, 251) to spend a year in servitude to a woman for the treacherous murder of Iphitus. The reason is that in this one instance alone he contrived to take a life by guile. And the gods, adds Lichas, do not love *hybris*. Now, Deianeira too departs from her nature just once, likewise to practice guile, and, if she does not commit *hybris*, her own apprehension concerning wicked daring reveals that, within her system of values, she is embarking on a course that risks the heinous. Though we are not to suppose that, like Heracles, she thus also hazards the wrath of Zeus, a major point yet inheres. The path that she takes is distinctly her own; but, as Sophocles now first leads us to understand outside her own condemnation of it, it is a wrong path.

Our last consideration, a concrete crime of Deianeira's, both crowns her dissociation from heaven and reduces the suggestion of divine abuse to the merest shadow. The heroine's deliberate deception of Lichas makes him ineluctably her personal victim. More crucially, he is as helpless, indeed, as naively innocent a pawn in her larger scheme as she is in Zeus'. Yet, if his destruction causes Deianeira regret, she gives no indication of it. The lucid, ironic parallel to her own use at the hands of the gods is, I suggest, Sophocles' way of laying the matter to rest. If we protest that Deianeira could know nothing of Lichas' or anyone else's perils, whereas Zeus knew everything, we but enter the mansion of the *Tyrannus*.

We cannot close without noting that the play offers two moments of epiphany which light its central, polar opposition. One, obviously, is the hero's apotheosis. The other, I dare say, equally as bright, is the ethical splendor of Deianeira's mortal judgment against herself. They shimmer with absolute loyalty, these moments, the one toward the supreme father, the other to the ideal self, and the tragic difference which separates them matches the distance between not only heroine and hero but between the human and the divine.

Richard Minadeo
Wayne State University

Notes

[1] P. E. Easterling, *Sophocles: Trachiniae* (Cambridge, 1982), "Introduction," 17, 23, fixes the first reflection of Heracles' apotheosis on Oeta at roughly the middle of the fifth century and the date of the play at any time "between 457 and, say, 430," with the proviso that the tradition may be much older than the mid-century reflection. All in all, these estimates leave ample opportunity for the play to incorporate the tradition.

[2] R. C. Jebb, ed. and trans., *Sophocles: The Trachiniae* (Cambridge, 1908), ad loc. Translations of the Greek, unless otherwise indicated, are my own.

[3] See, e.g., J. C. Kamerbeek, *The Plays of Sophocles: The Trachiniae* (Leiden, 1959), ad loc.

[4] C. Fuqua, "Heroism, Heracles and the *Trachiniae*," *Traditio*, 36 (1980), 59, n. 155.

[5] Most critics deny the manuscript tradition by ascribing this sentiment to the chorus leader. The dramatic gain of such a maneuver is dubious, the loss palpable, as the emotion behind the sentiment changes from a presumptuous exasperation continuous from 1264ff. to, at best, a rueful acceptance.

[6] Jebb, *Trachiniae*, ad loc., counsels against this interpretation, but not, surely, on grammatical grounds.

[7] Easterling, *Trachiniae*, "Introduction," 5f., it is true, cites a number of reversals in the exodos, but these are of a lesser order.

[8] For the latter, see H. D. F. Kitto, *Poiesis* (Berkeley, 1966), 177ff.

[9] Among her exclamations, one—"What secret bane have I taken into my house?" (376f.)—stands out for its unconscious, ironic correspondence to Nessus' gift, long hidden in the house. *Hypostegon* (376) also bears an ironic affinity to *eu stegometha* (596), where the motif of secrecy potently reappears. See n. 14.

[10] See my "Plot, Theme and Meaning in Sophocles' *Electra*," *Classica & Mediaevalia*, 28 (1967), 114–42; "Characterization and Theme in the *Antigone*," *Arethusa*, 18 (1985), 133–54; "Sophocles' *Ajax* and *Kakia*," *Eranos*, 85 (1987), 19–23; "The Thematic Design of the *Oedipus at Colonus*," *Studi Italiani di Filologia Classica*, 8 (1990), 60–85; "Plot and Theme in *Oedipus the King*," *La Parola del Passato*, 45 (1990), 241–76; "Theme and Plot in *Philoctetes*," forthcoming in *Studi Italiani di Filologia Classica*; "The Thematic Design of *Ajax*," forthcoming in *Dioniso*.

[11] Karl Reinhardt, *Sophocles*, trans. Hazel Harvey and David Harvey (New York, 1979), 46f. and 243, n. 11, while detecting that Deianeira dissembles at 436ff., finds it not a calculated deception, but a "pitiful delusion."

[12] Jebb's observation, *Trachiniae*, ad loc., that προσαρμόσαι, 494, betrays a hint of the love-charm is surely right, and so corroborates that Deianeira has decided upon its use by this time.

[13] This is to exclude the forced alternative reading, no doubt resulting from shock, adopted by Cedric Whitman, *Sophocles: A Study of Heroic Humanism* (Cambridge, 1951), 266, n. 37.

[14] Cf. Easterling, *Trachiniae*, ad loc.

[15] On another level, the darkness motif also alludes pathetically to Nessus' gift. See n. 17.

[16] G. H. Gellie, *Sophocles: A Reading* (Melbourne, 1972), 76.

[17] We shall see that this assumption concerning the unprecedented nature of her guile, safe enough in any case, is made implicitly certain in the course of the play.

[18] Easterling, *Trachiniae*, ad loc.

[19] Kamerbeek, *Trachiniae*, "Introduction," 26.

[20] The one exception—and Sophocles stresses the singularity—is his treachery against Iphitus (277f.).

[21] Cf. Easterling, *Trachiniae*, ad loc.

[22] It might be argued that the tradition, which names Poeas or Philoctetes as applying the brand, forces Sophocles' hand here, but the argument functions equally well in the other direction: the existence of the tradition allowed Sophocles to work in one small act of *charis* on Heracles' part.

[23] See my "Sophocles' *Ajax* and *Kakia*."

[24] Perhaps the factor of transference also explains his demand (which becomes lost in the controversy) that Hyllus refrain from tears of mourning at the pyre (1199ff.). Unconsciously, meanwhile, it foreshadows the apotheosis.

[25] For the irony, cf. Gellie, *Sophocles: A Reading*, 76.

[26] It will be seen that these delicate semblances of the divine are dramatically disastrous if Heracles' fate is merely to die a common death.

[27] Deianeira's turning away from the gods after the identification of Iole contrasts notably with the abrupt turn of Heracles' thoughts heavenward at the mention of Nessus.

Euripides' Medea: Woman or Fiend?

Ever since the invention of theater few plays have been discussed as much as Euripides' *Medea*, and very few have had an equal impact.[1] Yet, strangely, despite all this, the play's meaning today still remains unclear. Ever since its composition, the *Medea* has been interpreted in a variety of ways, and has often become the battlefield on which critics have defended diametrically opposite points of view. For example, Medea's powerful speech on the plight of womanhood (*Med.* 230–66) has been understood by some as expressing the dramatist's own intent to support women and to speak himself on their behalf.[2] Others, however, have considered Medea's passionate vengefulness as indicating that Euripides did not act as women's champion here.[3] Again, certain critics have considered parenthood to be the focal theme of the play.[4] Others have regarded Medea's murder of the children as being more pivotal.[5] Furthermore, there are those who have maintained that Medea herself has been presented as a witch in this play,[6] whereas others—supporting her humanity—have staunchly opposed this view.[7] Others, again, have stressed the heroic aspect of her nature.[8] Finally, although the *Medea* has been considered as one of the greatest and most powerful plays ever written,[9] there have been those who have considered its structure as faulty, and even Aristotle himself has characterized it as "impossible," "irrational," or "against the artistic correctness" (*Poetics* 1453a36–b2, 1461b19–21).

So what are we to make of all this, and how are we to understand the *Medea*? Is it really a good play, and whose view are we to follow? What is the meaning of this drama, and how are we to explain its structural "irrationalities" or the strange way in which it ends? Was this drama pertinent to the Athenian society of the late fifth century, and why should we be concerned with it now? Finally, what does it really have to offer—if anything—to us, here, today?

My intention here is not to try to analyze the whole gamut of problems that have tantalized the critics of the *Medea* throughout the centuries; for such an attempt could prove to be futile and would, most probably, lead nowhere. I suggest instead that, for a moment, we adopt a different attitude towards the play, and we begin to look at the *Medea* from a different angle, from which the play's structure and its characters may appear to be more deeply connected than previously believed, and from which its shockingly unexpected ending may prove to be less puzzling.

Among other critics, Knox is troubled by the fact that "Medea is presented to us not only as a hero, but also, at the end of the play, by her language, action, and situation, as a *theos* or at least something more than human. She does not start that way, but that is how she ends."[10] So the crucial question is this: if she does not start that way why does she end up so; or what could have been Euripides' motive for turning her into "something more than human?" Fairly recently, Pucci provided us with a good and thorough survey of the modern criticism addressing this question.[11] There is, however, a major problem here. Most critics have approached *Medea*'s spectacular coda as something that, by definition, cannot be explained by the rest of the play, and, therefore, as something that has to be understood as the dramatist's attempt to create theatrical effect, or, perhaps, as his effort to explain the existing cult or the ritual. In other words, these critics, unable themselves to find any connection between Medea the character and Medea the θεός of the end, adopt a condescending attitude towards Euripides, whom they try to excuse for having created something dramatically and structurally unjustifiable! But Euripides was too good of a dramatist not to know any better and, therefore, it would be much more reasonable on our part to assume that he created the drama as he did for a purpose.[12] To be sure, he never missed a chance of using ritual, cult, music, language, psychology, scenery, or spectacular theatrical effects in order to serve his dramatic purposes. But these things were always the means to his end, not what his plays were deeply about. So the question remains. What was Euripides' dramatic purpose behind Medea's *ex machina* appearance? Pondering on this, and keeping the ancient Athenians in mind, Knox has observed: "It is very hard to imagine what it meant to them (and what it should mean to us), for there is no parallel to it in Attic drama."[13]

It is a well known fact, of course, that many Euripidean plays conclude with the appearance of a *deus ex machina*, a device that the dramatist used quite extensively. What is different in the *Medea*, however, and what Knox means by saying that "there is no parallel to it in Attic drama," is that the *deus* here is no other than the heroine herself who had acted throughout as one of the play's main characters. In that respect, Medea as a *deus ex machina* is different from Apollo in the *Orestes*, Athena in the *Suppliants*, or Dioscuri in both the *Helen* and in the *Electra*, to mention only a few. But even so, Knox's statement is only partially true because, in fact, there is a parallel to the *Medea*, and this is to be found in Euripides' *Bacchae*. In that play, Dionysus, like Medea, begins as a slighted, weak character, but at the end, like Medea again, he turns destroyer, and mocks *ex machina* the people and circumstances that had earlier tried to suppress him. Now, the existence of the parallel shows that what happens in the *Medea* cannot be considered accidental, and that Euripides must have had a purpose in adopting the same pattern again at the end of his dramatic career. In order to discern this purpose, I suggest that we look closely for a moment at both of these plays. Our understanding of the *Bacchae* can enhance our understanding of the *Medea*. In other words, our understanding of what the dramatist does with the character of Dionysus can also help our understanding of the character of Medea, who is our main concern here because, as W. Arrowsmith said, "Upon our understanding of her depends the final interpretation of the play."[14] So let us begin our comparison, and observe how Medea emerges from it.

In the opening of both plays, both characters are presented as being utterly slighted and wronged, and they win our sympathy at once. Dionysus complains that Pentheus, the new young Theban king (*Bac.* 43–44), has declared war on him (ὃς θεομαχεῖ τὰ κατ' ἐμέ, 45), that he thrusts him from his offerings (καὶ σπονδῶν ἄπο ὠθεῖ μ', 45–46), and that he does not mention Dionysus' name in his prayers (ἐν εὐχαῖς τ' οὐδαμοῦ μνείαν ἔχει, 46). Similarly, Medea, in the beginning of the *Medea*, is described as slighted and dishonored (ἠτιμασμένη, *Med.* 20; cf. 33, 111–12), unfortunate and unhappy (δύστηνος, 20; cf. 96–97). Wronged by her husband (πρὸς ἀνδρὸς ἠδικημένη, 26; cf. 165 and 207), she lies without food (κεῖται ἄσιτος, 24), and not moving her face from the ground (οὔτ' ὄμμ' ἐπαίρουσα, 27), she wastes away her time in tears (συντήκουσα δακρύοις χρόνον, 25).

But the similarity between these two characters is not limited to the fact that they are both slighted and rejected. Their reactions to their situations are similar as well. Dionysus strongly indicates that "like it or not, the city of Thebes must learn its lesson" (δεῖ γὰρ πόλιν τήνδ' ἐκμαθεῖν κεἰ μὴ θέλει, 39). His tone is menacing, and the obsessive repetition of words indicating necessity and revelation throughout the prologue is ominous.[15] He has armed the hand of women with shafts of ivy (κίσσινον βέλος, 25); he has stung them with frenzy (ὤστρησ' ἐγὼ μανίαις, 32–33); he has hounded them to the mountains where they wander crazed of mind (παράκοποι φρενῶν, 33); he has forced them to wear the livery of his orgies (σκευήν τ' ἔχειν ἠνάγκασ' ὀργίων ἐμῶν, 34); and he has driven them from home, mad (ἐξέμηνα δωμάτων, 36). In the *Medea*, the nurse's description of her mistress is ominous, too. She says that she knows that Medea has a violent heart and she will not put up with the ill treatment she receives (βαρεῖα γὰρ φρήν, οὐδ' ἀνέξεται κακῶς πάσχουσ', 38–39). In the nurse's mind Medea is δεινή (44), a fearful, terrible, dreadful, arbitrary, strange woman, and in her excess of passion she may murder the king, the new-wedded groom, or even herself (39–42). You cannot make an enemy of her and hope to come out triumphant (44–45), says the nurse, knowing well (σάφ' οἶδα, 94) that Medea will not stop her rage before she has struck at someone (πρὶν κατασκῆψαί τινα, 94).

This passionate raging, which is a distinct characteristic of both Medea and Dionysus, vividly projects an animal-like nature. In both plays, this is described in a language evoking the world of animals, and this imagery is often pushed to a level where the characters are seen as monsters rather than humans. So in the *Bacchae*, the chorus calls Dionysus a bull-horned god (ταυρόκερων θεόν, 100); and, later on in the play, they pray to him:

φάνηθι ταῦρος ἢ πολύκρανος ἰδεῖν
δράκων ἢ πυριφλέγων ὁρᾶσθαι λέων.
(*Bac.* 1016–17)

O Dionysus, reveal yourself a bull! Be manifest
a snake with darting heads, a lion breathing fire![16]

Similarly, Pentheus, right before he is destroyed by Dionysus, experiences him as a bull:

καὶ ταῦρος ἡμῖν πρόσθεν ἡγεῖσθαι δοκεῖς
καὶ σῷ κέρατα κρατὶ προσπεφυκέναι.
ἀλλ' ἦ ποτ' ἦσθα θήρ; τεταύρωσαι γὰρ οὖν.
(Bac. 920–22)

And you–you are a bull
who walks before me there. Horns have sprouted
from your head. Have you always been a beast?
But now I see a bull.

On the other hand, in the Medea, the heroine is described as casting around savage glances—literally the glances of a bull (ὄμμα νιν ταυρουμένην, 92) or of a lioness (δέργμα λεαίνης ἀποταυροῦται δμωσίν, 187–88)—at her children and her servants. Moreover, the manner in which Jason experiences Medea's power at the end is similar to that in which Pentheus experiences Dionysus' in the Bacchae, and his language evokes savage bestiality as he describes his marriage to Medea. To him, she is a bitter, hateful, destructive sorrow, a lioness, not a woman, a beast wilder in nature than monstrous Scylla (κῆδος ἐχθρὸν ὀλέθριόν τ' ἐμοί, οὐ γυναῖκα, τῆς Τυρσηνίδος Σκύλλης ἔχουσαν ἀγριωτέραν φύσιν, 1341–43).

Medea and Dionysus are similar as well in that they both are non-Greek, oriental, and new to Corinth and Thebes respectively. In the beginning of the Bacchae, Dionysus painstakingly enumerates each and every one of the Asiatic countries he has left behind before arriving in Greece, thus placing a special emphasis on his barbarian origin. In addition, throughout the play, he is called "stranger" (ξένος, 233; cf. 247, 642) and "the latest divinity" (τὸν νεωστὶ δαίμονα, 219; cf. 256), epithets that, in the cultural context of revolt and unrest in the Greek world of the second part of the fifth century, could not but have sounded by themselves sinister. The same holds true of Medea; for the nurse (35, 431 ff., 441 ff.), the chorus (131–32, 209–12) and even Medea herself (166–67, 222, 256, 313–14, 328, 386) repeatedly, almost obsessively, remind us that Medea is a foreigner and a newcomer to Greece.

In addition to their barbarian origin, their female nature (effeminate in the case of Dionysus) is also perceived as undesirable. Both the Theban and the Corinthian rulers are excessively fearful of and perplexed by Dionysus' and Medea's nature. They cannot understand what this nature is, and with good reasons, since the way in which Euripides depicts both of these characters dictates that there must be no clear line between the male and the female, the Greek and the barbarian, the strong and the weak, the divine and the human, the loving and the hating, the old and the new, the meek and the savage in them. In some mysterious and enigmatic way, Medea and Dionysus personify the fusion of all these opposites, and the ambiguity of their nature threatens to upset the old Greek, aristocratic, male-dominated world in which everything was once neatly defined. In their struggle to cope with such a threat, traditional leaders like Pentheus, Creon, and Jason appear frightened, confused, and upset. Their first reaction is to reject outright the newcomers and eliminate them, Medea through banishment, Dionysus through imprisonment and death. In such a way, they believe, they can keep control of their power and protect themselves and their cities from Medea's and Dionysus' dangerous influence. So Creon, the king of Corinth, sure of his authority, enters the stage and orders Medea to leave the country:

> σὲ τὴν σκυθρωπὸν καὶ πόσει θυμουμένην,
> Μήδειαν, εἶπον τῆσδε γῆς ἔξω περᾶν
> φυγάδα, λαβοῦσαν δισσὰ σὺν σαυτῇ τέκνα·
> καὶ μή τι μέλλειν· ὡς ἐγὼ βραβεὺς λόγου
> τοῦδ' εἰμί, κοὐκ ἄπειμι πρὸς δόμους πάλιν,
> πρὶν ἄν σε γαίας τερμόνων ἔξω βάλω.
> (Med. 271–76)

> You, with the angry look, so set against your husband,
> Medea, I order you to leave my territories
> An exile, and take along with you your two children
> And not to waste time doing it. It is my decree,
> And I will see it done, I will not return home
> Until you are cast from the boundaries of my land.

Similarly, in the *Bacchae*, Pentheus, the young Theban ruler, in a fit of rage, orders his attendants to capture Dionysus:

οἳ δ' ἀνὰ τὴν πόλιν στείχοντες ἐξιχνεύσατε
τὸν θηλύμορφον ξένον, ὃς ἐσφέρει νόσον
καινὴν γυναιξὶ καὶ λέχη λυμαίνεται.
κἄνπερ λάβητε, δέσμιον πορεύσατε
δεῦρ' αὐτόν, ὡς ἂν λευσίμου δίκης τυχὼν
θάνῃ πικρὰν βάκχευσιν ἐν Θήβαις ἰδών.
(*Bac.* 352–57)

As for the rest of you, go and scour the city
for that effeminate stranger, the man who infects our women
with this strange disease and pollutes our beds.
And when you take him, clap him in chains
and march him here. He shall die as he deserves–
by being stoned to death. He shall come to rue
his merrymaking here in Thebes.

In turn, both Creon and Pentheus have a long dialogue with Medea and Dionysus respectively in which, once again, they try to prove their own authority. They continue to threaten them (*Med.* 335, 351–56; *Bac.* 509–14), but, at the same time, enchanted and bewildered by them, they begin to fall into their net of influence by weakening their resistance and giving in to Medea's and Dionysus' wishes. So Pentheus becomes extremely curious to learn about the mysteries of Dionysus (εὖ τοῦτ' ἐκιβδήλευσας, ἵν' ἀκοῦσαι θέλω, *Bac.* 475); and Creon, although he admits that Medea frightens him (δέδοικά σ', *Med.* 282), finally consents to her request that she may stay one additional day in Corinth (εἰ μένειν δεῖ, μίμν' ἐφ' ἡμέραν μίαν, *Med.* 355). Until the end, the rulers of Thebes and Corinth respectively remain determined to suppress and expel what Dionysus and Medea represent. But despite their determination, their efforts are futile, their threats sound empty, and their victims remain untouched. Little by little, the enchanting power of Medea and Dionysus completely enfolds the Corinthian and the Theban rulers, who, spellbound and confused, now experience this power as an unfamiliar Necessity ('Ανάγκη); the necessity that, against their will, finally leads them to bleak, utter destruction. Medea, for instance, speaking of Jason's new bride, says that it is a necessity for her (ἀνάγκη, Med. 806) to die a most terrible death by Medea's spell and enchantment. And, in the Bacchae, Pentheus—entangled by Dionysus, whom he sees and experiences as a bestial force—is told that he now sees what he must (νῦν δ' ὁρᾷς ἃ χρή σ' ὁρᾶν, Bac. 924).

This confusing enchantment and destructive necessity is dramatically described in both plays by means of miraculous events. Through a miracle Medea destroys everything that is important to Jason (συγχέασα, Med. 794), and through a miracle Dionysus takes revenge on Pentheus and the Thebans by turning everything up side down (ἄνω κάτω, Bac. 602). Although the words used in each play are not exactly the same, the imagery is identical, and the effect of Medea's and Dionysus' progressively destructive actions absolutely the same. In order to destroy Jason's new bride, for instance, Medea sends her a robe and crown of irresistible beauty and charm to wear. And, in the Bacchae, Dionysus assists Pentheus to enfold himself in splendid female attire before leading him to his final doom at Cithaeron.

Similarly, Medea's and Dionysus' ruinous charms are experienced in both plays as a demonic possession by Jason's bride and by Pentheus' mother Agave respectively. In the Medea (1174–75), this is vividly described by the messenger whose intense language brings to life Glauke's final suffering spasms, her foaming lips, her bloodless face; and, in the Bacchae (1122–24) as well, the delirious Agave is strikingly depicted as "foaming at the mouth, her eyes crazed rolling with frenzy, stark mad, possessed by Bacchus."

Moreover, the magical destructive powers of Medea and Dionysus manifest themselves through light and fire in both plays. So, in the Medea, Glauke's destruction is described by the messenger to Medea and the chorus:

χρυσοῦς μὲν ἀμφὶ κρατὶ κείμενος πλόκος
θαυμαστὸν ἵει νᾶμα παμφάγου πυρός,
πέπλοι δὲ λεπτοί, σῶν τέκνων δωρήματα
λεπτὴν ἔδαπτον σάρκα τῆς δυσδαίμονος.
(Med. 1185–88)

> The wreath of gold that was resting around her head
> Let forth a fearful stream of all-devouring fire,
> And the finely woven dress your children gave to her,
> Was fastening on the unhappy girl's fine flesh.

In the *Bacchae*, this sinister destructive light appears twice at the play's most crucial moments. For the first time, during the miraculous collapse of the palace–the dramatic and theatrical representation of Pentheus' inner collapse–Dionysus' voice resounds:

> ἅπτε κεραύνιον αἴθοπα λαμπάδα·
> σύμφλεγε σύμφλεγε δώματα Πενθέος.
> (Bac. 594–95)

> Launch the blazing thunderbolt of god! O lightnings, come! Consume with flame the palace of Pentheus!¹⁷

And at the end, a short moment before Pentheus' final crash, this sinister light appears again, this time on the mountain, as Dionysus urges revenge upon the ignorant young king. "And as he spoke," the messenger described in awe, " a flash of awful fire bound heaven and earth" (*Bac.* 1082–83).

Finally, when the destruction is complete, both Medea and Dionysus leave the stage and, this time *ex machina*, manifest themselves in full glory for what they really are: the demonic personification of nature's insensible, invincible, and indestructible power, kindly to friends and grievous to enemies (*Med.* 807–10; *Bac.* 860–61), whose bleak devastation they both mock.

From all this it follows that, despite external differences, Medea and Dionysus are very similar. Before having observed them closely together, perhaps one could have reasonably argued that Dionysus' *ex machina* appearance was in a way understandable—because he was a god after all—whereas Medea's divine transformation was troublesome and, in the play's context, made no sense. The close comparison between these two characters, however, proves that making such an argument would be equal to misunderstanding both plays. Despite what we may know from the myth, in their respective plays, Dionysus is not more divine than is Medea; and, by the same token, Medea is not more human than Dionysus. Blood relations seem to matter a lot to both (Dionysus wants to vindicate his mother, Medea is tortured by her decision to kill her children), and both demonstrate human qualities that attract our attention and win our sympathy. Right from the beginning, however, both of these characters are depicted ambiguously.[18] Dionysus, for instance, says that he is a god, but he acts like a human. He comes from the East, but he claims to be the son of the Theban princess Semele. He is a man, but he looks like a woman— much to Pentheus' annoyance. He is weak and, at the same time, most powerful. He causes extreme joy to the Bacchanals and terrible sorrow to the king. He is presented as a newcomer to Greece, and yet he represents what is old, immutable, and unchangeable in the world. He is simultaneously sweet and harsh, enlightening and confusing, loving and hating, divine and bestial. Similarly, the same opposites describe Medea's nature as well. She is a woman, and yet she acts like a man. She is a barbarian, but she behaves like a Greek. She is slighted and weak and yet she is able to destroy everything. She says she loves, but the power of her hatred comes through with equal intensity. She is human, but she possesses powers that go beyond human limits. In short, both of these characters are impossible to define. Throughout the action of both plays, Euripides depicts them as true daemons, constantly moving from one level of experience to its opposite, passionate and yet detached, victims and yet spellbinding. In that respect, their *ex machina* appearance at the end can be viewed as nothing more than the theatrically exaggerated culmination of their earlier depiction—a culmination which, no matter how shockingly sudden it may have appeared for a moment, nevertheless remained truly connected to the progressive development and purpose of both dramas.

What then? Am I, in all seriousness, proposing that Medea is not a woman here? Not exactly. Because she is that too, just as she is also a mother, a wife, a witch, a lover, a killer, a friend, an enemy, a barbarian, a Greek, a victim, a destroyer, a mortal, and an immortal. Any attempt to separate these roles in her, and to focus attention on one and one only, could result in destroying the picture that Euripides had created of her. For centuries, however, in their interpretations of the *Medea*, critics have repeatedly attempted this separation, offering and defending many different pictures of Medea. In a way, all these interpretations are valuable but, at the same time, terribly shortsighted and inadequate. Each one of them has described one side of Medea at a time, allowing us to see only part of her true picture. Consequently, through such interpretations, her image emerges fragmented, as though through the broken glass of a mirror that can no longer reflect wholeness.

In my view, we should try to see Medea as Euripides had depicted her, ambiguous and elusive, and try to understand the play without breaking the wholeness of her image. The natural question, then, is why is Medea so ambiguous, and what lies behind her indefinable elusiveness? In order to answer this question we need to remind ourselves that the Greek theater was "a genuine *theater of ideas* ... a theater of dramatists who used its machinery as a way of *thinking*, critically and constructively, about their world."[19] And we need to remember, too, that the *Medea* was produced during the second part of the fifth century B.C. which, for the Greeks, was "a period of immense cultural crisis and political convulsion," a period of divisiveness and "lost innocence."[20] It is not unreasonable, then, to assume that the play reflects the Hellenic world of its era, a world divided and confused, chaotic and uncontrollable. And in this context, it is not unreasonable to perceive Medea as the dramatic representation of the force that had brought about this chaos.

In the play, Medea's nature—like the nature of Dionysus in the *Bacchae*—is not understood by the Greek, male, leaders. In both plays, these leaders are dramatically described as traditional kings with eyes fixed on the old order of things, on the aristocratic ideal of Greek male dominance, and on the status quo of high birth, wealth, and war-valor. But Medea and Dionysus bring confusion to this world. Their barbarian, oriental, effeminate, emotional, and magical nature threatens the stability of the world that was dominated by Greek, male, logical, and rationally understood forces. For this, Creon and Pentheus respectively attempt to eliminate the threat by expelling or reducing the power of Medea and Dionysus. The more they try to destroy that power, however, the more entangled they become in the net of Medea and Dionysus, whose nature they do not understand. Strong rulers though they are, in the presence of Medea and Dionysus they appear to lose their power. Unable to impose order, they grow increasingly fearful, and they prove ignorant as they try to reduce chaos with threats and violence; despite their frenzy, their victims remain miraculously untouched, remote, mocking, and ambiguous. Their ambiguity, their enchanting, unfamiliar, and inescapably dreadful and confusing magical power can then be understood as representing the power and omnipotence of Nature herself. And, like Nature, Medea and Dionysus have shown themselves to be kind to friends and dreadful to enemies (*Med.* 807–10; cf. *Bac.* 859–61). According to the myth, Jason had enjoyed Medea's extreme benevolence in the past for as long as he himself had honored her and respected her; but when he and Corinth's king Creon began to push her away—as they did in the *Medea*—they began to experience her ruthless wrath in place of the benevolence. In the *Bacchae* as well, Pentheus' punishment by Dionysus is similarly based, and it seems that, in both plays, Euripides' message and concern are one and the same: that we violate Nature at our own peril; and that, at the end, regardless of our sex, status, age, origin, power, or wealth, by sheer Necessity ('Ανάγκη) Nature will always emerge victorious, its sweeping power swallowing the guilty and the innocent alike.

In conclusion, I believe that Medea's relevance to late fifth-century Athenian society—and to ours—is tremendous, but not simply because she is presented as a woman or because she rebels against the suffering of the female condition.[21] By creating his *Medea* the way he did, Euripides does not appear to have aimed at defending women or blaming them. If that were his goal, he would have certainly depicted the heroine as less violent and more sympathetic. But Euripides seems to be taking no sides. Jason may be intolerably calculating, base, and unjust,[22] but Medea is excessive, murderous, and wicked, too. If, however, behind her violence we recognize the rebellion not only of an abused woman, but rather of the Natural Law itself, then the play gains more meaning, and its structure appears as having more unity. In this light, there is nothing strange about Medea's murderousness, extreme violence, or her god-like appearance on the Sun's chariot at the end. After all the destruction, she remains untouched, just as fire or water remains pure, natural, and even beneficial still after a conflagration or a storm. Fire and water are simply elements, not the cause of destruction, and this is true of Medea here as well. The destruction in the play takes place through her, not because of her. So the real cause of her violent outburst is to be sought in the world that betrays her, and in the circumstances that push her beyond her limits. The desperate efforts of Creon and Jason to expel Medea from Corinth can then be seen as a metaphor of a world that tries to expel what is feminine, foreign, different, emotional, and instinctive—a metaphor of a world that tries to reduce life itself or, at least, most of the elements that make it vital.[23] The Hellenic world of the late fifth century resembled such a world. According to Thucydides (3.82–85), it was a world divided by greed, reckless ambition, uncontrolled violence, mistrust, betrayal, unleashed vengeance, and restless convulsion. The *Medea*—like the *Bacchae*—simply reflects this world. It depicts vividly the disaster to which the overemphasis of the Greek, aristocratic, male *nomos* ("custom," "tradition," "law") at the expense of *physis* ("nature") could lead.[24] At the time of Euripides, this unnatural overemphasis had reached extreme proportions in the Greek culture; so the implied message of both the *Medea* and the *Bacchae* seems to have been that if the culture were to survive, the gaping rift between these two poles had to be closed, and harmony and balance had to be quickly restored. In both plays, Creon, Jason, and Pentheus respectively were destroyed and devastated because they remained callous and ignorant to the end. But Euripides might have at least hoped that the Athenians could perhaps learn from those miserable examples and could avoid the outburst of disaster he saw galloping down upon them.

Lena Hatzichronoglou
Wayne State University

Notes

[1] For a short bibliography of works on the *Medea*, among others see K. J. Reckford, "Medea's First Exit," *TAPA*, 99, (1968), 329, n. 1; P. Pucci, *The Violence of Pity in Euripides' Medea* (Ithaca, 1980), 157–58, 226–29.

On the play's impact, cf. Albin Lesky, *Greek Tragic Poetry*, trans. M. Dillon (New Haven, 1983), 217; B. M. W. Knox, "The *Medea* of Euripides," in his *Word and Action: Essays on the Ancient Theater* (Baltimore, 1979), 295 and n. 3.

[2] According to John Ferguson, *A Companion to Greek Tragedy* (Austin,

1972), "Euripides wrote most powerfully when he was stirred by a cause, and here he has two causes. The first is the status of women. Let us again remind ourselves that this is the Athens in which Pericles proclaimed that the greatest glory of woman is not to be spoken of by men for good or bad. Euripides is out to attack this Victorianism; he would have enjoyed Philip Barry's definition of man as 'the second strongest sex'" (249). Cf. Stavros Zorbalas, Ο Ουμανισμός στο Έργο του Ευριπίδη (Athens, 1987), 76–100.

[3] "When Medea was revealed as obviously a wicked woman," writes Gilbert Murray, *Euripides and His Age* (Oxford, 1965), "the plain man thought that such women should simply be thrashed, not listened to" (41).

Cf. Reckford, "Medea's First Exit": "This is not to say that Euripides is acting as the women's champion (consider the allusions in Aristophanes), or writing social criticism or pleading for some reform of Athenian custom-law that might brighten the women's situation and reduce domestic pressure to a minimum" (339–40). See also Knox, "The *Medea* of Euripides," who claims that "Euripides is concerned in this play not with progress or reform. ...The *Medea* is not about woman's rights; it is about woman's wrongs, those done to her and by her" (306).

[4] J. March, "Euripides the Misogynist?" in *Euripides, Women and Sexuality*, ed. Anton Powell (London, 1990), 36.

[5] E. A. McDermott, *Euripides' Medea: The Incarnation of Disorder* (University Park, 1989), 9.

D. Page, *Euripides: Medea* (Oxford, 1938), curiously, with a simple sentence dismisses the importance of the murder of the children for the play itself and for the Athenian audience: "Such an act is outside our experience, we—and the fifth-century Athenian—know nothing of it" (xiv). Unfortunately, Page does not wonder at all as to why Euripides chose to make Medea commit such an action.

[6] According to Knox, "The *Medea* of Euripides," "this is especially true of critics writing in English and French" (320, n. 60, with extensive bibliography). Cf. P. Pucci, *The Violence of Pity*: "... the chariot of the Sun on which Medea stands untouchable suggests also the wild magic powers that have helped her to her goal" (158).

[7] Cf. March, "Euripides the Misogynist?": "Medea is clever, certainly, as she herself admits—σοφή—a woman of great intellectual capacity (294 ff., 539). And she has φάρμακα, drugs or poisons; so she has destructive powers with these φάρμακα, as any woman might have. But she seems to have no powers of creative magic, else she would not be in the state she is, with a husband lost and a sentence of exile on her head" (38–39). Knox, "The *Medea* of Euripides," argues against the argument that Medea is a witch in Euripides (306–9; cf. n. 60: "In recent German [and more rarely Italian] literature, the

normal, human aspects of Euripides' Medea have been emphasized.").

[8] For Medea's heroic nature and her similarity to the Sophoclean heroes see Knox, "The *Medea* of Euripides," 296–302. Cf. B. M. W. Knox, *The Heroic Temper* (Berkeley, 1964), where he describes the nature of the Sophoclean hero by saying: "Sophocles presents us for the first time with what we recognize as a 'tragic hero': one who, unsupported by the gods and in the face of human opposition, makes a decision which springs from the deepest layer of his individual nature, his *physis*, and then blindly, ferociously, heroically maintains that decision even to the point of self-destruction. Once again, the example of Euripides serves to reinforce the point. Except for Medea, the characteristic Euripidean hero suffers rather than acts" (5).

[9] E.g., Ferguson, *A Companion to Greek Tragedy*, 247–48.

[10] Knox, "The *Medea* of Euripides," 304. Cf. M. Cunningham, "Medea ΑΠΟ ΜΗΧΑΝΗΣ," *CP*, 49 (1954): "The important thing is that Medea appears aloft in the place and after the manner of a *theos*. She appears as a *theos* appears; she acts as a *theos* acts; and she says the sort of thing a *theos* says even to announcing the future establishment of a cult and the manner of the coming death of one of the characters" (152).

Regarding the manner of the production of Medea's divine appearance, T. B. L. Webster, *Greek Theater Production* (London, 1956), supports the view that the whole thing was presented through the help of the crane rather than by an appearance in the *theologeion* (12, 19).

[11] Pucci, *The Violence of Pity*: "Modern criticism is divided in its appreciation of this extravagant ending. Some scholars maintain that the striking theatrical effect of Medea's appearance on the Sun's chariot justifies the scene (Grube, Bates). Others underscore the religious significance of Medea's last appearance, pointing at her return into the realm of legend and at Euripides' desire to connect his drama to the Corinthian cult (Murray, Erbse, Garzya, Webster). By removing Medea from the human realm, other scholars argue, Euripides offers a symbolic representation of what happens to her after the murder (Cunningham, Schlesinger, Conacher). In my view, the last image of Medea on the Sun's chariot is symbolic of the success of her sacrificial self-mutilation, of the *pharmakon* that she has gruesomely applied to herself" (157–58; cf. also 226–29 and nn. 26–30).

[12] For an interesting and well-argued discussion on the subject see T. B. L. Webster's "Euripides: Traditionalist and Innovator," in *The Poetic Tradition: Essays on Greek, Latin, English Poetry* (Baltimore 1968), 27–45.

[13] Knox, "The *Medea* of Euripides," 304.

[14] W. Arrowsmith, "A Greek Theater of Ideas," *Arion*, 2 (1963), 48.

[15] For more on the vocabulary of necessity and revelation here see my "The Role of Dionysus in Euripides' *Bacchae*," in *The Many Forms of Drama*, ed. K.

Hartigan (New York, 1985), 60, 67, n. 9.

[16] For translations of Euripides, I have used William Arrowsmith, *The Bacchae*, and Rex Warner, *Medea*, in the Chicago Series, *Complete Greek Tragedies*, eds. D. Grene and R. Lattimore, vols. 5 and 1.

[17] In his translation of the *Bacchae*, Arrowsmith adds some stage directions here, describing vividly what must be happening on the stage: "A burst of lightning flares across the facade of the palace and tongues of flame spurt up from the tomb of Semele. Then a great crash of thunder" (180).

[18] For the ambiguity involved in the way that the Corinthian princess experiences Medea's power see R. M. Newton, "Medea's Passionate Poison," *Syllecta Classica*, 1 (1989), 17–18. Cf. R. Girard, *Violence and the Sacred* (Baltimore, 1979), 95, on the ambiguous meaning of the word *pharmakon* in classical Greek, meaning both poison as well as the antidote for poison.

[19] Arrowsmith, "A Greek Theater of Ideas," 32.

[20] Ibid., 33.

[21] Eva Cantarella, *Pandora's Daughters: The Role of Status of Women in Greek and Roman Antiquity*, trans. Maureen B. Fant (Baltimore, 1981): "Medea does not lament a personal unhappiness nor does she weep about her individual fate—speaking in the name of all women, for the first time in Greek literature, she rebels against the suffering of the female condition" (68).

[22] Cf. Murray, *Euripides and His Age*, "When Jason had to defend an obviously shabby case, no gentleman cared to hear him" (41). Cf. the opinion of S. B. Pomeroy, *Goddesses, Whores, Wives, and Slaves: Women in Classical Antiquity* (New York, 1975), that "Euripides structures these plays so as to leave us doubtful whether the men for whom the women sacrificed themselves were worth it" (110).

[23] On the subject of masculine versus feminine elements in the culture, Pomeroy, *Goddesses, Whores, Wives, and Slaves*, observes: "*Antigone* and many other tragedies show the effect of overvaluation of the so-called masculine qualities (control, subjugation, culture, excessive cerebration) at the expense of the so-called feminine aspects of life (instinct, love, family ties) which destroys men like Creon" (103).

[24] I owe the definitions of the words *physis* and *nomos* to W. Arrowsmith, "A Greek Theater of Ideas," 34.

Women and Power in Classical Athens

It is easy enough to say that women were excluded from power in classical Athens. After all, they had no political rights: they could neither vote nor hold political office. Legally, they were perpetual minors, unable to perform any legal or economic function without the express approval of their trustees (κύριοι). They could not own, inherit, or dispose of property. Nor could they sue, plead, or even appear in a court of law. With these facts in mind, the reader might justifiably think that any discussion of women and power in classical Athens will be brief indeed. Is there, in fact, anything to say on this subject?[1]

One approach has been to speak of Athenian women's power as resistance to male authority—or even outright rebellion. But the expression of this putative resistance stems from literature, principally dramatic literature. As a product of the imagination, though drawing on the social and cultural context, literature often imagines situations, quite deliberately, that are the reverse of the norm and the contrary of the possible. Thus, the words and deeds of Antigone, Clytemnestra, Medea, or Lysistrata are often taken too literally or simplistically. These fictional words and deeds are almost impossible to judge as social commentary not only because they are utterly fictional but also because they are totally and solely the product of Athenian men. Active or reactive, they articulate a male world view in the dominant language of men. For these and other reasons, the words and deeds of these literary heroines cannot be used to explain social reality. In fact, the reverse is the case. It is first necessary to understand the social reality in order to come to grips with the meaning of dramatic literature.[2]

In any case, the question of women's power in classical Athens for all practical purposes turns out to be the question of whether women had the power to influence men to a course of action or to achieve an objective in the male world of public life. We simply don't know enough, if anything at all, about the private and domestic world of

Athenian women to say anything meaningful about women's power in that realm. However, if we restrict ourselves to women's expressions of power in the male world, there is something to say. But we must bear in mind that such power and its exercise needs must always have been indirect. As such, it is heavily contextualized and often requires us to read a lot into a small amount of evidence.

To have power often means to have a say in things, quite literally. More than just having a say, it also often means being persuasive by displaying eloquence in what one says. In a society where women were systematically excluded from the world of men, unlettered, and barred from political and public life, one might at first dismiss outright any possibility that Athenian women could have spoken at all, much less with eloquence, to achieve a goal in a man's world. However, it so happens that there survives an outstanding example of female eloquence from Athens, c. 400 B.C. It is preserved in Lysias *Oration* 32, which was itself preserved (in part) by the ancient critic of rhetoric, Dionysius of Halicarnassus (*De Lysia* 23–27).[3] In this speech the wealthy Diogeiton is sued for embezzling over an eight-year period the prodigious inheritance of his two wards. As will become clear, the prime mover in bringing this suit was Diogeiton's own daughter. Through a remarkable kind of ventriloquism, she in fact managed to have her say in court and to indict her father before the jurors, even though women were excluded from Athenian courts.[4] In order to understand how this happened and why it was effective, it is first necessary to recount what led up to the trial. As the family relations and the legal background are, in any case, somewhat complex, a brief rehearsal of the facts will be doubly useful.

As to the family, one can do no better than to begin with Lysias:

> Diodotus and Diogeiton, gentlemen of the jury, were brothers born of the same father and mother, and they had divided between themselves the liquid assets but continued to hold the real property in common. When Diodotus had made a large fortune in shipping, Diogeiton induced him to marry his daughter, the only child he had. By her Diodotus had two sons and a daughter. (Lysias 32.4)

Although this relationship might seem incestuous to us, it was not uncommon among wealthier Athenians.[5] Indeed in this case, as in many others like it, it served a particular economic purpose. Diogeiton's daughter was in Athenian legal parlance an ἐπίκληρος, a term commonly but inaccurately translated as "heiress." If an Athenian man died without male issue, his surviving daughters were ἐπίκληροι and legally assignable (ἐπίδικοι) for marriage to his nearest male kin.[6] If the ἐπίκληρος was already married, the one she was assigned to could insist upon her divorce so that he might marry her. Conversely, if the nearest kinsman was himself married, he might divorce his current wife in order to marry the ἐπίκληρος (cf. Isaeus 3.64; Demosthenes 57.41). From our point of view, she served as a conduit for transmission of the estate, for she herself could not inherit. The purpose of this arrangement was to produce a male heir. Indeed, the husband himself did not inherit, although it might well be to his economic advantage to marry an ἐπίκληρος for he would be trustee of the heir, his son, and his fortune in the interval until the latter came of age.[7] Accordingly, in the case at hand, Diogeiton's daughter would have been "assignable" to Diodotus in the event of Diogeiton's death. Hence, it was in this sense natural that Diodotus marry the girl. Indeed, it made even more economic sense than might appear *prima facie*. The one case where an ἐπίκληρος was not "assignable" was where she had already produced a legitimate male heir or was pregnant with a legitimate male heir before her father's death.[8] Thus, if Diogeiton's daughter had married another and produced an heir, Diodotus would not have been able to claim her should his brother have died. Hence, the marriage between Diodotus and his niece both followed the rule of the ἐπίκληρος, if we may so call it, and in fact preempted the one eventuality where it would have been countervailed.

This discussion may appear to be an unnecessary, if interesting, digression. In fact it is important in the following analysis. In the general case, it is worth pointing out that the status of the ἐπίκληρος gave her importance. Although this status did not by itself give her power (for she could not determine who would become her husband) it made her an object of desire, albeit more probably economic than emotional desire. Or put another way, the ἐπίκληρος gained in value and, we may assume, in personal esteem. Secondly, as we shall see in the particular case at hand, the status of Diogeiton's daughter as his sole offspring had potentially great significance for the future of her sons.

In the summer of 409 B.C. Diodotus, despite his great personal wealth, was called up for military service (Lysias 32.5, 7). This was in the last stage of the Peloponnesian War. Before embarking on a military expedition that would take him across the Aegean to Asia Minor, Diodotus made a disposition of his property. This disposition (διαθῆκαι) cannot be called a will, for Athenian men with male offspring necessarily died intestate; their estates passed immediately and directly to their heirs. But as his sons were minors, Diodotus had to make provision for their future, in particular by appointing a trustee. Further, he had to provide for the future of his wife and his daughter, should anything befall him. That is, he had to provide for their dowries (so they could marry) and for any small legacies to be given them out of the estate. This Diodotus did, making his brother Diogeiton trustee (κύριος) of his sons, wife, and daughter and giving him a written account of his assets and the amounts to be apportioned to his wife and daughter for dowries and legacies. Later that year Diodotus was one of four hundred hoplites who died at Ephesus under the command of general Thrasyllus (Xenophon, *Hellenica* 1.2.6–9). In this situation, Diogeiton's daughter occupied a special position. Should her father now die too, she would *not* become ἐπίδικος, "assignable," because she had already given birth to legitimate sons. Instead, her sons by her deceased husband Diodotus would become heirs to Diogeiton's wealth as well. The family fortune would be united, making it one of the largest known at Athens in this period. What in fact came to pass proved to be a bitter disappointment to her.

After her husband's death, both Diogeiton's daughter (the widow) and his granddaughter were given in marriage, the former to an otherwise unknown Athenian named Hegemon, the latter to the man who eventually pronounced Lysias' 32d *Oration* in court, whom I shall refer to from now on for the sake of convenience as the συνήγορος, or advocate.[9] By the time Diodotus' elder son came into his majority in 400 B.C. his uncle informed him the estate of 15 talents 2600 drachmas left by Diodotus had been reduced through expenses to a mere 2600 drachmas. According to the speaker of Lysias 32, Diogeiton had embezzled the rest. What followed shows the remarkable strength of

Diogeiton's daughter in bringing her father to account.

When informed that they had been left virtually destitute, Diodotus' sons were reduced to helplessness and tears:

> On hearing these words they went away aghast and weeping (δακρύοντες), to their mother and brought her with them to me. ... The poor wretches wept aloud (κλάοντες) and begged me not to let them be robbed of their patrimony. (Lysias 32.10)

It is worth noticing Diodotus' sons' first action was to turn to their mother. It was her advice they sought, and we may imagine that it is more likely she took them in tow to see her daughter's husband than the other way around. At that meeting it was she who took the lead: "In the end, their mother implored and entreated me to assemble her father and friends" (Lysias 32.11). Such a family conclave was a common first step in trying to settle a dispute informally before resorting to the legal process. As a woman, Diogeiton's daughter could not convoke it, and therefore she prevailed on her son-in-law to do so. Remarkably, Diogeiton's daughter wanted the family meeting because she intended to take the lead in speaking and to indict her father before his assembled kinsmen and friends! She in fact did so, delivering a powerful and damning invective (Lysias 32.12–17). Indeed, she did more than denounce her father; she systematically proved before those assembled exactly the amounts and the manner in which he had defrauded his wards. According to the συνήγορος no one else spoke at this meeting. In fact, the others in attendance, all men, were literally struck dumb.

> No one among us, gentleman, was able to utter a word, but weeping no less loudly than those who had been wronged we went our several ways in silence.
> (Lysias 32.18)

Diogeiton refused to make restitution, and so the matter proceeded to formal arbitration and, as that failed as well, eventually to court. Diodotus' elder son brought suit but turned his speaking time over to his brother-in-law, who spoke as his advocate. Behind these proceedings

I believe we should see the insistence and powerful personality and intellect of Diogeiton's daughter. She had contrived to have a family conclave called at which she was the only speaker. She could not, however, appear in a court of law. Women were barred. Nonetheless, she managed to make an appearance. For her son-in-law reproduced in court the words she had spoken in the family meeting. In a sense she was like a ventriloquist who spoke through the mouth of her son-in-law, or, if another metaphor will help, she projected herself into court like some hologram, extending her presence into an arena which she was forbidden to enter physically.

Finally, let us note a telling contrast. It is Diogeiton's daughter who propels events and speaks with vigor. The men are curiously passive and mute. Her husband Hegemon does nothing. Her elder son is reduced to tears and looks to his mother for help. Male kin and friends can only weep and leave in silence. In effect, the roles we traditionally expect of Athenian men and women in such a situation have been reversed. Perhaps this is all Lysias at work, deliberately contriving this reversal for rhetorical effect. Perhaps, too, we should not always expect the stereotype. We should bear in mind that Lysias' aim was to win the case for which he had been paid to write this speech. It was incumbent upon him to present a picture that was both believable and appealing to the jurors who heard it. The force of personality and the eloquence of Diogeiton's daughter are striking; the passivity and inarticulateness of her men folk, unexpected. But I believe this depiction could not have found its way into an Athenian court unless it had at its core both credibility and verisimilitude. To put it less abstractly, Lysias decided to present to the all-male jury this woman's vigor and eloquence in the company of men because it rang true, because they had seen and heard or could imagine something similar happening in their own lives.[10]

Now, Lysias' speech was pronounced a masterpiece in antiquity (Dionysius of Halicarnassus, *De Lysia* 21–7; Photius, *Bibliotheca* 262), and moderns echo that sentiment. No small part of the speech's power and success lies in bringing the words and personality of Diogeiton's daughter into court. Adams pronounced this maneuver a "stroke of genius," and his opinion is generally echoed by those who comment on this speech.[11] But what has not been adequately appreciated is the way in which Diogeiton's daughter was able to motivate events in her male-dominated world, indeed to take control of events, not the least of all by having her say. She is, therefore, much more than "simply a good mother and decent woman" as Carey describes her.[12]

Good mother and decent woman she may well have been, but is it possible that more than motherhood and decency motivated her? A clue appears in her speech within a speech. While railing against her father for turning her children out of their own home without shoes, bedding, furniture, attendants, coats, or money, she draws this comparison: "and now you are bringing up the children you have by my stepmother in all the comforts of affluence" (Lysias 32.17). Now the motif of the stepmother who hardens her husband against her stepchildren was current in ancient Greece, too, and so this is a nice rhetorical ploy.[13] But we learn something important in addition. Diogeiton had remarried and had had more children since the death of his brother. These children were sons (τοὺς ἐκ τῆς μητρυιᾶς). This fact had a stunning consequence. As long as Diogeiton had had no more children, his wealth would have passed on his death to the sons of Diodotus (his grandsons). In that situation, his defalcations from his wards would eventually have been rectified and recouped as a matter of course. But Diogeiton had added insult to injury: not only did he defraud his daughter's children of their patrimony, he also remarried and had by his new wife male offspring; these cut off his daughter's sons from any possibility of recovering their inheritance except through legal action. In the same way, the status and importance of the daughter herself was diminished. While she remained her father's sole child, she was to be a conduit of family wealth to her sons: not an ἐπίκληρος after all, to be claimed by another, but no less important in securing the economic future of her sons. Diogeiton's remarriage and subsequent offspring reduced her status and undercut her importance. We may expect that her disappointment at least in part motivated her remarkable response.

By now the reader has doubtless grown tired of the cumbersome periphrasis "Diogeiton's daughter." Of course we must use this indirect designation because we do not know the actual name of Diogeiton's daughter. This is because in classical Athens it was not proper to use in public the name of a decent woman. The exceptions are women of low status or no status, or the dead. Correspondingly, to use a woman's name publicly was to characterize her as "common" in both senses of the word, as cheap and low and as a woman every man could have access to.[14] To do so was an insult not just to her but to her κύριος, whether husband, father, or brother.[15] Good examples of how this worked are Elpinice, sister of Cimon, and Aspasia, Pericles' second wife.[16] The fact that we know their names means that they were notorious. Each was impaired as to marriage, and that impairment opened the way for a litany of abuse about their sexual conduct. Ultimately, it was Cimon and Pericles, prominent politicians, who were the objects of those attacks.

Elpinice and her brother were probably born within a few years of each other, c. 510.[17] In 489 her father Miltiades was put on trial for his failure at Paros, convicted and fined 50 talents (Herodotus 6.136; cf. Nepos, *Miltiades* 7–8). Too ill to speak at the trial, Miltiades died a short time after his conviction from wounds received in the siege of Paros. The fine was immense. Annihilating to any other family, it staggered even the wealthy Cimonids. Herodotus noted that Cimon, Miltiades' son, paid off the fine. Such a blow would have had serious consequences for Elpinice's marriage eligibility because conceivably her dowry would have been too small for one of her class, or else non-existent. This probably lies behind the story that she committed incest with her brother (Plutarch, *Cimon* 4.5; Eupolis, *Poleis* frag. 208). Its basis can be understood by comparison with its milder variant, that "Elpinice did not live secretly with Cimon, but openly in a state of matrimony (φανερῶς γημαμένην συνοικῆσαι), since her poverty made her despair of a marriage worthy of her high birth" (Plutarch, *Cimon* 4.7; Nepos, *Cimon* 1.2). As Nepos noted (*Praefatio* 4; *Cimon* 1.2), this relationship may not have been incestuous at Athens as siblings born of the same father but of different mothers were permitted to marry. But there is no evidence that Cimon and Elpinice had different mothers, and that explanation, followed by some modern writers, seems a conjecture designed to mitigate the slander against Elpinice. What is more likely is that Elpinice was forced to live at home (συνοίκησις) with her κύριος, namely her brother Cimon, until the family could recoup some of its losses and afford her a proper dowry. While she lived at home, nubile but unmarried, she was subject to slander, slander ultimately aimed at impairing the politically aspiring Cimon.[18] Another slam at her family is that Callias rescued Cimon from financial ruin by paying off Miltiades' fine on condition he obtain Elpinice in marriage. This he would do because he was infatuated (ἐρασθείς, Plutarch, *Cimon* 4.7) with Elpinice. There are three damaging implications to this story. First, it is stated Callias made his offer because he was "in love" with Elpinice. Erotic passion was an improper basis for marriage among the Athenians.[19] Secondly, for Callias to be in love, he would have had to have prior contact with Elpinice, an impermissible situation for a decent woman. Finally, in effect Callias would have been buying the marriage of Elpinice, the exact reverse of dowry, and a huge insult to her brother. It would have made Elpinice a παλλακή, a kept woman.[20] But it is hard to believe that Callias in fact paid Miltiades' fine in exchange for Elpinice. The conversation would have had to take place in prison (in Nepos' version, Cimon was in prison because he could not pay his father's fine), and it is hard to imagine how the details of such a jailhouse negotiation could have gotten out, for the action derogated both Cimon and Callias.

As for Aspasia, she is typically characterized as a prostitute, "the most famous woman in fifth-century Athens ... who started as a *hetaira* and ended as a madam."[21] Assessments like this rely mainly on Plutarch who uncritically repeated slanders of the comic poets and the Socratics.[22] In fact, the calumnies of Aspasia were actually indirect attacks on Pericles by his political enemies. For instance, it was also alleged of Aspasia that she instigated Pericles to precipitate both the Samian and the Peloponnesian War (Plutarch, *Pericles* 24.1, 30.3; Aristophanes, *Acharnians* 524–27), in the first case because the Samians would not stop hostilities with Miletus, her native city, and in the second because some Megarians had raped two of her prostitutes.[23] Aspasia's vulnerability lay in her status as an alien.[24] Thus, though Pericles lived with Aspasia (beginning some five years after the divorce of his first wife) until the end of his life, she could not be his wife, but only his concubine (παλλακή). This status made her marginal and opened the way to slanders that she was also a call girl (ἑταίρα), a whore (πόρνη), and panderer and madam.[25] In other words, a convenient way to attack Pericles and his political policies was to attack Aspasia, and the way to attack her was to say she was a loose woman. That is why we know her name but not the name of Pericles' first wife.

On the other hand, the names of decent women were virtually taboo, and it was proper to address or refer to them only obliquely, for example as the wife or daughter or sister of their guardians (κύριοι). Much has been made of this indirect naming of decent women, how it defined their identity in terms of their male kin, how it stripped them of personality, how it emphasized their status as property of their κύριοι. Or so it may seem from a modern Western perspective. Such an analysis is too simple, biased by our own cultural perspectives. Looked at from the Athenian perspective, such nomenclature was thought to show women honor and respect and can only be properly understood in terms of the entire social system. To prove that claim is clearly beyond the scope of this paper. But it may prove profitable to examine some cases of "named women" from the corpus of Attic oratory. These turn out, naturally, all to be women on the margin. They are on the margin because they are in one sense or another "public" women who are trying to cross the social boundary and become "private" women. The common thread in these cases is that by seeking respectability each woman tries, with varying success, to ensure legitimacy and citizenship for her offspring, a legitimacy and citizenship which are precisely in doubt because of their mother's marginal status and her (alleged) sexual availability.

Perhaps the simplest case to begin with is that of Alce, the former slave-prostitute and freedwoman of Euctemon of Cephisia (Isaeus 6.18–26). As one of his business ventures Euctemon owned a bordello in Piraeus which was run by a freedwomen of his. One of the prostitutes employed there was a slave by the name of Alce. After she became too old for prostitution, Alce was freed and put in charge of a tenement in the Ceramicus. There she lived with Dion, another ex-slave, by whom she had two sons. Dion left Athens to avoid arrest, and Euctemon began to spend more and more time at the tenement until he finally moved in, abandoning his children and wife of many years. According to the speaker of Isaius 6, "he was reduced to such a state by drugs, disease, or whatever, that he was persuaded by the woman to introduce the elder of her two sons into his phratry under his own name" (6.22). At first the phratry brothers, at the insistence of Euctemon's legitimate son Philoctemon, refused, but eventually under coercion (Euctemon threatened to marry the sister of Democrates of Aphidna and produce more heirs if he didn't get his way), the family convinced Philoctemon to drop his objections. And so Alce's elder son entered Euctemon's phratry, but his inheritance was to be limited to a single farmstead. Aside from various interesting legal issues (e.g., whether such a phratry induction was legal when the result of extortion or whether a son could be a partial heir), what is important for the present study is how Alce, despite her sordid background, managed to get one of her sons recognized as an heir of Euctemon. His induction into the phratry would have cleared the way for his eventual citizenship, although the speaker does not elaborate on this possibility.[26]

A similar case is provided by the story of Neaira ([Demosthenes] 59). Purchased as a young girl, Neaira worked for many years as a slave prostitute for the brothel keeper Nicarete in Corinth. In the course of her career she had many famous and wealthy lovers and toured most of Greece plying her trade. After many escapades she took up with Stephanus the Athenian. Stephanus took Neaira with her three children to Athens where they lived together supporting themselves largely through her prostitution. In fact, her fees were higher because she passed herself off as Stephanus' wife. Eventually, Stephanus claimed Neaira's daughter Phano as their legitimate offspring and betrothed the girl to Phrastor of Aigilia with a dowry of one-half talent. After living with her for a while, Phrastor found out about her true background and expelled the pregnant Phano, at the same time refusing to return her dowry on the grounds that Stephanus had deceived him. Lawsuits followed on each side but were dropped. Eventually Phrastor fell deathly ill, and Neaira and Phano saw their opportunity.

Phrastor, we are told, had no children and was at odds with his relatives. Thus alone and extremely sick he was susceptible to the ministrations of Neaira and Phano. As they nursed Phrastor back to health, they convinced him to acknowledge Phano's son as his own (the child she had been carrying was now born). Phrastor agreed and attempted to introduce the boy into his phratry and into his clan. His clansmen, the Brytidai, however, balked, on the grounds that Phano was not an Athenian woman and hence not legally married to Phrastor. Phrastor sued, but when challenged to swear before the arbitrator that "he recognized the child as his own son, born of a citizen woman and one betrothed to him in accordance with the law," Phrastor backed down and refused the oath.[27]

There were further adventures for Stephanus, Neaira, and Phano of a similar type (and with similar outcome), but we may restrict ourselves to the above episode. It is very like the story of Alce. In both cases these marginal women attempt to get some of their offspring accepted as legitimate Athenians. We hear nothing of the fate of Neaira's two sons, Proxenus and Ariston, but there was a consistent effort to integrate Phano into Athenian society by marrying her with a dowry to an Athenian (after her encounter with Phrastor, Phano was married to Theogenes of Erchia under the same pretenses), and very certainly an effort to get Phano's son by Phrastor accepted as an Athenian. In the case of Phrastor, it is noteworthy that the two women were the ones who took the initiative and did their best to get Phano's son legitimized. We will have more to say on what this means after considering the case of Plangon.

Before moving on to that case, however, we should first remark on a law among the Athenians that a man without sons could not bequeath his property as he saw fit if his reason had been impaired by madness, senility, drugs, or disease or if he had acted under the influence of a woman (γυναικὶ πιθόμενος).[28] Allusion is made to this law in both the case of Euctemon (Isaeus 6.22) and the case of Phrastor ([Demosthenes] 59.55–6), that each acted under the influence of a woman to introduce a "son" into his phratry.[29] One might be inclined to pass over this regulation without much reflection as yet another negative assessment of women by Athenian men. But we can glean something more important from it than just that. First, the law clearly groups the influence of women on men with the irrationality caused by insanity, drugs, or senility. What is meant cannot be persuasive rhetoric (that appeals to reason) but rather female sexuality and eros, for the Greeks a well-known source of irrational behavior. Secondly, a law that takes notice of women's influence upon male decisions by that very fact shows that this was something that happened or could happen with some frequency. We should, therefore, not regard the cases we are examining as isolated instances. They are rather indices of how women could exercise power, by using their sexuality to achieve goals in their dominant male world. The case of Plangon is a star example.

Unlike Alce or Neaira, Plangon was an Athenian, in fact the

daughter of the wealthy and prominent Pamphilus of Ceiriadai.[30] Born near the end of the Peloponnesian War she was married to Mantias of Thoricos in the early 380s with a dowry of 100 minas. Her father served as general at Aegina in 389/8, but failed in his commission (Xenophon, *Hellenica* 5.1.2, 5) and was cashiered. Convicted of embezzlement, his estate was confiscated, and his family forced into economic ruin: he still owed 5 talents on his death.[31] The politically ambitious Mantias divorced his wife either while she was still pregnant or not long after the birth of her first son Boiotus, for one of the main arguments of Demosthenes 39 and 40 is that Mantias had not introduced his firstborn son to his phratry within the first year of birth, as was customary. This omission is confirmed by the boy's name, Boiotus. He was named after his mother's brother and not after his father's father, Mantitheus, which would have been the case had he been acknowledged at the δεκάτη naming ceremony and introduced to his father's φράτορες. Subsequently, Mantias married the daughter of Polyaratus, the widow of Cleomedon, son of Cleon (Demosthenes 40.6, 24–5), with a dowry of one talent. Around 380 Mantias had a son by her, whom he did name Mantitheus.

With their family saddled with a staggering debt to the state (which still had not been paid off some forty years later, Demosthenes 40.22), Pamphilus had been ruined, and so were his three sons, Boiotus, Euthydemus, and Hedylus. None appeared in public life. Plangon, too, faced a bleak future. Divorced, with a son her former husband would not acknowledge, she could not remarry: either Mantias had failed to return her dowry, or else when returned it was seized by the state in partial payment of her father's fine. Without a dowry she would not be able to find another husband.[32] In a very similar situation, Theomnestus noted of his sister-in-law:

> [Apollodorus'] other daughter would never have been given in marriage, for who would ever have taken to wife a undowered girl from a father who was debtor to the treasury and without resources?
> ([Demosthenes] 59.8)

But Plangon was resourceful. She was good-looking (εὐπρεπὴς τὴν ὄψιν, Demosthenes 40.27), Mantias was sexually attracted to her (ἧς ἐρῶν ἐτύγχανε, Demosthenes 40.27), and he consorted with her even after their divorce and his remarriage to the daughter of Polyaratus. As Mantitheus was forced to admit,

> My father, having thus married my mother, maintained her as his wife in his own house ... But with Plangon, the mother of these men, he still kept up a sexual relationship (ἐπλησίαζεν) of some sort or other: it is not for me to say what that was.
> (Demosthenes 40.8)

This relationship lasted a number of years. In fact, it resulted in yet another son, named Pamphilus (after his maternal grandfather), born sometime in the 370s. Even after the death of his second wife, which occurred when Mantitheus was a young boy (40.9, 27, 50), Mantias continued his liaison with Plangon. Properly speaking Plangon was a παλλακή, a mistress or kept woman.[33] This was apparently the fate of many Athenian women who could not bring a dowry with them for marriage. Still, this relationship, although less than the ideal, provided for Plangon and her children. If it was no longer possible for Plangon to be a "good" woman, then at least it was possible for her to use her looks and sexuality to secure her future and the future of her children.

But Plangon still had one task ahead of her, to legitimize her sons. As it was, Mantias had steadfastly refused to acknowledge his paternity. Consequently, they had not been inducted into his phratry, and upon coming into their majority they would not gain entrance into his deme. Potentially, Boiotus and Pamphilus would be non-persons, disinherited and disenfranchised. When Boiotus came of age, c. 370, he besought his father to acknowledge his paternity. Mantias refused and a suit was in the offing when Plangon offered a deal.

> If she were paid thirty minas, she would get her brothers to adopt these children, and for her own part, if my father challenged her before the arbitrator to swear that the children were in very truth his sons, she would decline the challenge. (Demosthenes 40.10)

Of course, her brothers' adoption of her sons would hardly be totally satisfactory. Although they would become citizens, Boiotus and Pamphilus would share in the ruin of her family, and their prospects would be nil. However, Plangon actually had something else in mind. When challenged to the oath by Mantias in the presence of the arbitrator, Plangon swore in the temple of Apollo Delphinius that not only Boiotus (who had been born in wedlock) but also Pamphilus were in fact the sons of Mantias (Demosthenes 39.3–4, 40.11).[34] Plangon double-crossed her ex-husband and longtime paramour. Fearing harassment by his political adversaries, Mantias caved in and enrolled the two youths in his phratry. Through her persistence, and, it is true, her duplicity, Plangon had achieved her goal of many years: she secured the legitimacy of her children and guaranteed that they would be heirs to a wealthy estate and secure from the financial ruin and degradation that beset her own family.

Elpinice, whom we discussed briefly above, presents a special case. There circulated three stories about her sexual availability that fit the pattern we have just examined: a woman exploits her own sexuality to restore or normalize the status of her male kin. What makes the case special is that the stories are very likely spurious. They cannot, therefore, be directly used to illustrate the hypothesis that has been offered. However, they do reveal how the Athenians used this model of female sexuality to make events intelligible to themselves.

In the first example, we return to the story of Cimon in his jail cell, unable to pay his father's fine to the state. He is confronted by Callias who will pay the fine if he can obtain the object of his passion, Elpinice. In this version, Cimon refuses with indignity. But Elpinice intervenes, saying she would not allow Miltiades' son to die in prison when she could prevent it by marrying Callias (Nepos, *Cimon* 1.4; cf. Plutarch, *Cimon* 4.7). In the second example, Cimon was brought to trial in 463 on the charge of being bribed by a foreign power. It is said his sister secured his acquittal by appealing personally to Pericles, his principal accuser. In fact, she went to his house to make her plea, highly unorthodox behavior for an Athenian matron (Plutarch, *Cimon* 14.4). Pericles' response was patronizing: "You're an old woman, you're an old woman to try something like this."[35] What did Elpinice try that was so inappropriate? To plead for her brother? That would seem appropriate, no matter how old she was. Rather, it is implied she was making a sexual advance—and got turned down. No matter. Pericles' role in the prosecution turned perfunctory, and Cimon was acquitted. Still, the political attacks continued, and two years later Cimon was ostracized (Plutarch, *Pericles* 9.5, *Cimon* 17.2). Some five years afterwards the Athenians recalled him. Most of our sources say this was because the Athenians needed his abilities as general in their conflict with the Spartans (e.g., Plutarch, *Cimon* 17.8–18.1, *Pericles* 10.4). But Antisthenes the Socratic gave the scurrilous alternative: "Pericles took as the price for Cimon's return from exile having sex with Elpinice" (Athenaeus 589d).

The consistent thread in these stories is that time after time Elpinice used sex to bail her brother out of trouble. It is very likely that these reports are spurious, for we have versions, based on good sources, that relate the same episodes without reference to Elpinice's charms. Instead, what we have are tendentious attacks on Cimon that work by smearing his sister's reputation and by implying that he couldn't handle the problems he got into by himself: his sister had to prostitute herself for him to get out of trouble. In a sense it is no matter that the stories are false; they illustrate for us a perceived model of female behavior in classical Athens, that a woman can exercise power in the male world (here of politics) by using her sexuality. Typically her objective is to restore or normalize the status of important males in her life.

In most instances, the power we see women exercising is in terms of the male world. In each instance, mothers strive to help their children, in particular their sons. We don't see these women acting for personal or selfish motives. But within the status definitions of the Athenian world it could hardly have been otherwise. An Athenian woman received social validation by being a wife and mother (and in a special case by being an ἐπίκληρος). In particular, she validated herself by securing the future of her husband's οἶκος, "household," through the legitimate male offspring she produced.

Diogeiton's daughter, the respectable woman, could operate in an above-board manner. Where her menfolk shrank from action, either through personal inability or fear of her wealthy father, she pushed, prodded, or shamed them to action. She used her eloquence powerfully, though not in a public setting: her words were spoken in a private family gathering. It was up to her son-in-law and his speech-writer (one likes to think at her suggestion) that her words made it into court.

Aside from the special case of Elpinice, the other women we have considered were in a much weaker position. They were public women and outside the social structure.[36] As such their status was marginal—or even beyond the margin. As a consequence, they could not work within the system, for in fact they were by definition outside the system. Instead, they used their sexuality and sometimes outright duplicity to achieve their goals. But these goals ultimately were defined in terms of the dominant male world, to move their children into the kinship structure, thereby legitimizing them and securing their future. They were, in effect, striving to demarginalize their children and to reintegrate them into the mainstream. Their values and goals, then, were not aberrant, but rather consistent with the social norm. Whatever their methods, we must admire their fortitude, their courage, and their persistence.

K. R. Walters
Wayne State University

Notes

[1] Seminal is J. Gould, "Law, Custom and Myth: Aspects of the Social Position of Women in Classical Athens," *Journal of Hellenic Studies*, 100 (1980), 38–59. See also D. MacDowell, *The Law in Classical Athens* (Ithaca, 1978), 84–97; S. B. Pomeroy, *Goddesses, Whores, Wives, and Slaves: Women in Classical Antiquity* (New York, 1975), 57–119; W. K. Lacey, *The Family in Classical Greece* (Ithaca, 1968), 100–176; A. R. W. Harrison, *The Law of Athens* (Oxford, 1968), vol. 1, 1–160.

The translations of the Greek passages are, with some modifications, taken from the Loeb editions.

[2] For the debate on this issue see Pomeroy, *Goddesses, Whores, Wives, and Slaves*, 58–60, 93–119.

[3] Particularly useful are C. Carey, ed., *Lysias, Selected Speeches* (Cambridge, 1989), 204–224, and J. K. Davies, *Athenian Propertied Families* (Oxford, 1971), under 3885 *Diodotus*. Old but still helpful in some places is H. Frohberger and T. Thalheim, *Ausgewaehlte Reden des Lysias*, (Leipzig, 1892), vol. 2, 190–206.

[4] Harrison, *The Law of Athens*, vol. 1, 84, vol. 2, 136–37, 150–51; MacDowell, *The Law in Classical Athens*, 243. Women could take oaths before

arbitrators (Demosthenes 39.3, 40.10; Isaeus 12.9).

⁵ E.g., [Demosthenes] 59.2, where Theomnestus married the daughter of his sister who was the wife of Apollodorus, son of Pasion, the enormously wealthy banker; or Demosthenes 44.10, where Meidylides of Otryne wished to marry off his daughter (and sole child) to his brother Archiades.

⁶ On the practice as a whole, see Harrison, *The Law of Athens*, vol. 1, 9–12 and passim; MacDowell, *The Law in Classical Athens*, 95–98.

⁷ Cf. the case of the poor man Protarchus who "inherited" the right to a wealthy heiress (Demosthenes 57.41).

⁸ Cf. Harrison, *The Law of Athens*, vol. 1, 309–11, appendix A.

⁹ Although the elder son was obliged to be the one to bring suit and thus to speak in court, he gave the bulk of his time to his brother-in-law to speak for him. See MacDowell, *The Law in Classical Athens*, 250–51.

¹⁰ Cf. the lively cross-examination and angry response Theomnestus imagines for the jurors from their women folk if they acquit Neaira, [Demosthenes] 59.110–12. Virginia Hunter, "Women's Authority in Classical Athens," *Échos du Monde Classique/Classical Views*, 33 (1989), 39–48, sees in Demosthenes' mother Cleobule a "head of household ... [who] does make decisions about her own and her children's lives. ... [I]t is an authority that no law gives, and no law protects. Its sway is familial and private, and its modes uncodified" (47). Unfortunately, Hunter is not able to adduce much direct evidence for her claim.

¹¹ C. D. Adams, *Lysias, Selected Speeches* (1905; rpt. Norman, 1970), 288. Cf. the words of Carey, *Lysias*, 211.

¹² Carey, *Lysias*, 211.

¹³ E.g., Euripides, *Alcestis* 304ff., *Ion* 1329; Herodotus 4.154.1; Plato, *Menexenus* 237b.

¹⁴ D. Schaps, "The Women Least Mentioned: Etiquette and Women's Names," *CQ*, 27 (1977), 323–30; Gould, "Law, Custom and Myth," 45–46. A. H. Sommerstein, "The Naming of Women in Greek and Roman Comedy," *Quaderni di Storia*, 6 (1980), 393–418, extends Schaps' work, noting, "[O]n a closer examination it becomes apparent that the characters of comedy—the free male characters, that is—are almost as reticent in this respect as speakers in the courts" (393).

¹⁵ Such a practice is deeply encoded in the culture, so deeply it is often transparent to members of the culture and therefore (explicit comment from the culture often lacking) almost invisible to us. A parallel may help illustrate the point. In the well-known story of the *tyrannoktonoi*, Hipparchus, brother of Hippias, tyrant of Athens, was rebuffed in his sexual advances to Harmodius. To get revenge, Hipparchus and Hippias rejected Harmodius' sister as a basket carrier (κανηφόρος) in a religious procession, saying she was "not worthy" (διὰ

τὴν μὴ ἀξίαν εἶναι). The result of this calculated insult was a bungled assassination attempt on the tyrant and his brother, in which only Hipparchus died. (The principal sources are Thucydides 6.54–57 and [Aristotle], *Athenaion Politeia* 18; other sources are cited by the commentaries, A. W. Gomme, A. Andrewes, and K. J. Dover, *A Historical Commentary on Thucydides*, vol. 4 [Oxford, 1970], and P. J. Rhodes, *A Commentary on the Aristotelian Athenaion Politeia* [Oxford, 1981].) At first glance, the murderous response may seem all out of proportion to the insult given. But precisely what was the insult? Thucydides says the tyrants rejected the girl on the grounds she was not "worthy." Harpocration, under κανηφόροι, cites Philochorus (*FGrHist* 328 F8) to the effect that it was first during the reign of Erichthonius that virgin girls in high regard (αἱ ἐν ἀξιώματι παρθένοι) were appointed to carry the baskets in the Panathenaia and other festivals. Hesychius, under κανηφόροι, and the scholia to Aristophanes, *Acharnians* 242, as cited by F. Jacoby ad loc. to gloss ἐν ἀξιώματι, define "basket carriers" as "citizen females of high birth (εὐγενεῖς)" and "virgin girls of high birth." This misleads. What is at stake is not so much high birth as virginity. Harmodius would have been insulted with an aspersion on the former; the latter was an unendurable outrage. Note as a parallel in usage that at [Demosthenes] 59.113 the speaker specifically contrasts the "worth and high repute of free-born women" (τὸ τῶν ἐλευθέρων γυναικῶν ἀξίωμα) with the status of prostitutes. Cf., too, Thucydides 6.15.2.

[16] In general, Judeich's article in *RE*, *Aspasia*, is still relevant. See also E. Cantarella, *Pandora's Daughters* (Baltimore, 1987), 53–55.

[17] Davies, *Athenian Propertied Families*, under *Cimon (II)*, *Miltiadou (IV)*, *Laciades* 8429.

[18] Cf. the story that Elpinice must have had an affair with Polygnotus of Thasos because he gave Laodice the features of Elpinice in the mural "The Sack of Troy," which he painted in the Stoa Poikile c. 462 (Plutarch, *Cimon* 4.5). It is far more likely that Elpinice was represented to suit Cimon, who seemed to have an ideological interest in the murals in the Stoa. See L. H. Jeffery, "The *Battle of Oinoe* in the Stoa Poikile: A Problem in Greek Art and History," *Annual of the British School at Athens*, 60 (1965), 42. If so, it was a bold depiction, for publicizing a woman's features in a wall painting could not have been much different from bandying about her name in public.

[19] There is an implicit criticism of Pericles that his love for Aspasia was amatory (ἐρωτική τις ... ἀγάπησις) and excessive (ἔστερξε διαφερόντως), Plutarch, *Pericles* 24.5.

[20] Cf. R. Sealey, "On Lawful Concubinage in Athens," *Classical Antiquity*, 3 (1984), 111–33.

[21] Pomeroy, *Goddesses, Whores, Wives, and Slaves*, 89.

[22] E.g., Plutarch, *Pericles* 24, 30.3. Much of the modern prejudice stems

from U. von Wilamowitz-Möllendorff, Aristoteles und Athen (Berlin, 1892–3), vol. 1, 263, n. 7; vol. 2, 99, n. 35. F. Frost, Greek Society, 2d ed. (Lexington, 1980), 127–29, even embroiders the remarks of the comic poets and the Socratics.

[23] Apart from the absurdity of such charges, it is worth pointing out that Plutarch has reversed the order of the marriages of Pericles' first (unnamed) wife. According to him she had first married Hipponicus and then Pericles (Plutarch, Pericles 24.8), whereas it has been shown that only the reverse order makes chronological sense. See Davies, Athenian Propertied Families, Pericles (III) 11811 and Callias (XII) 7826. This hardly helps Plutarch's credibility.

[24] The daughter of Axiochus of Miletus (Diodorus, FGrHist 372 F40; Plutarch, Pericles 24.3).

[25] ἑταίρα: Athenaeus 12.533d derived from Herodes Ponticus περὶ ἡδονῆς; πόρνη: Plutarch, Pericles 24.6; panderer and madam παιδίσκας ἑταιρούσας τρέφουσαν: Plutarch, Pericles 24.3, 32.1; Aristophanes, Acharnians 527; Athenaeus 569f.

[26] For a good discussion of this case and the issues involved see Sealey, "On Lawful Concubinage in Athens."

[27] [Demosthenes] 59.50–61.

[28] Demosthenes 46.14, 16; Isaeus 4.16, 6.9, 11; Hyperides 3.17; Plutarch, Solon 21.4, Aetia Romana et Graeca 265e; [Aristotle], Athenaion Politeia 35.2.

[29] The scope of the law itself was narrow and probably did not strictly apply in these cases; hence, the point was not pressed.

[30] The principal sources for this case are [Demosthenes] 39 and 40. There the facts are presented in deliberately garbled fashion. They have been largely unraveled by J. Rudhardt, "La reconnaissance de la paternité, sa nature et sa portée dans la société athénienne," Museum Helveticum, 19 (1962), 39–64. See also Davies, Athenian Propertied Families, under 9667 Mantias Manitheou Thorikios, and the excellent introduction to Demosthenes 39 in C. Carey and R. A. Reid eds., Demosthenes: Selected Private Speeches (Cambridge, 1985), 160–68.

[31] Aristophanes, Plutus (Wealth) 174ff. and schol. ad loc.; Plato, frag. 14; Demosthenes 40.22.

[32] Cf. [Demosthenes] 59.113, who refers to "the daughters of citizens, who through poverty cannot marry."

[33] Cf. Sealey, "On Lawful Concubinage in Athens."

[34] For a parallel see Isaeus 12.9. In general, Harrison, The Law of Athens, vol. 2, 150–53.

[35] Plutarch, Cimon 14.4, Pericles 10.5. In fact, Elpinice was probably in her mid-forties. Davies, Athenian Propertied Families, believes Pericles' similar response to Elpinice when she rebukes him for the death toll following the

Samian War (439) is a doublet of this event, and that the original story goes back to Stesimbrotus of Thasos.

[36] On the phrase "public woman" as meaning in the eighteenth century a loose woman, see *Oxford English Dictionary* under *public*, 4d; M. DeForest, "Eighteenth-Century Women and the Language of Power," *Classical and Modern Literature*, 12 (1992), 195; and C. Gallagher, "Who Was that Masked Woman? The Prostitute and the Playwright in the Comedies of Aphra Behn," *Women's Studies*, 15 (1988), 25–31.

Propertius, Poetry, and Love

This paper deals, in a sense, with the old question of the identity of the Cynthia of the Monobiblos.[1] Some have observed that Propertius supplies her with an incoherent mix of character traits unlikely to be found in a single person.[2] One could argue that the incoherence results from his exploration of love from various angles, but this theory suggests a fairly mechanistic approach to poetry. It also leaves out of account a huge matrix of lexical and literary clues to the real subject of the poems. A better explanation is available.

One of the most important contributions of recent criticism has been to discourage readers from confusing poetry with autobiography.[3] For Latin poets in general A. W. Allen's work on authorial voice should discourage literal readings. For Propertius in particular Joy K. King has demonstrated that the decision to compose love elegy and not epic makes a political point as well as an artistic one. Propertius restricts himself to love not just because Callimachus counselled against epic, but also because the kind of epic that Propertius is expected to write— epic celebrating the achievements of Augustus—is personally abhorrent.[4] Cynthia, the beloved at the center of the Monobiblos, thus has symbolic importance: she, not Augustus, controls the poet's work. In this paper I shall build on the work of King and Allen and demonstrate that Cynthia is in every detail an allegory for the kind of poetry that Propertius *is* willing to write. The story of his supposed love affair, that is, is a meditation on the poetic process and on the composition of poetry in the political environment in which Propertius lived. If I am right, then Cynthia's conflicting character traits, even the question of whether her name was Cynthia or not,[5] have diminished importance in and of themselves: Propertius' literary intention was not just to document the course of a real-life love affair. Superficially Cynthia may be his mistress, but in the allegorical dimension the mistress is poetry. With either reading, as the poems make clear, the force exerted upon the poet dominates every aspect of his life.⁶

This matching of poetry to love is a happy invention. Both the composition of perfect poems and the winning of a difficult woman are efforts marked by devotion and passion, often irrational. When a lover in these poems laments the lapses of the beloved, it is inspiration lost temporarily to the poet. When he discusses her appearance, his subject is poetic style. When he recalls his efforts at seducing her and the exhilaration of success, he describes a poet's exertions for perfection and his exalted feelings when the right words finally come. The evidence for this reading is ready to hand, I think. I set out some of it in detail in the second part of this paper, while in the final section I try to extend the work of Joy King by suggesting explanations for the apparent disparity between the elegies and the funerary epigrams that conclude the *Monobiblos*. First, though, for reasons that have more to do with critical history than with Propertius himself, it will be useful to review what we know about the kind of poetry he wrote. My thesis requires that we accept first of all that the *Monobiblos* is about much more than love.

David Ross has demonstrated with great clarity just what it is about.⁷ The poet's objective, as he makes clear, is that of all the Alexandrians since Callimachus: to compose poetry exquisite in form, novel in approach, and erudite. He also is sensitive to earlier poetic tradition, and eager both to claim that heritage and to leave on it his own personal stamp. Indeed, the *Monobiblos* is a kind of extended response to the work of poets who preceded him. Their poetic principles are as urgent and significant a force in the poems as Cynthia herself.

Gallus, or to be precise, Vergil, was one of Propertius' most significant conduits for the idea of the continuity of great poetry.⁸ In the culminating scene of Vergil's *Eclogue* 6, Gallus is initiated into a highly diverse poetic fraternity that stretches back to Apollo. He returns in *Eclogue* 10, here as a lovesick poet utterly despondent at his mistress' departure to follow an army, and driven even to the ends of the earth to find a cure. This image of the heartsore poet is, of course, Propertius' starting point, and the very first poem of the *Monobiblos* contains so many allusions to this stricken Gallus of *Eclogue* 10 as to make it quite clear that Gallus is for Propertius a force to be reckoned with.⁹ For the reader, the cumulative effect of the Gallan allusions in this poem and elsewhere in the Monobiblos[10] is to identify Propertius very closely with Gallus—not only in his choice of love as a subject but also in his stature as a poet who is as fit as the Gallus of Eclogue 6 to take up the mantle of tradition. The poems of the Monobiblos ratify Propertius in this position because they resound in nearly every line with the poetry of the past.

The list of other poets whose work Propertius incorporates or responds to is long.[11] Two however, Callimachus and Catullus, are so frequently invoked in the elegies that their significance for the poet clearly equals that of Vergil's Gallus, if it does not surpass it. Propertius' standards of composition throughout the Monobiblos keep to the criteria set out in the programmatic prologue of Callimachus' Aetia. There Apollo dictates his terms to the poet: poetry should be delicate and "thin" (θρέψαι τὴν Μοῦσαν λεπταλέην, "Keep your Muse slender," Aetia frag. 1.1.24). "A few subtle lines"—αἱ κατὰ λεπτόν—are preferable to bloated ones (Aetia frag. 1.1.11). Among Latin poets, Vergil indicated his compliance very early, in the critical Eclogue 6:

> cum canerem reges et proelia, Cynthius aurem
> vellit et admonuit: "pastorem, Tityre, pingues
> pascere oportet ovis, **deductum dicere carmen**."
> (Ecl. 6.3-5)

> When I was singing kings and battles, Cynthius pulled
> My ear in admonition: "A shepherd, Tityrus,
> should feed his flock fat, but recite a thin-spun song."

Deductum, his rendering of Callimachus' λεπταλέην, is his encapsulation of the principle of delicacy. Along with uncompounded duco, the word acquired in Propertius' hands the character of a technical term. He uses it to signify that his own poetry also was written to this Callimachean standard: *at tibi saepe novo* **deduxi** *carmina versu*, "but for you I have often spun songs in new verse" (1.16.41). The literary meaning of duco and its compounds also imports a literary subtext into passages that seem to describe only erotic actions. Thus Propertius can represent the slow process of composition as the desultory conversation of lovers and their languid sighs (*longa **ducere** verba mora*, "drawing out words with a long delay," 1.10.6; *raro **duxti** suspiria motu*, "You have drawn out sighs with a rare movement," 1.3.27). He can liken a poet's exhilaration in successful composition to a lover's pleasure in days and nights of love (*facili totum **ducit** amore diem*, "she spends the whole day in easy love," 1.14.10; *nostri cura subit memores a! **ducere** noctes?* "has care for me brought—ah!—nights full of memory?" 1.11.5). Even the enslavement of the poet to his art can be equated with the subservience demanded of a lover (*hoc ... assueto **ducere** servitio*, "to spend in this accustomed servitude," 1.4.3–4).[12]

Poetry so refined leaves no room for bombast: Callimachus (and later Vergil) explicitly rejects the long-windedness of traditional epic.[13] Propertius similarly insists on the delicate, gentle, unobtrusive nature of his poems. Sometimes he is explicit, as when he describes what he writes as *mollis ... versus*, "gentle verses," (1.7.19), *blandum carmen*, "sweet song" (1.8.40), or *arguta carmina blanditia*, "songs of poignant sweetness" (1.16.16). Elsewhere the poetic reference is implicit, for example in comments on the winsome words of the beloved—that is, of Propertius' kind of poetry: *assiduas a fuge blanditias*, "flee—ah—the constant sweetness," 1.9.30; or in the description of a delicately composed Cynthia: *molliter in tacito litore compositam*, "gently arranged on the quiet shore," 1.11.14; or finally in the image of words themselves wafting through gentle shadows: *a quotiens teneras resonant mea verba sub umbras*, "ah, how often do my words resound under the delicate shadows," 1.18.21.[14]

Callimachus also attributed to Apollo advice that the poet should avoid the broad highway of poetry and seek instead the untrodden track—that he should turn, that is, from familiar but tired subjects and seek the unfamiliar:

> ... τὰ μὴ πατέουσιν ἄμαξαι
> τὰ στείβειν, ἑτέρων ἴχνια μὴ καθ' ὁμά
> δίφρον ἐλᾶν μηδ' οἷμον ἀνὰ πλατύν, ἀλλὰ κελεύθους
> ἀτρίπτους, εἰ καὶ στεινοτέρην ἐλάσεις.
> (*Aetia* frag. 1.1.25–28)

Follow trails unrutted by wagons,

don't drive your chariot down public highways,
but keep to the back roads though the going is narrow.

Generations of Alexandrian poets followed this advice, turning to subjects previously too humble or too personal for fine poetry. Likewise Propertius. He chooses an entirely new approach for elegy—taking for his ostensible and sole subject the personal effects of love—and he indicates his compliance with Callimachean principles by adapting the same Callimachean metaphor of the common highway: [*Amor*] *nec meminit notas ut prius ire vias*, "Love does not remember the familiar ways as before" (1.1.18).

Epic is out, in keeping with the Callimachean code,[15] and is replaced by love poetry. In Propertius' hands this becomes a new kind of "epic," in which amatory exploits and sufferings assume the importance of stories of war and the poet suborns the terminology of battle, siege, and military hardship to describe them.[16] The *Monobiblos* begins, in fact, with an image of conquest. Cynthia has captured, not just captivated the poet (*Cynthia ... me cepit*, 1.1.1), and Love stands in the posture of a victor, with the lover under his feet (*et caput impositis pressit Amor pedibus*, "and Love bears down with his feet on my head," 1.1.4). Throughout the elegies the beloved is *dura*, a term traditionally appropriate to epic warriors (*quamvis dura, tamen rara puella fuit*, "although she is hard, nevertheless she is a rare girl," 1.17.16; *aliquid duram quaerimus in dominam*, "I look for some approach to a hard mistress," 1.7.6). In fact, in an image borrowed from the *Iliad*, her iron rigidity exceeds that of Homer's Achilles at his most awful, in the act of killing Hector (*sit licet et ferro durior et chalybe*, "let her be harder than iron and steel," 1.16.30).[17] Love himself shows signs of the same military harshness (*hac Amor hac Liber, durus uterque deus*, "on this side Love, on that side Wine, each a hard god," 1.3.14), and Venus is a match for the strength of heroes:

> Illa potest magnas heroum infringere vires,
>   illa etiam duris mentibus esse dolor.   (1.14.17–18)

> Venus can lay the might of heroes low,
> And be to hearts of stone a cause of woe.

The ironic conversion of war-talk to love-talk and the standard refusal to write epic suits Propertius' Alexandrian principles nicely, but it also fits his own particular program in the *Monobiblos*. In the final epigrams of the book, as I shall argue more fully below, he directs the reader's attention to the devastating effect of real war on human life and love.

Learned mannerism, obscure allusion, adumbration of meaning rather than explicit statement: these are the stock in trade of Callimachus, of his Alexandrian and neoteric followers, and of Propertius. Yet in the *Monobiblos* one finds none of the conventional, explicit signs that the poet is following the standard of Callimachean poetics. Callimachus himself is not mentioned in the entire book (although he is invoked at 2.1.40, in Propertius' backward look at Book 1). There is no explicit *recusatio* of epic poetry.[18] There is no parade of poetic initiation like that with which Vergil graced Gallus. Still, a careful reading of Propertius' poems—the only kind of reading appropriate if the poetry is properly Alexandrian—discloses these Callimachean principles at the very foundation. Propertius, having mastered the essential elements of Callimachean poetry, here puts them to work, not pausing in the conventional way to say he is doing so. What Ross observes of his debt to Catullus applies as emphatically for Callimachus too: Propertius "has no need to point to or proclaim his indebtedness ... the poem itself obviously would have been impossible without his precedent."[19]

Catullus did acknowledge a debt to Callimachus and also embraced the refinement called for by the Callimachean code.[20] He put it to a new use and demonstrated the power of poetry to express what Callimachus had largely ignored, namely the deepest of human emotions: hatred, kindness, friendship, bereavement, amorous passion. Both his Alexandrianism and his subject inspire Propertius in his effort to render love into poetry, and allusions both to Catullus' epigrams and to his longer poems permeate the *Monobiblos*.[21] Propertius' elegies share special common ground, however, with a single poem of Catullus, the long "Allius" elegy of 68.[22] Links range from verbal reminiscences to evocations of particular scenes;[23] their cumulative effect is to highlight the poets' common concerns.

Catullus 68, like the whole *Monobiblos*, is focussed entirely on the twin themes of love and loss of a loved one. It begins with the poet's claim that mourning for his brother prevents him from sending poems to Allius, who himself suffers a kind of bereavement after the recent departure of his lover. The poem ends with the poet's bitter reflections on a love affair of his own, concluded now that his mistress has run after other men. Between these personal narratives Catullus introduces Homer's story of Laodamia and her husband Protesilaus—their deep and passionate love and his meaningless death, which brings with it the premature rupture of their union. The single myth thus illustrates both the traumas described in the more personal passages of this poem (and indeed in much of Catullus' work): namely the love and loss of a lover, and the loss of a loved one to death. Propertius, in his last poem to Cynthia in the Monobiblos (1.19), invokes the same obscure story and casts it the same way: he emphasizes not Homeric heroics but the strength of Protesilaus' love, potent enough even to bring his shade back to the world of the living. By adopting Catullus' unconventional and un-epic reading of an obscure myth, he emphasizes their shared interests both in subject (the interaction of love and death) and in style (an Alexandrian taste for riddling refinement of obscure myth).

Both in Catullus 68 and in the Monobiblos, moreover, there is an obsession with a particular Callimachean problem: the elevation of an unheroic, personal experience to a status previously enjoyed only by epic subjects. Propertius' conscious replacement of epic bombast by the sweetness of love poetry has been mentioned already. Catullus similarly, in 68, robs heroics of their traditional values. In telling of Protesilaus' death at Troy, the narrator's obsessive concern is the agony it occasions for the wife Laodamia, not any heroism linked to Protesilaus' participation in the expedition. Indeed, his death has no glory about it in Homer's description:

τὸν δ' ἔκτανε Δάρδανος ἀνὴρ
νηὸς ἀποθρῴσκοντα πολὺ πρώτιστον Ἀχαιῶν
(Il. 2.701–2)

A Dardanian man had killed him as he leapt from his ship, far the first of all the Achaeans, …

Protesilaus' opportunity for the kind of heroic experience celebrated in the Homeric poems—daunting risks undertaken for the sake of everlasting glory (κλέος)—evaporated with this premature death.[24] For this very reason he is important to Catullus, whose only interest in the story is emphatically its unheroic elements, namely thwarted love and the eternity of death. The story of Laodamia and Protesilaus ties together the predominant subjects of Catullus' poems, loss of Lesbia and loss of a dear one to death. In telling it Catullus pointedly excludes the kinds of detail conventional in epic poetry, and by so doing asserts a Callimachean dislike for the poetry of war. When Propertius invokes the same story in 1.19, therefore, he is drawing the reader's attention to the Catullan conjunction of love and death. In the *Monobiblos*, as in Catullus 68, the primary subject is love and loss of love—although Catullus' second sort of loss, the loss of kin, is one that Propertius keeps muted until the closing poems of the book. But he is also making a poetic statement like Catullus': he is asserting his own Callimachean rejection of war and heroics as appropriate subjects.

Propertius is not, of course, the first Latin poet since Catullus to compose elegies that bring these subjects together. *Eclogue* 10 strongly suggests that Gallus also wrote poems about love and thwarted love, perhaps in a mock-epic vein.[25] (What remains of his work actually makes scant overt reference to love.[26]) Propertius' innovation is rather one of scale, not subject, and owes much to Catullus: he is the first to offer elegy with love as its solitary subject. But human love is not the whole point: however effective the elegies may be as love poems, they also constitute a running commentary on Alexandrian poetics. Those that purport to describe love affairs involving Propertius, Cynthia, and various of the poet's friends need not be anchored in any real series of sexual encounters in order to be read with meaning. Within each disconnected study of the trials of love are coherent and reiterative statements about what poetry can and should—and, as we shall see, what it should *not*—accomplish. In Propertius' view it should be marked by learning, craft, playfulness, minimalism, and a concern with the everyday rather than the grand. It should eschew hackneyed bombast. It should investigate, as Callimachus, Catullus, and evidently Gallus did, the nature and the power and the range of poetry. The poet's special challenge for himself is to test whether he can concentrate within small compass—within the context of elegies on this single narrow subject of love—the full nature and power and range of which poetry is capable. Cynthia, on the level of allegory, is a literary convenience which serves this poetic program. This interpretation has not previously been articulated as far as I know, probably because of the strong inertial force that has inclined readers to find only romance in these poems. As Ross observes, "Our literary reactions are still colored by Romanticism more than we care to admit."[27]

¶

Language and expression throughout the *Monobiblos* bring home these points, as Propertius concocts his studies of human love from the figures and terminology of poetry—or, to put it differently, sets out a description of fine poetry in the form of love poems. Each trial of love that he presents is simultaneously a statement about the poet's experience in composition. All the issues taken up—physical appearance, the conversation of lovers, physiological and mental conditions peculiar to those in love, characteristic physical movements, situations typical of love—are expressed in the language of poetry, so that in a sense the poems constitute an extended riddle. More seriously, the love/poetry identification indicates the depth of Propertius' own involvement with poetry. His thoroughness in working this equation into the poems of the *Monobiblos* has not received comment. In this section I assemble some of the evidence supporting these claims.

The mistress' very name, first, suggests that the poems range beyond mere personal experience. Cynthia is the feminized Cynthius, the epithet borne by Apollo as he tweaked Vergil's ear and redirected him from epic to elegy (*Ecl.* 6.3). Nor is this kind of word-play Propertius' innovation. Other Latin elegists also chose Apolline pseudonyms for their poetic "mistresses." Gallus' Lycoris takes her name from Apollo Lycoreus, an epithet deriving from Lycoreia on Mount Parnassus.[28] Varro's Leucadia got her name from Apollo's temple in Leucas.[29] Tibullus had Delia.[30] "Cynthia" is meant to keep the poet's program alive for readers. She signifies Propertius' own personal and beloved experience of poetry, and derives from Apollo, the source of all poetry. As Ross suggests (with greater caution), Cynthia is "[Propertius'] sort of elegy."³¹ As I am arguing, all description of her is simultaneously a description of Alexandrian poetics.

Consider physical appearance: *forma* in the context of a simple romance refers to looks, but in a discussion of poetry it is a technical term denoting style of composition. Propertius exploits the pun, for example when he places his mistress' *forma* above that of the heroines of Troy (1.19.13–14), or of Antiope and Hermione (1.4.5–6). There he essentially claims the superiority of elegy to epic as literary form. Allegorically expressed, they stand in place of more direct statements about refined vs. grand poetry such as were offered by Propertius' Alexandrian predecessors (Callimachus, *Aetia* frag. 1.1.3–5; Vergil, *Ecl.* 6.3).

Propertius' style of composition—Cynthia's appearance—is itself the subject of the entire second poem. He prefers it without adornment, simple, unsullied by gaudy and expensive ornament: an extended statement of Callimachean poetics, and in more than one sense. The call for simplicity is itself arranged with Callimachean care, replete with elaborate symmetries and mythological exempla.³² His involvement with Cynthia's looks (the finish of his poetry), in fact, is intense enough to induce madness, a subject I shall return to.³³

Puns flourish which refer to specific aspects of Cynthia's looks. Hair, a conventional motif in erotic poetry, also figured prominently in Callimachus and Catullus.³⁴ The former composed an adulatory poem about the metamorphosis (as constellation) of the lock of hair that Berenice dedicated against the safe return of her husband Ptolemy III from war (*Aetia* frag. 4). Catullus' translation of Callimachus, poem 66, is a tour de force that demonstrates Callimachean poetic principles. It is a playful but learned exercise, long but not epic, incorporating Catullan themes developed in greater depth in poem 68—particularly faith and faithlessness in love, and the emotional effect of separation and reunion on lovers divided (as Protesilaus and Laodamia are in Catullus 68) by war. For a poet so indebted as Propertius is to Callimachus and Catullus, allusions to the hair of the beloved recall and reinforce the artistic principles that he shares with those poets.

In the *Monobiblos* the preoccupation of the lover and the beloved with coiffure refers specifically to the writing of poetry—to the difficulty, that is, that Callimachean poets face in trying to interweave different strands of meaning in a well-composed unity. Propertius' lover (poet) takes pleasure in composing the beloved's coiffure (his poetry) and arranging the fallen strands (*gaudebam lapsos formare capillos*, "I enjoyed shaping her fallen locks," 1.3.23; *componere crines*, "to arrange her hair*,"*1.15.5). Like a good Callimachean, he deplores excessive ornament (*ornato ... capillo*, 1.2.1). He anticipates that when he dies, her locks (his poetry) will be his memorial (*illa meo caros donasset funere crines*, "she would have dedicated her locks at my funeral," 1.17.21). Appropriately, the elegiac Cynthia appears neatly composed (*molliter in tacito litore compositam*, "gently arranged on the quiet shore," 1.11.14) while the epic Calypso, represented as emphatically unlike Cynthia, is unkempt (*multos illa dies incomptis maesta capillis/ sederat iniusto multa locuta salo*, "for many days she sat sadly with uncombed hair and said many things to the cruel sea," 1.15.11–12). In these parallel scenes, moreover, Cynthia significantly appears to be resting on quiet lakeshores, far from the roar of the sea that Calypso faces.[35]

Propertius takes special note also of Cynthia's *figura*, a term which can refer to looks but also stands for a figure of speech or for style (1.2.7, 1.4.9); her *color* (complexion, whether physical or as a feature of style and diction: 1.2; 1.6.6, 1.15.39, 1.18.17);[36] her *membra* (limbs but also clauses: 1.2.6); her *pedes* (feet or meter, 1.18.12), which are too delicate to support the rigors she will undergo if she goes to war (turns to epic: 1.8.7).[37] Hands are important, too. When Propertius envisions Cynthia at Baiae, she is swimming with an elegiac stroke, parting the water with alternating hand (*alternae ... manu* 1.11.12). Love himself deals rewards with hands that alternate like lines in elegy (1.9.24). The lover's (poet's) hands are also busy, of course, although contact (writing) comes seldom. When the mistress is asleep (and inspiration dormant) she rests on her own unsteady hands (*Cynthia non certis nixa caput manibus*, 1.3.8). Soon he gains confidence and is tempted to move a hand toward her, as if to write (*admota ... manu* 1.3.16). And when he makes her an offering of fruit (the product of contemplation?), his hand curves around it as if around a stilus (*furtiva cavis poma dabam manibus*, "I gave stolen apples in hollowed hands," 1.3.24). Only when a lover and his beloved are completely united does a poet finally have his hands fully in control of his craft (*vidi ego te ... flere iniectis, Galle, diu manibus*, "I saw you ... weep a long time, Gallus, your hands thrown about her,"

1.13.16).

The poet also plants special meaning in his references to the conversation of lovers. Language, of course, is a primary vehicle of both love and poetry. Propertius goes beyond trite love talk, however, and makes language itself, that is to say poetry, a player in the affairs he describes. When in poem 6 the poet considers abandoning his girl (his kind of elegy), she wraps herself around him to restrain him (*complexae ... puellae*). The modifier *complexae*, significantly, may refer to the combination of words in a group (i.e., to literary composition) as well as to a physical embrace. Propertius exploits the ambiguity. In fact, we scarcely notice that it is actually words that restrain the poet here, rather than her physical action: *sed me **complexae** remorantur **verba puellae***, ("But the words of the clinging girl hold me back," 1.6.5).

The image from 1.6 of the girl (poetry) enveloping the lover (poet) inevitably dictates our interpretation of *complexa ... puella* when it recurs at 1.10.5. The latter passage, moreover, is exactly parallel to the former in arrangement (an initial conjunction followed by—in this order—a pronoun, a derivative of *complexus*, a verb, a noun, and a form of *puella*) and leads into another, unmistakable reference to composition, namely a repetition in the following line of the programmatic *ducere verba*:

>   cum **te complexa** morientem, Galle, **puella**
>   vidimus et longa **ducere verba** mora ...
>
>   (1.10.5–6)
>
>   I saw you swooning in her arms, and heard
>   Between long silences the lingering word ...

The poet's friend Gallus languishes here in the arms of a girl, but he is simultaneously in the grip of poetic composition, as Anna Benjamin has compellingly argued.[38] Surely, then, the Gallus of the *Monobiblos* represents the poet Gallus—or at least an author of Alexandrian poetry very much in his image.[39]

The poet warns others of the difficulty of talking with a mistress, but in such a way that his references to attempted or abortive conversations are also references to the difficulties of composition. Gallus is cautioned that once smitten (devoted to composing love elegy) he will find himself at a loss for words (*quaecumque voles **fugient tibi verba** querenti,* "whatever words you want will escape you as you seek them," 1.5.17). Similarly Ponticus, who turns to love (i.e., to elegy) in 1.7 later finds his language restricted (*dicebam tibi venturos, irrisor, **amores**,/ nec tibi perpetuo **libera verba** fore,* "I told you, mocker, that love would come and that your words would not always be free," 1.9.1–2). Ideally, the poet's words should restrain others from his own rash course (*heu referet quanto **verba** dolore mea,* "alas, with how much sorrow will he recall my words," 1.1.38). But for those who would attempt it anyway, Propertius' prescription is his own words, that is, they should work at the kind of poetry that he himself creates (*nec levis **in verbis** est medicina **meis**,* "strong medicine is in my words," 1.10.18).[40]

Conversation with Cynthia and discourse about love are recounted in language versatile enough to describe both romance and Alexandrian poetry simultaneously. Recurring words based on the root *argut-*, for example, effectively convey the ambiguity. This term is too uncommon to pass without drawing attention to itself. In fact, Propertius goes out of his way to ensure that it is noticed by using its verbal form, which is rarer than the adjective or noun and by giving it—apparently for the first time in Latin—a transitive meaning:

> illa mihi totis **argutat** noctibus ignis
> et queritur nullos esse relicta deos   (1.6.7–8)

> All night she'll pitch her passion high, and moan:
> "There are no gods, if I am left alone,"

The argumentative tone conveyed by *argutat* in this passage is present also in the commoner term *argutus*, which can refer to any sharp or clear noise, for example the penetrating sound of the songs offered by an *exclusus amator* (**arguta** *referens carmina* **blanditia**, "uttering his songs of shrill sweetness," 1.16.16) or the whine of a hen-pecked lover (*omnia consuevi timidus perferre superbae/ iussa neque* **arguto** *facta* **dolore** *queri*, "I was accustomed to endure all your haughty commands, and not to complain at your deeds with shrill grief," 1.18.25–26). As the oxymoron *arguta ... blanditia* suggests, however, the adjective describes not only the shrillness of a lovers' quarrel or lover's lament, but also the eloquence of fine poetry. In other authors it connotes the adroit use of language, delicacy of expression, even wit and word play, all prized Alexandrian qualities; likewise the more widely encountered noun *argutiae*, which is absent from the *Monobiblos* but contributes its nuances.

In Propertius, however, *argut-* carries even greater significance than its lexical meaning suggests. This is the very term used by Catullus at the most crucial moment of poem 68, the poem that the *Monobiblos* so repeatedly echoes (above, n. 23). In 68, when the poet's mistress crosses the threshhold and comes to him for the first time—the crisis of the poem and also of Catullus' whole poetic effort, since by doing so she initiates their affair—he makes her sandal squeak with this very adjective (*innixa **arguta** constituit **solea***, "she stood still, poised on a squeaking sandal," 68.72). That Propertius repeatedly uses an unusual term featured so ominously in a critical passage of Catullus' poetic/love life is, of course, important. It brings the reader's attention once again to the interplay of the two themes that dominate and intertwine in Catullus 68 and also in the *Monobiblos*, namely the personal experience of love and of death.

Cynthia, in appearance and conversation so like a poem, not surprisingly has other characteristics suited just as well to a book as to a living woman. Works of literature were regularly identified in antiquity by their opening phrases—a principle first applied in the Alexandrian Library by Callimachus himself in his *Pinakes*[41]—so it is significant that her name begins the *Monobiblos* (*Cynthia prima* 1.1). "Cynthia" did in fact serve in antiquity as a kind of title for this book, the poems being known collectively as the "*Cynthia Monobiblos*".[42]

On occasion Cynthia herself is explicitly something written or read.[43] In a passage from one of the most obviously programmatic poems of the *Monobiblos*, the poet envisions her name written on the bark of trees (*A quotiens teneras resonant mea verba sub umbras,/ **scribitur et vestris Cynthia** corticibus*, "Ah! How often do my words resound under your delicate shadows, and Cynthia is written on your trunks," 1.18.21–22).[44] Her written properties are more evident still in Book 2, where he promises to write epic once his girl "is written" (*bella canam, quando **scripta puella mea est**,* "I shall sing of wars when my girl has been written," 2.10.8), and foresees a time when Cynthia will be widely read

(*Tu loqueris, cum sis iam noto fabula libro/ et tua sit toto* **Cynthia lecta** *foro*, "Do you talk like this when you are already a story yourself because of your famous book, and your *Cynthia* is read all through the forum," 2.24.1–2). The same Cynthia/book equation is also hidden in the riddle *Cynthia causa fuit*, "Cynthia was the reason," at 1.11.26, where the common noun is the Latin equivalent of αἴτιον. The passage refers, that is, to the *Aetia* of Callimachus and serves as a reminder of the poetic principles to which Propertius subscribes.[45]

There are also miscellaneous bookish puns. The poet finds himself pinned between Love and the god of wine (*hac Amor hac Liber*, "on this side Love, on that Liber," 1.3.14)—the title of Bacchus here being chosen, I think, to suggest books and writing in general. Cynthia will never be a *nobilis historia* (1.15.24): the epic paradigms of Calypso, Hypsipyle, Alphesiboea, Evadne have no effect on her character (1.15.9–22). Nevertheless her fame is *perspecta* (1.11.17), "well scrutinized", a reference to the complexity of this poetry. The ambiguity of *lego* provides still other puns. One can pick (read) his way along the rivers of song (*sive* **leges** *umbrosae flumina silvae*, "whether you pick your way along the streams of a shady wood," 1.20.7);[46] and Propertius finds he can collect (read) all the wealth he needs when Cynthia is present and compliant (**legitur** *Rubris gemma sub aequoribus*, "and a jewel is plucked from under the Red Sea," 1.14.12).

Various experiences and attitudes of lovers are also explored for their poetic content. In real life, for example, love can bring misery and pain. Grief characterizes the uncertain life of the lover and accompanies his efforts to ensnare the beloved. From the first line of the *Monobiblos* the lover's wretchedness is central (*Cynthia prima suis* **miserum me** *cepit ocellis*, "Cynthia was the first to capture wretched me with her eyes," 1.1.1). Sorrow may be so intense that he can even wish the affair never begun (*me dolor et lacrimae merito fecere peritum,/ atque utinam posito dicar amore rudis*, "grief and tears have deservedly made me an expert; would that I be called a novice, with love set aside," 1.9.7–8). Love here is a metaphor for poetry, however, and the lover's (poet's) misery derives on the literary level from the struggle to compose exquisite, properly Alexandrian elegy. Appropriately, therefore, like-minded poets are similarly afflicted. Gallus, for example, weeps when he finally reaches union with his mistress, i.e., succeeds in composing a poem to meet Alexandrian standards (*vidi ego te* *toto vinctum languescere collo, et flere iniectis, Galle, diu manibus*, "I saw you droop, clinging right around her neck, and saw you weep a long time, Gallus, your hands thrown about her," 1.13.15–16).[47]

The struggles of a lover, or of a poet, are hard and unremitting. This way madness lies. Love indeed brought madness to Vergil's Gallus (*Galle, quid insanis?* "Gallus, what madness is this?" *Ecl.* 10.22), and so it does to lovers in the *Monobiblos*. The mythological lover Milanion wanders in frenzy in the very landscape that attracted the maddened Gallus (*nam modo Partheniis **amens** errabat in antris*, "for at times he wandered raving in the Parthenian caves," 1.1.11; cf. *Ecl.* 10.56–57).[48] And from the first poem of the *Monobiblos*, the lover/poet stresses his own maddened state (*et mihi iam toto **furor** hic non deficit anno*, "and for me now this madness has not diminished in a whole year," 1.1.7). When Gallus considers courting the poet's mistress (attempting Propertius' kind of poetry) Propertius calls him insane, and warns him away from the kind of madness he himself endures (*quid tibi vis, **insane**? meos sentire **furores**?*, "what do you want for yourself, madman, to feel my madness?," 1.5.1–6).

This is the proverbial madness of poetic inspiration.[49] In the *Monobiblos* the *furor* that has afflicted the poet for a year derives from his love, which is to say from his effort to produce poetry of the highest order, and grief defines his condition from the first line.

> haec sed forma mei pars est extrema furoris
>   sunt maiora, quibus, Basse, perire iuvat:
> ingenuus color et multis decus artibus, et quae
>   gaudia sub tacita dicere veste libet.   (1.4.11–14)

> Yet visual charm is not my passion's core,
> But things of greater note, worth dying for:
> Breeding, distinction, gifts with grace allied,
> And joys that secret-keeping bedclothes hide.

The very style (*forma*) he has chosen, its simple poetic coloration (*ingenuus color*), his efforts to implant hidden meaning in his words (*gaudia sub tacita dicere veste*), and the need to maintain an appropriate standard of decorum (*decus*) all exacerbate his frenzy (*pars ... extrema furoris*). The beloved's hold on her lover and poetry's control of the poet, that is, are the same.

Both love and inspiration are fitful as well. At times the poet finds himself denied access to his source of inspiration. He tells his troubles in anguish to the mistress' unresponsive door (1.16.18, 18.24), or beats on it with unworthy hands (1.16.6). At other times he suffers the painful insomnia of thwarted lovers—or of blocked authors who face a bleak dawn after a night devoid of inspiration (*me mediae noctes, me sidera plena iacentem,/ frigidaque Eoo me dolet aura gelu*, "midnights, the full panoply of stars, and the cold wind from the Eastern frost give me pain as I lie here," 1.16.23–24; for long sleepless nights, see also 1.12.13–14). The composition of fine poetry so controls the poet as to leave him little peace, and he finds only a difficult kind of quiet in an inhospitable landscape:

> pro quo divini fontes et frigida rupes
>   et datur inculto tramite dura quies.   (1.18.27–28)

> In return for this are given the divine fountains and
> cold cliffs and harsh quiet on rough track.

It is at least a poetically correct landscape, for the track here is rough and Callimachean (cf. κελεύθους ἀτρίπτους, "untrodden roads," *Aetia* frag. 1.1.27–28). It winds beside divine springs that recall the scene of Gallus' poetic initiation (Vergil, *Ecl.* 6.64ff). The terrain is also frigid and rocky, like the wilderness where Gallus wandered when love went wrong:

>   non me ulla vetabunt
> **frigor** Parthenios canibus circumdare saltus.
> iam mihi per **rupes** videor lucosque sonantes
> ire.   (Vergil, *Ecl.* 10.56–59)

>   No frosts will hinder me
> From drawing coverts on Parthenium with hounds.
> Already I see myself explore the sounding rocks
> and groves.

The worst may loom, if the beloved threatens to desert the lover's bed (1.8a). Inspiration, then, is in danger of fading forever. Despair reigns, because in her absence (its absence) there can only be indolence:

> quid mihi desidiae non cessas fingere crimen, ...
> tam multa illa meo divisa est milia lecto,
>   quantum Hypanis Veneto dissidet Eridano.
>   (1.12.1, 3–4)

> You charge me, friend, with sloth ...
> But Cynthia's sundered from my bed, you know,
> The leagues that part the Volga from the Po.

Here is a passage to bring us back again to both Gallus and Catullus. Not only is the Hypanis the river of the solitary non-papyrological fragment of Gallus; there also are resemblances in sound and word placement between the Propertian and the Gallan passages.[50] The Catullan connection, more shadowy, lies in the experience of serious emotional loss. In Propertius when the beloved leaves, poetry will cease. Similarly Catullus claims that the death of his brother was crushing enough to stop the flow of poetry, with the result that he had no consolatory pieces to send to his friend Allius (Catullus 68.1–30). Both the Gallan and the Catullan allusions, recondite as they are, call our attention again to Propertius' poetic program, specifically to the composition of spare, elegant, and artful poetry that is expressive of the most significant of human emotions.

When the beloved finally decides against departure, however, the lover-poet's contentment is restored. He joyously welcomes her back to his narrow bed, no ordinary one:

> illa vel **angusto** mecum requiescere **lecto**
>   et quocumque modo maluit esse mea ... .
>   (1.8.33–34)

> At any cost she'd rather (so she said)
> Be mine, and share with me a narrow bed ... .

This is a bed that Callimachus could happily lie in, because Propertius' punning use of *lecto* ("bed/ something read"), together with the modifier *angusto* ("narrow"), suggests refinement, selectivity, and careful reading (*angusto, lecto*). Indeed, two passages from the first poem of Book 2 confirm the Callimachean reference. One, an obvious echo of 1.8.33, plays with the now familiar notion of the *militia amoris*. The second, with *angusto* again occupying the second and third feet, refers to Callimachus himself:

> nos contra angusto versantes proelia lecto:
> qua pote quisque, in ea conterat arte diem.
> (2.1.45)

> To each his art—this subject tasks my day:
> The battle-field of bed, the lovers' fray.

> Sed neque Phlegraeos Iovis Enceladique tumultus
> intonet angusto pectore Callimachus.
> (2.1.39–40)

> Some mighty-breasted bard might thunder thus
> On Phlegra's plain—but not Callimachus.

When trials abate and love (inspiration) does come easily, the lover (poet) and his beloved (his poetry), can enjoy days and nights of harmony and be at peace. A quiet day with the beloved (i.e., a day spent successfully in composition) is as valuable as the gold of Lydia (*nam sive optatam mecum trahit illa quietem,/ seu facili totum ducit amore diem,/ tum mihi Pactoli veniunt sub tecta liquores*, "for whether she draws out quiet pleasures with me or spends the whole day in easy love, then waters of Pactolus come under my roof," 1.14.9–11). This is sweet food for reflection (*nostri cura subit memores a! ducere noctes?* "has care for me brought—ah!—nights full of memory?" 1.11.5). The atmosphere of 1.11 is enriched by association with Catullus 50, although there is no verbal link. In Catullus' poem, the poet savors a recent night of pure delight and sport—not making love with a woman (despite his erotic language), but composing poems with a friend. Propertius, by suggesting the Catullan scene and its linkage of love-making and the writing of poetry, again appropriates the love/poetry equation for himself. In Propertius, even the observation of another's success with a woman (i.e., reading Gallus' fine love poetry) induces the same sensation (*O iocunda quies, primo cum testis amori adfueram*, "O sweet peace, when first I was present as a witness to your love," 1.10.1–2).[51]

In a general but consistent way, Propertius also equates the poet's feelings toward his work with the feeling of a lover toward the beloved. The word for either is *cura*, a term useful for its flexibility. In the sense "concern" it typifies the ideal mutual attitude of lover and mistress: she is his *cura* and, he hopes, he is hers. On the poetic plane, however, *cura* can refer to the care in composition that was a primary concern of Alexandrian poets. This ambiguity is exploited in Vergil's *tua cura Lycoris*, "your concern/ mistress, Lycoris,"[52] a reference literally to Gallus' mistress, but a term which also suggests the trouble he took over the book of *Amores* addressed to her. For Propertius, too, *cura* has this double meaning: the amount of care lavished on a demanding mistress equals that spent on the finest poetry. He encourages lovers (poets) to cherish their mistresses, i.e., cultivate their own styles (*sua quemque moretur/ cura*, "let each one's care/mistress delay him," 1.1.35–36); warns prospective lovers (poets) of the troubles they face (*at tibi curarum milia quanta dabit*, "but how many thousands of cares will she give you," 1.5.10); and protests that his efforts at love (poetry) appear ineffectual in keeping his mistress (inspiration) at home by his side (*tune igitur demens, nec te mea cura moratur?* "Are you mad then, and does not my care make you pause?" 1.8.1).[53]

Finally, Propertius goes so far as to characterize his poems as riddles requiring solution, in a choice pun that links the break-up of his love affair with discovery of the meaning of his poems (*quo magis et nostros contendis solvere amores*, "the more you try to break apart our love," 1.4.15). Various other images further strengthen the association of complex poems and lovers' secrets. A lover's gifts are brought with hidden hands (*occultis ... manibus* 1.16.44), just as the poet's hand in secret hides meaning in the text. Love (composition) brings troubles that the lover (poet) keeps hidden from other people (1.18.3). The beloved reposes in silence (*molliter in tacito litore compositam*, [Cynthiam], "Cynthia gently arranged on the quiet shore," 1.11.14), like the delights of poetry that lie hidden in well-composed verse (also silent as it lies on the page). The lover also knows the joys that lie under the mistress' unrevealing clothing (*gaudia sub tacita dicere veste libet,* "it is pleasing to speak of joys under a concealing dress," 1.4.14), just as the poet knows the pleasures to be found in the discovery of his secret meanings.

The evidence for allegory assembled above is not exhaustive. I hope, however, it is sufficient to convince readers that love in the *Monobiblos* is a metaphor for poetic composition—that Propertius here is as deeply concerned with the nature of fine poetry as he is with the psychological effects of passion. From the beginning of the book almost to the end the language of love expresses simultaneously his principles of composition. Sexual passion represents the passion of poetic inspiration; the physical traits of the ideal mistress have the same description as fine poetry; the stress and frustration of a love affair are like the anxieties of a poet who aspires to Alexandrian standards of excellence in poetry. A significant achievement here, in fact, is that through the methodical application of allegory, Propertius has managed to apply Alexandrian principles to his poetry without exegesis, without formal announcement. Callimachus would approve of the subtlety.

¶

A question hovers, however, regarding the strange final poems of the *Monobiblos*. They are utterly dissimilar from those that precede. One wonders how a poet of such finesse, after so artfully composing and arranging[54] elegies of such elegance, could append two seemingly irrelevant poems. Neither contains a single reference to Cynthia or even to love between man and woman. Both in fact are funerary in form and subject. One purports to be the words of a dying Gallus. The other passes for a kind of *sphragis,* "seal," identifying the author in terms of his homeland and a kinsman who has died in war. Either would be more at home on a gravestone than in a book of love poems.

This affinity to funerary epigram is mainly significant for the shift in genre that it entails. Such a shift would naturally bring with it an alteration of the reader's expectations, because what a person anticipates in an epitaph is naturally different from one's expectations when reading poetry in any other genre. Specifically, a reader will look for the epigram to be more or less direct. Rhetorical polish has its place, but an epitaph is unlikely to be as riddling and arcane as elegy in the manner of Callimachus. It may exaggerate the agreeable characteristics of the dead and suppress the distasteful. But it would be unlikely to mask them in the kind of elaborate and learned literary flourishes that we have observed in the elegies of the *Monobiblos*. Propertius, by drastically altering his genre in these last two poems, has deliberately altered his voice. It is a signal to the reader that poems 1.21 and 1.22 should be read more as direct statements than as allegories. The poet here has put aside the love/poetry equivalencies of the preceding twenty poems. These are to be read straight. Yet surely in poetry as carefully crafted as Propertius' there is some significant connection between these and the preceding poems, despite their disparity of subject. The connection, not surprisingly, is the issue of poetry. The preceding elegies dwelt particularly on the process of composition. These face the paramount question of subject: what is it appropriate for a Callimachean poet to compose? The answer returns in the negative: "not epic."

We have seen already that Propertius supplied no formal Callimachean *recusatio* of epic poetry in the preceding poems. Yet whole elegies and portions of elegies can be read as arguing the case. In the seventh poem, for example, the poet cheerfully wishes Ponticus well in his rivalry with Homer but affirms his own choice to continue writing love poetry. This, he is confident, will bring him precisely the kind of fame (κλέος) conventionally reserved for the heroes of epic (*haec mea fama est,/ hinc cupio nomen carminis ire mei./ me laudent doctae solum placuisse puellae*, "this is my glory, from here I wish the name of my song to proceed. Let them praise me that I alone pleased a learned girl, 1.7.9–11).[55] If he offers no clamorous statement here or elsewhere of his refusal to compose epic, this is entirely consistent with his posture in the preceding elegies. There, a chief concern clearly was to display his governing poetic principles *without* formally announcing them. Poems 1.21 and 1.22 also lack any explicit *recusatio*, yet each strongly makes the case against epic. Their drastic change of form and their allusions to two famous passages from Greek poetry on war—one an epigram of Simonides, the other a scene from the *Iliad*—throw into still starker relief Propertius' stance on this paramount Callimachean principle.

The statement in 1.21 is direct but not blatant. The poem subtly echoes one of the most famous of ancient funerary epigrams, Simonides' couplet (109) on the Lacedemonians who fell at Thermopylae:

> ὦ ξεῖν', ἀγγέλλειν Λακεδαιμονίοις ὅτι τῇδε
> κείμεθα τοῖς κείνων ῥήμασι πειθόμενοι.

> Traveler, take this word to the men of Lakedaimon:
> We who lie buried here did what they told us to do.
> (trans. R. Lattimore)

> tu, qui consortem properas evadere casum,
>   miles ab Etruscis saucius aggeribus,
> quid nostro gemitu turgentia lumina torques?
>   pars ego sum vestrae proxima militiae.
> sic te servato ut possint gaudere parentes,
>   ne soror acta tuis sentiat e lacrimis:
> Gallum per medios ereptum Caesaris enses
>   effugere agnotas non potuisse manus;
> et quaecumque super dispersa invenerit ossa
>   montibus Etruscis, haec sciat esse mea.
> (Propertius 1.21)

> Soldier, hot-foot your comrades' fate to shun,
> As wounded from the Etrurian lines you run,
> Why do you, when my groanings reach your ear,
> Glare so on me, a friend-in-arms most near?
> Go safe, to glad your parents' eyes; and shed
> No tears, to tell your sister how I bled;
> How Gallus came from Caesar's swords unscarred,
> And by base hands was taken off his guard.
> Let him that finds the scattered bones that lie
> On Tuscan hills, pass mine in ignorance by.

In each epigram a soldier who has fallen in battle in mountainous terrain addresses a passer-by and entrusts him with a message for home.

The Propertian poem is longer than Simonides', more developed, and more meticulous in detail, but there are striking similarities between the two, and Propertius surely meant his reader to recall the Greek. The power of that poem derives from the scene of heroic futility that it describes: the battle of Thermopylae was a noble endeavor, but a vain one. Through blind obedience to military orders three hundred souls were lost. Nothing was gained but fame. Persia's invasion was barely impeded, and certainly not stopped.

The occasion for the Propertian epigram was evidently another tragic military adventure, the Perusine war of 41 B.C.[56] This was an episode of the civil wars in which the army of Octavian besieged the consul Lucius Antonius, brother of Octavian's co-triumvir Mark Antony. The siege was occasioned by Lucius' attempted revolt against Octavian at a time when relations between Octavian and Mark Antony were less than the best. But since Lucius had no clear encouragement from Antony for his revolt, and since Octavian and Antony were allied as triumvirs, Lucius' revolt against Octavian was in a sense also a revolt against his own brother: that is, it was at least symbolically fratricidal in purpose. However that detail rests, there was no question in Appian's mind at least of the *civil*, and therefore potentially fratricidal nature of the Perusine war. He offers this moving description of the surrender of Lucius' army:

> [Octavian's] own army, either purposely ... or moved by sympathy as for their own relatives, broke from the formation in which they had been placed, crowded around Lucius' men as they approached their former fellow-soldiers, embraced them, wept with them, and implored Octavian in their behalf, and ceased not crying out and embracing them, the new levies sharing in the outburst of feeling, so that it was impossible to distinguish or discriminate between them.[57]

As at Thermopylae, the Perusine war involved a painful siege. At the end, similarly, innocent souls were lost. In fact, the loss at Perusia was at least double that at Thermopylae. Herodotus' three hundred dead Lacedemonians were doubled by Octavian in the punishments he meted out after the siege: three hundred senators and three hundred *equites*—the greater part of each group in Perusia—were sacrificially executed.[58] Propertius' adumbration here of the Simonidean epigram underscores his distaste for war and the poetry of war. The futility of both adventures and their fratricidal elements (it was Greeks who betrayed the Lacedemonians) diminish the grandeur of epic, the genre in which such exploits would normally be celebrated. Moreover, Propertius himself was native to the region of Perusia and, as he says, lost kin in the struggle. His personal investment in this position is therefore all the deeper.

This is a point seen already by Joy King:[59] Propertius had personal experience in a war that was fratricidal and without point. That it was perpetrated by the very man who after Actium tried through Maecenas to persuade him to write a celebratory epic gives its antimilitarism all the more poignant force. Epic is unacceptable for poetic reasons, as Callimachus prescribed and as Propertius elsewhere suggests. That it is also repugnant to him for personal reasons is a point that he can make here—in the relatively candid context of a funerary epigram—but could hardly force into the elaborately artificial context of the earlier elegies.

The final poem is more directly a lament, again in the guileless and unsubtle manner of tomb inscriptions. As for poem 1.21 the epigrammatic form indicates that there is a direct correlation here between meaning and content. The poem, in its sorrowful reference to a kinsman killed in war, appears to supply a specific, personal explanation for Propertius' refusal to write epic poetry. Once again the war was doubtless one of the series of civil conflicts engaged in by Octavian in Italy. Once again, in light of personal experience, poetry celebrating the kill is repugnant, and for more than poetic reasons: it would elevate the person responsible for the death of the poet's own kin.

This is not all. The final poem also provides an argument against epic from epic itself—indeed from Homer—which should be sufficient to justify any poet's *recusatio*. It opens with a simple query:

> qualis et unde genus, qui sunt mihi, Tulle, Penates,
>   quaeris pro nostra semper amicitia.   (1.22.1–2)

> Tullus, you ask in our long friendship's name
> What rank, what birth, what household gods I
> claim.

The question appears bland enough, providing as it does an opportunity for the poet to identify himself. But note the terms. A similar question opened the memorable conversation between Diomedes and Glaucus at *Iliad* 6.123ff., where they discover a relation of friendship deriving from the friendship of their fathers. By the tenets of their social code, therefore, they cease mutual hostilities. Glaucus' actual response in this passage is of particular importance for understanding the Propertian epigram. It is one of the most stunningly anti-heroic passages of the *Iliad* and prepares the audience for the more shocking elaboration of the same idea when Achilles confronts the embassy in Book 9. Here in Book 6 Glaucus, as later Achilles, denies any lasting value to the pursuit of κλέος:

> High-hearted son of Tydeus, why ask of my generation?
> As is the generation of leaves, so is that of humanity.
> The wind scatters the leaves on the ground, but the live timber
> burgeons with leaves again in the season of spring returning.
> So one generation of men will grow while another dies.
>   (*Il.* 6.145–49)

As proof Glaucus offers the story of his blameless and heroic ancestor Bellerophontes who, although he overcame one heroic challenge after another, ended his life in ignominy, for no known reason:

> But after Bellerophontes was hated by all the immortals,
> he wandered alone about the plain of Aleios, eating
> his heart out, skulking aside from the trodden track of
> humanity.   (*Il.* 6.200–202)

Like Glaucus and Achilles, Propertius sees that if κλέος earned by traditional heroic means is ephemeral, the heroic code is bankrupt.

In addition, then, to poetic convention that since Callimachus had frowned on the composition of traditional epic, Propertius has offered in 1.21 and 1.22 two other, irrefutable reasons for avoiding the poetry of heroics. One is his personal experience of the worst effects of war. The other is the unanswerable testimony of history, and indeed of Homer himself. Although the final epigrams of the *Monobiblos* appear to have no part in the elaborately worked exercises in poetry and love which precede, in fact the elegies are only fully intelligible once we have comprehended these concluding poems. The finality of death becomes one of the strongest forces behind the poet's writing, as it was for Catullus. Propertius will escape extinction, however, because Cynthia, more beautiful than any heroine of Troy and allegorically his poetry, will outlive him (1.19.13–16, 19). By avoiding epic and by concentrating on her, that is, on his poetry, he assures his own κλέος.

Kathleen McNamee
Wayne State University

Notes

The paper originated in a 1988 elegy seminar, and profited from the acute sensibilities of those students. I am grateful to Mary DeForest for more help and re-readings than she would probably like to recall, to Michael Giordano and Richard Minadeo for advice on argumentation, and to my former colleague, Joy K. King, for painstakingly reading a draft and giving gracious advice. I offer it to her with trepidation, since I am a newcomer in her territory.

[1] For the text of Propertius I follow the edition of E. A. Barber (Oxford, 1960), for Vergil that of R. Mynors (Oxford, 1969), for Callimachus that of R. Pfeiffer (Oxford, 1949–53). The shorter translations are my own; other translations are those of A. E. Watts (Harmondsworth, 1966) for Propertius; Guy Lee (Harmondsworth, 1984) for Vergil; S. Lombardo and D. Rayor (Baltimore, 1988) for Callimachus; J. Michie (New York, 1969) for Catullus; and Richmond Lattimore (Chicago, 1951) for Homer's *Iliad*. The emphasis added to the quotations in bold type is my own.

[2] L. Richardson, Jr., *Propertius: Elegies I–IV* (Norman, 1976), writes, "In the course of studying P. closely the attentive reader eventually comes to the point where he no longer believes in the absolute truth of what the poet tells him about Cynthia and his love affair with her" (3). To be sure, Cynthia (like the other nameless women of the *Monobiblos*) varies from whorish to wifely, clinging to fickle, shrewish to sweet-tempered.

[3] For the theory that Archilochus' biography derives from the lying tales Odysseus told on Ithaca, see B. Seidensticker, "Archilochus and Odysseus," *Greek, Roman and Byzantine Studies*, 19 (1978), 5–22.

[4] A. W. Allen, "'Sincerity' in the Roman Elegists," *CP*, 45 (1966), 145–60; Joy K. King, "Catullus' Callimachean *Carmina*, cc. 65–116," *CW*, 81 (1988), 383–92; "Propertius' Programmatic Poetry and the Unity of the *Monobiblos*," *CJ*, 71 (1975–76), 109–24.

[5] According to Apuleius (*Apologia* 10), Cynthia is a pseudonym for one Hostia.

[6] For a comparable phenomenon in Elizabethan sonnets, see A. Marotti, "'Love is not Love': Elizabethan Sonnet Sequences and the Social Order," *ELH* (formerly *Journal of English Literary History*), 49 (1982), 396–428; there love is a metaphor for political and social ambition.

[7] D. O. Ross, Jr., *Backgrounds to Augustan Poetry* (Cambridge, 1975), 36–37.

[8] J. Zetzel, "Gallus, Elegy, and Ross," (review article) *CP*, 72 (1977), 249–60, especially 258. The identification of the Gallus of Vergil's *Eclogues* 6 and 10 with the poet originates with Servius.

[9] Recollections of Gallus abound in Propertius 1.1:

(a) The mythological exemplum beginning at Propertius 1.1.9 places Milanion in Arcadia, lovesick, and hunting; in *Eclogue* 10 Gallus, sick of love, in Arcadia, wants to hunt;

(b) The hunt takes both Milanion and Gallus among caves, to encounters with wild animals: *nam modo Partheniis amens errabat in antris/ ibat et hirsutas saepe videre feras* (Propertius 1.1.11–12), *certum est in silvis, inter spelaea ferarum malle pati* (*Ecl.* 10.52);

(c) For both Milanion and Gallus the landscape is "Parthenian": Propertius 1.1.11 (see b); *Parthenios ... saltus*, *Ecl.* 10.57. This is a topographical label, of course. It is also an acknowledgment by Vergil and by Propertius of the influence of Parthenius, who is credited with having introduced Alexandrian poetry at Rome and who composed for Gallus a set of ἐρωτικὰ παθήματα—prose accounts of obscure and contorted love affairs—with the intention expressed in the dedication that he might "have at hand a storehouse from which to draw material, as may seem best ... for either epic or elegiac verse," (trans. S. Gaselee [Cambridge, 1978]);

(d) Love brings madness to each: *furor hic*, Propertius 1.1.7, *quaerite non sani pectoris auxilia*, Propertius 1.1.26; *nostri medicina furoris*, *Ecl.* 10.60;

(e) For each, *cura* designates the object of affection: *sua quemque moretur/ cura* (Propertius 1.1.35–6), *tua cura Lycoris*, *Ecl.* 10.22

(f) Finally Propertius 1.1.29, *ferte per extremas gentis et ferte per undas* evokes Gallus' journey to the ends of the earth to escape the effects of love at *Ecl.* 10.65–

67 (the passage, of course, contains even stronger reminiscences of Catullus 101). Surviving fragments of Gallus' poetry: *Fragmenta Poetarum Latinorum*, ed. W. Morel (Stuttgart, 1963), 99; for the new fragment, P.Qasr Ibrim inv. 78-3-11/1, see R. D. Anderson, P. J. Parsons, R. G. M. Nisbet, "Elegiacs by Gallus from Qasr Ibrim," *Journal of Roman Studies*, 69 (1979), 25-55.

[10] E.g., Propertius 1.4.8–10 *Cynthia ... / nedum ... / inferior duro* **iudice** *turpis eat* and Gallus, P.Qasr Ibrim 9 (referring to poetry written for a mistress) *non ego, Visce/ ..]........l. Kato,* **iudice** *te vereor* (with *iudice* in the same metrical position in each); Propertius 1.5.3 and *Ecl.* 10.20, 22 (love and insanity); Propertius 1.5.27–28 and *Ecl.* 10.60 (medicine for love-madness); Propertius 1.18.1ff and *Ecl.* 10.65–69 (seeking release from love in geographical distance); Propertius 1.18.22 and *Ecl.* 10.53–54 (writing *Cynthia*, writing *amores* on trees). Also Propertius 1.5.10 *at tibi* **curarum milia** *quanta dabit* and *Ecl.* 10.22 *tua* **cura** *Lycoris*; Propertius 1.13.33 *tu vero, quoniam semel es periturus amore* (addressed to Gallus) and *Ecl.* 10.10 (Gallus dying of love).

[11] Of the most significant, I may mention Lucretius, whose observations on love Propertius implicitly opposes (I owe the reference to Joy King). P. Fedeli, "Elegy and Literary Polemic in Propertius' *Monobiblos*," *Papers of the Liverpool Latin Seminar*, 3 (1981), 227–42, points to others.

[12] The same Callimachean meaning is implied in *ducere* in passages that have no reference to love: 1.1.19 **deductae** *quibus est fallacia lunae*, and 23–24 *tunc ego crediderim vobis et sidera et amnes/ posse Cytaeines* **ducere** *carminibus*. See Ross' discussion (*Backgrounds*, 19, 26–27, 65–66).

[13] For Callimachus' emphasis on the superiority of short and carefully composed poems, see his *Aetia* frag. 1.9–12 and 17–24.

[14] On the ambiguity of *arguta* (1.16.16), see below. Other references to delicacy in poetry/love: 1.3.7, 12, 34; 1.5.8; 1.7.4; 1.11.11; 1.14.1; 1.17.22; 1.20.22; 1.20.39; 1.20.42.

[15] ......]ας οὐκ ἐν ἄεισμα διηνεκὲς ἢ βασιλ[η/ ἢ .....]. ους ἥρωας, ἔπος δ' ἐπὶ τυτθὸν ἐλ[ίσσω/ παῖς ἄτ]ε ... ("[The malignant gnomes who write reviews in Rhodes/ are muttering about my poetry again ...] because I have not consummated a continuous epic/ of thousands of lines on heroes and lords/ but turn out minor texts as if I were a child," *Aetia* frag. 1.1.3–6); βροντᾶ]ν οὐκ ἐμόν, [ἀλλὰ] Διός ("Not I but Zeus owns the thunder," *Aetia* 1.1.20).

[16] P. Murgatroyd, "*Militia Amoris* and the Roman Elegists," *Latomus*, 34 (1975), 59–79.

[17] See Hector's words to Achilles, οὐδ' ἄρ' ἔμελλον/ πείσειν· ἦ γὰρ σοί γε σιδήρεος ἐν φρεσὶ θυμός, "I know that I could not/ persuade you, since indeed in your breast is a heart of iron" (*Il.* 22.356–57).

[18] The term is modern: W. Wimmel, *Kallimachos in Rom; die Nachfolge seines apologetischen Dichtens in der Augusteerzeit* (Wiesbaden, 1960), 1.

[19] Ross, *Backgrounds*, 56. P. Fedeli, "Elegy and Literary Polemic," also stresses the Callimachean essence of the *Monobiblos*. For a concise study of Callimachean allusions in a single poem, see F. Cairns, "Propertius i.18 and Callimachus, *Acontius and Cydippe*," CR, 19 (1969), 131–33.

[20] *Mitto/ haec expressa tibi carmina Battiadae,* 65.15–16; *saepe tibi studioso animo venante requirens/ carmina uti possem mittere Battiadae,* 116.2. Surely neither passage refers literally to poems of Callimachus. For evidence of Catullus' adaptation of Callimachean poetics see King, "Catullus' Callimachean Carmina."

[21] E.g., the first poem echoes with suggestions of prominent Catullan poems:

(a) Catullus 85.1 **odi et amo** ... , and Propertius 1.1.4–5 *caput ... pressit* **Amor** *pedibus,/ donec me docuit castas* **odisse** *puellas*;

(b) Catullus 101.1 **multas per gentes** *et multa per aequora vectus* ... , and Propertius 1.1.29 *ferte* **per extremas gentis** *et ferte* **per undas**;

(c) Catullus 68.5–6 *quem neque sancta Venus molli requiescere somno/ desertum in lecto caelibe perpetitur,* and Propertius 1.1.33 *in me nostra Venus noctes exercet amaras* (note the metrical position of *Venus* in each);

(d) Catullus 76.7–8 *nam quaecumque homines* **bene** *cuiquam aut dicere possunt/ aut* **facere**, *haec a te dictaque factaque sunt,* and Propertius 1.1.16 *tantum in amore preces et* **bene facta** *valent. Bene ... facere* in Catullus 76.8 is the climax of a series of references to kindliness in the poems immediately preceding, so Propertius' Catullan echo is in fact louder than it might appear from this excerpt alone.

[22] What follows owes much to John Sarkissian, *Catullus 68: An Interpretation* (Leiden, 1983).

[23] The climax of Catullus 68, for example, is the moment when the poet's mistress steps delicately across the threshold of the house where they will conduct their affair:

> *quo mea se* **molli** *candida diva* **pede**
> **intulit** *et trito fulgentem in* **limine** *plantam*
>   *innixa* **arguta** *constituit solea. ...*   (Catullus 68.70–72)

> Visiting me there,
> My white-skinned goddess, tiptoeing, would put
> Her bright sole on the smooth-worn threshold, foot
> Poised on a creaking sandal. ...

By the adroit use of detail—the seemingly divine foot crossing the worn threshold in a squeaky sandal—Catullus fixes attention on the precise moment that began the love affair. Propertius evokes the very scene in 1.18:

> sic mihi te referas, **levis**, ut non altera nostro
>   **limine** formosos **intulit** ulla **pedes**.   (1.18.11–12)
>
> Yet no new mistress—else be mine no more—
> Has set her pretty foot inside my door.

Because of the momentousness of the occasion in Catullus 68 and Propertius' clear interest in it, other occurrences in the *Monobiblos* of *limen*, for example, or of *argut-* can evoke the same scene. They are impressively numerous for terms so specific in reference: *heu nullo* **limine** *carus eris*, 1.4.22; *a, mea contemptus quotiens ad* **limina** *curres*, 1.5.13; *illa [Venus] neque Arabium metuit transcendere* **limen**, 1.14.19; also 1.8.22, 1.13.34, 1.16.3, 22; for *argut-*, 1.6.7, 16.16, 18.26 (and see below).

[24] G. Nagy, *The Best of the Achaeans* (Baltimore, 1979), develops the idea.

[25] *Omnia* **vincit** *amor: et nos* **cedamus** *amori*, ("Love conquers all: we also must submit to Love," *Ecl.* 10.69).

[26] References to love in Gallus: *tristia nequit[ia....]a Lycori tua; .....] tandem fecerunt c[ar]mina Musae/ quae possem domina deicere digna mea*, P.Qasr Ibrim lines 1 and 6–7. The poem addressed to Caesar shows that Gallus entertained other subjects.

[27] Ross, *Backgrounds*, 51.

[28] Apollonius Rhodius 4.1490; Callimachus, *Hymn* 2.19; *Orphic Hymn* 33.1. Others note the linkage to cults of Apollo: e.g., M. Wyke, "Mistress and Metaphor in Augustan Elegy," *Helios*, 16 (1989); M. Hubbard, *Propertius* (London, 1974), 12; Ross, *Backgrounds*, 59.

[29] Strabo 10.452, 461; cf. Propertius: *Leucadius versas acies memorabit Apollo* (3.11.69).

[30] Ovid's Corinna (Κόριννα) is different: perhaps a reference to the poet, whom Propertius mentions at 2.3.21, perhaps diminuated reference to the poet's obsession with his girl/craft (κώρα/*cura*): see below, n. 52. Catullus, of course, also employed a poetic pseudonym in Lesbia.

[31] Ross, *Backgrounds*, 102.

[32] L. Curran, "'Nature to Advantage Dressed': Propertius 1.2," *Ramus*, 4 (1975), 1–16; Ross, *Backgrounds*, 58–59; Richardson, *Elegies I–IV*, 150. Cicero, too, made the analogy between cosmetics and rhetoric (*Letters to Atticus* 2.1).

[33] For other ambiguous references to appearance in general, s.v. *facies*, *cultus* in J. S. Phillimore, *Index verborum Propertianus* (1905; rpt. Darmstadt, 1966).

[34] The image applied to the writing of prose as well: Dionysius of

Halicarnassus used hairdressing as an image for Plato's pains with composition, as he continued to comb and curl and rebraid his dialogues all his life: κτενίζων καὶ βοστρυχίζων καὶ ... ἀναπλέκων (De compositione verborum 208).

[35] This reflects the Callimachean image of the roaring sea of epic, which Apollo disdains, and which Propertius evokes elsewhere even more explicitly (see F. Williams, *Callimachus: Hymn to Apollo* [Oxford, 1978], 98–99); Callimachus, Hymn 2.105–7: ὁ Φθόνος 'Απόλλωνος ἐπ' οὔατα λάθριος εἶπεν·/ "οὐκ ἄγαμαι τὸν ἀοιδὸν ὃς οὐδ' ὅσα πόντος ἀείδει."/ τὸν Φθόνον ...ὡπόλλων ποδί τ' ἤλασεν ὧδε τ' ἔειπεν· ... echoed by Propertius:

> Maecenas, eques Etrusco de sanguine regum
>   intra fortunam qui cupis esse tuam,
> quid me scribendi tam vastum mittis in aequor?
>   non sunt apta meae grandia vela rati.   (3.9.1–4)
>
> Maecenas, sprung from Tuscan kings, yet not
> Ambitious to exceed your knighthood's lot,
> On what vast sea of writing would you float
> Me, with large sails ill-fitted to my boat?

[36] Likewise her *pallor*: 1.1.22, 5.21, 15.39.

[37] At 1.20.8 the poet employs a similar pun in addressing Gallus: he speculates on the possible influence on Gallus' meter of Horace's metrical innovations (suggested by mention of the Anio river that passes through Tibur, the site of his famous farm): *sive Anio tuos tinxerit unda pedes.*

[38] Anna S. Benjamin, "A Note on Propertius 1.10. O *Iucunda Quies,*" CP, 60 (1965), 178.

[39] The question is hardly resolved. Those who identify the Gallus of the *Monobiblos* with the poet include Ross, *Backgrounds*, 82–84; Joy K. King, "The Two Galluses of Propertius' *Monobiblos*," *Philologus*, 124 (1980), 212–30. The following do not so identify Gallus: Fedeli, "Elegy and Literary Polemic"; W. A. Camps, *Sextus Propertius: Elegies, Book I* (Cambridge, 1961), 57; Hubbard, *Propertius*, 25; Richardson, *Elegies I–IV*, 8.

[40] Other cases in which the language of lovers can also refer to the language of poetry: *tibi singultu fortia verba cadent* (1.5.14); *illa suis verbis cogat amare Iovem* (1.13.32); *desine iam revocare tuis periuria verbis [Cynthia]* (1.15.25); *at mea nocturno verba cadunt zephyro* (1.16.34).

[41] R. Pfeiffer, *History of Classical Scholarship* (Oxford, 1988), 129; cf. P.Oxy. XXVI 2455.

[42] Propertius 2.24.1–2; Martial 14.189; Richardson, *Elegies I–IV*, 8.

[43] M. Wyke, "Written Women: Propertius' *Scripta Puella*," *Journal of*

Roman Studies, 77 (1987), 47–61.

[44] The carving on trees in 1.18 is in conscious imitation of *Eclogue* 10, a portion of which (46–49) Servius says Vergil adapted from Gallus. Ross argues that Vergil chose a programmatic poem from Gallus (*Backgrounds*, 73; for carving, see also Cairns, "Propertius i.18"):

> A! tibi ne **teneras** glacies secet aspera plantas!
> ibo et Chalcidico quae sunt mihi condita versu
> carmina pastoris Siculi modulabor avena.
> certum est **in silvis,** inter spelaea ferarum
> malle pati **tenerisque meos incidere amores
> arboribus.** crescent illae, crescetis, amores.
>
> (*Ecl.* 10.49–54)

> Ah, may the rough ice never cut *your* tender feet!
> I'll go and tune to the Sicilian shepherd's oat
> The songs I put together in Chalcidic verse.
> The choice is made—to suffer in the woods among
> The wild beasts' dens, and carve my love into the bark
> Of tender trees: as they grow so my love will grow.

[45] I owe the observation to Mary DeForest.

[46] For *silva* as a collection of miscellaneous poems, see Quintilian 10.3.17.

[47] See also Phillimore, under *lacrim-, fle-, miser-, dolor-*.

[48] Even the topographical marker emphasizes the poetic subtext. The poet Parthenius was responsible for a surge of interest at Rome in Alexandrian poetry, and dedicated a collection of bizarre love-stories to Gallus with the express hope that he should use them as material for his poems. The use of *antrum*, a neoteric addition to Latin vocabulary from the Greek, also contributes to the Alexandrian coloration of the passage.

[49] Propertius, acknowledging the incomprehensibility of inspiration, credits the beloved (i.e., the poet's inspiration) with insanity as well: 1.4.17, *sciet haec insana puella*; 1.6.16, *Cynthia et insanis ora notet manibus*; 1.18.14–15, *non ita saeva tamen venerit ira mea,/ ut tibi sim merito semper furor* ... .

This link of poetic inspiration with insanity does not originate here, of course. Plato considers the inspired enthusiasm of the rhapsode in *Ion*; and cf. Horace, *Satire* 2.7.117, *aut insanit homo aut versus facit*. Propertius returns to the theme frequently in the *Monobiblos* (see Phillimore, under *furor, insan-, demen-*).

[50] Gallus, *uno tellures dividit amne duas* (*Fragmenta Poetarum Latinorum*, 99). Propertius' *illa*, separated physically from *lecto* by *divisa est*, and his *Hypanis* separated from *Eridano* by *dissidet* both recall the separation of Gallus' *tellures*

and *duas* by *dividit*. *Dividit* itself is echoed in both sound and placement by Propertius' *divisa est* and *dividit*.

[51] Benjamin, "A Note on Propertius 1.10."

[52] *Ecl.* 10.22. *Cura* is a playful conversion of κώρα (see Theocritus 1.81–83 and Ross, *Backgrounds*, 69).

[53] Other occurrences of *cura*: 1.3.46, 11.5, 11.22, 13.7, 15.31, 18.23.

[54] Joy K. King, "Propertius' Programmatic Poetry"; O. Skutsch, "The Structure of the Propertian *Monobiblos*," *CP*, 58 (1963), 238–39.

[55] Elegies 9 and 14 boast the superiority of elegy over other genres, in particular epic. Elegy 8, I think, deals specifically with the impossibility of epic. In 8a, Cynthia is on the verge of a journey which in its details matches Lycoris' pursuit of the troops (*Ecl.* 10.46ff) and in its language recalls Callimachus' description of the bombastic poetry of war (*tune audire potes vesani murmura ponti/ fortis?* 1.8.5–6; cf. Callimachus, *Hymn* 2.105–12). That is to say, the mistress (poetry) may turn to war (epic). In 8b she has chosen to stay. The poet and his ways (i.e., elegy) are preferred.

[56] Appian, *Bellum Civile* 5.32–49; Cassius Dio 48.14; cf. E. Gabba, "The Perusine War and Triumviral Italy," *Harvard Studies in Classical Philology*, 75 (1971), 139–60.

[57] Appian, *Bellum Civile* 5.46, trans. H. White (Cambridge, 1928).

[58] Cassius Dio 48.14.3–4.

[59] King, "Propertius' Programmatic Poetry," especially 122.

From a Sure Foot to Faltering Meters: The Dark Ladies of Tibullan Elegy

After the last appearance of Delia at the end of 1.6, and before the first glimpse of Nemesis in 2.3, there appear in the *Elegies* of Tibullus four abstract forces personified in female form and described in terms of how their feet move: *Aetas* ("Period of Life," in this case Youth), on a foot that is not slow (*primi temporis Aetas/ ... non tardo ... pede*, 1.8.47–48); Punishment, on silent feet (*tacitis Poena ... pedibus*, 1.9.4); Death, on a silent foot (*Mortem/ tacito ... pede*, 1.10.33–34); and Night, whose dark Dreams move on an uncertain foot (*Nox/ ... et incerto Somnia nigra pede*, 2.1.87–90). These personified phenomena portray various forms of suffering and loss embodied in female form and, as such, constitute part of a continuum of increasingly dark portrayals of women in the *Elegies* that begins with the relatively realistic and, at least initially, amenable figure of Delia and culminates with the unreal, fleshless figure of the cruel Nemesis.

Before I discuss these passages more closely, a word of explanation about my inclusion of the neuter *nigra Somnia* is in order. Though neuter plural, *nigra Somnia* are presented in 2.1 as part of the feminine Night (2.1.87–90). In a reference to her Hesiodic genealogy (*Theog.* 211ff.; *Works and Days* 223–24), *Nox* is depicted here as the mother of both *Somnus* and *Somnia*,[1] leading her offspring in a procession that brings a close to the day of ritual purification—the central topic of the poem—and brings darkness to the amorous play that is introduced with the mention of *Cupido* at line 67. *Somnia*, Hesiod's φῦλον Ὀνείρων, among the parthenogenetically produced offspring of Night, are *part* of the night, one of its many aspects. The metonymic logic of the genealogy invites us to consider the attributes of Night's children, such as the unsure foot of the *nigra Somnia* at 2.1.90, among the attributes of Night herself. Further, the structure of the four-line vignette, which opens with *Nox* at 87 and closes (as does the poem) with *pede* at 90, supplies a poetic linkage between Night and the unsure foot. I thus regard *nigra Somnia* as part of the female *Nox* and include them in the present discussion.

I will argue in this paper that these figures constitute a continuation of the elegiac love theme, in part because two of them appear in the context of the Marathus affair, but, more significantly, because they are depicted as women who, like other women in elegy,[2] inflict suffering and loss.[3] The impact of each of these forces is described in terms of how her feet move, recalling the feet of lovers in the previous Delia poems (1.2.20, 1.2.37, 1.3.92, 1.6.62) and foreshadowing the poems' final expression of the forbidding female in the figure of Nemesis, whose feet we never see, but whose cruelty inspires a displacement of the poet/lover's erotic energies into the creation of metrical feet of poetry (2.5.109–12).

Age

In poem 1.8 the poet-lover (who loves Marathus) speaks to Pholoe (whom Marathus loves), urging her not to treat Marathus badly. In a speech that contrasts youthful love with the love of old age (27ff.), asserting the superiority of the former and denouncing the latter as the proper domain of love-gifts (and the female greed that demands them), he warns Pholoe that the springtime of life slips away with a foot that is not slow:

>   at tu dum primi floret tibi temporis Aetas[4]
>   utere: non tardo labitur illa pede.   (1.8.47–48)

>   But you, while the Age of first time flowers for you,
>   enjoy it: not with a slow foot does she slip away.

The personification of Youth, *primi temporis Aetas*, is achieved with the ambulatory foot, and its feminine gender emphasized with *illa* in line 48.

Youth's swift foot here recalls two previous instances of swift feet in the poems, both in fantasies of happier times: one of Delia running to meet the poet-lover at 1.3.92, the other of the swift foot that presses grapes at 1.5.24. Here in 1.8 Youth is personified as a woman slipping away on a swift foot, an image that identifies the too swift passage of time with a woman's elusiveness. This deployment of Youth as a woman presents elusiveness as an aspect of her gender, and her consequent power as agent of deprivation casts retrospective gloom on the previous instances of swift feet. Swift feet that run to meet a lover, swift feet that press grapes: these youthful pleasures, like swift-footed Youth herself, are ephemeral and will not stay long. Pleasure thus thwarted constitutes one version, one construction, of desire in these poems.

Punishment

At 1.9.4 the poet scolds Marathus for broken promises with the threat that, in the end, Punishment comes on silent feet.

> a miser, et si quis primo periuria celat,
> sera tamen tacitis Poena venit pedibus. (1.9.3–4)

> Oh wretched one, even if someone at first hides perjuries, late nonetheless does Punishment come on silent feet.

Here the severe *Poena*, a Greek goddess of punishment and revenge, and essentially equivalent to the Hesiodic Nemesis,[5] stalks deceitful lovers. The silence of her approach—described in terms of her feet— adds stealth to severity, combining the traits of an elegiac *domina* with those of a traditional Roman *severa mater*. We recall the foot that at 1.2.20 slips out of bed silently, *nullo sono*, where silence facilitates an elegiac encounter by deceiving the established partner.[6] Here in 1.9 the poet-lover is the injured party—the beloved Marathus has sold out to a rich lover—and he calls upon the threatening *Poena* in a desperate and, we sense, doomed attempt to preserve the integrity of his own erotic interests by casting blame on Marathus' treachery. *Poena*, with her silent, unannounced feet, is deployed not in amatory anticipation but as an agent of revenge upon Marathus for his infidelity. In this, the last of the four Marathus poems, Punishment's silent feet recall that earlier, happier construction of elegiac love in a contrast that suggests that elegiac love has begun to sour. *Poena*, in her dark, forbidding presence, recalls the brighter presentation of the early Delia, while she anticipates the darker, denying figure of the Tibullan Nemesis in the poems of Book 2.

Death

Also on silent feet comes *Mors*, Death, at 1.10.33.

> quis furor est atram bellis accersere Mortem?
> imminet et tacito clam venit illa pede.
> (1.10.33–34)

> What madness is it to summon dark Death with wars?
> She hangs over us and comes secretly on a silent foot.

This passage recalls not only the silent feet of *Poena* at 1.9.4 and of the lover at 1.2.20, but also a previous appearance in the *Elegies* of Death personified as a woman. With her head veiled and accompanying creeping Age, Death appears at 1.1.70–71, where together the two crones threaten to interrupt, all too soon, the pleasures of youthful love. Here in 1.10 Death, summoned by wars, is portrayed as a threat not to erotic pleasures but to the simple pleasures of an idealized rustic existence.[7] Smith compares these two appearances of Death (1.1.69–70 and 1.10.33–34), and remarks on the ancients' "keen perception of these relentless figures, dogging our footsteps unseen, unheard, unsuspected, and, when they finally reach us, always a surprise."[8] I would add to Smith's observation that very often these "relentless figures" are women.[9] An analysis of the ancients' feminization of life's dark forces is beyond the scope of this discussion, but I do call attention to Tibullus' appropriation of the phenomenon in his *Elegies*, where much of what is unpleasant and inevitable in life takes female form.[10] The silent steps of Death here, like those of Punishment at 1.9.4, embody in female form forces that thwart pleasure, in the former case erotic pleasure, in the latter, the pleasures of rustic peace.

Night's Dark Dreams

As discussed briefly above, dark Dreams, offspring of Night and part of a procession led by her, come in the last line of 2.1 on an uncertain foot, *incerto pede*.

> ludite: iam Nox iungit equos, currumque sequuntur
>   matris lascivo sidera fulva choro,
> postque venit tacitus furvis circumdatus alis
>   Somnus et incerto Somnia nigra pede.
>   (2.1.87–90)

> Play around: already Night yokes her steeds, and upon their mother's car follow the yellow stars in a lusty band, and behind comes silent Sleep encircled by dark wings and dark Dreams on an unsure foot.

In this poem of ritual purification in which the erotic is specifically prohibited (11ff.), a rustic Cupid intrudes (67) in a clever fusion of the agricultural with the erotic. The poet makes an appeal to enjoy youth (85ff.), for looming in the near background is Night followed by Sleep, silent and encircled by dark wings, and dark Dreams on an unsure foot. The unsure foot of Night's dark Dreams here recalls the sure foot of the farmer earlier in the poem:

> agricola adsiduo primum satiatus aratro
>   cantavit certo rustica verba pede
> et satur arenti primum est modulatus avena
>   carmen, ut ornatos diceret ante deos ... ,
>   (2.1.51–54)

> The farmer, sated with constant plowing first sang rustic words with a *sure step* and when sated was the first to play on the dry reed a song, so that he might speak before decorated gods ... ,

His life in a proper and pleasurable rhythm, the farmer works in the daylight and sings and dances when his work is done. His sure step, *certo pede*, signifies the confidence and appropriate balance of ideal georgic existence. By contrast, the unsure step of black Dreams at the end of the poem, following a reinstatement of the erotic with the entry of *Cupido* at 67,[11] is part of Night and all that she implies: fears of time's passage and uneasy apprehensions associated with the world of dreams, which, as Putnam suggests, in this context are probably nightmares.[12] Desire, as Tibullus constructs it, invades every sphere of life; even a rite of rustic purification is not safe from its effects. The sure foot of the farmer (who is, significantly, a poet, *cantavit rustica verba ... et modulatus est carmen*, 52–54) near the center of the poem, has by the end of the poem become the unsure foot of dark Dreams. Controlled rustic rhythms have been thrown off-balance by desire, portrayed here as a mischievous, boyish and, at the same time, mature Cupid, under whose generalship (*hoc duce*, 2.1.75), a secret rendezvous of lovers (complete with feet groping for paths in the dark) is carried out. Just as the feet of the robust farmer dance in rustic pleasure, the feet of lovers find one another in the dark in a stock scene of elegiac love. The unsure foot of dark Dreams at the close of the poem, by contrast, threatens those pleasures by reminding us that they are ephemeral and by calling up the dark side of psychic life that dreams signify. While it is the introduction of Cupid that transgresses the stated boundaries of the poem (lines 11–12) and diverts the narrative from the agricultural to the sexual, Cupid himself becomes comfortably incorporated into the rustic setting and revered as one of its gods (line 83). It is the dark Lady Night who constitutes a threat to human pleasures, both sexual and domestic.

In summary, these abstract phenomena, personified as women and characterized in terms of how their feet move, form part of a continuum of elegiac women who bring unhappiness and thwart pleasure. This continuum, which begins with the initially bright figure of Delia and culminates with the dark and denying figure of Nemesis, exposes an identification between the female forms depicted and the poet's political and literary anxieties, expressed in the four passages just discussed as so many of life's dark forces. As a site for the expression of such concerns, each of these feminized phenomena, by thwarting erotic pleasure or disrupting rustic peace, comes as an agent of unfulfilled desire. Delia and Nemesis, the two "mistresses" of the elegies who frame this continuum of elegiac women, similarly represent not real-life beloveds of the poet, but subjects of literary discourse through which the poet articulates political position and poetic program. From the seemingly "real" feet of Delia to the metonymically displaced feet of poetry that Nemesis, in her cruelty, inspires (2.5.109–12), female flesh serves as the referent of erotic endeavor (sexual, agricultural, political) and its literary construction.

Brenda H. Fineberg
Knox College

Notes

[1] Pointing to a poetic unity among all four of the personified figures under discussion, Night is also the mother of Age, Punishment, and Death: corresponding to Tibullus' *Aetas, Poena,* and *Mors,* are Hesiod's *Geras, Nemesis,* and *Thanatos* (*Theog.* 211ff.).

The translations of the Latin passages are my own.

[2] I follow Maria Wyke's use of the term "elegiac woman" to identify elegy's female figures not as girl-friends or other "real" people but as narrative subjects. See Wyke's "Reading Female Flesh: *Amores* 3.1," in *History as Text: The Writing of Ancient History,* ed. Averil Cameron (London, 1989), 117.

[3] Not all women in elegy, of course, are portrayed as causes of suffering and loss. However, the "good women" in elegy tend to be idealized for maternal and other nurturing qualities, and thus represent not a more positive presentation of women but, rather, one that is as polarized and as fictional as are the representations of the *durae puellae.* An example of such a positive female force is *Pax* at 1.10.45–50 and 1.10.67–68, whose idealized portrayal as a nurturing caretaker of agrarian affairs constitutes a deployment of woman as political signifier that is as polarized as the depictions of the darker female forces under discussion. As Lauren Berlant has said, "America, post-Utopia: Body, Landscape, and National Fantasy in Hawthorne's *Native Land,*" *Arizona Quarterly,* 44, Number 4 (Winter 1989), of the Statue of Liberty, "... the political deployment of the female icon often thematizes her 'power' as a quality of her gender" (21). For an insightful discussion of the range of elegiac women and their various political significances as narrative subjects, see Maria Wyke, "The Elegiac Woman at Rome," *Proceedings of the Cambridge Philological Society,* 213, n.s. 33 (1987b), 153–78.

[4] Editorial convention seems rather arbitrary in the capitalization of personified forces such as these. *Aetas* occurs four times in Tibullus and none is capitalized in available editions; *Poena* occurs six times, capitalized in Postgate's 1915 edition only at 1.9.4 (among the passages presently under discussion), and by Kirby Flower Smith (using Hiller's 1885 recension) not at

all; *Mors* occurs nine times, of which Postgate capitalizes three, not including the one under discussion here, while Smith capitalizes this instance (1.10.33) and four others, leaving only three uncapitalized; *Somnia* (occuring only here in Tibullus) and *Somnus* at 2.1.90 have been capitalized by both Postgate and Smith. *Somnus* occurs seven times elsewhere in the poems, none of them capitalized in modern editions. With one exception (the capitalization of *Mors* at 1.3.65), Putnam's capitalization follows that of Postgate. In keeping with a convention that seems to allow (but does not consistently require) the capitalization of personified phenomena, I have capitalized each of the four figures under discussion.

[5] *Poine*, the goddess of retribution, while not among the deities featured in the *Theogony*, appears in tragedy (Aeschylus, *Eum.* 323, *Choe.* 947; Euripides, *Iphigenia in Tauris* 200). As Smith, 360, and others have noted, *Poena* in Tibullus 1.9 is a metaphor for Nemesis, Retribution, whom Hesiod identifies as one of the offspring of Night at *Theogony* 223. *Poena* also appears in Horace at *Odes* 3.2.31 where, in spite of a lame foot, *pede claudo*, she rarely forsakes the guilty.

[6] Within the context of elegiac love, silence is essential to the success of illicit encounters, while the *sound* of approaching feet often signals a lover's arrival, as at 1.6.62 and 1.8.66.

[7] It is interesting that the pre-iron Golden Age described in lines 15–28 of 1.10 is inhabited by the poetic Ego as a young child. In psychological terms, of course, (but always only in retrospect) childhood *is* the pre-iron, pre-erotic, Golden Age(cf. Ament's essay in this volume). Also noteworthy is the intrusion of the erotic near the end of the poem, lines 53–66, where *bella* (cf. lines 7, 13) are now wars of Venus. The ages of human history, from Golden Age to savage wars, in other words, seem to have their analogue in the psychological ages of the individual.

[8] Kirby Flower Smith, *The Elegies of Albius Tibullus* (Darmstadt, 1971), 382.

[9] If we take Hesiod as an example, the line of descent that begins with the feminine Night includes thirteen female offspring (nine of them decidedly negative or unpleasant), and six male ones.

[10] While my present discussion is limited to passages that depict such personified figures explicitly "on foot," they appear elsewhere in the poems as well. In the case of *Mors* alone, for example, a personified presentation could be argued for 1.3.4–5, 1.3.65, and 2.4.43 (in addition to 1.1.70–71 and 1.10.33–34).

[11] Recall the similarly abrupt entrance of the erotic near the end of 1.10, note 7 above.

[12] Michael Putnam, *Tibullus: A Commentary* (Norman, 1973), 162–63.

Horace, *Satire* 1.8: Whence the Witches? Thematic Unity within the Satire and within the Satires of Book 1

Within Horace's first book, *Satire* 8 seems unique. In it Horace presents no Romans rooted in the realities of day-to-day existence, as he does in his other satires. We meet instead characters of a very different ilk: Priapus, a nervous garden god who speaks the monologue that is the satire, and the witches Canidia and Sagana, who emerge in the dark of the night to work their magic in the garden Priapus is supposed to protect. These three—Priapus, the witches, and the garden in which they converge—have something crucial in common. At the time we meet them, all have attained a new and different identify, an identity that is, superficially at least, more impressive than their former, original identity. Through their parallel stories, the rise from lowly origin to prestigious position becomes the primary theme of *Satire* 8. The same theme, moreover, is pivotal in Horace's own life. From his obscure birth as the son of a lowly freedman, Horace rose to the lofty position of trusted member of Maecenas' charmed circle. This paper will examine the theme of newly acquired identity within *Satire* 8 and will demonstrate the means by which this theme causes the satire to achieve unity within Book 1 of Horace's *Satires*. It will answer the question, "Whence the witches?" From what impetus has Horace drawn the unruly invaders of the gracious garden? What, in the end, is their purpose?

The figure of Priapus is central in *Satire* 8. In its first section (1–7), the garden god describes the circumstances of his rise to his current position. He began life as a mere stick of fig wood, and this base origin not only frames the satire (*ficulnus*, 1 and *ficus*, 47), but also supplies the central joke. Despite the fact that he has been carved into a *deus* (3), a transformation that resulted from the whim of a craftsman who decided against making the log into a footstool, Priapus' initial description of himself as a "useless stick of wood" (*inutile lignum*, 1) remains true. Fig wood holds no appeal to woodworkers because it is soft and prone to split, and, true to his nature, Priapus eventually splits with an onomatopoetic fart (*pepedi*, 46), caused by his abject shuddering at the magic rites of the witches. Thus the garden guardian inadvertently fulfills the purpose for which he has been created: he scares off the nocturnal invaders and a good laugh is enjoyed by all.

The second section of the satire (8–16) delineates a comparable transformation in identity on the part of the garden Priapus guards. This garden was located on a section of the Esquiline Hill outside the city walls of Rome and formerly used as a common graveyard (*commune sepulcrum*, 10) for the dregs of society: slaves, criminals, and the poor. According to Porphyrio, the site had been purchased by Maecenas and planted with attractive new gardens. Horace's description of the idyllic retreat of the present (14–15) is sandwiched between two longer, more detailed descriptions of the burial ground of the past (8–13, 16–20), and the repetition of *agrum* at the ends of both lines 12 and 16 draws attention to the fact that the gracious new garden is the very same place as the gruesome graveyard, only transformed. By means of analogous stories, then, and the temporal adverbs *olim* (1), introducing Priapus' origin, and *prius* (8), introducing the origin of the garden, Horace draws a parallel between the wooden figure and the plot that he guards. From lowly, even abject, beginnings the two have attained the impressive positions of god and garden.

The stories of Priapus and the Esquiline garden prepare the way for the arrival of the apparently frightening witches, Canidia and Sagana, who barge into the garden in the dead of night to collect bones and herbs and to perform their magic rites. When they first appear, in bare feet, with their hair streaming down and their black dresses hitched up, they are formidable. The frightened Priapus would like to stop them, but he admits that he is helpless (*has nullo perdere possum/ nec prohibere modo*, "These can I neither destroy nor prevent," 20–21). In this way Horace prepares us for the episode that follows, the visit of Canidia and Sagana as witnessed by the inept Priapus (23–45).

Two important story lines comprise this section. The magic rites of the witches traditionally receive attention, but the response of Priapus is equally important. The witches arrive, pale and horrible to see. They scrape the earth with their fingernails, tear apart a black lamb with their teeth, pour its blood into a ditch, and call forth ghosts of the dead that are attracted by the smell of the fresh blood, hoping to drink of it and thereby recover some of the lost vigor of life. Next they produce two figurines, one of wool and one of wax. The larger, woolen figure probably represents Canidia, the younger of the two witches and the leader in the rites; the smaller, waxen one represents a man whom she wishes to charm, probably a lover.[1] The rest of the witches' ceremony is dedicated to the accomplishment of their magic spell. They make the waxen image stand like a suppliant, cringing in the manner of a slave about to die while the woolen image towers above and inflicts punishments. As Canidia and Sagana shout out for Hecate and Tisiphone, Priapus claims he can see serpents and hell hounds wandering about. The witches' rites are indeed horrifying and repulsive, but since their ceremony is paralleled in magical papyri,[2] we see that Canidia's and Sagana's activities in Horace's vivid depiction are all aspects of practical magic performed in Rome at the popular level. Canidia and Sagana are doing what witches do—no more, no less.[3]

Priapus, for his part, is horrified at what he sees. The role of the god as witness to the scene frames this section; *vidi egomet*, "I myself saw "(23) starts it and *non testis inultus*, "no helpless bystander" (44) ends it. According to Priapus, the moon, who first had helped Canidia and Sagana find their bones and herbs (21), now blushes and hides behind tall tombstones so as not to witness all the gory details of their ceremony (*ne foret his testis*, 36). Priapus, therefore, claims he alone is left to tell the morbid story, and, to make sure we believe him, he interrupts his narration to swear an oath that he is telling the truth: "But if I am lying about anything," he vows, "may my head be dirtied by the white droppings of black crows, and may Julius and the weakling Pedatia and the thief Voranus come to urinate and defecate on me" (37–39). The vulgarity of this oath, alas, gives Priapus away. Instead of the solemn and austere language of a formal oath, he uses vocabulary straight out of the city cesspool. Instead of invoking a string of deities or the names of one deity, he calls upon three urban good-for-nothings. Regardless of the form he has taken, Priapus reveals that he is not by nature divine.

Priapus' abject shivering at the witches is fortunate in the end because it causes the fart that frightens Canidia and Sagana into running away. As they run, Canidia drops her false teeth, Sagana loses her wig, and they both let go of the magic herbs and the laces they had been carrying. As a result, the two initially formidable creatures, who only moments before were a source of terror to Priapus, are revealed to be mere women dressed up as witches. Moreover, since Canidia has lost her teeth and Sagana her hair, they now appear ugly and old. The witches, therefore, turn out to be analogous to Priapus and his garden. They are really abject creatures who had assumed a false and far more impressive identity.

The theme of the upstart, then, links Priapus, the garden, and the witches within *Satire* 8. All three derive from origins inferior to those a Roman would consider common or ordinary. The original idenitities of all three—fig wood, a paupers' burial site, and ugly, old women— were regarded by the Romans as worthless and even repulsive. The thematic structure of the stories of Priapus and his garden prepare for and necessitate the understanding of Canidia and Sagana as unwanted creatures masquerading in witch costumes rather than as powerful and horrifying agents of the underworld. Their primary role in *Satire* 8 is to reinforce the theme that creates unity within the satire, the theme of the upstart.

The thematic links between *Satire* 8 and the other satires of Book 1 have long perplexed analysts. Sometimes *Satire* 8 is dismissed. Both it and *Satire* 7 have been viewed as bits of fluff composed solely for entertainment and yielding little insight into Horace's life or opinions.[4] More recently, however, analysts have argued that the contrast between past and present in *Satire* 8 carries both political and literary significance. The garden belongs to Horace's patron, Maecenas, who, though not mentioned directly, is conjured up by the careful explanation of the setting, and by his implied presence establishes an autobiographical link for the satirist. Fraenkel, Rudd, Coffey, and Anderson understand Horace's reference to Maecenas as a form of tribute from poet to patron.[5] Anderson, furthermore, reads the satire as an expression of Horace's poetic program (disagreement with Lucilius and belief in the efficacy of laughter over invective) and proposes that "the rather genial, easily shocked Priapus may suggest ... some of the positive values of Maecenas' circle, whereas the malevolent witches suggest the literary opponents who are too devoted to the dead, destructive past."[6] In his zeal for finding opposition within the satire, however, Anderson disregards the strong thematic links among Priapus, the witches, and the garden within *Satire* 8 and mistakenly views Canidia and Sagana as frightening and inimical.

Canidia and Sagana are no more malevolent or threatening than is Priapus or his garden; all, instead, bear repugnant attributes. The witches do indeed frighten Priapus with their get-ups and their carryings-on, but Priapus himself, armed with his red phallus (*ruber ... palus*, 5) and reed stuck in the top of his head (*in vertice harundo/ ... fixa*, 6–7) delights in being a supreme source of fear for thieves and birds (*furum aviumque/ maxima formido*, 3–4). All remember the garden as formerly loaded with white bones (*albis ... ossibus*, 16), the remnants of which even now draw the witches to the site. At the end of *Satire* 8, morover, Horace explicitly directs his readers to regard Canidia and Sagana as laughable, not frightening. After he has uncovered their true identity, the satirist invites us, through Priapus, to share in recognition of the humor-filled reality of the situation (*cum magno risuque iocoque videres*, "you would see with great laughter and joking," 50).

This conclusion summons to mind Horace's self-proclaimed hallmark of his satiric style (*ridentem dicere verum*, "speaking the truth with a laugh," 1.1.24), and it becomes possible to see Horace's purpose in creating the analogous upstarts of *Satire* 8. Horace is smilingly telling the truth about himself. The satirist, too, acquired a new identity when he left behind his humble birth as the son of a freedman and entered into the circle of close personal friends of the lofty Maecenas. Maecenas, as we know from the dedication of *Satire* 1 and the personal tributes of *Satires* 4, 6, and 8, set the standard of excellence in Horace's life.

In *Satires* 4 and 6 Horace provides the most information about himself, and two of the themes he emphasizes in his own biography recur in his depiction of the upstarts of *Satire* 8. Most important is the theme of his humble origin, a theme granted center stage in *Satire* 6. At the opening of the piece Horace comes quickly to this theme by praising Maecenas' willingess to judge men on the basis of their character rather than their birth. This openness, after all, was what allowed the great man to accept Horace into his circle despite the fact that the poet was the son of a lowly ex-slave (*libertino patre natum*, 6.6), a label that is repeated as a derogatory chant in 6.45 and 6.46. The second theme, which Horace mentions in both *Satires* 4 and 6, is that of personal flaws.

Horace admits that he possesses moderate personal flaws, but claims that he is free of those faults that bring disaster (4.129–31, 137–40; 6.65–70). The satirist thereby acknowledges that he possesses the same flawed profile as does each of the players in Satire 8. All then—Priapus, the garden, Canidia, Sagana and the satirist—are analogous. Each is an upstart who can appear quite impressive in a newly acquired identity, but who can also be "unmasked" because he or she derives from lowly beginnings and retains a number of residual flaws from this base origin. The question "Whence the witches?" can therefore be answered. The dramatically memorable witches, just as Priapus and the pleasant garden in which they all meet, are elements in the satirist's self-ironical, implicit treatment of his own inferior birth and subsequent rise to stature.

Barbara Hill
University of Colorado

Notes

An earlier version of this paper, adjusted for oral presentation, was presented at the 1989 RMMLA meeting. I would like to thank Professors Emily Batinski and Elizabeth Holtze for their encouragement and astute suggestions concerning this work.

The translations of the Latin passages are my own.

[1] E. C. Wickham, *The Works of Horace*, vol. 2 (Oxford, 1891), 89.

[2] *Papyri Graecae Magicae: Die griechischen Zauberpapyri*, ed. Karl Preisendanz (Stuttgart, 1973–74), vol. 1, no. 4.

[3] P. LeJay, *Oeuvres d'Horace* (Hildesheim, 1966), 211–15, demonstrates an objective attitude toward the witches and their rites in his introduction to *Satire* 8: "La satire peint la réalité populaire et prend volontiers ses modèles dans la vie galante où la magie intervient" (211). LeJay also lists additional references to magic in Latin poetry.

[4] For example, W. S. Anderson, "The Roman Socrates: Horace and His Satires" in *Critical Essays on Roman Literature*, ed. J. P. Sullivan, (London, 1963), writes, "S. 1.7 and 8 exhibit considerable wit, but the personality of the satirist gains little from them" (25). See also D. L. Sigsbee, "The Disciplined Satire of Horace," in *Roman Satirists and Their Satire* (Park Ridge, 1974), who writes, "This satire should be taken as sheer entertainment. ... Horace ...

hardly wants his reader to spend a lot of time analyzing the poem. The whole thing is a comic story with a surprising, almost blasphemous ending" (75).

[5] E. Fraenkel, *Horace*, (Oxford, 1957), 123; N. Rudd, *The Satires of Horace* (Cambridge, 1966), 72; M. Coffey, *Roman Satire* (New York, 1976), 78; and W. S. Anderson, "The Form, Purpose and Position of Horace's Satires I,8." *AJP*, 93 (1972), 10–11, 13.

[6] Anderson, ibid., 10–11.

Julia in Lucan's Tripartite Vision of the Dead Republic

Although Julia makes only one appearance *propria persona* in Lucan's *Bellum Civile*, she is implicitly present each time Caesar and Pompey are called father-in-law and son-in-law.[1] The thematic importance of these social bonds is established in the proem to the epic in which Lucan defines civil war (*cognatae acies*, 1.4) as the destruction of normal family relationships. Representing the societal and personal relationships imperiled by the Civil War, Julia, as Thompson points out, allows the poet to express the impiety of war between kinsmen.[2] Critics have naturally focused on her one appearance in the epic, when she comes to Pompey in a dream just after he has embarked from Brundisium (3.9–35). This scene Lucan has enriched with echoes from the *Aeneid*, namely those where Aeneas speaks with the dead Creusa and Dido. The echoes underscore the differences between Pompey and Aeneas, illustrating Pompey's inability to subordinate personal concerns to the demands of the state.[3]

The apparition of Julia, moreover, belongs in a structural design encompassing the themes of the epic by contrasting the figures of Cato, Caesar, and Pompey. Morford has correctly understood that Pompey's dream of the dead Julia balances Caesar's vision of Roma confronting him at the Rubicon (1.185–203).[4] The third general, Cato, is also visited by a woman, his former wife Marcia (2.326–91). These female figures, Julia, Roma, and Marcia, appear only once, in scenes whose interconnections signal both their thematic relationship with each other and their importance for interpreting the poem as a whole. Of these three figures, Roma, the first to appear, establishes the paradigm that informs the reading of Marcia and Julia as representing aspects of the dying Republic. These three episodes, moreover, united by similar structure and repeated images, appear successively near the beginning of the first three books as Caesar, Cato, and Pompey enter the narrative.

Echoes of Aeneas' farewell to Creusa (*Aen.* 2.738–95) add additional commentary to the crucial moments when each general irrevocably enters the Civil War. How the generals respond to these very different figures shows their disparate attitudes toward Republican Rome.

A brief survey of the historical tradition demonstrates that Lucan moulds his raw material to form a unifying triptych. Concerning Cato, Plutarch mentions in passing that this stern Republican remarried Marcia just before departing from Rome to share Pompey's exile (*Cato Minor* 52.3). Caesar was said to have met an unearthly figure before committing himself to marching on Rome. Suetonius records that while Caesar deliberated the consequences of crossing the Rubicon, the apparition of an enormous man urged him on (*Iulius* 32). Plutarch reports that on the night before crossing the river, Caesar dreamt that he had slept with his mother (*Caesar* 32.9).[5] Pompey's dream about Julia's apparition, however, seems to be Lucan's invention.[6] The historical tradition provided the poetic impetus for Caesar's and Cato's encounters, but Lucan has transformed these reports, in conjunction with the appearance of the dead Julia, into events that echo one another and help to characterize these generals. The poet's manufacture of Pompey's dream to form a structuring device indicates a deliberate invitation to his reader to contrast how Caesar, Cato, and Pompey respond to direct confrontations with personifications of traditional Republican Rome.

Before examining Pompey's dream of Julia and her relation to Roma and Marcia, I will discuss the three other passages in which Julia is explicitly named, because they define her role in the *Bellum Civile*. These passages have not received significant scholarly attention, but they underscore the thematic importance of her appearance in the dream. In the introduction, she is identified as the person who could have prevented the war between her father and husband (1.115–16). After the Battle of Pharsalus, Cornelia prays that Julia will not exact punishment on Pompey for remarrying (8.103–5). Finally, the poet rebukes Caesar for his affair with Cleopatra and for giving Julia a bastard brother (10.77–78). As will be seen, in each of these passages, Julia emerges as an emblem of Republican *virtus*. Images of death and marriage, moreover, which dominate her visitation to Pompey, are integral to her presentation throughout the epic.

The first mention of Julia establishes her role as an emblem of traditional Roman *virtus*. Lucan links her with the illustrious moral paradigm of the Sabine women. Julia's familial connections parallel those of these early Roman women: she, too, stands between her potentially warring father and husband. Addressing Julia, Lucan claims that after the death of Crassus, she alone was capable of averting the war between Pompey and Caesar (*tu sola furentem/ inde virum poteras atque hinc retinere parentem*, "you alone were able to restrain your raging husband and father," 1.115–16).[7] If she had lived, she would have emulated these Sabine women (*ut generos soceris mediae iunxere Sabinae*, "just as the mediating Sabine women united sons and fathers-in-law," 1.118). Her association with this exemplum of female Roman virtue in the introduction of the poem identifies her with the Republic, now moribund. By likening her potential role to that of the women at Rome's origin, Lucan draws together the beginning of the Republic with its end. Julia, whose death prevented her from taking on the role of peace-maker, is not only the historical figure but also the symbol of the dead Republic.

In his introduction, furthermore, Lucan associates Julia's marriage with death and guilt for the Civil War. Her death destroyed the pledge that joined the families of Caesar and Pompey:

> nam pignora iuncti
> sanguinis et diro ferales omine taedas
> abstulit ad manes Parcarum Iulia saeva
> intercepta manu.   (1.111–14)

> For when Julia's life had been cut short by the cruel
> hand of the Fates, she carried off to the shades the
> pledges formed by marital bonds and the wedding
> torches made deadly with ill omen.

The marriage torches were ill-omened and foreboded death (1.111–13): they predicted not only Julia's early death but also the slaughter of citizens in the Civil War that her death precipitated. Even though Julia may seem a victim of fate, the poet signals her responsibility for the acts of cruelty growing out of her early death. *Saeva* (1.113), while syntactically agreeing with the hand of fate that causes Julia's early demise, is associatively linked with Julia herself by position. This cruel aspect of Julia will later be developed in the speeches of Pompey's wife Cornelia and of Julia herself.

Lucan first mentions Julia in his list of the causes for the war (1.67–182) and thus makes her, in part, responsible for the Civil War, a charge that he reinforces by ascribing to her alone the ability to avert it. With Julia's death in 54 B.C., the societal and personal bond between Caesar and Pompey disintegrates. Lucan employs her death as the point at which *fides* is broken, when it is now permitted for her father and husband to wage war (1.119–20). Like Valerius Maximus and Velleius Paterculus, Lucan credits Julia's marriage to Pompey as a principal factor that had inhibited these two generals from warring against each other.[8] No ancient historian, however, holds Julia responsible for the consequences of her death. Lucan has perversely altered the tradition found in histories: Julia assumes retroactive guilt in his epic.

Julia's guilt is a paradox that reflects Lucan's interpretation of the Civil War.[9] Once the war begins, the norms of society are inverted. Republican virtues no longer preserve traditional Rome; to the contrary, they assist in destroying the world that has fostered them. Lucan draws attention to the perversion of *virtus* in his assessment of Scaeva's bravery at the conclusion of his *aristeia* in Book 6. Although Scaeva triumphs gloriously over Pompey's men like a warrior in the *Iliad* or the *Aeneid*, his courage is directed toward replacing the Republic with tyranny (*infelix, quanta dominum virtute parasti*, "unfortunate man, with your great courage you have paved the way for a tyrant," 6.262). As Scaeva's heroic *virtus* is used to establish a dictator, so Julia's unfortunate death produces a conflict that stains her husband and father with kindred murder, a microcosm of the Civil War.[10] Julia has, moreover, established a familial bond between Caesar and Pompey by making them father and son-in-law. Her death had severed the *fides* between Caesar and Pompey, but Lucan, as shown earlier, repeatedly evokes this *socer/gener* bond throughout his epic. Therefore, Caesar and Pompey are not merely generals battling one another. Julia's marriage is responsible for transforming their conflict into a family war (*cognatae acies*, 1.4), an element essential to Lucan's definition of the Civil War.

The second mention of Julia occurs in Cornelia's speech after the Battle at Pharsalus. Like the narrator, she implies that Julia is responsible for the war, but goes further by attributing to her an active role. She accuses Julia of using the war to exact vengeance upon herself and Pompey:

> "ubicumque iaces civilibus armis
> nostros ulta toros, ades huc atque exige poenas."
> (8.102–3)

> "Wherever you lie dead, you avenge yourself on our bed. Come here and exact your punishments."

To underscore her plea to Julia on Pompey's behalf, Cornelia threatens suicide and begs Julia to have mercy on Pompey ("*Iulia crudelis, placataque paelice caesa/ Magno parce tuo*," "Cruel Julia, appeased with the death of your rival, spare your Magnus," 8.104–5). Although Cornelia complains of Julia's cruelty, she concedes her right to take revenge on Pompey for his new marriage.[11] By identifying herself as a *paelex*, "a concubine," Cornelia sanctions Julia's position as the irreproachable Roman matron and the embodiment of Republican virtue.

The third reference to Julia places her in relationship to her father. The poet charges Caesar with disgracing his daughter when he gives her a bastard brother from Cleopatra.[12]

> pro pudor, oblitus Magni tibi, Iulia, fratres
> obscaena de matre dedit.   (10.77–78)

> Shameful act! He forgot Magnus and gave to you, Julia, a brother from a disgraceful mother.

Julia has been betrayed by her father, as well as by her husband. The traditional family ties bound up in her have completely disintegrated. The ramifications of Caesar's betrayal and the implied rejection of Roman *virtus* emerge in his neglect of politics and the military, traditional concerns of a Roman general. Caught up in his affair with Cleopatra, he ignores Cato's forces gathering in Libya. Mindlessly, he turns Egypt over to his paramour instead of conquering the country as a traditional Roman general would have done (10.78–81).

Each time Julia is explicitly named, she functions as an emblem of the social bonds that the Civil War destroys. The destruction of these personal bonds, moreover, infects both the political and military spheres. *Fides* between Caesar and Pompey has been broken by her death. Both her husband and her father have dishonored her: Pompey, by a second marriage, Caesar, by giving her a bastard step-brother, Caesarion, which endangered both his own safety and Rome's. Julia emerges as a harsh, inflexible representative of Republican *virtus*. Her retroactive guilt for the war underscores Lucan's interpretation of this period: traditional Roman values that had built the Republic now paradoxically serve only to define the war that establishes tyranny. Ironically, Pompey is later accused by Lucan of failing to pursue his military advantage after Dyrrachium because he is lenient toward his father-in-law (6.303–5).

Pompey's dream of Julia dramatically confirms her image as the savage emblem of Republican *virtus*. In this scene, Lucan reiterates images and themes he associates with her elsewhere in the *Bellum Civile*. She appears to Pompey on the night he sails from Brundisium to Greece, when he commits himself and his followers to war.

> diri tum plena horroris imago
> visa caput maestum per hiantis Iulia terras
> tollere et accenso furialis stare sepulchro. (3.9–11)

> Then Julia, a fierce specter, seemed to raise her mournful head through the gaping earth and to stand like a fury upon the burning pyre.

As in the introduction and in Cornelia's address to her, Julia is associated with death. Here, too, she is a frightening figure, rising like a Fury (*furialis*, 11) from her funeral pyre. The grimness of the apparition suggests that she will demand from Pompey vengeance for his impiety in remarrying.[13] Implicitly and explicitly, the narrator and Cornelia had charged her with causing the Civil War. Paradoxically, Julia blames Pompey for her role in causing the civil war and at the same time revels in it. Now that the war has begun, she has been driven from the Elysian Fields of the blessed to the shadowy Styx, the abode of the guilty spirits:

> "sedibus Elysiis campoque expulsa piorum
> ad Stygias" inquit "tenebras manesque nocentis
> post bellum civile trahor."　　　　　　(3.12–14)

> "I am driven," she said, "from the Elysian Fields and the abode of the virtuous. After the beginning of the Civil War, I am dragged to the gloomy realm of the Styx and the guilty shades."

Her death precipitated the war and, therefore, she is guilty. She forecasts the disastrous results of the war: while in the region of the Styx, she had seen the fearsome agents of the Underworld prepare for the legions of the dead who will soon be arriving (3.14–19).

Julia denounces Pompey for attempting to sever their marriage bonds, emblematic of the societal values that Republican Rome had kept intact. She identifies herself as his only lawful wife when she pronounces Cornelia a *paelex* (3.23), a charge which, as already seen, Pompey's new wife accepts. (To maintain Julia's privileged role as the embodiment of traditional *virtus*, Lucan has omitted any reference to Pompey's first wife, Mucia.) Julia vows that she will continue to haunt his nights as her father will continue to torment his days in order to prevent him from making love to Cornelia and to insure that he remain faithful to her. In her boast that the Civil War will make him hers again (3.25–30), Julia appears as both wife and lover.

Pompey rejects Julia's prediction of disaster, an act which underscores the self-delusion consistent with Lucan's presentation of him in the epic. He ignores the divine and spectral warning of disaster with a quasi-philosophic assurance that death is meaningless.

> ille, dei quamvis cladem manesque minentur,
> maior in arma ruit certa cum mente malorum,
> et "quid" ait "vani terremur imagine visus?
> aut nihil est sensus animis a morte relictum
> aut mors ipsa nihil."　　　　　　(3.36–40)

Although the gods and the dead threaten defeat, he
rushed to arms more savagely with his mind ready for
troubles. "Why," he said, "am I terrified by the image of
an empty vision? Either no sensation remains for the soul
after death, or death is nothing."

Julia, however, has forecast not just Pompey's death but the slaughter of countless soldiers. He responds to her warning as directed only toward him and not toward Rome and his men. Although Pompey believes that he is fighting to preserve traditional Republican Rome, the poet and Cato repeatedly confront the reader with Magnus' self-deception. In the introduction, Pompey is described as trusting in his former greatness as a triumphant general, but as doing nothing to reinforce his reputation.

> nec reparare novas vires, multumque priori
> credere fortunae. stat magni nominis umbra.
> (1.134–35)

He does not expand his power, and he trusts greatly in
his former fortune. He stands as a shadow of his own
great name.

Cato condemns Pompey as no better than Caesar: no matter who wins the war, the result will be tyranny (2.319–23). He assures Brutus that his alliance with Pompey will be formed to remind this general that he should be fighting for Rome and not for himself (2.323). Pompey's opposition to Caesar superficially casts him in the role of defending the Republic. It is only after Pompey's death, however, that Cato can become *Pompeianus* (9.24). At that time Cato can assert that Pompey's espoused concern for Rome will never again be used as a pretext by any general seeking to rule Rome as a tyrant (*nunc et ficta perit. non iam regnare pudebit,/ nec color imperii nec frons erit ulla senatus*, "now even the fiction is destroyed. It will no longer be shameful to rule as a king. There will be neither pretense of legitimate power nor any façade of a senate," 9.206–7).[14]

Pompey's response to Julia echoes Vergil's account of the dead

Creusa coming to Aeneas as Troy is sacked by the Greeks.[15] Pompey, like Aeneas, attempts to embrace his dead wife who vanishes within his grasp (*umbra per amplexus trepidi dilapsa mariti*, "the specter slipped through the embrace of her alarmed husband," 3.35). The efforts of both Aeneas and Pompey signify their desire to cling to the past. Vergil and Lucan, however, have invested the past with different values. For Aeneas, Troy, as represented by Creusa, has been destroyed, and the future lies in abandoning this dead world. Creusa orders her husband to leave her and their razed city. He must go to Italy to remarry and to establish a new kingdom (*Aen.* 2.768–95). For Pompey, the past, as symbolized by Julia, is the moribund Republic. Like Creusa, Julia appears to Pompey as he leaves his homeland for the last time. Unlike Creusa, however, she vows that she will reclaim him as her husband.[16] Yet, ironically, the future that Creusa urges Aeneas to enter is identical with the past that Roma and Julia urge Caesar and Pompey to honor. It is identical with the Rome represented by Cato and Marcia. Lucan has inverted his Vergilian model. The past is now the goal.

Pompey's futile embrace of Julia's ghost, moreover, underscores his role as Rome's lover. Lucan's treatment of his Vergilian model, furthermore, recalls Propertius' appropriation of this epic scene into elegiac poetry. In 4.7, the ghost of the dead Cynthia comes to Propertius and denounces his new mistress. Like Julia, Cynthia contends that she alone is his love and, when Propertius dies, she will reclaim him in his grave. A grisly picture emerges as Cynthia foretells how she will grind her skeleton against his ("*mecum eris, et mixtis ossibus ossa teram,*" "you will be with me, and I shall grind your bones mingled with mine," 4.7.94).[17] Propertius' reaction to this macabre promise is to try, like Aeneas, to embrace the fleeting ghost. Like Propertius, Pompey also tries to grasp the image of Julia who has sworn that once dead he will be hers again.

Pompey's dream on the eve of the Battle of Pharsalus illustrates the erotic nature of his relationship with Rome. In his sleep he sees himself again in his theater at Rome receiving adoring applause for his past triumphs (7.7–24). Lucan's description of Rome's eventual loss of her Pompey in Egypt evokes the torment of a wife who will never see her husband's grave (7.29–39). As Morford notes, "their relationship can only be described by the vocabulary of love."[18] It is Pompey's role as lover, however, that compels him to confuse devotion to his new wife with concern for the Republic. After Pharsalus he hastens to Lesbos to assure himself of Cornelia's safety. Because this island has protected his wife, he calls it his Rome: *"hic mihi Roma fuit"* ("here was my Rome," 8.133).

Comparing Pompey's dream of Julia and Caesar's confrontation with Roma brings the two generals into sharp contrast. The circumstances of the two episodes are similar and signal the reader to regard them as thematically comparable. Roma appears at the critical moment at which Caesar is about to cross the Rubicon and begin the Civil War. Contrary to the conventional time for military movements and the historical testimony (e.g., Suetonius, *Iulius* 31–33), Caesar is about to lead his army across the river at night. This oddity indicates that Lucan has constructed the scene to parallel Pompey's dream.

> ingens visa duci patriae trepidantis imago
> clara per obscuram voltu maestissima noctem
> turrigero canos effundens vertice crines
> caesarie lacera nudisque adstare lacertis
> et gemitu permixta loqui.   (1.186–90)

> A huge vision of his alarmed country appeared to the general. [She appeared] shining through the dark night with a most sorrowful expression, and her white hair was loosened and falling from her head on which she wore a crown with turrets. With her hair disheveled and her arms bare, she stood and spoke with a groan.

Like Julia, Roma is threatening and sorrowful. Her disheveled hair and her bare and bruised arms testify to her grieving and repeat the death imagery that surrounds the ghost of Julia.

Aeneas' farewell to Creusa also informs Caesar's encounter with the personified Roma. Roma challenges Caesar and demands to know where he is leading her standards (1.190–91). Momentarily terrified, he stands on the banks of the Rubicon. He is unable to speak (1.192–94). Likewise, Aeneas, filled with fear or awe upon seeing Creusa, remained silent (*Aen.* 2.774). Caesar's subsequent prayers to the Trojan gods and the Julian clan reinforce the comparison with Aeneas (*Phrygii penates/ gentis Iuleae*, 1.196–97).[19] This Vergilian reminiscence, as Thompson and Bruère have shown, emphasizes that Caesar is the antithesis of the Julian clan that Vergil celebrates in the *Aeneid*.[20]

Just as Julia reflects Pompey's role as Rome's lover, so Roma corresponds to Caesar's relation to the city. Roma also demands that Caesar revere the past and her laws: he must remain where he is. Demanding to know where Caesar is going with her emblems (1.190–91), she brands his plan to cross the Rubicon as illegal and beyond established Roman behavior. It is the City, the embodiment of the public and political, who approaches him. Caesar calls upon the gods who have protected Rome and his family, asking Roma to sanction his march across the Rubicon. He defends himself by accusing Pompey of being the cause of the war in that he made Caesar an enemy of Rome. Whereas Julia addresses Pompey like a jealous elegiac mistress and demands his fidelity, Roma asks Caesar and his men if they intend to obey the law and act as citizens ("*si iure venitis,/ si cives,*" "if you come in accordance with law, if you come as loyal citizens," 1.191–92). Political/public concerns govern Caesar as opposed to the personal concerns motivating Pompey's actions in the epic. This contrast between Pompey and Caesar is strengthened when Caesar makes no attempt to embrace the personification of Rome.

Marcia comes to Cato under circumstances similar to those surrounding the appearances of Julia and Roma. As in those scenes, it is still dark, but dawn is only now just breaking (2.326). She too appears at a moment of decision, and her arrival echoes those decisive moments when Caesar crossed the Rubicon and Pompey departed from Italy. Here, Cato has just proclaimed to Brutus that he will ally himself with Pompey and follow him into exile (2.286–321). Marcia, like Roma and Julia, is sorrowful (*maesta*, 2.337) and appears with the trappings of death, for she is still mourning her dead husband Hortensius (2.327–28). These elements establish the parallel of Marcia with Roma and Julia.

Cato's response to Marcia, however, is diametrically opposed to that of Pompey's to Julia and Caesar's to Roma.[21] Marcia had initially left her home and marriage with Cato at his bidding to provide Hortensius with children. She has performed her duty. Now she returns to share Cato's troubles. Unlike Julia, she is not tied to her husband by erotic love (2.340–41). Cato, moreover, obeys Marcia's request and accepts her into his house again in a marriage that will produce no children, but will preserve Marcia's reputation (2.338–41). She wishes to omit from her tombstone any mention of her marriage to Hortensius, wishing at least in appearance to conform to the Roman ideal of the woman married to only one man.

Ahl persuasively argues that this marriage functions as an allegory and points out the echoes in this scene with Creusa's farewell to Aeneas. The Republic is dead; Marcia, no longer able to bear children (2.340–41), will be married to Cato, "the true father of the country" (9.601).[22] Cato unhesitatingly accepts this responsibility. Like Cato, Marcia is bound by duty; like Creusa, she belongs to a world irretrievably gone. As with the Roma and Julia episodes, moreover, this Vergilian echo achieves an antithetical effect. Whereas Aeneas must abandon the past in order to insure continuation, Cato must embrace what is dead, as represented by Marcia, in order to preserve *libertas*. The *Bellum Civile* looks backward for its hope.[23] Just as Marcia desires only the empty name of marriage (*"da tantum nomen inane/ conubii,"* "grant only the empty name of marriage," 2.342–43), so Cato follows the empty shadow of freedom (*"nomen, Libertas, et inanem persequar umbram,"* "Liberty, I shall follow your empty name and shadow," 2.303). Now, only the past contains the ideal that cannot continue into the future.

The apparition of Julia in conjunction with the appearances of Roma and Marcia forms a tripartite, thematic, structuring device. The circumstances, imagery, and Vergilian echoes unite these episodes into a triptych. When examined together the interconnections between the episodes amplify the import of each. These female images of Republican Rome articulate the antithetical perspectives of Caesar, Cato, and Pompey. Each general responds to a personification of Rome that reflects his own response to and understanding of the Republic: Caesar confronts the public/political; Pompey, the private/personal; Cato, the public/private in his Stoic acceptance of Republican duty. The repeated Vergilian echoes also signal the reader to be alert to a comparison between the *Aeneid* and the *Bellum Civile*. Roma, Marcia, and Julia are either dead or suffused with funereal imagery because they represent the moribund Republic and its *virtus*. Unlike Creusa, they embody a dead past that should be embraced even if the embrace is futile.

Emily E. Batinski
Louisiana State University

Notes

[1] According to R. Deferrari, M. Fanning, and A. Sullivan, *A Concordance of Lucan* (Washington, 1940), *gener* appears 24 times, and *socer* 33 times. These terms always apply to Caesar and Pompey with the following exceptions: *gener* 1.118 and 6.364; *socer* 1.118. See also L. Thompson and R. T. Bruère, "Lucan's Use of Virgilian Reminiscence," *CP*, 63 (1968), who discuss Vergil's account of Juno calling Aeneas and Latinus *socer* and *gener*, which confirms the importance of these concepts in the foundation of Rome (4).

[2] L. Thompson, "A Lucanian Contradiction of Virgilian *Pietas*: Pompey's *Amor*," *CJ*, 79 (1984), 207–15.

[3] W. Rutz, "Die Träume des Pompeius in Lucans *Pharsalia*," in *Lucan*, ed. W. Rutz (Darmstadt, 1970), 509–24; first published in *Hermes*, 91 (1963), 334–45; F. M. Ahl, *Lucan: An Introduction* (Ithaca, 1976), 188. See Thompson, "A Lucanian Contradiction," 207 n. 2, for an excellent bibliography of the Vergilian echoes in the *Bellum Civile*.

[4] M. P. O. Morford, *The Poet Lucan: Studies in Rhetorical Epic* (Oxford, 1967), 79. L. Eckardt, "Exkurse und Ekphraseis bei Lucan" (diss. Heidelberg, 1936), 1–34, demonstrates that Lucan establishes a balance between Books 1 and 3 by means of the catalogues of Caesar's and Pompey's forces (1.392–465; 3.169–297). This structural parallel underscores the polemical roles of the generals in the *Bellum Civile*.

[5] See Morford, *The Poet Lucan*, 77–78, for a discussion of the historical sources for Caesar's vision.

[6] There is, however, historical evidence for Pompey's dream of the adoring Roman crowds on the night before the Battle at Pharsalus. See H. Cancik, "Ein Traum des Pompeius (Lucan, *Pharsalia*, 7.1–47)," in *Lucan*, ed. Rutz, 546–52, for historical references and analysis of Lucan's poetic transformation of this evidence.

[7] A. E. Housman, M. *Annaei Lucani Belli Civilis Libri Decem* (Cambridge, 1926). All subsequent citations are to this edition. All the translations of Lucan are my own.

[8] Velleius Paterculus 2.47.2; Valerius Maximus 4.6.4. This theory was continued by later historians: Florus 2.13.13; Plutarch, *Caesar* 23.6; Dio

Cassius 40.44.2–3. But see E. S. Gruen, *The Last Generation of the Roman Republic* (Berkeley, 1974), 450–53, who demonstrates that substantial ancient testimony discredits this thesis as a possible reason for the war.

⁹ Paradox is a stylistic feature of the Silver Age, which, as C. A. Martindale argues in "Paradox, Hyperbole and Literary Novelty in Lucan's *De Bello Civili*," *Bulletin of the Institute of Classical Studies of the University of London*, 23 (1976), 45–54, reflects Lucan's interpretation of events. See also G. Moretti, "Formularità e techniche del paradossale in Lucano," *Maia*, 36 (1984), 37–49, who contends that paradox in the *Bellum Civile* indicates the poet's denunciation of the Civil War as a breakdown in logical order.

¹⁰ Julia's death as a cause for the war is striking because neither Pompey nor Caesar assumes responsibility. Caesar charges that Pompey will make him an enemy of Rome (1.203), and Pompey insists that Rome has ordered him to stop the raging Caesar (2.551–2). Lucan, moreover, explicitly condemns these generals for starting the war (1.125–26).

¹¹ In his first explicit reference to Julia, Lucan also suggests cruelty: *Iulia saeva/ intercepta manu*, "Julia cut off with a savage hand" (1.113–14). Although syntactically *saeva* agrees with *manu* in the following line, momentarily in the reader's mind this adjective is linked with the adjacent Julia until the chiastic structure appears between lines 113 and 114.

¹² Cf. Cicero, *Philippic* 2.24–28, in which he contrasts Antony's licentious behavior with the virtues of the Republic. For the function of Caesar and Cleopatra in the *Bellum Civile*, see R. Mayer, *Lucan: Civil War VIII* (Warminster, 1981), 20, 23, and especially 100–101, in which he discusses Lucan's contrasting the fidelity of Pompey and Cornelia with the licence of Caesar and Cleopatra; and M. G. Schmidt, *Caesar und Cleopatra. Philologischer und historischer Kommentar zu Lucan 10.7–171*, Studien zur klassische Philologie, 25 (Frankfurt, 1986).

Although tradition holds that Cleopatra had one son by Caesar, even in antiquity Caesarion's paternity was disputed (Suetonius, *Iulius* 52). This controversy has continued among modern historians. See J. Carcopino, "César et Cléopâtre," *Annales de l'École des Hautes-Études de Gand*, 1 (1937), 37–77; J. P. V. D. Balsdon, "Cleopatra," *CR*, n.s. 10 (1960), 68–71; H. Heinen, "Cäsar und Kaiserion," *Historia*, 18 (1969), 181–203.

¹³ See Morford, *The Poet Lucan*, 80.

¹⁴ Cf. 9.19–28.

¹⁵ Rutz, "Die Träume des Pompeius," 519, has argued that the main purpose of the Julia episode is to underscore the ironic parallel between Pompey and Aeneas.

¹⁶ This threat has caused Rutz, "Die Träume des Pompeius," 521, to liken Julia to Dido.

[17] W. A. Camps, *Propertius: Elegies Book IV* (Cambridge, 1965), suggests that this line may imply only a tight embrace. He concludes, however, that the "primary meanings of the words composing it are hard to escape from" (125).

[18] Morford, *The Poet Lucan*, 82.

[19] Ahl, *Lucan*, 211.

[20] Thompson and Bruère, "Lucan's Use of Virgilian Reminiscence," 7.

[21] Ahl, *Lucan*, observes that there is a "pointed contrast between Pompey's relationship with Cornelia and Rome, and that of Cato with Marcia and Rome" (181).

[22] Ahl, *Lucan*, 249.

[23] H. -P. Syndikus, "Lucans Gedicht vom Bürgerkrieg," (diss. Munich, 1958), 89–90, characterizes the *Bellum Civile* as a *Gegenbild* of the *Aeneid*.

The "Master Mistress" of My Passion: The Lady as Patron in Ancient and Renaissance Literature

In this paper, I will discuss the reconceptualization of the female lover as the "patron" of the poet in the Roman elegiac poetry of the first century B.C.E, focusing particularly on Propertius. From there I will move on to an examination of how Shakespeare used and transformed the "lover as patron" theme in his sonnets of some sixteen centuries later.

Although women were accorded a subordinate role in Greek and Roman society, the Roman elegists portray the female figures who are represented as their erotic interests—Catullus' Lesbia, Propertius' Cynthia, and Tibullus' Delia—as *dominae* (employing a word that appears to be the feminine counterpart of the Latin for "master") and as the ostensibly superior members of their partnerships.[1] In order to strengthen this image of female dominance, these poets address these women with language usually reserved for their patrons—men of wealth, nobility, and power who were truly dominant in the traditional patron-client relationships. Constructed as female patrons, the female lovers of the Roman elegists thus seem to be accorded a social standing and degree of power that the ordinary woman in Rome did not enjoy.

Scholarship on the ancient world commonly maintains that Roman women occupied a far stronger position socially, politically, and economically than did their Greek counterparts. The role that women are given in Roman poetry of the elegiac period certainly supports this scholarly position. But if we look carefully at the way in which these women are portrayed and compare the position of the male patron with that of the female patron/lover, we have cause to challenge another standard assumption: that Roman women achieved substantial power in their own right during the late Republican and early Imperial periods.

In order to examine the position of women in first-century B.C.E.

Rome and the construction of women as patron/lovers in Roman poetry, I will first look at several women during this period who were indeed patrons in the traditional sense of the word.[2] They will illustrate the type of historical persons upon whom the poetic constructs in Roman elegy might have been based. I will then look at one particularly interesting and well-developed example of such a patron-lover in literature: the Cynthia of the Roman elegiac poet Propertius (even the way the description of this woman is framed says something about Cynthia's and Propertius' respective positions of power). Finally, I will take a look at the further development of the patron/lover idea in some poetry of the Elizabethan era. The situation in Shakespeare, who addresses many of his sonnets to two addressees, a youth and a "Dark Lady," is particularly difficult, and I will not fully explore it. However, Shakespeare surely saw in his Roman literary predecessors interesting ways of portraying the lover as patron, and he transformed this convention, splitting this image into a feminized male and a dark, mysterious female.[3] His use of the earlier convention representing the female as patron is helpful to the classicist reader since Shakespeare's lover/patron can be interpreted partly as a comment on earlier poetic practice and partly as a contrast to the Roman poets' apparent elevation of the female lover. A comparison of Shakespeare's introduction of a male patron/lover into this situation with Roman elegiac practice might alter considerably our view of the position of women in Roman elegy. At the very least, it will reveal how different the circumstances are when a man takes the position of patron.

My starting point will be a definition of the conventional Roman understanding of "patronage." I will use the following as a working definition: a continuing reciprocal exchange relationship between two people of unequal status.[4] Taken in its usual sense, patronage always involved two elements: an exchange of some sort, whether material or spiritual, and inequality of social rank or status between the two partners in the relationship. Such conditions normally existed only between two men, since women were rarely in a position to give or receive substantial gifts. Furthermore, the question of the social rank and status of any woman vis-à-vis any man in classical Roman society is obscured by the fact that women generally seem to have been considered first in terms of gender and only secondarily in terms of social status.⁵ Within the ranks of the freeborn, at least, women were not regarded as equal to men even if they held the same social status. The issue of gender was always dominant, taking precedence even over social class. For example, in the situation involving interactions between a well-born woman such as a Cornelia or Servilia and a freeborn but lower-class man, there must always have existed with both parties some awareness that the woman had certain limitations because of her sex. Such limitations applied even if she possessed through her family or her husband a superior social standing and perhaps greater wealth.⁶

Therefore, it is difficult to conceive what a relationship between two people of unequal status might mean if one of these was a woman. How high did the status of a woman have to be before she was regarded as the superior of a man? There is also the problem of the public nature of patronage. Patronage between two men often involved political activities and was therefore carried out in the public sphere. Even when there was a private exchange, for example between poet and patron, it was made public by the poet's acknowledgment of the gift and by the public nature of the poems produced. If, on the other hand, two women ever exchanged gifts, it was a private act and was not likely to have been recorded publicly or recognized by society. Rarely did a woman have a public role or a public voice.⁷

There is, however, one situation in which women could make public benefactions and for which they received open acknowledgment: patronage of cities and guilds. This was an area in which it was permissible for a wealthy woman, whether nobly-born or freedwoman, to bestow gifts. Much historical information, in the form of inscriptions, attests to such benefactions and gives prosopographical information about the women and families in question. Many women in Rome, unlike women in fifth-century Athens, were entitled to keep control of their own property and to obtain a divorce by mutual consent or by action initiated by either party. In the mid-to-late Republican period, there were many powerful, well-born women in Roman life who not only exerted control over domestic affairs, but over political events as well. If we can trust the ancient sources, Servilia had a powerful effect on her son, Marcus Brutus, the assassin of Julius Caesar. Fulvia, married in succession to three powerful men (P. Clodius Pulcher, C. Scribonius

Curio, and Marcus Antonius), can be accurately described as the power behind the throne, who arranged summit meetings, influenced political proscriptions, and guided military affairs.[8] Such women are thought to have either directly or indirectly affected the course of Roman politics; Cato is reported to have inveighed against the influence of strong-willed and gossipy mothers on their young sons, who in turn spread this deleterious influence to the larger world of *Realpolitik*.[9]

While all or at least part of this may be true, there is an ambiguity inherent in the position of women at Rome.[10] The purported influence of Roman women over their sons, husbands, and other male kin and hence over the tide of Roman affairs was not grounded in any true political power of their own. They could not vote, and legally they were at a great disadvantage, always under the control of a male relative (until they had three children, even under Augustan legislation). The main locus of power for women, even those from elite families, was the household. In external, public affairs, the direct impact of women was slight and their unmediated participation was almost nonexistent. Women did not attend assembly or senate meetings, and they could not hold office; thus their influence over daily political events was at most indirect. Scholars like Hallett and Dixon have recently argued that many women of the Roman elite were able to gain increased political power, but only because the blurred distinction between the political and the social spheres in the late Republic and the identification of elite Roman women with men of their blood families allowed women at times to function in similar roles and to display similar qualities.[11]

While Roman women, then, were always in an ambiguous position in terms of the political power they wielded, there is no doubt that they were heavily implicated in the Roman politics of the late Republic and early Empire, often had some economic clout, were granted a certain amount of personal freedom, and could have been in a position to act as patrons. There are many impressive examples of such women from various parts of the Empire; I will concentrate on two from Pompeii.[12]

Inscriptions from tombs, houses, and temples indicate that Pompeian women were heavily involved in the religious, political, and business activities of the city. In these public roles, they obtained the position, stature, and wealth they needed to act as benefactors, at least to the city as a whole, if not in a more private capacity. Two such women, Mamia

P. f. and Eumachia L. f., were born of the highest municipal aristocracy. Mamia, who lived in the first century C.E., is somewhat of a puzzle and her origins unclear.[13] She is one of only two members of her *gens* known for Pompeii, but the family was prominent in Herculaneum. She rose to the position of public priestess and, in that role, dedicated a small temple near the forum of Pompeii to the *genius* of the emperor Augustus. The inscription reads: M(am)ia P f sacerdos public geni(o aug s)olo et pec ("Mamia, daughter of Publius, public priestess, [built this] to the *genius* of Augustus on her own land and with her own money," CIL 10.816). Probably in return for this benefaction, the local senate of Pompeii gave land for her burial on the Via dei Sepolcri. Her *schola* (tomb) is in the shape of a semi-circular bench and is just outside one of the city gates. The size of her tomb as well as its prominent position indicate that a singular honor was paid to her. The inscription on the tomb reads: *Mamiae P f sacerdoti publicae locus sepultur datus decurionum decreto* ("To Mamia, daughter of Publius, public priestess, the burial place was given by decree of the decurions," CIL 10.998).

Another prominent Pompeian benefactor in the first century C.E. was Eumachia, a public priestess of Venus. Her father, Lucius Eumachius, perhaps a descendent of early Greek colonists in southern Italy, had built up a thriving business in wine and pottery. Eumachia used her respectably inherited wealth to marry into one of Pompeii's older families, and she herself became prominent not only in her religious role, but also as a businesswoman.

A large and rather puzzling building connected to her, now called the Aedificium Eumachiae, has been found next to the temple dedicated by Mamia near the Forum of Pompeii. The importance of the building is evident from its prime location on one of Pompeii's main streets, the Via dell' Abbondanza, its large size, and its magnificence. The building is dedicated to Concordia Augusta and Pietas, both associated with Livia, mother of Tiberius and wife of Augustus. An inscription on the architrave reads as follows: *Eumachia L f sacerd publ nomine suo et / M Numistri Frontonis fili chalcidicum cryptam porticus concordiae / Augustae Pietati sua pecunia fecit eademque dedicavit* ("Eumachia, daughter of Lucius [Eumachius], public priestess, in her own name and that of her son, Marcus Numistrius Fronto, built with her own funds the porch, covered passage, and colonnade and dedicated them to Concordia

Augusta and to Pietas," *CIL* 10.810). The purpose of the building is not clear, but it is thought perhaps to have been a meeting hall and headquarters for the guild of fullers (cleaners, dyers, and cloth-makers), one of Pompeii's most influential trade-guilds.[14] The connection between Eumachia and the fullers is made from a statue of her that stood in the middle of this building. On the base of the statue we read: *Eumachiae L f sacerd publ fullones* ("To Eumachia, daughter of Lucius, public priestess, the fullers [dedicated this statue]," *CIL* 10.813).

One other monument has been found in Pompeii that indicates Eumachia's important position and status there. Her tomb, which, like Mamia's, is near one of the city gates, is the largest found in Pompeii. Unlike Mamia's tomb, however, Eumachia's was not erected at city expense, but at her own. The inscription on it says *Eumachia L f sibi et suis* (Eumachia, daughter of Lucius, [built this] for herself and for her household).[15]

There is a large amount of epigraphical evidence for many other prominent and wealthy women in Pompeii and in other cities in Italy, and we may assume that such women often took an active role in the life of their communities.[16] Unlike Greek inscriptions, which conflate women's domestic and public roles and use the same kind of language to describe both their public benefactions and their private virtues, Italian inscriptions differentiate more clearly between these two roles and create a different image for female benefactors than we find in Roman literary depictions and in funeral epitaphs. Such female benefactors were honored more and more prominently as the number of willing benefactors decreased in the second century C.E.[17]

Now that we have established the potential for women to be considered as patrons in Italy, let us turn to women who were portrayed as "patrons" of a very different sort, the poets' beloveds in Roman elegiac poetry. The traditional male patrons of literature differed from civic patrons partly in the nature of their gifts. A patron such as Maecenas might give to a writer a tangible gift—for example money or a house or farm—but of equal importance were the intangible kinds of support he could offer: inspiration, encouragement, potential audience, publicity, and subject matter for the verse. In return for such gifts, a poet could offer to celebrate his patron's name and to magnify his great deeds in words that would become monuments to the patron's talents;

in other words, the poet could immortalize the patron. When one considers this trade-off in temporal terms, it hardly seems balanced. For the duration of one's life on earth, surely money, houses, and an introduction to the right people count for more than the vague hope of immortality from a poem that may or may not survive. But from the longer perspective, such tangible, earthly rewards are of little consequence when measured against the gift of immortality (cf. Propertius 4.7; Horace, *Odes* 3.30; Ovid, *Tristia* 3.7).[18] And this of course had to be the poet's argument if he was to convince the patron that he had anything to offer in return for the more tangible presents he received.

But how could the poet make a good case for the potential gain of immortality when he was writing an admittedly inferior genre of poetry? As Catullus had already conceded in poem 1, lyric and elegiac poems were *nugae*, trifling, frivolous, and of dubious importance; later poets such as Propertius, Tibullus, and Ovid spilled much ink over apologies for such lightweight offerings (e.g., Propertius 1.6, 1.7, 2.1, 2.10, 3.3, 3.9; Tibullus 1.1; Ovid, *Amores* 1.1). To make matters worse, these poets not only avoided acceptable and appropriately serious philosophical and epic themes but actually went out of their way to make fun of such material. War, courage, physical prowess, business, politics, and standard morality were belittled, compared unfavorably with the life of love, parodied, and finally rejected. Traditional writers in the more serious genres were able to make the case that they were reimbursing their patrons by writing panegyrics, whether these works were openly laudatory and sometimes embarrassingly servile, as in the case of the poet whom the dictator Sulla paid so that he would stop writing panegyrics (Cicero, *Pro Archia* 25), or more accomplished, subtle, and pleasing, such as Vergil's *Aeneid* or Horace's Roman Odes. Here there was ample opportunity to mention the patron prominently and to make him the centerpiece of one's work.

In elegiac poetry, however, the poet could hardly praise a patron such as Maecenas by celebrating his deeds when the patron's major accomplishments and activities (politics and war) were the very object of the poet's criticism.[19] Propertius tries to compensate for this difficulty by emphasizing, as Horace does in his famous epilogue to Book 3 of the *Odes* (3.30), the physical nature of his poems. Like Horace, Propertius says that his poems are monuments that will survive the Egyptian pyramids and the great Mausoleum (3.2.18–26). Propertius claims to have the power to confer fame on the person lucky enough to be celebrated in his verse (2.5.27–30, 2.25.1–4, 3.2.17–18, 3.24.3–8), or conversely to withhold this power (2.11). All these grandiloquent claims for the almost magical powers of his verse somehow obscure the fact that it is not really the patron who is the object of praise in the elegists. When the patron is mentioned at all, it is usually by way of an apology, a rejection, or even a satirical parody (e.g., Propertius 1.6, 1.14, 2.1, 3.9; Tibullus 1.1, 1.3). The person who does benefit from the life-giving and life-preserving powers of the verse is the poet's lover. It is she who embodies all the aspects and qualities that the poetry requires for its very existence: charm, wit, beauty, softness, elegance, and sensuality. And it is she who stands as a kind of substitute patron, a literary construct who in a sense becomes Propertius' poetry.

I will first detail how Propertius substitutes his beloved for his male patrons and then examine what exactly Propertius had in mind when he gave his lover this apparent power over himself and his verse. The importance of the lover over the patron is suggested in the poems addressed to Propertius' two male patrons, Tullus and Maecenas.[20] Propertius' first poem to Tullus (1.6), for example, has puzzled commentators because, although it purports to be the initial approach to Tullus, his first patron, and to be a praise of Tullus' family and military career, it clearly centers on Cynthia, Propertius' lover, with Tullus coming in a poor second. The patron appears to be merely an excuse to introduce the lover. Similarly, in a poem to his second and more famous patron, Maecenas (2.1), Propertius spends the first sixteen lines giving the reasons why Cynthia is his inspiration and ends the poem by asking Maecenas to deliver the following epitaph at his grave: *Huic misero fatum dura puella fuit* ("A hardhearted woman was the end of this poor man," 2.1.78).

From the beginning of Book 1, Cynthia, Propertius' lover, is clearly his main subject and his inspiration. Thus he says: *Cynthia prima suis miserum me cepit ocellis* ("Cynthia was the first woman to capture me and make me wretched with her glance," 1.1.1). In each succeeding poem, Cynthia is identified with another aspect of his elegy (1.2: nature, luxury; 1.3: mythology, banquets, drinking, infidelity, sexuality), until in poem 1.6, Propertius openly rejects his patron, Tullus, using Cynthia as the excuse.

Slowly, throughout Book 1, the very essence of Propertius' poetry comes to be identified with Cynthia, just as in Horace's *Satires* and *Odes*, his patron Maecenas becomes the focal point of all Horace's major themes.[21] Thus, in a very important dedicatory poem to Maecenas, Propertius answers the question, "What is the source of your love poetry?" by claiming: *ingenium nobis ipsa puella facit* ("My lover herself is the source of my genius," 2.1.4). Her every look, word, and deed produce, according to Propertius, his own version of the *Iliad* (2.1.5–16).

This creative impulse, of course, ought to be the *patron*'s function. It is the patron, along with the Muses and Apollo, who is traditionally regarded as the inspiration for a poet's work, the patron who provides the main theme and all of its corollaries, and the patron to whom, in return, the poet promises fame on earth and hereafter.[22] But Propertius makes no such promises to his avowed patrons, Tullus and Maecenas, because his poetry cannot by its very nature celebrate such men and their deeds. It would, therefore, be a poor and totally inappropriate gift to offer them, since it is incompatible with them in both tone and matter. But it is the dictate of most ancient poets' personal needs and of literary convention that they have both a human and a divine source of inspiration. Since the elegiac poets could no longer find in a conventional patron such inspiration, a substitute had to be found; this substitute was the lover.

Like a patron, the lover was able to give support to the poet in the form of inspiration and subject matter for poetry. Cynthia takes on a thousand different roles at once: lover (passim), teacher (1.10.19–20), household and parents (1.11.23), literary critic (2.3.21–22, 2.13A.14), source of happiness (1.11.24), wife (2.6.41–42), sister and mother (2.18.33–34), and partner after death (1.19.11–12, 2.15.36, 4.7.93–94). In the end, she is all things to Propertius: his family, lover, teacher, theme, and inspirer. It seems logical that her role should be expanded one step further, to patron.

There are, of course, problems in turning a lover into a patron. She is, after all, only a substitute patron, and substantial differences exist between a woman like Cynthia and a male patron. The first difficulty is her gender. Since she is a woman and perhaps of lower social status, she would have been regarded as inferior to the poet, and it was awkward to have a patron inferior to his or her client. The second difficulty is her status as *libertina*, "freedwoman," a liminal position that would have placed her in limbo in respect to Roman law and society and made her dependent on her lover for protection. She is thus in an equivocal position, which Propertius cannot mention but which we always have in the backs of our minds. The third problem is her sexuality, an aspect that cannot be ignored and that distinguishes her from a patron like Maecenas.

How does Propertius handle these two aspects of his newly created "patron"? In elegy, the poets pretend to turn the common social disparity of male and female on its head, and there seems to be a bold reversal of gender roles.[23] From the time perhaps of Catullus (68.68, 156) and certainly of Propertius and Tibullus, the mistresses of elegiac poetry played the role of general in the war of love, cruel tyrant in the master-slave relationship. The well-known rules were sharply reversed by the poets so that the lover became the *domina*, the controller, and the poet, her lover, was presented as the weak and inferior partner.[24] The elegists described a whole new social order: the male became submissive, describing himself as a wounded, unsuccessful hero *manqué* (Propertius 1.1.9–14), a child and a brother (1.11.21–24, 2.18.33–34), dependent on his lover not only for sexual favors, but also for nurturing, inspiration, and encouragement.

By this seeming reversal, the elegists elevated women to a new status and circumvented the problem of the natural inferiority imputed to women. The word used to describe these women, *domina*, appears to be (but is not) the direct analogue to *dominus*, master. Using this obvious, but false, analogy, Propertius describes an unequal relationship like any other patron-client relationship, in which his lover becomes the superior and he becomes her inferior. By using this semantic sleight-of-hand, the poet is able to put the woman in what appears to be the more powerful position. But in terms of actual usage, the word *domina* is not the direct female analogue to the word *dominus*, but rather a domestic word that usually describes an overseer of slaves.[25] Thus the subtext of this analogy conveys an ambiguity in the new superior role assigned to the patron/lover, putting her back into the domestic sphere and undercutting the new public power that the word *dominus* would have assigned to her.

If Cynthia is to be portrayed as a patron, she must have something to offer which would give her a source of power over her inferior. A patron such as Maecenas had many such *beneficia* or gifts he might offer; a *domina* such as Cynthia had only one: her sexual power. Often she might threaten to withhold her gifts, using as her excuse a trip to the country, another man, the festival of Isis, or simple pique. In such an unequal relationship, it is the ability to withhold his or her gift that puts one party in the superior position. Cynthia's femininity and sexual charms put her in a dominant position; she is constructed as, at once, the nurturing mother and the seductive lover. She is given the power to nurture and to inspire her poet/lover both by her maternal presence and her sexual charms, or to enervate, emasculate, and destroy the poet and his verse by withholding her gifts. As *domina*, she is like the mother goddesses, who were described with such words as *genetrix* (cf. Venus in Lucretius, *De Rerum Natura* 1.1). Her powers of inspiration and her status as patron are as inextricably tied to her feminine characteristics as a traditional patron's status was bound up with his masculinity. Her gifts were seen as domestic or sexual in nature; his were public, economic, or social.

It is interesting to follow Propertius' trail as he turns his lover into his substitute patron, while at the same time rejecting the more conventional figures of his male patrons. The reversal is accomplished by the careful transference to Cynthia of the traditional language associated with male patrons. One important characteristic of a patron-client relationship is loyalty. In the two poems to Maecenas (2.1, 3.9) an analogy is drawn between Propertius' putative loyalty to Maecenas and his principles, and Maecenas' loyalty (*fides*) to the emperor Augustus (2.1.35–38, 3.9.33–34).[26] It is not jarring when we hear the same sentiment expressed in poems to Cynthia; after all, one can be loyal to one's lover as well as one's patron. In poem 2.20, Propertius swears eternal loyalty to Cynthia, hoping that *una fides* ("one faithful love") will take them both to their deaths, and he says that his loyalty will endure from start to finish (2.20.15–18, 34–36).[27] The kind of language used of Cynthia and the sentiments expressed remind us not only of Propertius' assurances to Maecenas, but also of Horace's statements to Maecenas throughout his works. Compare for example, Propertius to

Cynthia: *Cynthia prima fuit, Cynthia finis erit* ("Cynthia was my beginning, Cynthia will be my end," 1.12.20) with Horace to Maecenas: *prima dicte mihi, summa dicende Camena* ("you who were sung in my first poem and shall be sung in my last," *Epistle* 1.1.1).

The declaration of loyalty by Propertius to both Maecenas and Cynthia would not in itself compel us to draw an analogy between them as patrons. But we should note the language in the rest of poem 2.20: *nec mihi muneribus nox ulla est empta beatis:/quidquid eram, hoc animi gratia magna tui* ("I have not bought a night with you by means of rich gifts; whatever I have been, for this I am in your debt," 25–26). The themes of gifts, wealth, and indebtedness are fully developed in the poems to Cynthia and to Propertius' male patrons, and they act as another transitional device between the two. In 1.14, one of Propertius' important poems to Tullus, Propertius sets up an elaborate comparison between wealth and love. The poem is a *recusatio* or refusal of Tullus' way of life. Tullus may be wealthy, says Propertius, but he himself is wealthier still because *nescit Amor magnis cedere divitiis* ("Love will not give way before great riches," 8). If Propertius wins over his lover, he has all the wealth of the world; conversely, if one is unhappy in love, one is poor (15–16). When Cynthia is cooperating, in fact, Propertius can afford to scorn *munera* and *regna* (23–24). By the same token, material gifts are often devalued as crass, corrupting, and unworthy.

In poem 2.16, where Cynthia has transferred her affections to a certain wealthy praetor, Propertius advises Cynthia to take all the *munera* she can get, since he assumes (or pretends to assume) that no real love is involved (7–10). Here, then, we have a material exchange described: Cynthia's favors for the praetor's gifts. Propertius regards this kind of exchange as shameful (cf. 2.24.11–16), whereas the exchange between Cynthia and Propertius is conducted on a higher level, according to Propertius, with Cynthia supplying ideal love in return for his ideal poetry.

As Propertius describes it, then, he and Cynthia are involved in a mutual exchange relationship similar to that between patron and client, in which each has something to offer the other, but less on a material than a spiritual level. In their relationship, Cynthia is described throughout as the superior. According to Propertius' idealized account of the relationship, Cynthia reigns over Propertius and his poetry (3.10.17–18, 4.7.50) and she is his *ingenium*, his inspiration, the fount of his talent (2.1.4). In her role as patron, she "breathes inspiration into" (*spiraret*) Propertius and makes the shameful appear seemly (2.24.5–8).[28] Propertius offers in return the power of his poetry to give her fame and a measure of immortality. In a poem strongly reminiscent of Horace's epilogue to his first three books of *Odes*, 3.30, Propertius claims that his poems will bring good fortune to anyone celebrated in them (3.2.17–26); his *ingenium*, he claims, is deathless, immortal (*sine morte*, 26).

Nevertheless, by calling his *ingenium* deathless, Propertius has problematized the situation. If Cynthia is identified as his *ingenium*, how can his *ingenium* be immortal? Cynthia is a real woman and real women grow old and die—so Cynthia is represented as doing in Propertius' poetry. But, when we read the poems, we come to realize that Cynthia has no identity as a real person; rather, she becomes identified completely with Propertius' poetry and therefore with Propertius. When he mentions her name, he is denoting not Cynthia the woman, but Cynthia the subject of his poetry. When an imaginary friend says, *Tu loqueris, cum sis iam noto fabula libro/et tua sit toto Cynthia lecta foro?* ("Do you say this now that your book is famous and your Cynthia is read all over town?" 2.24.1–2), he is not referring to a person independent of the text. Even when Cynthia is given a more human and objectified form, she begins to take on the characteristics of his poetry. She reads his poems *deducta voce* ("in a refined and delicate voice," 2.33.38); *deduco* is a verb used to describe the Callimachean style of poetry that Propertius writes (1.6.41).[29]

Further, her actions, dress, words, and accomplishments are only important as fodder for his verse (2.1.5–16, 2.3.9–22); Cynthia quickly becomes a story (*historia*, 2.1.16; cf. 1.15.23–24). In her various roles, Cynthia is said to have the power of life and death over both Propertius' poetry and his very existence. If she withholds the nurturing force of her favors, he and his poetry suffer (1.12.5–6); if she grants such favors, she is like a god who has the power to make Propertius immortal (2.15.39–40). She becomes so much a part of his being that, if she is hardhearted (*dura*), he will die (2.1.78). Propertius even refers to their relationship continuing beyond the grave. In an abstract reference to Cynthia as inspirer and lover, he claims, *huius ero vivus, mortuus huius ero* ("hers I will be while I am alive, hers I will be when dead," 2.15.36; cf. 1.19.11–12, 2.13a).

More graphically, he pictures Cynthia appearing from beyond the grave and delivering a lecture on his faithfulness while pointing her skeletal finger at him (4.7.11–12). At the end of her grisly diatribe, Cynthia declares, *mox sola tenebo:/mecum eris, et mixtis ossibus ossa teram* ("Soon you will be all mine: you will be here with me and I will grind my bones against yours," 93–94). In her anger, she instructs him to burn his poetry and to stop capitalizing on the fame he derives from using her in his verse. She claims that his ivy, the standard adornment of poets, is choking her grave and her bones (79–80).[30] Here we have perhaps the ultimate identification of Cynthia with Propertius' poetry. Propertius cannot escape Cynthia even after death, but, by the same token, Cynthia's bones are choked by the ivy adorning Propertius in his poetic guise. Even after her death (and we could argue that she has been dead for him all along), he is choking her.

And of course she cannot escape Propertius because "she" is a figment of his imagination (whether she is real or not), his poetic construct. Although Propertius makes great claims for her power, his language often belies these claims. One example of this occurs in a passage where Propertius employs a standard metaphor from the world of agriculture. In poem 2.11, Propertius is angry at Cynthia, and he threatens her with the worst possible punishment: not receiving any notice in his poetry. He will not write of her, he says; rather, let another praise her, one who is stupid enough to "sow his seeds in a sterile ground" (*laudet, qui sterili semina ponit humo*, 2.11.2). Unlike Ovid, who often takes such traditional male/female metaphors and turns them on their head, Propertius maintains the standard posture of the male in the aggressive, dominant act of sowing and the female as the passive, weak receptor.[31] But here, Cynthia cannot even receive; she is sterile. Propertius has appropriated her most female characteristic, her childbearing capabilities, by picturing her as sterile and then investing in her a bogus substitute creativity that gives birth only to *his* poetry.[32]

Cynthia, then, is portrayed as a shifting figure—sometimes a literary construct, the creature of Propertius, sometimes the personification of inspiration and poetic power.[33] Propertius flirts with the idea of Cynthia offering immortality to him, but quickly denigrates her power to immortalize by frequent references to her death. In her capacity as the embodiment of Propertius' poetry (a capacity granted to her by Propertius), she can offer to him and to it eternal life, but, in her role as woman and lover, she cannot. Propertius kills off any corporeal, external aspect of this figure and removes any power he has invested in her by identifying her completely with his own poetry. She is allowed no subjectivity, no consciousness, no point of view. She is a vague composite of qualities, a figure who never existed.[34] And, as this is true, Propertius can easily manipulate her and appropriate her putative powers so that she becomes an embodiment of the traditionally constructed female: fickle, weak-minded, and easily swayed by gifts, wantonly destructive, a witch and a crone (Propertius 3.25, 4.7). She is also set apart from the male patrons whom she replaces in one important aspect. Male patrons always possess (or at least are given by their poet/clients) an identifiable, stable character and a power external to the poetry. Cynthia is a poor substitute, having no external identity or power and no integrity. She is wholly a creature of the poet, who has appropriated her power as a woman and used it to dominate and to change her.

¶

Propertius' identification of his lover with his patron appealed to later, postclassical poets who adapted this idea in interesting ways.[35] One writer in particular gives this idea an odd twist: Shakespeare. Many of Shakespeare's earlier sonnets (1–126) are addressed to a male patron who is tentatively identified by the publisher of the Sonnets, Thomas Thorpe, as Mr. W. H.; I shall refer to him here as the "fair youth."[36] Most editors regard the youth as a patron figure, and Shakespeare himself uses language that gives credence to this characterization (e.g., *Sonnet* 78). I will not argue here that the fair youth is in any real way parallel to a figure such as Cynthia; rather, we can view him as a contrast to the female lover/patron that reveals the essential difference between assigning the position of lover/patron to a man and to a woman.

Arguments over the identity of Shakespeare's fair youth abound. A large number of candidates have been proposed, including the 3d Earl of Southhampton (Henry Wriothesley, W. H. in reverse), William Herbert, Earl of Pembroke, and even Shakespeare himself (W. H.= "William Himself"), a symbolization of himself or his poetry.[37] A precise identification cannot be made (just as we cannot identify the Dark Lady), and surely Shakespeare has purposely left the identities and figures of these addressees vague. What makes the fair youth interesting for our purposes is that this lover/patron figure, who is in some ways analogous to Propertius' Cynthia, is cast as a feminized male and an androgynous figure. C. S. Lewis' reaction to this fair youth betrays his confusion over Shakespeare's feeling for his friend and patron which was "too lover-like for that of ordinary male friendship." "Yet," he claims, "this does not seem to be the poetry of full-blown pederasty."[38]

But it should not surprise us to find such androgynous figures in Shakespeare's poetry. Gender identities are kept fluid throughout Shakespeare's works. In the sonnets, he sometimes successfully imagines himself in the place of the female and crosses gender boundaries; we could, for example, identify the Dark Lady as a symbolization of Shakespeare and his poetry. His plays are full of characters who "play the other."[39] Most of these, however, reverse the situation of the fair youth, playing masculinized women or women dressed as men (e.g., Rosalind in *As You Like It*) rather than feminized males.[40] In the plays, the gender situation is usually normalized at the end, when disguises are removed and the woman disguised as a man is revealed to be a woman and is married to a male character. The fair youth, however, comes to no such resolution.

I would like to look at some of the sonnets in which the youth appears, where the language and imagery are reminiscent of Propertius' poems to Cynthia, and then draw some conclusions about his place in Shakespeare's poetry, drawing comparisons with Cynthia's role in Propertius' verse. First, two sonnets in which Shakespeare describes the youth's beauty:

> If I could write the beauty of your eyes
> And in fresh numbers number all your graces,
> The age to come would say "This Poet lies—
> Such heav'nly touches ne'er touched earthly faces.
> (17.5–8)[41]

or

> Shall I compare thee to a summer's day?
> Thou art more lovely and more temperate. (18.1–2)

The fair youth has beauty of the sort generally attributed to a woman. He is also the poet's muse, patron, and inspiration:

> So oft have I invoked thee for my muse,
> And found such fair assistance in my verse,
> As every alien pen hath got my use,
> And under thee their poesy disperse.
> Thine eyes, that taught the dumb on high to sing
> ....
> Have added feathers to the learned's wing,
> ....
> Yet be most proud of that which I compile,
> Whose influence is thine, and born of thee,
> ....
> But thou art all my art, and dost advance
> As high as learning my rude ignorance.
> (78.1–5, 7, 9–10, 13–14)

There is a conscious merging in these sonnets of the separate identities of lover and patron into one figure as there is in Propertius, but here the patron/lover is male. Shakespeare makes this fusion of the two gender-associated roles explicit when in 20.2 he calls his friend "the master mistress of my passion" (passion indicating here both his ardor and his love poetry). He is attracted sexually by the man's feminine charms, yet there is between them the kind of friendship that can exist only between men. His friend is "mistress" in that he fulfills the function of a lover (one who attracts and inspires by her beauty), yet he is superior to a lover such as Cynthia because he can master the poet's passion. So too, unlike Cynthia, whose female gender is linked with the lack of a genuine point of view, of a stable personality, or even of a serious bond with the speaker, he is represented as possessing a monolithic character that threatens the integrity of the poet himself.[42]

In return for the inspiration given by the youth, Shakespeare confers immortality upon his friend:

> 'Gainst death and all oblivious enmity
> Shall you pace forth; your praise shall still find room,
> ....
> So till the judgement that yourself arise,
> You live in this, and dwell in lovers' eyes.
> (55.9–10, 13–14)

Indeed, the youth will have two chances at immortality: his children and the poems in his honor:

> But were some child of yours alive that time,
> You should live twice in it and in my rhyme.
> (17.13–14)[43]

Never does Propertius mention Cynthia's child-bearing capabilities as connected with the potential for what Shakespeare sees as the real immortality; in fact, Propertius completely rejects the idea of having children (2.7; 2.15). Propertius removes from Cynthia her biological ability to bear children, appropriating the procreative talent for himself and vitiating her femaleness, her identity, and her maternal power. In any case, it would have been difficult for a woman to conceive of achieving personal, individual immortality through children in a society with patrilinear descent.[44] Shakespeare, on the other hand, feels perfectly secure in granting to his patron/lover all possible powers, since he participates in a close male-male relationship that is unthreatened by the unmanning posed by a woman such as Cynthia.

In his promise of immortality to his patron/lover, Shakespeare rings a remarkable change on his classical predecessors. Whereas Propertius concentrates as much on his own poetic immortality as on his power to bestow it upon his lover,[45] Shakespeare dismisses his own future reputation as insignificant and confers the hope of poetic immortality on his patron/lover alone:

> Or shall I live your epitaph to make,

> Or you survive when I in earth am rotten
> From hence your memory death cannot take,
> Although in me each part will be forgotten.
> Your name from hence immortal life shall have.
> Though I, once gone, to all the world must die,
> The earth can yield me but a common grave,
> When you entombed in men's eyes shall lie.
> Your monument shall be my gentle verse.
> ....
> You still shall live—such virtue hath my pen—
> Where breath most breathes, ev'n in the mouths of men.
> (81.1–9, 13–14)

Because Shakespeare's patron and the object of his devotion is a man, he never merges with the writer's poetry. In contrast, Shakespeare often alludes to his real identity (as opposed to the portrait presented of him by various poets), and he firmly indicates a sharp separation between the person and the poetic construct:[46]

> There lives more life in one of your fair eyes,
> Then both your poets can in praise devise.
> (83.13–14)

The fair youth is credited by the poet/lover with a clear identity and an integrated and monolithic character. There is an ease expressed about this relationship that is absent in the presence of a woman. Such a male-male involvement is set (very like Greek male friendships) within a structure of institutionalized social relations that are accomplished through women but depend on the bonds that exist between males.[47] By way of contrast, Shakespeare's poems to the Dark Lady betray a very different set of parameters. She has no point of view, no subjectivity, and no integrated personality. She is defined by doubleness and by deceit, and remains, like Cynthia, an uneasy and indistinct character.

In adapting, then, some of Propertius' forms of address to his patron/lover, Shakespeare radically reformulates the terms of the relationship by making a male the object of his poetry and his affections. Unlike

Propertius, who grants powers to his lover only to strip them away from her and deny her any real identity at all, Shakespeare successfully combines in his male addressee/lover/patron the sensual and inspirational qualities of a female lover with the dominance and articulated character and identity of a man. Shakespeare's "master mistress" has an intriguingly androgynous personality that Propertius' Cynthia cannot have. Although ostensibly constructed as male, Cynthia's female gender precludes the characterization of her as an independent and powerful individual.

Roman elegy is often said to be proof that Roman women were in a stronger position than their Greek predecessors, and this may indeed be the case. But Roman elegy at the same time points up the illusory nature of women's so-called dominance in its creators' literary imaginations. The power seemingly invested in these elegiac women to give immortality and inspiration is not granted to them as individuals but to a poetic, muse-like image created and manipulated by the male poet. Shakespeare's poems to his "master mistress," a male figure who, unlike Cynthia, has a true integrity apart from the poetry and shares a bond with the poet, are important for our understanding of Roman elegy. They help us to see in the male-produced and male-dominated poetry of first-century B.C.E. Rome the deeply-felt difference between a female "patron" such as Cynthia, who is essentially powerless to accomplish anything without the poet to manipulate her, and a real patron such as Maecenas, who has true political and personal power to advance his own and the poet's interests.

Barbara K. Gold
Hamilton College

Notes

I would like to thank Judith Hallett, Lawrence Richardson, jr and Carl Rubino for their comments on this paper.

[1] On the figure of the lover as slave in Roman elegy, see Frank O. Copley, "*Servitium Amoris* in the Roman Elegists," *TAPA*, 78 (1947), 285–300; R. O. A. M. Lyne, "*Servitium Amoris*," *CQ*, n.s. 29 (1979), 117–30.

² The female patrons I will examine will be drawn largely from first-century C.E. Pompeii because this period and place offer the most striking examples. Clearly, however, such powerful women existed in the period during which elegiac poetry was written as well; Republican literature such as Cicero's and Sallust's works offers us myriad examples.

³ It is difficult to know exactly what classical literature Shakespeare had read, but it is quite clear that he was deeply influenced by Roman and Greek literature. Frank Wadsworth, "Shakespeare's Life," in *William Shakespeare: The Complete Works*, ed. A. Harbage (1969; rpt. New York, 1986), speculates that at the Stratford grammar school, the curriculum consisted "almost entirely of Latin—grammar, reading, writing, and recitation." He continues: "It is probable ... that he [Shakespeare] would have been allowed to act out scenes from Terence and Plautus; there were, too, the wonders of Ovid, particularly of the *Metamorphoses*" (12). Shakespeare's early plays are laced with Latin, and his familiarity with the classics is apparent throughout. See, for example, *Titus Andronicus* IV.i, where Lucius comes in with some Latin books. Among these is Ovid's *Metamorphoses*, which Lavinia picks up. In her mutilated state, she manages to find in it the story of Philomela, which illustrates Lavinia's horrible tale. See also *The Taming of the Shrew* II.i, where Baptista receives a "small packet of Greek and Latin books" for the education of his daughters.

⁴ See Richard P. Saller, *Personal Patronage under the Early Empire* (Cambridge, 1982), 1; Saller, "Martial on Patronage and Literature," *CQ*, 33 (1983), 256. Saller takes his terms from J. Boissevain, "Patronage in Sicily," *Man*, n.s. 1 (1966), 18.

⁵ Judith Hallett, however, has argued in her article, "Women as Same and Other in the Classical Roman Elite," *Helios*, 16.1 (1989), 59–78, that blood line can at times transcend gender in aristocratic women, at least in how they are perceived as family representatives.

⁶ Cf., for example, the noble Servilia and wealthy Fulvia and their relationship to the equestrian Atticus (Nepos, *Life of Atticus* 9 [Fulvia], 11 [Servilia]); Cornelia's acquiescence when Scipio Aemilianus gave her mother's estate to his mother and his adoptive father's sisters (Polybius 31.26–28).

⁷ This is not to deny that women in Rome seem to have had a certain amount of influence on public events. See Skinner's remarks on Clodia, who "maintained a wide network of contacts and acquaintances and was known as a wealthy woman of some influence" (285); also notable are Brutus' mother, Servilia, who attempted to have a Senate decree changed (Marilyn B. Skinner, "Clodia Metelli," *TAPA*, 113 [1983], 285 n. 31; cf. Cicero, *Atticus* 15.11.2, 15.12.1); Antony's wife Fulvia (Appian, *Bellum Civile* 4.32–34; Judith P. Hallett, *Fathers and Daughters in Roman Society: Women and the Elite Family* [Princeton, 1984], 233–34; n. 9 below). See also Elizabeth P. Forbis, "Women's Public Image in Italian Honorary Inscriptions,"

AJP, 111.4 (1990), 493–512; Judith P. Hallett, "*Perusinae Glandes* and the Changing Image of Augustus," *American Journal of Ancient History*, 2 (1977), 151–71; Hallett, "Women as *Same* and *Other*," 59–78; Ramsey MacMullen, "Woman in Public in the Roman Empire," *Historia*, 29 (1980), 208–18; A. J. Marshall, "Roman Women and the Provinces," *Ancient Society*, 6 (1975), 109–27; and John Nicols, "*Patrona Civitatis*: Gender and Civic Patronage," *Latomus*, 206 (1989), 117–42, who discusses women as municipal *patronae* in the Roman empire. MacMullen, "Woman in Public," emphasizes the importance of the network of connections that such women were able to build because of their high social standing (217); Marshall, who denies that Roman women were ever given the chance to "make a distinctive contibution to Rome's imperial mission" (126), stresses that the women under Roman rule in Greece and Asia Minor owed any power they had to "the social class and inherited wealth of which civic office was ... merely the outward token ..." (125). For discussions of women's access to speech, see the essays of Kenneth Walters, Judith de Luce, and Elizabeth Holtze in this volume.

[8] For Servilia, see Tom Hillard, "On the Stage, Behind the Curtain: Images of Politically Active Women in the Late Roman Republic," in *Stereotypes of Women in Power: Historical Perspectives and Revisionist Views*, eds. Barbara Garlick, Suzanne Dixon, and Pauline Allen (New York, 1991), 53–55; for Fulvia, see Charles L. Babcock, "The Early Career of Fulvia," *AJP*, 86.1 (1965), 1–32, who argues that Fulvia had political involvements before her marriage to Antony, and Hallett "*Perusinae Glandes*," 151–71. For women in general who crossed into the political realm, see Garlick, Dixon, and Allen, *Stereotypes of Women*, especially the chapter by Arlene W. Saxonhouse, "Introduction—Public and Private: The Paradigm's Power," 1–9.

[9] See Aulus Gellius 1.23; Macrobius, *Saturnalia* 1.6.19–25; Hallett, *Fathers and Daughters*, 249–50. On the negative perceptions of politically active women, see Hillard, 37–64; Amy Richlin, "Julia's Jokes, Galla Placidia, and the Roman Use of Women as Political Icons," in *Stereotypes of Women in Power*, eds. B. Garlick, S. Dixon, and P. Allen, 65–91.

[10] See Marilyn Arthur, "From Medusa to Cleopatra: Women in the Ancient World," in *Becoming Visible: Women in European History*, eds. Renate Bridenthal, Claudia Koontz, and Susan Stuard, 2d ed. (Boston, 1987), 97–102, especially 98.

[11] See Suzanne Dixon, "A Family Business: Women's Role in Patronage and Politics at Rome 80–44 B.C.," *Classica & Mediaevalia*, 34 (1983), 91–112; Hallett, *Fathers and Daughters*, 29; Riet Van Bremen, "Women and Wealth," in *Images of Women in Antiquity*, eds. Averil Cameron and Amélie Kuhrt (London, 1983), 235–37, for Greek women in the Hellenistic and Roman periods. Anthropologists disagree over where exactly the locus of the greatest power for women lies.

Some argue that, when the distinction between public and private is highly developed, women have a lower status, being more segregated and kept from public power. Others would argue that women in this situation have a separate sphere of power and thus greater dominance than in societies where the public/private distinction is weak. See *Gender and Power in Rural Greece*, ed. Jill Dubisch (Princeton, 1986), 12–13 and the essay of Bella Zweig in this volume. It should be noted, however, that Roman women were not segregated in the same way that many Greek women were. A further kind of power is suggested by Ernestine Friedl, "The Position of Women: Appearance and Reality," *Anthropological Quarterly*, 40 (1967), whose article on contemporary rural Greece describes a disruptive, negative power that women have over men when they disrupt orderly relationships by refusing to behave in a chaste and modest fashion (108). I would like to thank Joseph Russo for this reference.

[12] For wealthy and powerful Greek female benefactors from the second century B.C.E. to the third century C.E. who formed part of the important system of "euergetism," see Van Bremen, "Women and Wealth," 223–42. She argues that women in many Greek cities in this period went beyond their usual religious roles and encroached on traditionally male areas of public life and politics. She mentions two particular examples of such women, Euxenia of Megalopolis (second century B.C.E.) and Menodora of Sillyon (first century C.E.). See also Sarah B. Pomeroy, who links the improved position of women largely to their education and their acquisition of economic power and subsequently of legal rights, *Goddesses, Whores, Wives, and Slaves: Women in Classical Antiquity* (New York, 1975), 126; and her "Technikai kai mousikai: The Education of Women in the Fourth Century and in the Hellenistic Period," *American Journal of Ancient History* (1977), 51–68. Van Bremen maintains that there was a continuum rather than an evolution in the prominence of some women and argues that only the size of their wealth increased in the Hellenistic period.

[13] I would like to thank Lawrence Richardson, jr, for his comments on Mamia and Eumachia; as always, he has been a great help to me.

[14] W. Moeller, "The Building of Eumachia: a Reconsideration," *American Journal of Archaeology*, 76 (1972), has suggested that this building served several purposes for both the fullers and the wool-traders (323–27); Lawrence Richardson, jr, "Concordia and Concordia Augusta: Rome and Pompeii," *La Parola del Passato*, 33 (1978), argues against this interpretation (269 n. 13). Richardson says that the building is too splendid for a cloth market and that there is not adequate access for the public. He suggests that it was a public *porticus* providing shelter, space to walk and to converse, and a bazaar area (268–69). Jean Andreau, *Les affaires de Monsieur Jucundus* (Rome, 1974), proposes that the building was a meeting place for the business men of Pompeii,

particularly those associated with maritime trade (294). See also Paavo Castrén, *Ordo Populusque Pompeianus: Polity and Society in Roman Pompeii* (Rome, 1975), who believes that the building "served more general political or social purposes" and was not necessarily connected to the activities of the fullers (101).

[15] For more information on these and other prominent women in Pompeii, see Castrén, ibid., 71, 95, 96, 101–102; Michele D'Avino, *The Women of Pompeii*, trans. M. Jones and L. Nusco (Naples, 1967), 20–21; Elizabeth Lyding Will, "Women in Pompeii," *Archaeology*, 32.5 (Sept./Oct., 1979), 34–43. For detailed information on the buildings of Mamia and Eumachia, see Andreau, *Les affaires de Monsieur Jucundus*, 78–79, 293–94 (Eumachia); Michael Grant, *Cities of Vesuvius: Pompeii and Herculaneum* (New York, 1971), 199 (Eumachia); Amedeo Maiuri, *Pompeii*, trans. V. Priestley, 5th ed. (Rome, 1961), 24–25 (Eumachia); August Mau, *Pompeii: Its Life and Art*, trans. F. W. Kelsey, 2d ed. (New York, 1904), 110–18 (Eumachia), 410 (Mamia); Moeller, 323–27 (Eumachia); Richardson, "Concordia and Concordia Augusta," 267–69 (Eumachia); Richardson, *Pompeii: An Architectural History* (Baltimore, 1988), 191–94, 254 (Mamia), 194–98, 256–57 (Eumachia).

[16] Van Bremen, "Women and Wealth," 223–42, and MacMullen, "Woman in Public," 213–18, discuss evidence for female patrons in Greek inscriptions; Forbis, "Women's Public Image," 493–512, examines Italian inscriptions and lists many of the numerous inscriptions that praise women for their own public benefactions (e.g., *CIL* 10.3703; 10.6529; 14.2804) and women for benefactions of male relatives (e.g., *CIL* 9.330; 11.405; 11.5270). Joseph C. Rockwell, *Private Baustiftungen für die Stadtgemeinde auf Inschriften der Kaiserzeit im Westen des römischen Reiches* (Jena, 1909), discusses female patrons of temples, baths, theaters, libraries, and other public buildings (84–88). Russell Meiggs, *Roman Ostia*, 2d ed. (Oxford, 1973), has only a brief section on women, but he mentions a particularly interesting inscription about a woman who bequeathed a sum of money for the upbringing of one hundred girls (229; cf. *CIL* 14, Supp. 1, 4450).

[17] Forbis, "Women's Public Image," 494–96.

[18] See Judith Hallett, "Catullus on Composition," *CW*, 81.5 (1988), in which she suggests that Catullus, in poems 50, 65, and elsewhere, compares his poetry to the engendering of progeny (395–401).

[19] The relationship of the elegists to their patrons is highly problematic. A poet like Propertius, who was from a wealthy family, did not require material support from his patrons, but may have wanted publicity, introductions, and similar non-material gifts. Furthermore, Propertius' predecessors had dedicated their works to patrons, and thus it was conventional to have a patron. Nevertheless, it was also becoming controversial by Propertius' time to take an

ironic stance and to reject the very public issues that such patrons stood for. Propertius, therefore, coopts men like Tullus and Maecenas, confounding the public and private worlds by his use of language and making good use of the *recusatio*, in which he could acknowledge the importance of epic and public values while rejecting them for himself at the same time.

[20] For a discussion of Propertius' relationship with his male patrons and of how the patronage system in Rome worked in general, see *Literary and Artistic Patronage in Ancient Rome*, ed. Barbara K. Gold, (Austin, Texas, 1982); Barbara K. Gold, *Literary Patronage in Greece and Rome* (Chapel Hill, N.C., 1987).

[21] Gold, *Literary Patronage*, 115–41. Horace's major themes, exemplified by Maecenas, are contentment, simplicity, and poetry.

[22] See, e.g., Catullus 1; Horace, *Odes* 1.1; Vergil, *Georgics* 2.39–41; for a case study of a close relationship between patron and writer (Horace and Maecenas), see M. Santirocco, "The Maecenas Odes," *TAPA*, 114 (1984), 241–53.

[23] For an important treatment of this matter, see Judith P. Hallett, "The Role of Women in Roman Elegy: Counter-Cultural Feminism," *Arethusa*, 6.1 (1973); rpt. in *Women in the Ancient World: The Arethusa Papers*, eds. John Peradotto and J. P Sullivan (Albany, 1984), 241–62.

[24] For a discussion of the word *domina*, see Hallett, "The Role of Women," 249–52 and n. 43.

[25] On the meaning of *domina*, see A. Ernout and E. Meillet, *Dictionnaire étymologique de la langue latine*, 3d ed. (Paris, 1951), s.v. *dominus*; Saara Lilja, *The Roman Elegists' Attitude to Women* (Helsinki, 1965), 81.

[26] Housman would transpose 3.9.33–34 after 2.1.38.

[27] Cf. also 2.20.4 and Cynthia's protestations of her loyalty in 4.7.51–54.

[28] For similar passages of gods or patrons inspiring the works of poets (and using the verb *adspiro*), see Vergil, *Aen.* 9.525; *Ciris* 99; Ovid, *Metamorphoses* 1.3.

[29] For a discussion of the meaning of *deduco* in the Roman poets, see David O. Ross, Jr., *Backgrounds to Augustan Poetry: Gallus, Elegy and Rome* (Cambridge, 1975), 19, 26, 65–66.

[30] See Horace, *Odes* 1.1.29–30 for a more traditional use of ivy as a poet's adornment.

[31] See Ovid, *Ars Amatoria* 1.449–50 and the comment on this passage by Laurie J. Churchill, "Magisterial Voice and the Pleasure of the Text: Irony in the *Ars Amatoria*," *Pacific Coast Philology*, 20 (1985), 33–38. As Churchill points out, the gender roles are reversed in Ovid, with the woman becoming the *dominus* and the lover himself figured as the sterile field that withholds its gifts (34–35). Cf. also Catullus 1.11.21–24 for the plough/field image. Page duBois, *Sowing the Body* (Chicago, 1988), discusses the developing metaphors used of women's bodies in antiquity. First figured as earth, they are subsequently described as field and then furrow, a space in the field that is "marked,

cut into, and ploughed by the cultivator" (65).

[32] Cf. Catullus' figuring of his poetry as his children in e.g., poem 65; see Hallett, "Catullus on Composition," 395–99.

[33] For other aspects of Cynthia, see Barbara K. Gold, "But Ariadne Was Never There in the First Place: Finding the Female in Roman Poetry," in *Feminist Theory and the Classics*, eds. A. Richlin and N. Rabinowitz (New York, 1993).

[34] Cf. the article of Kathleen McNamee in this volume.

[35] Cf. also Petrarch's representation of Laura.

[36] This term is used by Eve Kosofsky Sedgwick in *Between Men: English Literature and Male Homosocial Desire* (New York, 1985), 28–48.

[37] See M. Seymour-Smith, *Shakespeare's Sonnets* (London, 1963), 14–19.

[38] C. S. Lewis, *English Literature in the Sixteenth Century Excluding Drama* (Oxford, 1954), 503.

[39] For this phrase, see Froma I. Zeitlin, "Playing the Other: Theater, Theatricality, and the Feminine in Greek Drama," *Representations*, 11 (1985), 63–94.

[40] It bears notice here that these roles were written for male actors playing female parts, just to make matters even more confusing.

[41] I have used throughout the edition of Shakespeare's sonnets by Stephen Booth (New Haven, 1977).

[42] See Sedgwick, *Between Men*, 41–43.

[43] Cf. Sonnet 16, where Shakespeare extols physical procreation as a path to immortality superior to his "barren rhyme."

[44] See, e.g., Propertius 4.11, where Cornelia will achieve "immortality" only through her male-dominated bloodlines, but not through her own individuality as a creator.

[45] Propertius here echoes Horace, who is interested more in his own immortality than in that of his patron, Maecenas (Horace, *Odes* 2.20, 3.30). See the remarks of J. Fineman, *Shakespeare's Perjured Eye* (Berkeley, 1986), on the tendency of certain poets to turn poetry of praise into praise of poetry itself and of the poet himself. Although Fineman is discussing Renaissance sonnets, his remarks apply equally well to Roman lyric and elegy (8–9 and passim). Fineman argues that Shakespeare too essentially effaces the objects of his praise, including the youth, by refocusing the attention of his epideictic poetry on himself, his poetry, and his own admiration for the youth (209) and by throwing both himself and the youth into a "space of ontological indeterminacy" (219).

[46] Cf. also Sonnets 16, 82, 84.

[47] Sedgwick, *Between Men*, 35. I would distinguish the type of relationship represented in Shakespeare from a typical male-male patron/client paradigm because of the erotic nature and the shift of power in the former.

"O for a Thousand Tongues to Sing": A Footnote on Metamorphosis, Silence, and Power

In discussing American women poets revising traditional stories, Alicia Ostriker has written that "mythology seems an inhospitable terrain for a woman writer."[1] Greco-Roman mythology, which in its literary versions rarely tolerates the voices of women, is particularly inhospitable. We read of men's experiences, men's lives, in men's words. Even the story of an Andromache or a Dido is conveyed through the extant voices of male authors. In this sense, then, the woman of myth is truly the silent woman. Yet in literary treatments of a particular myth motif she is also the "silenced" woman when she is raped and thereafter rendered incapable of speech. It is with the silenced woman, in particular, Callisto, Io, and Philomela, that the current study begins.

Three scholars have already examined this motif with admirable thoroughness but in so doing have either left aside the profound silence of the victims or have not discussed its significance in light of Greco-Roman assumptions about language use. They have not articulated convincingly the link between speech and what it means to be human. Leo Curran anticipated by some years the work of later feminist critics when he explored in detail the rape stories in the *Metamorphoses*.[2] Relying in part on Susan Brownmiller, Curran noted the provocative correspondence between Ovid's representation of the trauma of rape and contemporary analyses of the psychological costs for the victim.[3] Curran concludes that by the time he wrote the *Metamorphoses*, Ovid was beginning to see that rape is "less an act of sexual passion than of aggression and that erotic gratification is secondary to the rapist's desire to dominate physically, to humiliate, and to degrade."[4] With his usual perceptiveness, Curran does note in the transformation of Io the connection between rape, dehumanization, and the loss of speech as a reminder of that dehumanization. I will build on Curran's work and develop the connection between the dehumanization of transformation and the traditional association of speech with humankind.⁵

Kathleen Wall has studied one example of the motif, treatments of Callisto's story from Ovid to Atwood. In this expanded study of the myth, Wall applies the lessons of feminist critical theory, including the work of Annis Pratt and Sherry Ortner.⁶ In her study, Wall draws together the implications of a pattern that includes an independent virgin, isolation or exile in the deep woods, echoes of a *hieros gamos* or sacred marriage, hints of initiation into mature female sexuality, and patriarchal interpretations of all these elements. Wall writes convincingly of the connection between women and nature, but fails to note that one of the most striking features of the rape stories is the silencing of the women, a silencing that may serve to isolate women within the non-human world.

Most recently, Elizabeth Forbis has studied voicelessness in Ovid's exile poetry, relating it to the motifs of voice and voicelessness in the *Metamorphoses*.⁷ Her study encompasses more than the rape stories, including individuals who are punished for speaking. She contrasts the muted victims in the *Metamorphoses* and the powerful narrator/poet who had controlled their stories, with the powerless and muted poet in exile who refers to those very individuals whose stories he told in the earlier poem. In spite of the comprehensiveness of the study, Forbis does not connect voicelessness with the traditional assumption in Greek and Roman tradition that language distinguishes human beings from other animals.⁸ My essay will serve as a footnote to these previous discussions by establishing the connection between the stories of silencing and humankind's alleged monopoly on language. At first I will consider the motif as if it were specific to women.

We should not ignore how many of Ovid's stories in the *Metamorphoses* involve the consequences of speech or its denial. In the approximately 250 stories of the poem, containing some 600 individuals, males outnumber females roughly 2:1. We must observe a caveat here, however, because the mere appearance of a name does not tell us much about the length of the story, its placement, or its importance in the poem. Moreover, there are reasons why so many men appear in the poem: for example, the Trojan War is essentially a story about men, with male heroes and male gods. Of those 250 stories, however, there are some 40 stories distributed throughout the poem that bear directly on issues of voice and silence: that is, someone gets into trouble for speaking; or we are reminded of the power of speech; or someone is rendered speechless through physical mutilation or transformation.

The accomplished speakers of the *Metamorphoses* include Nestor (12.160), Orpheus (10.148–739), and Ulysses (Books 12–14, passim). Of the women narrators, Arethusa and Galatea tell their own stories (5.572, 13.738), while Arachne and the Emathides tell the stories of others (6.5, 5.669). Cassandra reminds us of the plight of a speaker who is not believed (13.410); and Medusa, or at least her head, silences those who look upon her by turning them into stone (4.655). There are also ample reminders that speaking can get the speaker into trouble: a boy becomes a lizard after challenging Ceres (5.451); Galanthis, who enables Alcmena to give birth by tricking the goddess of childbirth into standing up, becomes a weasel (9.306); Echo, who detains Juno during Jupiter's liaison, loses her body (3.358); Niobe watches all her children killed, after she has boasted of her superiority as a mother because she has fourteen children and Latona has only two (6.165).

Although male characters outnumber female ones in the poem as a whole, in the forty stories reflecting some aspect of the silence/speech motif, women outnumber men 3:1. While the same caveat needs to be applied here, that the mere mention of a name does not tell us very much about the significance of the story, it is also true that a number of these stories are especially memorable and told at considerable length: Echo, Daphne, Io, Callisto, Niobe, Arachne, Procne, and Philomela.[9]

Contemporary feminist criticism has shown increasing interest in the very issues implied by these stories of silenced women, particularly the relationships among gender, silence, language, and power. Lacanian perspectives as well as the analyses of language patterns by Lakoff, for example, point to the social context within which men and women use language, and to what effect. Literary analyses of women's writing by Heilbrun, and Ostriker, among others, all suggest that we need to reread literature by and about women with as much attention to the opportunities for and conditions of speech as to what is actually said.[10]

Greek and Latin writers traditionally identified language use (and the concomitant ability to reason) as species-specific, that is, as a uniquely human characteristic absent in non-human animals. The examples that follow are by no means exhaustive, but they suggest the range and persistence of this assumption.

According to Plato in the *Politicus* (272c), human beings were once able to understand other animals during the Golden Age but lost that ability along with the Golden Age itself. Melampus derived his reputation as a seer in part from his ability to understand the speech of animals, although it is not necessarily clear whether he only understood their language or whether they also spoke his. At any rate, the ability to understand non-human language clearly marks him off from other people, including a number of other seers. Part of the humor of Plutarch's *Bruta animalia ratione uti*, (*Moralia*, Loeb vol. 12), of course, derives from our surprise that an animal can not only speak in human language but also can debate. In Plutarch's version, Circe had promised to change all his men back into human beings if Odysseus would discuss with a very eloquent pig and former crew member, Gryllus, the issue of whether human beings are happier than other animals and whether non-human animals can reason.

Traditionally, language use distinguished human beings, primarily because it allowed for the development of culture, generally assumed to be superior to the rest of the animal world's lack of culture. In *Antigone*, for example, Sophocles' chorus (332–72) links language, reason, and civilization. "Many the wonders, but nothing walks stranger than a human being." After enumerating the discoveries made by human beings such as hunting and fishing, domestication of animals and the practice of agriculture, the chorus muses on speech: "Language, and thought like the wind and the feelings that make the town."[11]

Lucretius, too, regards language as a critical step in the development of human culture. When the earth was still young, human beings lived in caves; they wore no clothing, built no fires; there was no agriculture; there was no society and no law; they might die because an animal attacked them during a hunt, but they did not die in war or on the sea.

> Then, too, neighbors began to form friendship one with another, longing neither to hurt not to be harmed, and they commended to mercy children and the race of women, with cries and gestures they taught by broken words that 'tis right for all to have pity on the

weak. ... But the diverse sounds of the tongue nature
constrained men to utter, and use shaped the names of
things.   (*De Rerum Natura* 5.1019–23, 1028–29)[12]

Language facilitates civilization in part because it eliminates the necessity for each community to "reinvent the wheel." With language, we can negotiate with our neighbors, hand on information, refer to the past, discuss those who are absent, and plan for the future.

Language, more specifically speech, bestows power on individuals. A non-Classical example is appropriate here: as Adam names the inhabitants of the world around him (Genesis 2.19–10), he arrogates the means to control that world. Belief in the relationship between the name and the person or object named leads to the belief that a person can be harmed if his or her name is known to another. This belief underlies the story of Odysseus and the Cyclops: as "Nobody" Odysseus was safe (9.366); only when Odysseus finally reveals his true name can Polyphemus curse the Greek hero.

In the *Iliad*, Homer also reminds us that power entails both action and speech. When Achilles and his companions take turns speaking in assembly, for example, they must take hold of the scepter, which authorizes them not only to speak, but also to initiate action. In the *Iliad*, Antenor describes to Helen the power of Odysseus' speech:

> "But whenever Odysseus of many wiles arose, he would
> stand and look down with eyes fixed upon the ground,
> and his staff he would move neither backwards nor
> forwards, but would hold it stiff, in semblance like a
> man of no understanding; thou wouldest have deemed
> him a churlish man and naught but a fool. But whenso
> he uttered his great voice from his chest, and words like
> snowflakes on a winter's day, then could no mortal man
> beside vie with Odysseus; then did we not so marvel to
> behold Odysseus' aspect."   (*Il.* 3.216–24)[13]

This is the same Odysseus who, in Ovid, cheats Ajax of the armor of Achilles in part because of his eloquence, which proves more persuasive among the Greeks than Ajax's tough loyalty (*Met.* 13.2–384). Moreover, it is Odysseus himself who tells us most of his adventures in the *Odyssey*. By controlling the narrative, by telling his own story, Odysseus manipulates his listeners in such a way that his truth becomes our own.

But this powerful use of language, of controlling the narrative, of initiating action, is not ordinarily granted to women in mythology or in literature based on that mythology. In Euripides' play, Hippolytus rails at women:

> "I hate a clever woman! ... We should not suffer servants to approach them, but give them as companions voiceless beasts, dumb ... but with teeth, that they might not converse, and hear another voice in answer."[14]   (*Hippolytus* 640, 645–48)

In Xenophon's *Oeconomicus*, Socrates is discussing the importance of a husband training his wife: after all, she was a mere child when they married and therefore requires instruction. He asks if there is any individual to whom the husband entrusts more matters of importance yet to whom that same husband talks less? The answer is no to both questions (3.12–13).

Other ancient sources may be less exuberant than Hippolytus in their condemnation of articulate women but as strong in their insistence that public speaking is the province of men. In the *Politics*, Aristotle quotes with approval, the sentiment of Sophocles' Ajax, that "silence is a woman's glory," and according to Pericles in Thucydides' history of the Peloponnesian war, women should not even be talked about (2.45). Little wonder, then, that Creusa in Euripides' *Ion* appears very much the sister of Io, Callisto, and Philomela. Raped by a god, she was compelled to abandon her son at birth and, until the action of the play, had never been able to tell anyone what had actually transpired.[15]

An equation emerges from this tradition. Language use is specific to the human species; men use language and are therefore human. Much of the non-human world is silent (that is, it does not use language); women are [supposed to be] silent; therefore women are not human. Moreover, men as users of language are associated with culture and civilization, while silent women are associated with the absence of culture, with nature. The stories of rape in the *Metamorphoses* rely on and reinforce this equation. The association of woman with nature and of man with culture is not an unfamiliar one, of course, but my own formulation of the equation relies on language use rather than on biological function, as in Ortner's work.[16]

It remains to see the connection between the traditional view of language and the motif with which I began this essay. I want to begin with three examples of this motif (Io, Callisto, Procne and Philomela), concentrating on the details that focus on speech and silence. These stories share other features, of course: sexual violence implied or enacted; a challenge to authority or the exercise of power; isolation of the victim; mutilation or transformation that enforces the victim's silence.

Io (Ovid, Met. 1.611–747), walking by herself in the heat of the day, is accosted by Jupiter, who tries to persuade her that he will escort her safely to her destination. She runs, he follows and rapes her. Then, to hide it all from Juno, who has already figured it out, he changes Io into a cow. When Juno asks for the cow as a present, Jupiter delays only briefly over the dilemma of revealing his guilt to Juno or abandoning Io as cow. In the end he abandons Io.

Transformation in the *Metamorphoses* takes a variety of forms. A few individuals can change their shape at will, but in most cases change occurs in one of two ways. Either someone or something is changed radically, so that the original is rendered physically unrecognizable, or else some secondary feature is changed, for example, the color of mulberries (4.125–27). In radical transformations, the real dilemma lies in the fact that while the physical appearance may undergo such alteration that the original individual cannot be identified, the personality of that individual usually remains untouched. So an Io, for example, finds that she must get on in a world that assumes, on the basis of her external appearance, that she is a cow and treats her accordingly, a condition for which the real Io is quite unprepared. In fact, Io's adjustment to life as a cow is a hard one: she cannot supplicate because she has no arms; she cannot speak and is frightened by her lowing; grass is bitter; she has no soft pillows to lie on; she is afraid of other animals. When she encounters her father and wants to tell Inachus who she is, she cannot address him, but scratches her name in the dust with a hoof. Inachus had been thinking that he needed to find her a husband; now he will have to find her a bull. When she is finally changed back into a woman, after much suffering, Io will still be afraid to speak. Curran says of this transformation, "That rape has robbed her of her very humanity is shown less eloquently in her external bovine shape than in her terrible isolation and inarticulateness."[17] He is, of course, perfectly correct. It is not bad enough that she no longer looks human, but now she cannot even speak.

The story of Callisto (2.409–528) follows this pattern as well. The favorite of Diana, Callisto is a virgin huntress. It is around noon, in an untouched forest, when Callisto takes a nap. Jupiter takes advantage of her vulnerability and appears as Diana. He is even pleased when Callisto tells "Diana" that "she" is greater even than Jupiter himself. The god does not let her tell her story of her hunt, however, but interrupts her, appears in his true form, and rapes her. Nine months later, Callisto's pregnancy is discovered when the nymphs are all bathing in a stream, and Diana drives Callisto away. Juno changes Callisto, who has given birth to a son, Arcas, into a bear, as penalty for having been beautiful enough to attract the roving eye of Jupiter. As a bear, she cannot speak but can only growl. Ovid tells us that her feelings do not change: although now an animal in form, she feels no kinship with them and in fact is frightened of the other wild beasts. The hunter becomes the hunted: Arcas nearly kills her before Jupiter intervenes and changes both of them into the Bears, the constellation which, because of Juno's undying enmity, can never set in the Ocean.

Kathleen Wall has written extensively about this story, and at the risk of oversimplifying her argument, let me identify a few of the most provocative parts. In the first place, Wall identifies Callisto with the goddess herself, a "psychological" virgin, that is, someone not owned by anyone else.[18] The elements of the story relating to sex and pregnancy, as well as the reminiscence of the *hieros gamos*, remind us that Diana herself was connected with fertility and with childbirth. Thus, we could see in Callisto a story of initiation into what it means to be a sexually mature woman.

But we can also look at the story from another perspective. The rape motif recalls the reality of marriage customs, of the fact that the first sexual encounter for a young woman may well have seemed like a rape. Wall also suggests that the detail of Diana's driving Callisto from her band of nymphs may be both a reflection of an initiation ritual and a patriarchal interpretation of the entire story.[19]

As we have seen in the cases of Io and Callisto, Juno punishes women who have fallen prey to Jupiter. By acting in rage, she can feel powerful, not rejected. That is, to sympathize with, to acknowledge the victimization of the woman is to acknowledge her own possible victimization. In the end, Callisto becomes a bear, and must live as one until, at the last crucial moment, Jupiter returns and saves her. His salvation asserts the power of male dominance as much as his original rape.

Still, Wall does not go on to remark that Callisto is rendered speechless, and without acknowledging that silence we do not have the full picture. Callisto not only cannot tell of Jupiter's guilt, she cannot tell her own story. She cannot even recognize, certainly not express, that she was not at fault, that the guilt was not hers. I am reminded of when the University of Michigan first published a brochure on sexual harassment in which persons who thought they had been victims of that behavior were urged to "tell someone." Rape victims often struggle with the tension between the need to tell someone (as distinct from filing charges) and the persistent cultural suspicion that rape is the victim's fault and that it is shameful to talk about it.[20] This is not to suggest that Ovid prefigures any number of therapeutic models but that in his hands the motif of silencing women rings true, and that our current experience with treating victims of rape, sexual harassment, and so on, stems from a similar recognition of the need to speak about the unspeakable, and of the consequences, including psychological consequences, of remaining silent. In the end, Callisto is reduced to the non-human, exiled from human society by virtue of her appearance and her silence.

The story of Procne and Philomela (6.428–668) departs slightly from the motif because their transformations into birds occur after the women have been driven to reject their humanity. The story begins with a woman who is raped and rendered speechless. Philomela's dehumanization through rape is foreshadowed by metaphorical references to the animal world. Whereas the other women's losses of humanity were simultaneous with their transformations, Ovid connects Philomela's story with theirs through the imagery of the similes. Procne had begged her husband to visit her father and ask his permission to bring back her sister, Philomela. Tereus makes the trip and becomes inflamed by Philomela's beauty, which is likened to that of a naiad or a dryad in the deep woods. From the start, therefore, Philomela exists in the realm of nature, that sphere which is without speech. In his account of her victimization, Ovid employs three animal images to describe her plight. Callisto and Io had been Jupiter's literal victims, but Philomela, at least metaphorically, is not free of the god either.[21] On the ship Tereus "never turns his eyes from her, as when the ravenous bird of Jove has dropped in his high eyrie some hare caught in his hooked talons; the captive has no chance to escape, the captor gloats over his prize" (6.515–18).[22] Again, when she has been raped by Tereus, "she trembled like a frightened lamb, which, torn and cast aside by a grey wolf, cannot yet believe that it is safe; and like a dove which, with its own blood all smeared over its plumage, still palpitates with fright, still fears those greedy claws that have pierced it" (6.527–30). Curran notes the "predatory appetite of the rapist, and the dehumanizing reduction of a woman to the level of a hunted animal."[23] The images of the rabbit, the lamb, and the dove point ahead to the woman dehumanized through lack of speech.

Tereus imprisons Philomela in an isolated hut where he continues to rape her. Philomela calls on her father, her sister, the gods. Like Callisto, she blames herself, "I have become a concubine, a sister's rival. ... Now Procne must be my enemy" (6.537–38). She warns Tereus that he will pay for his violence, and calls down the gods' wrath on his head; if she gets the chance, she will tell people; and if she can't get out of the hut to tell people, then she will shout it to the trees. Tereus silences her by cutting out her tongue. Ovid's lurid description of the severed tongue, flopping about at the feet of its mistress, serves as a grave digger's speech, to underscore the horror. The scene of Io pawing her name in the dust, while less grotesque, served a similar purpose.

Io had found an alternative to speech; so does Philomela. A year later Philomela manages to tell her story by weaving it into a tapestry that she persuades her guard to take to Procne. Her sister, understanding the tapestry, is struck silent as well, but this time out of anger and grief. When Procne manages to free her sister from the hut, Philomela is ashamed to look at her. When Procne sees that her son Itys can prattle charmingly to her, but her own sister is mute, Procne is torn by the demands of mother-love and sisterly affection. Yielding to sisterly affection, Procne kills the boy and feeds his flesh to Tereus. In the end, the transformation of Tereus, Procne, and Philomela into birds is an anti-climax: in a sense they had become non-human long before the actual change.

It would be tempting to argue further for the relationship between the threat that vocal women pose and their ultimate exclusion from human society through silence. If we turn, however, to one final example that nearly mimics the motif as we saw it in the Callisto story, then we must reconsider the full implications of the motif. In fact, the motif is not gender-specific.

When human beings are punished for their speech, or for the stories they tell, they have usually challenged the authority of the gods by undermining the dignity of those deities, or otherwise showing that they did not know their place. Sometimes the challenge to authority is accidental, as in the account of Actaeon which Ovid chose to tell (3.147–98). At the end of a morning's hunt, Actaeon tells his companions to go on home in the heat of the day. In mythology, mid-day is a dangerous time, especially for anyone out alone in the forest (Io, 1.588–92; Callisto, 2.417); in this case, the hour is fatal. When Actaeon stumbles on Diana and her nymphs bathing at a secluded spring, the goddess is offended by his blunder, and spattering him with water says, "Now you are free to tell that you have seen me all unrobed—if you can tell" (Met. 3.192–93). With that he is turned into a stag. When he sees his reflection in a pool, he tries to speak and discovers that he can only groan, yet like Callisto his mind remains intact. When his dogs come upon this unknown stag, they attack. We would be less distracted from the plight of Actaeon if Ovid hadn't paused here to name thirty-six of his dogs, but he does, perhaps in part for the same reason that he had Io scratch her name in the dust and Philomela's tongue flop at her feet. At any rate, at that time when Actaeon most needs to speak, he cannot, although Ovid says that he groaned with a sound not quite human, but not quite what a deer would make either. His friends, of course, urge on the dogs and call for the missing Actaeon. In the end, the hunter Actaeon, who like Callisto had become the hunted himself, succumbs to the wounds inflicted upon him by his own dogs.

It is always difficult to generalize about the *Metamorphoses* precisely because the poem is itself so protean that no general statement can stand without acknowledging a host of exceptions. Nonetheless, the stories that follow this motif share enough common features that we can draw some conclusions with reasonable confidence. I originally described the motif as involving the silencing of a woman, yet except for Actaeon's gender and the absence of rape, clearly his story matches that of a Callisto or an Io or a Philomela. If all the examples of this motif were rape stories of independent women, then one might be inclined to interpret the motif as being concerned primarily with gender politics, with misogyny. But all the examples cited here include specific references to the power of speech, to the frustration of not being able to speak, to the ingenious alternatives that the voiceless invent to compensate for the loss of their voices. Io and Philomela manage to write or to convey meaning by symbols and in so doing resemble the poet/narrator, whereas Actaeon, perhaps because he is a male and inexperienced in women's powerlessness, is utterly helpless when put in a situation many women could on some level recognize and deal with.[24]

I have no intention of suggesting here that the rapes are not relevant or that they can be discounted, but I would argue that the motif is really dealing with issues of power that extend beyond male/female antagonism. I mean power as defined by Carolyn Heilbrun: "Power is the ability to take one's place in whatever discourse is essential to action and the right to have one's part matter."[25] She is not discussing mythology or classical civilization when she writes this. Instead, she is exploring the ways a woman writes her life or tells her own story, and the extent to which a woman is discouraged, disadvantaged, or perhaps even prevented from doing so by patriarchal conventions, by speech patterns that are not sufficiently expressive, by a vocabulary that is inappropriate or inadequate.

That so many of the examples involve women does not undercut my argument that power is at the base of the story.[26] Are these women silenced by the powerful because they are women? Probably so. And because they threaten the status quo? Certainly so. As with the "slasher" movies so popular in the 1980s in which independent young women were mercilessly stalked and spectacularly killed, we need to ask what was the connection between the political, social, economic status of real women and the spate of movies that blithely dismembered women who appeared to defy certain traditional assumptions about women's place, women's roles.

That rape dehumanizes need hardly be argued. That rape is an act of aggression, a show of power, is hardly debatable either. What an Io or a Philomela experiences is literally unspeakable. In all the versions of this motif the victim is finally reduced to the non-human and denied the opportunity to engage in the one activity that is associated most specifically with humankind. The question remains, why does this happen? What do the victims do to merit this isolation from human society?

All of these individuals are independent of urban living and of any number of constraints that might impede their freedom (they are either actually seen alone in the woods or, in the case of Philomela, likened to a dryad in the woods); in their independence they threaten the status quo; they are brutalized in some fashion and then rendered speechless. They cannot, as Heilbrun would have them, take their "place in whatever discourse is essential to action."[27] Indeed, they cannot take any action at all. Moreover, their isolation from the human is even more profound because not only do most of them not appear to be human, but by virtue of their new shape they are rendered even more profoundly non-human because they cannot speak. This silencing would not be so powerful were it not for the traditional assumptions that the human animal is *homo loquens*.

I have argued in another context that Ovid uses metamorphosis as a metaphor for the psychological change that attends pathological grief.[28] For example, the loss of her entire family brutalizes Hecuba who witnessed the deaths of many of those family members, and who finally discovers not just the death of her remaining son but the perfidy of the alleged friend who had been charged with keeping the boy alive (*Met.* 13.485). In the wake of this litany of loss, Hecuba howls with grief. The distance between the woman brutalized by sorrow and the dog that she finally becomes is very short. The physical transformation reminds us of how isolated she is, how inconsolable she is, and in fact how absent any source of comfort is to her. In the face of her grief, the physical change serves as a metaphor for the psychological effect of acute grief. So in the stories of silencing, the metamorphosis (real and metaphorical, as with Philomela) underscores the dehumanization, the isolation, which these victims suffer. The transformation becomes a metaphor for the consequences of violating boundaries. The motif raises questions about what it means to be human, not just whether human beings really are the only talking animals, but what are the limits of human behavior, the boundaries of power that we violate at considerable cost.

I chose Ovid's *Metamorphoses* as the source for the myths discussed here not because his are the only versions, but because in many instances his are the most complete, the least problematic, or the most influential. But I also chose Ovid because he understood what it meant to be silenced by the powerful. When he was exiled to Tomis, separated from family and friends, sent to a community that was not only physically dangerous, but where they did not speak Latin or Greek, he was as isolated from the human associations that had defined his life as all those victims of transformation in his poem are isolated from what it means to be human. Transformation is a form of exile too, one characterized by silence. In his poems written from Tomis, Ovid describes his need to break his own kind of silence:

> An exile's voice is this: letters furnish me a tongue, and
> if I may not write, I shall be dumb.
> *(Letters from Pontus* 2.6)[29]

I am not here suggesting that the *Metamorphoses* is prophetic, that Ovid is anticipating his own fall from grace, but I am suggesting that the poet could not have been unaware of the consequences of alienating the politically powerful.

I will leave to Forbis and others the provocative suggestion that the *Metamorphoses* may have played a part in Ovid's exile. For the purposes of this essay, however, I cannot resist pointing out the obvious. In a poem in which speakers can be punished for overstepping the bounds of their humanity, for not knowing their place; in a poem in which an Io or a Callisto or an Actaeon, in the face of ultimate power, is rendered voiceless and therefore non-human, Ovid's epilogue to the *Metamorphoses* takes on even more force.

This reader finds it immensely gratifying that Ovid's prophecy was accurate. Even in exile, the poet was not silenced by the power of Augustus, and the final word of the *Metamorphoses* still holds true: *vivam*.

Judith de Luce
Miami University

Notes

Hymn text of the title is taken from Charles Wesley, 1739. I have presented various parts of this thesis orally: at the annual meeting of CAMWS, 1990; at colloquia at the University of Hartford, Miami University, and Northwestern University. A leave from the College of Arts and Science at Miami enabled me to do the original work on this project. I am indebted to the persistently startling insights of my students in "Feminist Revisions of Classical Mythology" at Hofstra University and to Jenny Winkler's helpful comments on contemporary issues of empowerment and violence against women. With his inexorable precision, Lee Horvitz has taught me how to entertain questions and identify connections that can illuminate an author as complex as Ovid. Any infelicities of thought or language are, of course, my own.

[1] Alicia Ostriker, "The Thieves of Language: Women Poets and Revisionist Mythmaking," *Signs*, 8 (1982), 68–80.

[2] Leo C. Curran, "Rape and Rape Victim in the *Metamorphoses*," *Arethusa*, 11 (1978), 213–41.

[3] Susan Brownmiller, *Against Our Will: Men, Women, and Rape* (New York, 1975).

[4] Curran, "Rape and Rape Victim, " 236.

[5] Amy Richlin, "Reading Ovid's Rapes," in *Pornography and Representation in Greece and Rome*, ed. Richlin (Oxford, 1992), 158–79.

[6] Kathleen Wall, *The Callisto Myth from Ovid to Atwood: Initiation and Rape in Literature* (Kingston, 1988).

[7] Elizabeth Forbis has kindly shown me her 1991 manuscript, "Voice and Voicelessness in Ovid's *Metamorphoses* and Exile Poetry."

[8] Language use, rather than the ability to reason or the manufacture of tools, has become increasingly important in discussions of the characteristics of the human and the non-human. For a discussion of the issues involved, see the introduction to *Language in Primates: Perspectives and Implications*, ed. Hugh T. Wilder and Judith de Luce (New York, 1983), 1–17.

[9] I have reserved for another time a discussion of Arachne's weaving, weaving as a metaphor for narrative, her transformation, and her kinship with the likes of Io and Callisto. Arachne's story represents a bridge between the tales of an Io and an Actaeon and a Niobe, and as such highlights the motif of silencing. For a discussion of artists in Ovid, including Arachne, see Eleanor Winsor Leach, "Ekphrasis and the Theme of Artistic Failure in Ovid's Metamorphoses," *Ramus*, 3 (1974), 102–42.

[10] For a wide-ranging discussion of women and language, see Sally

McConnell-Ginet, Ruth Borker, and Nelly Furman, eds., *Woman and Language in Literature and Society* (New York, 1980). See also Carolyn Heilbrun, *Writing a Woman's Life* (New York, 1988); Robin Lakoff, *Language and Women's Place* (New York, 1975); M. Landy, "The Invisible Woman," in *Monster* (New York, 1972); Elizabeth Meese, *Crossing the Double-Cross* (Chapel Hill, 1986); Barrie Thorne and Nancy Henley, eds., *Language and Sex: Difference and Dominance* (Rowley, 1975).

[11] Sophocles, *Antigone*, trans. Elizabeth Wyckoff, in *Sophocles I*, eds. David Grene and Richmond Lattimore (Chicago, 1954).

[12] Lucretius, *De Rerum Natura*, vol. 1, trans. Cyril Bailey (1947; rpt. Oxford, 1966).

[13] Homer, *Iliad*, trans. A. T. Murray, (Cambridge, 1978).

[14] Euripides, *Hippolytus*, trans. David Grene, in *Euripides I*, eds. David Grene and Richmond Lattimore (1955; rpt. New York, 1968). See also Nancy S. Rabinowitz, "Female Speech and Female Sexuality: Euripides' *Hippolytus* as Model," in *Rescuing Creusa: New Methodological Approaches to Women in Antiquity*, ed. Marilyn Skinner, *Helios*, 13.2 (1986), 127–40.

[15] I am indebted to Susan Guettel Cole and Francis Dunn for their reminders that Creusa belongs in a discussion of the motif of rape and silence. See Frances Dunn, "The Battle of the Sexes in Euripides' *Ion*," *Critical Studies in Greek and Roman Literature*, 19 (1990), 130–42.

[16] Sherry B. Ortner, "Is Female to Male as Nature Is to Culture?" in *Woman, Culture, and Society*, eds. Michelle Zimbalist Rosaldo and Louise Lamphere (Stanford, 1974). For additional discussion of these issues, see Carol McCormack and Marilyn Strathen eds., *Nature, Culture and Gender* (Cambridge, 1980); Susan Griffin, *Woman and Nature* (New York, 1980).

[17] Curran, "Rape and Rape Victim," 225.

[18] Wall, *The Callisto Myth*, 12–14.

[19] Ibid., 19–20.

[20] Anna Clark, *Women's Silence, Men's Violence: Sexual Assault in England 1770–1845* (London, 1987), considers the role of rape as control over women, the blurring of distinctions between rape and seduction (citing the use of military metaphors in this regard) and above all, the "double trauma" of the rape itself and the culturally imposed shame for women of speaking of sex. Moreover, by defining "sexual assault as an expert preserve, legal and medical discourses repressed women's ability to define rape and protest against it" (8). Callisto, too, would have understood this kind of silencing, would have felt the effect of the absence of language with which to talk about one's own experience. In the wake of the Clarence Thomas/Anita Hill hearings on sexual harassment in 1991, the rape trials of William Kennedy Smith and Mike Tyson in 1992, we are beginning to recognize that the pressure exerted on women to

remain silent and the tendency to discount a woman's credibility when she does speak out is only slightly reduced since the eighteenth and nineteenth centuries.

[21] I am indebted to Mary DeForest for suggesting this link among the stories.

[22] Ovid, *Metamorphoses*, trans. Frank Miller (Cambridge, 1968).

[23] Curran, "Rape and Rape Victim," 233.

[24] I am again indebted to Mary DeForest for this suggestion.

[25] Heilbrun, *Writing a Woman's Life*, 18.

[26] For a discussion of "women's speech" and its connections with the language of the powerless, see William M. O'Barr and Borman K. Atkins, "'Woman's Language' or 'Powerless Language,'" in *Woman and Language in Literature and Society*, eds. McConnell-Ginet et al., 93–110. O'Barr and Atkins examine the language of female witnesses in jury trials, but their observations and conclusions apply directly to the thesis of this essay.

[27] Heilbrun, *Writing a Woman's Life*, 18.

[28] See my "Metamorphosis as Mourning: Pathological Grief in Ovid's *Metamorphoses*," *Helios*, n.s. 9 (1982), 77–90.

[29] Ovid, *Tristia and Epistulae ex Ponto*, trans. Arthur Wheeler (Cambridge, 1939).

Martial's Sulpicia and Propertius' Cynthia

I. Introduction

The political resurgence of the feminist movement during the past two decades has transformed the study of literature throughout the academy. Within the discipline of classics, feminist concerns and perspectives have manifested themselves in a number of important research projects.[1] Not surprisingly, the foci of such research have prominently included the women poets of ancient Greece and Rome.

Classicists have reaped numerous benefits from the efforts of such scholars as Marilyn Skinner and Jane Snyder to define and appreciate what is distinctive about the body of Greek poetry composed by women.[2] The mere presence, however fragmentary, among our extant classical works of verses by Sappho, Corinna, Praxilla, Erinna, Nossis, and Anyte have made it possible to compare these Greek women poets with one another and to identify features and concerns common to all or most of them. Snyder, for example, observes as a result that "the women poets represented in The *Greek Anthology* ... treat the subject of emotional attachment and commitment between women in a way that is almost wholly absent from the works of their male contemporaries."[3] Scholarly investigations into women's poetry-writing in the ancient Greek world, among them my own, have also tried to elucidate the social contexts which nurtured and responded to female literary expression in various periods of Greek history.[4]

Similarly, learned studies have lately offered a variety of insights on a less extensive but equally thought-provoking collection of Latin poems by and about an Augustan woman who refers to herself as Sulpicia. Eleven elegies which feature this Sulpicia as their subject, and more often than not as their first-person speaker, are preserved in the corpus of her male contemporary Tibullus. While scholars concur in assigning Sulpicia the authorship of six of these poems, they also continue to disagree over whether or not she herself wrote the other five. Those who view all or part of this quintet as the work of an unknown, presumably male, poet have hence needed to explain why this male poet would have adopted Sulpicia's female *persona* and amatory themes. Stephen Hinds and Holt Parker have recently added new arguments to this longstanding debate.[5] But other aspects of Sulpicia's poetry have attracted the attention of Matthew Santirocco, H. MacL. Currie, N. J. Lowe, Snyder, and myself.[6] We have reflected upon what is distinctive about Sulpicia's language and themes, and in particular upon how her poetry resembles and differs from the work of Catullus and her fellow Augustan elegists—not only Tibullus but also Propertius and Ovid.

So, too, classical scholars have been sharing the benefits of their research with the wider community of non-specialists interested in literary works by women. Two books designed for use as classroom texts in undergraduate courses on women in classical antiquity have allotted a conspicuous place to Greek and Roman women writers: Pomeroy's 1975 historical survey on women in classical antiquity, and the source book in translation by Lefkowitz and Fant on women's lives in Greece and Rome, first published in 1977 and revised in 1982.[7] Snyder's 1989 book, *The Woman and the Lyre: Women Writers in Classical Greece and Rome*, provides English translations as well as extended discussions of the major Greek and Latin poetic texts composed by women. Diane Rayor's new study, containing translations of the Greek women poets, constitutes a further attempt at inviting a more general audience to look closely at the female poetic tradition in ancient Greece.[8]

For obvious reasons, both specialist and more general studies on ancient Greek and Roman women writers have concentrated on the better-attested Greek female poets—Sappho, Praxilla, Corinna, Erinna, Anyte and Nossis—and the Latin elegist Sulpicia. Indeed, little notice has been accorded to another, later, Roman woman poet, also named Sulpicia, who is known to us largely through the testimony of her contemporary, the late first century A.D. epigrammatist Martial. Santirocco merely mentions that "under Domitian, a Sulpicia wrote about her husband Calenus, and earned Martial's praise (10.35, 38). None of this literary production, however, has survived." Snyder merely states that "Martial ... refers to a contemporary of his named Sulpicia as a poet who sings not of mythological themes like the banquet of Thyestes, but rather of 'pure and honest love, amusements, delights and jokes.'" Both Santirocco and Snyder mention the seventy hexameter lines attributed to this Sulpicia, with Snyder noting that they treat the expulsion of the philosophers during the reign of Domitian, and Santirocco asserting that they are of "dubious authenticity." But Santirocco and Snyder do so only in their footnotes.[9]

In a new contribution to *Classical World*, entitled "The Other Sulpicia," Carol Merriam has gone some distance toward remedying this neglect. Here, Merriam reviews in some detail the efforts by earlier scholars first to identify and eventually to reject this later Sulpicia as the author of this 70-line "satire." After quoting—in Latin—Leo's claim that the poem was written by one Caecius, she cites such authorities as Knoche, Coffey, and Bardon in maintaining that it dates from about the fourth century A.D. Furthermore, through an examination of relevant passages in Martial 10.35, in which Martial praises this Sulpicia's poetry, and 10.38, in which Martial extols the wedded bliss of this Sulpicia and her husband Calenus, Merriam successfully challenges the claim of the later poet Ausonius in the *Cento Nuptialis* that Sulpicia wrote in a sexually provocative, obscene style likely to offend the sensibilities of tasteful readers (*prurire opusculum Sulpiciae, fronte caperare*).[10]

In the discussion to follow, I would like to correct what I believe to be a major error in Merriam's article, to consider some important evidence about Sulpicia which Merriam has omitted, and to supplement Merriam's observations about the "other" Sulpicia by placing Martial's depiction of her in a wider literary context. I will focus upon the way in which Martial has characterized Sulpicia by connecting her with two illustrious female figures in earlier Latin erotic poetry—Catullus' Lesbia and particularly Propertius' Cynthia. In so doing, I would not only like to explore how Martial utilizes this connection to characterize Calenus as well as Sulpicia. I would also like to consider how this connection is related to the content and concerns of Sulpicia's own writing, and why Martial's choice of a Propertian model over a Catullan model when extolling the mutual love of Sulpicia and Calenus is anomalous both in itself and in terms of Martial's own poetry.

II. Martial's Sulpicia: Some Clarifications

Pace Merriam, who twice maintains that Martial uses Sulpicia's *persona* and her "own poetic voice" when addressing Calenus in 10.38, Martial never assigns Sulpicia any words of her own.[11] In 10.38 Martial merely speaks, evidently in his own person, of Sulpicia as "your beloved" (*cum Sulpicia tua*, 2) to Calenus. Furthermore, Martial adopts a similar expository strategy in an earlier poem, 7.69. It is addressed to one Canius (perhaps the poet from Gades whom Martial mentions at 1.61.9, 3.20 and 64, 7.87 and 10.48) and praises the poetry written by Canius' female partner. Since 7.69 shares features with 10.35 as well as with 10.38, it now merits our close attention.

In the opening line of 7.69, Martial calls this woman by the Greek name Theophila and identifies her as Canius' fiancee (*haec est illa tibi promissa Theophila, Cani*), much as he identifies Sulpicia as Calenus' wife at the close of 10.35 and the beginning of 10.38. To be sure, some of Martial's comments about Theophila have no counterpart in his representation of Sulpicia in 10.35 and 38. He attributes to Theophila an "Attic voice" (*Cecropia voce*, 2), stating that the major Athenian philosophical schools—"the Attic garden of the great old man and the Stoic throng"—would rightly claim her (*hanc sibi iure petat magni senis Atticus hortus/ nec minus esse suam Stoica turba velit*, 3–4); he predicts that her work will live—since it is "not like a woman's writing or aimed at popular tastes" (*vivet opus quodcumque per has emiseris aures;/ tam non femineum nec populare sapit*, 5–6); so, too, he judges Theophila almost the equal of an unknown woman poet Pantaenis. Nevertheless, in comparing Theophila to Sappho, Martial asserts "Sappho—a woman of erotic inclinations—used to praise someone composing poetry" (*carmina fingentem Sappho laudabat amatrix*) and proceeds to judge Theophila to be more virtuous (*castior haec*, 8) and Sappho not to have been more learned (*non doctior illa fuit*, 8). This comparison resembles Martial's statement at 10.35.8 that Sulpicia "teaches virtuous and respectable passions" (*castos docet et probos amores*), and Martial's assertion at 10.35.16 that "you would be more learned and sexually well-behaved, Sappho" (*esses doctior et pudica, Sappho*), if Sappho had studied under or with Sulpicia.

There are, however, major differences between 10.38 and 7.69.

The latter is written in the elegiac meter, about a woman whom the addressee has not yet wed. Like 10.35, 10.38 is in the hendecasyllabic meter and proclaims that Sulpicia and Calenus have already shared fifteen years of married life: "O, the fifteen years of marriage with your Sulpicia, pleasurable to you, Calenus, which the god has generously allowed and accomplished" (*O molles tibi quindecim, Calene,/ quos cum Sulpicia tua iugales/ indulsit deus et peregit annos!* 1–2). Indeed, as Parker argues, the past tense of the verbs in 10.38 and the overall tone of Martial's words most likely indicate that 10.38 is meant as a *consolatio* to Calenus on Sulpicia's death.[12] If we interpret Martial as extolling Calenus' love for his dead wife in 10.38, we are additionally reminded of a celebrated poem by Catullus: 96, a consolatory elegy to Licinius Calvus on the loss of his wife Quintilia.[13] Inasmuch as we can point to further similarities, and dissimilarities, between 7.69 and the two poems about Sulpicia and Calenus, as well as to elements in 7.69 which help to illuminate Martial's message in the two poems about Sulpicia and Calenus, we will be visiting 7.69 again later in our discussion.

We should also consider the evidence on Sulpicia's writing provided by two authors of the fifth century A.D., Sidonius Apollinaris and Fulgentius. At *Ad Felicem* 9.261–62 Sidonius mentions her as a poet he will not try to imitate, with *non quod Sulpiciae iocus Thaliae/ scripsit blandiloquum suo Caleno*. At *Mythologiae* 1.4.1 Fulgentius refers to *Sulpicillae procacitas* and at 13.3 states that *Sulpicillae Ausonianae loquacitas deperit*.[14] These references to a *iocus*, "playful remark," in Sulpicia's poetry and to the *procacitas*, the erotically-charged but merely suggestive self-assertiveness, of Sulpicia's style recall Martial's comment at 10.35.13 that *tales Egeriae iocos fuisse*, "such were the playful jests of Egeria," and that *nullam dixerit esse nequiorem,/ nullam dixerit esse sanctiorem* at 10.35.11–12, "[one reading Sulpicia's verses] would say that no woman is naughtier, he would say that no woman is more honorable." These references, of course, would further undermine Ausonius' claim that Sulpicia expressed herself in an offensively coarse and ribald fashion.

Most crucially, we should examine the two lines of Sulpicia's own poetry, in iambic trimeters, which do survive: they are quoted by Giorgio Valla of Piacenza (c. 1430–1499) in his 1486 Venice edition of Juvenal's *Satires*. Valla attributes this quotation to 'Probus,' a manuscript now lost, containing scholia which are thought to derive ultimately from a late antique commentary written at approximately the end of the fourth century A.D. Here, commenting on Juvenal 6.537, *magnaque debetur violato poena cadurco*, "a great punishment is owed for the violated *cadurcum*," and in particular on the rare word *cadurcum*, ("*de cadurco*"), Valla remarks: "*membrum mulieris (inquit Probus) intelligitur; cum sit membri muliebris velamen. vel, ut alii, est instita qua lectus intenditur. Unde ait Sulpicia: Si me cadurci restitutis fasciis/ nudam Caleno concubantem proferat.* "The female genital (says Probus) is understood, since it is the covering of the female genital. Or, as others claim, it is a strip on which a bed is stretched. Whence Sulpicia says 'If, after the bindings of my bed frame have been put back in place, [it] would bring me forth, nude, lying down with Calenus.'"[15] A century after Valla, the reference to Calenus prompted Pierre Pithou of Troyes, author of a 1585 edition of Juvenal (and owner of the ninth-century Montpellier manuscript of Juvenal known as P in Pithou's honor), to identify the author as the Sulpicia mentioned by Martial in 10.35 and 38.[16] The identification has been widely accepted since; accordingly, several standard reference works cite these lines as an authentic fragment of Sulpicia's writing.[17]

III. Martial's Sulpicia and Catullus' Lesbia

Merriam's discussion merits commendation for pointing out Martial's skillful comparison between Sulpicia and Catullus' Lesbia in 10.35, and for noting the way in which this comparison operates to the detriment of Catullus' celebrated beloved. After quoting Martial 10.35.19–21, where Martial states that Sulpicia would live neither as the spouse of [Jupiter] Thunderer nor as the beloved of Bacchus or Apollo if Calenus were taken away from her, Merriam comments that "Martial's expression of Sulpicia's fidelity may recall Catullus' report of Lesbia's protestations" in poem 70 that she would prefer no one, not even Jupiter himself, to Catullus as a marriage partner. Merriam proceeds to comment: "But Catullus is only quoting Lesbia"; she then argues that Catullus has "no faith in [Lesbia's] fidelity, while Martial is expressing his own opinion of Sulpicia's loyalty to Calenus."[18]

Yet one might detect additional Catullan allusions in Martial's two poems about Sulpicia, both of which are in the hendecasyllabic meter popularized by and closely associated with Catullus.[19] Like the allusion to Catullus 70, these evocations of Catullan verse serve to contrast Sulpicia and Calenus sharply, and favorably, to Lesbia and Catullus as lovers. Martial 10.38 depicts every night and hour—*nox omnis et hora* (4)—shared by Calenus and Sulpicia as "marked with precious pearls," and states that Calenus would rather have *lucem unam* (13), one day of their married life, than four times the old age of Nestor. He thus recalls Catullus' statement at lines 4–6 of poem 5: *soles occidere et redire possunt;/ nobis, cum semel occidit brevis lux,/ nox est perpetua una dormienda*, "suns are able to set and rise again; for us, when our brief light has once set, there is one everlasting night which must be slept." Catullus, then, emphasizes both the brevity of the *lux* and perpetuity of the *una nox* to be experienced by himself and Lesbia. He views both spans of time, short life and long death, as grounds for defying conventional moral strictures, and for obfuscating the process of quantification through incalculable kisses. Martial, however, stresses only the short temporal units—*omnis nox* and *una lux*—shared by Calenus and Sulpicia, representing these periods of time as to be treasured in spite of their brevity.

In defining the fifteen years of Calenus' marriage to Sulpicia as a period of time "counted as your entire life," and in asserting that "you number only the days you have spent as a husband" (*aetas haec tibi tota conputatur/ et solos numeras dies mariti*, 10.38.10–11), Martial may also be recalling two of Catullus' statements: Catullus' promise to confuse the calculations of his and Lesbia's kisses (*conturbabimus*) at 5.11, and Catullus' threat to make it impossible for the overly inquisitive to count up these kisses (*pernumerare*) at 7.11. Here, too, Martial would be emphasizing the importance placed by Calenus on quantification, or at least on quantifying the span of time which he and Sulpicia have devoted to their mutual, and legally sanctioned, passion. Such an emphasis, therefore, implicitly contrasts Calenus' time-honoring values with Catullus' disregard for keeping count. So, too, if one takes into account the picture that Catullus' poetry furnishes of his relationship with Lesbia as a whole, Martial is emphasizing Calenus' and Sulpicia's mutual achievement at sustaining an enduring bond and contrasting their enduring bond with Catullus' futile efforts to maximize the pleasures of a short-lived and unhappily ending love affair.

Additionally, one might interpret 10.35.15–18 as another allusion to Catullus' poetry, and as likewise representing the love of Sulpicia and Calenus as superior to that of Lesbia and Catullus. We have already discussed this allusion, inasmuch as it resembles a statement which Martial makes about another woman poet, Theophila, at 7.69, by its favorable comparison between Sulpicia and Sappho. Here, though, Martial addresses Sappho directly: in so doing, he asserts that acquaintance with Sulpicia would have improved the mind and morals of the Greek female poet, even if the sight of Sulpicia and Sappho together would have prompted Phaon, Sappho's legendary and hard-hearted young male lover, to love Sulpicia instead.

Merriam aptly observes that Phaon's preference for Sulpicia "would be vain, for (returning to the main reason for Martial's encomium of Sulpicia and her work) Sulpicia is *univira*: completely devoted to her husband Calenus."[20] Yet Martial's address to Sappho in this context should additionally remind us that Catullus not only links his beloved with Sappho by choosing the adjective for that which is connected with Sappho's native island, "Lesbia," as the metrically-equivalent pseudonym for his beloved's actual name. By his translation of Sappho's *phainetai moi* and use of her distinctive meter in poem 51, by his use of Sapphic metrics in poem 11 as well, and by his adaptation and evocation of Sappho's celebrated marriage songs in poem 62, Catullus also associates Sappho with his own literary innovations and contributions.[21] And at 8.73.8, Martial himself—with *Lesbia dictavit, docte Catulle, tibi*, "Lesbia inspired you, learned Catullus"—gives substantial credit for these literary achievements to the woman Catullus calls Lesbia.[22]

Furthermore, at 35. 16–17 Catullus compliments the beloved of his fellow poet Caecilius by referring to her as a *Sapphica puella/ Musa doctior*, "a girl more learned than the Sapphic Muse." It is not altogether clear what the phrase "Sapphic Muse" signifies. We have some justification for interpreting *Sapphica Musa* as a soubriquet for Sappho herself, inasmuch as Sappho was hailed in antiquity as "the tenth Muse."[23] Nevertheless, even if Catullus is merely referring to the mythical patroness of poetry who inspired Sappho herself, the phrase "Sapphic Muse" might well denote his own beloved Lesbia in addition: after all, Catullus himself assumes Sappho's *persona* in poem 51, and adopts Sappho's distinctive meter there and elsewhere.

What is more, Martial's use of the adjective *doctus* for Catullus himself at 7.99 and 8.73 may well recall Catullus' application of this word to a woman, like his Lesbia, somehow linked with the "Sapphic Muse." The associations between *doctus* and Catullus may also resonate in Martial's use of the same adjective when praising Sulpicia and another female poet.[24] And whatever the enigmatic Catullan phrase "*Sapphica ... Musa doctior*" in poem 35 signifies, whether it does or does not imply a direct comparison with Sappho or Catullus' Lesbia or both, it echoes in Martial's descriptions of both Theophila in 7.69 (*Sappho .../ ... non doctior illa fuit*) and Sulpicia in 10.35 (*hac condiscipula vel hac magistra,/ esses doctior et pudica, Sappho*, "with [Sulpicia] as your fellow student or as your teacher, Sappho, you would be more learned and sexually well behaved").

The differences between these two Catullan echoes, moreover, warrant attention. To be sure, Catullus 35 superficially resembles Martial 10.35 (and 38) more closely than it does Martial 7.69 in its hendecasyllabic meter and its direct address to the woman to whom the word *doctior* refers. 7.69 is in elegiac couplets, speaks of Sappho in the third person, and to some extent distances *non doctior* Sappho from Theophila by placing the words *Sappho* and *doctior* in two successive lines. Yet whereas 7.69 applies the comparative *doctior* to Sappho in order to attribute equal erudition to Sappho and Theophila, 10.35 applies this same word to Sappho in a contrary-to-fact condition, to assert that Sappho's erudition would have increased by exposure to Sulpicia. In 10.35, therefore, Martial characterizes Sulpicia not merely as no less learned, but indeed as more learned than Sappho.

Similarly, by employing the comparative adjective *castior* when contrasting Theophila and Sappho in 7.69, Martial merely indicates that Theophila is superior to Sappho in her moral conduct. He does not explicitly criticize Sappho's moral behavior here. But by using the positive *pudica* in 10.35 to describe a "contrary-to-fact" Sappho influenced by Sulpicia, Martial characterizes Sappho as *impudica*, as engaging in unacceptable sexual conduct, and Sulpicia as correspondingly *pudica*.

And Martial does not merely suggest that Sappho, whom Catullus admired and associated with his Lesbia, a poet whom Martial himself judges intellectually equal if somewhat morally inferior to Theophila, is far inferior to Sulpicia on both intellectual and moral grounds. Just as Martial's references to Sappho call to mind Catullus' poems about his Lesbia, so Martial's use of *pudica* here specifically evokes Catullus' description of his rupture with his beloved at 76.28. There, while asking for divine help in curing himself of his passion, Catullus painfully acknowledges that it is impossible for his beloved to wish to be *pudica*.[25] Martial is hence attributing to Sulpicia a quality that is not only absent in Sappho, the poet Catullus admires, but also a quality that holds no attraction for Catullus' beloved Lesbia, whom Catullus honored by associating with Sappho's poetry. Lastly, in representing Calenus' beloved Sulpicia as morally and intellectually superior to Sappho, and by implication to Catullus' Lesbia, Martial implicitly characterizes Calenus as in this major respect superior in fortune to *doctus Catullus*. While Martial may praise, imitate, and invoke Catullus as a literary model, he represents Calenus as surpassing Catullus in amatory achievement.

IV. Martial's Sulpicia and Propertius' Cynthia

Merriam regards Martial's description of Sulpicia as *doctior* than Sappho "a reminiscence of the *doctae puellae* of Propertius and Ovid."[26] But Merriam does not deal with Martial's various echoes of Propertius' elegies, and especially of Propertius 2.15, in 10.38 and 35. These echoes warrant our scrutiny next. For these Propertian resonances implicitly liken Propertius' poetic portrayal of himself and his beloved Cynthia to Calenus and Sulpicia just as Martial's Catullan resonances in these poems compare Catullus and Lesbia to Calenus and Sulpicia. By recalling Propertius' poetry, Martial is to some degree contrasting the erotic relationship between Calenus and Sulpicia with the amatory partnership attributed to Propertius and Cynthia, just as Martial's echoes of Catullus contrast the love affair of Calenus and Sulpicia with the erotic ties ascribed to Catullus and Lesbia. Still, for the most part these Propertian echoes stress the similarities of Calenus and Sulpicia to Propertius and Cynthia. Most strikingly, the surviving scrap of Sulpicia's own poetry shares affinities in theme and language with the very Propertian poems—2.15 and a later elegy pointedly recalling 2.15—which Martial seems to evoke in honoring Sulpicia and her work.

The opening couplet of Propertius 2.15 contains three phrases of increasing length, each beginning with the word "*o*": *o me felicem! o nox mihi candida! et o tu/ lectule deliciis facte beate meis!* "O fortunate me! O night bright for me! and O you little bed, made blessed by my delight!" Martial 10.38 similarly opens with three phrases beginning with "*o*" as well, albeit phrases running for three, two, and three hendecasyllabic lines respectively. Addressing Calenus, he first invokes the years of his marriage with Sulpicia, "*O molles tibi quindecim, Calene,/ quos cum Sulpicia tua iugales/ indulsit deus et peregit annos!* "O, the fifteen years of marriage with your Sulpicia, pleasurable to you, Calenus, which the god has generously allowed and accomplished!" Martial then pays homage to the individual temporal units constituting these years, and to the passionate erotic couplings in which the couple has engaged:

> o nox omnis et hora, quae notata est
> caris litoris Indici lapillis!
> o quae proelia, quas utrimque pugnas
> felix lectulus et lucerna vidit
> nimbis ebria Nicerotianis!   (10.38.4–8)[27]

Words from each of the three Propertian phrases recur in Martial's poem: *felicem* resounds in line 7, in the nominative form *felix*; *nox*, in line 4; *lectule* is also echoed in line 7, with the nominative form *lectulus*. Propertius uses *lucerna*, which Martial employs in apposition to *lectulus* at 10.38.7, in the third line of 2.15: *quam multa apposita narramus verba lucerna,/ quantaque sublato lumine rixa fuit!* "How many words we spent in conversation after the lamp had been placed nearby, and how great a struggle there was when the light had been taken away!" It perhaps warrants attention, too, that while Propertius' term for his physical pleasure with Cynthia, *deliciae*, does not appear in Martial 10.38, the word is used in 10.35.9 to describe the contents of Sulpicia's poetry as *lusus delicias facetiasque*. *Lusus* here may likewise echo *ludere*, Propertius' verb for his and Cynthia's erotic play at 2.15.2.[28]

To be sure, Propertius addresses a *lectulus* as the site of his and Cynthia's shared joys; Propertius associates the light shed by a *lucerna* with pre-coital conversation, the physical act of making love with the removal of that light. Martial, however, represents both a *lectulus* and a *lucerna* in the third person, and as together witnessing Calenus' and Sulpicia's love-making. By the same token, Propertius describes his and Cynthia's lovemaking as physical struggle with *rixa*, "brawl" (4) and *est luctata*, "she wrestled" (5). Martial uses stronger language for the erotic activity of Sulpicia and Calenus, terms from the realm of war: *proelia*, "battles," and *pugnans*, "fighting" (6).[29] Yet these descriptions are similar enough to establish that Martial is seeking to evoke Propertius' erotic scenario at 2.15 here. And while there are indubitably minor differences between the respective erotic scenarios and vocabulary of the two passages, these differences do not—unlike the evocations of Catullus' poetry—sharply differentiate Calenus and Sulpicia from the pair of well-known literary models called to mind. Such differences merely point out that the marital relations of Calenus and Sulpicia have often been less restrained and more passionate than even the one night of fervent lovemaking celebrated as an extraordinary and joyous occurrence by an earlier and renowned erotic poet.

Martial 10.38 also recalls Propertius 2.15 in its emphasis on the units of time shared by the lovers in question, and by the association of these units of time with the power of divinity. Propertius returns to the subject of the poem's opening lines, the *candida nox* of lovemaking which he shared with Cynthia:

> quod mihi si secum tales concedere noctes
>   illa velit, vitae longus et annus erit.
> si dabit haec multas, fiam immortalis in illis:
>   nocte una quivis vel deus esse potest.
>   (2.15.37–40)

> But if she would be willing to grant me such nights with her, even one year will be life-long. If she will give me many years, I will become immortal in those years: by one such night any man is able to become a god.

Martial begins 10.38 by invoking the years of marriage (*iugales annos*) which a god (*deus*) has generously given to Calenus and Sulpicia and brought to completion; he next invokes each individual night and hour (*nox omnis et hora*) that Calenus and Sulpicia have treasured. In 9–11 he identifies Calenus' life, the only days Calenus counts, with his three *lustra* (fifteen years), of married life (*vixisti tribus, o Calene, lustris:/ aetas haec tibi tota conputatur/ et solos numeras dies mariti*, "you have lived three *lustra*, Calenus: this is reckoned your entire lifetime and you number only the days you have spent as a husband"); Martial concludes in 12–14 by avowing that Calenus would prefer that one of the Fates allot him one such night (*lucem redderet Atropos vel unam*) rather than four spans of the mythic Nestor's lengthy old age.

Here, too, the differences between the representations of time units by Propertius and Martial warrant both explication and explanation. But here, too, these differences are not as pronounced as those between Catullus and Martial. Propertius depicts the possibility of enjoying many passionate nights with Cynthia as a gift from Cynthia herself, and one such night as capable of rendering him a god. Martial describes the years of passionate nights actually shared by Calenus and Sulpicia as a gift bestowed by a god, and one such night as theoretically preferable to long periods of time. Martial is thus characterizing Calenus and Sulpicia as less erotically empowered than are Propertius and Cynthia: Calenus' time with Sulpicia has been subject to the control—and is not said to elevate him to the status—of a god; this god—and not his female beloved—has been capable of granting them time together.

Yet it bears emphasis that if Martial is depicting the relationship of Calenus and Sulpicia as severed by her death and thus physically irretrievable, he is therefore emphasizing the divine control over their lives as well as over their love. More importantly, Martial also represents the time already spent together by Calenus and Sulpicia as similar to that shared by Propertius and Cynthia, albeit as of longer duration and as a lived reality incapable of repetition. The two couples are alike in cherishing experiences of mutual, memorable, physically expressed passion, but Calenus and Sulpicia have enjoyed such experiences in greater abundance.[30]

Martial's use of a word—the diminutive *lectulus*—from the opening couplet of Propertius 2.15 in 10.38 is also striking because *lectulus* appears in only one other Propertian passage: at 4. 8.35–36, in a poem that seems to evoke 2.15 in various ways. There Propertius—piqued that Cynthia has abandoned him to participate in a religious festival—says he made love to two women at once on a *lectulus: unus erat tribus in secreta lectulus herba./ quaeris concubitus? inter utramque fui,* "There was one little bed for three on a hidden lawn. You ask what sexual positions we took? I was between the two" (4.8.35–36). Propertius' term for "sexual positions" in this particular passage, *concubitus*, does not appear elsewhere in his poetry. Significantly, though, one of the two instances in which Propertius uses a form of the verb from which *concubitus* derives occurs in 2.15. Here Propertius likens his own and Cynthia's nude bodies to those of legendary mythological figures:

> ipse Paris nuda fertur periise Lacaena,
>   cum Menelao surgeret e thalamo;
> nudus et Endymion Phoebi cepisse sororem
>   dicitur et nudae concubuisse deae.   (2.15.13–16)

> Paris is said to have perished of love at the sight of Helen of Sparta naked, when she rose from the bedchamber of Menelaus; naked Endymion is said to have captured the sister of Apollo, and to have lain with the naked goddess.

Additional resemblances between Propertius 2.15 and 4.8 include the opening line of 4.8 itself: like that of 2.15, it introduces the poem's subject as the events of a particular night (*disce, quid Esquilias hac nocte fugarit aquosus*). Some of the linguistic and thematic similarities between the two elegies involve the use of words, and metaphors, from the earlier poem to describe contrasting situations in the latter. Propertius' description of ocular pleasure in love-making at 2.15.11–12 (*non iuvat in caeco Venerem corrumpere motu;/ si nescis, oculi sunt in amore duces*) resonates at 4.8.47–48, where he depicts his lack of pleasurable response to his female companions, *nudabant pectora caeco*, "they bared breasts to a blind man." Propertius concludes 4.8 by describing how his quarrel with Cynthia was resolved when they made love on a couch, *et noto solvimus arma toro*. Here, as in 2.15, he applies language literally referring to physical struggle and warfare to his interactions with Cynthia: but to a quarrel that ceased, not to the love-making that commenced.[31]

Most importantly, though, Propertius' emphasis on his and Cynthia's nudity—his use of the adjective *nudus* three times in two consecutive couplets—in 2.15, and Propertius' description of his indifference to the nude breasts of his partners in 4.8, resemble Sulpicia's own emphasis on her own nudity in the surviving fragment of her poetry, where she wishes that she might be placed *nudam Caleno concubantem* in their repaired marriage bed. Sulpicia's use in this same context of the participle *concubantem*, from an otherwise unattested verb *concubare*, similarly recalls Propertius' use of *concubuisse* when emphasizing erotic nudity in 2.15 and of *concubitus* when depicting the activities on a *lectulus* in 4.8. Such resemblances between Sulpicia's own words about her connubial passion for her husband and the language of two related poems by Propertius (one of which is clearly echoed by Martial in extolling the connubial passion of Sulpicia and her husband) would suggest that Martial chose to evoke Propertius 2.15 in 10.38 because the poet it praises, Sulpicia herself, had done so already.[32]

Admittedly, Sulpicia's apparent debt to Propertius would not have been Martial's sole motivation for alluding to Propertius' poetry in verses about her and her husband: Martial's poems contain two explicit references to Propertius that voice a high regard for the Augustan elegist's achievements. These references themselves may also help account for Martial's decision in 10.38 to echo Propertian language and themes. For each of these two poems paying tribute to Propertius' literary accomplishments stresses Propertius' own debt to his beloved Cynthia.

The first poem, 8.73, is one which we have mentioned earlier in connection with Martial's homage to Catullus' Lesbia, and is written in Propertius' own elegiac meter. Here Martial tells his addressee Instantius that if Instantius wishes to give strength and spirit to Martial's Muse, and seeks poems that will live, he should give Martial something to love (*si dare vis nostrae vires animosque Thaliae/ et victura petis carmina, da quod amem*, 3–4). Martial next addresses Propertius as *lascive*, "erotically playful," and says that Cynthia made him a poet (*Cynthia te vatem fecit, lascive Properti*, 5). In the second poem, 14.189, also in elegiacs, Martial claims that "Cynthia, [who inspired] the youthful poetry of the eloquent Propertius, received fame and gave no less herself" (*Cynthia, facundi carmen iuvenale Properti,/ accepit famam; non minus ipsa dedit*). As Martial credited Cynthia for giving literary renown to as well as receiving literary renown from Propertius, through inspiring Propertius' poetry, he may have found Cynthia a particularly apt model for

Sulpicia, who had exalted both Calenus and herself through writing her own poetry.

The analogy between Propertius' Cynthia and Sulpicia is, admittedly, somewhat flawed. It would be more accurate for Martial to view not Cynthia, who merely inspired Propertius' poetry, but rather Propertius himself as a literary model for Sulpicia. Propertius himself, however, offered Martial strong grounds for equating Cynthia and Sulpicia by representing Cynthia as herself a writer of poetry. Indeed, Propertius 2.3 foreshadows Martial's comparison of Sulpicia to Sappho, since at 21–22 he compares Cynthia to two earlier Greek women poets, Corinna and Erinna: *et sua cum antiquae committit scripta Corinnae/ carminaque Erinnes non putat aequa suis*, "and she challenges with her own verse the writings of ancient Corinna, and does not think the poems of Erinna equal to her own." In arguing for Sulpicia's superiority to Sappho in morals, erudition, and lovability, Martial may be not merely recalling but elaborating upon Propertius' claim that Cynthia's poetry was, at least in her own eyes, better than that of two Greek female literary antecedents.

It warrants attention that in his representation of Cynthia as herself a poet, and in associating Cynthia's poetry with that of Corinna and Erinna, Propertius differs sharply from Catullus on yet another score. Catullus, after all, does not portray his beloved Lesbia as composing poetry herself; Catullus celebrates Sappho when paying tribute to the poetic inspiration and sensibilities of his female beloved, as well as in embracing earlier Greek literary models for his own work. This particular difference between Propertius' portrayal of Cynthia and Catullus' portrayal of Lesbia may help account for Martial's decision to assimilate Calenus and Sulpicia more closely to earlier portraits of Propertius and Cynthia than to depictions of Catullus and Lesbia. Martial's decision to depict Propertius and Cynthia as having more in common with Calenus and Sulpicia than with Catullus and Lesbia may additionally help account for Martial's disparagement in 10.35 of Sappho, whose poetic accomplishments were so valued by Catullus.

Whatever factors prompted Martial to associate Sulpicia and Calenus more closely with Cynthia and Propertius than with Lesbia and Catullus, Martial's association of Sulpicia and Calenus with Cynthia and Propertius seems an anomalous choice on several grounds. For one thing, the illicit, extramarital passion which Propertius ascribes to himself and Cynthia would appear to have little in common with the sanctioned marital love which Martial ascribes to Sulpicia and Calenus. To be sure, in 4.7 Propertius represents his often turbulent love affair with Cynthia as enduring, in its fashion, beyond the grave: he does not depict himself as emotionally devastated by a final rupture with his beloved in the way that Catullus does in such poems as 76. Yet, as both 4.7 and 4.8 document, Propertius also depicts both himself and Cynthia as involved with other partners during the course of their affair: the bond which Propertius claims to have shared with Cynthia is a far cry from the sexual exclusivity and mutual fidelity Martial attributes to Calenus and Sulpicia. For another, Martial not only invokes Catullus as his own literary model in several poems. While Martial would seem to echo Propertius' language approximately twenty-five times in his poetry, his specific and laudatory references to the work of Catullus are far more numerous than his comparable references to the poems of Propertius.[33]

Furthermore, several of Martial's poems—among them 10.35, his tribute to the literary accomplishments of Sulpicia—would appear to voice some strong criticisms of Propertius' work. Most obviously, Martial states that in Sulpicia's verses,

> non haec Colchidos adserit furorem,
> diri prandia nec refert Thyestae;
> Scyllam, Byblida nec fuisse credit:
> sed castos docet et probos amores,
> lusus delicias facetiasque.   (10.35.5–9)

> She does not claim as her subject the frenzy of Medea, nor does she relate the banquets of dreadful Thyestes, nor does she believe that Scylla and Byblis have existed, but she teaches virtuous and respectable passions, playful erotic encounters, sensual pleasures, and witty remarks.

Now several of the mythic characters here cited by Martial as excluded from Sulpicia's poetry figure in the elegies of Propertius, and do so to illustrate actual female misbehavior. At 3.19, for example, Propertius faults the lustful conduct of both Medea and Scylla. While Propertius does not mention Thyestes' banquet, he does refer to the adultery of Clytemnestra—with Aegisthus, Thyestes' son by his own daughter—and to the disgrace it brought to the household of Pelops, to which Thyestes belonged (*quidve Clytemestra, propter quam tota Mycenis/ infamis stupro stat Pelopea domus?* 19–20). While Propertius does not mention the incestuous passion of Byblis for her brother here (or elsewhere in his poetry), he does refer to Myrrha's incestuous passion for her father (*crimen et illa fuit, patria succensa senecta/ arboris in frondes condita Myrrha novae,* 15–16).

By asserting that Sulpicia excludes these mythic characters from her poetry *but* instructs about proper amatory sentiment and conduct, Martial obviously implies that these mythic characters exemplify improper amatory sentiment and conduct. Nevertheless, it is also significant that Martial singles out both Scylla and Byblis—two characters known in Roman literary circles from the works of Hellenistic writers, two characters immortalized in learned Latin poetry that conspicuously embodies Hellenistic literary principles—as rightfully excluded from Sulpicia's poems. These references suggest that Martial may also be disparaging the learned Hellenistic subject matter of poets such as Propertius, who not only glorifies the work and principles of the Alexandrian poet Callimachus, but even calls himself the Roman Callimachus at 4.1.64.[34] Such an interpretation is strengthened by Martial's statements in 10.4. Here Martial explicitly faults the *Aetia* of Callimachus as lacking relevance to contemporary Roman life; in so doing, he contrasts the *vana ludibria,* "empty bits of nonsense," of works concerned with outlandish mythic topics, to his own poetry, which "tastes like a human being" (*hominem pagina nostra sapit,* 10).

Significantly, when exemplifying the kinds of mythological topics that interest a reader attracted to Callimachus in 10.4, Martial first mentions three of the characters he also specifies as missing from Sulpicia's work: Thyestes, Medea and Scylla (*Qui legis Oedipoden caligantem Thyesten,/ Colchidas et Scyllas,* 1–2). Martial then cites Hylas, who figures prominently in Propertius 1.20, then Parthenopaeus and Attis. Finally, Martial cites Endymion, whom Propertius mentions only once—but at 2.15.15, in a poem we have observed Martial evoking in 10.38, in a passage we have argued that Sulpicia herself evokes in the sole surviving fragment of her work, in lines that celebrate Propertius' and Cynthia's nudity by recalling that of three mythological lovers. In the light of Martial's negative comments about the arcane nature, and irrelevant mythological topics, characterizing the kind of poetry Propertius embraced, and in view of Martial's negatively illustrative use of a mythological figure featured in Propertius 2.15, Martial's decision to evoke Propertius 2.15 in praising the mutual love of Sulpicia and her husband seems particularly incongruous.

Martial's evocations of Propertius' poetry when extolling Sulpicia and Calenus are incongruous for another reason as well: in 10.35 Martial is praising Sulpicia for celebrating female conduct and personal values rejected by Propertius in his poetry. In asserting that Sulpicia's poetry is for all women who want to please *uni viro* as well as for all husbands who want to please *uni nuptae*, Martial not only emphasizes that Sulpicia herself is *univira*. In so doing, Martial likens Sulpicia to the noble matron Cornelia eulogized by Propertius in the final poem of his final book, 4.11. For Propertius represents Cornelia as justifying her own life, and in that context proclaiming to her husband *in lapide hoc uni nupta fuisse legar*, "I will be read on this tombstone as having been married to one man" (36) and advises her daughter *fac teneas unum nos imitata virum*, "Make sure that you, following my example, hold on to one man" (68).[35]

Yet Propertius has also included Cynthia in two poems of Book 4, and portrayed her and Cornelia as extremely dissimilar in their conduct and values: particularly in his respective portrayals of the newly dead Cynthia as swearing to her love for Propertius, and of the newly dead Cornelia as boasting at length about her illustrious male ancestors and virtuous female ways but saying nothing about her love for her husband. Through this implicit contrast between Cynthia and Cornelia, he makes it clear that Cynthia and not Cornelia is his kind of woman.[36] In an earlier poem, 2.13, he even appears to be describing Cornelia's lack of attraction for him when he states that beauty and pride in noble ancestry in a woman are not enough to please him:

> non ego sum formae tantum mirator honestae,
> nec si qua illustres femina iactat avos:

> me iuvet in gremio doctae legisse puellae
> auribus et puris scripta probasse mea.
>
> (2.13.11–14)

I am not only an admirer of handsome form, nor if any woman boasts of distinguished male ancestors: it pleases me to have read my writings in the arms of a learned girl and for these writings to have tested discriminating ears."[37]

Perhaps more significantly, and more obviously, Martial's assertion in 10.35 that Sulpicia's work *castos docet et probos amores,* "teaches virtuous and respectable passions," recalls a statement made by Propertius in the very first poem of his first book: that, after he was first captured by Cynthia, *Amor ... improbus* taught (*docuit*) him to hate *castas puellas* (1.1.4–6). By describing Sappho's beloved Phaon as *durus,* hardhearted, Martial also utilizes what is virtually a Propertian buzz-word. Propertius employs this adjective—in a variety of meanings, of course—seventeen times in Book 1 alone, and nearly fifty times in his entire corpus.[38] It often carries the same emotional connotations with which Martial invests it, and frequently refers to Cynthia. At the close of 2.1, for example, Propertius asks his patron Maecenas to honor him posthumously with the words *Huic misero fatum dura puella fuit,* "A hardhearted girl was the cause of this poor man's death" (80).

Martial's evocations of Propertius when celebrating the mutual love of Sulpicia and Calenus in 10.35 and 38, and Martial's representation of Sulpicia and Calenus as similar to Propertius' portrayals of Cynthia and himself, then, are not merely anomalous: anomalous in view of Martial's relatively few references to Propertius as compared to Catullus, anomalous in view of Martial's disparaging statements about the learned, inaccessible Hellenistic mode of writing which Propertius embraced. More incongruously still, Martial even echoes Propertius' language and uses Propertian themes to praise what Propertius criticizes and to criticize what Propertius praises. Again, I would attribute these Propertian evocations, both laudatory and critical, to the influential role evidently played by Propertius' poetry in Sulpicia's own work, and to Propertius' representation of his beloved Cynthia as—like Sulpicia—

a poet in her own right who had elevated both herself and the man she loved in the eyes of others.

I would, moreover, cite as an analogical phenomenon to Martial's anomalous evocations of Propertius Martial's characterization of Sappho as a standard of poetic measurement for both Sulpicia in 10.35 and Theophila in 7.69. In both poems Martial not only compares Sappho unfavorably with female poets of his acquaintance on moral grounds, and female poets of his acquaintance favorably with Sappho on intellectual grounds. He also makes highly unflattering remarks about Sappho in each poem. In 10.35, he characterizes Sappho as *impudica*, and as far less appealing to males—or at least to the one male with whom she was erotically linked in literary tradition—than Sulpicia. In 7.69 he refers to Sappho by the negatively-charged noun *amatrix*, "woman who engages in carnal acts," when acknowledging that she praised "a person who wrote poems."[39] Martial's praise of Theophila's poems in 7.69 as immortal because they are not like a woman's writing (*tam non femineum*) even suggests that Martial was uncomfortable with women poets generally as well as with Sappho in particular.

But Martial's poetic predecessors Catullus and Ovid had assigned an influential literary role to Sappho, the latter when setting standards for women's poetry: at *Tristia* 3.7.20, for example, Ovid compliments the work of his literary protégée Perilla by according it the potential of being surpassed only by Sappho's.[40] Inasmuch as Sulpicia's own work seems to evince a literary debt to Propertius' poetry, it is not impossible that Sulpicia had been influenced by Sappho's lyrics as well. Whatever the case, whether or not Sulpicia actually identified with Sappho in her poetry, a long-standing literary tradition, which represented Sappho as a role model for women of poetic sensibilities and as a standard of achievement for later female poets, put Martial under pressure to invoke Sappho in praising Sulpicia.

V. Martial's Sulpicia and Feminist Literary Criticism

Ovid's reading recommendations for women desirous of erotic success at *Ars Amatoria* 3.329ff. begin with Callimachus and include the erotically playful Sappho (*quid enim lascivius illa*, "for what is more playful than she?" 331). Two lines later, he advises *et teneri possis carmen legisse Properti*, "You should be able to have read a poem by youthful Propertius" (333). The unmistakable Propertian echoes in Martial's poetry about Sulpicia, and the apparent Propertian echoes in what remains of Sulpicia's, imply that at least one educated and erotically successful woman living in Rome a century after Ovid actually accorded to Propertius' poetry the special status which Ovid sought to obtain for it. But what does the respect for Propertius' writing by this actual Roman woman poet have to do with the issues that inform feminist scholarship on classical antiquity? Has, for that matter, our inquiry on Martial's Sulpicia qualified as a feminist project?

As I began my discussion by recognizing the important contributions of feminist approaches to the study of Greco-Roman antiquity, I would like to conclude by considering how these efforts to situate Martial's representation of Sulpicia in a wider literary context relate to some larger concerns of current feminist scholarship. One of these concerns stems from the recognition that "literary language has traditionally encoded male privilege" and thus cannot adequately describe or express women's experience. Feminist scholars have thus stressed the need for women to "seize speech, and make it say what we mean," to become— in the words of the French feminist and classicist C. Herrmann, "*voleuses de langue*," thieves of language. Solely on the basis of words used by Martial to characterize Sulpicia's poetry, Parker has contended that Sulpicia has proven herself precisely such a thief, "appropriating masculine language" in her erotic discourse, albeit a discourse rendered respectable to Martial "by placing her desire in the context of marriage and fidelity."[41] Martial's and Sulpicia's specific echoes of Propertius would support, indeed strengthen, Parker's contention. By evoking a Propertian portrayal of extramarital passion when celebrating her own marital devotion, moreover, Sulpicia's writing challenges at the same time that it conforms to norms of social respectability. Martial may judge Sulpicia *casta* and *pudica* for extolling her love for her husband. But other ancient Roman critics may have found her resemblance to Cynthia and her debt to Propertius troublingly defiant and consequently socially deviant; such reactions to Sulpicia's work may even explain why Martial goes to such lengths in contrasting her and her poetry with Sappho.[42]

However Martial and his various contemporaries may have viewed

Sulpicia's similarities to Propertius' Cynthia, however they interpreted Sulpicia's apparent echoes of Propertius, I believe that we are justified in interpreting Sulpicia's challenge to accepted societal norms—a challenge she would seem to voice by appropriating masculine language associated with the celebration of extramarital love—as, in Sulpicia's own particular Roman milieu, a feminist gesture. The acceptance of these societal norms denied Roman women the right to express themselves and describe their erotic activity as men did; Sulpicia's challenge would seek to assert that right when utilizing her own form of literary expression.[43] An issue important to feminist interpretation also arises in addressing the question of why Sulpicia chose to evoke this particular male poet. I have furnished what I regard as the most plausible answer: that Propertius portrays his female beloved Cynthia as, like Sulpicia, a writer of poetry herself who enhanced the life and reputation of her male partner.

But we should not rule out further explanations for Sulpicia's decision. By adopting a feminist literary stance through her appropriation of Propertius' language and her evocation of Propertius' erotic scenario, Sulpicia additionally would have been emphasizing the similarity between her own literary self-representation and Propertius' representation of both himself and Cynthia. In so doing she would implicitly characterize Propertius' own work as feminist as well. The attraction of Propertius's poetry for an actual feminist writer residing in early imperial Rome, of course, challenges a recent scholarly claim that Propertius' portrayal of Cynthia, his milieu, and his values should not be regarded as a feminist statement. This argument has been advanced on the grounds that the Augustan elegists do not provide or demand a consistent political role for the female subject in focusing on the portrayal of "their first-person heroes as displaced from a central position in the social categories of Augustan Rome."[44]

Sulpicia's evocation of Propertius to map out an unconventional poetic role for herself, though, has profound political implications if we define "political" as feminist thought has urged us to do. That is, if we understand the term not merely in the narrow sense of having to do with the state, with human government, and other institutional structures of behavioral control, but as of wider import, pertaining to the distribution of rights and power in all human interactions. Presumably Sulpicia used her own writing, and certainly Martial used Sulpicia's writing, to impress upon an audience composed of both males and females the positive aspects of erotic literary self-expression by women: hence Martial's enjoinder that all brides eager to please one man and all husbands eager to please one bride read Sulpicia; hence Martial's favorable comparison of Sulpicia to Sappho, whom he depicts as having given such writing a bad name. By affecting larger social assumptions about women's sexual behavior and public speech, such a message had the potential of affording women greater opportunity to conduct themselves as men did in two particular spheres of human activity, marital relations and artistic production. The poetical is also and always the political.

Martial's two poems about Sulpicia, however, pose serious obstacles for those of us engaged in feminist inquiry and recovery. Martial, however supportive he may be of Sulpicia's potential literary contribution to both marital relations and artistic production, does not do Sulpicia's actual literary contributions full justice. Propertius represents his beloved Cynthia as speaking in a number of his poems: at line 8 of 2.15, for example, in the very poem which we have argued that Martial and Sulpicia sought to evoke, Propertius reports that Cynthia sought to arouse him sexually with the words *sicine, lente, iaces*, "do you lie down so inertly, you dawdler?"[45] But, as I have emphasized above, Martial's Sulpicia is silent in both of his poems that pay tribute to her as poet and as loving wife. Even if he does not quote her actual verses, he could still assign her some words of her own. So, too, Martial's evocation of Propertius in 10.38 may assimilate both Calenus and Sulpicia to the roles of earlier literary figures remembered for their expressions of mutual passion. Yet in view of the poem's single allusion to Sulpicia and nine references to Calenus, this evocation seems motivated primarily by a desire to extol and elevate Calenus, albeit by associating him with a poet who defied Roman conventions in his writing and in the life style that it represented.

Furthermore, by likening Sulpicia's *ioci*, "witticisms," to those of Egeria in the cave of king Numa, Martial implicitly likens Calenus to Numa, an esteemed Roman monarch who upheld and indeed established Roman conventions. By way of contrast, in characterizing Egeria's remarks as mere *ioci*, Martial trivializes a tradition reported, for example, at Livy 1.19.5 and 21.4, about this woman of Roman legend with whom Sulpicia is equated: that Numa credited Egeria and her sister goddesses, the Camenae, with the advice by which he "established sacred practices most welcome to the gods, and appointed priests to serve each god." While we owe Martial our gratitude for bearing witness to the existence, and literary contributions, of an otherwise almost silenced female voice from classical Roman antiquity, we feel resentment, too, at the obvious limitations of his testimony, testimony which at best would have been no substitute for Sulpicia's own voice.

Judith P. Hallett
University of Maryland, College Park

Notes

This paper has appeared in essentially the same form in *CW*, 86 (1992), 99–123.

All the translations are my own.

[1] See, for example, Sarah B. Pomeroy, "Selected Bibliography on Women in Classical Antiquity (Part I, to 1973, Part II, 1973–81)," in *Women in the Ancient World: The Arethusa Papers*, eds. J. Peradotto and J. P. Sullivan (Albany, 1984), 315–72; L. Goodwater, *Women in Antiquity: An Annotated Bibliography* (Metuchen, 1975); J. Hallett, "Classics and Women's Studies," Working Paper No. 119, *Wellesley College Center for Research on Women* (Wellesley College, 1983); P. Culham, "Ten Years after Pomeroy: Studies of the Image and Reality of Women in Antiquity," in *Rescuing Creusa: New Methodological Approaches to Women in Antiquity*, ed. M. B. Skinner, special issue, *Helios*, 13.2 (1986), 9–30; M. B. Skinner, "Expecting the Barbarians: Feminism, Nostalgia, and the 'Epistemic Shift' in Classical Studies," in *Classics: A Discipline and Profession in Crisis*, eds. P. Culham and L. Edmunds (Lanham, 1989), 199–210; R. Meyer, "Neuere Entwicklungen und Tendenzen der Frauengeschichte im Bereich der klassichen Altertumskunde (1973–1989)," *Schriftliche Hausarbeit zur ersten Staatsprüfung für die Laufbahn der Studienrate an Gymnasien* (Kiel, 1991).

[2] M. B. Skinner, "Corinna of Tanagra and her Audience," *Tulsa Studies in Women's Literature*, 2 (1983), 9–20; "Sapphic Nossis," *Arethusa*, 22.1 (Spring 1989), 5–18; and "*Nossis Thelyglossos*: The Private Text and the Public Book," in *Women's History and Ancient History*, ed. S. B. Pomeroy (Chapel Hill, 1991),

20–47; J. Snyder, *The Woman and the Lyre: Women Writers in Classical Greece and Rome* (Carbondale, 1989), and "Public Occasion and Private Passion in the Lyrics of Sappho of Lesbos," in *Women's History and Ancient History*, ed. Pomeroy, 1–19.

For some other recent feminist analyses of Greek women poets, see, for example, M. B. Arthur, "The Tortoise and the Mirror: Erinna PSI 1090," *CW*, 74 (1980), 53–65; J. Winkler, "Gardens of Nymphs: Public and Private in Sappho's Lyrics," *Women's Studies*, 8 (1981), rpt. in *Reflections of Women in Antiquity*, ed. H. P. Foley (New York, London, and Paris, 1981), 63–89; E. Stehle, "Sappho's Private World," *Women's Studies*, 8 (1981), rpt. in *Reflections of Women*, ed. Foley, 45–61, and "Sappho's Gaze: Fantasies of a Goddess and Young Man," *Differences*, 2 (1990), 88–125.

[3] *The Woman and the Lyre*, 98, citing "Erinna in her expression of affection for Baukis" as particularly noteworthy in this regard. On the women poets in the Greek anthology, see also S. Barnard, "Hellenistic Women Poets," *CJ*, 73 (1978), 208–10.

[4] C. Calame, *Les Choeurs de jeunes filles en Grèce archaïque*, 2 vols. (Rome, 1977); J. Hallett, "Sappho and her Social Context," *Signs*, 4 (1979), 447–64; Snyder, *The Woman and the Lyre*, 2–4.

[5] Stephen Hinds, "The Poetess and the Reader: Further Steps Toward Sulpicia," *Hermathena*, 143 (Winter 1987), 29–46; Holt Parker, "Sulpicia, the *Auctor de Sulpicia* and the Authorship of 3.9 and 3.11 of the *Corpus Tibullianum*," forthcoming in *Helios*, 1992.

[6] Matthew Santirocco, "Sulpicia Reconsidered," *CJ*, 74 (1979), 229–39; H. MacL. Currie, "The Poems of Sulpicia," *Aufstieg und Niedergang der römischen Welt*, 2.30.3 (1983), 1751–64; N. J. Lowe, "Sulpicia's Syntax," *CQ*, 38 (1988), 193–205; Snyder, *The Woman and the Lyre*, 128–36; Hallett, "Contextualizing the Text: The Journey to Ovid," *Helios*, 17.2 (1990), 187–95.

[7] S. B. Pomeroy, *Goddesses, Whores, Wives, and Slaves: Women in Classical Antiquity* (New York, 1975), 53–56, 137–39, 173–74; M. R. Lefkowitz and M. B. Fant, *Women's Lives in Greece and Rome: A Source Book in Translation* (Baltimore and London, 1982), 4–10, 131–32.

[8] Diane Rayor, *Sappho's Lyre: Archaic Lyric and Women Poets of Ancient Greece* (Berkeley, 1991).

[9] Santirocco, 229 and n. 3; Snyder, *The Woman and the Lyre*, 128 and n. 14. See also A. E. Richlin, *The Garden of Priapus: Sexuality and Aggression in Roman Humor* (New Haven and London, 1983), 232 n. 4, who discusses Martial's references to this Sulpicia and identifies her as "the Sulpicia who wrote iambics on the breakup of her marriage to Calenus" on the basis of Probus Vallae *ad Iuv.* 6.537 (discussed below).

[10] Merriam, "The Other Sulpicia," in "Scholia," *CW*, 84.4 (March-April 1991), 303–5, responded to in three articles *CW*, 86 (1992): my "Martial's Sulpicia;" Holt Parker, "Other Remarks on the Other Sulpicia," 89–95; and Amy Richlin, "Sulpicia the Satirist," 125–40.

[11] Merriam, "The Other Sulpicia," 303 and 305. Parker, "Other Remarks," also corrects Merriam on this matter.

[12] Parker, ibid.; cf. also Martial 1.99, addressed to a Calenus, observing that even though four deaths within seven months brought this Calenus a huge sum of money, he entertains his friends in a cheap fashion.

In "Sulpicia," however, Richlin advances several arguments in support of the claim, which she made earlier in *The Garden of Priapus*, that 10.38 may not represent Sulpicia's and Calenus' marriage as terminated by her death. 10.38 may, for example, be "a working out for Calenus of the sentiment sketched more briefly for Sulpicia at the end of 10.35: as she would not wish to live, even as the wife of a god, were Calenus to be taken from her, so Calenus would not wish even for the long life of Nestor, if he could have back only one day of his life with Sulpicia—the implication being, *if* she were taken from him."

[13] It bears reflection that the surviving fragments of Licinius Calvus' poetry, collected in *Fragmenta Poetarum Latinorum*, ed. W. Morel (Stuttgart, 1963), 84–87, include one fragment which has certain verbal and thematic similarities to Martial's descriptions of Sulpicia in 10.35 and 38. Cited by a scholiast to Vergil, *Aeneid* 4.58, it describes the goddess Ceres: *et leges sanctas docuit et cara iugavit/ corpora conubiis et magnas condidit urbes*, "and she taught honorable laws and joined cherished bodies in marriage and founded great cities." Martial utilizes Calvus' word for Ceres' laws, *sanctas*, in stating at 10.35.12 that whoever would think well of Sulpicia's poems *nullam dixerit esse sanctiorem*, "would have said that no woman is more honorable." *Cara* is echoed by *caris* and and *iugavit* by *iugales* in Martial's praise of Calenus' marital life at 10.38.5 and 2 respectively. Such echoes raise the possibility that Martial is here evoking Calvus' own poetry as well as Catullus' encomium to Calvus on his marriage to Quintilia. However, unlike numerous other Latin authors—among them Propertius (2.25.4), Ovid (*Amores* 3.9.62), Horace (*Sat.* 1.10.19), Velleius Paterculus (2.36.2), and the younger Pliny (*Epistulae* 1.16.5)—Martial does not couple Calvus with Catullus when referring to the latter, or even mention Calvus at all. For Martial's references to Catullus, see T. P. Wiseman, *Catullus and His World: A Reappraisal* (Cambridge, 1985), 246–58.

[14] On the diminutive "*Sulpicilla*" here as contemptuous, see Parker, "Other Remarks," and Richlin, "Sulpicia." Merriam, "The Other Sulpicia," concludes her summary of Martial's and Ausonius' evidence on Sulpicia's writings with the statement, "Such are our only witnesses to the writings of Sulpicia"; her omission of the testimony on Sulpicia furnished by Sidonius Apollinaris and

Fulgentius is surprising, since their statements strengthen her own thesis.

[15] On *cadurcum*, see Richlin, "Sulpicia," who observes, "The scholiast is not quite right in his definition; as we know from attestations elsewhere, this *cadurcum* was a kind of bedding linen, named after its makers, the Gallic tribe of the Cadurci (see Mayor *ad Juv.* 7.221)."

[16] See the discussion of Parker, "Other Remarks," and *inter alia*, W. S. Anderson, "Valla, Juvenal and Probus," *Traditio*, 21 (1965), 383–424; J. E. G. Zetzel, *Latin Textual Criticism in Antiquity* (Salem, 1981), 179–80, 184–86, and R. J. Tarrant in *Texts and Transmission: A Survey of the Latin Classics*, ed. L. D. Reynolds, (Oxford, 1983), 19, 202.

[17] Most obviously W. Kroll, "Sulpicius" 114, *RE*, 4A, 880–82 [1932]; M. Schanz and C. Hosius, *Geschichte der römischen Literatur* (Munich, 1935), vol. 2, 560; Morel, *Fragmenta Poetarum Latinorum*, 134. Inasmuch as Merriam, "The Other Sulpicia," cites the paragraph on Sulpicia in Schanz and Hosius, her failure to mention these two lines of Sulpicia is particularly striking.

[18] Merriam, "The Other Sulpicia," 304. As Wiseman (164) remarks, Catullus 70 imitates a poem of Callimachus, 9 (Gow-Page). As we will observe below, at 10.4 Martial explicitly compares the topics of his own verses to those of Callimachus. By claiming in 10.35 that Sulpicia's work does not treat themes he associates with Callimachus in 10.4, Martial also implicitly contrasts Sulpicia's subject matter to Callimachean themes. Since neither the comparison in 10.4 nor the comparison in 10.35 favors Callimachus, Martial may also be disparaging Catullus' erotic scenario merely by alluding to a Catullan poem with an obvious Callimachean model.

[19] For Catullus and the hendecasyllabic meter, see Wiseman, 250 (citing Caesius Bassus) and 254–56; and Richlin, "Sulpicia," who persuasively argues for the influence of the hendecasyllabic Catullus 45—depicting the mutual love of Septimius and Acme—on 10.35.

[20] Merriam, "The Other Sulpicia," 304. Parker observes, in "Other Remarks," that Sulpicia is only "allowed an open expression of sexuality" because she conforms to the type of *univira*. He likens Martial's representation of Sulpicia to Plautus' characterization of Alcmena at *Amphitryo* 635–41, 735, 802–8 and 840 (where her desire is called "becalmed," *sedatum cupidinem*) and likens Sulpicia's own celebration of marital love to Calvus' elegy for his wife Quintilia and Parthenius' elegy for his wife Arete. Richlin, "Sulpicia," also contrasts Martial's defense of Sulpicia's poetic and moral reputation with Sulpicia's self-exposure, with her "daring reappropriation" of literary strategies honed by male satirists, and with the "transgressive force" of her writing.

[21] For Catullus' debt and similarities to Sappho, see R. Jenkyns, *Three Classical Poets: Sappho, Catullus and Juvenal* (Cambridge, 1982), 20ff., 44–53, 73, and 80ff.

[22] As Wiseman's appendix—which provides all known references to Catullus in ancient authors—indicates, Martial also refers to both Catullus and Lesbia at 6.34.7–8, 7.14.1–6, 12.44.5–6 and 14.77.

[23] For references to Sappho as the tenth Muse, see the *Palatine Anthology* 7.14, 9.66 and 571; 9.506 (by Plato) and Plutarch, *Amatorius* 18. For the possible implications of such a statement, see Hallett, "Sappho and her Social Context," 447–48. Wiseman assumes that "Caecilius' girl friend is compared" to Sappho (148); Jenkyns' book, notwithstanding its focus on the relationship between Sappho and Catullus, does not discuss poem 35.

[24] Catullus refers to Nepos' volumes as *doctis* at 1.7; to Caecilius' beloved as *doctior* at 35.17; to the Muses as *doctis virginibus* at 65.2. But he does not apply the adjective to himself, although it is so applied by Horace (*Sat.* 1.10.19), Ovid (*Amores* 3.9.62), Lygdamus (at Tibullus 3.6.41), and Terentianus Maurus (=*Grammatici Latini* 6.401 Keil) as well as by Martial; for the relevant passages, see Wiseman, 246ff.

[25] *Pudicus* and its antonym, *impudicus*, are frequent and loaded Catullan terms: Catullus, for example, refutes the charge that he himself is *parum pudicum*, while acknowledging that his verses are *parum pudici*, in poem 16. Catullus also employs the noun *pudicitia* in the context of female sexual fidelity at 61.217.

[26] Merriam, "The Other Sulpicia," 304; she does not, however, provide any examples of Propertius' or Ovid's references to *puellae* as *doctae*. Furthermore, she fails to explore the implications of the direct address to Sappho, the contrary-to-fact condition, and the comparative *doctior* in 10.35.15–16; she merely quotes H. Bardon's statement in *La Littérature latine inconnue* (Paris, 1956), vol. 2, 228, that "Martial means that her 'talent serait comparable à celui de Sappho.'"

[27] It was not until several months after I independently discerned these echoes of Propertius 2.15 in Martial 10.38—and analyzed the literary significance of these echoes in a paper I presented in honor of Joy King's retirement at the University of Colorado in May 1991—that I discovered two earlier articles which had similarly identified these lines as Propertian echoes: D. R. Shackleton Bailey, "Echoes of Propertius," *Mnemosyne*, 5 (1952), 318, who has listed Propertius 2.15.1–4 as echoed by Martial 10.38.4–8; and A. La Penna, "De Marziale Properti imitatore," *Rivista di Filologia e di Istruzione Classica*, 33 (1955), 136–37, who has listed Propertius 2.15.1–4 as imitated by Martial 10.38.4–8 and Propertius 2.15.37–40 as imitated by Martial at 10.38.9–14. In his extensive list of Propertian echoes in later authors, however, Shackleton Bailey does not mention Sulpicia's own two-line fragment. I would like to thank John P. Sullivan for providing me with bibliographical information about these two articles, which he discusses in *Martial: The Unexpected Classic*.

A *Literary and Historical Study* (Cambridge, 1991).

[28] Martial, however, also echoes Catullus' use of *ludere* in a literary sense—to describe writing amatory verse—in poem 50, and frequently uses *lusus* and *ludere* to describe his own erotic poetry. At 1.35.12, for example, Martial asks his reader to spare his *lusibus* and *iocis*; at 1.113 Martial refers to his youthful writing of light verse with the verb *lusi*; at 4.49 Martial complains that someone who would only call epigrams *lusus iocosque* does not know what epigrams are; and at 7.12.9 Martial claims that his poems are harmless, *ludimus innocui*.

[29] Martial may, however, be evoking Propertius 2.1.45, *nos contra angusto versantes proelia lecto*, "we on the other hand writing poetry about lovers' wars on a narrow couch." Parker, "Other Remarks," argues that the words *lusus, delicias, facetias* (10.35.9), *proelia, pugnas*, and *felix lectulus* (10.38.6) are all attributed to Sulpicia's own poetry by Martial and are "all part of the erotic vocabulary well known from Catullus and the elegists"; he concludes from these arguments that Sulpicia has "appropriated masculine language and become a true *voleuse de langue*." I would not interpret Martial as here attributing these exact words to Sulpicia's writing; I will, however, argue below that Sulpicia's use of Propertian language in her one surviving fragment makes it likely that she employed other vocabulary associated with the Latin love elegists and hence appropriated—as does the earlier Augustan elegist Sulpicia—masculine language. On this last point, see also Richlin, "Sulpicia," who remarks that "… following the first Sulpicia, Sulpicia the satirist is committing a double breach of barrier. Where the first Sulpicia both broke into a male job (writing) and a male genre (elegy), turning the lover's gaze back on a male object, the second Sulpicia broke into writing and into the shoes of Priapus."

[30] The descriptions of time in Propertius 2.15, it should be noted, themselves seem to evoke those of Catullus 5. Lines 23–24 of the Propertian elegy, *dum nos fata sinunt, oculos satiemus amore:/ nox tibi longa venit, nec reditura dies*, "while the fates allow us, let us fill our eyes with love: long night comes to you, nor is the day about to return," call to mind Catullus' *soles occidere et redire possunt/ nobis, …/ nox est perpetua una dormienda* (4–6); Propertius' *errat, qui finem vesani quaerit amoris;/ verus amor nullum novit habere modum*, "he is mistaken, who seeks an end to frenzied love; true love knows how to have no limit" (29–30), recalls Catullus' concern with losing count of kisses in both 5 and 7; Propertius' *omnia si dederis oscula pauca dabis*, "If you will have given all of your kisses, you will give few" (50), evokes Catullus' emphasis on innumerable quantities of kisses as well.

[31] It perhaps merits note that Martial's phrase at 10.38.5 for the precious pearls marking each night and hour shared by Calenus and Sulpicia, *caris litoris Indici lapillis*, and particularly the diminutive word *lapillus*, recall Propertian descriptions: 1.2.13, *litora nativis persuadent picta lapillis*, and 1.15.7 *nec minus*

Eois pectus variare lapillis.

[32] Observing that Sulpicia's language leaves "the impression of a strong writer, a stylistic link between Persius and Juvenal," Richlin, "Sulpicia," argues that Juvenal himself may be imitating Sulpicia when he twice uses the word *cadurcum* (at 7.221 as well as at 6.537), once in close proximity to the word *concubitus*. On Martial's possible imitation of Sulpicia here, see also Richlin, "Sulpicia," who cites the *RE* article by Kroll.

[33] For Martial's echoes of Propertian language, see Shackleton Bailey, "Echoes of Propertius." Wiseman's appendix of passages in ancient authors which refer to Catullus by name lists nineteen such passages in Martial (246–61). In six of these passages Martial explicitly compares his work to (or at least associates his work with) the poems of Catullus, and in so doing represents Catullus' literary efforts in an extremely positive light: the preface to Book 1, 2.71, 4.14, 7.99, 8.73, and 10.78.

[34] On the Hellenistic literary sources for and learned associations to the stories of Scylla, Byblis, and Myrrha, see, for example, B. Otis, *Ovid as an Epic Poet*, 2d ed. (Cambridge, 1966), 62–65, 206, 226, 366–86, 391–92.

[35] Curiously, Shackleton Bailey's list of passages in Propertius' poetry echoed by Martial, in "Echoes of Propertius," cites three echoes of 4.11, more than those in any other Propertian elegy.

[36] For this interpretation of Propertius' contrasting representations of Cynthia and Cornelia, see my "The Role of Women in Roman Elegy: Counter-Cultural Feminism," *Arethusa*, 6.1 (1973), 103–24, rpt. in *Women in the Ancient World*, eds. Peradotto and Sullivan, 241–62, especially 257–58.

[37] Propertius' statement, that Cynthia *splendidaque a docto fama refulget avo*, "basks in the glory of her illustrious male ancestor" (3.20.8), is also relevant in this regard, since it implies that Cynthia—like Cornelia—has distinguished male forebears of whom she could boast. Cynthia's ancestor is thought to be the earlier epic poet Hostius on the basis of Apuleius' claim at *Apologia* 10 that Cynthia was a pseudonym for Hostia. On Hostius, see Morel, *Fragmenta Poetarum Latinorum* 33, with *testimonia* from a scholiast to Vergil, *Aeneid* 12.121 and Priscian 1.270H; and Macrobius 6.3.6 and 6.5.8. The last of these fragments, containing the phrase *invictus Apollo/ arquitenens Latonius* may also be echoed by Propertius at 4.6.55–57, *dixerat, et pharetrae pondus consumit in arcus:/ proxima post arcum Caesaris hasta fuit./ vincit Roma fide Phoebi.*

[38] J. S. Phillimore, *Index Verborum Propertianus* (Oxford, 1905), 25.

[39] Two earlier uses of *amatrix* by Plautus—at *Asinaria* 511 and *Poenulus* 1304—mark it as a pejorative term. In the first passage, it is applied by a procuress to her insolent courtesan daughter(*satis dicacula es amatrix*, "you are an impudent streetwalker"), who responds, *Mater, is quaestus mihi est:/ lingua*

poscit, corpus quaerit, animus orat, res monet, "Mother, it is my meal-ticket. The tongue demands, the body goes looking, the mind begs, the situation prompts." In the second quotation, *amatrix* is also applied to a courtesan accused of shameless behavior.

[40] Ovid also acknowledges Sappho's literary importance at *Tristia* 2.365, *Ars Amatoria* 3.331, *Remedia Amoris* 761, and *Heroides* 15.

[41] Alicia Ostriker, "The Thieves of Language," *Signs*, 8 (1982), 68–90, rpt. in *The New Feminist Criticism*, ed. E. Showalter (New York, 1985), 314–38, citing C. Herrmann, *Les Voleuses de Langue* (Paris, 1976); Parker, "Other Remarks;" and Richlin, "Sulpicia."

[42] On this point see also Richlin, ibid., who argues, "The savage and angry voice, the petulant spleen, that characterized her fellow satirists, seems also to have characterized her work."

[43] So also Richlin, ibid.

[44] M. Wyke, "Mistress and Metaphor in Augustan Elegy," *Helios*, 16.1 (1989), 43–47, responding to, *inter alias*, Hallett, "The Role of Women in Roman Elegy: Counter-Cultural Feminism."

[45] Although Propertius thereby uses the character of Cynthia to voice his own sentiments; for this phenomenon of "literary ventriloquism," see Richlin, "Sulpicia."

Women in Ancient Science

The role played by women in Greco-Roman science was certainly limited but by no means non-existent. On historical, literary, and divine levels, women contributed to at least three scientific fields: philosophy, alchemy, and medicine. Female philosophers, especially Pythagoreans and Neoplatonists, read, lectured, and wrote on mathematics, number theory, and astronomy. Female names appear also in lists of alchemists, and one, Maria the Jewess, made significant contributions to her field. Literary and inscriptional sources, furthermore, name women who practiced and wrote on medicine. Although much of the evidence is late and most of it scant, a general survey may reveal the extent and importance of female scientific activity in Greco-Roman antiquity. It is, finally, less important to determine quantitative contributions (an impossible task) than to acknowledge that women contributed at all to any field in a society which at first glance appears so male-dominated.

Philosophy

Several learned women in antiquity were active in philosophy. Educated women from privileged families occasionally followed the literary and philosophical careers of male relatives.[1] The schools of Pythagoras, Plato, and Epicurus accepted female students. Aristotle, who thought that the female mind lacked full development of rational ability and claimed that the male was by nature superior (*Politics* 1254b; 1259–60), counted no women among his adherents. Nor did women pursue careers in Stoic philosophy, although Arnold sees no inequality in the Stoic treatment of the two sexes.[2] Manning argues that, in Roman society, women's social position differed from that of men and that this difference underlies Stoic treatises (those of Cicero and Seneca, for example).[3] The Stoic philosopher Epictetus (c. A.D. 100), emphasizing the physical differences between men and women, argues that, because of these differences, male and female roles are distinct and ought not be confused (1.16.11–4). Philosophy is appropriate for men; motherhood and housekeeping are the duties of women, according to Epictetus.

Many female students, teachers, and writers followed the precepts of Pythagoras (c. 525 B.C.). Iamblichus (fourth century A.D.) mentions seventeen women in a list of 235 of Pythagoras' students (*Lives of the Philosophers* 235).[4] Philochorus (d. 260 B.C.) may have written a book on learned Pythagorean ladies.[5] Pythagoras (525 B.C.) thought that women must set the highest value on goodness, not honor the gods with bloodshed and death, and not oppose their husbands (Iamblichus, *Lives of the Philosophers* 54). The so-called Speeches of Pythagoras (fifth/fourth century B.C.) concerning the appropriate behavior for men and women indicate that the philosopher considered both sexes important in fulfilling his precepts. In his (spurious) address to the women of Croton, Pythagoras argues that the male should by nature be more easily able to control his sexual desires, and, on the request of the women, that men should be faithful to their wives (Iamblichus, *Lives of the Philosophers* 54–57). It is an unusual emphasis for this time that marriage be presented as a religious commitment.[6] Callicratidas of Sparta (third/second century B.C.) went so far as to say that marriage is a harmony of opposites, just as much of Pythagorean philosophy was based on the theory of the attraction of opposite forces.[7] Because of the communal aspect of Pythagorean life, it was necessary that both men and women understand philosophy, and it was therefore reasonable for women to practice and teach it.[8]

In most cases, we have nothing more than the names of female Pythagoreans. Writings have been attributed, however, to five women. All the extant treatises are brief (from 5 to 100 lines), and most of them deal with the proper behavior for women. Thesleff dates all these works to between the third and first centuries B.C.[9] Myia wrote on the care of infants.[10] Melissa, outlining the duties of women, advised refraining from luxury. Perictione suggested how a woman can achieve excellence through self-control and moderation. She also discussed the duties of woman to god, parents, husband, and home. Phintys wrote on female chastity and temperance with respect to ritual duties. Theano wrote on the care of infants, how a woman should behave towards an unfaithful husband, and on subjects not related to gender: as well as writing on the immortality of the soul, and on numbers, she is credited with works on mathematics, medicine, and physics. In *Concerning Piety*, Theano argues that Pythagoras stated that things did not come into being from number but rather through number. The *Suda* attributes to Theano several works whose titles alone survive: *Pythagorean Apothegms, Address to Women, Concerning Excellence, On Pythagoras, Philosophical Notes*. Her works seem to have been more ethical and philosophical than scientific, but their fragmentary state makes it difficult, if not impossible, to determine her value as a scholar.

A few women philosophers appear, likewise, in the ranks of the Platonists. In Book 5 of his *Republic*, Plato discusses the role and education of women. Women should have the same education as men of the same class. Both male and female animals, Plato argues, are expected to perform the same duties and must receive the same training. Dogs of both sexes guard the flocks and help in the hunt, for example. It is reasonable, Plato surmises, to expect women to help protect the city. The only difference between the sexes is the female's ability to bear children, and thus the same code of virtue should apply to both men and women. Although the average man may be superior to the average female, the superior woman is preferable to the inferior man.[11]

Plato did accept female students, among whom were Lastheneia of Mantinea and Axiotha of Phlius, who wore men's clothing (Diogenes Laertius 3.46). Both women then studied under the biologist Speusippus, Plato's successor as head of the Academy (Diogenes Laertius 4.2). Nothing extant indicates the nature of the studies of Plato's female students. Were they mathematicians and astronomers? Plato encouraged the study of abstract mathematics (geometry) and astronomy as useful in guiding the soul to invisible realities: the immortal and eternally existing Form or Idea (*Timaeus* 27d–28c).[12] Did these women study biology like Aristotle and Plato's nephew Speusippus? Or did they simply continue their studies at the Academy because of continuity and convenience?

In addition to Plato's two female students, the names of other female philosophers are preserved by Diogenes Laertius, who dedicated his collection of biographies of eminent philosophers to an unnamed female Neoplatonist (3.47).[13] Arete of Cyrene (c. 400 B.C.) studied under her father Aristippus, who was an itinerant lecturer (Diogenes Laertius 2.86). Hipparchia (c. 300 B.C.), whose brother was Theophrastus' student Metrocles of Maroneia (Diogenes Laertius 6.94), warrants her own brief biography (Diogenes Laertius 6.96–98). She was charmed by the teachings of Crates the Cynic, whom she married. No writings are known. Diogenes Laertius (8.88) anecdotally mentions also Actis, Philtis, and Delphis, the daughters of the astronomer and geometer Eudoxus (c. 407–357 B.C.). There is no mention of how these young women were educated or of Eudoxus' attitude concerning their mental abilities. Epicurus (341–271 B.C.) kept the company of women including the *hetairai* Mammarion, Hedia, Erotion, and Nikidion (Diogenes Laertius 10.7). Because of the better education of these prostitutes, it is reasonable to assume that they could contribute to philosophical and scientific discussions.[14]

Perhaps the most famous female philosopher and scientist of antiquity is the Neoplatonist Hypatia (c. A.D. 370–415) whose fame, unfortunately, rests primarily on her dramatic death.[15] The ancient sources for her life include the *Suda* (4.644), Damascius' *Life of Isidore*, Socrates' *Ecclesiastical History* (8.9), and the letters of her student Synesius of Cyrene.[16] She was the daughter of Theon of Alexandria, a mathematician associated with the Alexandrian museum. Hypatia studied mathematics, astronomy, and Neoplatonism. According to the *Suda*, her publications included commentaries on the first six books of the *Arithmetica* of Diophantus of Alexandria (A.D. 250), an astronomical canon that may have been a commentary on Ptolemy's astronomical works (fl. A.D. 150), and a commentary on the *Conic Sections* (geometry) of Apollonius of Perga (fl. 210 B.C.).[17] She also helped her father revise a commentary on Ptolemy's *Almagest*[18] and may have assisted Theon in revising his commentary on Euclid's *Elements* of geometry. Only the title of the third book of Theon's commentary on the *Almagest* indicates Hypatia's involvement, and, indeed, Rome notes a slight difference in style between this and the preceding books.[19] Rome reserves judgment on the extent of Hypatia's involvement but suggests that she may have revised only the third book, which is not included in many manuscripts of the commentary.[20] Alic, from her reading of the letters of Synesius (especially letter 159), suggests that Hypatia developed instruments for distilling water, measuring water level, and determining specific gravity of a liquid (hydrometer).[21] In addition, Alic credits Hypatia with the construction of a plane astrolabe that measures the position of the sun, stars, and planets and is used to calculate time and the ascendant sign of the zodiac (fig. 1).

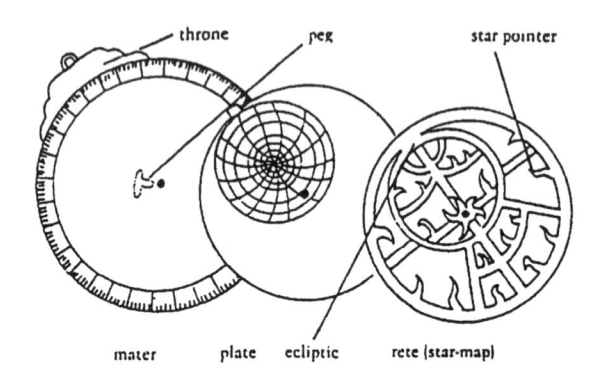

Fig. 1: Plane Astrolabe, from Alic, *Hypatia's Heritage*, 46.

Although Hypatia may very well have worked on and developed such instruments, the evidence in Synesius is not convincing. During an illness, he asks his friend and teacher to have a hydroscope made for him. Synesius describes the instrument in great detail (letter 15). It is a cylindrical device about the size of a flute. Notches in a perpendicular line allow the weight of a liquid to be tested. A cone at one end provides a lid. Its base is called a baryllium. In water it remains erect so the notches remaining above the water level can be counted easily to determine the specific density of a liquid. Such a description implies that Hypatia was not familiar with the device, else she would not have needed so detailed an account. Unlike other female philosophers, Hypatia seemed more concerned with matters of hard science than of proper feminine behavior. All of her works are lost.

Hypatia was an influential lecturer; she was charming, beautiful, and had a reputation for vast learnedness. She was chaste and virginal, according to the *Suda* and Socrates. She had no desire for marriage and tried to keep suitors away. She may have held an official post through which she delivered her well-attended lectures on Plato and Aristotle.[22]

Among her most famous students are the Christian Synesius and Proclus of Byzantium, who headed the Platonic Academy in Athens in the late fifth century A.D.[23]

Hypatia's death at the hands of a Christian mob has been much discussed and debated. The *Suda* implies that our scholar owed her death to her knowledge of mathematics and astronomy. Socrates suggests, without supporting evidence, that Hypatia followed the Neoplatonic teachings of Plotinus, a school hostile to Christianity. The *Suda* tells us that Cyril, the archbishop of Alexandria, was jealous of Hypatia's large number of students but gives no evidence of his involvement in her death. Socrates puts the murder into its proper and complicated context, explaining that strife between Jews and Christians led to rioting and a political dispute. The prefect Orestes and Cyril took opposite sides, and rumors arose that Hypatia was using her influence to prevent a reconciliation. Synesius, however, implies that she never exploited her political power, even though he asks her as a special favor to use her influence to help restore Nicaeus and Philolaus to their property (letter 81).

Gibbon saw the situation in black and white: Cyril was the villain; Hypatia the heroine.[24] Rist argues that Hypatia probably never spoke with hostility in public about Christianity and that danger to her life arose not so much from her learning or "anti-Christian" teachings (one of her closest friends was Christian) but from the fact that philosophy was the pursuit of aristocrats unsympathetic and potentially hostile to Christianity.[25] These aristocrats comprised the bulk of her friends and students, and, according to Rist, it was because of her association with such people that her life was taken.[26]

Hypatia was a popular scholar who lectured on philosophy and commented on mathematical and astronomical treatises. But what was her worth as a scientific mind? Crawford's judgment, that she was not an original thinker, seems speculative.[27] Gibbon seems to have blind admiration for her. One is forced to agree with Fitzgerald in that it is impossible to assess Hypatia's philosophy, much less her value as a scientist, when all examples of her work have been lost.[28] Yet the notices of the crowds she attracted with her lectures, her scholarly reputation, and the admiration of Synesius, who was himself a fine scientist, suggest her brilliance.[29] Synesius refers to her as "the lady who legitimately presides over the mysteries of philosophy" (letter 137).

Alchemy

In the area of mathematics and astronomy, and philosophy in general, female contributions are clouded by lack of solid evidence in all cases, by legend, as with Theano, and by speculation, as with Hypatia. The female contributions to alchemy may prove more satisfactory. Considered a science in antiquity, alchemy provided the basis of chemistry and yielded advances in metallurgy as well as chemistry. Taylor suggests that alchemy may have arisen from the traditional knowledge of the Egyptian priesthood.[30] Because of the deeply religious tone of alchemical texts (many are accompanied by mythological tales), Taylor argues that the authors of these texts attempted to restore or rediscover secrets of the past. Alic argues that women were instrumental in the development of alchemy and that the science arose from the manufacture of cosmetics and perfumes (by women) and from the Egyptian artistic tradition (involving the mixing of dyes and the production of jewelry).[31] Greco-Roman sources cite Hermes as the mythical founder of the science; Egyptian sources cite Isis. The alchemist tried to produce gold, silver, or purple from ordinary materials, being more interested in the resultant color than in chemical makeup. Alchemy, nonetheless, yielded advances in the technology of sublimation, distillation, and fusion, and improvements in the instruments necessary for chemistry and metallurgy.

Taylor includes three female names in his lists of the Greek alchemists. Isis (first century A.D.) studied in the school of pseudo-Democritus, which is characterized by an interest in the superficial colorings of metals and by the use of fusion in preparing alloys.[32] Democritus was the pen name for Bolus (c. 200 B.C.), the author of *Physical and Mystical Matters*, containing recipes for the production of purple dye and the imitation of gold.[33] Isis' text, entitled *Isis the Prophetess to her son (Horus)*, exists in two forms, in which the mythology varies slightly but the alchemy is identical.[34]

Cleopatra (first century A.D.) used distillation and sublimation as was typical in the school of Maria and Comarius.[35] Three of her works survive in part. Her *Chrysopoea* exists as a single page of drawings and symbols (fig. 2).[36]

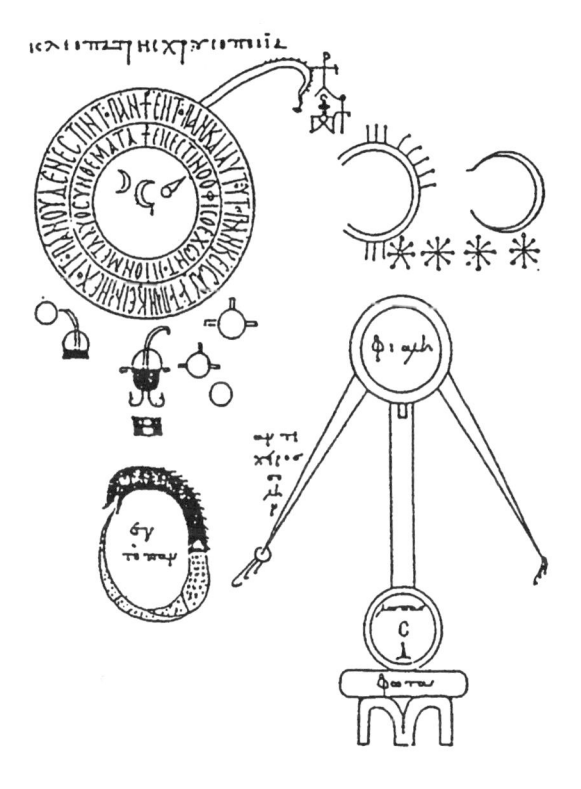

Fig. 2: Cleopatra's *Chrysopoea*, from Berthelot, *Collection des Anciens Alchimistes Grecs*, vol. 1, 132.

The symbols for mercury, silver, and gold are found in the center of a double circle from left to right (upper left).[37] The inner circle contains the aphorisms "In all and everything through itself and everything to itself and if it does not have all, nothing has all"; the outer ring is inscribed with "One is the serpent having poison after two compositions." Coming up from the outer ring is a figure that Berthelot interprets as symbolic of a mystic serpent.[38] Also depicted at the lower left of the illustration is a tail-eating serpent (Ouroboros) with the inscription "One is the all." The first aphorism must imply the alchemical philosophy, that all matter is basically the same, which enables the alchemist to do the job of converting one material into another. The second aphorism is a mystery.[39] To the right of the concentric rings is a series of odd symbols. The incomplete double circle may symbolize the transmutation of lead and silver (into gold?).[40] Just below these circles lie the symbols for alchemical operations. Below the concentric rings, one finds various instruments: a still with a "balloon" to receive vapor; a *kerotakis* (reflux vapor phase reaction chamber); and tripods placed on heat sources (left to right). Cleopatra also included a sketch of a still with two condensing arms (lower right). She is credited, in addition, with a treatise on weights and measures and a spurious *Dialogue between Cleopatra and the Philosophers*.[41]

Finally, Maria the Jewess, "the founding mother of alchemy," is one of the most important alchemical writers, although her work survives only in quotations in the writings of Zosimus of Panopolis (third/fourth century A.D.).[42] Her alchemical doctrine was, for the most part, traditional. The Hermetic art rests on the premise that all substances are basically the same and that anything can be produced with the still, as Cleopatra's aphorisms indicate.[43] Maria also drew analogies between human beings and metals. Copper must receive nourishment before it can be converted into gold, just as people need food to exist.[44] Metals consist of four elements and result from the association of liquid, solid, and spirit, as do people.[45] Maria also saw in metals two sexes: "Join the male and the female and you will find that which is sought."[46] Metals, like people, die destroyed by fire. Copper only assists in making gold, and its body, through chemical treatment, becomes useless in death, so Maria thinks.[47]

Maria's work also included the description, improvement, or invention of several alchemical devices. She lives today in her *balneum Mariae* (*bain marie*, *Marienbad*, or double boiler). An outer vessel containing water permits slow heating of a substance within an inner vessel. Lippmann argues that the double boiler was known to Hippocrates and Theophrastus (*De odoribus* 22) and that the credit for its invention goes to Maria by chance.[48]

Maria provides the earliest description of the *kerotakis* (fig. 3).[49] The device has three parts: a container where material to be distilled is heated; a section to condense the vapor; and a receiver. It was used for softening metals and mixing them with pigments.[50]

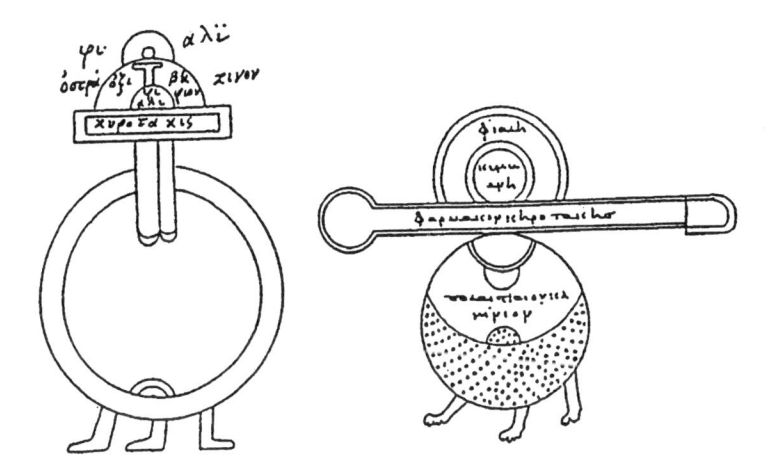

Fig. 3: *Kerotakis*, from Taylor, "A Survey of Greek Alchemy," 134 (Ms. Marc. 299)

Presented in the sources as Maria's own invention is the tribikos, a more complex still made of three copper tubes, an earthenware pan for sulfur, and glass flasks (fig. 4). Maria seems to be one of the earliest scientists to work with blown glass. She preferred working with glass because it permitted her to observe reactions and it was safer for moving dangerous materials.[51]

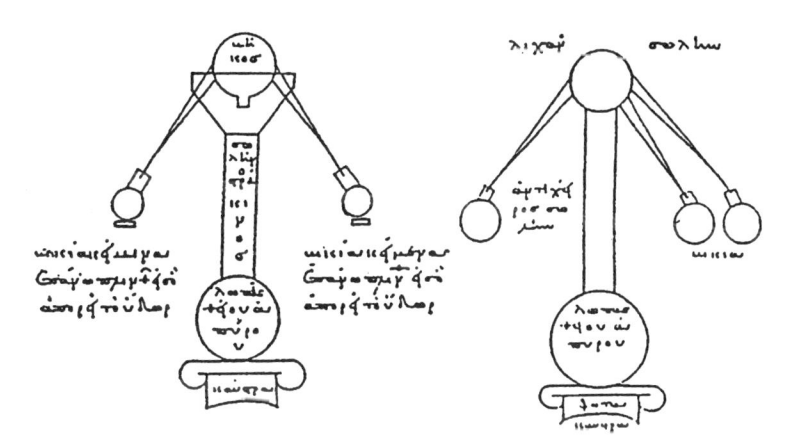

Fig. 4: Distillation Apparatus, from Taylor, "A Survey of Greek Alchemy," 136 (Ms. Marc. 299)

To make gold, Maria would take the tetrasomia (a mixture of copper, iron, lead, and tin) and heat and burn it with sulfur, mercury, arsenious acid or with "divine water" (derived from the smoke of sulfur or arsenic-containing materials). Because of the sulfuric content of the "divine water," silver would blacken while mercury and lead would lighten to yellow or white.[52] The modern reader should remember that the alchemist in antiquity was more concerned with a color than a chemical change. Maria also used the application of organic substances (plant oils, resins, juice of jellyfish) to make precious stones glow in the dark.[53]

The obscurity of the primary sources makes it difficult to distinguish Maria's inventions from her improvements of existing devices. Her legendary reputation further clouds the facts (as with Hypatia). She has been associated with Moses' sister Miriam and has been accredited with visions of Christ.[54] Some have made her a student of Xerxes' brother-in-law Ostanes (d. 465 B.C.), who was supposed to have taught botany, alchemy, mineralogy, and medicine at Memphis in Egypt. Called Maria the Copt, our alchemist was supposed to have carried the baby Jesus on her shoulder.[55] Many influential figures of antiquity (Pythagoras, especially) enjoyed similarly productive *Nachleben*. Maria's reputation and lasting legacy, nonetheless, reveal that she was a productive and influential alchemist.

Historical Evidence for Medicine

Historical female figures practiced obstetrics and midwifery. The mythographer Hyginus (second century A.D.) relates the story of Hagnodice (Agnodice) in *Fabula* 247. According to his story, before there were midwives in Athens, women died in childbirth from shame. Therefore, Hagnodice disguised herself as a man and completed a medical apprenticeship under a certain Herophilus. Since she became so popular with her female patients, who knew that she was a woman, Hagnodice was accused of seducing and corrupting them. In court she revealed the truth of her gender. The Athenians thereby amended a law permitting free-born women to learn the science of medicine.[56] Von Staden views the tale with scepticism, as belonging to the genre of the *fabula*, to be included with mythical inventors and discoveries.[57] Plato

(c. 350 B.C.), living several generations before Herophilus (c. 270 B.C.), knows of female midwives (*Theaetetus* 149a1–2). Yet Herophilus' *Midwifery* is our earliest known treatment of the subject. Midwives traditionally handled uncomplicated deliveries, while trained physicians took care of more difficult births. Artistic evidence indicates the tradition of female midwives. A stone relief from Sparta, for example, shows two women assisting in the delivery of a baby.[58] As von Staden suggests, Hagnodice's achievement may have been in "challenging the exclusion of women from the ranks of physicians."[59]

Plato declares that the midwife should be beyond childbearing years (*Theaetetus* 149). Since Artemis, the goddess of childbirth, is childless, the midwife, who can no longer bear children, honors the goddess by being like her. Midwives, Plato continues, use drugs and chants to arouse labor, make difficult labors easier, and even induce miscarriages. Plato's view reflects the attitude of mysticism and the association of magic (chants) to medicine that many Greco-Roman men felt towards female physiology and the natural process of childbirth.

The role of midwives is discussed by Soranus of Ephesus (A.D. 98–138), perhaps the most important gynecologist of antiquity, whose *Gynaeciorum Commentarii* (four books) survive in fragments.[60] He gives a scientific account of the qualifications and duties of a midwife (1.4–5). The midwife must be literate and must study methodically. In support of the fact that female practitioners of medicine must study, Krug cites a tomb relief (second/first century B.C.) depicting a physician with a scroll in her hand.[61] Soranus advises the midwife that she must also have good understanding and memory. She must enjoy her work. She must be honorable, strong and steady, and have sound sense. Practical experience is necessary, and the midwife should not be superstitious or easily alarmed. Her hands should be gentle, her nature kind and sympathetic. She should not talk too much or be susceptible to bribes from those wishing to obtain illegal abortions.[62] The Hippocratic oath (fourth century B.C.), dedicated to Apollo, Asclepius, Hygieia, and all the powers of healing, forbids its adherents from practicing surgery, helping a patient commit suicide, or helping a woman procure an abortion, even though suicide and abortion were not illegal in antiquity.[63]

The duties of the midwife include assisting in the delivery, declaring the sex of the baby, and convincing the mother that the child is worth raising. Soranus includes instructions for cutting the navel cord with nails, shells, and steel surgical instruments. He also gives advice for bringing out a retained afterbirth. Soranus includes qualifications for wet-nurses and instructions for the care of the newborn.

Epigraphical and artistic sources indicate that women also practiced obstetrics, which requires greater formal education than midwifery. A funeral stele at Acharnae in Attica shows a seated woman, identified as Phanostrate, reaching to a veiled standing woman. Phanostrate, the wife of a Milesian citizen, was a midwife (*maia*) and a physician (*iatros*) according to a late fourth century B.C. inscription.[64] Antiochis (first century A.D.) followed her father Diodotos into the medical profession. The community of Tlos in Lycia set up a statue to Antiochis in honor of her medical knowledge and experience.[65] Galen names her as the inventress of medicines for pains in the spleen, for sciatica, and for rheumatism.[66] A funerary epigraph names Pantheia of Pergamon (second century A.D.) as a physician and praises her skill. Pantheia's husband, Glykon, was the son of the physician Philadelphus.[67] A terracotta relief at Ostia (second century A.D.) shows a Scribonia assisting in the delivery of a baby.[68] In Cilicia Tracheia (near Anemourion) an inscription was dedicated to Obrimos (second/third century A.D.) and his wife Ammina, both physicians.[69] Krug notes that women occasionally follow male relatives into medical careers (as do female poets and philosophers).[70] An epitaph in honor of the physician Domnina shows that she was highly esteemed. She lived in the second/third century A.D. at Neoclaudiopolis (Phazimonitis in Asia Minor).[71] Cleopatra, who lived in Rome in the second century A.D., wrote on cosmetics and skin diseases. Her contemporary Aspasia also wrote on gynecology and obstetrics. In many cases, inscriptional evidence does not reveal the nature of the medical practice of these women (Antiochis, Ammina, Domnina), although we may assume that they practiced obstetrics and gynecology.

Pliny (*Natural History* 28.81–84) names a few female medical writers. Lais and Elephantis, who lectured in Rome, disagree on the effects of burning cabbage root, myrtle, or tamarisk if extinguished by menstrual fluid. The process causes either fertility or barrenness. Salpe of Lemnos suggested that the bites of wild dogs, tertians, and quartans can be cured by the flux on the wool of a black ram if contained in a silver bracelet. The midwife Sotira adds that rubbing the patient's feet with the flux is most effective if the patient does it herself and without her own knowledge. Pliny's wording makes little sense. This method can also revive an epileptic who has fainted. Pliny (and his readers both ancient and modern) find these and other remedies incredible. Olympias of Thebes (fl. c. A.D. 25) wrote on remedies to prevent miscarriage and to induce abortion (*Natural History* 20.226). In most cases, only the names of these women, as Pliny presents them, survive. Elephantis, however, was a poet admired by Tiberius (Suetonius, *Tiberius* 43).[72] Martial mentions her (12.43.4), and Galen knows her as a medical writer (*On the Compounding of Drugs* 12.416k). Metrodora (second century A.D.), finally, composed a treatise entitled *Concerning the Female Suffering of the Mother*, in which she discusses diseases affecting the uterus, stomach, and kidneys.[73]

Conclusion

This survey on female scientific activity in antiquity reveals that several women contributed significantly to some areas of science and technology. Many women entered scholarly fields on the heels of successful male relatives. In philosophy (mathematics and astronomy) the modern student is burdened by the fact that so much of the written evidence did not survive. Even a few fragments would help in assessing Hypatia's contribution. It is unfortunate also that many of these women are simply names in a manuscript or inscription. It is clear that the activity of women is greatest in medicine. Cults were established in honor of goddesses whose concerns were restricted to matters of female health (Artemis and Eileithyia) and to goddesses concerned with the health of the general population and with purity (Athena and Hygieia). That Athena, a desexed divinity of technology and civilization, holds this duty is not surprising. In contrast, female physicians, like female philosophers, restricted themselves to the health concerns of women (reproductive physiology and childbirth). Even Hagnodice's patients were only women. Women whose interests were broader (Hypatia and Maria the Jewess) lived in Egypt. Perhaps because they lived outside the bounds of traditional and average Greco-Roman society, these women did not restrict themselves to female concerns. The attitude of the typical or average Greek woman concerning appropriate areas of activity may have been expressed by Euripides. When Phaedra has been struck by Aphrodite and is suffering from love-sickness, the concerned nurse says to her mistress:

> If you are sick and it is some secret sickness
> here are women standing at your side to help.
> But if your troubles may be told to men,
> speak, that a doctor may pronounce upon it.
> (*Hippolytus* 293–96)[74]

Georgia L. Irby-Massie
University of Colorado

Notes

With thanks to Professors Harold Evjen, Tad Maslowski, and Eckart Schütrumpf, and to Barbara Hill and Paul Keyser for reading drafts of this paper and offering helpful and insightful suggestions. This paper is humbly dedicated to Professor Joy King, an inspiration to scholars of both sexes and of all times.

[1] Sarah B. Pomeroy, *Women in Hellenistic Egypt: From Alexander to Cleopatra* (New York, 1984), 65.

[2] Edward Vernon Arnold, *Roman Stoicism* (New York, 1911), 270.

[3] C. E. Manning, "Seneca and the Stoics on the Equality of the Sexes," *Mnemosyne*, 26 (1973), 175.

[4] Iamblichus, a Neoplatonist born in Syria, is a late source and perhaps not so reliable. Walter Burkert, *Lore and Science in Ancient Pythagoreanism* (Cambridge, 1972), 193–96, finds Iamblichus messy in his use of sources. Using a single source in two places, Iamblichus introduces contradictions, for example.

[5] *FGrH* 3.B328, frag. 91, nos. 25–26.

[6] Gillian Clark, trans., *Iamblichus: On the Pythagorean Life* (Liverpool, 1989), xviii.

[7] Hogar Thesleff, "The Pythagorean Texts of the Hellenistic Period," *Acta Academia Aboensis, Humaniora*, 30.1 (1965), 102–7. Callicratidas is preserved only in Stobaios (4.28.16–18). It is interesting to note that Empedocles' brother was named Callicratidas (Diogenes Laertius 8.53). Empedocles (fl. c. 445 B.C.) proposed the four element theory (everything exists as a combination

of earth, air, fire, and water) and argued that change is possible because of the opposing forces, Love and Strife, which guide the universe.

[8] Pomeroy, *Women in Hellenistic Egypt*, 65.

[9] Hogar Thesleff, *An Introduction to the Pythagorean Writings of the Hellenistic Period*, Acta Academia Aboensis, Humaniora 24.3 (1961), 99 and 113. Thesleff dates the works of Theano and Myia to the third century B.C. in southern Italy. Melissa and Perictione worked in Alexandria in the first century B.C.

[10] Pythagoras' daughter was a Myia, his wife's name was Theano. These writers, of course, could not have been the daughter and wife of the philosopher since they lived several centuries later. Pomeroy, *Women in Hellenistic Egypt*, 64, argues that the names are authentic. Even today, parents name their children in accordance with religious convictions.

Thesleff, "The Pythagorean Texts," provides Greek texts with brief commentary. A useful introduction to and French translation of the works of the Pythagorean women is Mario Meunier, *Femmes Pythagoriciennes: Fragments et Lettres de Théano, Périctioné, Phintys, Mélissa, et Myia* (Paris, 1932).

[11] Dorothea Wender, "Plato: Misogynist, Paedophile, and Feminist," in *Women in the Ancient World: The Arethusa papers*, eds. John Peradotto and J. P. Sullivan (Albany, 1984), 213. Wender notes contradictions in Plato's attitude towards women.

[12] G. E. R. Lloyd, *Early Greek Science: Thales to Aristotle* (New York, 1970), 67–69. Although Plato has been accused of hostility towards specific scientific disciplines, he clearly encouraged abstract thought, necessary for mathematics.

[13] See P. Von der Muhll, "Was Diogenes Laertios der Dame, der er Sein Buch Widmen Will, Ankundigt," *Philologus*, 109 (1965), 313–15. Diogenes Laertios mentions no names in this passage, and the identity of this woman is debated.

[14] Sarah B. Pomeroy, "Technikai kai Mousikai," *American Journal of Ancient History*, 2 (1977) 58.

[15] Praechter, "Hypatia," *RE*, 9 (1916), 242–49.

[16] Socrates was an historian of the Byzantine church. Born in Constantinople c. A.D. 380, his history continued after Eusebius, covering the years A.D. 305–439. J. M. Rist, "Hypatia," *Phoenix*, 19 (1965), 215.

[17] T. L. Heath, *A History of Greek Mathematics* (Oxford, 1921), vol. 2, 448, 519. The dates of Diophantus (the father of algebra) are disputed. The last seven books of his *Arithmetica* have been lost. Heath suggests that the first six books survive partly because of Hypatia's commentary. She never worked on the latter half. For her commentary on Ptolemy, see P. Tannery, "L'article de Suidas sur Hypatie," *Ann. de la Fac. des Lettres de Bordeaux*, 2 (1880), 199. Apollonius of Perga devised the system of epicycles to explain the irregular orbits of the planets.

[18] The Arabs renamed Ptolemy's work the *Almagest* (*The Great Book*). Ptolemy himself called it A *Mathematical Treatise in Thirteen Books*. Its contents consist of a systematic treatment of astronomy and mathematics.

[19] A. Rome, *Commentaires de Pappus et de Théon d'Alexandrie sur l'Almagest* (Vatican, 1936), vol. 2, lxxxiii. In this work, Theon calls his daughter a philosopher, not a mathematician.

[20] Ibid., vol. 2, 317.

[21] Margaret Alic, *Hypatia's Heritage: A History of Women in Science from Antiquity through the Nineteenth Century* (Boston, 1986), 44. For the numbering of Synesius' letters, I follow R. Hercher, ed. *Epistolographi Graeci* (Paris, 1873).

[22] C. Lacombrade, *Synesios de Cyrene* (Paris, 1951), 44–45.

[23] Rist, "Hypatia," 222.

[24] See the description of Edward Gibbon, *The Decline and Fall of the Roman Empire* (New York, 1914) "In the bloom of beauty and in the maturity of wisdom, the modest maid refused her lovers and instructed her disciples; the persons most illustrious for their rank or merit were impatient to visit the female philosopher; and Cyril beheld, with a jealous eye, the gorgeous train of horses and slaves who crowded the door of her academy" (vol. 5, 117).

[25] Rist, "Hypatia," 222.

[26] Ibid., 224.

[27] W. S. Crawford, *Synesius the Hellene* (London, 1901), 138, 395.

[28] Augustine Fitzgerald, *The Letters of Synesius of Cyrene* (Oxford, 1926), 15.

[29] Consider Synesius' description of the hydroscope (letter 15) and his discussion of astronomy and the astrolabe (letter 159).

[30] F. S. Taylor, "A Survey of Greek Alchemy," *Journal of Hellenic Studies*, 50 (1930), 110.

[31] Alic, *Hypatia's Heritage*, 36.

[32] Taylor, "A Survey of Greek Alchemy," 114.

[33] M. Wellmann, "Bolos (3)," *RE*, 3 (1897), 676–77; M. P. E. Berthelot, *Collection des Anciens Alchimistes Grecs*, vol. 2, 41–56.

[34] Berthelot, ibid., vol. 2, 28–33.

[35] Taylor, "A Survey of Greek Alchemy," 114.

[36] Berthelot, *Collection des Anciens Alchimistes Grecs*, vol. 1, 132.

[37] Ibid., vol. 1, 133.

[38] Ibid., vol. 1, 133.

[39] Paul T. Keyser, "Alchemy in the Ancient World: From Science to Magic," *Illinois Classical Studies*, 15.2 (1990), asks, "But what does it all mean?" (361–62). Others do not even address the problem.

[40] Berthelot, *Collection des Anciens Alchimistes Grecs*, vol. 1, 133.

[41] Taylor, "A Survey of Greek Alchemy," 116; Friedrich Otto Hultsch,

Metrologicorum Scriptorum Reliquiae (Leipzig, 1864), vol. 1, 253; Berthelot, *Collection des Anciens Alchimistes Grecs*, vol. 2, 290.

⁴² Raphael Patai, "Maria the Jewess: Founding Mother of Alchemy," *Ambix*, 29 (1982), 177–97. Her dates are disputed. Patai, 192, would date her to the second or third century A.D. Keyser, "Alchemy in the Ancient World," 362, prefers an earlier date (first century A.D.) because her earlier stills were made from copper, later ones from glass. It is scholarly convention that glassblowing was practiced early in the Christian era after the discovery of the blowpipe (perhaps in Syria). See G. Mariacher, *Italian Blown Glass: From Ancient Rome to Venice* (London, 1961), 8.

⁴³ Berthelot, *Collection des Anciens Alchimistes Grecs*, vol. 3, 168.

⁴⁴ Ibid., vol. 3, 169–70.

⁴⁵ Ibid., vol. 3, 170.

⁴⁶ Ibid., vol. 3, 196.

⁴⁷ Ibid., vol. 3, 153.

⁴⁸ Edmund O. von Lippmann, "Zur Geschichte des Wasserbades," *Abhandlungen und Vorträge zur Geschichte der Naturwissenschaften*, (Leipzig, 1906–13), vol. 2, 185, and *Enstehung und Ausbreitung der Alchemie* (Berlin, 1919), vol. 1, 50. Keyser, 362, suggests that Maria may have improved the *kerotakis*.

⁴⁹ Patai, "Maria the Jewess," 179.

⁵⁰ Berthelot, *Collection des Anciens Alchimistes Grecs*, vol. 2, 225–26; vol. 1, 139.

⁵¹ Patai, "Maria the Jewess," 178.

⁵² Ibid., 181.

⁵³ Ibid., 181.

⁵⁴ Epiphanius (A.D. 315–402), a bishop of Salamis, describes Maria's vision. She worked with sulfur and is also associated with a "white flower of the mountain" (perhaps morning glory, as suggested by a student at the University of Colorado, Ronnie Seward). Sulfur fumes and hallucinogenic drugs may have induced her visions.

⁵⁵ Patai, "Maria the Jewess," 188–89.

⁵⁶ Heinrich von Staden, *Herophilus: The Art of Medicine in Early Alexandria* (Cambridge, 1989), 38–40.

⁵⁷ Ibid., 40–41.

⁵⁸ Pieter Herfst, *Le Travail de la Femme dans la Grèce Ancienne* (Utrecht, 1922), 53. Herfst provides no clue on the date.

⁵⁹ Cf. von Staden, *Herophilus*, 41.

⁶⁰ Marbach, "Soranus," *RE* 2d ser., 3 (1929), 1113–33. Muscio or Moschion in the sixth century A.D. composed a *Midwife's Catechism* (questions and answers in two books) derived largely from Soranus' *Gynaeciorum*

Commentarii (discovered in the sixteenth century). Moschion received credit for the writing of this Greek text. In 1837, F. R. Dietz noticed that Oribasios' (A.D. 325–405) description of the female genitalia followed the wording of the Commentarii. Oribasios had named Soranus as his source, and thus it was determined that Soranus, not Moschion, wrote these influential works on gynecology. It is thanks to Moschion that the shorter work survives at all in translation.

[61] Antije Krug, Heilkunst und Heilkult: Medizin in der Antike (Munich, 1985), 196.

[62] Aristotle went so far as to condone abortion. He thought that the state, a living organism, had a natural limit, an optimal size. Aristotle argued that abortion was preferable to the exposure of unwanted infants, both practiced in antiquity (Politics 1326a35–1335b19). Soranus discusses even late-term abortions, which must have been practiced at least occasionally.

[63] In some cases, abortion could be prosecuted since a father's right to progeny had been violated because of the mother's actions (Lysias frag. 10; Cicero, Pro Cluentio 11.32). Ludwig Edelstein, Ancient Medicine (Baltimore, 1967), 16, emphasizes that not the rights of the unborn child but those of the father are protected.

[64] N. Firatli and L. Robert, Les Stèles Funéraires de Byzance Gréco-Romaine (Paris, 1964), 176; H. W. Pleket, Epigraphica: Texts on the Social History of the Greek World (Leiden, 1964), vol. 2, 1.

[65] J. Benedum, "Antiochis" (8), RE suppl. 14 (1974), 48–49; Firatli-Robert, 175, 178; Pleket, vol. 2, 12.

[66] Krug, Heilkunst und Heilkult, 197.

[67] Pleket, Epigraphica, vol. 2, 20.

[68] Krug, Heilkunst und Heilkult, 196.

[69] Pleket, Epigraphica, vol. 2, 27.

[70] Krug, Heilkunst und Heilkult, 197.

[71] Firatli-Robert, Les Stèles Funéraires, 175; Pleket, Epigraphica, vol. 2, 26.

[72] Crusius, "Elephantis" (3), RE, 5 (1905), 2324–25.

[73] Deichgraber, "Metrodora," RE, 15 (1932), 1474. The text survives in the manuscript Laur. 75.3f.4–33.

[74] Hippolytus, trans. David Grene (Chicago, 1942).

Images of Iphigenia

Conflicting versions of the myth have left us with two Iphigenias: the girl sacrificed to Artemis at Aulis, with her father's consent, whose death became the reason—or excuse—for Clytemnestra's murder of Agamemnon; and the woman who, miraculously rescued and transported to the land of the Taurians by the Black Sea, served as priestess in the rite of human sacrifice to the same goddess.[1] The more dominant image has been that of Iphigenia as the innocent victim of mistaken religious belief. Lucretius saw in her the symbol of all the crimes that have been committed in the name of religion, making of her, as it were, the patron saint of his own Epicurean gospel.

At first thought, the myth of Iphigenia at Aulis might appear to be gender neutral inasmuch as it closely parallels other stories in which the sex of the victim appears to be inessential. In the Old Testament we have Abraham's intended sacrifice of Isaac and Jephthah's sacrifice of his daughter (Genesis 25; Judges 11). Less well known are two characters from Euripides' plays, both of whom died at an oracle's command: Menoeceus, Creon's son (in *The Phoenician Women*), and Macaria, Heracles' daughter (in *The Children of Heracles*).[2] All of these tales obviously reflect an earlier phase of religious belief in the history of peoples who first practiced and then abandoned human sacrifice. Indeed, the account of the ram that suddenly appeared as the surrogate for Isaac and the mysterious substitution of a slain deer in place of Iphigenia dramatically point to the moment in religious history when the deity was believed to have ratified the acceptability of animal rather than human sacrifice. According to Cyrus Gordon, the tales derive as well from the established custom, in the ancient Near East and Mediterranean world, of requiring that a military leader sacrifice one of his children so as to insure success in battle.[3] With one possible exception, each of our examples implies some such historical precedent. Jephthah had vowed that if he and his men defeated the

Ammonites, he would sacrifice whatsoever first met him on his return home. Agamemnon killed Iphigenia in order that the fleet might sail to Troy. Menoeceus died so that Creon might win the war for Thebes. The case of Macaria is just a bit less obvious. She was sacrificed so that the Athenians, as the protectors of Heracles' refugee family, might prevail over its Argive pursuers. But Macaria's grandfather, Iolaus, had asked for Athenian protection; after her death, his youthful vigor was renewed as he became one of the leaders in the battle won by the Athenians. The one true exception is Abraham's interrupted sacrifice of Isaac. No battle is involved. Still, we recall that Abraham was about to lead the members of his household out of their own land to take over territory inhabited by people hostile to them.

Looked at in this light, all of these stories glorify male, patriarchal values. Except for Isaac, the children are killed directly for the sake of military victory. Their lives are the price for it. Among the fathers, Creon alone refuses to consent to the death of his child or grandchild, and he continues to fight in the hope he will conquer anyway. The mothers are not consulted. Of them, only Clytemnestra's reactions have been recorded, and that was because she wickedly dared to reject the masculine priorities and became a murderess. What of the victims? Isaac's feelings are not described, though one likes to imagine what he told Sarah when he got home. Jephthah's daughter, never mentioned by name, requested and obtained from her father a reprieve of two months during which she and her companions might roam the mountains and mourn her wasted virginity; she apparently did not seek to escape her death.[4] Menoeceus patriotically killed himself against Creon's wishes and in his absence. Macaria volunteered to be the "young woman of noble birth" whom the oracle demanded. It appears that all of them accepted and internalized the ruling male values without question. The case of Iphigenia is more complex. Today's readers of Aeschylus' *Agamemnon* may view her less as Lucretius looked on her and more as she was seen by Clytemnestra and the Erinyes: as the female victim of male aggression.

Euripides, at separate dates, chose Iphigenia as the heroine for two of his tragedies, one set at Aulis, the other by Artemis' temple in the land of the Taurians on the coast of the Black Sea. Since both plays assume that Iphigenia was snatched from the altar by Artemis, there is no glaring discrepancy in plot. But for all practical purposes we may treat them as deriving respectively from two separate traditions. Both works inspired numerous later creations and interpretations, including those of at least one philosopher and one film artist. I want to examine a few of these images of Iphigenia, looking at them solely from the vantage point of contemporary feminism. I will begin with the girl brought on her father's orders to Aulis.[5]

Iphigenia speaks for herself in Euripides' *Iphigenia in Aulis*, but some critics have argued that the playwright has put words in her mouth that do not properly belong to her. Aristotle was the first, but not the last, to complain that the child who piteously begs for her life when she first learns of her sentence is abruptly transformed before our eyes into a self-confident young woman ready, almost eager, to die for Greece—without adequate motivation or any explanation for the change (*Poetics* 1454a32). To my mind, Aristotle failed to read Euripides with the care that the subtle tragedian deserved. One would expect that Iphigenia's first reaction would be terror, her first recourse an appeal to a father's love in the hope that he would and could make everything right again. Agamemnon's reply that he was powerless in the face of the divine command, the army's will, and the Greeks' need to avenge Helen's abduction might make Iphigenia see her father differently. It would hardly be enough by itself to persuade her to take a broader view in which her death would be a meaningful part of a communal enterprise—a sacrifice rather than a murder. The attainment of such a heroic vision would of itself signify the movement from child to young adult. The two are, in fact, inseparable. But Euripides has not left us in the dark as to how it came about. Between the scene of Iphigenia's pathetic appeal to Agamemnon and her resolve to go willingly to her death, Achilles has declared his intention of fighting the entire army on her behalf, valiantly but hopelessly, with his own death a certainty.[6] In asserting that she will not accept his offer, Iphigenia at the same time sees all of the Greek warriors as ready to give their lives for Greece. Why should she alone refuse? She will die, not a victim, but a heroine. In a sense she, too, will prove herself a warrior, equal in courage to a man. Euripides may well have intended to underscore Iphigenia's superiority to the men in the play. Even Achilles is motivated primarily by the affront to his honor and admits that he might conceivably have consented to let his name be used in luring Iphigenia to the camp by a false promise of marriage—if only he had been consulted by those who concocted the plot. Agamemnon's inner conflict is great enough to lead him, a little late, to send a secret message ordering his daughter to return home without completing her journey; but when Menelaus, out of sympathy for his brother, is willing to go along with this plan, Agamemnon is quick to find reasons why it will not work. Menelaus' cynical picture of Agamemnon's unscrupulous struggle to become the commander of the Greeks, and Clytemnestra's revelation that he had already, out of jealous rage, killed a child of hers by an earlier marriage prevent our having any admiration for the man who may have genuinely loved his child but whose dominant desire was "to bear the scepter and to lead armies," as his wife charged (*Iphigenia in Aulis* 1194–95).

Strictly speaking, the divine command to kill Iphigenia was hypothetical, not categorical. She must be slain *if* the fleet is to sail against Troy. Although nobody in the play, not even Iphigenia, raises the question of the justice of the war itself, Euripides' unfavorable depiction of the Greek leaders, his obvious sympathy for Clytemnestra, and the fact that Iphigenia alone shows herself capable of selfless idealism have led some critics to conclude that *Iphigenia in Aulis*, like *The Trojan Women*, is intended as an anti-war tragedy.[7] Even if that is the case, it is the playwright and not the play's heroine who challenges the prevailing ethos of war. As a symbol for feminists, this Iphigenia would be decidedly limited. Plato might have valued her as one of those rare women who, if given the opportunity, show themselves equal to the best of men. She decides to go to her death willingly, but her action is in the name of precisely those male values which have condemned her. It follows naturally that she would beg her mother not to blame Agamemnon. Iphigenia is as much a man's heroine as a woman's. She comes dangerously close to exemplifying the ancient masculine ideal of a woman who will readily sacrifice her own interests if this will further whatever goal a man has found worth pursuing.[8]

In later tradition the Iphigenia of Aulis continues to be more victim than active agent. Cacoyannis' film, *Iphigenia* (1978), carries still further the idea, perhaps implicit in Euripides, that Iphigenia was inexcusably the victim of mistaken male ambitions. At least in Euripides' version the wind does blow after her sacrifice. Cacoyannis turns the oracle into a lie invented by the priest Calchas, who is offended by Agamemnon's slaughter of a sacred animal. The calm was already holding up the ships before this episode. Iphigenia is killed *after* the wind has risen. Thus her death is not only unjustified but useless. Iphigenia does not act out of even misguided patriotism and reverence for the goddess. She wants to prevent Achilles from dying needlessly. Mostly, she simply recognizes that she is powerless to alter the situation. There is no use in wanting the impossible, she says. She must die, but at least she can determine *how* she will die. She opts for dignity in accepting the inevitable. Despite this resolve, she is the sympathetic but helpless victim she was for Aeschylus and Lucretius. Clytemnestra's bitter resentment is an appropriate response.

I have mentioned Cacoyannis' film first among later treatments since despite Cacoyannis' modifications, it remains an adaptation of Euripides' tragedy rather than a complete rewriting of the story. Jean Racine's *Iphigénie* (1674) alters the story line and presents us with an entirely different image of Agamemnon's daughter.[9] As he explained in his preface, Racine was aghast at the idea of defiling the stage "with the horrible murder of a person so virtuous and lovable" as Iphigenia. He therefore had recourse to a variant on the myth which said that the girl sacrificed at Aulis was another Iphigenia, the secretly born child of Helen and Theseus. Since the identity of the Iphigenia intended by the oracle is not revealed until the very end of the play, the basic conflict faced by the principal characters remains the same, and Racine has, in fact, borrowed many details from Euripides. Yet, by bringing in the second Iphigenia, who had been known by the name Eriphile, he totally transforms the play, using her to introduce a fatal triangle: Eriphile is in love with Achilles who, in this version, has been publicly recognized as the affianced lover of Iphigenia. Dominated by jealous hatred, Eriphile is so evil and so treacherous a person that her death at the altar scarcely seems unjust. By contrast, other characters are elevated. Clytemnestra is resolved to give her own life if that will save her daughter, and she shows none of the resentful hatred of her husband which, in both Euripides' tragedy and Cacoyannis' film, foreshadows the later murder. Achilles retains his men's support and actually succeeds in fighting off the rest of the Greeks and saving Iphigenia before Calchas announces that it is not she but Eriphile whose sacrifice is required. Agamemnon, too, is somewhat redeemed. Moved by his daughter's pleas and his wife's reproaches, he decides to send Iphigenia secretly back to Argos; Eriphile prevents her escape by revealing the plan. But, if less cruel, Racine's Agamemnon remains weak and is more petty than Euripides' character. He does not draw his own sword on behalf of Iphigenia when the fight breaks out. Even worse, angered when Achilles refuses to accept Agamemnon's original order for Iphigenia's death, he spitefully declares afterward that if he does decide to save Iphigenia, it must be on condition that her planned marriage to Achilles be canceled.

Racine's Iphigenia is more fully developed as a character than Euripides' heroine, but this does not mean that she is either any more lifelike or more heroic. Unlike the Greek Iphigenia, she does not internalize and seek to realize for herself the values for which men fought. Rather, she is the incarnation of those feminine virtues which the men of Racine's period valued in women. She is unwavering in her filial obedience. Her plea to Agamemnon begins with her acceptance of his right to do with her whatever he wishes. "My life is yours. You wish to take it back?" (1177) She is ready, she declares, to "Give back to you my blood that is your own." She says that she would not even attempt to persuade him to change his purpose if it were not for the sorrow her death would bring to her mother and to her betrothed. She half apologizes even for asking for her life for their sakes.

> He knows your plans. Imagine his alarm.
> My mother stands before you, bathed in tears.
> Forgive my pleading, for its only aim
> Is to prevent the tears they'll shed for me.
> (1217–20)

Obedience to her father so dominates Iphigenia that she comes close to quarreling with Achilles when he proposes to save her against her father's will. Her lover is even moved to doubt the depth of her attachment to himself.

> Give to your father a heart in which I see
> Less of respect for him than hate for me.
> (1599–1600)

Achilles is wrong, of course. The heroine of a baroque drama acts out of duty, but her only hope for happiness rests in her lover. Iphigenia shows anger on her own behalf only once—in her vehement verbal attack on her treacherous rival. Later she tells Achilles that her dismay at learning of her father's consent to her death was as nothing compared to her anguish when she mistakenly believed her fiancé had come to prefer Eriphile. At the point when she believed that she might live but be forbidden to see her lover again, she no longer wanted her life.

> The kinder gods asked only for my life.
> Let me obey and die.   (1515–16)

Willing to die to please her father and because she can't have her lover, Iphigenia does not need the consoling thought that her sacrifice will benefit her country. Intellectually and emotionally, she is totally dependent on the men in her life. If she can be said to think for herself at all, it is only when duty to father and love for the fiancé originally picked by her father come into conflict. Agamemnon is finally shamed into reconciliation with Achilles. Thanks to the revelation of the true meaning of the oracle, the perfect daughter will be granted the privilege of becoming the respected, selfless wife—the epitome of the male ideal of what constitutes fulfillment for "the second sex."

In Racine's play, Iphigenia at least holds the stage as the central character: her feelings, her ultimate fate are the focus for our sympathy. Whatever we may think of her as an image for feminism, her creator regards her as important in herself and as worthy of our high admiration. In Søren Kierkegaard's hands, Iphigenia virtually disappears as a person. In *Fear and Trembling* (1843) Kierkegaard directly compares the account in Genesis of Abraham and Isaac with Euripides' drama, bringing them together in a bold metaphor that defies geography.[10] Abraham is "the solitary man who ascends Mount Moriah, which with its peak rises heaven-high above the plain of Aulis." The image encapsulates Kierkegaard's intention, which is to show that Agamemnon, the tragic hero, acts on a lower level than Abraham, the Knight of Faith. This is because Abraham, as Kierkegaard sees him, acts solely on the basis of his belief that he has received God's bewildering command that he must kill his son. Prompted by this inner conviction, he is ready to perform an act which goes against all ethical reasoning, and to do it solely because of his nonrational faith that somehow for him to sacrifice his son must be right on a higher religious plane even though God had earlier made the promise that, through Isaac, Abraham's seed would multiply forever. This "teleological suspension of the ethical," as Kierkegaard calls it, does not come into play for Agamemnon for two reasons. First, the oracle was a public declaration, vouched for by the priest, not a personal communication to Agamemnon. "Such a relationship to the deity paganism did not know" (70), the Christian Kierkegaard says, a little complacently. Kierkegaard explicitly denies that even Socrates might be thought of as a Knight of Faith, despite Plato's many references to Socrates' "divine voice" and his mystic trances. Second, Kierkegaard takes as given the assumption that it is right for the individual to be sacrificed to the interest of the State. Once the divine pronouncement is made that the expedition to Troy cannot be carried out unless Iphigenia is killed, Agamemnon knows what he ought to do. Whatever his personal anguish, there is no moral conflict. "He lets one expression of the ethical find its telos in a higher expression of the ethical; the ethical relation between ... daughter and father, he reduces to a sentiment which has its dialectic in its relation to the idea of morality" (69). Comfortably ensconced in the Universal, his lower duty to his child is redeemed in the higher duty of service to the community. Agamemnon's self-righteousness is guaranteed.

As for Iphigenia, Kierkegaard says almost nothing about her. Her decision to let herself be sacrificed without resistance Kierkegaard presents, even more narrowly than Racine did, as a pure act of filial submission. "Iphigenia bows to her father's resolution, she herself makes the movement of infinite resignation, and now they are on good terms with one another" (124). In Kierkegaard's view, apparently, this is an adequate reward for her. Primarily, Iphigenia's role is to be the temptation which Agamemnon overcomes to his glory. Kierkegaard would have liked it even better if Iphigenia's conduct had been such as to test her father still more severely.

> In the play Iphigenia had leave to weep, really she ought to have been allowed like Jephthah's daughter two months for weeping, not in solitude but at her

father's feet, allowed to employ all her art "which is but tears," and to twine about his knees instead of presenting the olive branch of the suppliant. (97)

It has long been recognized that *Fear and Trembling*, while it contains an essential core of Kierkegaard's religious philosophy, reflects the author's concern with an immediate emotional crisis of his own. In speaking of Abraham's sacrifice of Isaac, Kierkegaard had in mind his decision to break off his engagement with Regina, which he regarded as a painful but necessary step he must take in order to fulfil his highest religious commitment. Modern readers, although ready to grant that Regina was probably happier in the long run to have married someone other than Søren Kierkegaard, are frequently appalled to see how little thought he gave to the feelings of either Isaac or the young woman he dismissed. Lucretius would probably have seen in Regina yet another, though much less injured, victim of the evil deeds committed in the name of religion.

¶

The images inspired by the Iphigenia of the alternate tradition, the one who served as Artemis' priestess among the Taurians, are understandably quite different from those of the victim slain at Aulis. Interestingly enough, no writer whom I know has portrayed this Iphigenia as vindictive or vengeful as she might easily have been imagined to be. Euripides' *Iphigenia in Tauris*, not a sequel, of course, but written some years before *Iphigenia in Aulis*, presents a woman who is strong, capable of initiating action, compassionate, and entirely without bitterness.[11] She does not even reproach her father, excusing him with the explanation that he had unwittingly trapped himself and her by vowing to Artemis that he would sacrifice to her the fairest creature born in his house during the year in which Iphigenia fatefully came to birth. Following the custom of her new country, Iphigenia has reluctantly assisted at the sacrifices of the strangers made captive by the Taurians. She now finds herself asked to offer to the goddess two Greeks, whom she discovers to be her brother, Orestes, and his friend, Pylades, come at the command of Apollo so that Orestes may carry off to Greece the temple's sacred statue. It is Iphigenia who invents and makes possible a plan by which all three of them may steal the statue and escape. By itself this might show her cleverness and strength while still leaving her open to the charge that she is indefensibly ungrateful to one who has befriended her—as she appears to the eyes of Thoas, King of the Taurians, when he learns of the plot. Euripides prevents this judgment—or at least softens it—by having Iphigenia refuse to follow Orestes' suggestion that they simply kill Thoas. She is willing to deceive him and to steal the statue because that is the only way to save the two men and because she believes it is the will of Apollo (and of his sister, Artemis) that the goddess' likeness be conveyed to Greece.

For Iphigenia this act is more than simple obedience to an oracle. Euripides has bestowed on her what the Greeks would have deemed a "masculine" intellect, the ability to reason philosophically. Iphigenia detests the human sacrifices, not just because, as a woman, she shrinks from bloodshed, but because she believes the rite is inconsistent with the nature of the deity. She even questions the truth of the traditional myths.

> And what does Artemis ask of me here?
> She who forbids approach by any man
> Whose hand is stained with blood or with touch
> Of childbirth or of burial, finds him
> Unclean and bans him. She so delicate
> In all these ways will yet demand the blood
> Of human beings on Her altar stone!
> It cannot be. How could Latona bear
> To Zeus so cruel a daughter? It is not true.
> It is as false as tales of Tantalus
> Feeding the Gods a child. O Artemis,
> These people, being murderers themselves,
> Are charging Thee with their own wickedness.
> No! I will not believe it of a God.   (380–91)

Even so, Iphigenia bows to the seeming evidence that the goddess, however inexplicably, must approve of the sacrifices since she has placed her here. When Iphigenia learns that the new captives are being brought to the temple, she says,

> Once more I must believe that Artemis
> Desires this worship, once again I serve her.
> (466–67)

The epiphany of Athena at the end of the play persuades Thoas to let Iphigenia and her companions leave, thus ensuring the success of Orestes' mission. Iphigenia sets sail for Greece, taking the goddess in her material representation to a country where she will be worshiped without the taking of human life, with the offering of only a single drop of blood pricked from a human throat as a memorial of the ritual's barbarous origin. The divine will is now perceived to be in harmony with Iphigenia's own religious beliefs.

There are suggestions in the play of what are today often called feminist values. Iphigenia's appeal to the chorus of Greek women, themselves captive servants in the temple, is an appeal to women's solidarity.

> A woman knows how much her weakness needs
> The sympathy and help of other women,
> Their understanding and their loyalty. (1059–61)[12]

She promises to send help to these women later if she herself escapes, and Euripides, via Athena, makes sure that Thoas will not take reprisal on them. The author seems to share women's rejection of the military heroic idea. At least he has Orestes declare that the whole Trojan expedition was a wicked war, with evil waste its only consequence. Iphigenia, to be sure, cherishes a desire for revenge against Helen and Menelaus, as those responsible for the disasters, and wishes that *they* might be brought to the altar for her to sacrifice. But one doubts that she would have been willing to carry through if chance cooperated. Deluded by a false interpretation of her dream, at the beginning of the play, she believes that Orestes has died, and she announces that, hopeless now, she will no longer be reluctant to perform the sacrifices. Actually, she is moved to pity for the two captives, even before she learns their identity. The mood of *Iphigenia in Tauris* is one of reconciliation. Lattimore notes the play's stress on the ideals of friendship and "the love of Greek for Greek" in "a wider Hellenism."[13] Its heroine is an intelligent woman, understanding and able to forgive, sensitive to others' suffering, ready for defiant action when the situation demands it. She is no revolutionary, but she merits a prominent niche in feminism's Hall of Fame, albeit her place is with the precursors.[14]

In Goethe's *Iphigenia in Tauris* (1779), a play both modeled on and radically departing from Euripides' drama with the same name, we find an Iphigenia who embodies one man's (her creator's) ideal without becoming, like Racine's heroine, an ideal for men only. Like Racine, Goethe resolved to work out an ending which would not require a divine epiphany, yet relied on a reinterpretation of an oracle the authenticity of which is never questioned. But whereas Racine's revelation of a second Iphigenia is metaphorically as much a *deus ex machina* device as Athena's appearance is literally so for Euripides, Goethe brings about the reinterpretation as the result of a deeper understanding; and he uses it to facilitate a psychological reconciliation of all parties. As Orestes explains to Iphigenia, the oracle had said,

> "If you will bring to Greece the sister who
> On Tauris' shore now tarries in the temple
> Against her will, the curse will be removed."
> This we construed to mean Apollo's sister,
> While he had you in mind!   (2113–17)[15]

This happy solution, which enables Thoas to keep the statue while allowing Iphigenia to leave with her brother and Pylades, is possible only because the influence of Iphigenia's personality and her actions have brought about the requisite changes in Thoas and Orestes so that they are open to compromise.

Paradoxically, in Iphigenia Goethe sought to incarnate both the ideal woman and the essence of Hellenism (not as it was historically, but as it had been recreated by eighteenth-century German writers).[16] Such a composite figure inevitably suggests a certain androgyny. Here perhaps is the source of my claim that regardless of what she may have been to Goethe, we today may find in her a positive image for feminism. Let us look more closely at what she says and does.

This priestess, who will finally declare proudly that she is "as freeborn as any man" (1858), has successfully persuaded King Thoas to abandon the ancient rite of human sacrifice. His decision after years of lapse to renew it by killing Orestes and Pylades is made out of pique: Iphigenia has rejected his offer of marriage, declaring that she believes that to marry him would be against the will of the goddess who had brought her to the temple. Iphigenia is strong enough to defy Thoas by saying that she will not carry out an order she holds to be wrong. Like Euripides' Iphigenia, she can reason clearly and effectively. She tells Thoas to his face that she is better able to see what is best for him than he is. Under her calming influence, Orestes, in a mystical dream, sees himself accepted by his parents and other ancestors in Hades, themselves finally at peace with each other. He awakens, cured of his madness. In a debate with Pylades and later in deliberations with herself, Iphigenia spells out for us the moral code by which she lives and will act in the present crisis. She rejects Pylades' pragmatic appeal to self-interest. She has her own principles. A lie, she maintains, injures the liar as well as the one lied to. Ingratitude remains an evil even if it is seemingly justified by necessity. She recognizes that these convictions of hers derive as much from emotions as from reason. When principles conflict, "I do not analyze, I merely feel" (1650). Most remarkable, perhaps, is the way in which Iphigenia herself regards her final decision. Instead of deceiving Thoas and escaping with the stolen statue, she will remind the King of his former promise to send her home to Greece if she ever found the means to go there; in short, she will appeal to what is best in him, offering trust in exchange for trust. She sees her act as a new kind of heroic daring.

> Do men alone, then, have the right to do
> Unheard of feats? Can only men clasp things
> Impossible to their heroic bosoms?   (1892–94)

After hearing her revelation, Thoas hesitates when Orestes interrupts with a request to settle the matter by a duel. Again Iphigenia challenges the male code of values:

> By no means! For such bloody testimony

> There is, O king, no call! Withdraw hands from
> Your swords, and think of me and of my fate.
> A quick fight may immortalize a man,
> And even if he falls, the songs will praise him.
> But the unending tears thereafter shed
> By the surviving and deserted woman
> No future age will count, and poets speak
> No word about the thousand days and nights
> Of weeping when a silent soul consumes
> Itself in vain with yearning to bring back
> The lost and suddenly departed friend.   (2064–75)

Iphigenia wants no victory and no defeat for either man. Even when she has elicited Thoas' grudging consent to let them go so long as he may keep the statue, she is still not satisfied.

> Not this, my king! Without your blessing,
> With your ill-will, I shall not part from you.
>   (2151–52)

Thoas at last extends his hand so that they may part in friendship and wishes them well (*Lebt wohl!* 2174).

Some readers might complain that in her very perfection Goethe's Iphigenia resembles the goddess Athena more than Orestes' sister. Pylades speaks of her as "godlike" (*göttergleiches Weib*, 772). Orestes actually addresses her as "great soul" (*große Seele*, 1076), and even as "divine" (*Himmlische*, 1127).[17] This impression is reinforced by Goethe's emphasis on her reluctance to marry Thoas. Granted, Iphigenia felt that she was pledged to the goddess. But one does not feel that there is any conflict here between her emotions and her sense of religious duty. Dramatically, of course, an Iphigenia who chose to be a Taurian wife and mother would be disastrous. It would be as if Snow-White decided to stay with the Dwarfs. The Greek myth which told how Artemis first demanded Iphigenia's sacrifice, then literally snatched her from her death was psychologically sound in representing the rescued victim as gladly devoting her life to the deity's service. I admit, however, that Goethe is possibly open to the suspicion that his ideal woman stands on a pedestal, aloof from sex. Going beyond Euripides, he has his heroine not only allow her understanding to pardon Agamemnon, but even express the hope that the goddess might preserve her to be the comfort of her father's old age, a destiny familiar to many oldest daughters!

In every other way Goethe's Iphigenia seems to me to epitomize the new feminist ethics. In place of adversarial tactics, she puts conflict resolution. Her goal is harmonious communal relations, based on the understanding and valuing of everyone's needs. As a woman who explicitly says that she wants her life to be useful, she rejects the prevalent male values based on violence. True, she does not fulfil herself sexually. She is not total Woman. But her decision not to accept the offer of a conventionally glorious marriage because she holds something else to be more important and satisfying for her is an affirmation of a woman's right to make herself after her own pattern. Iphigenia at Tauris, unlike the victim at Aulis, does not sacrifice herself for anyone, but she realizes her power, in saving herself, to raise others to a higher level. If Iphigenia at Aulis is an example of the crimes men have committed in the name of religion, Iphigenia at Tauris offers a vision of what human beings might do if they learned to act mutually on trust and with compassion.

¶

From the point of view which I have adopted here, my chosen examples do not show any enlightened progression in the depiction of Iphigenia at Aulis. Racine and Kierkegaard are blatantly retrogressive in this respect. Cacoyannis' Iphigenia is more lifelike, possibly more appealing than her Greek predecessor since she is more fully developed. She is perhaps more pitiful than tragic inasmuch as she finds no reason for dying other than brutal necessity. Artemis' priestess among the Taurians grows in stature under the pen of Goethe, but the possibilities for such a development were already planted in Euripides' version. Although I have not elaborated on the fact, it should be obvious that all of the Iphigenias reflect to considerable degree the preoccupations of the period in which their authors lived. Yet in every case the artist had been, if not at variance with the prevailing attitudes of his age, at least distinctively positioned within it, speaking to it as well as from it. Critics today mostly frown upon any attempt to establish an author's intention, and sometimes go so far as to argue that all interpretations of a creative work are equally valid. I myself believe that, within broad limits, an intelligent reader can perceive or sense the attitude which creative artists wanted their audience to assume toward fictional characters. The favorable opinion held by Dickens for Nell in *The Old Curiosity Shop* is not less discernible than Kierkegaard's marveling admiration for Abraham.[18] To me the most interesting result of our brief survey of accounts of Iphigenia is the perception of the difference between our judgment on the Iphigenia we find when, with "willing suspension of disbelief," we think of her as a real person and what we imaginatively reconstruct as the author's view of her.

Hazel E. Barnes
University of Colorado

Notes

[1] Various reasons were offered by the Greek tragedians to explain Artemis' demand for Iphigenia's sacrifice: (1) Agamemnon had angered her by killing an animal under her protection (implied in Aeschylus' *Agamemnon*, stated explicitly in Sophocles' *Electra*, 566–72); (2) Agamemnon had on an earlier occasion made a vow to offer to her the fairest thing born in that year (Euripides, *Iphigenia in Tauris*, 20–21); (3) the oracle is given without explanation (Euripides, *Iphigenia in Aulis*, 89–93, 358–60, 879). In this case one may consider it mere caprice on the goddess' part or a deep-laid plan to put into motion all of the events involving the House of Atreus after the fall of Troy. But the second alternative would seem in itself to require an explanation.

[2] There are, of course, other examples of human sacrifice in Greek literature; for example, the Trojan captives slain at the funeral of the dead Patroclus, and Astyanax and Polyxena, who were killed to give honor to the dead Achilles. These are not close parallels since they do not involve any belief that a specific supernatural command was involved.

[3] Cyrus H. Gordon presented this thesis in a lecture at the University of Colorado in Boulder. I have not tried to find a full discussion of it in Gordon's published work. He makes a brief reference to the idea in *Before the Bible: The Common Background of Greek and Hebrew Civilizations* (New York, 1965), 255, n. 1.

⁴Barbara Meldrum has drawn to my attention a discussion of Jephthah's daughter by Harriet Beecher Stowe. She claims that the early Hebrews provided for an "order of women who renounced the usual joys and privileges of the family state, to devote themselves to religious and charitable duties" (125). Therefore, Stowe claims, Jephthah's daughter was deprived of life only in the sense of having to give up the normal expectations of becoming a wife and mother in her husband's home—like later nuns. That this is intended in the passage in Judges I seriously doubt. It is true, however, that in many places the practice of human sacrifice preceded and probably led to the later custom of allowing, or compelling, a person to dedicate his or her life to the service of God. In the same way, eunuch priests might be considered the forerunners of celibate priests. See Stowe's "Jephthah's Daughter," in *Woman in Sacred History* (New York, c. 1873), 123–26.

⁵I make two disclaimers: (1) I have never attempted to trace the story of either of the Iphigenias through the centuries of literary history. I have simply chosen a very few of what I have found to be the most interesting examples. (2) My strictly limited and admittedly one-sided approach of necessity ignores those qualities which in each of my selections make it an artistic masterpiece. I have chosen to concentrate on an aspect which would appear as a footnote, if at all, in a full literary criticism of the work.

⁶There is an interesting parallel here with what happens in *Philoctetes*. Sophocles' hero refuses to be reconciled with the Greek leaders until he is so commanded by Heracles, who suddenly appears from heaven. If we interpret the epiphany as representing Philoctetes' own inward change, then it is significant that this comes immediately after his realization that Neoptolemus is willing to risk his life and his honor on Philoctetes' behalf.

⁷Perhaps the strongest case for this interpretation is made by Dimock in his introduction to his and Merwin's translation of the play. Dimock reads into Iphigenia's acceptance of the necessity for the Greeks to punish the Trojans a covert reference to a speech by the Sophist Gorgias in 408 B.C. which exhorted the Greeks to give up their internecine struggles with one another and to embark together on a war against Persia. Euripides, in Dimock's view, was condemning the proposal. Bernard Knox, in a review of this book (and of Cacoyannis' film, *Iphigenia*) makes an opposing suggestion: that Euripides might well have felt that a union of Greeks against their common enemy was at least "the lesser evil." I would find it difficult to believe that Euripides would use the Trojan War, which he unmistakably condemned in other tragedies, to stand for a project of which he approved. But even if we could be certain of his attitude, my point here is that the fictional Iphigenia has accepted her father's position as valid. See Euripides, *Iphigeneia at Aulis*, trans. W. S. Merwin and George E. Dimock, Jr. (New York, 1978); Bernard Knox, "A Four

Handkerchief Tragedy," *New York Review of Books*, February 9, 1978, 16–17.

[8] I am omitting here all reference to the play's supposedly happy ending in which a messenger reports that Iphigenia had mysteriously disappeared from the altar, a dying deer left in her place. Even if this section was written by Euripides, which some scholars have doubted, and assuming that we do not join Clytemnestra in suspecting that the account is a false story invented by Agamemnon to placate her, the supernatural intervention in no way affects our judgment on the previous behavior of the characters, none of whom had cherished the faintest hope of a miracle.

[9] Racine explains his intention and his Greek source for the story of a second Iphigenia in his preface to the play. Quotations are from John Cairncross' poetical translation of *Iphigénie* in Jean Racine, *Iphigenia / Phaedra / Athaliah* (Baltimore, 1963). In a few instances I have very slightly altered Cairncross' translation with consultation of the French text.

[10] Søren Kierkegaard, *Fear and Trembling* and *The Sickness unto Death*, trans. Walter Lowrie (Princeton, 1941), 71.

[11] Here, as with the other plays from which I quote, I have chosen to use a translation in poetry: *Iphigenia in Tauris*, trans. Witter Bynner, intro. Richmond Lattimore, *Euripides II* (Chicago, 1956).

[12] It is true, of course, that the needs of the plot require the silence of the always present Chorus—as in a number of other Greek tragedies. Still I believe that Euripides' attribution of these words to Iphigenia represents more than a dramatic device.

[13] "Introduction," *Euripides II*, 119.

[14] There is an interesting exchange between Iphigenia and her brother. In arguing with him that his escape is the most important thing to insure, she says, much like the Iphigenia at Aulis:

> If a man die, a house, a name is lost,
> But if a woman die, what does it matter?   (1005–6)

To which Orestes responds rather grimly,

> It mattered when my mother died!   (1007)

[15] Johann Wolfgang von Goethe, *Iphigenia in Tauris*, trans. Charles E. Passage (New York, 1963). Goethe and his translator follow the common custom of treating *Tauris* as a place name although it is properly the name of a group of people, the Taurians. This practice is convenient in contrasting the heroine "at Aulis" with the one "at Tauris," and I follow it insofar as Goethe's play is concerned.

[16] Goethe may have borrowed certain details of plot from other eighteenth-century plays on this theme, but the character of Iphigenia is certainly his own creation. Critics have usually assumed that she is in part an idealized reflection of Charlotte von Stein. Ulrich K. Goldsmith has argued persuasively that the humane, virginal Iphigenia was inspired by Goethe's younger sister, Cornelia, to whom he was deeply attached, and that the play, examined in light of psychoanalytic theory, is among other things the "embodiment of a sublimated brother-sister relationship." See his "The Healing of Orestes in Goethe's *Iphigenie auf Tauris*," *Far Western Forum* (May 1974), 209–19 (reprinted in Goldsmith's *Studies in Comparison* [New York, 1989], 75–86).

[17] C. Passage translates this as "Immortal One," which may be going a bit too far.

[18] I realize that technically the one whose voice is heard in *Fear and Trembling* is the pseudonymous Johannes De Silentio. But he is Kierkegaard in the same sense that the omniscient narrator in *The Old Curiosity Shop* is the "authorial Voice" (to use Wayne Booth's term) of Dickens and not the voice of the Dickens who lectured in America. The same might be said of Euripides, the author of *Iphigenia in Aulis*, as compared with the Euripides who strolled through the streets of Athens. To the extent that we may meaningfully speak at all of "the author's intention," it is always within the confines of a particular work.

Sirens and Their Song

> What song the Sirens sang, or what name Achilles assumed when he hid himself among women, though puzzling questions, are not beyond all conjecture.
>   Sir Thomas Browne, *Hydriotaphia*

Homer is our first source for Sirens, as he is a source for the collocation of the verb *to sing*, ἀείδειν, with the recitation of epic poetry.[1] The latter observation becomes a commonplace since poetry is one of the arts that enjoys the patronage of the Muses and the verb *to sing* often describes the composition or recitation of poetry. It is noteworthy, however, that in the twelfth book of the *Odyssey* the monstrous Sirens also possess the power of song, a most often male prerogative. Perhaps this very power to appropriate male voice makes the Sirens monstrous—or at least as consistently compelling as any other female monsters from antiquity.[2]

What female figures in ancient literature have this gift of song? The Muses do, to be sure, but their gift serves their father Zeus through his male bards.[3] In the *Odyssey* mortal women like Penelope, Nausicaa, and Arete only listen to the songs of bards and heroes in contrast to Circe (10.221), Calypso (5.61), and the Sirens (12.183), who themselves sing songs. In addition to their ability to sing, Circe, Calypso, and the Sirens all possess both the power to impede Odysseus' journey home, should they choose to do so, and knowledge beyond that of human beings: Circe tells the hero how to evade the dangers he will encounter (among them, the Sirens); both Circe and Calypso[4] know what lies ahead of Odysseus when he leaves their shores; and it is knowledge of what happened at Troy and afterward rather than sensory delights that the Sirens promise Odysseus in their singing. Thus these more-than-mortal feminine figures share knowledge, the power to seduce the unwary male traveler, and song.

The Sirens are both dangerous and alluring because they have voice.[5] What and how they sing, however, depends very much upon the author who tells their story. In the nineteenth and twentieth centuries, three common approaches to the problem of the Sirens' voice prevail in poetry, and examples in the work of three poets—Matthew Arnold, W. H. Auden, and Margaret Atwood—illustrate these three approaches. Matthew Arnold's "The New Sirens," first published in 1849, is a perhaps not-so-new view of Sirens as representing the seductions of the senses; W. H. Auden's clerihew "Lord Byron," published in 1972, uses a stereotype, narrowing the idea of Siren so far as to eliminate her power of song altogether; and Margaret Atwood's "Siren Song," published in 1976, tells the story from the point of view of a Siren herself rather than from that of the male adventurer. Arnold, Auden, and Atwood, along with additional examples illustrating each approach, demonstrate the diversity of this classical image even in contemporary poetry, but for me Atwood's approach is the most challenging. When poets like Atwood shift the narrative point of view to that of the Sirens, two dramatic things happen. First, the Sirens cease to be defined only in terms of what the male protagonists see and feel: our opinion of both the singers and their songs changes along with our perspective. Second, new possibilities arise as poets record modulations in the Sirens' song through time. We are only beginning to read the stories that poets—particularly women poets—will write about these women singers.[6]

Before the twentieth century the diversity in the image of Sirens and their song extended to almost every twist of plot or dialogue but never shifted the point of view to that of the Siren herself. These creatures, sometimes pictured as bird-women but always as luring hapless sailors to their deaths by the power of song, are one peril that Odysseus (*Od.* 12.39–54, 166–200), Aeneas (*Aen.* 5.864–65), and the Argonauts (Apollonius of Rhodes, *Argonautica* 4.891–920) all survive, although both their encounters and their methods of escape vary.[7] Hesiod and Homer both mention that their island abode is a flowery meadow; Sophocles says that their father was Phorcys, while Apollonius of Rhodes maintains that their parents were Achelous and the muse Terpsichore; Alcman associates them with the Muse, while Euripides and Erinna associate them with mourning; Plato turns the Sirens' song into celestial music (one Siren for each of the eight spheres); Cicero understands that their temptations are based on the lure of knowledge rather than that of the senses[8]; Ovid gives them wings, and Pausanias tells how they came to lose all of the feathers from those wings. The fascination with this image continues in the later years of the Roman Empire in the writings of Clement of Alexandria, Origen, Eusebius, St. Jerome, and Cyril of Alexandria. Later still, Sirens appear in Dante, Petrarch, and Boccaccio, in medieval bestiaries, and in English letters as early as Chaucer, Trevisa, and Gower. In all of these ages, including our own, psychological or allegorical or rational readings of the Sirens are myriad—and varied. However, the point of view is that of the male adventurer; the Sirens are always viewed as Other.

In recent years in the popular culture, Sirens have appeared in plays[9] and novels[10] where the connection to classical Sirens is seldom if ever anything other than metaphoric. The word in a very generalized sense becomes a way of describing a variety of human enchantresses as disparate as Clara Bow and Anne-Sophie Mutter.[11] The word has also spread into fields other than pure fiction, such as literary criticism,[12] diaries,[13] personal reminiscences,[14] historical travelogues,[15] art,[16] and psychology.[17] For writers of fiction and nonfiction in the years since Homer, Sirens sometimes appear as a powerful feminine archetype; at other times they are simply stereotypes. In either case, however, they continue to be seen as Other.

The image of Sirens and their fatal song was well established when Matthew Arnold entitled his thirty-four-stanza poem "The New Sirens,"[18] and his Sirens are indeed new in several important ways. They still lure hapless men away from their true pursuits (37–39) but "The uncouthness/Of that primal age is gone" (49–50), presumably because they no longer cause physical death. They still sing (57–88), but their message is one of romantic love that by its very nature cannot last. Their song still has allure but not its ancient power: the speaker of the poem, a poet himself who has forsaken his Muse to share with the Sirens their peculiar alternations of "Fits of joy and fits of pain" (206), is able to reject the Sirens' song even after hearing and participating in it. Some modern critics have seen the rejection of the Sirens as a rejection of Romanticism.[19] Whether or not the poem can be glossed as simply as that, these "pale maidens" (275) are pallid shadows of the Sirens of earlier time.[20] They move from bower to palace, from excitement to ennui and back, and seem hardly a danger since the poet-speaker can reject them so handily.[21] Most interesting is Arnold's ability to reshape the image of the Sirens so dramatically to fit his personal and cultural concerns. One recent critic goes further when he sees in Arnold's poetry an example of how "archetypal myth perpetually re-enacts itself, not only in cultural history, but in the individual consciousness attuned to history."[22]

Arnold's myth gives voice to the Sirens. It is they who utter the Romantic dictum, "Only, what we feel, we know" (84). However, the poet-speaker is actually retelling their words, and so what appears to be direct quotation we get second hand. The speaker also exhorts the Sirens to relinquish song for presumably mute action ("Pluck, pluck cypress, O pale maidens" [113, 269, 275]), and his rebuttal to their four-stanza song (57–88) is twenty-three stanzas in length (89–276), hardly equal time. These Sirens could be perfectly cast as Victorian ladies: twice they are called Graces (9, 243), and their appearance, action, and gesture all denote the utmost gentility. The mood and movement of the trochaic stanzas are highly crafted and perfectly suited to their content.[23]

Not all Victorians pictured Sirens in quite the same way, however, even when the Sirens remained embodiments of sensory seduction. In the contemporaneous libretto "The Doom of the Sirens,"[24] Dante Gabriel Rossetti produces the "fierce, sensual lovers of antiquity" to whom Arnold refers in his letter to Clough,[25] but who never appear in his poem. Rossetti's Sirens, embodiments of paganism, first tempt and then destroy two generations of Christian princes. To the Prince in the first generation, the three Sirens offer first wealth, then greatness, and finally love in a series of offers reminiscent of the Judgment of Paris but with more immediately fatal consequences. Rossetti's "lyrical tragedy" recounts in Act I the temptation of the Prince and his death by the Siren Ligeia: "in her arms, as she sings, under her poisonous breath" (610). In Act III the son of this first foolish Prince, grown to adulthood, challenges the Sirens,

> and when, at his last word of reprobation, the curse seizes her [Ligeia] and her sisters, and they dash themselves headlong from the rock, he also succumbs to the

>doom, calling with his last breath on his Bride to come
>to him. (613)

Thus at the conclusion of the libretto, the three Sirens are dead; the young Prince and his bride are dead; his parents, the first Prince and his queen, are dead; the hermit who reared him is dead; even the pagan oracle that first told of the curse bestirs itself to speak one last time, only to fall silent forever. Rossetti uses the same image to further his emotional, romantic plot that Arnold used to unmask the deficiencies of Romanticism; he also presents a two-dimensional, stereotypical view of Sirens whereas Arnold's picture expands and complicates what we thought we understood.

A different appeal to the senses is present in James Russell Lowell's "The Sirens,"[26] first published in 1840 and so antedating Arnold's "The New Sirens" by six or seven years. In four long and irregularly shaped stanzas, the Sirens make an appeal to a body exhausted from labor and danger. Their song sounds more appropriate to Lotus Eaters than Sirens:

>"Here mayst thou harbor peacefully,
>Here mayst thou rest from the aching oar;
>Turn thy curved prow ashore,
>And in our green isle rest forevermore!
>Forevermore!" (30–34)

The text of this poem is a verbatim transcription of the Sirens' song, without even one line of frame or introduction. But the reader does not identify with the Siren-narrators. Rather, the reader directly experiences their allure, as it is envisioned by Lowell.

Another nineteenth-century American poet, Mary E. Hewitt, pictures the Sirens as seductresses who rely upon both visual and oral enticements. In Hewitt's "Myth,"[27] three beautiful Sirens sing a song to two audiences, the mariners whom they entice and the fishermen who recognize the peril:

>Beware! beware their treacherous wile!
>Destruction lurks their smile beneath—

> Their song is guile—their clasp is death! (105–7)

However, the mariners obey the call of the Sirens as the horrified fishermen watch:

> They [mariners] swim the sea—the waves they ride—
> With giant strength they breast the tide—
> They gain the shore—Oh! veil our eyes,
> Ere we behold the sacrifice! (118–21)

Hewitt's poem, although typically nineteenth century in its Romanticism and its rhyme, differs in significant detail from other uses of the myth. Here the "flowing locks of gold," "blue eyes," "fair feet," and "beauteous hands" of the Siren Parthenope (65–76) seem at least as important an enticement as her song. She and her two sisters sing of a life of ease and revelry, not on the green isle of Lowell's poem but in caverns filled with riches under the sea (87–102). And although both mariners and fishermen see and hear the Sirens, only the mariners succumb. The fishermen, each like a latter-day Ulysses, remain determined to return home, and Hewitt's poem ends as they are greeted off the coast of Sicily not by the guileful voice of the Sirens but by "soft voices ... glad voices" (140–41) welcoming them home. Although Hewitt's picture of the Sirens is highly individualized, she continues to portray the Sirens as Other and writes a poem in which the reader—male or female—still identifies with the point of view of the male wayfarers.

In some twentieth-century poetry the Sirens continue to represent, as they do in Arnold, the seduction of the senses. In contrast to Arnold's pallid Sirens or Hewitt's lovely but fatal Parthenope, Laurence Binyon describes monstrous creatures in his 1931 poem "The Sirens."[28] Their "voluptuous throats" create

> ... the extreme ache to press
> Lips on those lips, that thirst to suck the breath,
> The heart's blood, into theirs, till eyes grow dull,
> Till lips be lips no longer, and only a skull

> Roll from your feast of death,
>   O sated Sirens! (336–37)

Binyon's "malignant Sirens" use both spiritual and fleshly lures, but the Sirens are not the real subject of the poem; the real subject is "Man, predestinate" (350), about whom Binyon goes on and on (323–51).

Thirty years later Robert Graves uses the Sirens as an image of fleshly temptation for a hero whose life was a series of such temptations. In "Ulysses,"[29] the hero is never done with women, "whether gowned as wife or whore" (2). Penelope and Circe represent a tempestuous dichotomy that metaphorically extends to natural phenomena, such as the Symplegades or Scylla and Charybdis or the Sirens:

> They [Penelope and Circe] multiplied into the Sirens' throng,
> Forewarned by fear of whom he stood bound fast
> Hand and foot helpless to the vessel's mast,
> Yet would not stop his ears: daring their song
> He groaned and sweated till that shore was past.
>   (11–15)

Graves's Ulysses finds that the "one pleasure" of the flesh does not help to solve the multiple problems that are the lot of human kind. Despite his reputation for cleverness and wit, he remains trapped in a preoccupation with the sensory.

Arnold and Lowell present the Sirens as fleshly temptation (albeit of different kinds) and give them voice. Rossetti, Binyon, and Graves mention the Sirens' seductive song, but the reader knows of it only by reputation and in off-hand descriptions. W. H. Auden presents a picture of Sirens in a four-line clerihew, "Lord Byron,"[30] that is the logical conclusion of this movement: his Siren, the quintessential femme fatale, has no voice at all. Instead, a pen-and-ink drawing (fig. 1) occupies the page facing the four-line clerihew and gives the reader a literal picture of a Siren. The effect is very different from that in Arnold. Where Arnold was serious and self-absorbed in his classicism, Auden is witty and holds his subject at arm's length. Where Arnold took 276 lines to describe the poet's relationship to the "pale maidens," Auden compresses his entire poem into a total of thirteen words:

Lord Byron
Once succumbed to a Siren:
His flesh was weak,
Hers Greek.

Here in neither the text nor the accompanying illustration is a seductress who promises either knowledge or inspiration. This Siren has no song. Instead, Auden presents us with a very factual, very corporeal series of three statements. The humor of the lines comes from the juxtaposition of the facts in the last two of these statements, from the suddenness of the rhyme, and from the purposefully superficial treatment of the image of Sirens.

Fig. 1: From ACADEMIC GRAFFITI by W. H. Auden, Filippo Sanjust illustrator. Illustration copyright © 1972 by Filippo Sanjust. Reprinted by permission of Random House, Inc.

The clerihew seems to be the ideal form for such statement. Gavin Ewart, who has critiqued clerihews written by the inventor of the form, Edmund Clerihew Bentley, finds that they often exhibit the following characteristics: a sense of absurdity, an absence of malice, the challenge of ingenious rhymes, a tone "both civilized and dotty," and anachronistic elements.[31] "Lord Byron" exhibits all of these characteristics and, as such, might be recommended as an example of the light verse that Auden admired and at which he excelled.[32] It displays "the fencing wit of an informal style"[33] in its form, its rhymes, its juxtapositions. Indeed, Byron's exuberant phil-Hellenism and the fact that he actually died in Greece make the chance rhyme of *Byron* and *Siren* all the more witty.

For all of its cleverness, however, this clerihew holds a very narrow view of Sirens. It ignores much of the legend surrounding them, focusing only on the seductiveness of a single Siren and assuming that that seductiveness is purely physical. It does not speculate beyond the moment described: are there consequences for Lord Byron's indiscretion? It does not give the Siren voice. Even the humor of the final couplet depends upon a juxtaposition in the understanding of the word *flesh* whereby Byron is granted emotion and the Siren is seen as object. When the accompanying illustration is also considered (fig. 1), the reader sees a single female figure, singularly unattractive and with the tail of a medieval mermaid. If we laugh, we are laughing at a stereotype (just as in Rossetti or Binyon we are fearing a stereotype).

Like Auden's clerihew, a recent *New Yorker* cartoon uses the image of Sirens in a humorous context that turns on the use of anachronism (fig. 2). Where the former transposes the classical monster and the nineteenth-century poet into the same context, the latter shows a Siren using language a director of marketing might use when speaking to a new member of the sales staff. As a ship sails past on the horizon, one attractive and completely anthropomorphic Siren says to another, "Basically, we're aiming at an audience of adventuresome, outdoor-oriented, upwardly mobile young males."

As light as its treatment of the subject, this *New Yorker* cartoon takes one step that is rare among the many uses of the figure of Sirens: it shows a glimpse of the Siren's inner self, allowing us to overhear language she directs at an audience other than her victims. Here the focus of a reader is upon the Siren herself, a rare occurrence.[34] Always before the twentieth century, whether the source is classical, medieval, or modern, and whether the poet is a man or a woman, the focus is upon the man who must confront and somehow best the Siren, and our sympathy and interest are presumed to lie with him. Indeed, the masculine point of view is assumed to be a universal one.

"*Basically, we're aiming at an audience of adventuresome, outdoor-oriented, upwardly mobile young males.*"

Fig. 2: Drawing by D. Reilly; © 1991 *The New Yorker Magazine*, Inc.

Even in the twentieth century, when almost everything else about this image undergoes change, the view of Siren as Other predominates. Two sonnets, one by C. Day Lewis, the other by John Manifold, may serve as examples. In Lewis's "Nearing Again the Legendary Isle,"[35] the weary wayfarers who give the first-person account feel no temptation.

Everyone in the poem feels instead the ravages of "gnawing" time: the Sirens appear as "chorus-girls ... surely past their prime" (5)[36] and the speakers are too exhausted to do anything more than mock the idea of an appeal to their numbed senses. Even the day is near its end. In Manifold's "The Sirens,"[37] a wayfarer may feel temptation but is soon distracted. The octet begins with what Odysseus hears, the sestet with what Odysseus sees of the Sirens. In both parts anachronistic elements call attention to the fact that this world is a contemporary one, not Homer's. The troubles of such a world are so immediate and so pressing that Odysseus can hear the Sirens sing madrigals of Thomas Morley or *Lieder* of Hugo Wolf and in twenty minutes forget them. The appearance, the songs, and the power of the Sirens all change, but the Sirens themselves remain the female antagonists whom the male protagonist must confront.[38]

A notable exception to the masculine point of view is "Siren Song" by Margaret Atwood,[39] a poem of nine three-line stanzas. Here only the middle section (stanzas 4 through 8 plus part of the following line) contains the second person—presumably singular—pronoun "you"; only this section is necessarily addressed to the intended victim. Before and after the middle section and enclosing it come lines of statement that could, perhaps, be addressed to the "you" of the middle section but all or part of them could also be either soliloquy or addressed to some unnamed third party. In all three sections the focus is on the Siren and her song, not the adventurer who is tempted by it.

> This is the one song everyone
> would like to learn: the song
> that is irresistible .... (1–3)

The word *song* appears in the first line of each of the opening three stanzas (1, 4, 7), and three more times (2, 21, 26), along with *singing* (17), before the end of the poem. The Siren describes her song as "fatal and valuable" (18) and, in the middle section, she gives the reader an example of such a song. Atwood remains faithful to the details of the classical myth: the three Sirens (although Homer mentions two[40]) are bird-like creatures[41] located on an island littered with "beached skulls" and they sing an irresistible song that ends in death for all who hear it.

The song that is reproduced in the poem itself is remarkable for its contemporary language and the clarity with which the Siren sees much of her situation:

> Shall I tell you the secret
> and if I do, will you get me
> out of this bird suit?
>
> I don't enjoy it here
> squatting on this island
> looking picturesque and mythical .... (10–16)

One cannot imagine that the Siren's song would have been irresistible had it remained always in this vein, but subsequent stanzas shift into flattery, claiming that the hearer, who hears the word *you* six times in six lines, is "unique":

> you are unique
>
> at last. Alas
> it is a boring song
> but it works every time. (24–27)

"Unique/ at last" is, alas, a lie, and the idea that the Siren herself feels lonely and bored, simultaneously victimizer and victim,[42] comes as a revelation. Nowhere else, I think, do we so effectively learn how the Siren feels about her circumstance. Trapped in a role predetermined by a mythological tradition that focuses on a male hero, the female Other is left only the roles of helpless heroine or monster. The Siren as female Other always seems monstrous because she uses her voice, in this case the prerogative of song, in destructive ways.[43] The fact that there is a radical difference between what her song says and what it does only increases the irony.[44] Atwood can simultaneously make us feel the pull of the Siren as archetype and help us feel compassion for the Siren as a sentient, suffering individual.

Another contemporary poet who allows the reader to see events from the point of view of the Sirens is Donald Finkel, but in "The

Sirens"[45] this new perspective only reinforces the traditional image of these female monsters. Here the Sirens are too "busy with the fugue" (12) to bother to observe Odysseus' agony. And besides, they have no need to do so, knowing not only what happened as he sailed past but also what he continues to endure because of the experience:

> Now in a sea
>
> of wheat he rows, reconstructing.
> In his ridiculous, lovely mouth the strains
> Tumble into place. Do you think
> Wax could have stopped us, or chains?   (15–19)

In the very process of rewriting the conclusion of Odysseus' journey, Finkel reinforces the archetype of Sirens as fatal seductresses by suggesting that Odysseus only appeared to have escaped. His ability to pass their bone-circled island physically is unimportant because he remains psychologically trapped in the snare of their song.

But is the Siren's role predetermined by the mythological tradition? From the evidence one can argue either yes or no. In support of an affirmative response there are critics who maintain that one method "to affirm male space over female space, to affirm the conviction that 'nothing can change'" is to appeal to the authority of classical mythology.[46] Mythology affirms stasis because of its stories, which cannot be rewritten. In an Atwood prose poem sequence "Circe/Mud Poems," the goddess's words support the argument for stasis when she says, "Don't evade, don't pretend you won't leave after all: you leave in the story and story is ruthless."[47] On the other hand, support for the idea that the Siren's role is not predetermined by the mythological tradition is also present. In the extreme case we can point to examples of revisionist mythologies that write stories as the author wishes them to be rather than the way in which they have come down to us.[48] An extreme but not isolated case of this practice is found in Hélène Cixous's "The Laugh of the Medusa"[49]

> Wouldn't the worst be, isn't the worst, in truth, that
> women aren't castrated, that they have only to stop

> listening to the Sirens (for the Sirens are men) for history to change its meaning? You only have to look at the Medusa straight on to see her. And she's not deadly. She's beautiful and she's laughing. (885)

But not all revisions of this image go to the extreme of seeing the Sirens as men. Less extreme cases of revisionist mythology occur in any literary work in which the image of Siren is seen afresh—as it is in Arnold, Atwood, and others—rather than seen as a simplistic shorthand for an easily categorized, static, two-dimensional female seductress, a convenient stereotype.

Another example of the richness of the image of Siren comes in a poem by Joyce Carol Oates that is almost contemporaneous with Atwood's Siren poem. In "The Sirens,"[50] Oates recasts the images of rocks and sea, male and female, language and betrayal, in a context set in a library. The siren is wordless (and lacking an upper-case letter) but the narrator says of her, "Oh it is my truest self" (23) because an inarticulate siren resides within the body of every woman in the library who confronts "civilization/like a hill of rocks/in a sea" (5–7). Once again, as in Atwood's "Siren Song," the focus is on the female speaker. For Oates, however, the Siren inside the speaker is without voice because civilization, time, and language are all pervasively male-centered. This internal Siren, the poet's "truest self," is silenced as effectively as is Auden's songless but otherwise stereotypical Siren.

Both Atwood and Oates shift the point of view from that of the adventurer/hero to that of the Siren herself. Just that shift in point of view does not, however, resolve the problems associated with the role that has been traditionally assigned to the Sirens. Revisioning of the whole context, perhaps along the lines of that suggested by Cixous, would be necessary for that. Indeed, Cixous's idea that the Sirens are really men appears in a recent *New Yorker* cartoon featuring a determined woman and a grinning bird with the face—and necktie—of a man. But no seduction occurs. The woman greets the bird-man with the pithy rejoinder, "Forget it" (fig. 3).

"Forget it."

Fig. 3: Drawing by C. Barsotti; © 1991 *The New Yorker Magazine*, Inc.

Yet another example of role reversals occurs in Marilyn Hacker's sonnet "Mythology,"[51] published in 1986. Penelope is a *"garçon manqué"* weaving sonnets, Persephone is a "Telemaque-who-tagged-along," and Ulysse-Maman

> plugs into the Shirelles[52] singing her song
> ("What Does a Girl Do?"). (8–9)

Hacker posits here a cast of human characters who have all switched gender. In this world with a female hero, the Siren figures sing a song that asks a question rather than promises to bestow knowledge.[53] To the Siren/Shirelles' question, the narrator is the one with at least a partial answer:

> ("What Does a Girl Do?") What *does* a girl do
> but walk across the world, her kid in tow,

stopping at stations on the way, with friends
to tie her to the mast when she gets too
close to the edge? And when the voyage ends,
what does a girl do? Girl, that's up to you.   (9–14)

Both the solution to the question of what a girl protagonist might do and expressions of the consequences of those deeds remain open-ended in this poem. As Hacker reminds us, "Ours/is not the high-school text" (3–4). In her poem, as in the *New Yorker* cartoon (fig. 3) and in Cixous's "Laugh of the Medusa," the traditional point of view has shifted, as have the roles of singer and listener, monster and hero, victimizer and potential victim. But the more things change, the more they may stay the same. Even when the point of view shifts to the Siren herself (as in Atwood), or when the gender roles of all human characters are reversed (as in Hacker),[54] the relationship between singer and listener remains polarized—antagonistic and dangerous.[55] We may understand more about the dynamics of human relationships as a result of this gender awareness, but there is no concomitant resolution to the problems presented by the situation. The voice of the Other, however defined, remains simultaneously alluring, antagonistic, dangerous.

It is impossible to predict how poets, both male and female, may use the image of Sirens in future works of literature. It is, however, possible to look back over the past two centuries and anticipate that future uses of this image will be as provocative, numerous, and diverse as its past uses. Our traditional view of Sirens, the first source of which is that wily sophist Odysseus, is no longer the only view. This archetype continues to provide for us new songs alongside the old ones.

Elizabeth A. Holtze
Metropolitan State College of Denver

Notes

For the quotation by Sir Thomas Browne, for the information that the "'puzzling questions" alluded to were first enunciated by Tiberius (see Suetonius, *Tiberius* 70), and for many other thoughtful suggestions, I wish to thank Mary DeForest. I also owe a debt of gratitude to Hannah Kelminson of the University of Colorado-Denver for close reading of and helpful direction on this paper; and to the Denver Area Teaching and Research Colloquium, where I presented an earlier draft of this work.

[1] E.g., Μῆνιν ἄειδε, θεά, Πηληϊάδεω 'Αχιλῆος, "Sing, goddess, the anger of Peleus' son Achilleus," (Homer, *Il.* 1.1, trans. Richmond Lattimore [Chicago, 1951], 59).

[2] Medusa is another female monster who exerts a continuing fascination. See, for example, poems entitled "Medusa" by Louise Bogan, Rachel Blau DuPlessis, Vincent O'Sullivan, and Sylvia Plath; poems entitled "Perseus" by Robert Hayden and Louis MacNeice; other poems such as "The Medusa" by Guy Davenport, "Medusa's Hair Was Snakes. Was Thought, Split Inward," by Kathleen Fraser, "Near the Ocean" by Robert Lowell, "Aspecta Medusa" by Dante Gabriel Rossetti, "The Muse as Medusa" by May Sarton, "On the Medusa of Leonardo da Vinci in the Florentine Gallery" by Percy Bysshe Shelley, "Women of Perseus" by Ann Stanford, "Head of Medusa" by Marya Zaturenska; "Persiad," the middle of three sections of the novel *Chimera* by John Barth; "The Laugh of the Medusa" by Hélène Cixous, *Signs*, 1 (1976), 875–99; and criticism such as Annis V. Pratt's "'Aunt Jennifer's Tigers': Notes towards a Preliterary History of Women's Archetypes," *Feminist Studies*, 4 (1978), 163–94, and Karin Elias-Button's "The Muse as Medusa" in *The Lost Tradition*, ed. Cathy Davidson and E. M. Broner (New York, 1980), 193–206.

Other winged female monsters include Gorgons, Harpies, the Sphinx, and the Erinyes, whose similar characteristics are discussed on 415ff. of Henry Alden Bunker's "The Voice as (Female) Phallus," *The Psychoanalytic Quarterly*, 3 (1934), 391–429.

[3] Pietro Pucci, "The Song of the Sirens," 126–28 in *Arethusa*, 12 (Fall 1979), 121–32, enumerates the ways in which the Sirens are like the Muses. J. R. T. Pollard, "Muses and Sirens," *CR*, 11 New Series (June 1952), 60–63, refutes the arguments of Buschor (*Die Musen des Jenseits*, Munich, 1944) that the Sirens were an underworld double of the heavenly Muses. W. Compton Leith, *Sirenica* (London, 1924), says, "The Muses and the Sirens together mean all art and the Sirens alone romance" (170).

[4] Like the Sirens, both Circe and Calypso have inspired authors since the classical era. See the poems entitled "Circe" by Lord De Tabley, William Gibson, H. D., A. D. Hope, Richard Kell, Louis MacNeice, and Beulah May; other poems entitled "The Strayed Reveller" by Matthew Arnold, "Circe/Mud Poems" by Margaret Atwood, "Ulysses and Circe" by Robert Lowell; the description of Circe and the Italianate gentleman in "The First Book for the Youth" from *The Schoolmaster* by Roger Ascham; the short story "Circe" by Eudora Welty; and "Circe's Palace" from *Tanglewood Tales* by Nathaniel Hawthorne. See, also, poems "Calypso Speaks" by H. D., "Calypso's Island"

by Archibald MacLeish, and "Calypso's Song to Ulysses" by Adrian Mitchell.

[5] Their allure is, in fact, so great that wayfarers willingly risk—indeed endure—death in order to hear it. As great as the admiration may be for the songs of Phemius (*Od.* 1.325–27), Demodocus (*Od.* 8.72–82, 266–367, 499–521), or Odysseus himself (*Od.* Books 9–12), the listeners render up tears and tripods, not their lives.

[6] Diane Purkiss, "Women's Rewriting of Myth," in *The Feminist Companion to Mythology*, ed. Carolyne Larrington (London, 1992), reviews a number of recent rewritings, focusing on the theoretical difficulties and concluding with the suggestion "that *no* possible strategy of rewriting myth or anything else can really constitute the kind of absolute, clean and revolutionary break with discourse and order sought in the days of feminism and poststructuralism's greatest confidence" (455).

[7] For sources of Sirens from Homer through the Renaissance, I am indebted to Jane Ellen Harrison's *Myths of the Odyssey in Art and Literature* (London, 1882) and Siegfried de Rachewiltz' *De Sirenibus: An Inquiry into Sirens from Homer to Shakespeare* (New York, 1987).

[8] W. B. Stanford, *The Ulysses Theme*, 2d ed. (Ann Arbor, 1968), 76–78, maintains that the Sirens, combining flattery and the lure of knowledge through the medium of song, tailor their temptation specifically for Ulysses: "If an Agamemnon or a Menelaus had been in his place, they might have changed their tune" (78).

[9] E.g., "Siren" by David Williamson and "Siren Tears" by Veronica Francis.

[10] David Beaty, *The Siren Song* (London, 1964); Sarah Caudwell, *The Sirens Sang of Murder* (New York, 1989); Heather Graham, *Siren from the Sea* (New York, 1987); Kathryn Kramer, *Siren Song* (New York, 1990); Stephen Pett, *Sirens* (New York, 1990); Leslie Stone, *Siren Song* (New York, 1985); Kurt Vonnegut, Jr., *The Sirens of Titan* (1959; rpt. New York, 1974); Irving Wallace, *The Three Sirens* (New York, 1963).

[11] "Sirens without Sound" by Andrew Sarris, *Village Voice*, 33 (11 October 1988), 76, profiles Clara Bow. "Siren Songs at Center Stage" by Michael Walsh, *Time*, 131 (11 April 1988), 104–8+, discusses a group of female violinists.

[12] Maurice Blanchot, *The Sirens' Song: Selected Essays of Maurice Blanchot*, ed. Gabriel Josipovici, trans. Sacha Rabinovitch (Bloomington, 1982); Jimmie E. Cain, Jr. "Women: The Siren Calls of Boredom" *The Review of Contemporary Fiction*, 5 (1985), 9–14.

[13] Charles Ritchie, *The Siren Years: Undiplomatic Diaries: 1937–1945* (London, 1974).

[14] Edward John Moreton Drax Plunkett, Lord Dunsany, *The Sirens Wake*

(London, 1945).

[15] Norman Douglas, *Siren Land*, rev. ed. (New York, 1923). Among other things, Douglas tells anecdotes about the Sirens and the Emperor Tiberius (7, 71ff.), geographically locates the home of the Sirens (270ff. and elsewhere), and reproduces a dialogue among three prehistoric human beings: the hapless sailor, the seductive—and human—Siren, and her cannibal mate:

> Sailor: Opopoi! I do begin to fear mightily. How he rolls his eye under those cavernous brows; and she, with wolfish clashings of teeth—Ai, Ai! Papaiax—they seize me—attatai, papai, pai, io, moi, moi, omoi, otototoi—
> Woman: They [the sailor and other wayfarers] sing wrong.
> Man: They eat right. (274)

[16] Chris Achilleos, *Sirens: Women of Fantasy Art* (United Kingdom, 1988).

[17] Jon Elster, *Ulysses and the Sirens: Studies in Rationality and Irrationality*, rev. ed. (New York, 1984).

[18] Matthew Arnold, "The New Sirens" in *The Poems of Matthew Arnold* (London, 1979), 50–58.

[19] E.g., Warren D. Anderson, *Matthew Arnold and the Classical Tradition* (Ann Arbor, 1965), 20.

[20] Of Circe in "The Strayed Reveller," Anderson, *Matthew Arnold and the Classical Tradition*, says, "But Arnold has not merely conventionalized his classical subject and made it Victorian. He has sought unconsciously to weaken its force, as in so many other instances, and thereby he reveals a characteristic which is primarily personal" (26).

[21] Some critics see these new Sirens as still powerful. Lionel Trilling, for example, *Matthew Arnold*, 2d ed. (New York, 1949), says of them, "They are gentler and more lawful, if actually no less dangerous ..."(101).

[22] William E. Buckler, *On the Poetry of Matthew Arnold* (New York, 1982), 44.

[23] George Saintsbury, *Matthew Arnold* (1899; rpt. New York, 1967), was one of Arnold's early critics. In the most extraordinary mixture of praise and censure, he described the verse form thus:

> The scheme is trochaic, and Mr. Arnold ... was happier than most poets with that charming but difficult foot. The note is the old one of yearning rather than passionate melancholy, applied in a new way and put most clearly, though by no means most poetically, in the lines—

> Can men worship the wan features,
> The sunk eyes, the wailing tone,
> Of unsphered, discrowned creatures,
> Souls as little godlike as their own?
>
> The answer is, "No," of course; but, as someone informed Mr. Arnold many years later, we knew that before, and it is distressing to be told it, as we are a little later, with a rhyme of "dawning" and "morning." Yet the poem is a very beautiful one .... (18)

[24] Dante Gabriel Rossetti, "The Doom of the Sirens," in *The Works of Dante Gabriel Rossetti* (London, 1911), 610–13. For a discussion of Rossetti's libretto and his pastel drawing *Ligeia Siren*, see Dianne Sachko Macleod's "Rossetti's Two Ligeias: Their Relationship to Visual Art, Music, and Poetry," *Victorian Poetry*, 20 (Autumn—Winter 1982), 89–102.

[25] Quoted in Arnold, *The Poems of Matthew Arnold*, 49.

[26] James Russell Lowell, "The Sirens," in *The Poetical Works of James Russell Lowell* (Boston, 1978), 2–3.

[27] Mary E. Hewitt, "Myth," in *Poems: Sacred, Passionate, and Legendary* (New York, 1853), 172–78.

[28] Laurence Binyon, "The Sirens," in *Collected Poems of Laurence Binyon* (London, 1931), 323–51.

[29] Robert Graves, "Ulysses," in *Collected Poems* (Garden City, 1961), 97.

[30] W. H. Auden, "Lord Byron," in *Academic Graffiti*, illus. Filippo Sanjust (New York, 1972), #11.

[31] Gavin Ewart, "Introduction" to *The Complete Clerihews of E. Clerihew Bentley* (New York, 1981) xii–xv.

[32] John G. Blair, *The Poetic Art of W. H. Auden* (Princeton, 1965), quotes Auden's "Letter to Lord Byron" (*Letters from Iceland*, 202) as proof of the poet's admiration of light verse:

> You must ask me who
> Have written just as I'd have liked to do.
> I stop to listen and the names I hear
> Are those of Firbank, Potter, Carroll, Lear. (128)

[33] A statement by Auden about his own art quoted by Marianne Moore, "W. H. Auden," in *Auden: A Collection of Critical Essays*, ed. Monroe K. Spears (Englewood Cliffs, 1964), 52.

[34] Thom Gunn performed a similar shift of focus in his poem "Moly," in

Moly and My Sad Captains (New York, 1973), 6–7, in which the speaker is one of Odysseus' men recently transformed by Circe and yearning to be human again:

> From this fat dungeon I could rise to skin
> And human title, putting pig within.   (25–26)

John Gardner also shifted focus when he wrote *Grendel* (New York, 1971), a novel told from the point of view of the monster of the same name, not the traditional hero, Beowulf.

[35] C. Day Lewis, "Nearing Again the Legendary Isle," in *Modern British Poetry* (New York, 1962), 421–22.

[36] Another contemporary poem in which the Sirens appear aged is Edwin Arlington Robinson's "Veteran Sirens," in *The New Oxford Book of American Verse*, ed. Richard Ellmann (New York, 1976), 385–86.

[37] John Manifold, "The Sirens," in *Modern British Poetry* (New York, 1962), 513.

[38] Two additional contemporary examples of Sirens as Other can be found in Elliot Coleman's "Sirens," in *From A to Z: 200 Contemporary American Poets* (Chicago, 1981), 33, and Donald Finkel's "The Siren of Solitude," in *The Wake of the Electron* (New York, 1987), 28.

[39] Margaret Atwood, "Siren Song," in *Selected Poems* (Toronto, 1976), 195–96.

[40] Harrison, *Myths of the Odyssey*, 150–51 and figure 37, and de Rachewiltz, *De Sirenibus*, 263 and figure 2, reproduce a red-figure vase painting from an amphora of the fifth century, now in the British Museum, that shows three Sirens with female heads attached to the bodies of birds; De Rachewiltz names the three Sirens who were worshiped on the southern Tyrrhenian coast of Italy: Parthenope, Leucosia, Ligeia (55).

[41] Sharon R. Wilson, "Sexual Politics in Atwood's Visual Art," in *Margaret Atwood: Vision and Forms*, ed. Kathryn VanSpanckeren and Jan Garden Castro (Carbondale, 1988), 205–14, discusses an untitled watercolor, archive-labeled "Atwoods as Birds," 1974, signed (pl. 8). Wilson recounts that Atwood in a taped interview identified the three figures in the watercolor as a mother harpy and chicks because she "is interested in the idea of women (chicks) as birds" (212). I would like to suggest an additional allusion—Atwoods as Sirens. The figures in the watercolor resemble in number and shape both the Sirens on a fifth-century amphora cited by de Rachewiltz and the Sirens in Atwood's "Siren Song." Atwood published "Siren Song" in *You Are Happy* in 1974, the same year the watercolor was painted. The coincidence seems remarkable. As Wilson says, "Like Atwood's poetry and fiction, the watercol-

ors present recurrent, archetypal images of power politics, in which women and men may not only oppose but also represent aspects of one another, playing roles evoking fairy tales, gothic stories, myths, television, comic books, and nursery rhymes" (208).

[42] David Buchbinder, "Weaving Her Version: The Homeric Model and Gender Politics in *Selected Poems*," in *Margaret Atwood: Vision and Forms*, ed. Kathryn VanSpanckeren and Jan Garden Castro (Carbondale, 1988), 122–41, discusses both the Siren and Circe in the double role of victim and victimizer.

[43] Alicia Suskin Ostriker, *Stealing the Language: The Emergence of Women's Poetry in America* (Boston, 1986), sees the situation in a related but different way: "What Atwood implies, as do other women who examine the blackness that has represented femaleness so often in our culture, is that the female power to do evil is a direct function of her powerlessness to do anything else" (222).

[44] On this point, see Buchbinder, "Weaving her Version," 128–29.

[45] Donald Finkel, "The Sirens," in *New Poets of England and America* (Cleveland, 1957), 66.

[46] Frank Davey, *Margaret Atwood: A Feminist Poetics* (Vancouver, 1984), 21.

[47] Atwood, *Selected Poems*, 221.

[48] Numerous scholars have investigated the ways in which Hesiod and other classical authors rewrote mythology, e.g., Michael Gagarin's "'Flow Backward Sacred Rivers': Tradition and Change in the Classics," *CJ*, 87 (1992), 361–71. Today rewriting the traditional stories continues in works such as Hélène Cixous's *The Book of Promethea*, trans. and intro. Betsy Wing (Lincoln, 1991) and Monique Wittig's *Les Guérillères*, trans. David Le Vay (1971; rpt. Boston, 1985). For a similar development in the field of fairy tales, see Anne Sexton's *Transformations* in *Complete Poems* (Boston, 1981) 221–95, and Wolfgang Mieder's *Disenchantments: An Anthology of Modern Fairy Tale Poetry* (Hanover, 1985).

[49] Hélène Cixous, "The Laugh of the Medusa," trans. Keith Cohen and Paula Cohen, *Signs*, 1 (1976), 875–99.

[50] Joyce Carol Oates, "The Sirens," in *Love and Its Derangements* (Baton Rouge, 1970), 8–9.

[51] Marilyn Hacker, "Mythology," in *Love, Death, and the Changing of the Seasons* (New York, 1986), 48.

[52] The three Shirelles released "What Does a Girl Do" in September of 1963. The song was in the top 100 hits for five weeks, but never above 56. See Frank Hoffmann, comp., *The Cash Box Singles Charts, 1950–1981* (Metuchen, 1983), 534.

[53] What we have seen in Atwood's "Siren's Song" and Hacker's "Mythol-

ogy" are techniques that Rachael Blau DuPlessis, *Writing beyond the Ending: Narrative Strategies of Twentieth-Century Women Writers* (Bloomington, 1985), calls "displacement" and "delegitimation": displacement in Atwood's "Siren Song" and both displacement and delegitimation in Hacker's "Mythology." DuPlessis explains, "Narrative displacement is like breaking into the sentence, because it offers the possibility of speech to the female in the case, giving voice to the muted. Narrative delegitimation "breaks the sequence": a realigment that puts the last first and the first last has always ruptured conventional morality, politics, and narrative" (108).

[54] The difficulty of the Sirens remaining female when all other characters switch gender dissolves if this text and a second sonnet, "La Sirène," published on the facing page (49) of the same volume, are read from the point of view of a lesbian speaker.

[55] Antagonism and tension remain as long as the duality of singer and listener remain. Lou Lipsitz, "The Sirens," in *Leaving the Bough: 50 American Poets of the 80s*, ed. Roger Gaess (New York, 1982), 98, removes the violence by removing the antagonist. His Sirens exchange their songs directed toward others for conversations among themselves as they collect rocks, carve, and tie fish nets (18–25).

Select Bibliography

Alic, Margaret. *Hypatia's Heritage: A History of Women in Science from Antiquity through the Nineteenth Century*. Boston, 1986.
Arthur, Marilyn B. "Cultural Strategies in Hesiod's *Theogony*: Law, Family, Society." *Arethusa*, 15.1/2 (1982): 63–82.
———. "The Dream of a World Without Women: Poetics and the Circles of Order in the *Theogony* Proemium." *Arethusa*, 16 (1983): 97–116.
———. "Early Greece: The Origins of the Western Attitude Toward Women." In *Women in the Ancient World*, 7–58. See under Peradotto and Sullivan.
———. "From Medusa to Cleopatra: Women in the Ancient World." In *Becoming Visible: Women in European History*, edited by Renate Bridenthal, Claudia Koonz, and Susan Stuard, 79–105. 2d edition. Boston, 1987.
———. "Politics and Pomegranates: An Interpretation of the *Homeric Hymn to Demeter*." *Arethusa*, 10 (1977): 7–47.
———. "The Tortoise and the Mirror: Erinna PSI 1090." *CW*, 74 (1980): 53–65.
Babcock, Charles L. "The Early Career of Fulvia." *AJP*, 86.1 (1965): 1–32.
Balsdon, J. P. V. D. "Cleopatra." *CR*, n.s. 10 (1960): 68–71.
Barnard, S. "Hellenistic Women Poets." *CJ*, 73 (1978): 208–10.
Bergren, Ann L. T. "Language and the Female in Early Greek Thought." *Arethusa*, 16 (1983): 69–95.
Blok, Josine, and Peter Mason, eds. *Sexual Asymmetry: Studies in Ancient Society*. Amsterdam, 1987.
Bonnafé, Annie. *Eros et Eris. Mariages divins et mythe de succession chez Hésiode*. Lyon, 1985.
Bremen, Riet Van. "Women and Wealth." In *Images of Women in Antiquity*, edited by Averil Cameron and Amélie Kuhrt, 223–42. London, 1983.
Brownmiller, Susan. *Against Our Will: Men, Women, and Rape*. New York, 1975.
Buchbinder, David. "Weaving Her Version: The Homeric Model and Gender Politics in *Selected Poems*." In *Margaret Atwood: Vision and Forms*, edited by Kathryn VanSpanckeren and Jan Garden Castro1, 22–41. Carbondale, 1988.
Calame, Claude. *Les choeurs de jeunes filles en Grèce archaïque*. 2 vols. Rome, 1977.
Cantarella, Eva. *Pandora's Daughters*. Translated by Maureen B. Fant. Baltimore, 1987.

Carcopino, J. "César et Cléopâtre." *Annales de l'École des Hautes-Études de Gand*, 1 (1937): 37–77.
Carson, Anne. "Putting Her in Her Place: Woman, Dirt, and Desire." In *Before Sexuality*, 137–45. See under Halperin, Winkler, and Zeitlin.
Christ, Carol, and Judith Plaskow, eds. *Womanspirit Rising: A Feminist Reader in Religion*. New York, 1979.
Churchill, Laurie J. "Magisterial Voice and the Pleasure of the Text: Irony in the *Ars Amatoria*." *Pacific Coast Philology*, 20 (1985): 33–38.
Cixous, Hélène. *The Book of Promethea*. Translated by Betsy Wing. Lincoln, 1991.
———. "The Laugh of the Medusa." Translated by Keith Cohen and Paula Cohen. *Signs*, 1 (1976): 875–99.
Clay, Jenny Strauss. *The Politics of Olympus: Form and Meaning in the Major Homeric Hymns*. Princeton, 1989.
Culham, P. "Ten Years after Pomeroy: Studies of the Image and Reality of Women in Antiquity." In *Rescuing Creusa*, 9–30. See under Skinner.
Cunningham, M. "Medea APO MHCANHS." *CP*, 49 (1954): 151–60.
Curran, L. "'Nature to Advantage Dressed': Propertius 1.2." *Ramus*, 4 (1975): 1–16.
———. "Rape and Rape Victim in the *Metamorphoses*." *Arethusa*, 11 (1978): 213–41.
Currie, H. MacL. "The Poems of Sulpicia." *Aufstieg und Niedergang der römischen Welt*, 2.30.3 (1983): 1751–64.
D'Avino, Michele. *The Women of Pompeii*. Translated by Monica H. Jones and Luigi Nusco. Naples, 1967.
Deichgraber. "Metrodora." *RE*, 15 (1932): 1474.
Delcourt, Marie. *Hermaphrodite: Myths and Rites of the Bisexual Figure in Classical Antiquity*. London, 1961.
Dexter, Miriam Robbins. *Whence the Goddesses: A Source Book*. New York, 1990.
Dixon, Suzanne. "Conclusion—The Enduring Theme: Domineering Dowagers and Scheming Concubines." In *Stereotypes of Women in Power*, 209–25. See under Garlick, Dixon, and Allen.
———. "A Family Business: Women's Role in Patronage and Politics at Rome 80–44 B.C." *Classica et Medievalia*, 34 (1983): 91–112.
Dubisch, Jill, ed. *Gender and Power in Rural Greece*. Princeton, 1986.
duBois, Page. *Centaurs and Amazons: Women and the Pre-History of the Great Chain of Being*. Ann Arbor, 1982.
———. *Sowing the Body: Psychoanalysis and Ancient Representations of Women*. Chicago, 1988.
Dunn, Francis. "The Battle of the Sexes in Euripides' *Ion*." *Critical Studies in*

Greek and Roman Literature, 19 (1990): 130–42.
DuPlessis, Rachael Blau. *Writing beyond the Ending: Narrative Strategies of Twentieth-Century Women Writers*. Bloomington, 1985.
Easterling, P. E. *Sophocles: Trachiniae*. Cambridge, 1982.
Ehrenberg, Margaret. *Women in Prehistory*. Norman, 1989.
Elias-Button, Karin. "The Muse as Medusa." In *The Lost Tradition*, edited by Cathy Davidson and E. M. Broner, 193–206. New York, 1980.
Foley, Helene P. "'Reverse Similes' and Sex Roles in the *Odyssey*." *Arethusa*, 11 (1978): 7–26.
———, ed. *Reflections of Women in Antiquity*. New York, 1981.
Forbis, Elizabeth P. "Women's Public Image in Italian Honorary Inscriptions." *AJP*, 111.4 (1990): 493–512.
Friedl, Ernestine. 1967. "The Position of Women: Appearance and Reality." *Anthropological Quarterly*, 40 (1967): 97–108. Reprinted in *Gender and Power*, 42–52. See under Dubisch.
Gagarin, Michael. "'Flow Backward Sacred Rivers': Tradition and Change in the Classics." *CJ*, 87 (1992): 361–71.
Garlick, Barbara, Suzanne Dixon, and Pauline Allen, eds. *Stereotypes of Women in Power: Historical Perspectives and Revisionist Views*. New York, 1991.
Gilligan, Carol. *In a Different Voice: Psychological Theory and Women's Development*. Cambridge, 1982.
Gimbutas, Marija. *The Goddesses and Gods of Old Europe, 6500–3500 B.C.: Myths and Cult Images*. Berkeley, 1982.
———. *The Language of the Goddess*. London, 1989.
Göttner-Abendroth, Heide. *Matriarchal Mythology in Former Times and Today*. Translated by Lise Weil. Freedom, 1987.
Gold, Barbara K. "But Ariadne was Never There in the First Place: Finding the Female in Roman Poetry." In *Feminist Theory and the Classics*. See under Richlin and Rabinowitz.
———. "Dionysus, Greek Festivals, and the Treatment of Hysteria." *Laetaberis*, 6 (1988): 16–28.
Goodwater, L. *Women in Antiquity: An Annotated Bibliography*. Metuchen, 1975.
Gould, J. "Law, Custom and Myth: Aspects of the Social Position of Women in Classical Athens." *Journal of Hellenic Studies*, 100 (1980): 38–59.
Griffin, Susan. *Woman and Nature*. New York, 1980.
Hall, Nor. *The Moon and the Virgin: Reflections on the Archetypal Feminine*. New York, 1980.
Hallett, Judith K. "Classics and Women's Studies." Working Paper No. 119, *Wellesley College Center for Research on Women*. Wellesley College, 1983.

———. "Contextualizing the Text: The Journey to Ovid." *Helios*, 17.2 (1990): 187–95.
———. *Fathers and Daughters in Roman Society: Women and the Elite Family*. Princeton, 1984.
———. "The Role of Women in Roman Elegy: Counter-Cultural Feminism." *Arethusa*, 6.1 (1973): 103–24. Reprinted in *Women in the Ancient World*, 241–62. See under Peradotto and Sullivan.
———. "Sappho and her Social Context." *Signs*, 4 (1979): 447–64.
———. "Women as *Same* and *Other* in the Classical Roman Elite." *Helios*, 16.1 (1989): 59–78.
Halperin, D. M., J. J. Winkler, and F. I. Zeitlin, eds. *Before Sexuality*. Princeton, 1990.
Hanson, A. E. "Continuity and Change: Three Case Studies in Hippocratic Gynecological Therapy and Theory." In *Women's History and Ancient History*, 73–110. See under Pomeroy.
———. "Hippocrates: Diseases of Women 1." *Signs*, 1 (1975): 567–84.
———. "The Medical Writers' Woman." In *Before Sexuality*, 309–38. See under Halperin, Winkler, and Zeitlin.
Harrison, Jane Ellen. *Myths of the Odyssey in Art and Literature*. London, 1882.
Heilbrun, Carolyn. *Toward a Recognition of Androgyny*. New York, 1973.
———. *Writing a Woman's Life*. New York, 1988.
Henderson, Jeffrey. "Women and the Athenian Dramatic Festivals." *TAPA*, 121 (1991): 133–47.
Herfst, Pieter. *Le Travail de la Femme dans la Grèce Ancienne*. Utrecht, 1922.
Herrmann, C. *Les Voleuses de Langue*. Paris, 1976.
Hillard, Tom. "On the Stage, Behind the Curtain: Images of Politically Active Women in the Late Roman Republic." In *Stereotypes of Women in Power*, 37–64. See under Garlick, Dixon, and Allen.
Hinds, Stephen. "The Poetess and the Reader: Further Steps toward Sulpicia." *Hermathena*, 143 (Winter 1987): 29–46.
Humphreys, Sally. *Anthropology and the Greeks*. London, 1978.
Hunter, Virginia. "Women's Authority in Classical Athens." *Échos du Monde Classique/ Classical Views*, 33 (1989): 39–48.
Jenkyns, R. *Three Classical Poets: Sappho, Catullus and Juvenal*. Cambridge, 1982.
Judeich. *Aspasia*. RE, 2, 1716–18.
Jung, C. G. *The Archetypes and the Collective Unconscious*. Translated by R. F. C. Hull. Bollingen 20. *Collected Works* 9, Part 1. 2d ed. Princeton, 1968.
———, and Carl Kerényi. *Essays on a Science of Mythology: The Myth of the Divine Child and the Mysteries of Eleusis*. Translated by R. F. C. Hull. Bollingen 22. Princeton, 1963.
Just, Roger. *Women in Athenian Law and Life*. London, 1989.

Katz, Marylin A. *Penelope's Renown: Meaning and Indeterminacy in the Odyssey.* Princeton, 1991.
Kelly, Joan. *Women, History and Theory.* Chicago, 1984.
Kerényi, Carl. *Eleusis: Archetypal Image of Mother and Daughter.* Translated by Ralph Manheim. Bollingen 65. 1962; rpt. New York, 1967.
———. *Zeus and Hera: Archetypal Image of Father, Husband and Wife.* Princeton, 1975.
Keuls, Eva C. *The Reign of the Phallus: Sexual Politics in Ancient Athens.* New York, 1985.
Knox, B. M. W. "The *Medea* of Euripides." In his *Word and Action: Essays on the Ancient Theater,* 295–322. Baltimore, 1979.
Kunstler, Barton. "Family Dynamics and Female Power in Ancient Sparta." In *Rescuing Creusa,* 31–48. See under Skinner.
Lacey, W. K. *The Family in Classical Greece.* Ithaca, 1968.
Lakoff, Robin. *Language and Women's Place.* New York, 1975.
Lauter, Estella, and Carol Schreier Rupprecht, eds. *Feminist Archetypal Theory: Interdisciplinary Re-Visions of Jungian Thought.* Knoxville, 1985.
Lefkowitz, Mary R. *Women in Greek Myth.* Baltimore, 1986.
———, and M. B. Fant. *Women's Lives in Greece and Rome: A Source Book in Translation.* Baltimore, 1982.
Leith, W. Compton. *Sirenica.* London, 1924.
Lerner, Gerda. *The Creation of Patriarchy.* Oxford, 1986.
Lilja, Saara. *The Roman Elegists' Attitude to Women.* Helsinki, 1965.
Lincoln, Bruce. *Emerging from the Chrysalis: Studies in Rituals of Women's Initiation.* Cambridge, 1981.
Llonie, Iain M. *The Hippocratic Treatises "On Generation," "On the Nature of the Child," "Diseases IV."* Berlin, 1981.
Loraux, Nicole. *Tragic Ways of Killing a Woman.* Translated by Anthony Forster. Cambridge, 1987.
Lowe, N. J. "Sulpicia's Syntax." *CQ,* 38 (1988): 193–205.
Luce, Judith de. "Metamorphosis as Mourning: Pathological Grief in Ovid's *Metamorphoses.*" *Helios,* n.s. 9 (1982): 77–90.
MacMullen, Ramsey. "Woman in Public in the Roman Empire." *Historia,* 29 (1980): 208–18.
March, J. "Euripides the Misogynist?" In *Euripides, Women and Sexuality,* ed. by Anton Powell, 32–75. London, 1990.
Marquardt, Patricia. "Penelope Πολύτροπος." *AJP,* 106.1 (1985): 32–48.
Marshall, A. J. "Roman Women and the Provinces." *Ancient Society,* 6 (1975): 109–27.
May, Robert. *Sex and Fantasy: Patterns of Male and Female Development.* New York, 1980.

McConnell-Ginet, Sally, Ruth Borker, and Nelly Furman, eds. *Woman and Language in Literature and Society*. New York, 1980.

McCormack, Carol, and Marilyn Strathen, eds. *Nature, Culture and Gender*. Cambridge, 1980.

McDermott, E. A. *Euripides' Medea: The Incarnation of Disorder*. University Park, 1989.

Merriam, Carol. "The Other Sulpicia." "Scholia." *CW*, 84.4 (March–April 1991): 303–305.

Meunier, Mario. *Femmes Pythagoriciennes: Fragments et Lettres de Theano, Périctioné, Phintys, Mélissa, et Myia*. Paris, 1932.

Meyer, R. "Neuere Entwicklungen und Tendenzen der Frauengeschichte im Bereich der klassichen Altertumskunde (1973–1989)." *Schriftliche Hausarbeit zur Ersten Staatsprufung fur die Laufbahn der Studienrate an Gymnasien*. Kiel, 1991.

Moeller, Walter O. "The Building of Eumachia: A Reconsideration." *American Journal of Archaeology*, 76 (1972): 323–27.

Neumann, Erich. *The Great Mother: An Analysis of the Archetype*. Translated by Ralph Manheim. New York, 1955.

Newton, R. M. "Medea's Passionate Poison," *Syllecta Classica*, 1 (1989): 13–20

Nicols, John. "*Patrona Civitatis*: Gender and Civic Patronage." *Studies in Latin Literature and Roman History* V, edited by C. Deroux. *Latomus*, 206 (1989): 117–42.

O'Barr, William M., and Borman K. Atkins. "'Woman's Language' or 'Powerless Language.'" In *Woman and Language in Literature and Society*, 93–110. See under McConnell-Ginet, Borker, and Furman.

O'Brien, Joan. "Homer's Savage Hera." *CJ*, 119 (1991): 105–25.

Ortner, Sherry B. "Is Female to Male as Nature Is to Culture?" In *Woman, Culture, and Society*, edited by Michelle Zimbalist Rosaldo and Louise Lamphere, 67–87. Stanford, 1974.

Ostriker, Alicia. *Stealing the Language: The Emergence of Women's Poetry in America*. Boston, 1986.

———. "The Thieves of Language: Women Poets and Revisionist Mythmaking." *Signs*, 8 (1982): 68–90. Rpt. in *The New Feminist Criticism*, ed. E. Showalter, 314–38. New York, 1985.

Parker, Holt. "Other Remarks on the Other Sulpicia." *CW*, 86 (1992): 89–95.

———. "Sulpicia, the *Auctor de Sulpicia* and the Authorship of 3.9 and 3.11 of the *Corpus Tibullianum*." Forthcoming, *Helios*, 1992.

Patai, Raphael. "Maria the Jewess: Founding Mother of Alchemy." *Ambix*, 29 (1982): 177–97.

Peradotto, J., and J. P. Sullivan, eds. *Women in the Ancient World: The Arethusa*

Papers. Albany, 1984.
Pötscher, Walter. *Hera: Eine Strukturanalyse im Vergleich mit Athena*. Darmstadt, 1987.
Pollard, J. R. T. "Muses and Sirens." *CR*, 11 n.s. (June 1952): 60–63.
Pomeroy, Sarah B. *Goddesses, Whores, Wives, and Slaves: Women in Classical Antiquity*. New York, 1975.
———. "Selected Bibliography on Women in Classical Antiquity." In *Women in the Ancient World*, 315–77. See under Peradotto and Sullivan.
———. "Technikai kai Mousikai." *American Journal of Ancient History*, 2 (1977): 51–68.
———. *Women in Hellenistic Egypt: from Alexander to Cleopatra*. New York, 1984.
———, ed. *Women's History and Ancient History*. Chapel Hill, 1991.
Praechter, "Hypatia." *RE*, 9 (1916): 242–49.
Pratt, Annis V. "Spinning Among the Fields: Jung, Frye, Lévi-Strauss and Feminist Archetypal Theory." In *Feminist Archetypal Theory: Interdisciplinary Re-Visions of Jungian Thought*, edited by Estella Lauter and Carol Schreier Rupprecht, 93–136. Knoxville, 1985.
———. "'Aunt Jennifer's Tigers': Notes towards a Preliterary History of Women's Archetypes." *Feminist Studies*, 4 (1978): 163–94.
Price, Theodora Hadzisteliou. *Kourotrophos: Cults and Representations of the Greek Nursing Deities*. Leiden, 1978.
Pucci, Pietro. "The Song of the Sirens." *Arethusa*, 12 (Fall 1979): 121–32.
Purkiss, Diane. "Women's Rewriting of Myth." In *The Feminist Companion to Mythology*, edited by Carolyne Larrington, 441–57. London, 1992.
Putnam, Michael. *Tibullus: A Commentary*. Norman, 1973.
Rabinowitz, Nancy S. "Female Speech and Female Sexuality: Euripides' *Hippolytus* as Model." In *Rescuing Creusa*, 127–40. See under Skinner.
Rachewiltz, Siegfried de. *De Sirenibus: An Inquiry into Sirens from Homer to Shakespeare*. New York, 1987.
Rayor, Diane. *Sappho's Lyre: Archaic Lyric and Women Poets of Ancient Greece*. Berkeley, 1991.
Reiter, Rayna, ed. *Toward an Anthropology of Women*. New York, 1975.
Reuther, Rosemary R. *Sexism and God-Talk: Toward a Feminist Theology*. Boston, 1983.
———, ed. *Religion and Sexism: Images of Women in the Jewish and Christian Traditions*. New York, 1974.
Richardson, Lawrence, jr. "Concordia and Concordia Augusta: Rome and Pompeii." *La Parola del Passato*, 33 (1978): 260–72.
Richlin, Amy E. *The Garden of Priapus: Sexuality and Aggression in Roman Humor*. New Haven, 1983.
———. "Julia's Jokes, Galla Placidia, and the Roman Use of Women as

Political Icons." In *Stereotypes of Women in Power*, 65–91. See under Garlick, Dixon, and Allen.

———. "Reading Ovid's Rapes." In *Pornography and Representation in Greece and Rome*, edited by Amy E. Richlin, 158–79. Oxford, 1992.

———. "Sulpicia the Satirist." *CW*, 86 (1992): 125–40.

———, and Nancy S. Rabinowitz, eds. *Feminist Theory and the Classics*. New York, 1993.

Rist, J. M. "Hypatia." *Phoenix*, 19 (1965): 214–25.

Rubin, Nancy Felson, and Harriet M. Deal. "Some Functions of the Demophon Episode in the *Homeric Hymn to Demeter*." *Quaderni Urbinati di Cultura Classica*, 5 (1980): 7–21.

Ruddick, Sara. *Maternal Thinking: Toward a Politics of Peace*. Boston, 1989.

Rudhardt, J. "La reconnaissance de la paternité, sa nature et sa portée dans la société athénienne." *Museum Helveticum*, 19 (1962): 39–64.

Saliou, Monique. "The Processes of Women's Subordination in Primitive and Archaic Greece." In *Women's Work, Men's Property*, edited by Stephanie Coontz and Peta Henderson, 169–206. London, 1986.

Sanday, Peggy R., and R. G. Goodenough, eds. *Beyond the Second Sex: New Directions in the Anthropology of Gender*. Philadelphia, 1990.

Santirocco, Matthew. "Sulpicia Reconsidered." *CJ*, 74 (1979): 229–239.

Sarkissian, John. *Catullus 68: An Interpretation*. Leiden, 1983.

Saxonhouse, Arlene W. "Introduction-Public and Private: The Paradigm's Power." In *Stereotypes of Women in Power*, 1–9. See under Garlick, Dixon, and Allen.

Schaps, David M. *Economic Rights of Women in Ancient Greece*. Edinburgh, 1979.

———. "The Women Least Mentioned: Etiquette and Women's Names." *CQ*, 27 (1977): 323–30.

Schlegel, Alice. "Gender Meanings: General and Specific." In *Beyond the Second Sex*, 21–41. See under Sanday and Goodenough.

Schmidt, M. G. *Caesar und Cleopatra. Philologischer und historischer Kommentar zu Lucan 10.7–171*. Studien zur klassische Philologie 25. Frankfurt, 1986.

Sealey, R. "On Lawful Concubinage in Athens." *Classical Antiquity*, 3 (1984): 111–33.

Sissa, Giulia. *Greek Virginity*. Translated by Arthur Goldhammer. Cambridge, 1990.

Skinner, Marilyn B. "Clodia Metelli." *TAPA*, 113 (1983): 273–87.

———. "Corinna of Tanagra and her Audience." *Tulsa Studies in Women's Literature*, 2 (1983): 9–20.

———. "Expecting the Barbarians: Feminism, Nostalgia, and the 'Epistemic Shift' in Classical Studies." In *Classics: A Discipline and Profession in*

Crisis? edited by Phyllis Culham and Lowell Edmunds, 199–210. Lanham, Md., 1989.
———. "Nossis Thelyglossos: The Private Text and the Public Book." In Women's History and Ancient History, 20–47. See under Pomeroy.
———. "Sapphic Nossis." Arethusa, 21.1 (Spring 1989): 5–18.
———, ed. Rescuing Creusa: New Methodological Approaches to Women in Antiquity. Helios, 13.2 (1986).
Slater, Philip. The Glory of Hera. Boston, 1968.
Slatkin, Laura. "The Wrath of Thetis." TAPA, 116 (1986): 1–24.
Snodgrass, Anthony. Archaic Greece: The Age of Experiment. Berkeley, 1980.
———. The Dark Age of Greece. Edinburgh, 1971.
Snyder, J. "Public Occasion and Private Passion in the Lyrics of Sappho of Lesbos." In Women's History and Ancient History, 1–19. See under Pomeroy.
———. The Woman and the Lyre: Women Writers in Classical Greece and Rome. Carbondale, 1989.
Sommerstein, A. H. "The Naming of Women in Greek and Roman Comedy." Quaderni di Storia, 6 (1980): 393–418.
Stehle, E. "Sappho's Gaze: Fantasies of a Goddess and Young Man." Differences, 2 (1990): 88–125.
Stigers, Eva Stehle. "Sappho's Private World." Women's Studies, 8 (1981): 47–60.
Tran Tam Tinh, V. Isis Lactans: Corpus des monuments gréco-romains d'Isis allaitant Harpocrate. Leiden, 1973.
Tyrrell, Willam B. Amazons: A Study in Athenian Mythmaking. Baltimore, 1984.
Walker, Alice. In Search of Our Mothers' Gardens: Womanist Prose. New York, 1983.
Wall, Kathleen. The Callisto Myth from Ovid to Atwood: Initiation and Rape in Literature. Kingston, 1988.
Wender, Dorothea. "Plato: Misogynist, Paedophile, and Feminist." In Women in the Ancient World, 213–28. See under Peradotto and Sullivan.
Whitman, Cedric. "Hera's Anvils." Harvard Studies in Classical Philology, 74 (1970): 37–42.
Will, Elizabeth Lyding. "Women in Pompeii." Archaeology, 32.5 (September/October 1979): 34–43.
Winkler, John J. The Constraints of Desire: The Anthropology of Sex and Gender in Ancient Greece. New York, 1990.
———. "Gardens of Nymphs: Public and Private in Sappho's Lyrics." Women's Studies, 8 (1981). Reprinted in Reflections of Women in Antiquity. See under Foley.

Wittig, Monique. *Les Guérillères*. Translated by David Le Vay. 1971; rpt. Boston, 1985.
Wyke, M. "The Elegiac Woman at Rome." *Proceedings of the Cambridge Philological Society*, 213, n.s. 33 (1987): 153–78.
———. "Mistress and Metaphor in Augustan Elegy." *Helios*, 16.1 (1989): 25–47.
———. "Reading Female Flesh: *Amores* 3.1." In *History as Text: The Writing of Ancient History*, edited by Averil Cameron, 111–43. London, 1989.
———. "Written Women: Propertius' *Scripta Puella*." *Journal of Roman Studies*, 77 (1987): 47–61.
Zeitlin, Froma I. "Cultic Models of the Female: Rites of Dionysus and Demeter." *Arethusa*, 15.1/2 (1982): 129–57.
———. "The Dynamics of Misogyny: Myth and Mythmaking in the *Oresteia*." *Arethusa*, 11 (1978): 149–84.
———. "Playing the Other: Theater, Theatricality, and the Feminine in Greek Drama." *Representations*, 11 (1985): 63-94.
Zweig, Bella. "The Primal Mind: Using Native American Models to Approach the Study of Women in Ancient Greece." In *Feminist Theory and the Classics*. See under Richlin and Rabinowitz.

Index

Abraham 373–74, 379–81, 388
Achilles: in female dress, 19; questions heroism 133, 240; as infant 8, 95; savagery 110, 123–24, 219. *See also under* Iphigenia
Actaeon 315–16
Adam 309. *See also under* Eve
Aeschylus' *Oresteia* 129–42
Agamemnon: arrogance 134–35; contrasted with Abraham 379–81; loved by Hera 128 n 27. *See also under* Clytemnestra, Iphigenia
Agave 23, 185
Ajax 172, 309
Amazons 11, 12; and reversal of gender roles 21, 84–85; liaisons with heroes 20–21
androgyny 1–25; as aboriginal 2–3, 10, 13; of gods 5–13; of heroes 13–23; rationalized 9, 19–22; in ritual 8–9, 14–17, 18, 47
Antiope 13, 21, 224
Aphrodite: birth 95; and Hermes 21; as male 18
Apollo 382; birth 95–99, 120; demands Clytemnestra's death 138–39; and poets 216–218, 223, 287; as usurper 98–99, 105
Arachne 307, 319 n 9
Ares 21, 128 n 26; birth 6, 127 n 13
Aristophanes 24
Aristotle 375
Arnold, Matthew 394–95, 396, 397, 398
Artemis 312, 373, 374, 382; birth 95–98; as Earth goddess 15, 99, 103, 104–5, 312; wrath 134
Aspasia 201, 202
Athena 141, 142, 383, 384; birth 6, 10–12, 75 n 52, 111

Atwood, Margaret 402–5
Auden, W. H. 398–400, 405
Austen, Jane x, xii
Baubo dolls 131
Bellerophon 132, 154, 240
Binyon, Laurence 397–98
Cacoyannis, Michael 376–77, 387
Caesarion 269
Callimachus 96–97, 228; *Aetia* 217, 224, 229, 339; literary values vi, 215, 216, 217–19, 222, 235–36; misrepresented as writer of love poetry 342. *See also under* Catullus, Martial, Propertius
Callisto 13, 306, 312–13, 314
Calypso 225, 392
Cato 264, 265, 268, 271, 272, 274–75, 282
Catullus 288, 324, 327–31, 336–38; and Callimachus 224, 244 n 20; literary values 330. *See also under* Martial, Propertius, Sulpicia, Sappho
Cerberus 110
Ceres. *See* Demeter
children: obligations to the father 55–57, 171–73, 378; obligations to the mother 38, 45, 56–57, 129–30
Cimon 201–2, 208–9
Circe 392, 404
Cixous, Hélène 404–5
Cleopatra 265, 268
Clodia 299 n 7
Clytemnestra 339, 376; and Agamemnon 134–136, 139, 373; and Earth goddess 130–31, 135, 138; and Iphigenia 130, 373–77, 390; and Orestes 129–131, 136, 138–40, 142
Cornelia (wife of Pompey) 265, 267–68, 270, 273
Cronus 5, 8, 12, 62, 115
Cynthia 272, 279–80, 286–93, 331–47; as literary allegory 215–41; as poet 337
Cynthus 99, 101, 104–5
Deianeira 159–75; deceptiveness 164, 167–68
Deidameia 20–21

Delos 95–105
Delphi 103, 104
Demeter 7, 11, 54–67, 307
Demophoön 8, 60–61
Diana. *See* Artemis
Diomedes 95, 240
Dionysus 23–24, 128 n 26, 180–90; birth 7, 9; feminine qualities 21, 23–24, 183; rites 15, 17
Earth goddess (also Artemis, Athena, Demeter, Hera, Metis): creative and nurturing 105, 122, 130, 137–41; destructive 61–62, 65–66, 131, 135, 137–41; diminishment 12, 54–67, 98, 105; and earth 3, 61–62, 65, 102–5, 115; honors of 62–64, 66; pre-patriarchal 54–55, 76 n 56; powers 5, 9; sites sacred to 98, 102–5, 109, 128 n 27; and snakes 22, 110–12, 115, 120–21, 130, 136; taming of 58, 65, 116, 125; wrath 59, 61, 64, 65, 140–41
Elpinice 201–2, 208–9
Euripides: and anti-war tragedy 376; *Bacchae* 180–90; *Iphigenia in Aulis* 374–76; *Iphigenia in Tauris* 381–84; *Medea* 178–90
Eve: and Adam 10, 11, 13
evil eye 131–42
Finkel, Donald 403–4
Freud 2
Fulvia 281
Furies 140–42, 374
Gallus 222, 223, 232; as character in Vergil's *Eclogues* 216–17, 220, 222, 231, 234; as character in Propertius' *Monobiblos* 216–17, 225–27, 229–30, 234
Goethe, Johann Wolfgang von 384–87
Golden Age: and childhood 256 n 7; and communication with animals 308; androgyny in 4–5, 10, 13–14
Graves, Robert 398
Hacker, Marilyn 406–7
Hades 55, 60, 62, 63
Hecate 9, 54–67
Hector 110, 219

Hecuba 130, 317
Hephaestus 10; birth 6, 127 n 13; battle with river 118; Hera's champion 117, 119; son/lover of Earth 6; and Typhon 117–18, 120
Hera: and Heracles 118, 130; and Ocean 111, 120–23; as Earth goddess 5–6, 95, 109, 112; jealousy 9, 95, 118, 120, 307, 313; as mother and nurse of monsters 110, 112, 114–16, 122–24; as nurse of heroes 123, 130; as rebel against Zeus 114–17; Seduction of Zeus 113, 115, 121; wrath 123
Heracles 20, 21, 130, 159–75; in female dress 16–18
Hercules. *See* Heracles
Hermaphroditus 13, 21–22
Hewitt, Mary E. 396–97
Hippocratic corpus 78–86
Homeric Hymn to Demeter 54–67
Horace 257–62
human sacrifice 373, 382
Hydra 6, 110, 120, 122
Hypatia 357–60
Io 122, 311–12, 316
Iphigenia 373–88; feminism 384–86; and Achilles 375, 377–379; and Agamemnon 131–32, 134, 142, 145, 374–380, 387, 388; and Orestes 381–86. *See also under* Clytemnestra
Isaac 373–74, 381
Jason 128 n 27, 189
Jephthah 373–74, 380
Julia (daughter of Julius Caesar) 264–75
Julius Caesar 264–75
Jung 2, 4, 11, 13
Juno. *See* Hera
Jupiter. *See* Zeus
Kierkegaard, Søren 379–81
Klein, Melanie 137–38
Lesbia 222, 327–31
Leto 95–99, 104, 105, 120
Lewis, C. Day 401–2
Lowell, James Russell 396
Lucan 264–76

Lucretius 308, 373, 374, 377, 381
Maecenas 257, 260, 261, 284, 285–86, 287, 288, 289, 341
Maenads 23
Manifold, John 401–2
Marcia 264–65, 274–75
Maria the Jewess 362–64
Martial 322–46; disparagement of Callimachus 339, 349 n 18; and Catullus 327–31; and Propertius 331–42. See also under Sappho
Medea 179–90; as hero vi, 179; power over males 183–84, 188–89; vitality as mythic figure x
Medusa 137, 146, 307, 404–5, 408 n 2
Metis 9, 11–12, 57, 75 n 52
mystery religions 7, 65–67
mythology: historical strata 54–55, 65–66, 91, 92–93, 98–99, 115; and psychology 136–38; and ritual 8, 14–21, 312–13; women's rewriting x–xiv, 402–7
Nemean lion 6, 110, 120, 122, 124
Neptune. See Poseidon
Oates, Joyce Carol 405
Octavian 215, 238–39
Odysseus 19, 133, 151, 152, 308–10, 398, 404
Omphale 16–17, 20
Orestes. See under Clytemnestra, Iphigenia
Ostriker, Alice 305
Ovid 245 n 30, 285, 292, 299 n 3, 305–18, 323, 342–43; identification with women characters 306, 318
Penelope 149–56, 392, 398
Pentheus 23–24, 180–84
Pericles 1, 202, 208–9, 310
Persephone 54–67
Philomela 313–15, 316, 317
Plato 10
Pompey 264–75
Poseidon 7, 11, 72 n 29, 76 n 57, 92–94, 133
Priapus 13, 257–62
Procne 313–15

Prometheus 10, 13–14
Propertius 215–41, 285–93, 331–42; allusions to Callimachus 215–41, 291, 339; allusions to Catullus 215–41; literary values 216, 222, 224
Protesilaus 221–22, 224
Racine, Jean 377–79, 380, 384
rape: and domination 305; and silence of victims 66, 311–14; as metaphor for marriage 58, 76 n 57
recusatio (refusal to write epic poetry) vi–vii, 215, 219, 221–22, 239, 285, 290
Roma 264, 265, 272–76
Rossetti, Dante Gabriel 395–96
Sappho: and women poets 342; and Catullus 329–31, 342; and Ovid 342; disparaged by Martial 325, 329–31, 337, 342, 343, 345
Servilia 281
Shakespeare 279, 280, 293–98
Sirens 392–407; allure 394–98; in male literature 392–402; in female literature 402–7
Socrates 24, 33, 310
Solon 134
Sophocles: *Trachiniae* 159–75
speech and humanity 305–18
Sulpicia (Augustan) 322–23
Sulpicia (1st a.d.) 323–46; and literary tradition 335–36, 342–46
Teiresias 9, 22
Tereus 313–15
Theseus: in female dress 19–20
Thetis 8, 19, 120, 122
Tibullus 249–55, 285, 288, 322
Titans 8–9, 58, 66, 114
Typhon 6, 110, 115; and Python 110, 112, 124; war with Zeus 114, 117. See also under Hephaestus
Ulysses. See Odysseus
Venus. See Aphrodite
water as source of life: theory 111, 121, 147 n 41; theory rejected 81–84
Weldon, Fay x–xiv
women in men's books: representations

controlled by men ii–iii, 292–93, 325, 345–46; theatrical roles acted by men 129, 294; witches 249–55; in Euripides 23, 178; respected by Plato 24–25, 354; disparaged by Aristotle 32, 42, 81, 310, 354; of Roman elegy vi–vii, 215–41, 249–55, 279–93; ancient medical theories concerning 78–86, 104; as "implied readers" vii; as inspiration 286–87, 291–92; as peace-makers 64, 266, 387; and reversal of gender roles 84–85, 187, 288, 292, 294, 303; symbolizing stages of life 249–55; symbolizing poetry 215–41; classed with animals and barbarians 82–84, 110, 181–83, 310–11; cunning 113, 135, 138–39, 149–56, 166–68; as monsters 394–98

women in men's world: as commodities 56, 66; education vii, 310; economic power (in Sparta) 42, (in Italy) 281–84; eloquence in home 195, 198–200, 281–82, 310; goals 200, 203, 205, 208; isolation 55; marriage and death 55; as midwives 364–66; namelessness 200–201, 203; as pawns to hurt other men 202; permanent dependence 60; power in home 69 n 10, 198–200; power in single-sex communities (Native American) 36–40, 45–46, (Spartan) 41–48; contrast of Roman with Athenian 281–84; male bias against Spartan 32, 42; as transmitters of property 57–58, 66, 196–97, 200

women's fertility: claimed as male 6–10, 12, 55, 58, 62, 81–86, 292, 296; honored 38, 44–47; as incompatible with sexuality 57–58; male control of 55, 58; and human immortality 60, 65, 67; medical theory concerning 78–86; as conferring royal power 62; as separate from nurturing 58, 60, 64

women's sexuality: asserted by women 345; condemned and feared by men 205, 208–9, 289, 329–31

women writers: philosophers 354–57; poets (ancient) 322–46; scientists 357–64, 366–67; consciously seizing the pen 343–46, 392, 393, x–xiv, 402–7; male resentment of ix

Woolf, Virginia 1

Zagreus 6–9

Zeus 6–13, 21, 22, 55–64, 133, 134, 312, 313; and Earth goddess 5, 9, 11–12. See also under Hera